THE COMMUNIST CONTROVERSY
IN WASHINGTON

From the New Deal to McCarthy

THE COMMUNIST
CONTROVERSY
IN WASHINGTON

From the New Deal to McCarthy

EARL LATHAM

HARVARD UNIVERSITY PRESS

CAMBRIDGE, MASSACHUSETTS · 1966

To Margaret Latham

Preface

This book is one of several originally sponsored by the Fund for the Republic, Inc., under Professor Clinton Rossiter of Cornell University as General Editor. The title of the series is *Communism in American Life* and the following volumes are now in print: Theodore Draper, *The Roots of American Communism;* Robert W. Iversen, *The Communists and the Schools;* David A. Shannon, *The Decline of American Communism;* Theodore Draper, *American Communism and Soviet Russia;* Clinton Rossiter, *Marxism: The View from America;* Ralph Lord Roy, *Communism and the Churches;* Frank S. Meyer, *The Moulding of Communists;* Nathan Glazer, *The Social Basis of American Communism;* and Daniel Aaron, *Writers of the Left.*

Special thanks are owed to the Fund for the Republic, Inc., and to the Social Science Research Council for grants that helped to make this study possible.

Grateful acknowledgment is made to Professor Clinton Rossiter, Professor George Kateb of Amherst College, Professor Andrew Hacker of Cornell University, and E. M. Kirkpatrick, Executive Director of the American Political Science Association, for many valuable suggestions about substance and style; and to Jeane J. Kirkpatrick, Pio Uliassi, Peter Latham, and Maurice J. Goldbloom for indispensable research assistance and counsel. Former Ambassador Joseph C. Grew, former Secretary of State Dean G. Acheson, and John Carter Vincent supplied helpful information by interview or letter on the circumstances attending the assumption by Mr. Acheson of the post of Under Secretary of State in 1945.

The epigraphs from Aristotle's *Rhetoric* and *Poetics* are from the Modern Library edition put out by Random House in 1954. This translation was reprinted by Random House with the permission of the Jowett Trustees and the Clarendon Press, Oxford. The translators are W. Rhys Roberts and Ingram Bywater. Quotations from Aristotle's *Politics* are from the translation by Benjamin Jowett published by the Oxford University Press, 1926, first edition 1905. The quotations from

Medea are taken from the Everyman edition of the plays of Euripides. Quotations from the other Greek plays are from *The Complete Greek Drama*, edited by Whitney J. Oates and Eugene O'Neill, Jr., and published by Random House in 1938.

For patiently checking notes and citations, thanks go to Margaret and Susan Latham; and for typing service of skill and speed, to Mrs. Evelyn Cooley of Pelham, Massachusetts.

Any errors are mine.

Earl Latham

Amherst, Massachusetts
July 1965

Contents

THE COMMUNIST CONTROVERSY
IN WASHINGTON

From the New Deal to McCarthy

Introduction

There is a new generation of people who have no memory of the tensions about communism in the years from the confrontation of Hiss and Chambers to the condemnation of Senator McCarthy of Wisconsin by the United States Senate; and for whom the names of the principals in a hundred sensations are as faded in interest as in mind. It is not that they doubt the historicity of the events; they merely see the actors as figures flattened and blurred by the distance of a few years and therefore as unreal and two-dimensional as a page of text. But the reality was vivid enough, and there was abuse, and bitterness, and injury in political litigation over Communists in the Federal government in the 1940's and 1950's, and in the stress it created between the Congress and the Executive over serious issues of governmental trust and civil liberty.

The far-ranging controversy bred scores of incidents full of the variety of the human experience, brilliant and inept, sinister and sad, devious and naïve. There was the lawyer in a Communist unit of taxicab drivers whose pseudonym was "Hacker"; and a hunt for Communists in the National Labor Relations Board with the help of Communists in the National Labor Relations Board. And there was General Patrick J. Hurley telling Chiang Kai-shek that he had the personal assurance of Molotov that Chinese Communists were related to communism in no way at all. One responsible Federal official sincerely questioned whether Cohn and Senator McCarthy weren't Communists themselves because of the skillful and clever job of sabotage they were performing on the State Department. A McCarthy investigator who visited information centers in Germany and France reported that there were German girls in the German centers and French girls in the French centers. And it was the respectable Senator Robert A. Taft who urged, "If one case doesn't work, then bring up another."

For five years, beginning early in 1950, Washington officialdom and professional and intellectual circles throughout the country were in an uproar over communism, with fresh sensations almost every week. Alger Hiss was found guilty of perjury in January 1950 for denying that he had known Whittaker Chambers after a certain date in the 1930's. In February, Senator McCarthy charged that the Department of State knowingly employed Communists. For four months, the Tydings committee held hearings on these charges, months during which several other events contributed to the panic melee — for example, the refusal of the Supreme Court to review the contempt convictions of two Hollywood writers; the conviction on charges of conspiracy (later reversed on procedural grounds) of Judith Coplon of the Department of Justice and a Soviet representative at the United Nations; the arrest (at different times) of Harry Gold, David Greenglass, and Julius Rosenberg on various charges connected with espionage; a grand jury investigation into the *Amerasia* case; investigations by the House Committee on Un-American Activities into alleged communism in Hawaii and by the California Legislature Committee on Un-American Activities into matters entirely within the jurisdiction of the Federal government; and a chorus of denunciations, charges, counter-charges, demands for Executive documents, refusals to acquiesce, citations for contempt, and a Declaration of Conscience by Senator Margaret Chase Smith and six other Republicans. All this within the span of a few months in 1950.

In 1951, the turbulence continued. The McCarran subcommittee seized files of the Institute of Pacific Relations in February and began an investigation of alleged subversive influences in the Institute and the relations between the Institute and the Department of State. The Rosenberg-Sobell trial opened in March, and in April the Rosenbergs were sentenced to death. J. Edgar Hoover assured Congress that the FBI was ready to arrest 14,000 dangerous Communists in the event of war with the Soviet Union. Speaker Sam Rayburn in June said that the enemy would find it unnecessary to hire spies if congressional investigations, like that into the Truman-MacArthur controversy, were to continue. A foundation offered $100,000 to support research into the creation of a device for detecting traitors.

In 1952, Senator William Benton of Connecticut tried to have the United States Senate expel Senator McCarthy. In April, Senator McCarthy offered a resolution for a full-scale investigation into Senator Benton's official, business, and personal activities. The year was filled with newspaper stories about convictions, indictments, appeals, reversals, prosecutions, and charges as two committees in the Senate and two in the House pressed a spreading search for possible subversive influence in Federal agencies, local schools, the United Nations, philanthropic foundations, laboratories, and unions. As the presidential campaign lent license to extravagance in declamation, Richard Nixon said that Adlai Stevenson had disqualified himself for the presidency by giving a deposition in the Hiss case attesting to the good reputation of the defendant. Twenty-two prominent lawyers, including Eisenhower supporters, upheld Stevenson. Sixteen lawyers called the defense of Stevenson's deposition by twenty-two lawyers unsound. General Eisenhower charged that the Administration had permitted spies of the Soviet Union to steal secrets. Senator Wayne Morse of Oregon resigned from the Republican party, and McCarthy made a speech in which he used "Alger" for "Adlai" in faked mistake.

The year 1953 found Senator McCarthy at his peak, and at the beginning of his decline. He investigated the Voice of America, the overseas libraries, and other activities of the State Department in sensationalistic manner. The House Committee on Un-American Activities started an investigation of churches but was forced to give it up. Congressman Harold Velde of the HUAC said that churchmen had committed the "sin" of subversion when criticizing his proposal to probe the clergy. Julius and Ethel Rosenberg were executed. McCarthy began an investigation into military establishments and industrial espionage at military installations, and the denouement began. The Department of the Army, after first trying to placate Senator McCarthy, stiffened its resistance, and a showdown ensued in the spring of 1954 to determine the truth of contradictory charges and recriminations. In August of 1954, Senator Ralph Flanders of Vermont introduced a resolution to censure Senator McCarthy. The Senate delayed action on the resolution until after the congressional elections in November but then, within a month, adopted the resolution of condemnation that prudence had postponed.

The temper of the time was suspicious, excited, emotional, pathetic, and hard. There was rage and outrage, accusation and defiance, a Babel of shouting anger in these tense years. At the center of the storm of recrimination which blew so violently for so long there was a Communist problem, and there was a Communist issue. The *problem* was a matter of fact and law, and was dealt with (not inadequately) by the official agencies of the government — the removal of security and loyalty risks (however painfully and awkwardly accomplished) from employment, the prosecution of leaders of the Communist Party by the Department of Justice under the Smith Act of 1940, the prosecution and conviction of defendants charged with espionage activity, the discipline of recusant witnesses in the courts, and the conviction of defendants accused of perjury. These were, to repeat, matters of fact and law. The Communist *issue*, however, was a complex clash of attitudes and predilections, of dispositions and predispositions, of views about what should be and what should not be. It was a disagreement about the basic values of the American political system, in the course of which disclosures concerning Communists were used by partisans of various fealties to serve sectarian ends — Republicans against Democrats (or rather, most Republicans against most Democrats); conservatives against liberals; and Congress against the Executive. The Communist controversy in Washington bore with heavy stress upon the effective conduct of office and laid a costly tax upon that charity which assumes the good faith of decent men in government.

The nature of the stress may be seen in the organization of the public power within which it occurred. The Federal government is a structure of political and institutional elements fitted together to perform national functions in the political system. Each of the institutional elements must mesh with the others if government is not to be stultified, and there are gross procedures — like the veto and the over-rider — to solve extreme cases of blockage. There are other, more informal procedures for the encouragement of smooth cooperation, and political harmony is aided by many predisposing inclinations — the habit of familiar roles, an awareness of history, sense of need, patriotic feeling, the sheer inertia of grooved momentum. Soon after the founding of the Republic, however, it seemed that these were not, by themselves, enough to make the new system work easily, and the party system grew out of the need to organize, if not command, the cooperation of two legislative houses and the Executive in the conduct of governance.

But the party system which can promote political amiability can also disrupt it, and where the parties themselves lack unity, they aggravate the disorganization of the public powers. A breakdown in either of the major congressional parties encourages alliances among factions that may represent no common electoral constituency, and can give to a legislative junta presiding influence to enact some measures, and block others, without the salutary control that normal party discipline entails. It may be said, by the way, that although party idiosyncrasy in Congress is well known, the record shows, as Stephen Bailey has pointed out, that legislative party votes over a period of time, although not rigorously disciplined, are considerably more ideological and consistent in program than critics usually allow.

There are other centrifugal impulses in the legislature besides party disorder, the chief of which is a corporate interest as against the Executive. A Congress under the domination of a bipartisan coalition which feels disenchanted with the President can create a stalemate that only the electorate can ultimately resolve. Until there is such a solution there is an aching, and even disabling strain on the government, a state or condition of stress in the accomplishment of the most ordinary business, an abrasion and friction of the touching parts. The period from 1950 to the end of 1954 (roughly) was a period of such stress.

The stress in these years was a symptom, not a cause, and although it had many symbols, there was one that predominated. The symbol is what will be called in this book, "prescriptive publicity" — the exercise by Congress alone of powers normally thought to be shared with the Executive and with the courts, a procedure which made the Congress strongly competitive with the other branches of the government, and arrogated to the legislature control of certain ceremonials of legitimacy which normally require the acquiescence of the other branches for full validation. The nature of this power is discussed in Chapter Twelve. It was through the use of prescriptive publicity that the Communist problem developed as a political issue. The concept of prescriptive publicity did not originate with the conservatives of the forties and fifties but with the liberals of the thirties — still another of history's many depressing ironies. Its use in the earlier period had been in accord with the outlook of the Administration, however, whereas in the later period it was either in defiance of the Administration, or actively hostile to it.

It may be repeated that the stress created by the Communist controversy was a symptom but, if so, a symptom of what? Was the embroilment of five years — a complicated and embarrassing episode to thousands — merely the agitation of demagogues? Any demagogues? Some demagogues but not others? The "demagogues" came and went — Dies, the Democrat, removed himself from elective politics and J. Parnell Thomas, the Republican, went to jail, but the House Committee on Un-American Activities continued on and on in what seemed to be an independent life of its own. Was it a neo-Populist revolt, a flare of fascism in democratic America, a new political phenomenon referred to by some as "status politics," a clash of fighting faiths, each thinking the other heretic, as some conservative critics have alleged? Why did the stress occur when it did? A provisional answer might be put in general terms somewhat as follows: It may be said that the stress was a function of conservative politics, that certain inhibitions to a clear electoral mandate frustrated normal and expected political change, that the electorate did mandate change once but failed to affix the necessary authority for it, and that the resulting impasse produced the stress. When the electorate did mandate change and bestow the necessary authority upon its custodians, the impasse disappeared and the stress eased.

To put the matter more historically — from Grant to Eisenhower, the years which span the rise of unregulated capitalism and its eventual moderation by welfarism, the political parties served as the principal agency through which social change received popular and then legal ratification. The new class of business enterprisers who presided over the industrial revolution after the Civil War found political expression in the Republican party. Working in their favor was the presumption of continuous office which makes things a little easier for incumbents than for their challengers. The presumption can be rebutted when there is an accumulation of grievances but the case normally has to be made against the incumbent, and the program of the outs then is always reformist in some degree. The leader of the opposition wins when he has been able to forge a coalition of the discontented.

There was such an accumulation of grievances in the 1880's because the Republicans had governed with too narrow and sectarian a view of the public interest, but the leadership of the opposition — Cleveland and the Democratic party — was unable to forge this discontent into an effective and durable coalition. Cleveland was unable to do so because he did not appreciate the role of the opposition in the way it was to be perceived later. Instead of being broadly reformist he was about as business-minded as his predecessors, and he assumed much of their coloration. Dissatisfied, the casualties of the industrial revolution turned to other forms of political relief, hence the emergence of the Populists, the Alliance, and other protest organizations and parties. Their vigor and influence produced partial reforms but successful electioneering by the Republicans in 1896 and the return of prosperity eased the discontents.

Eased them, that is, but did not make them disappear. It was for Wilson to understand the historic role of the opposition and, with the help of a split among the Republicans, to produce the reforms of the New Freedom. The Democrats were like political referees in bankruptcy, acquiring authority from the court of the people (without gaining title to the properties they controlled) to redistribute the public assets in favor of creditors whose claims had not been satisfied. After the completion of the reform proceedings, the political estate was restored to its rightful owners. This function had been completed by 1916 but the trust was extended another four years, with a warning in 1918 that it would end in 1920, which it did. By 1932 a real bankruptcy had occurred, political creditors (the unemployed, farmers, small businessmen, and others) were gravely stricken, their discontents were again gathered as in 1912, and another program of social reform was inaugurated in the New Deal.

There was one change, however, that distinguished the 1930's from the previous six decades. Republicans had won most of the national

elections in the time from Grant to FDR and those they lost they lost
by small margins. Those they lost in 1932 and 1936 were lost mas-
sively. But as the reformism of the New Freedom was done by 1916,
so was the reformism of the New Deal done by 1938. The year 1938
was a hinge year in several respects: the New Deal domination at the
polls was cracked; the first anti-Communist prohibitions in Federal
employment were written into the Hatch Act; and the first investigating committee hostile to the New Deal (the Dies committee) was
established. As the relaxation of the reformist spirit had been accompanied by narrowing margins for the Administration after 1916, so
were there narrowing margins of electoral support for the New Deal
after 1938. The curves of statistical tendency for Roosevelt began to
close like scissors on the New Deal after 1936, in fact, and they might
have produced a change in the White House in 1940, or 1944 at the
latest.

They might have closed in 1940 if Roosevelt had not run for a
third term. They surely would have closed in 1944 if we had not been
at war. They did close on the Democratic margins in the Senate and
House in 1946, as soon as the war was over, and the Republican victories of 1946, like those of 1918, were widely assumed to forecast the
loss of the White House to the Democrats in 1948. But nobody "won"
the election of 1948 because nobody received a majority of the popular votes, although there was a majority in the Electoral College for
President Truman. The electorate seems to have wanted change of
some sort but had failed clearly to make up its mind about the nature
of the change and the party and candidates that should supervise it.
The Democratic Congress rejected the Fair Deal of the Democratic
President and the period of sharpest stress began, with the attendant
excitements over the Communist issue. By 1952, the electorate was
prepared to vote change and to entrust it to the Republican party and
Eisenhower, and the stress began to ease. By 1954, with the condemnation of Senator McCarthy, it disappeared.

This conception — that there was an increasing stress of government in the late forties and early fifties, with distal causes in the history of almost a century of social change through party action, and
proximal causes in a bipartisan conservative alliance in Congress, is
discussed in the closing pages of this book. It is mentioned here —
and at greater length there — to provide a frame for the exposition,
which is chronological. Part One deals with the 1930's; Part Two with
the 1930's and the 1940's; Part Three with the 1940's and the 1950's;
and Part Four with the 1950's. But although the sequence of the book
is roughly chronological, it is not a chronicle, and the account does
not attempt to deal with all events of interest, even where Federal

officials and employees are involved. For example, the use by the House Committee on Un-American Activities of the membership list of the American League for Peace and Democracy to embarrass the Administration in 1939 and 1940 is an interesting story that is mentioned only in passing. Certain matters like loyalty programs and their administration have been written about elsewhere in a degree of detail that does not need to be repeated. Loyalty programs are discussed here only to the extent to which they enlighten recognition of the political aspects of the Communist issue.

Although the book deals with the Communist problem and the Communist issue, many more of the chapters are concerned with the first of these matters than with the second. Perhaps there should have been two books, not one. To many it may seem that the emphasis is misplaced, that the treatment of the issue should have been greater and that of the problem, less. Other writers will distribute the weights as they think necessary, but here it is felt that a proper appreciation of the issue required as thorough a statement as I could make of the problem, the detail of which is perhaps less familiar than the rhetoric that obscured it. The problem, then, is the nature of the Communist presence in the civilian agencies of the Federal government, and the issue, which is considered at briefer length, is the political exploitation of the problem. It may be repeated that it is the civilian agencies with which the book is concerned, not unions, the movies, the schools, factories, churches, or military establishments, about which several good accounts have already been written.

The principal sources of the book are the written public records, and the principal records are the hearings of the congressional investigating committees. This circumstance presents difficulty. So involved did the committees become in the partisan controversy that attitudes towards the information spread upon the record of committee proceedings became fixed by strong emotion rather than by strong reason. The committees were perceived by liberal-left partisans as engines of anti-intellectualist reaction, vehicles for the self-promotion of committee chairmen, agencies of bitter revenge upon champions of the New Deal by spokesmen for a coalition of small town provincials, anti-Semites, business Babbitts, labor-baiters, Ku-Kluxers, hypocrites, political philanderers, and narrow-gauge bigots. The committees, on the other hand, were perceived by conservative-reactionary partisans as agencies of fearless, honest, Christian, simple, moral men crusading against atheistic, materialistic enemies of the American Way of Life, abused by smear and innuendo beyond toleration, but steadfast nevertheless, of oak and oxen strength because their hearts were pure and their cause just.

Even extensive legislative investigations are only crude and approximate instruments for ascertaining fact, as indeed are court proceedings and research teams in the social sciences. In an evaluation of committee material much depends upon which committee you are talking
about. The hearings of the Fish and the McCormack-Dickstein committees in the early and middle 1930's produced no such arousal as
those in the 1940's and 1950's. An explanation for this is suggested in
Chapter I, "The Strategy of Alienation." Among the later committee
hearings with which this book deals are those of the Smith committee
of 1939–40, the Hiss-Chambers hearings conducted by the House Committee on Un-American Activities in 1948, the Tydings committee
hearings in 1950, the hearings on the Institute of Pacific Relations held
by the McCarran Subcommittee on Internal Security in 1951, and the
McCarthy subcommittee hearings on the Department of State in 1953.
Many others are used but those named are dealt with at length. No
single judgment covers all these committees. The Smith committee
was largely an absurdity, bent upon union-busting by an attack upon
the National Labor Relations Board which, among other delinquencies,
was accused of harboring an employee who had exhibited "a strongly
exaggerated social consciousness." But this does not mean that the
Smith committee hearings are worthless to a researcher. There are
great quantities of material in the record, the validity of which does
not depend at all upon one's attitude towards Congressman Smith of
Virginia, upon the purity of his motives, or upon any judgment about
the wisdom of Federal policy in the field of labor relations.

The Tydings committee hearings are almost unique in that they
represent an inquiry from the "liberal" side into charges against one
of the agencies of the government, the Department of State, and the
general conclusion in this study is that the charges were not sustained,
a conclusion also reached by a few of the articulate defenders of
Senator McCarthy. One of the by-products of the Tydings inquiry,
however, is a quantity of information about the *Amerasia* case which
justifies either of two conclusions — that there was an unlawful traffic
in government documents centered in the State Department, or that
the security system must have been porous. In the investigation of the
Institute of Pacific Relations, there is a great deal of information which
officers of the Institute themselves supply about the activities of the
organization, which may be taken as reliable, and which supports the
conclusion that in its relation with the Department of State there was
something very considerably less than the subversive conspiracy the
Senate subcommittee tried to establish and more than the quiet routine that officers of the Institute argued. The McCarthy hearings on
the Voice of America and the overseas information centers were almost

unmitigated frightfulness, a wrecking operation of great destruction, without redeeming features. Even the Permanent Subcommittee on Investigations, however, did publicize some useful information about the Government Printing Office. So, it must be said that universal suspicion of the committees is no more justified than universal approbation. Some of the material they collated or developed is worthless and some is not.

But what of some of the witnesses? How reliable are they? The ideological bias that distorts perception of the committees also, of course, distorts perception of the witnesses who testify. The left-liberal tends to discount the testimony of witnesses that fails to accord with his preconception and the conservative-reactionary tends to find constructive truth in every false appearance. Picking one's way through the tangle of assertions and denials by zealots, informers, misinformers, compulsive egotists, sick neurotics, the muckrakers, the sly, the payers-off of bitter grudges, the political arsonists who start fires of slander and defamation so as to shine in the reflected glow, the authors of hatred and hurt — to try to guess the truth, if any, in what they say challenges reason itself. When words are used not to convey intelligence but to defeat it, when double-speak is a club to stun the senses and to confuse rather than inform understanding, the very rules for the communication of sense are abolished.

Another problem is the weight to be given to the testimony of former members of the Communist Party. Normally this question would be resolved by such rules as apply to the credibility of any witness. In the heat of debate over the Communist question, however, the partisans of both extremes of view have tended to infuse judgments about credibility with predilection. This was and is especially true about the testimony of Elizabeth Bentley and Whittaker Chambers concerning the existence of espionage activities in Washington, and the people they named. Elizabeth Bentley was a mere courier in Soviet espionage while her sweetheart, a Russian agent, lived, and she left the service when he died. She was not the "spy queen" that lurid headlines proclaimed. Chambers, on the other hand, was an operator in the underground, endowed with intellect and, until he broke away, a committed partisan of the power goals of the Soviet Union.

It is not too much to say that the testimony of these two and the sensations of the Alger Hiss case, produced such a violent agitation that most subsequent debate has been structured by the commitments of choice that their statements forced. Without the Alger Hiss case, the six-year controversy that followed might have been a much tamer affair, and the Communist issue somewhat more tractable. The hatred for Chambers that the Hiss case produced among the partisans of the defendant still animates comment almost two decades after the confrontation of the accuser and the accused in the Hotel Commodore in New York. In November 1964, one reviewer of a collection of notes, letters, and other small pieces by Chambers dismissed them as of little importance. But he then used hundreds of words to say, repeatedly, that Chambers was a liar and a perjurer, and that his testimony was largely responsible for the jailing of "a respected public figure, who denied and still denies his charges." It was admitted that "much in the Hiss case remains puzzling" and that critics of Chambers are "likely to be hit on the head with that Woodstock" but this seemed less important than the fact that Chambers had said that there are nine inflections of the Russian noun when it is a fact "universally recognized by grammarians" that there are only six or seven, depending on whether you count the vocative.

There are palpable inconsistencies and contradictions, both careless and deliberate, in the testimony of these two witnesses, and confusions about some individuals, but the working assumption of this book is that the accounts of Bentley and Chambers are substantially acceptable. There are two reasons that support my inclination to believe, as correct, the main features of the accounts of Bentley and Chambers about espionage activity. The first is subjective. In the outlook of some today, the shaping rule of moral behavior is style, and people who "practise the virtues," to quote Rebecca West, "are judged as if they had struck the sort of false attitude that betrays an incapacity for art." But the law assumes that persons who testify under oath on the public record will generally be more careful about the truth than they might if they could not be held accountable in the courts for what they say. This assumption is not always true, of course, and in the Hiss-Chambers controversy it was clear that one of them was not telling the truth, although both were sworn witnesses. The law provides for such a contingency, however, and the perjury trial that ensued emphasizes the risk taken by one who violates his sworn oath. In addition, there are penalties of law for injurious statements not made under oath, and both Bentley and Chambers were respondents in libel actions. The case against Bentley concerned a matter of identification and was settled out of court. The case against Chambers set in train the very proceedings that led eventually to the conviction of Hiss.

The second reason is less subjective than the first. This is that there is some corroboration of the probable correctness of the accounts of Bentley and Chambers. Although it does not appear that either ever knew the other, and their journeys through Soviet espionage went by different routes, they had dealings with several individuals in and out of the government whom they identified, separately from each other.

There is also the silent testimony of the documents that Chambers produced in his defense against the libel action initiated by Hiss. As Chambers corroborates Bentley in part, so in part was Chambers corroborated by Lee Pressman. The credibility of the main accounts of Bentley and Chambers does not depend entirely upon the mere statements of each. Moreover, both were talking about very real people, very specifically in much of what they said. Bentley was refuted when she was wrong in the case of the Golds and William Taylor. Chambers was sustained when he was said by Hiss to have been wrong. The "fantasies" of Chambers and Bentley were not peopled by "Mr. X" or "highly placed persons," or "important officials" of ambiguous reference.

Maybe Chambers and Bentley did not fake the people they talked about but couldn't they have faked all the action? The very matter of corroboration may be thought to be suspicious. Could it not have been collusively obtained? Did not the FBI manufacture the "evidence"? Wasn't Bentley an unconvincing and neurotic old maid? Wasn't there something abnormal about Chambers? Who is covering up for whom? The problem of proof is shared by both history and law and it may be said that few issues are resolved in an ultimate sense, that is, by the indisputable establishment of the facts in every particular.

But I have come across no argument against the credibility of the main stories of Bentley and Chambers that seemed to me convincing enough to suspend the tentative conclusion that most of what they said was correct. Critics of both would ask that any conclusion be permanently deferred, but there does not seem to be any more reason to do so than there is in comparable areas of intellectual concern or of social fact. This is especially the case where it is clear that judgment has often been the servant of bias, as in the persistent suggestion that President Kennedy was assassinated by a conspiracy which may have involved the CIA, or Texas oil millionaires, or the FBI, or the Dallas police, or the John Birch Society. Because the Bentley-Chambers stories were, in the main, coherent, and because there was some corroboration, they are accepted as substantially correct until new evidence refutes them. This does not mean, however, that all that they said is relevant or useful to this book. Insofar as necessary, the assertions of Bentley and Chambers are referred to as assertions and where these assertions are denied, the denials are also included. The aim of this book is to be analytical, not accusatory, and to ascertain with as much exactness as the evidence will allow, what was probably true.

There is one form of rejoinder to accusation from which no inference of admission can properly be deduced and none is made. This is the plea of the Fifth Amendment. A Fifth Amendment plea is an assertion by the testifier that he thinks that a truthful answer to the question put to him would incriminate him. But this is not an admission of the truth of whatever statement he refuses to testify about and, indeed, it is not even an answer. It is a refusal to answer. The Fifth Amendment plea was always acknowledged as a right of the witnesses. Interrogators frequently pressed witnesses to testify, re-framed questions in artful ways, asked whether the witness believed that a truthful answer to the questions put would really be incriminating, and otherwise conducted skirmishes along the borders between the right of the committee to hear and the right of the witness to refuse to speak, but the protection of the witness in his refusal is and was, ultimately, impregnable. The only question in court actions against witnesses who have pleaded the Fifth Amendment is not whether they have a right to do so, but whether they have waived the right, a troublesome but not insoluble problem of adjudication.

How then employ the testimony of witnesses who pleaded the Fifth Amendment? All that can be done is to report that they so pleaded. In some instances it will seem curious to the reader that the plea was made, as when a witness declines on Fifth Amendment grounds to say where he worked when committee counsel has an official employment record in his hand. Or he may refuse to say whether he knows an individual whose name he used as an employment reference or with whom, even, he shared quarters as a roommate. The fact that the witness pleads the Fifth Amendment, then, cannot be construed as an admission, because it is not.

It may be noted in passing that the exercise of Fifth Amendment rights during Senator McClellan's long inquiry into labor racketeering was not, later, to excite the same compassion for witnesses that the Communist controversy aroused. Senator McClellan of Arkansas appeared on national television standing in the well of the committee room over a seated witness, a St. George stabbing the dragon with taunts of "yellow" for pleading the Fifth Amendment. At a later point, Robert F. Kennedy, counsel for the committee, more quietly told the witness that he lacked "guts" in pleading self-incrimination. No national committees were formed to protest the barbarity. In February 1965, President Johnson condemned the KKK and called upon Congress to investigate it. Before any steps were taken to act upon his recommendation, a national magazine said of the witnesses to be called in public session that those "who hide behind the Fifth will brand themselves and their organization almost as surely as by open confession." Many might have thought so.

The Communist problem and the debate over the Communist issue in two respects require an extended discussion of the context in which they occur. Considerable detail is supplied in these two instances because of the importance of the subject, and because much of the discourse on these matters has been cast in glib generalization and shouted in slogans. The first is the period of the 1930's when the international Communist party line changed from hard to soft, from a policy of alienation to one of enticement, with important consequences both for the perception of the Communist Party held in this country and for its contribution to the Communist problem of the 1940's. Without the change of the party line, it is not too much to say that there would have been no Communist problem at all. It has been thought desirable to explain in some detail the changing face of communism in the United States — the effect first of the Sixth World Congress of the Communist Party and the modification of the appearance of the party after the Seventh World Congress. The account also serves to indicate the manner in which the Communist Party, USA, cooperated then and in 1939 and 1941 with the changing policies of the world Communist movement. The change in the character of the membership of the American party was a direct result of the change in the party line between the two world congresses, and the account of this development is intended to throw light upon the nature of the American Communist problem at the time, and to counteract the stereotype of the party member that has been standard in right-wing attacks upon liberals. For sophisticated readers the account may seem very elementary but it is offered (to students especially) to place in context some of the events of the 1930's. At the least it may show that the initial entry into the government of members of the Communist Party was not exactly the crafty premeditation of conservative imagination.

The second of the matters for which extended background has been provided is the development of the Chinese civil war between 1925 and 1941. The purpose of this account is to demonstrate the nature of the conflict between Chiang Kai-shek and the Chinese Communists which was misunderstood or ignored by many commentators and public officials during the Second World War, and by their conservative critics when the war was over. It was not always evident in the general debate over China policy that the Chinese conflict was most nearly like a war between two independent states — the Kuomintang and the Communist Republic of China — and that all solutions of the conflict were doomed to failure that supposed that the tension was one between two parties under one sovereign authority. There were "two Chinas" as early as 1931 and the issues between them were basically no more easily negotiable than those between North and South Korea and North and South Vietnam, because neither could agree to any terms that did not suppose the subjugation of the other.

The extended discussion of the background of the Chinese civil war is necessary also because of the importance attached to developments in China by critics of the Administration after the war, and the pains that some, like the McCarran Subcommittee on Internal Security, took to maintain the proposition that a sinister Communist cabal in the Department of State engineered the triumph of the Chinese Communists in 1949 for subversive and disloyal reasons. China fell to the Communists for reasons having their roots in the early 1920's and although there were differences of opinion among the Foreign Service officers of the State Department during the war about the policy that should be enforced as between the Kuomintang and the Chinese Communists, events that could not possibly have been manipulated by the FSO's determined the final outcome. The background on the Chinese civil war then may help to lend perspective on the McCarran committee hearings on the Institute of Pacific Relations and the activities of the Department of State in the China theater during the Second World War.

It is worth emphasizing the point of view from which the Communist problem and the Communist issue of the 1940's and 1950's are approached. To explain all the alarm, outrage, and polemical outpouring as a consequence of conservative paranoia or liberal paranoia, or the machinations of left-wing propagandists, or the righteous reaction of true liberals to the inquisitions of bigoted Congressmen out to "get" the New Deal and destroy civil liberties, is certainly to oversimplify an extremely difficult period in American history. Even more serious, from the point of view of political research, is to substitute name-calling for such facts as can be ascertained, to mistake a complex political conflict involving diverse groups for a Manichaean alignment of the good and the bad.

This study tries to avoid these pitfalls, and to regard all propositions as demonstrated or not demonstrated, probable or not probable. On this basis, the conclusion seems warranted by the evidence that there was a Communist "problem" in the 1940's — that members of the party and their supporters occupied numerous positions in the Federal service, that they helped and aided each other in getting into desirable positions and holding on to them, that some of these officials and employees were organized into groups, and that some of these groups had espionage functions. The evidence does not seem to warrant the conclusion that the influence of these functionaries was very substantial. In the National Labor Relations Board for a period of three or four years, there was an earnest effort to make the Board an instrumentality for the promotion of a left-liberal tendency in labor policy, but the public record fails to demonstrate the successful steering of the policy of any agency into unnatural courses for subversive reasons. The most serious effort to establish the existence of such influence in the making of public policy was the attack upon the Foreign Service officers of the Department of State and, as has been said, the demonstration does not come off. Most of the efforts to prove such influence succeed merely in demonstrating that members of the Communist Party, or those accused of such membership, or those who may have cooperated with such persons, held identifiable positions of responsibility. The rest is inference, much of it implausible.

It is possible that the success of the espionage groups in Washington was greater than that of those involved in the making of domestic policy, but this is not entirely clear. It seems to be established that quantities of information were obtained from a number of "sources," but even Whittaker Chambers remarked that political espionage was a "magnificent waste of time." Military espionage was, perhaps, another matter and industrial espionage was still another. Since the focus of this study is on the civilian agencies of the Federal government in Washington, there is no basis for making judgments about espionage activity in military units and industrial installations, even if the information were publicly available, which seems not to be the case.

The partisan arousal over the Communist "issue" in the 1950's provides much that is demonstrable but also leaves open choices of interpretation that are broader than those involved in the Communist "problem." As has been indicated, it is possible that the political elements in the imbroglio have not been sufficiently appreciated, because there is a tendency among the writers to explain the phenomenon of McCarthyism in terms of generous and sweeping abstraction. The final portion of this study considers several interpretations that undertake to establish the meaning of McCarthyism, McCarthyism being taken as the enclosing concept that symbolizes the turmoil of half a decade.

Part One　Two Faces of Communism

. . . I want all to have a share of everything
and all property to be in common;
there will no longer be either rich or poor;
no longer shall we see one man harvesting
vast tracts of land, while another
has not ground enough to be buried in,
nor one man surround himself with a whole army
of slaves, while another has not a single attendant;
I intend that there shall only be
one and the same condition of life for all.

THE ECCLESIAZUSAE

Revolutions are effected in two ways,
by force and by fraud.

ARISTOTLE, *Politics*

I The Strategy of Alienation

The 1940 Constitution of the Communist Party, USA, said that the organization was a "working class political party carrying forward the traditions of Jefferson, Paine, Jackson, and Lincoln, and of the Declaration of Independence" against the reactionary enemies who would destroy democracy and all popular liberties.[1] But the phrases in this political paternoster were mere pieties of distraction, drawing attention from certain anomalies in the party position. The first was that the party was unattractive to the working class it presumptuously bespoke; and the second was that it was the New Deal and not the Communist Party that was carrying forward the liberal progressive tradition in American politics. The Communists were the fellow travelers, and their effort to identify communism and liberalism was as fraudulent as were the efforts, among the Roosevelt-haters on the other side, to identify liberalism with communism.

In one very important respect, the American Communist Party differed from all political organizations that had preceded it in American history. This was its connection with the world Communist movement, making of the local party a piece of political and administrative apparatus in a larger structure of international organizations managed from the Soviet Union. Although the Communist Party in 1940 formally dissolved its connection with the Communist International, the activities of the party had been closely orchestrated with the world Communist movement before 1940, and were to continue so afterwards.[2] The relation of the American Communist Party to the Inter-

1. Eighty-fourth Congress, Second Session, House of Representatives, Committee on Un-American Activities, House Report No. 2244, *The Communist Conspiracy*, Part I, Section E, p. 1 (hereafter cited as *The Communist Conspiracy*).

2. The dissolution of the connection with the Third International was necessitated by the Voorhis Act of 1940 which required the registration at the discretion of the Attorney General of all organizations with international affiliations. See *The Communist Conspiracy*, Exhibit No. 21, p. 165, for the statement of Earl Browder explaining the need to disaffiliate from the Communist International, originally appearing in *World News and Views*, October 30, 1940, pp. 691–692.

national had been somewhat loose and organizationally untidy, but as Earl Browder said in testimony in 1939, although it might deviate from the International on some questions of organization, it never deviated on political questions.[3]

This close collaboration is of importance to an understanding of events in the 1930's and thereafter; for to lose sight of the conscious accommodation of the policies of the American Communist Party to the Soviet line in foreign affairs, is to make inexplicable the turns and tergiversations of the national policies of the party, for which no other objective explanation exists.[4] Although the American Communist Party was not a field office of the International, with the locals responding with push-button alacrity to the dictate of the home office, the American party did resemble a dealer agency through which propaganda products, centrally manufactured, were distributed; and after the Lovestoneite confusions of 1928 and 1929 had been settled in Moscow, the American party had an exclusive franchise under Stalinist management.[5] This change coincided with the inauguration by Stalin of a left-

3. Seventy-sixth Congress, First Session, House of Representatives, Special Committee on Un-American Activities, *Investigation of Un-American Propaganda Activities in the United States,* vol. VII, September 5, 1939. Browder, a member of the Executive Committee of the International, in reply to a question about the relationship of the American party to the Comintern said, "So far as the political essence of the problem is concerned, there is the closest harmony between the Communist Party of the United States and the Communist International." At another place, Browder spoke of the relation between the American Communist Party and the Comintern in response to the following question: "Mr. Whitley: In other words, your relationship to the Communist International was just the same as if there had been a formal approval of the constitution? Mr. Browder: In its political essence, yes; in its organizational forms, no." *Ibid.,* p. 4309.

4. It was often difficult for the American party to anticipate the turns that the Soviet line would take. See for example, John Gates, *The Story of an American Communist* (New York: Nelson and Sons, 1958) for an account of the strains created among American Communists by the Soviet-Nazi Pact of August 23, 1939 and the attack upon Russia by the Nazis in June 1941, pp. 74–77 and 80–82. Although later an editor of the *Daily Worker,* Gates at the time was a member of the Young Communist League, of which he was the New York State chairman in 1941.

5. After three years of disorder and factionalism among the American Communists, the unity of the party with the International was first established in 1922, with the help of the Comintern representative, Valetski. Theodore Draper, *The Roots of American Communism* (New York: Viking, 1957), p. 388. After Foster and Lovestone had cooperated in expelling Cannon and the "left opposition" from the party in 1928, leading to the organization of the American Trotskyist movement, Lovestone sought to establish the thesis of "American Exceptionalism," arguing that political tactics which were meaningful in Europe were not necessarily of any value in the exceptional American situation. The Foster line pressed for a radicalization of policy (in line with cues from abroad) while Lovestone stayed with Bukharin. He stayed too long, and although he repudiated Bukharin in 1929, he was himself thrown out of the American Communist Party by Moscow. See Irving Howe and Lewis Coser, *The American Communist Party, 1919–*

ward trend in Soviet domestic policy, the purge of the right devi-
ationists, the installation of the first Five Year Plan, and the final
entrenchment of his power as dictator within the Soviet Union and in
the world Communist movement. Thereafter — in the thirties, the
forties, and the fifties — the courses of the American Communist Party
were a reflection of the world strategies of the Soviet Union.

The Sixth World Congress

Two world congresses of the Communist Party charted courses that
the American party followed with especially important consequences
for the controversies in the 1940's and 1950's over subversion. These
were the Sixth World Congress in 1928 and the Seventh World Congress in 1935. The Sixth World Congress, held in Moscow from July
15 to September 1, 1928, produced a program that publicly and unequivocally set forth the purpose of the Communist International to
work towards the world of the Marxist dream — a universal unity of
social systems under Communist regulation — to be brought about by
the force and violence of revolution. The program of the Sixth Congress has been called "the definitive exposition of the strategy and
tactics of the Communist International" [6] and it takes its importance
from the fact already noted, that it coincided with the consolidation of
Stalin's power in the party in Russia and his hegemony over the parties
of the world.[7] At the same time it was the first attempt, as Bukharin
explained, to state in clear and concrete fashion the task of establishing
the dictatorship of the proletariat throughout the world. Unlike the
Communist Manifesto the program was thought of as a blueprint and
not a mere propaganda piece.[8]

Although calculations of historic time for the onset of capitalist decay had to be somewhat sketchy and impressionistic, both Bukharin

---

1957 (Boston: Beacon Press, 1957) for a short statement about the crosses and
intricate double-crosses of this episode, chap. iv. See also Theodore Draper,
American Communism and Soviet Russia (New York: Viking, 1960), p. 357.

6. *The Communist Conspiracy*, p. 177.

7. Although Bukharin led the International at the Sixth World Congress, and
was the author of theses and programs that were eventually adopted unanimously,
the power and force behind him were those of Stalin. See the account of the
Corridor Congress (the caucus operating behind the façade of the Sixth World
Congress) in Benjamin Gitlow, *The Whole of Their Lives* (New York: Scribner's,
1948), pp. 154–156. Stalin had used Bukharin to prevail over Trotsky. As Gitlow
says, "In 1928 Bukharin was considered, next to Stalin, the most powerful man
in the international communist movement. The following year he became an
outcast, a man hounded and despised by the communists who had fawned at his
feet during his presidency of the Comintern." *Ibid.*, pp. 163–164.

8. For the text of the program, and a brief headnote explanation of its significance, see *The Communist International, 1919–1943, Documents*, selected and
edited by Jane Degras (London: Oxford, 1960), vol. II, 1923–1928, p. 471 (hereafter cited as *The Communist International, 1919–1943*).

and Stalin displayed some certainty about the stage to which capitalism had come by 1928. The First Period of revolutionary attainment had succeeded in establishing and consolidating "the proletarian dictatorship in an immense country, created a new type of State, the Soviet State," and thus produced an acute capitalist crisis. This was followed by a Second Period in which capitalism had, with all its inner contradictions, nevertheless succeeded in partial stabilization. A Third Period had arrived (1928),[9] one in which the contradictions would deepen and become more acute, and which would lead inexorably to the final collapse of capitalism and the triumph of communism. It was not said when the final collapse would occur and the time was left in the indefinite future. What could be expected in this third phase was a series of imperialist wars.[10] It was Stalin's view, or at least his position, that the collapse of capitalism was imminent and not remote, and that realism demanded recognition of this fact in a turn to the left. In world policy, this was to mean the increasing radicalization of Communist Party programs; the organization of dual unions; refusal to collaborate with social-democratic elements; hostility and distrust of all non-Communist associations including — but surely and especially — Socialists, trade unions, and liberals (called "social fascists"); and preparation for the assumption of power to come after violent class struggles and war.[11]

The Third Period line of extremism and isolation was immediately followed by the American party under its new Stalinist leadership, headed by William Z. Foster. In August 1929, for example, the Trade Union Educational League met in Cleveland on the call of Lozovsky, Stalin's representative, denounced the American Federation of Labor

9. See *The Communist International, 1919–1943*, pp. 481–488, for an exposition of the three stages in the program. Although the third stage had come in 1928, Bukharin was never very clear as to when the second stage had ended.

10. The vision of the third phase was summarized as follows: "Thus the edifice of world imperialism is being undermined from a number of directions, and the partial stabilization of capitalism shaken, by the contradictions and conflicts among the imperialist powers, the rising of the colonial millions, the struggle of the revolutionary proletariat in the mother countries, and finally, by the leading force of the world revolutionary movement, the proletarian dictatorship in the Soviet Union. The international revolution is advancing. Against this revolution, imperialism is mobilizing all its forces: expeditions against the colonies, a new world war, and the campaign against the Soviet Union are now on imperialism's order of the day. This is bound to release all the forces of the international revolution, leading inexorably to the downfall of capitalism." *Ibid.*, p. 488.

11. Theodore Draper has pointed out that "The timing of Stalin's Left turn had little to do with the state of capitalism. At the end of 1927 capitalism showed no signs of collapse. The American crash was still two years away. Even when capitalist stabilization gave way to capitalist crisis, the Stalinist third period policies of extremism and isolation provided the conditions for a fascist rather than a revolutionary upsurge." *American Communism and Soviet Russia*, p. 305. Like many of the world policies of the Soviet Union, the external line is a reflection of internal circumstance.

as a fascist organization, changed its name to the Trade Union Unity League, and organized itself as a Communist federation of trade unions to rival the AFL. The Communist political program of the new organization was aimed "to sharpen, deepen, and unite the scattered economic struggles of the workers into a general political struggle aimed at the abolition of capitalism and the establishment of a workers and farmers government." [12] In all, the TUUL organized (or reorganized) thirteen national revolutionary unions, and some local organizations, including a Trade Union Unity Council in New York.[13]

As part of its policy of the "united front from below" the Communist Party discovered the Negroes of the South. Theodore Draper has pointed out that it seems to have been Lenin who first drew the attention of the American Communist Party to the Negro question, the previous line having been that of left groups in America generally, namely, that there was no need for a special Negro program.[14] Through the middle 1920's the International and the American party had found that their way to Negroes was blocked by "Garveyism," the program of Marcus Garvey which looked towards the migration to Africa of large numbers of American Negroes, a program disparagingly referred to as Negro Zionism. The Program of the Sixth World Congress had scalding words for Garveyism, which it listed among a number of objectionable social-democratic tendencies bearing marks of bourgeois degeneration.[15] The question of policy was whether the dominating line should be "self-determination" or "equality." The Sixth World Congress chose to adopt the first position[16] and the Executive Commit-

12. Benjamin Gitlow, *I Confess* (New York: E. P. Dutton, 1940), p. 478. William Z. Foster had originally organized the Trade Union Educational League as a center for all progressive elements in the trade union movement. It was strongly against dual unionism and trade union splitting. The forced submission of the progressive objectives of the League to the requirements of Communist Party policy, however, soon cost the TUEL its significance as a rallying point for progressive groups and individuals. J. B. S. Hardman (ed.), *American Labor Dynamics* (New York: Harcourt, Brace, 1928), p. 22.

13. For a partisan account of the accomplishments of the Trade Union Unity League, see William Z. Foster, *From Bryan to Stalin* (New York: International Publishers, 1937), pp. 216–281.

14. Draper, *American Communism and Soviet Russia*, p. 321.

15. *The Communist International, 1919–1943*, vol. II, p. 519. The Program said, "Similarly, Garveyism, at one time the ideology of the American Negro petty bourgeoisie and workers, and still with a certain influence over the Negro masses, today impedes the movement of these masses towards a revolutionary position. While at first advocating complete social equality for Negroes, it turned into a kind of 'Negro Zionism' which instead of fighting American imperialism advanced the slogan 'Back to Africa.' This dangerous ideology, without a single genuinely democratic feature, which toys with the aristocratic attributes of a non-existent 'Negro kingdom,' must be vigorously resisted, for it does not promote but hampers the struggle of the Negro masses for liberation from American imperialism."

16. Draper, *American Communism and Soviet Russia*, p. 349.

tee of the Communist International (ECCI) spelled it out. The earlier view was that class was decisive and race was not — that Negro workers had more in common with white workers than they had with the Negro bourgeoisie, and that the latter were to be classed with white capitalists. After the Sixth Congress, however, American Negroes became an oppressed "nation" within the territory of the United States, requiring its own revolutionary movement, somewhat like the Negroes of South Africa. But the policy was curiously bifurcated. There was one for the South and one for the North. As to the Negroes of the South the ECCI Resolution on the Negro Question, October 26, 1928, said,

> The various forms of oppression of the Negro masses, who are concentrated mainly in the so-called "Black Belt," provide the necessary conditions for a national revolutionary movement among the Negroes. The Negro agricultural laborers and the tenant farmers feel the pressure of white persecution and exploitation. Thus, the agrarian problem lies at the root of the Negro national movement.[17]

Systematic work in the South was to require special stress to be laid upon the "right of Negroes to national self-determination in the southern states, where the Negroes form a majority of the population," [18] and the local program was to organize active resistance against lynching, Jim-Crowism, segregation, and other forms of oppression of the Negro population. But the program for the Negroes of the North was more traditional, for what was called the "existence of a Negro industrial proletariat of almost two million workers" merely required that they be "organized under the leadership of the Communist Party, and thrown into joint struggle together with the white workers."

The most extensive study of the Negro in America scarcely mentions the Communist Party, except to say that it was not attractive to Negroes,[19] but the party was active in propaganda, and exploited several

17. *The Communist International, 1919–1943*, vol. II, p. 554.

18. *Ibid.* Even at the time of the ECCI Resolution of October 26, 1928, the social situation to which the International addressed itself was outdated by a decade at least. For, although the migration of Negroes north from the southern states was a trickle before the First World War, it became great after the war. Negro farm ownership and tenancy (the latter being greatly predominant, of course) declined in the South from 922,914 holders in 1929 to 881,687 in 1930, a decrease of some 3 per cent, while the total Negro population increased from 10.4 millions to 11.8, an increase of almost 15 per cent. Source: U.S. Bureau of the Census, *Statistical Abstract of the United States: 1957*, Seventy-eighth edition (Washington, D.C., 1957), pp. 32 and 630.

19. Gunnar Myrdal, *An American Dilemma* (New York: Harper and Brothers, 1944), pp. 508–510. After pointing out that "To many white people in America, apparently, it seems natural that they should turn Communist," Myrdal says,

opportunities. One of these — the Scottsboro case — was taken up by American Communists and turned into both an important piece of propaganda and a money-making enterprise at the same time. Nine Negroes were arrested in Alabama for the alleged rape of two white women on a train going from Chattanooga to Scottsboro. The women were of doubtful reputation and one later recanted the testimony which had helped to convict the defendants. Eight of the nine were found guilty at the first trial in which they were represented by lawyers of the National Association for the Advancement of Colored People. The Communist Party took up the case, forced out the NAACP after a bombardment of scurrilous nature against the organization and its counsel, added mass pressure to legal defense, held rallies, collected money for the defense, arranged for the stoning of American diplomatic embassies and consulates around the world, organized mass meetings of protest not only in the United States but in Europe and in Central and South America, and depicted white southern justice as a stew of cant, duplicity, cruelty, connivance, mendacity, prurient self-righteousness, and class hatred.[20] Eventually, none of the Scottsboro defendants was executed, and four were freed, although the fate of the victims was less important to the Communist Party than the conduct of the campaign by party means and for party purposes. One of the cultural mementoes of the campaign was a play by John Wexley, produced by the Theater Guild. The dramatic point of the play is the rejection by the defendants of the services of the NAACP (The American Society for the Progress of Colored Persons in the play) and the advent of the ILD (called the National Labor Defense), done in a vaudeville dialect that even Amos and Andy fans would have found grotesque and objectionable,[21] and which in the 1960's — the decade of freedom marches — strikes the ear with deadly insult.

But the campaigns against southern injustice towards defendant Negroes were only part of the agitation. The main line was the establishment of the Black Republic, and this activity got to the Supreme Court of the United States. Angelo Herndon was a Negro Communist organizer who had joined the party in Kentucky and was sent to Atlanta to call meetings, recruit members, disseminate literature, and establish

"Still, the Communists have not succeeded in getting any appreciable following among Negroes in America and it does not seem likely that they will." *Ibid.*, p. 508.

20. Howe and Coser, *The American Communist Party*, pp. 212–216. See also the account of the entry of the International Labor Defense (ILD) into the Scottsboro case in Henry Lee Moon, *Balance of Power: The Negro Vote* (New York: Garden City, 1948), pp. 129–130, also cited by Howe and Coser.

21. John Wexley, *They Shall Not Die*, published in 1934 and reprinted in Granville Hicks and others (eds.), *Proletarian Literature in the United States* (New York: International Publishers, 1935), pp. 306–320.

an organization.[22] Among the tracts he carried was a pamphlet called *The Communist Position on the Negro Question* which bore a map of the United States on its cover. Across some of the southern states was drawn a black belt and the legend, "Self-Determination for the Black Belt." [23] In accordance with the ECCI Resolution of October 1928, the text argued that a separate nation should be carved out of the South, a Negro state that would be ruled by Negroes, freed from class domination, made independent of the rest of the American Soviet Union, and put in control of its own foreign relations. When arrested in 1932, Herndon was carrying this brochure, and others, and membership blanks. Bundles of the material were found in his room. Georgia tried Herndon under a Civil War statute that punished by death anybody who attempted to set off an insurrection of the slaves, or even brought within the boundaries of the state printed matter calculated to excite an insurrection among slaves, few of whom could read. The statute was a legal weapon against the distribution of Garrison's *Liberator,* and other inflammatory Abolitionist publications.

Since the only evidence against Herndon under the statute was that he had enrolled five members (Justice Roberts thought there were more), and had possession of printed materials that the prosecution could not show he had distributed, the Supreme Court reversed the conviction in a statement of unintelligible confusion. It was never clear whether the reversal was on the ground that the offenses had not constituted a clear and present danger or that the statute was unacceptably vague, but the case started the Supreme Court towards a re-affirmation of freedoms that it was not to contract until it upheld the convictions of eleven top Communists under a Federal statute much later.[24]

Besides the tough line on trade unions and Negroes, the savage alienation and isolationism of the Third Period policy in America led the Communist Party into attacks upon Franklin Roosevelt and the New Deal. It had entered national American politics in 1924 under the name of the Workers' Party and had run William Z. Foster for President and Benjamin Gitlow for Vice President, but had managed to get on the ballot in only thirteen states and to poll only 33,316 votes. Foster

22. *Herndon* v. *Lowry,* 301 U.S. 242, 57 S.Ct. 732, 81 L.Ed. 1066 (1937).

23. Zechariah Chafee, Jr., *Free Speech in the United States* (Cambridge, Mass.: Harvard, 1941), p. 388.

24. *Dennis et al.* v. *U.S.,* 341 U.S. 494, 71 S.Ct. 857, 95 L.Ed. 1137 (1951). Although Angelo Herndon got to the Supreme Court with the help of the International Labor Defense, others were not so fortunate. See Earl Browder, *The People's Front* (New York: International Publishers, 1938), p. 173 for the acknowledgement of the part of the ILD in the defense of Herndon and of Dirk De Jonge in *DeJonge* v. *U.S.,* 299 U.S. 353, 57 S.Ct. 255, 81 L.Ed. 278 (1937). But Mary Dalton and other Communists indicted under a different statute did not get out of the Georgia courts. See *Dalton* v. *State,* 176 Ga. 645 (1933).

spent much of his time attacking La Follette as an enemy of the workers. In 1928, Foster and Gitlow were again the candidates and the party was on the ballot in thirty-four states, winning 48,228 votes. Although it doubtless could not have done very much better if it had pressed the campaign vigorously, it did not in fact press it vigorously, since a large part of the officialdom of the party was in Moscow during critical months, attending the meetings of the Sixth World Congress. In 1932 the party ran Foster and James Ford, a Negro, as its candidates for the two highest elective offices, and polled 103,000 votes, an extremely disappointing showing inasmuch as great effort had been made to conduct an extensive campaign.

The campaign did have one result of consequence for the development of the Communist Party — it attracted some support from a broader band of writers and intellectuals than it had previously, from those who in the 1920's had voted regularly for Norman Thomas as a protest against the feel and texture of the culture. Declarations of support were forthcoming from what have been called "the more romantic intellectuals" [25] who published testaments of impatience with the hypocrisy of the major parties and the unvirile reformism of the Socialists; and, with chins lifted and shoulders squared, raised clenched hands in fraternal salute to the other workers of the world.

The American Communist attack upon the New Deal after the election of Franklin Roosevelt was unsparing. The theory of the attack was that Roosevelt was a hypocritical Hoover, that his purpose was to shore up the crumbling defenses of the capitalist class, and that this reformism was at best palliatory, if it was not in fact the execution of a fascist design to exploit the misery of the toiling masses.[26] In 1934 the Eighth National Convention of the American Communist Party resolved that "The Roosevelt regime is not, as the liberals and Socialists claim, a progressive regime, but a government serving the interests of finance capital and moving toward the fascist suppression of the workers' movement." [27] William Z. Foster said of the New Deal in 1936,

It was calculated to preserve the capitalist system by relieving somewhat the economic and mass pressure. The center of it, the National Recovery Act (NRA), was contrived in Wall Street and was first enunciated by the U.S. Chamber of Commerce. Many capitalist

25. Arthur M. Schlesinger, Jr., *The Crisis of the Old Order* (Boston: Houghton Mifflin, 1957), p. 436.
26. One observer has said of Roosevelt and communism, "Roosevelt's attitude toward communism was always the disenchanted one of skeptic, the rigorous one of the believer in the soundness of the American tradition, the negative one of the statesman aware of its totalitarian character." Mario Einaudi, *The Roosevelt Revolution* (New York: Harcourt, Brace, 1959), p. 96.
27. Howe and Coser, *The American Communist Party*, p. 232.

theoreticians hailed it as the beginning of fascism. To call the New
Deal socialistic or communistic is nonsense; it had nothing in common with either.[28]

According to the *Daily Worker*, the NRA was a fascist slave program,
and the Wagner Act of 1935, which provided the first firm national
guarantees of the rights of workers to organize and bargain collectively, was said to be an "anti-strike" measure. Under this "anti-strike
measure," constituent unions of the CIO became the biggest and most
powerful union organizations in the world.

Perhaps enough has been said to draw a conclusion about the Sixth
World Congress and the new Third Period line as applied to trade
unions, Negroes, and the New Deal. The conclusion is that the Communist Party appeared, with graphic clarity, to be what it said it was
— a revolutionary party bent on making a revolution, abjuring reformism and parliamentarianism, scorning the soft formulas of the
Socialists, bitter about the crypto-fascism of the New Deal, antagonis-
tic towards orthodox labor unions, determined to break the power of
union bureaucrats and payrollers living off the toil of the masses, pressing forward racialist formulas for racial tensions, a party that every
day proclaimed its ambition to destroy the existing social system by
the force and violence of a proletariat that it had not yet succeeded in
arousing. The party in this period lacks no defining line — its hard
edge has the sharp clarity of a knife. It was not a liberal party, it said
that it was not a liberal party, and few could possibly have confused
it with liberalism. Liberals and reformers were mere social fascists who
would be destroyed in a dialectical Armageddon.

The Fish and McCormack-Dickstein Committees

The nature of the party as a revolutionary agency — perceived as
such by itself and by others — is demonstrated in the hearings of the
Fish Committee of 1930.[29] Hamilton Fish of New York was the sponsor

28. Foster, *From Bryan to Stalin*, pp. 246–247.
29. Seventy-first Congress, Second and Third Sessions, House of Representatives, Committee to Investigate Communist Activities in the United States, *Investigation of Communist Propaganda*, 1930–31 (hereafter cited as *Fish Committee Hearings*). House Resolution 220 of the Seventy-first Congress established
the special committee of five members of the House of Representatives to investigate Communist propaganda in the United States "and particularly in our
educational institutions," the activities and membership of the Communist Party,
the "ramification of the Communist International in the United States," the
Amtorg Trading Corporation, the *Daily Worker*, and all "entities, groups, or individuals" alleged to teach or advocate the overthrow of the Government of the
United States by violence. Seventy-first Congress, Second Session, *Congressional
Record*, May 22, 1930, pp. 9390–9397. The chairman of the committee was Hamilton Fish, Jr. of New York, Republican. The other members were John E.

of the resolution to set up the committee which he headed to investigate Communist Party activities in the United States. A graduate of Harvard College with honors in the class of 1910, and of the Harvard Law School, a football player and war hero, Fish entered politics as a New York State Assemblyman in 1914. He moved to the Congress of the United States in 1918, where his father and grandfather had preceded him. Somewhat of a patrioteer, a man of rather flamboyant personality, a silk-stocking Republican of independent temperament (he supported William Borah for the presidential nomination in 1936), Fish summoned an odd lot of witnesses to testify about Communist activities in the United States — a priest, policemen, labor leaders, businessmen, officials of various patriotic organizations like the American Legion and the Daughters of the American Revolution, and several spokesmen for the Communist Party. William Z. Foster was the sixteenth witness, testifying towards the end of the hearings.[30] The committee, in fact, spent most of its time with the patrioteers, the businessmen, labor leaders, and clergy. Therefore, the testimony and findings represented what others said about Communists, rather than what they said about themselves, with the principal exception of Foster's testimony.

The members of the committee were not very well qualified for their tasks. Representative Carl George Bachmann of West Virginia acted the role of the patriotic "old line American," placed great faith in the activity of patriotic and fraternal organizations as a shield of the people against the menace of communism, proudly referred to the fact that his "wife and a good many of my relatives are members of the D.A.R.," and regarded the Communist movement as a specialty of aliens with which real citizens would have no truck. The direction and depth of his insight may be gathered from his question to a witness from the D.A.R.:

> I notice from the photographs that most of the people in the mob have the appearance of foreigners . . . Would you not say from your studies that a majority of them are aliens?

Representative Edward Everett Eslick of Tennessee played only a small part in the proceedings. His main concern (one shared by Bach-

---

Nelson, Maine, Republican; Carl G. Bachmann, West Virginia, Republican; William J. Driver, Arkansas, Democrat; and Edward E. Eslick, Tennessee, Democrat. All of the members of the special committee were lawyers. Bachmann, the Republican whip, was 40 years old, Fish was 42, and the others were in their fifties. In 1930 all had served at least three terms in the House. Fish was to serve the longest — from 1918 to 1944 when he was defeated for reelection.

30. The hearings show that 14 others spoke after Foster but all the statements were short ones.

mann also) was the Negro membership of the Communist Party. His fears could hardly have been assuaged in the colloquy he conducted with Foster at one point:

> Eslick: Do you believe in the social equality of the Negro and the white man?
>
> Foster: I do, most assuredly.
>
> Eslick: . . . you believe in interracial marriage between Negroes and whites?
>
> Foster: [Yes]
>
> Eslick: So you make no distinction between races?
>
> Foster: No, sir.[31]

Neither Representative William Joshua Driver of Arkansas nor Representative Robert E. Hall, who replaced him, said a single thing that was published in the hearings. The most tolerant of the committee members was Representative John Edward Nelson of Maine, although like the others, he seemed to come to the hearings with a minimum knowledge of the subject he was investigating.

Fish was the dominating figure, as chairmen of congressional committees customarily are. Through the use of his power as chairman, he set the agenda, called the witnesses, stopped the witnesses, created a favorable tone for those he favored, created an unfavorable one for those he did not, and rode hard on the members of the committee as well as the witnesses. For example, after Roger Baldwin of the American Civil Liberties Union had made a statement condemning the committee, Representative Bachmann angrily said, "I refute the statement and ask that it not go into the record because it is not true." [32] Fish refused the suggestion and allowed Baldwin to proceed and finish his statement. With less important witnesses, however, Fish used his power somewhat arbitrarily. Two witnesses were Alexander Grube, an alien seaman who had escaped from a forced labor camp in the Soviet Union, and Reverend Thomas S. McWilliams, a professor at Western Reserve, who had just traveled in Russia. To Grube, who had a little difficulty expressing himself, Fish said, "Can you make it a little briefer? The committee is not interested in your travels . . . all of this you have told us so far amounts to nothing." [33] But the committee was allowed to listen to an extensive narrative by Professor McWilliams of his travels in Russia, although even McWilliams confessed that he was not

31. *Fish Committee Hearings*, vol. IV, p. 388.
32. *Fish Committee Hearings*, p. 407.
33. *Fish Committee Hearings*, pp. 85–87.

sure of its relevancy. Fish created a pleasant mood for William Green, president of the American Federation of Labor, when he said, before Green had testified, ". . . later on I propose to release a statement . . . as to the work that your organization has done in combatting . . . [Communist] activities . . . [you are] entitled to the gratitude of . . . the American people." [34] But when Roger Baldwin was testifying, the following exchange occurred:

> Fish: You mention here . . . what you think is in the best interests of the United States of America. Did you ever serve the United States . . . in the World War?
> Baldwin: I certainly did.
> Nelson: I do not think that is fair. We have no jurisdiction to inquire into the personal affairs of this witness.
> Fish: I do not press the question, but I ask the question.[35]

The lead-off witness was Father Edmund Walsh, the Vice President of Georgetown University, who talked about the history of the Communist movement. William Green of the AFL and Edward F. McGrady, Legislative Representative of the AFL, talked about the Trade Union Unity League. Walter S. Steele, the general manager of the *National Republic*, a right wing magazine, discussed the subversive intentions of the Communist Party. Ralph H. Burton, counsel for the Daughters of the American Revolution and other patriotic organizations, wanted legislation punishing even indirect advocacy of revolution, and the head of the DAR, Mrs. William Sherman Walter, spoke of the "gigantic force" that was now concentrating on "capturing little children," although the daughters of the Daughters were doubtless safe. Police Captain Edward J. Kelley of Washington, D.C., said that the white Communists he had observed were an illiterate class of foreigners, and Dr. William B. Reed told the committee how worried he was about a possible increase in syphilis because of the free love practiced by Communists.

Besides the crackpot, fright-wig testimony by patrioteers and others, there was testimony about the organization of the Communist Party, the activities of the TUUL, the strikes the party had promoted, disruptive economic competition by the Soviet Union, workers schools, the activities of Amtorg, the Soviet trading corporation, forced labor camps, and Communist missionary work among foreign born and foreign language groups in America. But the material was a hodge-podge,

34. *Fish Committee Hearings*, vol. I, p. 43.
35. *Fish Committee Hearings*, vol. IV, p. 412.

a miscellany of unconnected matters, bits of this and that about the Soviet Union and the Communist Party, swept into the record unchecked and unfocused. Most of the witnesses came to the hearings with panaceas of coercion to peddle, and although the facts might be disorderly, the prescriptions were loud and clear.

The most striking and incisive testimony of the hearings was that supplied by the principal Communist witness, William Z. Foster, at the time the head of the TUUL.[36] After being sworn in as an atheist, Foster read a long statement to the committee in which he said that the purpose of the Fish Committee was to outlaw the Communist Party. He said that the activity of the Communist Party was the protest and struggle of the masses against unemployment, low wages, and starvation, and observed, "If the Fish Committee wants to investigate the growth of Communism, let it investigate the miserable situation under which the masses live and from which only Communism shows them the way out." [37]

He said that the Communist Party had ten to twelve thousand dues-paying members in the United States, and that some 60 to 70 per cent were foreign born although a majority of these were naturalized citizens because the Communist Party had them naturalized in order to vote. The mission of the membership was perfectly clear — it was to serve the program of the Communist Party, to lead the proletariat to the inevitable dictatorship after the violent overthrow of the bourgeoisie. The workers of America and of the world, he said, have only one flag — the red flag. "All capitalist flags are flags of the capitalist class, and we owe no allegiance to them." [38] When he was asked whether Communists in the United States took orders from the Communist International, he regarded the question with a kind of contemptuous amazement. The Communists in the United States *work out policies* with the International, he said.[39] Foster's statements harbored no confusion about the differences between communism and liberalism. The party he described was a small, trained, compact vanguard of the proletarian revolution (which would inevitably come) with a leadership without illusions, a dedicated and committed cadre of the captain-priests of a new social vision, tough, relentless, unsentimental. It was a national agency joined to an international organization whose goal it was to free the workers of the world from the class exploitation of a

36. For a contemporary description of the appearance of Foster before the Fish Committee, see Edmund Wilson, "Foster and Fish," *The New Republic*, December 24, 1930, pp. 158–162.
37. *Fish Committee Hearings*, vol. IV, p. 352.
38. *Fish Committee Hearings*, p. 385.
39. Wilson, "Foster and Fish," p. 161.

decadent and corrupt capitalist oppression. It was not liberal but radical, not reformist but revolutionary. And it would prevail.

One of the best epitaphs for the supposed bankruptcy of liberalism was written by Edmund Wilson, then an editor of the *New Republic*. Writing at the time of the Fish Committee hearings, he said,

> I believe that if the American radicals and progressives who repudiate the Marxian dogma and the strategy of the Communist Party hope to accomplish anything valuable, they must take Communism away from the Communists, and take it without ambiguities or reservations, asserting emphatically that their ultimate goal is the ownership of the means of production by the government and an industrial rather than a regional representation. What we need in this country is a genuine opposition, and it is a long time since the liberals have been one. A genuine opposition must, it seems to me, openly confess that the Declaration of Independence and the Constitution are due to be supplanted by some new manifesto and some new bill of rights.[40]

This statement was published two weeks after an admiring account of the appearance of Foster before the Fish Committee.[41]

The Fish Committee after six months of hearings made a report with recommendations for legislation, and Representative Nelson made a report of his own.[42] The committee report said that the International was part and parcel of the Russian Communist Party and of the Soviet government, that American Communists owed allegiance to the International, and that the American party which had received more than 100,000 votes in the 1930 elections had probably some 500,000 to 600,000 sympathizers in the United States. It noted that industry was the principal point of penetration, that youth activities were centered in the programs of the Young Pioneers and the Young Communist League, that about 80 per cent of the membership of the summer camps was either alien or foreign born, that a large percentage of all known district organizers were of Jewish origin, but that the party had had little success with Negroes. It said also that there had been recruiting around army camps, that wheat, lumber, and manganese were being "dumped" in the United States, that Amtorg was not connected with subversive activities but that the American Civil Liberties Union as

40. Edmund Wilson, "An Appeal to Progressives," *The New Republic*, January 14, 1931, pp. 234–238, at p. 238.
41. Wilson, "Foster and Fish," 158–162.
42. Seventy-first Congress, Third Session, House of Representatives, Special Committee to Investigate Communist Activities in the United States, *Investigation of Communist Propaganda, House Report 2290*, January 17, 1931.

well as the International Labor Defense and the Garland Fund (the American Fund for Public Service) were closely connected with the Communist Party.[43]

Because the committee tended to perceive the party as an alien or-ganization — not only metaphorically but literally — it was recom-mended that the immigration laws be amended to prevent the admis-sion of Communists into the United States, that the naturalization of Communists be ended, that aliens who visited Russia for Communist training be denied re-entry into the United States, and that the naturali-zation of foreign-born Communists be canceled. All publications ad-vocating revolutionary communism were to be made unmailable. Such publications were also to be denied the channels of interstate com-merce, and the use of secret codes by governments and the trade agencies of governments with whom the United States had no diplo-matic relations was to be prohibited. The committee also recommended that the Communist Party be outlawed. Representative Nelson thought that more harm would be done to civil liberties by the recommenda-tions of the majority than his estimation of the danger would warrant.

In still one other forum, the revolutionary character of the Ameri-can Communist Party was affirmed by Communist Party officials with the force and clarity that characterized their public statements about themselves in the Third Period. This was in the McCormack-Dickstein Committee hearings of 1934–35 which, although concerned primarily with fascist and Nazi activities, nevertheless devoted some time and energy to the Communist movement.[44] Most of the witnesses on Nazi and fascist activities were directly involved in such movements as the

43. The inclusion of the American Civil Liberties Union with the International Labor Defense and the Garland Fund was a sad irony. Roger Baldwin had testi-fied that although William Z. Foster had been a member of the board of directors of the American Civil Liberties Union, he had recently resigned in a dispute with the ACLU about Communist bail-jumpers defended by the ACLU whose bail-jumping embarrassed the defense. He also testified that the only other Com-munist in the upper reaches of the ACLU organization was a representative of the International Labor Defense with which the ACLU cooperated, Anna Rochester. The congressional committee tended to regard the defense of Com-munists in legal actions as, in itself, Communist activity. The failure to make this distinction plagued the ACLU throughout the thirties and forties. The association of the American Civil Liberties Union with the Communist Party in a united front operation was ended in the period of the Stalin-Hitler Pact when the Union voted to oust its more notorious Communist Party members. See Eugene Lyons, *The Red Decade* (Indianapolis: Bobbs-Merrill Company, 1941), pp. 372–373.

44. Seventy-third Congress, Second Session, House of Representatives, Special Committee on Un-American Activities, *Investigation of Nazi Propaganda Ac-tivities and Investigation of Certain Other Propaganda Activities* (hereafter cited as *McCormack-Dickstein Hearings*). The committee was established by House Resolution 198 of the Seventy-third Congress. Seventy-third Congress, Second Session, *Congressional Record*, March 20, 1934, pp. 4934, 4949.

German-American Bund and the Friends of New Germany,[45] and most of the witnesses about the Communist movement were the clerics, policemen, businessmen, labor leaders, and patrioteers who had been the principal witnesses in the Fish Committee investigation.[46] The lead-off witnesses on the Communist movement were Earl Browder, Executive Secretary of the Central Committee of the Communist Party, and James Ford, organizer of the Harlem section of the CPUSA. Browder's estimate of the membership of the Communist Party in 1934 was 24,000 according to his report to the Communist International in 1935,[47] and the influence of the party was said to extend to hundreds of thousands who were not party members. He and James Ford reported that the recent convention of the party, the Eighth Convention, had adopted a resolution of the Comintern affirming the revolutionary nature of the

45. The Nazi witnesses were aggressive and hostile, as in later hearings in the 1940's and 1950's the left wing witnesses were to be. One of the witnesses in the McCormack-Dickstein investigation was Herbert Schmuck, president of the Friends of New Germany. He referred to Dickstein in the German press as the "representative of New York's Ghetto . . . the rottenest and the most shameful and the most impudent liar I have ever seen . . ." *McCormack-Dickstein Hearings*, December 29, 1934, pt. 2, p. 678. Another witness, Raymond Healey, the twenty-one-year-old editor of *Healey's Irish Weekly*, had the following conversation with Dickstein: Healey: "Don't you know that there is Communism in America?" Dickstein: "The least that you can do is to be respectable and try to cooperate with the government." Healey: "What government?" Dickstein: "The United States Government." Healey: "I thought you meant the International Finance Company." *McCormack-Dickstein Hearings*, November 30, 1934 and December 5, 1934, p. 4.

46. In fact some of the witnesses in the McCormack-Dickstein investigation had appeared in the Fish Committee investigation. Among these were Mrs. William Becker of the Daughters of the American Revolution, Rev. Edmund A. Walsh of Georgetown University, William Green and Matthew Woll of the American Federation of Labor, and Walter Steele who, by the time of the 1934 hearings, was appearing as head of an organization called The American Coalition. For his testimony, which was very comprehensive, and was to be presented again in the later Dies Committee investigations, see *McCormack-Dickstein Hearings*, December 17 and 18, 1934, p. 218.

47. Estimates of the membership of the CPUSA throughout this period and later are as confusing sometimes as the reported memberships of church organizations. In his 1935 report to the Communist International, however, Browder had estimated the membership as follows: 1931: 8–9,000; 1932: 12–14,000; 1933: 16–19,000; February 1933: 20,593; July 1933: 15,000; 1934: 24,500; and May 1935: 31,000. See Nathan Glazer, *The Social Basis of American Communism* (New York: Harcourt, Brace, 1961), p. 92. William Z. Foster's statement to the Fish Committee put the membership of the CPUSA in December 1930 at 10–12,000. Two decades later, Foster put the party membership in the period 1929–1933 as an increase "from somewhat less than 10,000 members to 18,000. . . ." William Z. Foster, *History of the Communist Party of the United States* (New York: International Publishers, 1952), p. 292. At the Eighth Convention of the Communist Party, USA, held in Cleveland, April 2, 1934, the breakdown of the membership enrollments was as follows: 1930: 7,500; 1931: 9,257; 1932: 14,475; 1933: 19,165; 1934: 23,467. Howe and Coser, *The American Communist Party*, p. 225.

party.[48] Meyer Baylin, educational director of the Communist Party in Los Angeles, said that there was nothing secret about the party; Pettis Perry, identified with the International Labor Defense, said that revolution was in *his* mind; Lawrence Ross, secretary of the Communist Party in Los Angeles, said that the time was not now; and Max Kitzes, identified as bookkeeper for the Communist Party, said that all his transactions were in cash and that he could not produce any books. The final report of the committee devoted ten pages out of the total of twenty-four to the activities of the Communist Party and, for emphasis, took out of the testimony certain excerpts from the Browder statement indicating that the CPUSA was a section of the Communist International.[49]

48. This assertion was in contrast to the undertaking of the Soviet Union when the United States resumed diplomatic relations in November 1933. In the Russian note to President Roosevelt transmitted by Maxim Litvinoff on November 16, 1933, it was said to "be the fixed policy" of the USSR to refrain "from any act tending to incite or encourage armed intervention, or any agitation or propaganda having as an aim the violation of the territorial integrity of the United States, its territories or possessions, or the bringing about by force of a change in the political or social order of the whole or any part of the United States, its territories or possessions." Jane Degras (ed.), *Soviet Documents on Foreign Policy* (London: Oxford, 1953), vol. III, 1933–1941, p. 36.

The American party was worried by the Litvinoff agreement. According to Benjamin Gitlow: "A private meeting was arranged between members of the Secretariat of the Communist Party, Litvinov, and the chiefs of the OGPU apparatus in New York. At this meeting, Litvinov assured the frightened communists that they had nothing to worry about. The agreement, he explained, was between governments and not between the United States government and the Communist International. Not having specifically referred to the letter, Litvinov went on to explain that the Comintern is not restrained by the Soviet government and is free to carry on whatever activities it deems necessary. 'After all, comrades,' he concluded, 'you should know by this time how to handle the fiction of the tie-up between the Comintern and the Soviet government. Don't worry about the letter. It is a scrap of paper which will soon be forgotten in the realities of Soviet-American relations.'" *The Whole of Their Lives*, pp. 264–265. The letter referred to was the note sent by Litvinoff to Roosevelt already cited.

49. Seventy-fourth Congress, First Session, House of Representatives, Special Committee on Un-American Activities, *Investigation of Nazi and Other Propaganda*, *Report*, H. Report 153, February 15, 1935. There were four Democrats and three Republicans on the McCormack-Dickstein Committee. Since the focus of the investigation was Nazi and Fascist activity, with Communist activity somewhat secondary, but by no means unimportant, the test of the competence of the committee should perhaps be judged by their awareness and understanding of the extreme right. Carl M. Weideman, Democrat, Michigan, was in his first and last term as a Congressman, a lawyer, of German descent, and at some pains to make it clear that the German-American population was not the Bund, or vice versa. Charles Kramer, Democrat, Kentucky, was in the first of what were to be five consecutive terms of service in the House of Representatives. The other two Democrats were seasoned Congressmen. Samuel Dickstein of New York had been in the House since 1923 and was to continue until 1945. Born in Vilna, Russia, he was also chairman of the House Committee on Immigration, and was especially well informed about the social and economic problems of

In the course of the investigation, Samuel Dickstein said to William Green, the president of the American Federation of Labor, about the Fish Committee, "It is my recollection, and I have studied the matter, that not a bit of legislation was presented as a result of the report [of the Fish Committee], nor was any recommendation made which would bring about the destruction of this un-American Communist movement." [50] At another time, he suggested that a permanent Committee on Un-American Activities be created,[51] but the Congress was not to accede to this proposal until 1945. Congress did later act on two of the proposals of the McCormack-Dickstein Committee — the recommendation that Congress enact a statute requiring the registration of foreign agents, and a recommendation to allow United States attorneys outside the District of Columbia to proceed against recusant witnesses.[52]

The efficiency and decorum of the McCormack-Dickstein Committee have been remarked upon by at least one writer studying congressional investigations of communism,[53] and there is some basis for forming such a judgment. In fact, the procedures of the committee were a model of scrupulous conduct. Executive sessions were held before the public sessions, care was taken to see that extraneous names were not mentioned casually to the detriment of private reputations, and witnesses succeeding each other supplied complementary information in a well-defined pattern. The counsel for the McCormack-Dickstein Committee was a sixty-two-year-old Democrat from Georgia by the name of Thomas Hardwick who had become a member of the Georgia House of Representatives at the age of eighteen, had

---

immigrant groups. John McCormack of Massachusetts, the chairman of the committee, had been in the House of Representatives since 1928. The Republicans on the committee had been in Congress from eight to fifteen years: U. S. Guyer of Kansas, Thomas A. Jankins of Ohio, and J. Will Taylor of Tennessee. They had virtually no role to play at all in the committee. Most of the hearings were in fact hearings held by subcommittees in the charge of the individual members of the majority. When the full committee met, the minority members were present about half the time, rarely spoke when present, and then on unimportant matters.

50. *McCormack-Dickstein Hearings*, December 17 and 18, 1934, p. 14.

51. *McCormack-Dickstein Hearings*, p. 77.

52. The McCormack Act of 1938 required the registration of all agents of foreign governments disseminating propaganda in the United States. 52 *Stat.* 631. Dickstein attempted to get the House of Representatives to establish a Committee on Un-American Activities in 1937 for the principal purpose of investigating Nazi activities but the House rejected his proposal. Seventy-fifth Congress, First Session, *Congressional Record*, April 8, 1937, p. 3289. At least part of the stated reason for rejection was the belief of some Congressmen that racial prejudice would be aroused — that is, that anti-Semitism would be stimulated.

53. August Raymond Ogden, *The Dies Committee* (Washington: Catholic University of America, 1945), p. 34.

served as United States Senator for one term, and as Governor of
Georgia for one term. His most remarkable service had been performed as counsel for the Communist defendants in the Gastonia strike,
where he appeared for the American Civil Liberties Union. It is
difficult to imagine that the Dies, Thomas, Wood, Velde, and Walter
leadership of later House investigations would have found this experience to be meritorious, but it is undoubted that his service contributed
much to the fair-minded efficiency of the committee proceedings.

American Images of the CPUSA in the Third Period

Despite Samuel Johnson's contempt for the dictum of George
Berkeley that the physical world has no reality independent of our
perception of it, the reality by which we regulate our behavior can
only be the one we perceive — the "pictures in our heads," in Walter
Lippmann's phrase. The alteration of these pictures may be full of
traumatic risks. Whittaker Chambers, in an account of his conversation
with Max Bedacht about leaving the open Communist Party and
entering upon underground work, said

> Every man to whom such a summons has come must have found
> it deeply unsettling. Just the implication of undefined power lurk-
> ing behind a figure like Bedacht and suddenly giving him ambiguous
> meaning, is disturbing. The terms "special institution" and "under-
> ground" could only mean secret, possibly dangerous party work.
> They could only mean that, somewhere beside the open Communist
> Party, there existed a concealed party which functioned so smoothly
> that in seven years as a Communist I had not suspected it. At that
> time, I thought of the underground as an underground of the
> American Communist Party.[54]

In accordance with his new perception of the party, and of his role
in it, the whole mode of Chambers' life changed, both in his relations
with members of the apparatus to which he belonged, and in his public
appearance.[55] Within the party itself there were different perceptions
of its role and mission; it was a different thing to those in the open
organization and to those in the underground. And even within the
open party there were contrasting images — what has been called the
"exoteric" image and the "esoteric" image,[56] the public impression
and the private experience.

54. Whittaker Chambers, *Witness* (New York: Random House, 1952), p. 276.
55. In the open party, carelessness of dress was tolerated, but when he went
into the apparatus underground one of Chambers' first acts was to buy himself
clothes with money given him for this purpose. Chambers, *Witness*, pp. 282–283.
56. See Gabriel Almond, *The Appeals of Communism* (Princeton: Princeton,
1954), pp. 5–6. Of this distinction Almond says: ". . . at the point of entrance

Perhaps enough has been said at this point to establish the nature of the public impression created by the leaders of the Communist Party in the political term known as the Third Period, but it may be summarized in a different way. Coinciding as it did with the solution of a divisive factional fight in the American party, and the triumph of the Stalinist elements, the Third Period in the United States was the stage for the Communist militant on the Leninist model. The Third Period Communist was no leader waiting for the inevitable collapse of capitalism and the accompanying rapid increase in the class consciousness of the proletariat, an agent merely leading and guiding the rise of forces determined by history and predicted by science. The Communist leader marching to the tune of the Sixth World Congress was one who was prepared to execute a tough and hard radicalization of the Communist Party and its programs, and to prepare for the assumption of power which the imminent collapse of capitalism was to make possible. The proletariat and other social formations were to be organized and brought under the control and direction of a tight, strongly knit, and centrally controlled Communist Party in which discipline and obedience were essentials.[57] There are many testaments to the depersonalization of the recruit and the creation of a new and dependent personality suitable to the needs of the party.[58] The goal of all this energy was the

---

into the movement, the party is all things to all men. It tempts the workman with an image of the alert and militant trade unionist, concerned with the pragmatic and immediate needs of the working class. It confronts the peasant with the ideal of the militant defender of the rights of the small farmer and farm laborer. It offers the intellectual the tempting model of the artist or writer employing his talents effectively in the cause of social justice. It offers the native colonial the image of the militant patriot driving the imperialists before him, wiping out the indignities of centuries of exploitation and humiliation. And before all potential party recruits and supporters, it holds up the generalized image of the militant and effective reformer locked in battle with injustice. These images are the public or exoteric images of the Communist movement; they are the tools of agitation especially fashioned to suit the susceptibilities of particular audiences. Once drawn into the movement, the neophyte is exposed in varying degrees to the esoteric model of the Communist militant. Perhaps for most of the rank and file of the Communist movement — and this is particularly true in the mass parties [abroad] — this exposure to the esoteric model is quite superficial, and in this sense they are not true Communist militants." *Ibid.*, p. 5.

57. "The Blanquist movement in France came closest to the later Leninist conception. It was a conspiratorial armed formation dedicated to the seizure of power by coup d'état." Almond, *The Appeals of Communism*, p. 11.

58. For one, see Frank S. Meyer, *The Moulding of Communists* (New York: Harcourt, Brace, 1961). The party spokesmen did not conceal the disciplinary nature of the control in the party. For example, Earl Browder in testimony in 1939 entered upon the following colloquy in a congressional investigation: "Mr. Matthews: A member must carry out all decisions of the party or be expelled from the party? The Chairman: Is that correct? Mr. Browder: Yes; that is correct. Mr. Starnes: A party member does not have any latitude or discretion in the matter — he has to carry out orders or get out? Mr. Browder: The party

conquest of power in which "all the capitalist parties — Republican, Democratic, Progressive, Socialist — will be liquidated, the Communist Party functioning alone." [59]

The public agitations of the Communist Party served to reinforce this image. For example, the *New Masses* in its first issue of 1934 said,

> In presenting this first issue of the *New Masses* as a weekly, we think we can best indicate our program in these concrete terms: The *New Masses* has friends and it has enemies. It supports the militant sections of the working class, the living core of which is the Communist Party. Its enemies are the enemies of the working class, the upholders of capitalism: bankers, militarists, imperialists, Fascists, labor fakers, Social Fascists, and all other open or hidden defenders and apologists of the capitalist order.[60]

John Strachey said that "an attempt to establish the Fascist form of the capitalist dictatorship in America is inevitable." [61] Congress was described as "Some five hundred bankers, corporation lawyers, Ku Klux Klansmen, factory owners, preachers, insurance brokers, vaudeville actors, and odd numbers such as a former representative of Machado, the Assassin, and gentlemen of unknown occupations. . . ." [62] And Michael Gold in the poet's corner of the literary barricade thought that

> It is better to be in jail for the Working Class
> Than in the White House for the capitalists.[63]

Subsequent issues in 1934 continued the familiar themes. Henry Ford would "no doubt" become "one of the financial angels of some fascist gang," and was doomed to go under to his rivals in automobiles "unless he can get a better set-up with the state apparatus." [64] James Burnham admired Lenin because Lenin identified himself with the working class: "Such an identification is the farthest extreme from demagogy: Lenin was not a Hitler nor a Roosevelt." [65] Because —

---

has to carry out orders." Seventy-sixth Congress, First Session, House of Representatives, Special Committee on Un-American Activities, Hearings on H. Res. 282, *Investigation of Un-American Propaganda Activities in the United States*, p. 4417.

59. William Z. Foster, *Toward Soviet America* (New York: Coward-McCann, 1932), p. 275.

60. *New Masses*, January 2, 1934, p. 3.

61. John Strachey, "Fascism in America," *New Masses*, January 2, 1934, p. 8.

62. Marguerite Young, "Congress — Who's In It and Who Owns It," *New Masses*, January 2, 1934, p. 16.

63. Michael Gold, "Tom Mooney Walks at Midnight," *New Masses*, January 2, 1934, p. 19.

64. *New Masses*, January 23, 1934.

65. James Burnham, "His Place in History," *New Masses*, January 23, 1934, p. 15.

presumably — of the profit-fattening, monopoly-swelling, labor-grinding programs of the Roosevelt Administration, the *New Masses* advised its readers to support the Communist Party platform and to vote for Communist candidates in the fall elections in 1934.[66] When the election was over there were references to "Roosevelt's post election offensive against labor." [67] and to the "Mussolini-schooled boys of the Administration." [68] On the literary and theoretical side, the readers of the *New Masses* were treated to a *corrida* in which three philosophers ran from communism while a fourth baited them for doing so.[69]

The extreme right of opinion honored the Communist Party image of itself. A good example of this was the statement of Walter Steele, editor of the *National Republic*, testifying before the McCormack-Dickstein Committee as a representative of the American Coalition. In the course of his presentation, he noted the reported and estimated membership of the Communist Party, which was certainly small, but said that the figures in themselves were misleading. There were six times as many Communists in the United States, he said, as there were in Russia at the time of the revolution in 1917.[70] The suggestion in this would seem to be that the danger in America from Communist subversion was at least as great as it had been in Russia in 1917. The suggestion failed to give fair weight, however, to objective differences between Russia in 1917 and America in the thirties. The American population was mostly literate and the Russian population had not been. Disaffection had fermented for three decades in Russia and was to explode in the heat of war. And the Russian political system had historically been antidemocratic, providing little or no opportunity for a peaceable redress of grievances.

Moreover, in 1917 the Bolshevik faction was represented in strategic places in the government. In 1934, the policy of extremism and isolation of the American party directed Communist action in the United States towards the trade unions, the youth, the Negro, and other minority populations — in short, the social formations, not the governmental. Even though some candidates ran for office, the effort was largely gesture. Government was to be conquered, not wooed; the administration was fascist in its tendency; and like the Socialists and the social fascists it was to be opposed, not joined. In the mood of the

66. "Why We Vote Communist," *New Masses*, October 30, 1934, p. 8.
67. *New Masses*, December 4, 1934, p. 4.
68. *New Masses*, December 11, 1934, p. 4.
69. John Dewey, Bertrand Russell, and Morris R. Cohen explained why they were not Communists, and Sidney Hook explained why he was. Paul Salter and Jack Librome, "Dewey, Russell, and Cohen," *New Masses*, July 17, 1934; July 24, 1934.
70. *McCormack-Dickstein Hearings*, December 17 and 18, 1934, p. 218.

party in the Third Period it is hard to imagine Communist participation in the Treasury Department of Ogden Mills and William Woodin, in the Democratic Party of John J. Raskob, John Nance Garner, and Alfred E. Smith, and in the Department of Agriculture of Arthur H. Hyde. The impending collapse of the capitalist system on which the resolutions of the Sixth World Congress had been predicated would bring power to the cadres of the Communist Party anyway.

Among the leaders and spokesmen of the prevailing middle class orthodoxy the Communist Party was seen less as an American agency of a foreign power than as an alien association of foreigners, a curious and fanatical enterprise of unassimilated immigrants, largely of Jewish birth and Russian or German nationality. In 1952 Attorney General Tom Clark gave a Senate committee the results of a study of the ethnic composition of the Communist Party leadership which had been prepared in 1947 by the Department of Justice.[71] The militants studied were a group of 5,000 or so who were active in party affairs, had held office, and so on. Of this group, 56.5 per cent were born in Russia or neighboring countries, born of one or both parents from this area, or married to a person of Eastern European origin. In addition, another 34.9 per cent were either from stock of other foreign countries or were married to stock from other foreign countries. Only 9 per cent of the militants were native-born of native stock, and married to native stock.[72] What was true of the late forties was true of the early and middle thirties. The organization report made to the Sixth World Congress by Jack Stachel said that the working class in America were foreign born. Immigrant groups made up the bulk of the working force, and the party was rooted in the immigrant groups.[73] Questions like those asked by Representative Bachmann in the Fish Committee hearings — don't the people in mob photographs look like foreigners? — reflected widely-held conceptions of the party as an association that was non-American, as well as un-American.

Still another evaluation of the Communist Party in the Third Period was that of those who thought that any mischief that the International might conceivably cause in America was not great enough to justify the risk of civil liberties they thought to be in jeopardy from the Fish and the McCormack-Dickstein investigations. The Fish investigation

71. Eighty-first Congress, First Session, United States Senate, Committee on the Judiciary, Subcommittee on Immigration and Naturalization, Hearings on S. 1832, pt. 1, p. 318.

72. Almond, *Appeals of Communism*, discusses these ratios at pp. 201–202. Morris L. Ernst and David Loth, *Report on the American Communist* (New York: Holt, 1952), at pp. 143–144, uses the same figures although there is no citation.

73. Glazer, *The Social Basis of American Communism*, p. 76.

had been opposed in Congress on the ground among others that it would provide publicity for communistic propaganda and that it would jeopardize basic freedoms — speech and thought.[74] Maury Maverick of Texas opposed investigations of the Fish kind up until the establishment of the Dies Committee, and thereafter, on the ground that the seriousness of the danger was not great enough to warrant the threats to basic freedoms that they entailed. The Maverick position, strongly libertarian, was adopted by many critics of the congressional investigations, from the Fish Committee throughout the 1940's and 1950's. Some did so for ulterior reasons, perhaps, but there was always a substantial element of vocal opinion that declined to accept the view of the committees and of the officials of the Communist Party — that the party was a revolutionary organization, and that it meant business.

Finally, there was the view that the subversive intention of the party should not be disregarded, since it was plainly to be a spur to acts, but that its results should not be overestimated. This was the opinion of Representative Nelson in his separate statement in the Fish Committee report. He warned that the Communists were to be taken seriously and that they were not to be dismissed as a disreputable company of "ignorant rogues and selfish adventurers." He added that

> The actual dues-paying members of the Communist party in the United States are, as a rule, men and women of foreign extraction, of unusual intelligence and ability, actuated by no hope of personal reward and absolutely devoted to the Cause, for which they are ever ready to sacrifice their time, health, and talent. . . . The communist is a zealot, supremely self-confident, and as devoid of compassion as an executioner. . . . All this gives them a strength and influence all out of proportion to their numbers, a kind of strength possessed, perhaps, by no other organization in this country.[75]

But although the Communist Party was to be taken seriously, it should not excite mindless panic but should be weighed and judged as to its results. Representative Nelson said that patriotic associations, "to encourage their financial support, do not minimize either the extent of radical activities or the consequent danger to the Republic." [76] In his opinion, however, the economic and world-wide threat of communism was greater than the political and national threat posed by the party in the United States. The committee had been able to uncover only two Communists in the Army, and twelve to fifteen in the Navy.

74. Ogden, *The Dies Committee*, p. 23.
75. Special Committee to Investigate Communist Activities in the United States, *Investigation of Communist Propaganda, Report*, p. 77.
76. *Ibid.*, p. 92.

Out of 810 schools in New York, only three had any noticeable Communist activity. Less than one per cent of the AFL was Communist. But despite this evidence, "Since this committee began its investigation . . . imaginative souls have ascribed to the Communists responsibility for nearly every untoward event that has disturbed our industrial and social life." [77] It was Representative Nelson's conclusion that communism constituted "no instant national threat"; and that "Freedom should be the rule in America rather than restrictive legislation, and we should approach with reserve the consideration of any criminal statutes that seek to fetter the operation of the human mind or to encroach in the slightest degree on those rights guaranteed in our Constitution to the lowliest individual in the United States." [78]

Thus the principal perspectives on the Communist Party which were to dominate in the decades thereafter were stated at the very beginning of the 1930's. The extreme left tended to treat the present in the Soviet Union as though it did not exist, and the future as though it had arrived;[79] while the extreme right spoke as though yesterday were eternal and tomorrow need never be born. The left and right gave each other unearned credentials as sinister forces of morbid malignancy; and simple facts were made to yield apocalyptic inference. The Communist movement was "un-American" less because its majority was foreign-born than because its social theory and political technique were alien in the American culture. On the other hand, the coercive prescriptions of the right were features of a philosophy more like the bitter conservatism of the post-Enlightenment than the tolerant optimism of the Jeffersonian ideal. Ignorance made the extremes unintelligible to each other, and their conversations across the hearing table were a dialogue of the deaf. It was true that

> Imagination frames events unknown,
> In wild fantastic shapes of hideous ruin,
> And what it fears creates.

The Third Period of isolation and extremism ended with the Seventh World Congress; and the relative clarity of the Communist Party was to disappear in a blur of confusion.

77. *Ibid.*, p. 96.
78. *Ibid.*, p. 79.
79. On this point see the statement of Louis Fischer in *The God That Failed* (New York: Bantam Books, 1952), p. 208. Although Fischer was not a member of the Communist Party, he was a supporter of the Soviet Union up until the Nazi-Soviet Pact of 1939.

II   *The Strategy of Enticement*

The typical Third Period line of Soviet, Comintern, and CPUSA spokesmen made it appear that Norman Thomas was more dangerous than Hitler. At the Eleventh Session of the Executive Committee of the Comintern in 1932, D. Z. Manuilsky said, "In order to deceive the masses, the Social Democrats deliberately proclaim that the chief enemy of the working class is Fascism. It is not true that Fascism of the Hitler type represents the chief enemy. . . ."[1] With the achievement of power by the Nazi Party and Adolf Hitler, however, the fantasies of the Third Period gave way to the political reality of the Third Reich. In the dream world of Third Period supposition, the workers were expected to rise and overcome their oppressors. They did not rise in Germany, and there was no civil war on the Marxian model. The regime did not collapse but grew strong. It did not pose a threat in domestic politics only, it menaced the shining homeland of the working class, the "only searchlight of hope that cuts through the deep gloom of the capitalist world."[2] The policy of isolation pursued by the Stalinist regime and the Comintern, and therefore the Communist Party USA in the Third Period — a policy of extremist alienation in domestic and international affairs — promised to leave the Soviet Union without friends or allies, aloof and vulnerable to its foes. The party line therefore changed, and with the change the magnitude, focus, and direction of the Communist problem in the United States also changed.

1. Quoted in Jan Valtin, *Out of the Night* (New York: Alliance Book Corporation, 1941), p. 352. The miscalculation made by the German Communists of the strength of the Hitler movement in 1932 — shared by many others — is evident in the opinion expressed to Valtin when he asked Ernst Thaelmann, "What will happen when Adolf Hitler seizes power?" Thaelmann's answer was, "Let him, he won't last long. The workers will rise. There will be civil war." *Ibid.*, p. 351.
2. Earl Browder, *What Is Communism?* (New York: Vanguard, 1936), p. 225.

The Seventh World Congress

The drive for collective security and the united front was announced at the Seventh World Congress of the Communist International held in Moscow, July 25–August 20, 1935, and the spokesman of the change was Georgi Dimitroff, a Bulgarian Communist, and defendant in the Nazi trial of 1933 for alleged conspiracy in the burning of the Reichstag.[3] The historic *démarche* was made by Dimitroff in a political report to the Congress which began with an attack on fascism, described as "the open terrorist dictatorship of the most reactionary, chauvinistic and most imperialist elements of finance capital." [4] In the face of this mortal threat, the "first thing that must be done" was the formation of a "united front," a unity of action among all elements of the working class in every country and all over the world,[5] a program that would ally the Communist Party in "joint action with Social-Democratic Parties, reformist trade unions and other organizations of the toilers" through "mass action locally, to be carried out by the local organizations through local agreements." [6]

In a review of "key questions" of united front action in various countries of the world, Dimitroff considered and commented upon the American situation. American fascism comes forward principally in the guise of opposition to fascism, "which it accuses of being an 'un-American' tendency imported from abroad," [7] he said, with some lack

3. In 1928, Stalin had assigned the leading role in the Sixth World Congress to Bukharin. In the Seventh World Congress, he assigned the leading role to Dimitroff, appearing at the Congress on only one occasion. It has been suggested that the Gestapo, unlike the Russian secret police, made the mistake in 1933 of failing to brainwash the defendant before bringing him to public trial. Before an assembly that included newspapermen from abroad, Dimitroff established an alibi, and the Nazis felt that they had to release him. For this view see Eighty-fourth Congress, Second Session, House of Representatives, Committee on Un-American Activities, House Report No. 2242, *The Communist Conspiracy*, Part I, Section C, *The World Congresses of the Communist International*, p. 292 (hereafter cited as *World Congresses of the Communist International*).

4. Georgi Dimitroff, *The United Front* (New York: International Publishers, 1938), p. 10. The theory of Norman Thomas was that fascism was a middle class phenomenon and not a conspiracy of the upper classes. In 1934 he said, "If we are to generalize, we can say only that Fascism is the last stand not only of capitalism, in an economic sense, but of the whole middle class culture and prestige, both of which had been warped and twisted by the passion and fear dependent on war, a disappointing peace, and economic collapse. . . . It was not, until the very end in Germany, the *first* choice of business interests, and certainly not of Hindenburg." *The Choice Before Us* (New York: Macmillan, 1934), p. 53. Dimitroff also rejected the theory of the "British Socialist Brailsford," that fascism was "the revolt of the petty bourgeoisie which has captured the machinery of the state." *The United Front*, p. 11.

5. Dimitroff, *The United Front*, pp. 30–31.

6. Dimitroff, *The United Front*, p. 37.

7. Dimitroff, *The United Front*, p. 41.

of clarity and specification. It tries to portray itself as the custodian of the Constitution and of American democracy, and although it had not yet become a directly menacing force, it might be one in the very near future. With something less than an adhesive grasp of American politics, Dimitroff proposed that fascism in America could be counter-vailed by a Workers' and Farmers' Party which would be one specific form of the mass people's front which was yet to be established.[8]

Dimitroff then proposed a political tactic that was to produce incomparable mischief. He was actually talking about the penetration of the mass organizations established in fascist countries — like the Hitler Youth Leagues, *Kraft durch Freude,* sports organizations, and the *Doppo Lavoro* in Italy — but the tactic he proposed had universal uses. As he stated it,

> Comrades, you remember the ancient tale of the capture of Troy. Troy was inaccessible to the armies attacking her, thanks to her impregnable walls. And the attacking army, after suffering many sacrifices, was unable to achieve victory until with the aid of the famous Trojan horse it managed to penetrate to the very heart of the enemy's camp.
>
> We revolutionary workers, it appears to me, should not be shy about using the same tactics with regard to our fascist foe, who is defending himself against the people with the help of a living wall of his cutthroats.[9]

Any comrade who might find the tactic of the Trojan horse deceitful and "humiliating" must be regarded as "a windbag and not a revolutionary," for unless he was willing to employ such methods as necessity forces, he would be unable to lead the masses to the overthrow of fascism.

Although Dimitroff drew inspiration from the Greek classics for part of his program, he drew freely on fascist models also. The piquant "putrefaction of capitalism" which was fascism supplied certain essences that the comrades were to appropriate for themselves. Nationalism was a big thing in Germany, Italy, France, and America; and the fascist authors of criminal activities in these countries had been at some pains to ally themselves with national heroes like Garibaldi, Joan of Arc, and Washington and Lincoln. The Communists must also identify themselves with national symbols and not hand over "to the fascist falsifiers all that is valuable in the historical past of the nation, that the fascists may bamboozle the masses." [10] With little inconven-

8. Dimitroff, *The United Front,* p. 42.
9. Dimitroff, *The United Front,* p. 52.
10. Dimitroff, *The United Front,* p. 78.

ience, Dimitroff fitted the new nationalist line into the orthodoxy of proletarian internationalism that the Marxian texts had prescribed.

The iron edge of Third Period policy was pounded flat by the thumping dictum that "Sectarianism finds expression particularly in overestimating the revolutionization of the masses, in overestimating the speed at which they are abandoning the positions of reformism, and in attempting to leap over difficult stages and the complicated tasks of the movement." [11] This had been precisely the Comintern policy in Germany and America and Dimitroff was aware that the new line contradicted the old, but new conditions made new tactics necessary, and "wiseacres who will sense in all this a digression from our basic positions" were dismissed with a proverb from Bulgaria.[12]

In the discussion which followed his report to the Seventh World Congress of the Communist International, Dimitroff applied the new formulas to the American situation. Whereas party functionaries in America for two years had been flogging the fascism of the New Deal, it now appeared that these comrades were guilty of stereotyped thinking. Dimitroff said,

> Even now we have survivals of a stereotyped approach to the question of fascism. When some comrades assert that Roosevelt's 'New Deal' represents an even clearer and more pronounced form of the development of the bourgeoisie toward fascism than the 'National Government' in Great Britain, for example, is this not a manifestation of such a stereotyped approach to the question? [13]

Although it had not previously been made very clear in the speeches and writings of Communist leaders that Roosevelt was really more victim than master, it was now evident that the real villain in the American piece was finance capital. Indeed one would have to be very partial to hackneyed schemes "not to see that the most reactionary circles of American finance capital, which are attacking Roosevelt, are above all the very force which is stimulating and organizing the fascist movement in the United States." [14] To fail to see this was to mislead the working class in its struggle against its worst enemy.

The Seventh World Congress adopted resolutions in keeping with the line laid down by Dimitroff, and proclaimed that "at the present historical stage it is the main and immediate task of the international labor movement to establish the united fighting front of the working class." [15] And with the new line laid down by the International, a new

11. Dimitroff, *The United Front*, p. 85.
12. Dimitroff, *The United Front*, p. 91.
13. Dimitroff, *The United Front*, p. 99. The remarks here quoted were from a speech made on August 13, 1935.
14. Dimitroff, *The United Front*, p. 99.

line appeared in the American Communist Party. As John Gates, former editor of *The Daily Worker,* described the excitement of the change:

> The [Communist] Congress approved the new policy of subordinating the ultimate goals of the Communist movement to the drive against fascism. Important new changes were made in Communist theory: Communists could now support their own capitalist-democratic governments, even participate in them; socialists were their brothers and comrades; unity was essential not only within the labor movement but also with the middle classes and even with capitalists who opposed fascism. This was the People's Front. . . .
>
> New impetus was given to the efforts of the American Communist Party to become a serious political trend in American life, an indigenous social organization.[16]

But before the new act could go on, there was a certain amount of scene-shifting to be done. The Trade Union Unity League was abolished, and the workers went into the unions of the American Federation of Labor.[17] Within the Federation, the growing disaffection over industrial unionism between William Green, Matthew Woll, and William Hutcheson of the Carpenters' Union on the one hand and John L. Lewis on the other resulted in the split at Atlantic City in October 1935, and members of the party entered the newly organized CIO in great numbers.[18] William Z. Foster's work which reflected the hard leftism of the Third Period, *Toward Soviet America,* written in 1932, was officially discarded by the party and by Foster himself, since he was faithfully submissive to the new party line.[19] The primer of the new policy was written by Earl Browder who said, "We Communists claim the revolutionary traditions of Americanism. . . . We are the Americans and Communism is the Americanism of the twentieth century." [20]

15. Resolution on the Report of Georgi Dimitroff, adopted August 20, 1935 by the Seventh Congress of the Communist International, in *World Congresses of the Communist International,* p. 351.

16. John Gates, *The Story of an American Communist* (New York: Nelson and Sons, 1958), p. 38.

17. Of the dissolution of the TUUL, William Foster some twenty years afterwards was to say, "Although it displayed some sectarian and dualist tendencies [one of the delicately phrased understatements of the time] the T.U.U.L. nevertheless played an important constructive role in the labor movement." *History of the Communist Party of the United States* (New York: International Publishers, 1952), p. 304. The TUUL disbanded in July 1935.

18. See Benjamin Gitlow, *The Whole of Their Lives* (New York: Scribner's, 1948), p. 261.

19. Gates, *Story of American Communist,* pp. 38–39.

20. Browder, *What Is Communism?* p. 19.

The swing from the hard line to the soft occurred on three main political fronts with varying results: overtures for unity with the Socialists; the establishment of a Workers and Farmers Party; and change in the Communist Party attitude towards the New Deal of Franklin Roosevelt.

In the program for unity with the Socialists, the Communist Party moved toward the right, the Socialists under Norman Thomas moved toward the left, but a juncture of the two left tendencies was never effected.[21] Earl Browder and Norman Thomas appeared in a series of debates in the fall of 1935, but Thomas continued to refuse proposals for a Popular Front on the general ground that the victory of socialism was the pre-condition for the defeat of fascism. He was lectured by Earl Browder for exhibiting symptoms of the infantile disorder — "left-wing" communism — against which Comrade Lenin had warned.[22] The Socialist Party in the years 1934 to 1938 was invaded, undermined, split, and re-split by factional controversies over policy and organization engineered by the Militant Group and the Revolutionary Policy Committee, Lovestoneites and Stalinists, Trotskyites and Communists. Under Thomas, although the Popular Front was rejected, certain collateral organizations like the Socialist Students' League for Industrial Democracy joined with the Communist American Student Union, and the Socialist Workers Alliance joined with members of the Communist Unemployed Councils when the latter organizations were abolished. The result in each of these cases was that the unified organizations came under Communist leadership and control. The Trotskyites were finally expelled from the Socialist Party in 1938 at which time they organized the Socialist Workers Party. The Socialists refused to join with the Communist Party in the May Day parades of 1938 and 1939, and thereafter the question of collaboration became moot when the Communist Party line changed again, following the Hitler-Stalin Pact of 1939.[23]

21. Irving Howe and Lewis Coser, *The American Communist Party, 1919-1957* (Boston: Beacon Press, 1957), p. 327.

22. Earl Browder, *The People's Front* (New York: International Publishers, 1938), p. 170. Browder thought the following passage from Lenin was especially pertinent to Thomas: "To tie one's hands beforehand, openly to tell the enemy, who is now better armed than we are, whether and when we shall fight him, is being stupid, not revolutionary. To accept battle at a time when it is obviously advantageous to the enemy and not to us is crime; and those politicians of the revolutionary class who are unable to 'maneuver, to compromise' in order to avoid an obviously disadvantageous battle are good for nothing." Browder twitted Thomas for his "extremism" although he said that it was an "extremism in words" for "we would never accuse him of being extreme in deeds." *Ibid.*

23. See Benjamin Gitlow, *I Confess* (New York: E. P. Dutton, 1940), pp. 578–584 for an account of the author's role in the politics of the Popular Front with the Socialists, and for his statements about the parts played by J. B. Matthews, former head of the Communist front group, the American League Against War

The effect of the Popular Front agitation on the Socialists, in short, was to split them into irremediable confusion and to compromise the Socialist Party as the traditional alternative it had been for intellectuals disaffected by the major parties.

The question of the Workers and Farmers Party that Georgi Dimitroff had raised in the Seventh World Congress was also handled with considerable clumsiness. The first reaction in the American Communist Party was to go ahead with the effort, and the leadership in this undertaking was taken by Earl Browder in the late winter of 1935–36.[24] Although the election of 1934 had shown that the support for the Roosevelt Administration among the people of the country was massive, presaging the most comprehensive presidential sweep in history that Roosevelt was to achieve in 1936,[25] the Communist Party acted as though it were now about to assume the political leadership of the masses. In the fantasy of the Dimitrovian strategy, the American party was to win the workers and farmers away from the major parties, the parties of reaction.[26] But in the late spring of 1936, this third party policy was abandoned and an ambivalent policy of support for Roosevelt was worked out instead.[27]

---

and Fascism, and Joseph P. Lash, at first head of the Students League for Industrial Democracy and later of the American Student Union. Although Gitlow uses phrases like "Then the Communists won over Joe," and "He became one of their secret agents" (*ibid.*, p. 581), John Gates, former editor of the *Daily Worker*, was later to refer to Lash as a "Socialist and head of the American Student Union," one of those who "broke with us" after the Hitler-Stalin Pact of 1939. *The Story of an American Communist*, p. 76.

24. At this time, Browder was the symbol of the new policy, and its principal spokesman. Foster was the symbol and principal spokesman of the tough anti-collaborationist policy of the Third Period. A sign of the change in policy in the Communist International was the new prominence given to Browder in Moscow and the role of second fiddle forced on Foster. Browder was to represent the soft line during the years of the Second World War also when the Communist Party became the Communist Political Association. When this line changed in 1945 Browder was deposed and Foster restored to prominence. In 1952 and therefore after the demotion of Browder, Foster, as required by the cold war line, was severely critical of Browder policies in the middle 1930's even though those policies were then in accord with the party line of the time. Thus, on the question of the farmer-labor party, Foster's later revisionist view was that Browder was saved from making a serious blunder when his proposal for such a party was not endorsed. Foster, *History of the Communist Party*, p. 336.

25. This was the only off-year election in the twentieth century when the party in the White House not only did not lose seats in the Congress but in fact increased the number by nine. It forecast the making of the famous Roosevelt coalition that was to last through 1948 when it began to crack.

26. Howe and Coser quote Alex Bittleman on this point in April 1936, "The real and immediate problem is: to win away the masses from the capitalist parties." *The American Communist Party*, p. 329.

27. Sandor Voros relates that he had been selected by the Comintern's American representative in the spring of 1936 to manage the national campaign for Earl Browder, the choice having fallen on him because of his success in 1935 in

The policy towards Roosevelt was ambivalent because it worked for his election without endorsing him as a candidate. The slogan of the party was "Defeat Landon At All Cost — Vote for Earl Browder." [28] As the party slogan indicated, the tactic was to attack Landon as the leader of the major forces of reaction and fascism, and to work for Roosevelt behind the scenes.[29] Confused comrades who asked how they could defeat Landon at all cost by voting for Browder just did not understand the iron laws of history.[30]

Thus on three major fronts of domestic political engagement the new Communist line was, at the most, mischievous and disruptive, divisive and confusing, but certainly not a major element in shaping the direction and courses of American political life. The policy of the Seventh World Congress was indeed a major re-orientation of Communist international tactics but much of the new thrust was directed to European rather than to American conditions. The new line was shaped by the foreign policy requirements of the Soviet Union in a context of imperial ambition on the Nazi side and a weak and unreliable system of alliances on the other. It was not a call to defend America and other free peoples from fascist aggression, but a call to defend the Soviet Union as the socialist fatherland. Although the terms "fascist" and "fascism" were freely applied to financial and other business groups by Communist orators, and picked up by imitators, the truth is that there was no "fascism" in America to combat.[31]

The curious lack of fit between the political prescriptions of Dimitroff for the United States and the conditions of American life was born in defects of understanding abroad that go back to Marx himself. As Earl Browder was to say many years later, after he had been de-

getting 55,000 votes for I. O. Ford, Communist candidate for governor of Ohio. Voros was asked whether he thought that the Communists would be able to poll three million votes for Browder in 1936 and he says that he replied, "At least that! Maybe even more than La Follette polled in 1924. With our new party line we can really go places!" By the time Voros prepared a scheme for the campaign, the decision had been made to concentrate on the defeat of the Republican candidate without endorsing Roosevelt. *American Commissar* (Philadelphia: Chilton, 1961), pp. 264–265.

28. Voros, *American Commissar*, p. 265.

29. Foster summarized the Communist Party position as follows: "The position of the Communist Party in the 1936 elections, in line with its general attitude toward the New Deal, was one of objective, but not official support for Roosevelt." *History of the Communist Party*, p. 333.

30. Sandor Voros has said that when he was asked the question how to put the party slogan into actual practice, he would reply, "By defeating Landon at all cost and by voting for Earl Browder." *American Commissar*, p. 265.

31. The best that Dimitroff could do in inventing a fascist bogey in America was to refer obliquely to the slogan "Share the Wealth" as a ruse of anti-capitalist demagoguery engineered — according to the analysis of fascism made by Dimitroff — by finance capitalists. *The United Front*, p. 14.

posed from leadership in the American Communist Party, "Karl Marx was a man of positive and sharply defined opinions. With regard to America, however, he displayed an ambiguity that was never overcome." [32] The ambiguity was that he saw America in two "quite different images, both of them clear but contradictory to each other." The first was a strong America, independent, and mature, a world leader in political and economic progress; and the other was that of an America still, economically, only a colony of Europe. But, alas for the ambiguity, Marx did not put America outside the doctrine of impoverishment as the "absolute general law of capitalist accumulation" — the doctrine that the capitalist rich get richer and the proletarian poor get poorer until the objective condition produces the overthrow of the bourgeoisie and the advent of the dictatorship of the proletariat. America stood outside the pattern at the time Marx wrote, yet "he did not ask if the pattern should be changed to make room for America, but only how America must change to conform to the pattern." [33] Although the subtitle of Browder's later statement, over two decades after the Seventh World Congress, was "Why Communism Failed in the U.S.," he was hard at work in the late thirties to make the patient fit the prescription.

The New Image of the CPUSA

The image of the American Communist Party which had been so clear and sharp in the Third Period of isolation and radical extremism softened and blurred, and one of those principally responsible for making the alteration was Earl Browder himself. In 1936, he explained in a major tract that most of the public notions about the Communist Party were false.[34] In the first place, the American Communist Party did not take its orders from Moscow,[35] although it was united with brother parties all over the world in the Communist International. Nor was the party one of revolutionary violence.[36] The transfer of power from the capitalists to the proletariat would doubtless be accom-

32. Earl Browder, *Marx and America* (New York: Duell, Sloan, and Pearce, 1958), p. 3. As William Z. Foster's revisionist American Communist Party history disparaged and degraded the work of Browder, so Browder, in these lectures, was able to pay his respects to Foster who had said in his *Outline History of the Americas* that the material prosperity of America was based upon the exploitation and robbery of other nations. Of this book Browder says, "This illiterate parody of Marxism was read by hardly anyone in America, but was extravagantly praised by Moscow publications, and translated into many languages all over the world." *Marx and America*, p. 6, n. 1.
33. Browder, *Marx and America*, p. 4.
34. Browder, *What Is Communism?*
35. Browder, *What Is Communism?* p. 205.
36. Browder, *What Is Communism?* p. 163.

panied by violence but it would not be initiated by the workers. It
would be launched by the exploiters to save their spoils. "Communists,
despite what their enemies say, do not advocate or idealize violence." [37]
The immediate aims of the Communist Party were reformist, and they
could join with others in a united front farmer-labor party to press for
higher wages, the right of workers to organize, adequate relief programs for the unemployed and the aged, public works, and union
wages on all public works projects. Browder and the Communist Party
were against sales taxes and they were for a veterans bonus, farm relief, civic rights for Negroes, the abolishment of judicial review, the
extension of the referendum and recall, the prohibition of professional
strike-breaking, the protection of the rights of women, and peace.[38]

Although the American Communist Party did not take its orders
from Moscow, nevertheless the example of the Soviet Union must always remain a beacon for the toilers of the world, and of America. No
demagogue like Father Coughlin need shed crocodile tears over the
workers in the Soviet Union who "are now busily building a great,
prosperous, strong, peaceful socialist society with the greatest democracy ever known in history. . . ." [39] The workers' paradise was a
standing rebuke to "rich capitalist countries like the United States"
where millions of the unemployed were being put on a wage just a
trifle too much to die on, but not enough to live on. The rallying center in the world fight for peace and decency was "the policy of the
Soviet Union"; and it was the revolutionary duty of every class-conscious worker "to defend the Soviet Union." [40]

Of such appeals to class-conscious workers to defend the Soviet
Union, Morris Ernst and David Loth were later to say:

> In the past, we have had our own spies in purely military ways —
> and some of them are national heroes. Our enemies had the same
> kind. Each side also had spies who were motivated entirely by
> money, and some who preferred the enemy and became deserters.
> But here is a spy whose fanaticism leads him to set himself entirely
> apart from national loyalties on either side. By some psychological
> gymnastics, he convinces himself that the welfare of mankind is
> linked to the success of another country.[41]

Although, as the authors of this comment also pointed out, it is obvious

37. Browder, *What Is Communism?* p. 166.
38. Browder, *What Is Communism?* pp. 115–117.
39. Browder, *What Is Communism?* p. 76.
40. Browder, *What Is Communism?* p. 173.
41. Morris L. Ernst and David Loth, *Report on the American Communist*
(New York: Holt, 1952), p. 112. The same theme is developed by Rebecca West
in *The New Meaning of Treason* (New York: Viking, 1964).

that not all members of the party enter this stage of bigotry and belief, the obligation laid upon the faithful to defend the Soviet Union as the highest priority of commitment certainly distinguished the Communist Party of the thirties from all others at the same time or before it in America.

The defense of the socialist fatherland was one of the prime political goals of the party but the rhetorical appeal concentrated on liberal reformist actions. The political orientation of Washington in the 1930's favored the Communist movement only insofar as the party identified itself with that orientation, and Browder was at some pains to make the identification. The re-touching of the Communist Party with a liberal coloration had one corollary effect that strengthened its new appeal. Anticommunism was widely associated by Communists and non-Communists alike with social reaction, international fascism, depression, Republicanism, anti-Rooseveltism, the American Legion, boosters, yellow-dog contracts, union-busting, munitions makers, the Daughters of the American Revolution, finks, and the American Liberty League. Many liberals and conservatives alike reinforced this identification — the liberals by attacking "red-baiters" as advocates of antisocial attitudes; the latter by lumping together (as being without substantial difference) socialists, atheists, pacifists, supporters of the American Civil Liberties Union, New Dealers, and Communists.

In still one other manner Browder blurred the image of the Communist Party which had been so clear in the Third Period — that is, by associating the public objectives of the party with the public objectives of radical Populist groups and organizations like the EPIC program of Upton Sinclair, the Townsendite movement, and others. This tactic sought to take advantage of the radicalization of national politics that the depression had encouraged — and to show that there was a substantive core of broad agreement in the aims of a variety of social groups. Of the Townsend movement Browder said that while it was not directly anticapitalist, it strongly attacked concentrated wealth and big bankers, criticized reaction, and called for strong support of the American democratic system. "It is clear that the Townsend movement contains great positive possibilities," he concluded.[42] In accord with the united front tactic, he said that the party approached "the rank and file of these organizations in the most friendly spirit," and he offered unity of action to end poverty and to secure the tranquillity of old age in the United States.[43] He made a similar offer to the EPICS,[44] explicitly disavowing the view of "some superficial critics" that the masses in

42. Browder, *What Is Communism?* p. 82.
43. Browder, *What Is Communism?* p. 84.
44. Browder, *What Is Communism?* p. 86.

these various movements were crackpots, a view he characterized as "political snobbery." [45]

The creation of a new vision of the Communist Party and of the Soviet Union as agencies for the attainment of social reforms and democratic values was assisted by the Soviet Union itself. The GPU was given a new name — the Commissariat for Internal Affairs — and so was made to disappear as a symbol of police ruthlessness and suppression. And a new constitution was devised for external consumption — a basic law to be the embodiment of everything that's democratically excellent, to paraphrase the Lord Chancellor, with Stalin embodying the law. One of the pleasantries of the new constitution was a statement of the right of member states of the Soviet Union to secede, that even the Constitution of the Confederate States of America did not provide.[46] The Bill of Rights was made especially attractive to liberals. It included among the fundamental rights and duties of Soviet citizens a right to work, to rest and to leisure, to maintenance in old age and sickness or disability, and to education; freedom of conscience, speech, press, assembly, street processions, and demonstrations; equal women's rights; and the secret ballot. The reception accorded this document in America by those in the party or susceptible to its rhetoric was affectionate; and doubtless many without a knowledge of the totalitarian context in which it should have been judged were dazzled by the splendorous sentiments it expressed. Anna Louise Strong wrote a whole book about it, and Louis Fischer proclaimed that "The Bolshevik dictatorship is slowly, almost imperceptibly, abdicating. When the change to democracy is completed, the world will wonder how it happened." [47] The second sentence is as true today as it was in 1935.

In the wonderland of utopian fantasy through which some traveled during and after the Seventh World Congress — from the darkness and

45. Browder, *What Is Communism?* p. 87. Browder did not have quite as much trouble with Huey Long and his "share the wealth" and "every man a king" slogans, which were characterized by Dimitroff as fascist capitalism operating as an anti-capitalist movement. Browder said of the demise of Long, ". . . the assassination was prepared by those forces in the ruling class which were determined to bring a halt to the share-the-wealth demagogy. They considered it too dangerous in the present economic and political state of the country." *Ibid.*, p. 62.

46. Article 17 of the Soviet Constitution of 1936 said, "The right freely to secede from the U.S.S.R. is reserved to every Union Republic." Russell F. Moore, *Modern Constitutions* (Ames, Iowa: Littlefield, Adams, 1957), p. 216. The Constitution of the Confederate States of America, adopted March 11, 1861, made no provision for the withdrawal of any state but, to the contrary, declared in its preamble that it was ordained and established in order "to form a permanent federal government." William MacDonald (ed.), *Documentary Source Book of American History* (New York: Macmillan, 1928), p. 425.

47. *Current History*, September 1935, quoted in Eugene Lyons, *The Red Decade* (Indianapolis: Bobbs-Merrill, 1941), p. 168. The Stalin Constitution was drafted in 1935 and went into effect in 1936.

coldness of the Third Period into the wonderful warmth of the Fourth — Americans would some day live in a Soviet America where there would be no slums, no poverty, and no profits. The material change would create other changes also. In a fine burst of prophetic declamation, Browder said,

> Socialism is not only a revolution in economic life. It makes an entirely new human race. It takes this man who has been brutalized and degraded through the ages by the violence and oppression of class societies, frees him from his woeful heritage, carries over from the past only the achievements of the human mind and not its crimes and stupidities, and remakes man, molding him in the heat of socialist labor into a new social being.[48]

With these and similar utterances, the Communists reversed the tactic earlier proposed by Edmund Wilson. Americans had not succeeded in taking communism away from the Communists, but the Communists were seeking to take democracy from the democrats and, by preempting its values, to monopolize — and to make squalid with ulterior intent — the decent impulses of democracy and humanism in the American culture. Whether coincidentally or causally, the membership of the American party grew rapidly in the Fourth Period of Communist International policy. As noted earlier, the best estimate put the membership figure at 24,500 in 1934. Reports to the Central Committee of the party put the figure at 31,000 in May 1935; 37,000 in January 1937; and 55,000 in January 1938.[49] The membership in the late thirties was four to five times what it had been earlier in the decade. What was it

48. Browder, *What Is Communism?* p. 234. The utopian expectation of a basic and radical change in human nature is referred to elsewhere as follows: "Socialism was an unbounded dream. Fourier promised that under socialism people would be 'ten feet tall.' Karl Kautsky, the embodiment of didacticism, proclaimed that the average citizen of the socialist society would be a superman. The flamboyant Antonio Labriola told his Italian followers that their socialist-bred children would each be Galileos and Giordano Brunos. And the high-flown grandiloquent Trotsky described the socialist millennium as one in which 'man would be immeasurably stronger, wiser, freer, his body more harmoniously proportioned, his movements more rhythmic, his voice more musical, and the forms of his existence permeated with dramatic dynamism.'" Daniel Bell, *The End of Ideology* (Glencoe, Illinois: Free Press, 1960), p. 265.

49. Nathan Glazer, *The Social Basis of American Communism* (New York: Harcourt, Brace, 1961), p. 92. The estimate made by Lyons is considerably higher than that of Glazer, by almost 50 per cent in fact. Lyons says that the public figure was 100,000 in 1938 and that the private figure claimed by party officials was 75,000 instead of the 55,000 stated by Glazer. The absolute figures are less important than the two inferences that can be drawn from all the figures, namely, that there was a substantial increase in membership in the Fourth Period of Communist International policy, and that the influence of these numbers far surpassed the figures themselves. Lyons, *The Red Decade*, p. 178.

that members saw in the party in the later years that they did not see
in the earlier ones? What fulfillments did they expect membership to
bring them?

Without foreclosing the question of motivation, skepticism slows
acceptance of statements that assert the existence of "certain specific
psychological structures" that are drawn to communism, although
psychological explanations of radicalism persist.[50] Two such explanations are provided in works based on samples of individuals once in
the party.[51] In the study by Ernst and Loth, the method seems by
academic standards at least somewhat casual and journalistic, without
notes, tables, or index. The findings were said to have been drawn
from interviews and written statements by "nearly 300 former Communists," and from information taken from the public record of testimony by cooperative witnesses in congressional committee hearings.
In a summary statement of conclusions, the authors outlined the characteristics of American Communists: they were more likely to join
the Communist Party between the ages of nineteen to twenty-three;
came from homes of luxury and comfort, and from the families of
professional men, successful businessmen, bankers, and ministers, where
there was a pattern of suicides, desertions, divorces, and aggressive
fathers of conservative politics. Those attracted to the party had a
high level of education and worked in nonmanual occupations. They
joined out of a mixture of motives in which the emotional value of
"belonging" rated high, and money and power incentives rated low,
but where the impulse was almost never moved by "bad company,"
poverty, Communist party literature, or party oratory. They showed
some personality traits in common, including a sense of personal inadequacy, preoccupation with intellectual matters, a sense of selfless dedication rather than pushing opportunism, often submissiveness, and
willingness to be told what to do or think. They tended to be urban
rather than rural, and were indifferent or hostile to religion. Men and
women were equally attracted to the party.[52]

One difficulty with this kind of survey is that the population measured is uncharacteristic. Even if the personality structures of the re-

50. See, for an earlier one, Henry de Man, *The Psychology of Socialism* (New
York: Holt, 1927), where the Marxian program is explained in terms of affective
dispositions, complexes, and compensations. The phrase "certain specific psychological structures" is that of Frank Meyer in *The Moulding of Communists* (New
York: Harcourt, Brace, 1961), p. 178. He rejects the view that there are specific
personality types who come into the Communist movement, and says that the
important thing is the *production* of a standard type after entry into the party,
by the process of moulding.
51. Gabriel Almond, *The Appeals of Communism* (Princeton: Princeton, 1954)
and Ernst and Loth, *Report on the American Communist*.
52. Ernst and Loth, *Report on the American Communist*, pp. 1–16.

spondents were exactly recorded and described, without bias or error in the accounts, the report nevertheless is not a report on the American Communist but a report on American Communists who left the party and then talked about their experiences. It is quite possible that the psychological characteristics of those who left the party are different from those who stayed. Moreover, the data are less persuasive in the absence of some statistics showing that there is a greater tendency for all upper class youths with aggressive fathers to enter the Communist Party than to enter upon careers of crime as a way of life, say, or juvenile delinquency, or to become President of the United States like John Quincy Adams, or make the Supreme Court like Oliver Wendell Holmes, Jr., both of whom had dominating fathers. The Ernst-Loth study makes the Communist Party sound like a sanitorium drawing its clientele from the physically handicapped, the emotionally and socially rejected, the guilty rich, and the resentful new poor.[53]

Of greater professional sophistication is the Almond study on the appeals of communism. Here the sample was smaller than the one used by Ernst and Loth but the design of the study was shrewder and the methods were more rigorous.[54] The investigators were interested to know whether the recruit to communism perceived the Communist Party in the model of militancy, whether he was aware of the power goals, which were central, and the extent to which he was made privy to the external and internal representations of the party, which are different from each other. The external representation, which is largely propaganda and agitation, varies with the audience. The internal representation of the party is the same the world around — that is, leaders of the party who have been recruited by various agitational means (help labor, abolish segregation, throw out the colonial oppressors, etc.) are taught from the same classics and are shaped to the design of the model Communist militant.[55]

53. Ernst and Loth, *Report on the American Communist*, pp. 128–129.
54. The Almond study was based on a sample of 221 former Communists in the United States and abroad, 64 of whom came from the United States. The study was cast in two parts: (1) an examination of the classics of Communist literature to establish a model of the militant Communist; and (2) depth interviews with the respondents. In the image of the Communist militant as the Communist classics describe him, ". . . all values save power have been squeezed out. It is all a matter of power and tactics. The world as at present constituted is incapable of realizing humane values. All the values advocated by groups (including the Communists) in the world here and now are false values used by power groups to conceal the sordid power reality. The only meaningful ethical orientation in the here and now is one which turns away from all short run and false humanitarianism and strives for a monopoly of power which will then lead to an era in which genuine values may be achieved. All non-power ends are suspended in the ideal image of the Communist militant." Almond, *Appeals of Communism*, p. 18.
55. Almond, *Appeals of Communism*, p. 69.

The evidence of the Almond study tends to support the conclusion that relatively few individuals at the time of joining the party perceived the power pattern in its doctrinal militancy. Not more than 27 per cent of the respondents had any acquaintance with the Communist classics before they were recruited or joined the party. Even among those who were exposed to the esoteric doctrine before joining, there were very few who registered and accepted it.[56] Almost all of the respondents perceived the party at the time of joining in terms of one or a combination of its agitational goals. This would seem to be closer to an explanation of what historically took place in the thirties than psychologizing about predisposing personality structures, for it takes into account the objective condition of the time. The agitational appeals of the Third Period were harsh, forbidding, and alien. The agitational appeals of the Fourth Period were a kind of liberal seduction. Presumably the psychotics and psychoneurotics were not less in number or proportion in 1933 than in 1936 or 1938 — at least the aggressive fathers who begat unstable offspring had done their creative and mutilating work some time before the Seventh World Congress. This suggests that the membership variable was more than likely the change in the party line and not a sudden increase in weak personalities.

The party of course was also perceived as a means of attaining personal and nonpolitical objectives. Almond says, "The typical perception involved a combination of one or more agitational goals with some conscious personal need and expectation." [57] It is this aspect — the satisfaction of conscious personal needs and expectations — that the Ernst-Loth statement emphasizes; and the Almond study tends to confirm some of the less sensational propositions of the Ernst-Loth report. Since the Almond sample included European Communists as well as American, it was possible to suggest ways in which American Communists are, or were, different from their European counterparts. The evidence tended to show that Americans and Englishmen, more so than the Europeans, did see the party as a means of solving personal problems of loneliness and isolation. Other organizations perhaps could have assuaged feelings of loneliness and isolation, but the Communist Party had an agitational appeal also; and the agitational appeal was attractive because it accorded with a widespread concern for the policy

56. Almond, *Appeals of Communism*, p. 102.
57. Almond, *Appeals of Communism*, p. 105. Almond also suggests that the reason for this among the Americans, possibly, was the large number of foreign born and immigrant-derived members in the American party. But the core of such members in the party — it was almost exclusively the membership of the party in the 1920's — brought their radicalism with them from abroad.

issues, independent of psychic difficulty, that the managers of the party manipulated.[58]

The evidence of these two studies of samples of former party members fails to demonstrate any necessary affinity between specific psychological structures and membership in the Communist Party. What is clear is that the party looked different and sounded different between 1935 and 1939, at which time the foreign policy of the Soviet Union changed again, and it resumed some of the stances of the Third Period. The Almond study tends to show that the exoteric members (not the hard core of the insiders) joined it not because it was revolutionary, nor even in the main because it was socialist, but because it seemed more strenuously reformist than the existing parties. In addition, although isolationist sentiment was strong in the mid-thirties in the United States, the neutrality legislation it fostered signified political and military neutrality, not moral neutrality. The Soviet Union and the American Communist Party prospered then in some degree as undeserving beneficiaries of the repulsion felt for Nazism and its works.

Even so, the party, to repeat, never had more than 100,000 members at the outside, and this figure is dubiously large. The Ernst-Loth statement concludes that the average length of membership was two to three years, while the Almond study (which included Europeans) found that it took one to seven years for defectors to break away, both estimates of course being limited to the samples which were studied.[59] Whatever may be the nearer figure, the turnover in the party was very great. Perhaps a close statement of the fact is the conclusion of Arthur Schlesinger, Jr. about the early years of the party:

> But Communism became the whole way of life for very few Americans. In 1930, the party claimed only six thousand members; by 1932 after two years of furious agitation in the midst of economic

58. In the professional prose of the Almond study, this point is put as follows: "In the United States and England, the political goals of the party were more often perceived as general social improvement and bettering of conditions than as specifically socialist aims. These differences [i.e., differences from the Europeans] may have two causes. In the first place, the party shapes its agitational goals to coincide with the already existing goal aspirations of the groups to which they appeal. And second, the new recruits at the point of joining tend to see the party in a relationship of continuity with their prior goal aspirations." Almond, *Appeals of Communism*, p. 104. As compared with the Europeans in the sample, however, the Almond study concludes that emotional maladjustment as a factor influencing adherence to the Communist movement seemed to be a more pronounced characteristic of American and British middle class intellectuals. *Ibid.*, p. 256.

59. Almond, *Appeals of Communism*, p. 337. Ernst and Loth, *Report on the American Communist*, p. 182.

collapse, only a meager twelve thousand. Many more signed membership cards in these years; but most passed through the party as through a revolving door, finding the discipline unbearable, the dialectic meaningless, and the vocabulary incomprehensible. Some left the party for the same reason they entered it — because they cared deeply about democracy and freedom. The Communist vision had been enticing; but the facts, even after three years of capitalist decay, remained dull — a clique of dreary fanatics and seedy functionaries, talking to themselves in an unintelligible idiom, ignored by the working class, dedicating their main efforts to witch hunts against liberals and Socialists. The party was sodden, contentious, bureaucratic, and feeble.[60]

To repeat, the public image of the party changed radically between 1935 and 1939. The basic party itself did not change, although its tactics did. When it seemed to some to be an agency through which liberal reformist aspirations could be achieved, its membership increased. When it was clear that its power goals were not those of liberal democracy, its membership decreased. The political context, and the adjustment of the party to the prevailing political disposition, are the keys to an understanding of the vogue that the party had for some. Although life in the party may have been a subculture in Europe and in small concentrated spots in the United States, membership in the party by and large was a passing aberration, limited to less than one-tenth of one per cent of the total population of the United States.

The Two Faces of Communism

The two faces of American communism in the Fourth Period are the traditional masks of the theater — the saturnine realism of the programs for the inner party and the strength-through-smiling-joy themes of the mass organizations manipulated by party members. The first served the goals of power and the second served the goals of propaganda where, in the words of Oliver Goldsmith, "Thus 'tis with all — their chief and constant care/ Is to seem everything but what they are." In the literature of the first, the party is self-regarding, that is, it is concerned with its organization and directives, the communication of policy and advice throughout the structure of the institution, the development of the mechanisms of control, the concentration of the organization effort, and the foraging for funds. The literature of the second is other-regarding, that is, it is concerned with the promotion of agitation and propaganda, the manipulation of the symbols of

60. Arthur M. Schlesinger, Jr., *The Crisis of the Old Order* (Boston: Houghton Mifflin, 1957), p. 22.

identification and rejection, the manufacture of slogans, the quick organization of causes, the orchestration of claques of defamation and reprisal, the production of sound effects of a clangorous multitude.

A useful document to illustrate the party's structure and definition of self in the Fourth Period is the manual of organization that appeared in July 1935.[61] J. Peters was "one of the most important Kremlin representatives to enter the United States." [62] He was known at various times as Alexander Stevens, Goldberger, Silver, Isidore Boorstein, Steve Lapin, and Steve Miller, and served as a link between the American apparatus and Soviet espionage in the United States,[63] right hand man to Comintern representative, Gerhardt Eisler,[64] and, as chief of the Communist underground, the man in charge of the "study circles" existing among governmental employees in Washington.[65] He was also the author of the manual of organization.

The ultra-left policy of the Third Period was a failure from the viewpoint of international communism because it isolated the movement from the masses it presumed to lead. It did not succeed in making the "united front from below" — the unity of the rank and file of socialist and labor organizations with the Communists — and it grossly underestimated the threat of fascism, as has been seen.[66] But there was one great gain for the international party — the purging of the party of such organizational diseases as automatism, and of reformist and legalist illusions.[67] As the transformation has been described,

> Out of this period of ultra-left phrases, revolutionary adventures, splits, purges, and intensive indoctrination there emerged the steeled movement we know today. This is not to say that the communist leaders designed it so. But the modern communist movement is a product of its history: it owes elements of strength, as well as of weakness, to the apparently irrational period of "social fascism" and "united front from below." [68]

61. J. Peters, *The Communist Party: A Manual on Organization* (New York: Workers Library Publishers, 1935). Excerpts from the Manual are reprinted in Eighty-fourth Congress, Second Session, House of Representatives, Committee on Un-American Activities, House Report No. 2244, *The Communist Conspiracy*, Part I, Section E, *The Comintern and the CPUSA*, pp. 120–134 (hereafter cited as *The Comintern and the CPUSA*).
62. *The Comintern and the CPUSA*, p. 119.
63. David J. Dallin, *Soviet Espionage* (New Haven: Yale, 1955), pp. 390, 407.
64. Dallin, *Soviet Espionage*, p. 412.
65. Dallin, *Soviet Espionage*, p. 412.
66. There was even tactical cooperation between the Communists and the Nazis in the German Parliament — against the "social fascists" of course — and in the strike of transportation workers in Berlin in 1932.
67. For a short statement on reformism, see R. N. Carew Hunt, *A Guide to Communist Jargon* (New York: Macmillan, 1957), pp. 139–143.
68. Philip Selznick, *The Organizational Weapon* (Glencoe, Illinois: Free Press, 1960), p. 137.

Although the appeals of the Fourth Period were addressed to the most
enduring and compelling values of western culture — reason, justice,
science, humanitarianism — the engine of power that stirred them was
a combat party bent upon the "continuous conquest of power through
full use of the potentialities of organization." [69]

As architecture is said to be frozen music, so the Communist Party
organization is sometimes supposed to embody a principle of philosophical grace — the principle of democratic centralism.[70] In the structure of the party, according to Peters' *Manual*, the unit or nucleus is
basic. The word "cell" is not a term in the nomenclature of the *Manual*
although its use in popular discussions is so widespread that it is by
now ineradicable. Not the "cell" but the unit or nucleus (shop or
street) was the most local form of organization, and the progression
moved up in the hierarchy through sections and districts to the national conventions and international congresses.[71] At each of the levels
— unit, section, and bureau — there was an organization of affairs in
fewer hands than the full membership. Thus there was a Section Committee that functioned when the convention was not meeting, and a
Section Bureau that wielded the power of the Section Committee.
There was a District Committee that functioned when the District
Convention was not meeting and a District Bureau that wielded the
power of the District Committee. And for the Communist Party
throughout the nation, there was a Central Committee that functioned
when the national convention was not in session, and a Political Bureau that wielded the power of the Central Committee.[72]

This organization illustrates the significance of the Communist Party
as a combat party, committed to revolutionary goals by the attain-

69. Selznick, *The Organizational Weapon*, p. 17.
70. Carew Hunt points out that there have been at least three forms of the
principle: obedience to orders of the leaders with discussion at the lower levels
restricted to ways and means of carrying them out; broad discussion of party
directives before they come into force, with the lower organs permitted to submit proposals until the issue is settled by the party congress, when it becomes
binding on all; and discussion of all issues by all ranks in the party with the party
congress bound to carry out the will of the rank and file. *A Guide to Communist Jargon*, pp. 54-55.
71. It should be noted that the establishment of the world congress of the
Communist International as the supreme organ of the world Communist movement is true as of the time of the Peters *Manual*. The Comintern, however, was
abolished during the Second World War. The communication of central decisions about world strategies has been less public and more clandestine since that
time; and with the emergence of polycentrism and the rivalry of Chinese factionalism, the monopoly of Soviet influence among the Communist parties of the
world has been limited.
72. See Wilbert E. Moore, "Sociological Aspects of American Socialist Theory
and Practise," in Donald Drew Egbert and Stow Persons, *Socialism and American Life* (Princeton: Princeton, 1952), vol. I, pp. 523-556, at p. 551.

ment of power, and the "necessity of tight discipline in a group engaged in conflict with established institutions." [73] The "centralism" is clear in the subordination of the lower parts to the higher. The "democracy" is less visible. The strict principle of numerical representation in this organizational system was not followed since greater weight could be given to some units, sections, and districts than others, as strategic and tactical considerations set by the leaders required. The initiative in policy did not bubble up from the bottom, but poured from the top. The structure of the organization then was designed primarily to communicate the policies of the leaders throughout the membership — it was a net of control and communication, intended to produce the maximum of understanding with the maximum of security, without generosity and without error.

The justification for the paramilitary organization of the Communist Party is that it is supposed to constitute the vanguard of the working class. As Stalin was to put the idea,

> The Party cannot be a real Party if it limits itself to registering what the masses of the working class think or experience, if it drags along at the tail of the spontaneous movement, if it does not know how to overcome the inertia and the political indifference of the spontaneous movement; or if it cannot rise above the ephemeral interests of the proletariat, if it cannot raise the masses to the level of the class interests of the proletariat.[74]

The party was to lead the mass, to instruct it in its real interests, to give form to its historic revolutionary will, and to keep it from pursuing what it thinks its interests are. The party was bound to the mass as the arm is to the lever, and the organization was the grasping hand, guided by the sentient brain of the leadership. The Leninist principle of going to the masses can scarcely be confused with the popular ethic of Lincoln, for it is a principle of power through the people rather than one of power of, by, and for the people.[75]

73. *Ibid.*, p. 550. Peters' *Manual* says "the number of delegates to Conventions is not fixed in the Constitution of the Party"; and further, "The Party committees elected at the conventions are composed of the best, most developed comrades in the given organization. Representation to the Section Committee is not on the basis of representation from each unit; nor does each section elect a representative to the District Committee." *The Communist Party: A Manual on Organization*, pp. 131–132. The elements of consideration in the forming of the committees are stated as follows: "The size of the Party committee always depends on the numerical strength of the organization which elects it, on the importance of the organization, and on the given situation." *Ibid.*, p. 132.

74. J. Stalin, *Foundations of Leninism* (New York: International Publishers, 1932), p. 105.

75. This point is well stated in Selznick, *The Organizational Weapon*, pp. 80–82.

The points of pressure and penetration in the "strategic aim of the Communist Party . . . to win the majority of the working class for the proletarian revolution" were located by J. Peters as follows: (1) big factories, mines, mills, docks, ships, railroads, and the like; (2) unions; (3) the ranks of the unemployed; (4) fraternal, cultural, and sports organizations; (5) Negro organizations; and (6) farms. No mention was made of government or governmental agencies.[76] Much more will be said presently about party organization and activity in agencies of the government,[77] but here it may be remarked that the "cells" could not perform the function of control in governmental agencies, as in unions and other mass organizations, because the structure of a federal agency is normally such that it does not lend itself easily to any but the most marginal kind of manipulation. Instead, the Washington groups became sources of information, a function that, in the beginning, was an incidental activity, but which became more useful and important.[78]

The power goals of the Communist Party were the concern of the organization. The agitational goals were the concern of the fronts. Others have pointed out that there is a difference between the "united front" in which the party did not conceal its presence but joined openly with other parties, as in France under Leon Blum, in a public political alliance, and the "front" in which it concealed its role.[79] The front was a device of deception trickier than the Biblical confusion perpetrated by Jacob; for while liberal hands of welcome opened membership to the mass, the voice of the fronts was a chorus of party inspiration. Estimates of the number of fronts run into the hundreds[80] and it is merely tedious to trace their changes of name and line through the many tortuous tactics of the Communist campaign. But one of them — the American League for Peace and Democracy — may be taken as surrogate for the rest, for the League was by far the largest, most seductive, and most successful of the front organizations.[81]

76. Peters, *The Communist Party: A Manual on Organization*, pp. 128–129.

77. On the problem of infiltrating federal agencies, see the comment in Ernst and Loth, *Report on the American Communist*, pp. 44–45.

78. Dallin, *Soviet Espionage*, pp. 440 and 443. The practice of espionage through "cells" was such a violation of the principles of espionage, which work to minimize the number of people who know each other, that "the men of the Soviet apparatus requested that the more important members of the Washington groups cease working through the American party and work directly for the apparatus." *Ibid.*, p. 443. After some resistance to the suggestion, it is said that Comrade Browder yielded. *Ibid.*, p. 444.

79. See Selznick, *The Organizational Weapon*, pp. 144–146, for discussion of different meanings of the word "front."

80. Lyons, *The Red Decade*, chap. xvi, "The Incredible Revolution Spreads," discusses the "riotous luxuriance" of old and new fringe organizations.

81. It was also one that the House Committee on Un-American Activities very

In 1939 the chairman of the League, Dr. Harry Freeman Ward, appeared before the House Committee on Un-American Activities to testify as a voluntary witness about the organization.[82] It was tart circumstance in the hearing that one of Ward's interrogators, the Director of Research of the Committee, was Dr. J. B. Matthews, a convert from radical causes who had himself been the chairman of the American League for Peace and Democracy when it was known as the League Against War and Fascism.[83] Ward was conscious of the irony and occasionally referred to the superior knowledge that Matthews had about certain aspects of the enterprise he was investigating.[84] The ALPD grew out of what was known as the Amsterdam World Congress Against War, which met in Holland on August 27–29, 1932, in response to a call over the signatures of Romain Rolland and Henry Barbusse.[85]

---

early used as a form of pressure on the Administration. On October 25, 1939, the Washington *Times-Herald* published the list made public by the committee of the names of members of the ALPD employed by agencies of the Federal government. This action was taken after the committee adopted a report (January 3, 1939) in which the ALPD was called a Communist front organization. This action, considered by Dies to be a warning to government employees to get out of the organization, failed to produce the result desired. The publication of the names was intended to produce the withdrawal that the mere castigation of the ALPD as a Communist front had failed to do. Hundreds of names were reported from numerous agencies and parts of agencies. A number of letters were sent to the newspaper, the committee, and to the Washington office of the ALPD by individuals who complained that they were not members of the ALPD, or who were not now such members, or whose names had been listed by the ALPD without their permission. The publication of the membership by the committee was protested by many figures in official and academic circles. See Thomas I. Emerson and D. M. Helfeld, "Loyalty Among Government Employees," 58 *Yale Law Journal* 1 (1948).

82. There was some dispute about whether the committee through its staff had seized records of the ALPD, but it seems clear, from the testimony of Ward himself, that permission to take the records was granted (by Ward) when the committee requested them. In fact, the Washington office of the ALPD itself delivered the records to the committee. Seventy-sixth Congress, First Session, House of Representatives, Special Committee on Un-American Activities, *Hearings on H. Res. 282*, vol. X, pp. 6215–6216 (hereafter cited as *Hearings on H. Res. 282*).

83. For a sketch of the career of J. B. Matthews, see Murray Kempton, *Part of Our Time* (New York: Simon and Schuster, 1955), chap. v, "O'er Moor and Fen."

84. *Hearings on H. Res. 282*, p. 6217, where the following exchange occurred: "Mr. Matthews: In other words, you assumed the chairmanship, Dr. Ward, about 5 or 6 months after the founding of the organization? Mr. Ward: Well, that I cannot say accurately, because I was not present at the founding of the organization. You know more about that Mr. Matthews. You were there."

85. Out of that Congress emerged the World Committee Against War. From the World Committee Against War derived the American Committee for the Struggle Against War. From the latter came the First United States Congress Against War which convened in New York City, September 29–30, 1933, and

The program of the ALPD under Dr. Ward was extremely broad. Among other things, it planned to stop the manufacture of munitions by mass picketing and strikes; to expose preparations for war; to demand the transfer of all war funds to relief of the unemployed and the creation of a system of social insurance; to oppose "American Imperialism" and support colonials against their oppressors; to oppose fascism; to win the support of the armed forces to the program of the League; and to recruit women and youth to the cause of the League. Of particular interest in the program was the statement of the preferred line with respect to the Soviet Union, where it was said,

> To support the peace policies of the Soviet Union for total and universal disarmament which today with the support of the masses in all countries constitutes the clearest and most effective opposition to war throughout the world; to oppose all attempts to weaken the Soviet Union, whether these take the form of misrepresentation and false propaganda, diplomatic manoeuvering, or intervention by imperialist governments.[86]

The central position given to the defense of the Soviet Union certainly distinguished the American League for Peace and Democracy from other benevolent or pacifist organizations. Indeed it was neither benevolent nor pacifist, although it drew to its ranks some who thought it was.

Also distinguishing the ALPD from other social organizations was the presence on the Executive Committee of leading members and officials of the Communist Party, among whom were Clarence Hathaway, the editor of the *Daily Worker*, Israel Amter, Ella Reeve Bloor, Langston Hughes, and Max Bedacht.[87] Some of the members of the Second Congress Against War and Fascism, held in New York City in 1934, expressed worry about the domination of the League by the Communist Party, so much so that Dr. Ward found it useful to make a speech on the matter. But the thrust of his speech was less to assure his audience that the comrades were not in control than to make an argument for more action. He said in discussing the Communists in the organization,

> Concerning the legitimate use of this organization by political groups, I will take a concrete case. You all heard the speech of Earl Browder last night. You heard him make a clear historical judgment that there was only one choice before mankind now and that was be-

organized the American League Against War and Fascism. *Hearings on H. Res. 282*, pp. 6217–6218.

86. *Hearings on H. Res. 282*, pp. 6238–6239.

87. *Hearings on H. Res. 282*, Appendix, vol. X, p. xxvi.

tween Fascism and Communism. When Earl Browder pointed out that humanity now has to choose between the Fascist and Communist type of organization of society, he neither meant nor implied that we all had to join the Communist Party if we were not going to turn Fascist. He then went on to point out with pardonable pride, as he was perfectly entitled to do, to the achievements of the Communist Party throughout the world in offering very effective resistance to the development of Fascism. [Applause] If other political groups whom we have invited here had taken part in that program, if their leaders had spoken as asked, they would have been entitled to do the same thing, if they could. [Applause] [88]

In the same mood of respectful — even admiring — and certainly conscious cooperation with the Communist Party and its leaders, Dr. Ward also told his audience,

> When it comes to the participation of different political groups in this movement, my own position is this: Legitimately, the group which can offer to this movement the most valuable suggestions concerning program and tactics, which can offer the most dynamic active force for carrying it out, will gain political activity in this League and are entitled to do so.[89]

To cheer up the fighters for freedom from fascist capitalist oppression, one of the last speakers at the Second Congress, an anonymous lieutenant of the United States Army (said to be, at least), opened his remarks with the salute: "The revolutionary soldiers of the Sixth Corps Area, which includes the Regular Army in Michigan, Wisconsin, and Illinois, extend revolutionary greetings." [90] It is possible to guess that these words may have stirred a thrill of historical recognition, uniting the Sixth Corps area with the guards who joined the mob in front of the Bastille, the Red Army, and the Kronstadt sailors of 1917.

Dr. Ward was also the presiding officer at the Third United States Congress Against War and Fascism, held in Cleveland, January 3–5, 1936.[91] Between the second and the third of the congresses, the Seventh World Congress of the Communist International had taken place, and a new line had been announced which ratified tendencies that had already been in movement in a number of countries in 1934. The new line was reflected in the ten resolutions adopted by the Cleveland Congress, some of which showed concern for legislation enacted by the Congress, or pending. For example, there was a demand for air-tight

88. *Hearings on H. Res. 282*, Appendix, vol. 10, p. iv.
89. *Ibid.*
90. *Ibid.*, pp. xxiii–iv.
91. *Hearings on H. Res. 282*, p. 6256.

neutrality legislation, and a call to oppose legislation regulating efforts to promote subversive disaffection in the armed forces, which the ALPD called programs "designed to secure peace, freedom, and justice."

Although Dr. Ward had denied predominant influence by the Communist Party in the First and Second Congresses, Earl Browder, in *What Is Communism?* published in September 1935, had said of the First Congress, that "The congress from the beginning was led by our party quite openly but without in any way infringing upon its non-party character." [92] When this statement was read to Dr. Ward in the proceedings conducted by the House Committee, his answer was that it did not apply to the League in 1939, any more than the Republican party of Lincoln was the Republican party of 1939. [93]

The change in tone presaged by the change in the resolutions at the Third Congress was ratified at the Fourth United States Congress of the League which was held in Pittsburgh, November 26–28, 1937, when the organization was renamed the American League for Peace and Democracy. [94] The Fifth United States Congress of the American League for Peace and Democracy took place in Washington, D.C., January 6–8, 1939, after which it became unnecessary to worry about peace and democracy, not because ruthless fascist imperialism had melted before the hot resentments of peace-loving progressives of the ALPD, but because the Soviet Union had entered upon an arrangement of convenience with Adolf Hitler. After the 1937 congress, the Communist Party, which had been a formal affiliate of the League, withdrew its affiliation. Although it no longer paid affiliation fees of about $2,000 a year (which had been the practice before 1937), it continued to contribute financially to the League thereafter at about the same rate. [95]

In its heyday the League claimed to speak for individuals and organizations with a total membership somewhere in the neighborhood of seven and a half million people, although, under pressure, Dr. Ward cut down this estimate to 19,000 individual members of the national organization, and an imprecise estimate of somewhere between three or four hundred local and other affiliated organizations. [96] Only the Communist Party ever paid its affiliation dues in full, although some contributions were received from other sources. [97] That the Commu-

92. Browder, *What Is Communism?* p. 148.
93. *Hearings on H. Res. 282*, pp. 6265–6266.
94. *Ibid.*, p. 6269.
95. See the testimony of Robert William Weiner, Financial Secretary of the Communist Party, on September 12, 1939, before the House Committee on Un-American Activities, *Hearings on H. Res. 282*, pp. 4805–4806.
96. *Hearings on H. Res. 282*, p. 6275.
97. *Ibid.*, p. 6276.

nist Party exercised a continuing influence in the activity of the League is evident in the action that the Executive Board took in refusing by a vote of 14 to 1 to condemn the Nazi-Soviet Pact, only LeRoy Bowman voting for the condemnation.[98] In the early years of the League some pretense was made that the organization was a forum for the union of several political parties and other groups, but when no other political parties had joined after some four years of existence, the Communist Party, as has been said, simply withdrew its public affiliation.[99]

The strategy of alienation put the Communist Party in a stance of antagonism against all American values and institutions. The strategy of enticement blurred the public appearance of the party and induced numbers to join who would have been and were repelled by its character as a combat party bent upon power goals of subversive design. The power goals did not recede; the Communist Party was a revolutionary party in the Third Period and a revolutionary party in the Fourth Period. In the Third Period it was quite clearly perceived as an ultimate weapon of group violence, self-described as such, and accepted as such by all partisans of factional dispute — right and left. In the Fourth Period the party was generally perceived as an instrument for the achievement of reformist and welfarist goals, talking (but not loudly) the rhetoric of revolution but discounted as a vehicle of violent social change because of its apparent rejection of immediate goals of revolution, and its benignity towards less catastrophic forms of protest.

The early (i.e., 1935) objects of party concern were the workers in industry and the mines and fields, the unions, the unemployed, the Negro, and cultural organizations. There is no evidence that the Communist Party had any master plan to infiltrate the agencies of the government of the United States with members of the party. Members of the party of course did come to occupy positions in the federal agencies, but the evidence seems to suggest that, for the most part, the party first found them in the government, and then found them something to do.

98. *Ibid.*, pp. 6282–6283. See *New York Times*, October 13, 1939, p. 10, col. 2, for the public statement of LeRoy Bowman on his resignation from the Board of the American League for Peace and Democracy and his reasons for doing so.
99. *Hearings on H. Res. 282*, p. 6319.

There are three qualifications required
in those who have to fill the
highest offices — first of all, loyalty
to the established constitution —

ARISTOTLE, *Politics*

III   The Future Comes

In 1933 Charles Beard and an associate published a book under the title *The Future Comes,* in which they hailed the advent of new concepts about the responsibility of government for social welfare that, after two decades, were to become the orthodoxy of even the Republican party.[1] Much has been written on and about the New Deal which fostered and gave force to these concepts, but there are some aspects of government in the thirties that have a special bearing on the "infiltration" of Communist officers and employees to which relatively little attention has been given, and which students of political science would think significant. Of central importance is the problem of bureaucracy under Roosevelt, because the need for competent staff and the consequent growth of the federal service after 1933 created opportunities for employment, and difficulties of management, unique in Washington history.

The Opening of the Government Service

Champions of the sovereignty of the states, a former President of the United States, and others concerned with the *salus reipublicae* spoke grave foreboding in the 1930's about the encroachments of the Federal bureaucracy upon the liberties of the people. A common figure of journalistic fun was the wild-eyed, New Deal, visionary, longhaired, crackpot, radical bureaucrat who had never met a payroll. To be sure many other Americans were not meeting payrolls either, and had not since 1929 when the "technical reaction" of the market drove prosperity around the corner from which it was expected, as was said in frequent bulletins, to emerge. The Beardian prophecy was forced to wait upon various analgesic palliatives which were tried by men

1. Charles A. Beard and George H. E. Smith, *The Future Comes* (New York: Macmillan, 1933).

who, as Talleyrand said of de Maistre, were prophets of the past, acting out memories as though they were premonitions.

The arrival of Roosevelt on the scene put the apparatus of the government at the service of other groups besides business enterprise, and the number and complexity of agencies did indeed wax and swell. Public loan and insurance agencies were created or enlarged — for example, the Federal Deposit Insurance Corporation, Federal Home Loan Bank Board, Federal Housing Administration, an expanded Reconstruction Finance Corporation, and credit agencies for agriculture.[2] There were new labor agencies like the National Labor Board, the National Labor Relations Board, National Longshoremen's Labor Board, National Steel Labor Relations Board, and expanded versions of existing agencies in the labor field. In the broad and sometimes inconsistent attack on general problems of the economy, there were the National Industrial Recovery Administration, Federal Emergency Administration of Public Works, Agricultural Adjustment Administration, Federal Emergency Conservation Work, Federal Emergency Relief Administration, and literally dozens of others, some of which became better known in their acronymic shorthand as CCC, WPA, PWA, and so on. There is no need to expand the long list. The point is that suddenly, indeed overnight, there was an increase in the number of agencies created by the Federal government to fulfill new concepts about government and society, and a consequent need for large numbers of competent people to fill the agencies.[3]

If the large number of new officials in the Federal government sometimes seemed to use energy and reformist zeal as a substitute for administrative competence, the conservative mourners of this result had only themselves to blame. For the country lacked a large and stable corps of professionally trained civil servants prepared to take on and administer the great governmental enterprises to which they had been appointed. Except for the military and, to some extent, the diplomatic service, there was virtually no professional bureaucracy on which to

2. For a contemporary account of the multiplicity of agencies, see Laurence F. Schmeckebier, *New Federal Organizations* (Washington, D.C.: Brookings, 1934).

3. The bureaucracy grew so great and so complex so quickly that it got out of hand. By 1936–1937, the disorder moved some friends of the President, including Louis Brownlow, to urge that he take steps to rationalize the confusion. Accordingly, Roosevelt appointed the President's Committee on Administrative Management to study the organization of the Federal government, and to propose measures for reorganizing it. This action led to the submission of reorganization plans. For a view of the problem somewhat different from that adopted by the President's Committee on Administrative Management, see Lewis Meriam and Laurence F. Schmeckebier, *Reorganization of The National Government* (Washington, D.C.: Brookings, 1939).

draw. English critics of English bureaucracy could deplore what they thought were dangers of officialdom at home, but the too-weak bureaucracy has risks as well as the too-strong.[4] In 1933, Washington took on some of the aspect of a frontier town as rapid recruitment created an officialdom to criticize.

The mourners had only themselves to blame because, from the beginning of the Republic, men of prudence and property had vested an interest in administrative idiosyncrasy — in that partition of the public power which the constitutional texts sanctified as the "separation of powers" — to the end that the decree of the Federal law should be narrowly drawn against the claims of national interest. Although this comparison is doubtless odious — as all are said to be — the men of 1789 anticipated by 170 years the "troika" principle favored by the Soviet Union as a disruptive tactic in the United Nations, and for roughly the same purpose, to prevent the concentration of effective central power, and to invest different social formations with a veto over the acts of others. The purpose of the eighteenth century partition of the public power was to prevent the Federal government from concentrating its political resources except in times of war or other national emergency. Each of the branches of the Federal government came to acquire a corporate interest in its own survival, and a watchful concern for the protocols of power and prestige.

On the part of the Congress this concern took the form of a rivalry with the Executive for the control of the executive establishment, and thus contributed to the retardation of the growth of a professional bureaucracy or, more politely, the career civil service. Certainly one of the historical high points in this duel was the Tenure of Office Act of 1867 through which a runaway Congress attempted to dominate the cabinet appointments of the President of the United States. At a less dramatic level, the Congress only very slowly consented to the establishment of a merit system, because it was reluctant to give up patronage.[5] Control of appointments and budgets by Congress split the Federal authority over the civil service, and helped to prevent the organization of a competent professional corps of superior function-

4. Lord Hewart of Bury, *The New Despotism* (London: Ernest Benn, Ltd., 1929).

5. The maintenance of the spoils system is usually regarded as the concern of the President who, as party leader, finds it necessary to reward deserving partisans. But patronage has also been the historic method by which Presidents have secured Congressional support for legislation. The negotiation of patronage has thus been a concern of Congress, and the practice of "senatorial courtesy" ritualizes one aspect of it. The Pendleton Act of 1883 was put on the books only when it appeared desirable to a Republican Congress to freeze Republican officeholders in their jobs when the Democrats made important gains almost two decades after the Civil War.

aries. It may seem farfetched to suppose that the Tenure of Office Act of 1867 had anything to do with the Communist Party and the New Deal but the underlying unity of political events makes them distant kin. The requirements of the public service in 1933 were so extensive that there was an immediate demand for over a quarter of a million new functionaries.[6]

Now where did all these people come from? Any history of the New Deal must impress readers with the casual, haphazard, even desperate way in which recruitment of the top and middle management positions proceeded. Perhaps the two callings more nearly professionalized than any other which also produced people capable of dealing with issues of public policy were the military establishment and the law. The administration of civilian programs by military figures is not unusual in the New Deal. General Hugh "Iron Pants" Johnson, for example, was given the task of making the National Recovery Administration operate successfully. Members of other professional elites were also drawn into government. Social workers were put in charge of the WPA and the Department of Labor. And lawyers and economists abounded. The 50 per cent increase in the size of the Federal establishment between 1933 and 1938 was recruited from the outside, and many were drawn into government service who, in more prosperous times, would have found their way into the ranks and files of the business world.[7]

The year 1933 marked the first time in American history (save for a year during the First World War) when entry into the government service was more desirable to many (and perhaps easier) than the employments they could get in the private sectors of the society. It is for this reason that the persistent word "infiltration" in the literature of the congressional investigations into communism is not entirely appropriate.[8] The conception conveyed is that of an insidious penetration of a resistant exterior, a military foray behind the lines of an enemy arrayed for combat, and on the alert. Nothing could be further from the actual circumstance of the first five years of the New Deal at least. The problem was not to keep the hostiles out but to get

6. On February 28, 1933, the Federal government employed 568,200 persons. By September 30, 1938, it was employing 870,031. Meriam and Schmeckebier, *Reorganization of the National Government*, p. 96.

7. For a comment on the new scope in the government for intellectuals, see Earl Latham (ed.), *The Philosophy and Policies of Woodrow Wilson* (Chicago: University of Chicago, 1957), Introduction.

8. See, for example, Eighty-second Congress, Second Session, House of Representatives, Committee on Un-American Activities, *Hearings on Methods of Communist Infiltration in the United States Government*, June 10 and 23, 1952 (hereafter cited as *Hearings on Methods of Communist Infiltration in the United States Government*).

enough people into the government to run it. And there were no loyalty or security programs. These were to come considerably later.[9]

The hospitality that the New Deal showed towards unmoneyed intelligence attracted a certain kind of new recruit — the bright young person with a social conscience, drawn into the public service not just because there was a job to be had, but because there was a job to be done. The reformist goals of the New Deal offered a challenge of change to a generation that was sick to the teeth with the nonsense that had been fed to the country by its leaders in the worlds of business and politics in the period from 1929 to 1933. To recall them even now is to test temper and indulgence. On November 22, 1929, Alexander Legge, chairman of the Federal Farm Board, said: "It looks as if industry would have to begin scraping around to get employees instead of laying off anybody." [10] This cheerfulness echoed the statement of John D. Rockefeller three weeks before that "fundamental conditions of the country are sound";[11] and anticipated the chirpy New Year's statement by Secretary of the Treasury Andrew W. Mellon five weeks later, when he said, "I see nothing, however, in the present situation that is either menacing or warrants pessimism." [12] On March 3, 1930, Robert P. Lamont, Secretary of Commerce, said, "Business will be normal in two months." [13] Hearst columnist Arthur Brisbane, author of the view that a gorilla could lick both Dempsey and Tunney, dismissed the depression on July 16, 1931, with the remark that "This country hasn't lost anything, except a few billion dollars." [14] Reed Smoot of Utah, chairman of the Senate Finance Committee, and co-author of the most disastrous tariff in American history, thought in 1931 that "One of the most powerful influences working towards business recovery is the tariff act which Congress passed in 1930." [15]

Despite the mild nature of the Roosevelt program — which, in Macaulay's phrase, was to "Reform in order to preserve" — Roosevelt came to be castigated by conservative elements, and this very castigation gave relish to the excitement of working for the New Deal. It was not that

9. 53 *Stat.* 1147–48, 18 U.S.C.A. #61a (August 2, 1939).

10. Edward Angly (ed.), *Oh Yeah?* (New York: Viking, 1931), p. 13.

11. *New York Times*, October 31, 1929, p. 1, col. 6. Rockefeller said, "Believing that fundamental conditions of the country are sound, and that there is nothing in the business situation to warrant the destruction of values that has taken place on the exchanges during the past week, my son and I have for some days been purchasing sound common stocks. We are continuing and will continue our purchases in substantial amounts at levels which we believe represent sound investment values." *Ibid.*, p. 2, col. 4.

12. *New York Times*, January 2, 1930, p. 30, col. 3; see also January 1, 1930, p. 4, col. 2.

13. *New York Times*, March 4, 1930, p. 1, col. 7.

14. July 16, 1931, in his column, "Today."

15. *New York Times*, April 18, 1931, p. 6, col. 3.

Roosevelt really arrayed class against class as his opponents charged; it was that his popular success gave social approval to the resentments of millions against the suave pieties of the business elites. It served to focus the sense of wrong that lay beneath the surface of a society in which the promise of economic opportunity and material plenty seemed to be contradicted by the event.[16] Some sections of the press encouraged the notion that identification with the New Deal was an adventurous flirtation with social danger. In support of Landon in 1936, for example, the Hearst papers called the Administration

> The Red New Deal with a Soviet seal
> Endorsed by a Moscow hand,
> The strange result of an alien cult
> In a liberty-loving land.[17]

Some scores of centuries earlier it had been put somewhat differently in the First Book of Samuel where of David it was said that "everyone that was in distress, and everyone that was in debt, and everyone that was discontented, gathered themselves unto him; and he became a captain over them. . . ." The sweeping victory of the New Deal in 1936 provided fresh confidence that its supporters were indeed embarked upon one of the greatest and most needed programs of social and economic reform in history.[18]

It is in this milieu that the "penetration" of the agencies of the Federal government and the "infiltration" of its offices by the Communists must be seen. The wonder is not that there were many who made careers in the government; the wonder is that the total membership of the party did not do so after the party line had changed from red to true blue. But there were certain inhibitions in the way. First, the party was hostile to the New Deal, as has been seen, until 1935 and 1936, and even then it was publicly somewhat less than enthusiastic. Second, the political work of the party before the lights changed had largely concentrated on the election of local Communist candidates despite talk about the mass parties and farmer-worker coalitions. Third, although the "Popular Front" was an important political tactic in Europe — associating the Communist Party at high levels of political responsibility with other groups — nothing like it was possible in this country. As was indicated earlier, the thought that Earl Browder

16. For a description of this outlook, see the remarks on populism by Daniel Bell, *The End of Ideology* (Glencoe, Illinois: Free Press, 1960), pp. 105–107.

17. As quoted in Arthur M. Schlesinger, *The New Deal in Action* (New York: The Macmillan Company, 1939), p. 38.

18. This attitude was accompanied by a great deal of naïve imperception of communism. See Leslie Fiedler, *An End to Innocence* (Boston: Beacon Press, 1955).

might have entered the cabinet of the New Deal in a Popular Front
display of the unity of "progressive" forces in the face of fascism is, as
John Marshall used to say, "an absurdity too gross to be insisted upon."
As was also said earlier, the public record of Communist maneuver
seems to suggest that the *party's* work was to concentrate upon the
unions, women, youth, Negroes, and the mass organizations of social
and cultural enterprise.

There were four principal levels of party activity of diminishing
public visibility: the agitational work in unions and other mass organizations; the conduct of more or less public party affairs (the open
party), with public congresses and conventions and a busy and shrill
press; the covert work of the party; and the espionage activity of
Soviet agents who sometimes worked through underground members
of the party and sometimes did not. Before 1934 or thereabouts, the attention of the American Communist Party to the agencies of the
Federal government seems to have been virtually absent; and even the
Soviet espionage apparatus seems not to have devoted much attention
to American affairs.

The Beginnings of Soviet Espionage in America

In the attention to American affairs given by the Soviet espionage
apparatus a distinction has to be made between the early period —
1927 to 1932 — and later.[19] Prior to 1927, Communist espionage in the
United States, if it existed, appears to have been sporadic and minor.
According to Jacob Spolansky, an American Communist named Peter-
son was sent by Ludwig C. A. K. Martens, the Soviet representative
in New York, to enter the service of the FBI in 1920, and was actually hired — but was kept under observation by other agents.[20] The
FBI obtained proof of his connection with the Martens office; and
when he was confronted with the evidence he broke down, confessed,
and was fired. To cover up his failure, he falsely reported to the party
that one of its leaders, Louis Fraina (Lewis Corey), was a secret agent
of the FBI. Theodore Draper's account of the case makes no mention
of any Communist attempt to penetrate the FBI but his account is
drawn from Communist and ex-Communist sources which might have
had no knowledge of the espionage elements in play, and might not
have cared to stress them if they did.[21]

19. It may also be noted that espionage was not the work of a single organization but that the Comintern, the GPU, and Soviet Military Intelligence all played
parts.
20. Jacob Spolansky, *The Communist Trail in America* (New York: Macmillan, 1951), pp. 143–145.
21. Theodore Draper, *The Roots of American Communism* (New York: Viking, 1957).

At various times Benjamin Gitlow has made statements indicating that some types of espionage did exist in the early years, although the value of the statements may be questionable. In his first exposé of the Communist Party there is no mention of espionage at all.[22] But in the same year that his book appeared (1940) he told the Dies Committee that Communists in unions were a potential source of espionage and sabotage.[23] In a reference to the possibility that Communist personnel in Navy yards might transmit military secrets to the party, Gitlow said, "Those things have been done." [24] When asked by Representative Starnes, "Has there been any effort made along that line in government employment?" Gitlow replied, "During my time there was a slight effort along the line of military and industrial secrets." [25] In general terms, he also referred to Communist efforts to penetrate the Army, although without indicating that the purpose was espionage rather than subversion.

The year 1927 is the earliest specific date mentioned by Gitlow in the Dies hearings for the initiation of Soviet espionage in the United States. The occasion was the recruitment into the Soviet espionage service of Nicholas Dozenberg,[26] an old member of the party, and indeed a member of the Lettish Confederation, a Communist group which antedated the American Communist Party. But the account of the beginning of espionage is somewhat expanded in another book by Gitlow, published in 1948, almost ten years later.[27] In *The Whole of Their Lives*, he told of the recruitment in Russia of one Carl John-

22. Benjamin Gitlow, *I Confess* (New York: E. P. Dutton, 1940).

23. Seventy-sixth Congress, First Session, House of Representatives, Special Committee on Un-American Activities, *Hearings on H. Res. 282*, pp. 4569–4570 (hereafter cited as *Hearings on H. Res. 282*). At the conclusion of his colloquy with Dies of Texas, Gitlow said: ". . . It was Stalin himself who told us that he would rather get one official of a trade union into the Communist Party than 10,000 rank and file members." *Ibid.*, p. 4570.

24. *Hearings on H. Res. 282*, p. 4585. Gitlow said that members of the Communist Party were chosen for such tasks as espionage, and in answer to a question by Representative Thomas as to whether employment of a Communist in "some munitions works, or in an industrial plant" didn't enable him to "become practically a spy for the Soviet Union," the following exchange occurred: "Mr. Gitlow: If he is designated for that purpose; yes. They have selected people for that, and wherever they want to use them, they do. Mr. Thomas: They are in key positions in the industry? Mr. Gitlow: Yes, sir. Mr. Starnes: Would that apply to the government service also? Mr. Gitlow: A Communist member has only one loyalty, and that is to the party, and that applies to every service in which they are engaged." *Ibid.*

25. After he had made the quoted remark, Gitlow was then asked by Dies, "During your time, they did not make any effort to place members in the Government service?" and Gitlow answered, "Not at that time." *Hearings on H. Res. 282*, p. 4585.

26. *Hearings on H. Res. 282*, p. 4675.

27. Benjamin Gitlow, *The Whole of Their Lives* (New York: Scribner's, 1948).

son as a spy in 1919, but the only specific activities he attributed to Johnson were connected with the smuggling of Soviet funds to subsidize the American party.[28] Gitlow also said, in his 1948 publication, that the party, during its underground period after the Palmer raids and other excitements of the early 1920's, had set up a Technical Aid Society which smuggled in spies and engaged in industrial espionage.[29] The 1948 account, then, is somewhat at variance with the statements before the Dies Committee, at least as to the time when the Soviet Union began espionage activities in the United States, but the discrepancy is not material. It seems clear that there was no systematic espionage before 1927, and perhaps none at all.[30]

Other sources tend to support this conclusion. There is a specific account of industrial espionage in 1925 by Jan Valtin (Richard Krebs),[31] but Valtin was sent to this country not by the Soviet Union but by the Comintern's seamen's organization in Hamburg. The industrial espionage in which he was engaged was not illegal, it had nothing to do with military matters but rather with whaling techniques, and it did not involve the American Communist Party in any way. Moreover, the main purpose of the trip was organizational and the espionage was incidental. Valtin also mentioned the existence of GPU representatives in the United States but he quotes the GPU men as saying, "We've no contacts with the Party in the United States." [32]

General Walter Krivitsky, after his defection from Soviet Military Intelligence, told the Dies Committee that Felix Wolf headed Soviet Military Intelligence in the United States from 1924 to 1929, and that Wolf was followed by Alfred Tiltin[33] from 1929 to 1933. This account

28. Gitlow, *The Whole of Their Lives*, p. 46.
29. Gitlow, *The Whole of Their Lives*, p. 84.
30. The discrepancy between the earlier and the later statements may have been essentially a semantic one. The general concern in the 1940's with espionage activities may easily have caused Gitlow to classify as espionage activities which he had previously not regarded in that light. There are other discrepancies that are somewhat less easily explained. For example, in his testimony before the House committee, Gitlow said that Dozenberg had been assigned to the GPU when it seems more likely that he had been assigned to Soviet military intelligence. He also told the committee that the technical advisers of the American Trade Union Delegation to the Soviet Union in 1927 "were all party people." *Hearings on H. Res. 282*, p. 4701. The only definite party man in the group, however, seems to have been Robert Dunn. Among the non-Communists in the group were Stuart Chase, Rexford Guy Tugwell, J. Bartlett Brebner, and Paul Douglas.
31. Jan Valtin [Richard Krebs], *Out of the Night* (New York: Alliance Book Corporation, 1941), pp. 109 and 124–125.
32. Valtin, *Out of the Night*, p. 163.
33. *Hearings on H. Res. 282*, p. 5742. The text of the hearings reports the name as Alfred Tilden but this is doubtless a stenographer's error since the name is given by almost all other sources as Tilton or Tiltin. Dozenberg, a native of Latvia, told the House committee that he learned Tiltin's real name in Moscow, and that the Tiltins were Latvians. *Ibid.*, pp. 570, 572.

is almost certainly in error in regard to dates. Dozenberg told the committee in 1940 that he entered the service of Soviet Military Intelligence under Tiltin's direction — apparently in 1927 — and that in 1928 Tiltin left for Moscow because, after two years service in the United States, he was entitled to be relieved. This would place Tiltin's arrival in the United States at some time in 1926, towards the end of the year. Given a reasonable time to establish himself, he should have been able to get his operation under way early in 1927. This, in fact, is the first significant evidence of an organized Soviet intelligence operation in systematic contact with the American Communist Party; and Tiltin is the first head of that operation whose contacts with the party can be proved.

Tiltin may have returned to the United States subsequently, since Dozenberg says that he came back from his trip of "a few weeks" to Moscow — he obtained the passport for this trip in November 1928 — to help Tiltin set up a shipping company as a front.[34] There may be some confusion of dates here also; it is possible that Tiltin left early in 1929, after Dozenberg's return, rather than before. In any case Dozenberg told the FBI that he used Tiltin's apartment in Moscow in 1932, and that at that time Tiltin was on active service with the Soviet Army.[35] Tiltin used the name "Joseph Paquette" and had a Canadian passport in that name, according to Dozenberg.[36]

Despite certain anomalies about dates, then,[37] Dozenberg was apparently recruited into what was already a going concern. Shortly after he started to work for Tiltin, the latter told him of having had the plans of the British warship, *Royal Oak*, stolen en route between New

34. *Hearings on H. Res. 282*, pp. 574–575.
35. *Hearings on H. Res. 282*, p. 617.
36. *Hearings on H. Res. 282*, p. 570. Tiltin's wife, who worked with him, was named "Maria" and both had Canadian passports in the name of Martin. There seems reason to believe that Mrs. Tiltin is the same person as the "Canadian" Mary Louise Martin, who was later to figure prominently in the Jacobson espionage case in Finland and the Switz case in France. Jacobson and the Switzes were Americans with whose recruitment she seems likely to have had some connection. See David J. Dallin, *Soviet Espionage* (New Haven: Yale, 1955).

37. Neither Dozenberg nor Chambers appears to have had a very good memory for dates. Frequently Dozenberg either said that he did not remember a date or gave one which the House committee, on the basis of documentary evidence, was able to show was wrong. When Committee counsel or members suggested that he was in error, he would tell them that they knew the dates better than he did. As to Chambers, in his initial testimony he gave an incorrect date for his break with the party. In *Witness* (New York: Random House, 1952), p. 295, he placed the arrest of Arvid Jacobson, a key event in the history of Soviet espionage, in 1935 instead of 1933. He also attributed important activity to the National Student League at a period before its birth. None of this seriously reflects on the general accuracy of the testimony given on matters of first-hand knowledge, other than dates.

York and Washington, photostated, and replaced.[38] Arrangements for Dozenberg's assignment were said to have taken place through the office of Jay Lovestone, the General Secretary of the Communist Party, and Lovestone gave him leave from his party duties for his new activities.[39] Asked by the committee whether he had been assigned to Soviet intelligence by the party, Dozenberg said that he was not sure, since Lovestone might have been acting in his personal capacity.[40] Dozenberg's testimony appears to involve no party leaders other than Lovestone. While he stated that he believed that Browder knew about his assignment, he had no personal contact with Browder and Foster because he and they belonged to opposing factions.[41]

Dozenberg spent only a little time in the United States after his induction into Soviet military intelligence; and he does not appear to have been much impressed by the way military intelligence operated, so far as he was able to observe it. According to his testimony, his associates shipped over tremendous quantities of publicly available material.[42] Dozenberg told the committee, "I feel sad. . . . You can buy these books in any bookstand and they were silly in buying them." Military intelligence was mainly interested at this time in material on army training and industry, little of which seems to have been secret, according to his testimony. He expressed doubt that any party members had supplied secret industrial information at that time.[43]

Much of the activity of Communist espionage centers in the United States in the early days seems to have been connected with the recruitment of agents for use in other countries. Dozenberg's own field of activity changed, and rather soon, so that most of what he did after 1929 is not of great relevance or interest at this place. However, in 1932 he did return to the United States to obtain equipment needed

38. *Hearings on H. Res. 282*, p. 595.
39. *Hearings on H. Res. 282*, pp. 565 and 570.
40. *Hearings on H. Res. 282*, p. 567.
41. *Hearings on H. Res. 282*, p. 565. The specific relation of the Lovestone faction to the early stages of Communist espionage is worth noting. It continued long after their expulsion from the party, as can be seen in Dozenberg's testimony. One of the first contacts of Whittaker Chambers with the underground was one John Sherman, who had entered the Soviet underground *after* his expulsion from the party. It is possible that Chambers himself was really a Lovestoneite. It is an important consideration in this connection that Henry Yagoda, who headed the GPU until 1937, had been connected with the Russian Right Opposition, with which Lovestone had been allied. At the same time, General Ian B. Gamarnik, executed along with Tukachevsky, headed Soviet Military Intelligence, and also maintained contact with the Communist Right-wing Opposition, at least outside of Russia. This fits in with the political support that Lovestone and his allies in other countries gave to the Soviet Union, including support for the first Moscow trials as long as Yagoda and Gamarnik were in power.
42. *Hearings on H. Res. 282*, p. 594.
43. *Hearings on H. Res. 282*, p. 596.

for a movie company which was to be set up as a cover for Soviet activities in Rumania. He was also to obtain the necessary money for this purpose.[44] He went to Lovestone, who had been expelled from the party in 1929, for assistance. Either Lovestone, or one of his followers, Dr. Valentine Burtan, who was also one of the incorporators of Dozenberg's film company, arranged an appointment for Dozenberg with Lowell Limpus of the New York *Daily News*, who gave him an introduction to Senator Burton K. Wheeler. Senator Wheeler who, of course, had no idea of Dozenberg's activities, helped him to get the information he needed on makers of movie sound equipment from the Department of Commerce. There was nothing out of the ordinary about such a request. Dozenberg's testimony does not indicate whether Limpus had any idea of what he was after, or whether any connection may have existed between Lovestone and Limpus.

Dozenberg never got the money he needed for this operation, so the supplies remained unbought. According to his testimony, he learned when he returned to Moscow that the money he was supposed to have received was to have come from the proceeds of a stock of counterfeit United States bills which the Russians had prepared, and which Dr. Burtan was to have distributed. Unfortunately for the enterprise, Dr. Burtan was caught before the distribution had progressed very far, and he was sentenced to a term of years in prison. There are a number of accounts of this incident which disagree on the allocation of responsibility for the counterfeiting operation. Dozenberg's testimony would seem to indicate that he had had no part in planning or conducting the operation, and only learned about it afterwards. He suggested to the House Committee on Un-American Activities that General Walter Krivitsky had arranged the whole thing.[45] On the other hand, Spolansky attributes the management of the affair to Dozenberg, and says that he used it to discredit the Lovestoneites.[46] Gitlow mentions Burtan and a German ex-officer, with Dozenberg perhaps concerned in the preliminaries of the counterfeiting itself.[47]

44. *Hearings on H. Res. 282*, pp. 566–567, 583, 585, 590–592.
45. *Hearings on H. Res. 282*, pp. 620–624. Dozenberg also suggested that Krivitsky was interested in getting money for the Trotskyites but this is highly improbable since, even after breaking with the Communists, Krivitsky was not a Trotskyite.
46. Spolansky, *Communist Trail in America*, pp. 166–168.
47. *Hearings on H. Res. 282*, pp. 4683–4685. A note of Lovestoneite factionalism enters Gitlow's account. Dozenberg's early connection with the counterfeiting is alluded to in the remark that in 1928 Dozenberg was assigned the task of finding "out the secrets of the serialization numbers of American currency bills." He once inquired of Gitlow where information could be obtained but Gitlow said that he did not know. In an earlier description of Earl Browder's activities in China in 1927, Gitlow mentions a sum of $10,000 received from Europe for transmission to Browder. The money was received by Dozenberg

Apart from the confusion about the roles of particular individuals, it is clear that the counterfeits were of official Soviet origin, and that their circulation was connected with the intelligence apparatus. A connection with the American party is established through Max Bedacht, at that time still a high official of the party, and at various times engaged in raising funds for Burtan's defense.[48]

Dozenberg subsequently operated in the Philippines, covering his operation by acting as a sales representative for various eminently respectable American companies. Most often, it appears that the companies were glad to be represented in areas where it would not have paid them to set up offices of their own. Whether this was always the only factor involved is not clear. Dozenberg told the committee[49] that the head of the camera division of one of the companies he represented was a one-time leading Communist who had been expelled as a Trotskyite, and it is quite possible that old friendship, if nothing more, served Dozenberg in this instance.[50]

Dozenberg finally broke with the Soviet intelligence apparatus in Moscow in 1939 when he was ordered to work in the United States and refused to do so.[51] His refusal seems to have been motivated primarily by the disappearance of most of his old Soviet contacts in the great purges of the thirties, although he indicated to the committee that he believed in the validity of the Moscow trials! [52] He was told that he would be permitted to return to the United States because the Russians did not want another Robinson case.[53] Of incidental interest is his statement that when he was asked to work in the United States

"and Dozenberg came to the national office, and asked us about it, whether we should send it all to China, or whether he should use it in his own way. Since he belonged to a different faction from the leaders of the party in this country, we were afraid if he got hold of a lot of money he might use it here for the American party. He immediately turned it over to Kitty Harris [then the wife of Earl Browder] who went with it to China." *Ibid.*, p. 4681.

48. *Hearings on H. Res. 282*, pp. 5874–5875. Also *ibid.*, Executive Hearings, pp. 591–593. See also Chambers, *Witness*, pp. 271, 280. Bedacht was a charter member of the American Communist Party and had held numerous offices including that of general secretary of the party in 1929 when there was a crisis of leadership, and Lovestone was expelled. Although he denied that he had contributed money directly to Burtan for his defense, he did admit collecting money for Mrs. Burtan. *Hearings on H. Res. 282*, p. 5875.

49. *Hearings on H. Res. 282*, Executive Hearings, p. 652.

50. Of course, even apart from businesses created for the purpose of cover, businessmen have sometimes consciously lent their names to firms to cover Communist espionage or other activities. See Boris Morros, *My Ten Years as a Counterspy* (New York: Viking, 1959), p. 28.

51. *Hearings on H. Res. 282*, Executive Hearings, pp. 614, 643–644.

52. *Hearings on H. Res. 282*, p. 650.

53. See Chambers, *Witness*, pp. 399–400, for an account of the Robinson-Rubens case.

he was told that it made no difference whether those he recruited to assist him were "Leninites, Fascists, Trotskyites, or anybody." After his break and return to the United States, he was arrested and convicted for passport fraud.[54] Dozenberg's pay for his work, he told the committee, averaged about $1,000 a year; the most he ever received in one year was $1,800, and his highest weekly salary was $50. Working for Soviet military intelligence was clearly not one of the more direct roads to wealth.

The creation in the United States of a base for operations in other countries and the recruitment of personnel for these operations seems to have been a substantial enterprise, perhaps because of the value of an American passport.[55] Dozenberg himself testified that he had recruited several persons for Soviet intelligence in 1929.[56] Chambers said that John Sherman entered the operation immediately after his expulsion from the party in 1929, and Chambers himself was recruited into an operation that was already complex, and that was apparently a separate subdivision from the one with which Dozenberg was involved. The careers of George Mink and Leon Josephson in the service of the GPU seem to have commenced at about this time, although they be-

54. Spolansky, *Communist Trail in America*, p. 153.

55. Neither the use of fraudulent passports nor the illicit transfer of funds is necessarily connected with espionage, although both are essential to it. American Communists have used false passports almost from the beginning in order to conceal their movements. Their methods, however, increased in sophistication. In 1921, Earl Browder went to Moscow on a passport taken out in the name of Dozenberg without the latter's knowledge. This was unwise since it served to display rather than to conceal the party's Moscow contacts, even aside from the fact that it landed both Browder and Dozenberg in jail many years later. By the time Dozenberg entered the service of Soviet intelligence, the techniques were much more highly developed. He tells, for example, of a trip he made to South Carolina to obtain necessary background information about a dead soldier whose passport was to be used by a Soviet agent in France. *Hearings on H. Res. 282*, Executive Hearings, pp. 578–579. Later a large-scale and systematic operation for obtaining passports in false names was developed. Passports of American volunteers in the Spanish civil war were also taken from their owners and given to Soviet agents for use in other countries.

Illicit transfers of funds also formed part of the Soviet operation from the beginning. Gitlow, Spolansky, and various witnesses before the Dies Committee and its successor have described some of the methods, such as jewel smuggling. Another method, and more difficult to detect, was the use of business channels. Thus for many years A. A. Heller, who headed the party publishing firm, International Publishers, and presumably met its deficits, was one of the principal sources of party funds. Heller had been a prosperous businessman even before his Communist days, and was generally regarded as a millionaire. He left the party with Earl Browder. According to the testimony of Alexander Trachtenberg before the House Committee on Un-American Activities, Heller's oxygen company had profitable contracts with the Soviet Union. *Hearings on H. Res. 282*, p. 4882. There is no evidence, however, that Heller was the channel for any of the funds used in the intelligence operation.

56. *Hearings on H. Res. 282*, Executive Hearings, pp. 610–611.

came much more important later on.[57] The migration of Henry F. Mins, Sr. from New York to Warsaw in 1928 also seems to have been connected with the operations of Soviet intelligence.[58]

There is, however, little evidence of any effort to secure United States official secrets during this period. General statements as to the existence of such an operation were made by the Finnish and French police in connection with the Jacobson and Switz trials but, at least as reported in the American press, they gave no details.[59] There was one case involving an American soldier in the Canal Zone named Osman. Arrested in July 1933, he was convicted August 30, subsequently received a new trial, and was acquitted.[60] Some of the evidence in this case suggested the existence of Communist espionage in the area before 1933.

Communists in Government Unions

The great influx of workers into the Federal government, indeed into governmental employment in the state and municipal agencies also, in the mid and late 1930's created opportunities for the development and spread of Communist activity and influence through organizations of these workers. The story of the Communist enterprise in this area is more properly part of union history, but mention may be made of the Communist venture into the organization of governmental workers because these organizations would seem to have been natural channels for the dissemination of the party line, for the placement of agents, and for the recruitment of agents for the underground. There is no evidence, however, that these organizations did any significant work in any of these areas. Rather, they seem to have been used by the party to promote certain agitational goals, and to serve as a source of some revenue.

It has been said that the Communist Party assigned Abram Flaxer, the eventual president of the United Public Office Workers, to "capture the Government agencies," [61] but in the context of the remark

57. Jan Valtin told the House Committee on Un-American Activities that Mink began in 1930. *Hearings on H. Res. 282*, p. 8498.

58. *Hearings on H. Res. 282*, Executive Hearings, p. 3417.

59. For an account of the Jacobson and Switz cases, see Dallin, *Soviet Espionage*, pp. 61–67.

60. For an account of the proceedings against Corporal Ralph Osman of the United States Army, see the *New York Times* as follows: August 26, 1933, p. 3, col. 5; August 28, p. 6, col. 2; August 29, p. 15, col. 3; August 30, p. 7, col. 7; August 31, p. 1, col. 2. Corporal Osman was convicted and sentenced to a fine of $10,000 and two years at hard labor.

61. Eighty-second Congress, First Session, United States Senate, Committee on the Judiciary, Subcommittee to Investigate the Administration of the Internal Security Act and Other Internal Security Laws, *Hearings on Subversive Control of the United Public Workers of America*, 1951, p. 36 (hereafter cited as *Hear-*

it could only have meant control of union organizations, and not the literal possession its words suggest. The United Public Office Workers of America was formed in April 1946 by the merger of the United Federal Workers of America and the State, County, and Municipal Workers of America, comprising a total membership of some 40 to 50,000 members. On February 16, 1950, the Congress of Industrial Organizations expelled the UPOWA because ". . . the policies and activities of the UPW are consistently directed toward the achievement of the program and the purposes of the Communist Party rather than the objectives and policies set forth in the CIO constitution." [62] It will be noted that the merger and the expulsion come rather late in the development of the Communist movement. At the time of its expulsion, the UPOWA had about one hundred local units of organization, most of which were in the states and municipalities. Only some 11 per cent of the members were thought to have been in the Federal government,[63] located for the most part in the Bureau of Engraving and Printing, Treasury Department, Post Office Department, and the Veterans' Administration. Of the membership in the state and municipal agencies, the concentration was greatest in New York. At the time of its greatest growth, then, the UPOWA does not seem to have had a very large following in the Federal government, nor to have been distributed throughout the Federal government, nor to have had listed in its membership the principal officers of the few agencies in which it had members at all.

Before the merger of the United Federal Workers with the State, County, and Municipal Workers of America, each of these organizations had had a considerable history of change. Flaxer had been executive secretary of the Association of Workers in Public Relief Agencies in 1936, the constituent parts of which were affiliated with the American Federation of Government Employees, one of the constituent unions of the American Federation of Labor. At the 1936 convention of the AFGE in Detroit, Flaxer was appointed to the executive board of the parent organization.[64] The contact between the AWPRA and the AFGE was in fact rather slight. The AFGE had given charters to the locals of the AWPRA without admitting the "parent" organization as a bloc, so, in effect there were two controls

ings on the United Public Workers of America). The accusation was made by Victor Riesel, a labor news reporter for the New York *Daily Mirror*.

62. *Hearings on the United Public Workers of America*, p. vi.

63. This is the outside estimate of the membership employed in the Federal government. Flaxer himself indicated that the percentage was closer to five. *Hearings on the United Public Workers of America*, p. 70.

64. See testimony of Henry W. Wenning, *Hearings on the United Public Workers of America*, pp. 41–46.

— one real and one paper. At the Detroit convention, the state, county, and municipal workers were permitted to leave the AFGE and to organize the American Federation of State, County, and Municipal Employees, with a separate charter from the AFL, and an equality with the AFGE. Within the new American Federation of State, County, and Municipal Employees, however, the earlier AWPRA group constituted a bloc against the formal leadership of the new union. The bloc, at the time of the formation of the CIO, moved over to the CIO and created the State, County, and Municipal Workers Organizing Committee. John L. Lewis had encouraged the move and Flaxer became the leading officer in the new committee.[65]

It seems clear that party members were active in the leadership of the State, County, and Municipal Workers of America. Although Flaxer refused to say whether he was a member or not, even at his trial before the executive board of the CIO at the time of the expulsion of the UPOWA, his wife, who said that she had been a member of the party, also testified as to his membership. And the national organizer of the SCMWOA, Henry Wenning, was an admitted member, having joined in 1934 and remained in the party a year when he was expelled, only to return again a year after that (in 1936), there to remain until 1941 when he quit again, to return with no questions asked, and to quit again, this time, finally, in January 1944. He wanted Flaxer's job and could not get it.[66]

In so much shuffling there were inevitable quarrels about office organization and staff. Jack Stachel, a top official of the Communist Party, and the man in charge of trade union matters, decided one dispute over the employment of a Negro union organizer whom the officers of the SCMWOA wanted to discharge. The officers were called to party headquarters, told that they were white chauvinists and that they did not understand the Negro question. They were also told that the replacement would not be allowed and that the officers would have to mend their ways in relation to the Negro organizer.[67] Wenning reported the incident to the Senate Committee but Flaxer, when asked whether he recalled the meeting with Stachel and James W. Ford in

65. The new union was organized July 1937 with two officers appointed by Lewis: Flaxer as executive vice-president of the SCMWOC, and Henry W. Wenning as national organizer. *Hearings on the United Public Workers of America*, p. 46.

66. *Hearings on the United Public Workers of America*, p. 62. Of his "break" Wenning said, "When I finally got ready to leave, in the very beginning of 1944, when I discussed it with Flaxer, I discussed it frankly with him. In fact, I remember his grinning at me and saying 'Well, what you are saying is if you could have my job you would stay.' I said, 'Well, I guess that is it and I am not prepared to split the union by having an open fight with you in the union.'"

67. *Hearings on the United Public Workers of America*, p. 63.

connection with William Gaulden, refused to answer the question.[68] Continuous contact between the newly formed CIO union and the Communist Party was maintained by various individuals at different stages of the development of the organization. Thus Rose Wortis, the trade union director for the New York District of the Communist Party, was the initial contact for local affairs, while Roy Hudson was the contact in the CPUSA for national questions.[69]

Officials of the UPOWA served the agitational causes of the party vigorously. Flaxer, for example, was a sponsor of many organizations and fronts;[70] the secretary-treasurer, Ewart Guinier, former American Labor Party candidate for the Manhattan Borough, was vociferous on the Smith Act trials conducted by Judge Harold Medina,[71] on Paul Robeson in Peekskill,[72] and on various other causes promoted by front organizations, although he was uncertain about the significance of the *Daily Worker*[73] and was not sure whether he was an Elk.[74] Members of the union distributed handbills outside the New York office of the Immigration and Naturalization Service, joined parades to protest the deportation of aliens,[75] and circulated petitions for peace because President Truman wanted peace.[76] The president of the UPOWA was authorized by his executive board to make contributions to various causes at his own discretion up to a limit of $1,200 a year, and sums were given to such organizations as the Willie McGee Defense Fund, the Committee in Defense of Carl Marzani, and activities for the repeal of the McCarran Act.[77]

On the question whether there was attempted procurement of confidential government information on behalf of the Communist Party, Abram Flaxer refused to say. He did say, however, that such questions were "filthy and dirty blows below the belt that I resent," "filthy," "dirty," and "invidious." [78] He did not say "no," but it is doubtful that the membership of the UPOWA was very much of a source of information of this kind. Although party members were active in the leadership of the union, it was not a union of Communist members. It was a noisy organization of some of the lower paid government workers, with little vogue in the Federal, state, and local governments, with-

68. *Ibid.*, pp. 98–99.
69. *Ibid.*, p. 57.
70. *Ibid.*, p. 81.
71. *Ibid.*, pp. 127, 129.
72. *Ibid.*, p. 133.
73. *Ibid.*, p. 128.
74. *Ibid.*, p. 121.
75. *Ibid.*, p. 139.
76. *Ibid.*, p. 165.
77. *Ibid.*, pp. 80–81.
78. *Ibid.*, p. 104.

out bargaining power (since it was impossible to bargain for hours and wages in government agencies), and without the acceptance among Congressmen that several unions of government employees had had for some time — such, for example, as the Postal Workers Union, the established labor unions working on government projects, and the uninfluential but decorous American Federation of Government Employees.[79]

What Is A Communist?

It is quite clear from what has been said that the Communist Party, even in the sensitive area of espionage, was not strongly interested in the colonization of the government before the thirties, and then not, probably, until after the middle thirties. In the investigations held by Hamilton Fish and the McCormack-Dickstein Committee, the presence of Communists in government agencies was not a problem; and neither the questioning nor the testimony in these hearings produced any serious evidence of colonization, as was later to be the case in certain agencies.

Before turning to the establishment of the first known units of the Communist Party in Federal agencies in Washington, a word needs to be said about the key term, "Communist." It is frequently of less importance to establish who was a Communist than to ascertain what the Communist Party did. The identification "Communist" is not without ambiguity, for the Communist Party worked through several influential persons who were not in fact members of the Communist Party.

The key term is ambiguous for a number of reasons. First, there were various degrees of commitment to the party, and various badges and signs of that commitment. Thus, a former New York newspaperman did not carry a card when a member of the party doing rather low-grade espionage work for the Soviet Union in Finland, Rumania, and Yugoslavia.[80] The wife of Abram Flaxer testified that she had

79. For an account of the steps in the development of the organization of the UPOWA, see the testimony of Bernice B. Heffner, national secretary-treasurer of the American Federation of Government Employees. *Hearings on the United Public Workers of America,* pp. 1–8.

80. Eighty-fourth Congress, First Session, United States Senate, Committee on the Judiciary, Subcommittee to Investigate the Administration of the Internal Security Act and Other Internal Security Laws, *Hearings on S. Res. 58,* July 28 and 29, 1955 (hereafter cited as *Hearings on S. Res. 58*). Winston Burdett said that he was a member of the party for a period of approximately two years, that he had been recruited for espionage abroad by Joseph North and given his instructions by Jacob Golos, who also recruited Elizabeth Bentley. Before taking the assignment to Finland, Burdett was required to surrender his party card to Golos. *Ibid.,* p. 1331. He also gave Golos photographs of himself for identification, and a short autobiography, also for the convenience of those abroad who were to contact Burdett in Finland.

seen his party card,[81] but Henry W. Wenning testified that from 1935, after his expulsion from the Communist Party,

> I never joined the party after that again. I never technically became a book-holding member of the Communist Party from 1935 on. At the same time, I must, in all honesty, state that I was virtually a member of the Communist Party in every sense of the word, let us say, from 1936. . . . When I came back in the fall, no one raised any question with me as to whether I was a member of the party or not. I think everyone presumed that I was, and I must in all honesty say that there was no reason why anyone shouldn't presume that I was.[82]

According to Wenning's testimony, even though he was not a "book-holding member" of the party after 1935, he participated in its affairs, responded to its direction, and had many meetings with party officials. The phrase, "card-carrying member of the Communist Party," has become through somewhat tedious repetition in the rhetoric of debate, the *ruban bleu* of affiliation, but although it is of significance, it is not of dominating significance.

Second, some of those caught in the swirls and eddies of Communist currents were scarcely models of the revolutionary ideal. Such a one was William Remington who, whatever the degree of his activity for party causes, never seems to have made up his mind whether he was fully in or out.[83] He seems to have been a protypical James Dean, a rebel without much of a cause, "beat" before the word became fashionable, riding the hills of Knoxville, Tennessee, on a motorcycle when he worked for TVA, unkempt in dress, unreliable in deportment. He denied that he had been a member of the Communist Party, and Kenneth McConnell, former Communist Party organizer for the Knoxville area, testified that he had never seen a party card of Remington's.[84] But Remington seems to have been regarded by the party as one of its own — a somewhat emotionally underdeveloped associate whom it urged to leave his employment in Knoxville and finish his education at Dartmouth. And Remington himself testified:

> It has been implied that some of the people with whom I worked most closely, people who were among my closest friends [he roomed with Pat Todd the organizer of the party cell in the TVA], were

81. *Hearings on the United Public Workers of America*, p. 15.
82. *Hearings on the United Public Workers of America*, p. 56.
83. Murray Kempton, *Part of Our Time* (New York: Simon and Schuster, 1955), pp. 223–224.
84. Eighty-first Congress, Second Session, House of Representatives, Committee on Un-American Activities, *Hearings Regarding Communism in the United States Government*, Part I, p. 1812 (hereafter cited as *Hearings Regarding Communism in the United States Government*).

Communists. I was not. I can understand that if there were secret
Communists engaged in the activities in which I was engaged as the
kid member of the party, kid member of the group, kid member of
the parties working in the union's organization there, that they
might have considered me as one of their own secret clique because
I was associated with them or with others whom they knew to be
members of their secret clique.[85]

Remington never failed to insist that he was not a member of the Communist Party; he was said by an agency board to have been part of
the Communist enterprise, was cleared by the Loyalty Review Board,
was convicted and sentenced for perjury in denying membership in
the party, and met death in prison as a result of a fight among inmates
in which he was apparently only a marginal spectator. In a grim kind
of way his death symbolized his life, close to violence, perhaps not a
committed agent of it, but caught up in it and destroyed, first professionally, and then physically.[86]

Third, some of those who had no obvious connection with the
party at all were more lethal instruments of its intention than those
who carried cards, paid dues, studied Karl Marx, sent telegrams to
Getulio Vargas of Brazil protesting his regime, and contributed to
various defense funds. These were the members of groups in Washington under the direction of J. Peters, and agents who held no official
position of any kind but worked for Soviet military intelligence or the
GPU like Whittaker Chambers and Elizabeth Bentley.

Although the kinds of identification, private and public, with party
enterprise are various, there is less mystery about the swift and varied
mobility of party fans in the Federal service. In part it was aided by
the practice of mutual reference and recommendation in which members helped each other to arrange employment, promotions, and transfers. The party was interested in the identity and location in the government of the relations of new recruits and requested this information
from prospects who had been signed up. This technique, however, may
have been less useful than the operation of professional and, what may
be thought of broadly as "class," factors in the recruitment and de-
ployment of members of the movement. Some were lawyers and
economists, and lawyers and economists tend to know something about
the composition and credentials of the members of their profession.
And they also tend to be graduates of a dozen or so schools. They
know each other or know about each other or know how they can
easily find out about each other. The professional elites thus have

85. *Hearings Regarding Communism in the United States Government*, p. 1813.
86. Kempton, *Part of Our Time*, p. 230.

superior resources of communication, and mobility is accordingly accelerated. That the mobility of party members within the Federal government should have been rather swift and easy, then, is by itself not astonishing. The work histories of the hundreds and thousands of professionals who were not in the Communist movement show a similar mobility for there were numerous new programs in the New Deal and war periods, and shifts and transfers were common all over the government.

But — having said so much — it can be further said that the supporters of the movement did help each other, and in the ways indicated. Whittaker Chambers testified that when he made up his mind to break with the Communist Party, as a matter of security to himself, he decided to obtain employment in the Federal government and asked George Silverman to assist him in this effort. According to Chambers, Silverman referred him to one Irving Kaplan who was said to have got him a job within twenty-four hours.[87] Kaplan declined to answer any questions about the Chambers assertion on Fifth Amendment grounds.[88] He himself had transferred from one branch of the government or from one agency to another several times, and in turn had endorsed such persons as Edward Fitzgerald, who declined on Fifth Amendment grounds to say whether he knew Kaplan, although Kaplan had been listed by Fitzgerald as a reference.[89] According to Elizabeth Bentley, Kaplan was a member of the Silvermaster group.[90]

In forming an opinion about the mobility of party members and their friends in the Federal government, then, account should be taken of the professional and class factors at work, and the assistance that fellow partisans gave each other. But there is still one other element. The promotions and transfers at increases in grade and pay were not a swindle by insiders to benefit incompetents whose only virtue was their association with Communist enterprise. By and large, the mem-

87. *Hearings on Methods of Communist Infiltration in the United States Government*, pp. 3375–3376.
88. *Ibid.*, pp. 3377–3407.
89. Eighty-third Congress, First Session, United States Senate, Committee on the Judiciary, Subcommittee to Investigate the Administration of the Internal Security Act and Other Internal Security Laws, *Hearings on Interlocking Subversion in Government Departments*, 1953, p. 249 (hereafter cited as *Hearings on Interlocking Subversion in Government Departments*).
90. *Hearings on Methods of Communist Infiltration in the United States Government*, p. 3388. When Miss Bentley was asked whether there were other members of the Silvermaster group she had left out, she was prompted by the remark, "You did not mention Mr. Kaplan. Where was he employed?" Her answer was, "He was employed in the War Production Board. He was in a very peculiar position because he was paying his dues to the Perlo group and giving his information to the Silvermaster group. Somehow the two groups got a little scrambled at that point." *Ibid.*

bers of the movement in the significant circles of agency responsibility
were men of considerable professional skills, and they worked hard.
The competence and hard work of the Communist elements in the CIO
were knowingly exploited by John L. Lewis and Philip Murray until
it was thought, in 1948, that the time had come to purge the unions.
And Ring Lardner, Jr., a former member of the Communist Party in
Hollywood, has said,

> I was at that time [1948] a member of the Communist Party, in
> whose ranks I had found some of the most thoughtful, witty, and
> generally stimulating men and women of Hollywood. I also en-
> countered a number of bores and unstable characters, which seemed
> to bear out Bernard Shaw's observation that revolutionary move-
> ments tend to attract the best and worst elements in a given society.[91]

Anthony Panuch, former Deputy Assistant Secretary of State, has
said of Carl Marzani, alias Tony Whales, a former member of the OSS
transferred to the Department of State after the war, that Marzani's
"record of war service had been glowingly praised by high officers of
the supersecret OSS and the War Department," that in some difficult
work required by State after the transfer, Marzani had been the "spark-
plug." [92] Thus did professional skill lead to advancements which enlarged the opportunity for devious service.

To sum up — in the late forties and fifties, it was easy for critics
of the New Deal to imagine that the Communist Party was the
engineer of a master plan of subtle complexity, contrived and cunning,
to work into and through the agencies of the government as soon as
Roosevelt took the oath of office, but the facts seem to be otherwise.
Members of the Communist Party did indeed enter the government in
the early months of the New Deal, but the entry seems to have occurred without plan, and it is even possible that the party bureaucracy
at first looked at it askance. It will be remembered that the Third
Period mentality was not favorable towards working for a capitalist
government.

It doubtless did not take long, however, for the party to realize that
it could make use of its members in Washington to gather information. However, there is no reason to suppose that the party was think-

---

91. "My Life on the Blacklist," *Saturday Evening Post*, October 14, 1961, p. 38.
92. *Hearings on Interlocking Subversion in Government Departments*, pp.
882–890, reprinting an article by Panuch titled, "The Inside Story of the Marzani
Case" from *Plain Talk*, October-March, 1947–48, pp. 884 and 883. Marzani was
convicted of fraud in the concealment of his Communist membership, affiliations,
and activities in connection with his employment in the Department of State.

ing of that information for other purposes than its own political ones
— albeit these were, at least theoretically, revolutionary. It is the suggestion of one anonymous student of communism that sometime in
1934 Earl Browder approached various people friendly to the Communist Party, but not members of it, with the request that they organize a sort of clearing house for information supplied by Communists
in government. If this did happen, it was an incidental use of fortuitous
opportunity rather than a maneuver planned in advance. That the
enterprise was casual is evident from the overt political way in which
some members of the party in useful positions in the government behaved, ending their usefulness for anything else. Thus, when the party
at one time had a number of people in the FBI identification section,
they used it to establish a union, and thereby got every member fired.
Certainly it seems they would not have behaved in such a way if their
primary interest had been in getting official secrets.

Not all members of the party in government, however, wished to
identify themselves publicly with agitational goals of the party. And
the party recognized the utility of keeping people in positions of influence — for instance in the National Labor Relations Board. Hence
it protected these people by permitting them to have secret membership, and by organizing secret groups for their convenience, or by letting them be members at large. This secrecy, although not initially
connected with espionage, was useful when the organization of espionage rings began.

The Communists in government positions did systematically bring
in more of their comrades. In part, this was a simple patronage operation. In this respect it was a matter of building up the party in accordance with principles laid down by President Andrew Jackson and
Senator Marcy, and faithfully followed by non-Communist politicians
before and since. There seems to have been a similar Communist
patronage operation in the motion picture industry, and every Communist-controlled union seems to have operated in the same way.

The war, even before our entry into it, revolutionized the structure
of the administration once again. Many new functions developed for
which the existing agencies — or at least their staffs — were completely
unqualified. This was true in the organization of the economy, in the
foreign policy field, and even in military activities. To these agencies
moved many of the Communists already in government — like thousands of others — and they brought into them friends from the outside.
There were many factors in the migration. Some were personal: salaries in the new agencies tended to be higher; promotion was easier
because of their rapid expansion — indeed, a transfer to one of them
usually involved an immediate promotion; and their activities were

more interesting to a politically-minded person than those of most of the old-line agencies. The opportunities for "infiltration" were also great because some of the people in charge of the new agencies were liberals who were accessible to Communist influence, although they might not have recognized it.

The shift in the party line in 1935 is often regarded as a mere adjustment of tactics — a period of temporary relaxation of open and hard antagonism towards the western democracies — but it may have been more. Selznick is of the opinion that the shift represented something more fundamental, that it represented the culmination "of the logic of Leninism, wherein deception became recognized as communism's most useful and characteristic tool." [93] And Leslie Fiedler has said of the Popular Front Communist that the ordinary Congressman is helpless to recognize him unless there is a "renegade" willing to make revelations. The one kind of Communist most likely to go unidentified and unremarked in the Popular Front period was the "genteel Bolshevik who keeps his nose clean and never even reads the *New Republic*." [94] Chambers, although speaking about the year 1932, described the new kind of person entering the Communist Party then and later in the 1930's, who was to find positions in the government:

> An entirely new type of Communist made his appearance, not singly but in clusters, whose members often already knew one another, influenced one another and shared the same Communist or leftist views. A surprising number came of excellent native American families. Nearly all were college trained from the top percent of their classes.[95]

And Nathaniel Weyl has said of the influx of the newcomers,

> Under Stalinist leadership the lineaments of the archetypal underground Communist had entirely changed. The resolute and romantic organizer of street war had been put away in a museum. Into his place had stepped the iron bureaucrat — the well-dressed, softspoken, capable executive who sat in the board room or on the Government committee. This man with a briefcase led a secret life of his own. If Communist rule should be proclaimed in this country, he would move to the head of the table.[96]

93. Philip Selznick, *The Organizational Weapon* (Glencoe, Illinois: Free Press, 1960), p. 145.
94. Fiedler, *An End to Innocence*, p. 19.
95. Chambers, *Witness*, p. 269.
96. Nathaniel Weyl, *Treason* (Washington, D.C.: Public Affairs Press, 1950), p. 425.

For numbers of these smooth, professionally competent, hard-working, deceptive partisans of the Popular Front, the future began when
they entered the employment of the Federal government in the thirties.
The discovery of their pasts in the late forties was to create a controversy of historical bitterness.

Part Two   The Compromise of Trust

> . . . And now less
> Than ever can I trust thee;
>   for 'gainst those
> Of hasty tempers with more ease
>   we guard . . . than the silent foe
> Who acts with prudence.
>   *Medea*

For the offices of a state
are posts of honor —
ARISTOTLE, *Politics*

IV The Ware Group

Julien Benda, more than a generation ago, rebuked the intellectuals of his day for not rising above the passions of class, nation, and race, which he said they had embraced; for not respecting their natural duty to act as moral men, detached from the strifes of the vulgar, guardians of values of mind and spirit; and for failing their destiny to shape and decide transcendental truth.[1] It could have been of Communists in the government service in America that Benda spoke when he said,

> The "clerks" have not been content simply to adopt political passions, if by this one means that they have made a place for these passions side by side with the activities they are bound to carry on as "clerks." They have introduced these passions into those activities. They permit, they desire them to be mingled with their work as artists, as men of learning, as philosophers, to color the essence of their work and to mark all its productions. And indeed never were there so many political works among those which ought to be the mirror of the disinterested intelligence.[2]

But of course he was writing about other groups in other times and places; and the appearance of followers of the Communist movement in the American government service was still some time in the future. They seem to have appeared first in the Department of Agriculture, they represented the Popular Front personality and not the Third Period attitude, and they seemed to have been primarily concerned

---

1. Julien Benda, *The Treason of the Intellectuals*, trans. Richard Aldington (New York: William Morrow, 1928). The translator confessed difficulty in producing an English equivalent for "clercs" in the original title, *La Trahison des Clercs*. The word "intellectuals" came closest to Benda's meaning when he said, ". . . I mean all those whose activity essentially is *not* the pursuit of practical aims, all those who seek their joy in the practice of an art or a science or metaphysical speculation, in short, in the possession of non-material advantages, and hence in a certain manner say: 'My kingdom is not of this world.'" *Ibid.*, p. 43.
2. Benda, *The Treason of the Intellectuals*, p. 67.

at first with agitational ends rather than espionage, although for a few this was to change.

Origins of the Ware Group

It was not until fourteen years after the establishment of the famous Ware cell in the Department of Agriculture that the news that it had existed became public.[3] It is a gentle entertainment in a world of mortal paradoxes that the founder of the cell, Harold Ware, got his start in government during the Coolidge and Hoover administrations.[4] Ware was a dedicated Communist, the son of a dedicated Communist,[5] a charter member of the Communist Party, a specialist in agriculture and its problems who had done work on American agriculture for Lenin himself, the husband of a Communist whom he wed in a ceremony performed by a Presbyterian minister by the name of Norman Thomas, and a driver of fast cars, who was to meet his death in one of them in 1935. In the early 1920's, Ware had been in the Soviet Union on a cooperative farm project, and when he returned to the United States he came convinced that the prospects for organizing American farmers were good. This, it has been said, was also the opinion of the Communist International, and so Harold Ware was entrusted with the task of organizing the farmers and given $25,000 by the International to get things going.[6]

The principal source for the statement about Ware's connection with the International is Whittaker Chambers, and although the assertion is clear enough, the supporting evidence is somewhat difficult to weigh. In his first public statement, made before the House Committee on Un-American Activities on August 3, 1948, Chambers said that the apparatus to which he had been attached was "an underground

3. See the statement of the chairman of the House Committee on Un-American Activities in 1955: "In 1948, the Committee on Un-American Activities of the House of Representatives heard, for the first time, testimony of Communist cells within the Government." Eighty-fourth Congress, First Session, House of Representatives, Committee on Un-American Activities, *Hearings on Investigation of Communist Infiltration of Government*, 6 pts., 1955–1956, p. 2955 (hereafter cited as *Fuchs Hearings*).

4. This was the occasion for a partisan comment by the chairman of the House Committee to one of his Republican colleagues. Eighty-first Congress, Second Session, House of Representatives, Committee on Un-American Activities, *Hearings Regarding Communism in the United States Government*, April-June 1950, p. 2898.

5. This was "Mother Bloor." Whittaker Chambers mentions the demotion of the mother of Benjamin Gitlow as "Mother Gitlow" and the installation of "Mother Bloor" as the matriarch of the American party after Gitlow had been expelled from the party as a Lovestoneite. *Witness* (New York: Random House, 1952), p. 204. Mother Gitlow was also expelled from the party for "incurable right-wing deviationism."

6. Chambers, *Witness*, pp. 333–334.

organization of the United States Community Party, developed, to the best of my knowledge, by Harold Ware, one of the sons of the Communist leader known as 'Mother Bloor'." [7] In response to questions, Chambers later said, "Harold Ware was, of course, the organizer." [8] Somewhat later the following colloquy occurred,

> Mr. Stripling: Harold Ware was employed in the AAA, was he not?
> Mr. Chambers: I don't know whether he was or not. If I have known, I have forgotten. My impression is he wasn't.[9]

Thereafter the hearings in August and September were concentrated rather more on the conflict of testimony between Chambers and Alger Hiss than on small points of identity about Harold Ware. In his subsequent book, *Witness*, Chambers was considerably more definite and detailed about Ware's antecedents and his connection with the Department of Agriculture, and about his role as a functionary of the International. There is no assertion that the organization of the Washington cells was on the specific instruction of the International in 1933 and, as indicated in Chapter Three, there is much to suggest that the first appearance of Communists in Federal employment was uncontrived.

But the interest of the International (and indeed of the GPU and Soviet Military Intelligence) in the development of various party enterprises in the United States in and around 1933 can be abundantly established. This was the year, for example, that Gerhardt Eisler, traveling on passports forged in the name of Samuel Liptzen, showed up as the top International representative in this country, where he was to stay for five years under such names as "Edwards" and "Brown." [10] He was to reappear in 1941 with a woman who became

7. Eightieth Congress, Second Session, House of Representatives, Committee on Un-American Activities, *Hearings Regarding Communist Espionage in the United States Government*, p. 565 (hereafter cited as the *Hiss Hearings*).

8. *Hiss Hearings*, p. 566.

9. *Hiss Hearings*, p. 575.

10. Eightieth Congress, First Session, House of Representatives, Committee on Un-American Activities, *Investigation of Un-American Propaganda Activities in the United States*, transcript of proceedings, February 6, 1947, p. 16 (hereafter cited as *Eisler Proceedings*). One witness who identified Eisler in these proceedings was William O'Dell Nowell, a minor official of the American Communist Party who attended the Lenin School in Moscow, an institution of the Communist International for the training of espionage agents. Hede Massing, in her book, *This Deception* (New York: Duell, Sloan and Pearce, 1951), pp. 96–97, also places Eisler in Moscow at the time Nowell said he was there. According to her account, Eisler had just returned from the mission to China that reestablished him in the favor of Stalin. Nowell was a man of flexible principles who had been associated with Gerald L. K. Smith. He was used as a witness for the government in the trial of eleven Communist leaders for violation of the Smith Act of 1940, although at least one critic was of the opinion that he should

his third wife, to deny that he was a member of any organization whatsoever, and of course, therefore, of any Communist organization, to be denounced by his sister in 1947, and to flee on the Polish ship *Batory* to Poland and to East Germany where he was to become the propaganda specialist for Ulbricht and the East German regime.[11] A German Communist who married Hede Massing (née Tune) from whom he separated in 1923, Eisler had incurred the disfavor of Stalin by opposing Ernst Thaelmann in Germany when Stalin was supporting him. But he climbed back into Stalin's favor after a mission to China in the late twenties, where he was said to have been distinguished for his ruthlessness in the service of the Kremlin.[12] Among those reporting to Eisler during his stay in the United States in the thirties was J. Peters, the author of the manual of organization that has been discussed, whose principal distinction, however, was not literary but managerial. He was the direct link between the Ware apparatus and the International through Eisler. He was also the man who introduced Whittaker Chambers to his superior in espionage, Colonel Boris Bykov.

The Communist International was not the only Soviet agency[13] interested in the establishment of party enterprises, including centers of information in the United States in 1933. Two others were the GPU and the Soviet Military Intelligence, and each of them maintained separate lines of communication and contact with its respective underground. That the GPU extended its effort in America at this time is established in the testimony of Hede Massing. Indeed, the GPU was

not have been so employed. Nathaniel Weyl, *The Battle Against Disloyalty* (New York: Crowell, 1951), p. 313.

11. Upon his entry into the United States in 1941 under his own name, Eisler denied that he was then or had ever been a member of any Communist organization, or even sympathetic to the "Communist cause," while in 1942 he denied that he had been a member of any organization. *Eisler Proceedings*, pp. 6 and 49.

12. Massing, *This Deception*, pp. 95–96.

13. Technically the Communist International was not an agency of the Soviet Union but an international organization theoretically independent of the Soviet Union, providing a common association for all the Communist parties of the world, the Soviet party being one of the constituent members. But the fact was that the Soviet party, certainly after 1929, dominated the International as it dominated the Soviet government, so that the International was then an agency of the Russian party as the Soviet government was another. The International was formally dissolved in 1943 when the American Communist Party was formally dissolved. The International later appeared as the Cominform and the American party resumed its earlier official identity after two years of existence as the Communist Political Association. This is not to say that the Cominform was a reincarnated Comintern, but it did exist as an instrument for transmitting the desires of Moscow to Communist parties throughout the world. The Cominform was dissolved in April 1956. For a discussion of the Cominform, see Thomas H. Stevenson, "International Communist Fronts," in George B. de Huszar and Associates, *Soviet Power and Policy* (New York: Crowell, 1955).

able, through its American leader, Valentine Markin, to force the
Soviet Military Intelligence to lie dormant in the early years of the
New Deal, after an appeal to Moscow over authority and precedence.[14]
Markin was found in a hallway in New York in 1934 with a head
wound from which he died, and his place as head of the GPU appa-
ratus was then taken by Walter Grinke, working under the name of
"Bill." [15] Throughout the thirties, the GPU also maintained surveil-
lance through an individual operating under the Armenian alias, Gaik
Badalovich Ovakimian.[16]

The third line of underground influence extending into the United
States from the Soviet Union was the Fourth Section of the Soviet
Military Intelligence which, despite its dormancy, seems nevertheless
to have maintained some activity in the early years of the New Deal
which was accelerated in the later years. Whittaker Chambers was
never sure for whom he was actually working and did not learn until
after he had broken with the Communist Party and deserted the underground in 1938 that he had actually been working for six years for
Colonel Boris Bykov, a Russian officer of the Fourth Section of the Red
Army.[17] He learned about Bykov, whom he had known only as "Peter,"
from General Walter Krivitsky, who had been the head of Fourth
Section activities in Europe.[18]

There is no established connection between the organization of the

14. Mrs. Massing's superior in Europe had been a man she knew only as
"Ludwig." "Ludwig" was Ignace Reiss, head of the European GPU, who was
assassinated in Switzerland in 1937. She was handed over to "Der Lange," the
Long Man, in Europe for instruction on her mission to the United States, the
Long Man being Paul Hardt, "the head of some apparatus, probably the GPU
in England." Massing, *This Deception*, pp. 136–137. Her first connection upon
her arrival in America, she said, was William Joseph Berman, who turned her
over to her first supervisor, "Walter." *Ibid.*, pp. 143–149. "Walter," according to
Mrs. Massing's account, was the "head of all GPU activities in the United States,"
a man by the name of Valentine Markin. *Ibid.*, p. 155. Markin, in fact, was the top
GPU agent, having established the priority of the GPU over the Soviet Military
Intelligence as the principal espionage control in the United States in 1933. This
he may have done by convincing Molotov that Soviet Military Intelligence had
bungled the counterfeiting operation through its functionaries, Nick Dozenberg
and Burtan. This account is confirmed by both Mrs. Massing, *This Deception*,
pp. 154–155, and David J. Dallin, *Soviet Espionage* (New Haven: Yale, 1955),
pp. 403–404. A note of skeptical caution towards this explanation is suggested,
however.

15. Massing, *This Deception*, p. 162.

16. *The Shameful Years: Thirty Years of Espionage in the United States*, prepared and released by the Committee on Un-American Activities, U. S. House of
Representatives, Washington, D.C., December 30, 1951, pp. 13–19. After his arrest in 1941 for violation of the Foreign Agents Registration Act, Ovakimian was
allowed to return to the Soviet Union by agreement between the United States
and the Soviet Union in exchange for Americans arrested by the latter.

17. Chambers, *Witness*, pp. 26–27.

18. Chambers, *Witness*, p. 27.

Ware group and the international agencies of Communist espionage. The most that the available evidence justifies saying is that the former was organized and the latter were stimulated into activity at roughly about the same time.[19] Agents for the Fourth Section were already in action; the GPU was shuffling its people between Europe and America; and the International was busy. Even though Dallin regards the level of espionage activity in 1933–34 as somewhat reduced (but not minor),[20] the instruments were on hand for the intensification of this activity as the exigencies of Soviet policy might require. After the formal change in the party line, which ratified trends already in being, the full development of the underground system occurred. In the fully developed system there were those who came from abroad to direct operations — men like Ware, J. Peters, George Mink,[21] and Jacob Golos,[22] who were members of the American party, and the "sources," not all of whom were party members, who worked in the agencies of the Federal government and supplied various kinds of information. Of them Chambers was to say,

> Those who lacked the hardihood or clarity to follow the logic of their position and become Communists clumped around the edges of the party, self-consciously hesitant, apologetic, easing their social consciences by doing whatever the party asked them to do so long as they did not have to know exactly what it was. . . . Within a decade, simply by pursuing the careers that ordinarily lay open to them, these newcomers would carry the weak and stumbling American Communist Party directly into the highest councils of the na-

19. Ralph de Toledano and Victor Lasky assert the connection flatly: "And along with other Comintern agents, he [Ware] was given the order to begin the systematic creation of Communist cells wherever possible. . . . Ware, because of a seven-year tenure (1925–1932) as a dollar-a-year man for the Agriculture Department, was assigned to Washington to direct operations there." *Seeds of Treason* (New York: Funk and Wagnalls, 1950), pp. 44–45. The authors, however, adduce no documentation or other evidence to support the assertion.

20. Dallin says that Soviet espionage in America had been reduced in 1933–34, but that after the Seventh World Congress it was "not only increased but pushed forward with unprecedented vigor." *Soviet Espionage*, p. 413.

21. George Mink was said to be an American agent of the GPU who, without waterfront experience, nevertheless was put in charge of the National Maritime Union with the help of the American party, and served with the GPU in its American Section in Spain during the civil war. See Eightieth Congress, First Session, House of Representatives, Committee on Un-American Activities, *Investigation of Un-American Propaganda Activities in the United States (Regarding Leon Josephson and Samuel Liptzen)*, pp. 39–41.

22. Jacob Golos, also an American agent of the GPU, was the head of World Tourists, Inc., a cover for illegal traffic in and out of the United States and elsewhere, and the man for whom Elizabeth Bentley worked as a courier in the underground. *Hiss Hearings*, p. 505.

tion, would subtly (or sometimes boldly) help to shape the country's domestic and foreign policies.[23]

Composition of the Ware Group

The composition of the Ware group in the Department of Agriculture illustrates Chambers' comment on the social and personal characteristics of the new Communist type. It included Lee Pressman, Nathan Witt, John Abt, Henry Collins, Charles Kramer, and Alger Hiss, according to Chambers.[24] Independent confirmation of four of the members has been supplied by Lee Pressman, who first refused to admit the fact and then recanted his testimony,[25] and of all of them by Nathaniel Weyl.[26] The head of the group was Harold Ware until his death in 1935, at which time his place was taken by Nathan Witt. All of these men were in the Agricultural Adjustment Administration whose counsel was then Jerome Frank, of whom Schlesinger has said, "He searched the law schools and the great firms of New York and Chicago to make up his staff. Knowledge of farming was, from Frank's point of view, the least of requirements; he had a lawyer's confidence that men trained in the law could master anything." [27] Among the men recruited by Jerome Frank from the Harvard Law School were Hiss, Pressman, Abt, and Witt. Although one account credits Pressman with being the principal force in drawing this group together,[28] the fact seems to be that it was not Pressman who brought Hiss to Washington but Hiss who urged Frank to bring Pressman; Pressman brought in Witt and Frank brought in Abt whom he had known in Chicago. This would seem to suggest that the group was originally brought to-

23. Chambers, *Witness*, p. 269.
24. *Hiss Hearings*, p. 565.
25. Pressman at first refused to say, on Fifth Amendment and other grounds, whether he was a member of the Communist Party (*Hiss Hearings*, pp. 1022–1028) or whether he knew a number of people about whom he was asked. But two years later he changed his mind and said that he had been a member of the Ware group and a member of the Communist Party. *Hearings Regarding Communism in the United States Government*, Part 2, pp. 2844–2901. Pressman made a curious slip of the tongue in the first hearing when he asked whether anyone had accused him of espionage. His question was: "Has there been any charge made by any witness that has appeared before this committee that I have participated in any espionage activity, either while a member — or rather an employee of the Federal government or thereafter?" *Hiss Hearings*, p. 1023. In fact there had not been any testimony that he had engaged in espionage.
26. Eighty-third Congress, First Session, United States Senate, Committee on the Judiciary, Subcommittee to Investigate the Administration of the Internal Security Act and Other Internal Security Laws, *Hearings on Subversive Influence in the Educational Process*, p. 711 (hereafter cited as *Subversive Influence in the Educational Process*).
27. Arthur M. Schlesinger, Jr., *The Coming of the New Deal* (Boston: Houghton Mifflin, 1959), p. 50.
28. De Toledano and Lasky, *Seeds of Treason*, p. 42.

gether in the AAA of the Department of Agriculture, not by the Comintern nor by Ware nor by any other agent or agency of the Soviet Union. They were brought together largely by the imagination of an able lawyer and civil servant responding to the requirements of the programs and of the service he was appointed to administer. But once on hand, they were fashioned into a left faction under the direction of their organizer, Harold Ware.[29] It was Ware who recruited Pressman into the Communist Party;[30] others may have been in the party when they were appointed to their posts.[31]

Although Pressman agreed with Chambers about the names of Witt, Abt, and Kramer, there was some difference of opinion between them about others. Chambers also named Henry Collins, Jr., who, he said, had been treasurer of the group collecting dues for the Communist Party, and Alger Hiss. Pressman said that Collins was not a member of his group, that Collins was not an employee of the Department of Agriculture, and that the House Committee's information was therefore wrong.[32] He also said that "Henry Collins was not present at a meeting during my participation in that group";[33] by reiterating that the members of the group were the four named and no others, he excluded Hiss; and he further said that he had "absolutely no recollection" of "having met Whittaker Chambers in Washington in connection with my participation in the group." [34] In his book, Chambers later indicated that the testimony of Pressman provided "an account of its [the Ware group's] organization which may well bear a sketchy resemblance to its first formative state." [35] By 1934, however, accord-

29. Although Chambers was reasonably clear about the faction and its membership, he seems not to have been so some three years before he made the news public, when he was reported by Raymond Murphy of the Department of State, who made memoranda of his conversations with Chambers, to have said that Lee Pressman was not a party member. Eighty-third Congress, First Session, United States Senate, Committee on the Judiciary, Subcommittee to Investigate the Administration of the Internal Security Act and Other Internal Security Laws, *Hearings on Interlocking Subversion in Government Departments*, 1953, p. 1183 (hereafter cited as *Hearings on Interlocking Subversion in Government Departments*). The conversation took place at Chambers' place in Westminster, Maryland, on March 20, 1945, and Murphy made his memoranda the next day. He may, of course, not have recalled the conversation accurately, but then, again, Chambers may have been misleading.

30. This is according to Pressman's testimony about himself. *Hearings Regarding Communism in the United States Government*, Part 2, p. 2853.

31. Nathaniel Weyl said that he was a member of the party before he came to Washington to work in the Department of Agriculture as an economist in the AAA. *Subversive Influence in the Educational Process*, p. 710.

32. *Hearings Regarding Communism in the United States Government*, Part 2, pp. 2853–2854.

33. *Ibid.*, p. 2879.

34. *Ibid.*, p. 2881.

35. Chambers, *Witness*, p. 335.

ing to the account of Chambers, the Ware group had developed into a "tightly organized underground, managed by a directory of seven men." But since Pressman was included in the seven, it must follow, if the account of Chambers is correct, that Pressman's own testimony was describing as the *only* phase of the organization an early situation which he may have known in its later phases also.

Henry H. Collins, Jr., named by Chambers, in fact was not in the Department of Agriculture but in the National Recovery Administration from 1933 to 1935, although he did join the Soil Conservation Service in the Department of Agriculture in 1935, staying there some three years or so. On August 11, 1948, he was questioned by the House Committee on Un-American Activities and refused, on grounds of possible incrimination, to say whether he was a member of the Communist Party. He also refused to say, on the same grounds, whether he had ever met with Abt, Hiss, Pressman, or J. Peters at his apartment at St. Matthews Court in Washington.[36] Although he had been questioned by the FBI in 1942 about his connections with certain organizations, he said that he could not remember whether he was asked about Communist connections. Throughout, he was willing to say that he never knew a man by the name of Whittaker Chambers but declined on grounds of possible incrimination to say whether he knew "Carl," the name Chambers used in the underground.[37] In 1953, the Senate Internal Security Subcommittee took him over the same ground,[38] with the same result. Although Nathaniel Weyl in February 1952 had corroborated the Chambers statement that Collins was a member of the Ware group, the latter continued to decline to answer the familiar questions about his acquaintance with members of that group on the ground of possible incrimination.[39] Chambers, however, said that he and Collins had been close personal friends, and that the latter had served "irrepressibly as a recruiting agent for the Soviet apparatus among members of the State Department," [40] whatever may be meant by the word "irrepressibly."

Charles Kramer (Krivitsky), identified by both Chambers and Pressman as an original member of the Ware group, when asked about his possible acquaintance with any of the others who had been named, declined to answer on grounds of incrimination.[41] He entered Federal employment in the AAA in 1933, worked with the Consumers Counsel in the Department of Agriculture, and helped to set up the first

36. *Hiss Hearings,* pp. 803–804.
37. *Hiss Hearings,* pp. 808–810.
38. *Hearings on Interlocking Subversion in Government Departments,* pp. 1–52.
39. *Ibid.,* p. 11.
40. Chambers, *Witness,* p. 31.
41. *Hiss Hearings,* pp. 818–835, for Kramer's testimony.

farm labor program under the Jones-Costigan Act. His service in the Department lasted until 1935 when he began to move around — first to the National Youth Administration, then to the La Follette Committee in 1936, the National Labor Relations Board in 1937, the Office of Price Administration in 1942, and to two Senate committees thereafter.[42] Elizabeth Bentley was to identify Kramer in testimony before the House Committee on Un-American Activities as a member of the Perlo group in the 1940's,[43] but she did not do so in her subsequent book and barely acknowledged him in one reference.[44] Herbert Fuchs, who confessed his Communist role in the National Labor Relations Board, could only say of Kramer that he had met him "once or twice on an introduction-basis only." [45] Chicago and Washington newspaper accounts had reported that Fuchs had stated he had known Kramer as a member of the Communist Party, but the reports were in error, and were corrected in the record of the committee hearings the next day.[46] Although the public record on Kramer is sparse, he was counted by the FBI in a "top secret" report to the White House as one of the sources through which information was passing from the government to Soviet agents.[47]

More will later be said about Alger Hiss and Nathan Witt and John Abt and about their activities respectively in the State Department and the National Labor Relations Board. As to their presence in the Ware group in the AAA, it may be said again that Chambers and Pressman agreed on the latter two, while Pressman declined to corroborate Chambers on the membership of Hiss in the group. Two others were named by Chambers in his public testimony on August 3, 1948 — Donald Hiss and Victor Perlo.[48] Donald Hiss, the brother of Alger

42. *Hiss Hearings,* p. 819, for a résumé of Kramer's Federal employment. The two Senate committees for which Kramer worked were the Subcommittee on War Mobilization (the Kilgore Committee) and the Subcommittee on Wartime Health and Education (the Pepper Committee). He was with the Kilgore Committee in 1943 and with the Pepper Committee in 1945 and 1946.

43. *Hiss Hearings,* p. 513.

44. Elizabeth Bentley, *Out of Bondage* (New York: Devin-Adair, 1951). The book was published three years after her public testimony before the House Committee on Un-American Activities. The only reference to Kramer appears at p. 239 in the sentence "Seated around the living room were four men, Victor Perlo, Charlie Kramer, and two others." This statement occurs in her account of a trip to the New York apartment of John Abt to take over the so-called Perlo group after arrangements to do so, she said, had been made by Earl Browder.

45. *Fuchs Hearings,* p. 3015.

46. *Fuchs Hearings,* pp. 3021–3022.

47. *Hearings on Interlocking Subversion in Government Departments,* p. 385. The FBI memorandum, or reference to it, appears in several places. In this place, the witness was Victor Perlo who refused to answer on grounds of incrimination when asked whether he knew Charles Kramer.

48. *Hiss Hearings,* p. 566.

Hiss, was an entirely different witness from any of the others named. He answered responsively all questions put to him after making a statement of denial of all charges to the press on the same day that Chambers made them.[49] In fact, Donald Hiss appeared at the hearing at his own request.[50] Although Chambers had accused Hiss of membership in the Ware group in the AAA when he testified before the House Committee, and had included his name in lists given to Adolf Berle in 1939 and to a State Department security officer in 1945, he did not include Donald Hiss as one of the members of the Ware group in *Witness*, which he published in 1952.[51]

Although he did not include Donald Hiss in the Ware group list, Chambers in *Witness* did, however, reprint parts of the testimony he had given before the House Committee. Part of the testimony contained mention of Donald Hiss, in which Chambers said that his relation with Donald Hiss had been a "purely formal one," that Donald Hiss had known Chambers as "Carl," and that Chambers had collected party dues from him although he was not clear where he had made such collections, supposing that it had been in Alger's house.[52] Chambers said that Donald Hiss had been in the Immigration Section of the Department of Labor, from where he transferred to the Department of State.[53] At that point in his testimony the questioning of Chambers by then Representative Richard Nixon was turned back to Alger Hiss, and Donald ceased to figure in the account. Congressman Karl Mundt also took the testimony about Donald Hiss without much apparent concern, and chose to pursue the matter of Alger Hiss instead.[54]

Despite the reprinted testimony, Chambers in *Witness*, to repeat, did not say that Donald Hiss had been a member of the Ware group. He merely referred to the testimony of Donald Hiss before the House Committee as "one brief piece of testimony . . . which in its consequences proved curiously important." [55] It was to be "curiously important" not because it had anything to do with Donald Hiss, but because it had something to do with Alger Hiss. After reciting the testi-

49. *Hiss Hearings*, pp. 928–933.

50. Alger Hiss, *In the Court of Public Opinion* (New York: Knopf, 1957), p. 137.

51. Chambers, *Witness*, pp. 334–335, contain the listing of the seven men Chambers said were members of the Ware group. Donald Hiss is not included, although in his 1948 testimony before the House Committee, Chambers had eight in the group, the extra man being Donald Hiss.

52. Chambers, *Witness*, pp. 569–570.

53. Chambers, *Witness*, p. 570.

54. Chambers, *Witness*, p. 689.

55. One commentator on the proceedings judged that the questioning of Donald Hiss was an example of "poor questioning" on the part of committee members. Robert K. Carr, *The House Committee on Un-American Activities* (Ithaca, N.Y.: Cornell, 1952), p. 292.

mony of Donald Hiss in which categorical and sweeping denials were
made of all charges laid against him by Chambers before the House
Committee, Chambers said, "Donald Hiss's forthrightness had a powerful impact on the public." [56] For Donald had said that he had never
known Chambers under any name. This had to mean, then, that he
had never known Chambers under the name of George Crosley, the
cognomen by which Alger Hiss was to say that he knew Chambers
as a free lance writer when he, Alger, was with the Nye Committee.
The argument of Chambers on this point seems to have been that if
Donald did not know Chambers as George Crosley, he was therefore
unable to "bear out his brother's testimony in any way at any time
upon that interesting character," who was presumably fictitious.

Although failing in his book to reiterate his charge that Donald
Hiss had been a member of the Ware group, Chambers did make some
further account of him. He reported that his superior in the Soviet
underground, Colonel Bykov, at one point wanted to know whether
Donald, who was then in the Department of State, would bring out
material. The question was said to have been raised in an inquiry by
Bykov to Alger Hiss through Chambers acting as interpreter, as to
whether Alger would himself act as a source of information, to which
Alger is said to have given his assent. The conversation then continued:

> "Ask him," said Bykov eagerly, "if the brother will also bring out
> material?" By "the brother," Bykov meant Donald Hiss, Alger's
> younger brother, who was a legal adviser to the newly created
> Philippines Division of the State Department. In his own way, Alger
> answered: no.[57]

There is no further mention by Chambers of any charge of subversion
or espionage against Donald Hiss.

In fact, Donald Hiss was never accused of espionage; the most even
Chambers could assert was that he was a member of the Communist
Party.[58] During the first trial of Alger Hiss for perjury, Chambers,
in his account of the meeting of Bykov with Chambers and Hiss,
testified that when Alger said his brother would not serve as a source
for the underground, he also said that "he was not sure his brother
was sufficiently developed for that." [59] Despite this clear indication

56. Chambers, *Witness*, p. 577.
57. Chambers, *Witness*, p. 418.
58. De Toledano and Lasky point out that Donald Hiss "was accused only of
membership in a Party cell—never of espionage." *Seeds of Treason*, p. 80n. And
Alger Hiss has said that Chambers had ever received any
documents from Donald Hiss. *In the Court of Public Opinion*, p. 183.
59. Alistair Cooke, *Generation on Trial* (New York: Knopf, 1950), p. 128

that Donald Hiss was not involved in espionage, one public account by a presumed expert (Dallin) listed him under a topic sentence that read, "During the war years the Soviet apparat had its men in at least the following agencies. . . ." [60] In this list Donald Hiss (and others) are down for the State Department "with access to the secret cable room of OSS." The author irresponsibly supplies no substantiation for the statement, and it seems likely that Donald Hiss was drawn into the wide-ranging turmoil over possible subversion only because his name was Hiss, not because there was any provable testimony against him.

Although there were some discrepancies in the charges against Victor Perlo, the account of his asserted involvement with the Soviet underground hung together with considerable consistency, since there was some corroboration and there were no real conflicts. One of the discrepancies concerns Perlo's employment at the time Chambers said that he knew him. In his testimony before the House Committee in August 1948, Chambers was asked where Perlo was employed at the time he (Perlo) was "a member of the apparatus" — presumably the Ware group — to which Chambers was assigned. Chambers said, "I believe at that time Victor Perlo was employed by the Brookings Institution." [61] But the record of employment of Victor Perlo that Chambers set out in his book showed that Perlo was employed by the Brookings Institution from 1937 to 1939. He could not have been at Brookings when Chambers was connected with the Ware apparatus by J. Peters in 1934; and since Chambers said that he had left the party and the underground in mid-April 1938,[62] the chances are good that he could not have known Perlo very well. In fact, in his testimony he admitted that he had not known Perlo very well, said that he did not like him, and thought him to have been "a rather sullen and shallow kind of man." [63] He also said that the only place he had seen him was at the house of Henry Collins and that in the Ware group Perlo "was a very minor figure."

Perlo did not cut a very admirable figure when he testified before the House Committee after Chambers had named him as a member of the Ware group. He tried to make it appear in the record that he had come voluntarily but it was established that he had not appeared on his own initiative, that he had never asked to appear, and that he was under subpoena.[64] Perlo was never employed by the Department of Agriculture but entered the Federal government in 1933 by joining

60. Dallin, *Soviet Espionage*, p. 441.
61. *Hiss Hearings*, p. 571.
62. *Hiss Hearings*, p. 575.
63. *Hiss Hearings*, p. 575.
64. *Hiss Hearings*, p. 701.

the National Recovery Administration as an economist and he stayed there until 1935. From NRA he went to the Home Owner's Loan Corporation until 1937, then to Brookings for two years, and into the Department of Commerce in 1939. From Commerce he moved to the Office of Price Administration where he was Chief of the Statistical Analysis Branch of the Research Division, and then to the War Production Board in 1943, and to the Treasury Department in 1945, where he was hired by Harry Dexter White, Assistant Secretary of the Treasury, on the recommendation of "various people" he said he could not identify.[65]

Except for vital statistics and employment data, Perlo declined to answer most of the questions put to him on grounds of possible self-incrimination. He refused on these grounds to say whether he knew Donald Hiss, although the latter was to deny the truth of Chambers' statements about him, without himself falling back on the defense of self-incrimination. Elizabeth Bentley, who was in the committee room while Perlo was testifying, was called upon to identify Perlo after his refusals to answer questions, and she did so, saying as she had earlier that he was the head of a group of government employees who were furnishing information for her as courier for the Soviet underground.[66] After this confrontation, Perlo was returned to the stand and asked whether he had furnished any information to Elizabeth T. Bentley. He refused to answer on grounds of possible self-incrimination.

At this point in his testimony, Perlo wanted to put into the record a statement that he had read to the committee when he had met with it in executive session previous to his public appearance. He was asked by committee members whether the statement he wished to read was the same as the one they had earlier heard, and he said that it was, with a trifling change. The original statement contained the sentence, "I vigorously deny the charges which have been leveled against me." [67] He was asked whether he intended to read that he vigorously denied the charges that Elizabeth Bentley had made, and he said that he did. The following exchange then occurred:

> Mr. Nixon: I again refer to your statement: "I vigorously deny the charges that have been leveled against me." One of the charges that has been leveled against you is that you gave secret Government information to Miss Bentley. Do I understand you to say now that you vigorously deny that charge?
>
> Mr. Perlo: On advice of counsel I stand on my rights under the fifth amendment to the Constitution and refuse to answer that

65. *Hiss Hearings*, p. 681.
66. *Hiss Hearings*, p. 687.
67. *Hiss Hearings*, p. 693.

question on the ground that it might tend to incriminate or degrade me.

Mr. Nixon: Then, you do not wish to keep this particular statement in, because this statement is not true; is that correct?

Mr. Perlo: I wish to keep the sentence in the statement.

Mr. Nixon: You vigorously deny the charges made against you and yet you refuse to testify on the ground that you may incriminate yourself when asked about a specific charge. Is that it?

Mr. Perlo: I decline to answer that question.

Mr. Nixon: On what ground?

Mr. Perlo: On the ground that it might tend to incriminate or degrade me.[68]

Perlo was allowed to make his statement to the committee and to get into the record reference to his role in "helping in my humble way to carry out the great New Deal program under the leadership of Franklin D. Roosevelt"; and to say that he was "particularly proud of my present opportunity to contribute to the great campaign of Henry Wallace for peace, against inflation, and for decent standards of living and full democratic rights for all people." He did not say that he vigorously denied the charges that had been leveled against him.[69]

Perlo's chief role in the underground scene was to be played after 1944, according to Elizabeth Bentley's account, when Browder made arrangements for her to take over a group of sources headed by Perlo.[70] She did not know him in the thirties when the Ware group was formed, and the information about his activities at that time is provided only in the testimony and book of Whittaker Chambers.[71] Although Cham-

68. *Hiss Hearings*, pp. 694–695.

69. Although he omitted from the statement the express denial of charges that he had included in the earlier version, he did use the following language: "I am a loyal American and I categorically assert that I have never violated the laws or interests of my country." If this was intended to mean the same thing as the sentence omitted, it may be wondered why any change was made. If it was intended to mean something different, the difference is not very clear. *Hiss Hearings*, pp. 699–700 for the Perlo statement. At the time of the hearing he was a paid worker for the Progressive Party.

70. Bentley, *Out of Bondage*, p. 239.

71. Five years after the hearings in August 1948 in which Bentley and Chambers both accused Perlo (but independently of each other) and Perlo also testified, he was taken over the same ground by the Senate Subcommittee on Internal Security. On this occasion, when asked "Are you presently a member of a Communist espionage ring?" he answered "No," unequivocally and without resort to the plea of self-incrimination, but when asked whether he was "presently a member of the Communist Party" he declined to answer on grounds of self-incrimination. *Hearing on Interlocking Subversion in Government Departments*, Part 7, p. 384. When asked whether he had been the head of an espionage ring during the war, Perlo refused to answer on grounds of self-incrimination. *Ibid.*, p. 385. A new witness to corroborate the testimony of Chambers about Perlo's member-

bers did not think that Perlo was more than a minor figure in the original Ware group, he did report an incident that would seem to indicate that Perlo thought of himself as something more. According to this report, when Harold Ware was killed in an automobile accident, it became necessary to decide who his successor as leader of the group would be. The majority of the group preferred Nathan Witt. J. Peters was for Witt, and so was Chambers. There were the necessary votes to carry the majority view easily but the members "did not wish to risk trouble in the Group by alienating him [Perlo]," and Peters "did not wish to use his authority to act against any member of the Group in favor of another member." The impasse was resolved eventually, and Perlo, it was said, "agreed to abide by discipline." [72]

Functions of the Group

The men organized by Harold Ware were young, highly educated men of capable talents and early achievement, people of wit and intelligence, smooth, assured, cool, and competent, unlike the agents of alienation in the Third Period style. The secrecy of their private lives was so well kept that even a sharp and unsentimental observer of Popular Front machinations like Eugene Lyons failed to mention them in a strong attack in 1941.[73] No member of the original Ware group had acquired — because all had avoided it — conspicuous association with the public causes of Popular Front agitation.[74]

The original Ware group of seven was young in years, ranging in age from Nathan Witt who was thirty in 1933, to Victor Perlo who

---

ship in the Ware cell had come forward since Perlo's 1948 appearance before the House Committee. This was Nathaniel Weyl. When asked whether he knew Weyl, Perlo refused to answer on grounds of self-incrimination.

72. Chambers, *Witness*, p. 379. Because of the part that Chambers played in resolving the difficulty over the succession to Ware's leadership, at the suggestion of J. Peters the relation between Perlo and Chambers, which had been formal, became more so. Chambers said that after the succession was settled, Perlo "would scarcely speak to me."

73. Eugene Lyons, *Red Decade* (Indianapolis: Bobbs-Merrill, 1941).

74. Lyons does devote some attention to Lee Pressman, whom he places close to party operatives, but this is in connection with Pressman's service as general counsel for the CIO, and not his term in the government. Lyons, *Red Decade*, p. 225. On August 25, 1948, during the taking of further testimony from Alger Hiss, mention was made in passing of an article by the columnist George Sokolsky, "These Days," which had appeared that day. From it, Representative Karl Mundt read two paragraphs, as follows: "Way back in 1941 I came across the existence of the Ware group in Washington, who were engaged in placing Communists in the most critical positions in the Federal government. I was then told who the original ten were, and among them was mentioned Alger Hiss." *Hiss Hearings*, p. 1157. Even if this claim of prior inside information is allowed, it remains that knowledge of the existence of the Ware group did not become public until 1948. The "Ware group," as such, did not exist in 1941.

was twenty-two in 1933. Alger Hiss and John Abt were twenty-nine, Henry Collins was twenty-eight, and Lee Pressman and Charles Kramer were twenty-seven and twenty-six respectively. In their education, some of the best undergraduate schools are represented — Princeton, Columbia, Johns Hopkins, Chicago, and New York University — and all had some graduate education at such places as the Harvard law and business schools, the graduate schools of Columbia and New York University, and the University of Chicago Law School. Of the seven, five were in the Department of Agriculture, and two — Collins and Perlo — were in the National Recovery Administration. By 1935, however, there had been some dispersal of the original seven: Witt was in the statutory National Labor Relations Board which Congress created after the Supreme Court invalidated the NRA (in 1934, he had joined the predecessor agency of the same title which had been established by executive order); Hiss was in the office of the Solicitor-General of the United States; Abt was in the Works Progress Administration; Collins was in the Soil Conservation Service; Kramer was in the National Youth Administration; Perlo was in the Home Owner's Loan Corporation; and Pressman was on his way to the CIO. By the time Chambers joined the group, or was attached to it, in 1934 it was already broader in agency representation than the nucleus in the AAA with which it started.

In all of the tension and public excitement about spies at the time the first public disclosures about the Ware group were made, sight was lost of an important fact. The Ware group was not an espionage group like the so-called Perlo and Silvermaster cells with which Elizabeth Bentley said she was connected. In the notes of his conversations with Chambers in 1945 and 1946, Raymond Murphy, political analyst with the Department of State, summarized the information on this point given him by Chambers as follows:

> This group did not exchange secret documents from the Government departments, but did give sealed reports on the membership of the groups and on policy. It was not a spy ring but one far more important and cunning because its members helped to shape policy in their departments. Henry Collins, as secretary or treasurer, delivered most of the sealed reports to my informant [Chambers].[75]

It may be wondered what the phrase "important and cunning" adds to the description of the group except an alarmist and rather im-

75. *Hearings on Interlocking Subversion in Government Departments*, p. 1182. Murphy's memorandum covered a conversation with Chambers on August 28, 1946.

plausible innuendo, since the professional responsibilities of the members involved them with hours, wages, employment, rural welfare, and similar questions of New Deal concern.

Chambers, in his book, however, repeated the description noted by Murphy, saying that the work of the group was not espionage, although some members of it were later drawn into espionage. Its routine functions, he said, were the recruiting of new members into the underground, and the staffing of government agencies with Communist Party members. The real power of the group, he said, was "a power to influence, from the most strategic positions, the policies of the United States Government, especially in the labor and welfare fields." [76] As will be seen in the next chapter, there was both opportunity and effort to influence "the policies of the United States Government." But the image of a Communist commandantura projected by words like "important," "cunning," and "strategic positions" is almost certainly overdrawn, since "the policies of the United States Government" tend to emerge only with great difficulty from the cross-pull of a thousand pressures. This is true even when the management of policy is in the hands of the President at a time when he is supported by majorities in Congress and a mandate at the polls, neither of which the Communists had.

When Lee Pressman decided to declare his part in the Ware group, he confined his disclosures to the four people he admitted were in the AAA, and he also described an enterprise of somewhat more limited scope than Chambers had outlined. When asked, "What was the function of or reason for having your group of four?" he said that he would confine his answer to the activities of the four and to the period during which he was a member of the group. "During that period what we did was receive literature of a Communist nature, daily newspaper, monthly magazines, books, and things of that nature, Communist literature; we would read the literature and discuss the problems covered by the literature." [77] He said that Harold Ware was the man who stood out clearest in memory as paper boy for the Communist press, but that J. Peters may also have made deliveries after the death of Ware. Peters participated in the discussions which were held once or twice a month.

Although the Ware group was not an espionage group, it may possibly have been more than the mere Marxist study group of Pressman's description. Where the public record is as spottily sparse as it often is in matters of security and subversion, the temptation is strong to sub-

76. Chambers, *Witness*, p. 343.

77. *Hearings Regarding Communism in the United States Government*, Part 2, p. 2855.

stitute supposition about "what must have been the case" for lack of
fact. But normal tests of credibility can be misleading when applied to
underground activity, and inferences about what constitutes "natural"
behavior can be belied by the fact.[78] Conclusions that begin with the
remark, "It does not seem likely that," suppose standards of judgment
derived from a context that may not exist or is irrelevant. But, having
said so much, "it does not seem likely" that a group like Pressman,
Witt, Abt, and Kramer — containing some extremely able lawyers —
would meet twice a month with Ware or Peters, the latter an important
functionary, to read Communist editorials only, or to scan the canons
of communism with exegetical patience. Although doubtless the fighting soldiers of a revolutionary faith must be freed of negativism, derogatory thought, and religious inclination, it is inconceivable that
they might not manage, now and then, to discuss the course of the
battle, and the tactics to try.

The impression that Pressman's testimony leaves about the narrowly
limited nature of the evenings together is not supported by the statements of Chambers which seem closer to expectation. Chambers, as
has been said, thought that Pressman might have "sketchily" described
an earlier stage in the development of the group than the one it had
reached when he joined it, and said that even in the later stage, J. Peters
would sometimes visit the group to lecture it on Communist organization and Leninist theory. But he also said that general policy and
specific problems were part of the agenda.

Nathaniel Weyl joined the Communist Party while at Columbia University in the winter of 1932–33, and left the Communist Party in
1939. He was a member of the original Ware group in the Department of Agriculture where he was employed as an economist in the
office of Consumers Counsel of the Agricultural Adjustment Administration. It was his duty to represent the consumer interest in market-
ing agreement hearings conducted by the triple A.

He identified as members of the Ware group all of those who had
been named by Whittaker Chambers with the exception of Donald
Hiss. Weyl became a member of the group in the fall of 1933 and
stayed in it only for a period of some nine months, leaving, he said,
when he found that being a member of the party and an employee of

78. For example, it would be an easy assumption that two individuals getting
into a subway car without looking at each other, riding in the same car without
talking, and disembarking without any public sign of recognition, probably did
not know each other. But this was the behavior of Judy Coplon and her Soviet
contact in the United Nations, Valentin Gubitschev. Her counsel, in denying
that the defendant was engaged in espionage, said that such encounters were
amorous trysts in which the lovers were fleeing the surveillance of detectives
hired by Gubitschev's wife.

the government created a "personally uncomfortable" situation. Feeling that he was primarily a Communist and "therefore could not resign
from the Communist Party," he resigned from the government and
left Washington. Eleven years after he left the Communist Party and
two years after the sensational disclosures of the summer of 1948,[79]
he talked with the FBI about his former membership.

Weyl said that at the time he was a member of the Ware group the
activity of the cell was largely confined to discussions of Communist
doctrine and of government policies insofar as they affected agriculture. There was no espionage, a point on which Weyl and Chambers
agreed. It is also a point worth emphasizing because of a widespread
assumption to the contrary. When asked whether Communist perspectives could be introduced into his work in the Department of Agriculture, Weyl said no. His training had been in classical economics and
the function of the Consumers Counsel was to protect consumer interests. "There was," he said, "no way in which Marxism could help
you particularly in that."

The Ware group did not stay intact, or limited, very long, nor did
the members remain in the original two agencies. Although various
circumstances — discharge, transfer, the organization of new agencies,
and personal choice — controlled the eventual movements of its members in Washington, the immediate cause for the dispersal of the group
was the action of Secretary of Agriculture, Henry A. Wallace, who
resolved a long-simmering power and policy dispute in the agency
by firing Jerome Frank, whose office had been the center of the tension.[80] A very active liberal, Gardner Jackson, who was a member of
the anticonservative group, is reported to have said that Alger Hiss
had known that the purge was coming at least a week before it actually
did, and is quoted as saying, "He undoubtedly told Pressman, and Lee
told him what to do in order to remain in the Department as his pipe-
line." [81] The purge occurred in February 1935. Witt had already gone
to the executive order labor board, Abt and Pressman went into the
WPA, and Kramer went into the National Youth Administration.
Perlo and Collins were not involved directly in the explosion in the
AAA since they were both in another agency — the National Recovery Administration.

79. Weyl's book, *Treason*, was published in 1950. Although the book refers
to the testimony of Chambers about the Ware group, Weyl does not discuss
the participation in it of anyone except Alger Hiss.
80. See Schlesinger, *The Coming of the New Deal*, pp. 79–80, for the final
confrontation. The spokesmen for the anti-conservative opinion were Jerome
Frank and Alger Hiss who went in to the Secretary of Agriculture to receive the
notice of dismissal.
81. Alger Hiss survived the execution. De Toledano and Lasky, *Seeds of
Treason*, p. 60.

The Spread of Influence

Alger Hiss was the only one of the original group left behind in the AAA; and he did not stay there very long, moving into the office of the Solicitor-General in 1935. Before his departure he did special service with one of the numerous congressional committees of the thirties among which other partisans of the extreme left were to find employment. In 1934 Hiss had been lent by his agency to the Nye Investigating Committee, named after Gerald Nye, isolationist Senator from North Dakota, which was bent upon proving that the First World War was largely the work of munitions makers who wished to make profits out of the disasters they promoted — "merchants of death" they were called in the steamy rhetoric of the hearings. The coincidence of the time and the subject of the hearing is of some interest. The time was the period of the strategy of alienation, the policy of extremism and isolation in the Communist Party, the cold front that was to anticipate the Cold War of a dozen years later, and which just preceded the warm fraternity of the policy of collective security and the Popular Front, soon to follow. Although Nye got his isolationism and suspicion of Wall Street out of the Populist imagination about the rich and their ways, independently of the Communist texts, the class themes of the hearings were well augmented in the orchestration supplied by Communist orators and the Communist press.

Other members of the original Ware group to find employments with an important Senate committee were John Abt who became chief counsel to the La Follette Subcommittee on Civil Liberties and Charles Kramer who became a field investigator for this subcommittee, preparing for hearings and the writing of reports. Two other individuals with the La Follette subcommittee whose activities will be discussed further in the next chapter were Charles Flato and Allan Rosenberg, the first serving as public relations officer. The latter was the first man hired under Abt on the committee.[82]

Senator Robert M. La Follette published an article in 1947 (shortly before his death) about his experiences with his staff during his chairmanship of the Senate Civil Liberties Committee.[83] The subject of the article was the infiltration by Communists and their abettors of four Senate committees, the other three, besides his own, being the Pepper Subcommittee on Wartime Health and Education, the Kilgore Subcommittee on War Mobilization, and the Murray Special Committee on Small Business. The staff director of the Senate Small Business Com-

82. *Report on Interlocking Subversion in Government Departments*, July 30, 1953, pp. 33–34.
83. Robert M. La Follette, "Turn the Light on Communism," *Collier's*, February 8, 1947.

mittee was Henry Collins. Kramer, while working for the Civil Liberties Committee, also had "final responsibility" for the reports of the
Senate Subcommittee on Technical Mobilization, and was attached to
the staff of the Senate Subcommittee on Wartime Health and Education.[84] The senator's comments covered all of these committees, but
he had a special word about his own, the Subcommittee on Civil Liberties. As he put it, "I was forced to take measures in an effort to stamp
out influences within my own committee staff." [85]

His charges of manipulation were severe. Although members of the
left faction frequently worked for "desirable legislation and worthy
objectives," they nevertheless were always ready to "further their own
cause at the expense of the legislation they were advocating." The staff
of the Pepper subcommittee "probably did great harm to the cause of
improved health in this country by its reckless activities." The staff
of this committee released a report under highly irregular procedures
that "prompted severe criticism on the floor of the Senate." The report had neither the approval of the subcommittee nor of the parent
Senate committee, but the staff released it as though it had had full
approval. Senator La Follette also complained that the staffs of the four
committees made illicit use of committee information. They often sat
in on and participated in the executive sessions of the committees, and
therefore had access to committee files that contained private documents that the committees had forced by subpoena on the recommendations of the staff. Senator La Follette said,

> On several occasions I have had the revealing experience of re-
> ceiving prompt protests and advice from strange and remote sources
> the day after I had voiced anti-Communist sentiments or voted con-
> trary to the prevailing Communist Party line in executive sessions
> that were wholly unreported in the press. Such reactions could not
> occur without an effective grapevine.

Even more insidious, he thought, was the practice of coloring the information that was disseminated. As to minimum wage and Fair Employment Practice Committee legislation, it was his feeling that the
"Communists and fellow travellers" who lobbied these bills "preferred
to get no bills at all."

Senator La Follette thought that the practice of "borrowing downtown personnel" from the executive departments in the staffing of congressional committees assisted the infiltration of committee staffs. There
were, of course, many legitimate uses for expert staff from the executive agencies, and occasions when the services of such temporary de-

84. *Report on Interlocking Subversion in Government Departments*, p. 34.
85. *Ibid.*, p. 33.

tails of executive experts to a congressional committee were valuable. But it became necessary to curb the practice. La Follette said:

> . . . when Senators felt that it had become the means whereby Communist sympathizers assembled their cohorts and placed them in a position to scheme from the inside on legislative activities, without any direct lines of responsibility to either the Senate or to the government agency on whose payroll they were carried — then, the Senate curbed the practice.

As a first step the Senate required all committees to publish regularly in the *Congressional Record* the names and assignments of all staff borrowed from the executive agencies. Later, provision was made that borrowed staff be paid out of congressional funds so that a closer check on staff borrowed from the agencies could be achieved.

As was said earlier, the process of formulating the public policy is a complex and intricate affair of many persons and groups, of split authorities and separated powers, of maneuver and design by caucuses, factions, alliances, and combinations, of blocs and parties and cabinet offices, of courts and constituencies, so that the product is not the work of one or even a few but of many, in formal and informal associations. Party members and their friends on committee staffs, then, could not control the output of the Senate, nor "make" the law, even if they had been able to vote on the floor. But they could and did make private information available outside, which was valuable in agitational activity that might influence the course of policy.

*...the weak-minded tendency of the hearer
to listen to what is beside the point.*

ARISTOTLE, *Rhetoric*

V   The National Labor Relations Board

Some of the investigating committees of the Congress in the thirties, like the La Follette subcommittee on civil liberties, became places of employment for party members who were between jobs in the executive branch, or who were temporarily on loan from one of the executive agencies. At least one of them, however, the Wheeler committee, was also a place for the original recruitment of individuals who were then to find their way into the executive establishment, and it was here that the leader of one of the cells in the National Labor Relations Board got his start in Federal service. Communist activity in the National Labor Relations Board occurred in a context of pressing conservative hostility to the agency which reached a climax in the Smith investigation of 1940, an inquiry which fairly illustrated the weak-minded tendency of some hearers to listen to what is beside the point. Certain aspects of this investigation resemble a burletta in which the leads were played by Vice and Folly.

The Wheeler Committee

The Wheeler committee,[1] so-called after its chairman, Senator Burton K. Wheeler of Montana, conducted an extensive investigation into propaganda, lobbying, and self-regulatory activities in the railroad industry which led to the passage of the Transportation Act of 1940.[2]

1. Seventy-fourth Congress, Second Session, United States Senate, Committee on Interstate Commerce, Subcommittee on S. Res. 71, Hearings under the title, *Investigation of Railroads,* 1938.
2. The Transportation Act of 1940 marked the end of an effort begun in 1920 to have the Interstate Commerce Commission develop plans for the ultimate consolidation of the railroads of the country into a limited number of systems. The Commission issued a preliminary plan in 1921, asked Congress repeatedly, beginning in 1925, to be relieved of the responsibility of preparing a "final" plan, issued a "final" plan in 1929 for the consolidation of the roads into 21 systems, granted a number of exceptions from the plan, and was finally relieved of the unwanted responsibility in 1940. For a discussion of patterns of railroad coordination — from the lack of which the railroads are slowly collapsing — see Earl

The Wheeler committee had a sizeable cell of Communist Party members, headed by an attorney by the name of Herbert Fuchs.[3] Although an attorney, Fuchs had been recruited into the party in New York late in 1934 by a taxi driver of whom he said, "I had a great deal of liking and respect for this man and I wanted to join the Communist Party and I wanted to work where he was working."[4] So he was assigned to a Communist Party group of taxicab drivers working in a union of taxicab drivers; and if "life seems a jest of Fate's contriving," some of the fateful humor certainly lies in the Communist pseudonym that Fuchs took — "Hacker," which was his mother's name and his recruiter's occupation.

In July 1936, less than two years after his recruitment, Fuchs left the New York Communist group, went to Washington, took employment with the Wheeler committee, and was re-integrated into the Communist Party, he said, by one Arthur Stein, an employee at the Works Progress Administration.[5] There was no cell in the Wheeler committee at the time Fuchs took employment, but there was one soon afterwards. According to Fuchs, Stein could have taken him into the unit at the WPA but preferred that he organize a new one in an agency of the government hitherto uncolonized. One of the asserted reasons for this — apart from the obvious desire to extend the brotherhood — was the policy of the party, or so Fuchs understood, to have groups limited to fellow employees as much as possible.[6] Although there was no group in the Wheeler committee staff, there was a member of the party, James Gorham, and he and Fuchs got together and organized the group. The Senate Committee staff was housed in the Interstate Commerce Commission building. According to Fuchs, the group organized included Ellis Olim, an employee of the Interstate Commerce Commission, and several members of the Wheeler committee.

Gorham had been sent from the WPA to the Wheeler committee on loan after a tour in a number of agencies, beginning in New York

Latham, *The Politics of Railroad Coordination, 1933–1936* (Cambridge, Mass.: Harvard, 1959), chap. v.

3. Herbert Fuchs was a volunteer witness before the House Committee on Un-American Activities in 1955, confessing freely his part in the Communist units in the Wheeler committee and the National Labor Relations Board. For his pains he was discharged from a teaching position at American University by the president of the institution, Hurst R. Anderson. See the editorial, "Why No Fuss When a Helpful Ex-Red Professor Is Fired?" in the *Saturday Evening Post*, December 10, 1955.

4. Eighty-fourth Congress, First Session, House of Representatives, Committee on Un-American Activities, *Hearings on Investigation of Communist Infiltration of Government*, 6 pts., 1955–1956, p. 2959 (hereafter cited as *Fuchs Hearings*).

5. *Fuchs Hearings*, pp. 2961–2962.

6. *Fuchs Hearings*, p. 2962.

in 1934 where he had worked in a Federal Emergency Relief Administration research project under the general administration of Joseph
B. Eastman, the Federal Coordinator of Transportation.[7] Unlike many
who joined the Communist Party without full knowledge of its program and methods, Gorham at Columbia had been an active Socialist
doing constant battle with the Stalinists on the campus. His failure to
unite liberals and socialists in a caucus against the Stalinists led him,
upon joining the staff of FERA where he found the Communists active, to give up the fight and join them.[8] He attended a closed party
meeting that planned to facilitate the movement of comrades from
New York into the Federal service in Washington, and received some
instruction on the proper conduct of a Communist functionary. In his
words,

> They also went, at some length, into an explanation of the Com-
> munist Party apparatus in Washington. They stated that there was
> what they described as an open party, which did not include Gov-
> ernment employees, and there was another party organization which
> they said was organized on a sort of a modified A B C system, which
> they explained to mean that the groups in one unit would have one
> person in the unit who would meet with similar individuals from
> other units, who in turn would have one person forming liaison to
> a higher unit, and the purpose of this was to prevent discovery or
> detection. As we went into Communist operations in Washington,
> we would be expected to counsel [sic] our membership in the party
> since they felt that our effectiveness would be destroyed if we were
> known to be Communists.[9]

The word "counsel" is doubtless a misprint for "conceal," but the
sense of the instruction was clear enough. Gorham went to Washington to work for the Railroad Retirement Board, and was attached to
the Communist group in the NRA. Although an energetic Communist,
Gorham never had a party card in Washington. As he said, "No one in
Washington held a card, to my knowledge. Cards may have existed in
our names, but no one in Washington held a card." [10] From the NRA,
Gorham went into the WPA and then to the Wheeler committee.

The Communist Party does not seem to have been interested in the

7. The project on which Gorham worked as a statistical clerk was a white
collar relief project under the immediate administration of the FERA, but doing
work for the Federal Coordinator of Transportation on a study of wages and
hours of railroad employees in connection with the need for retirement systems.
Fuchs Hearings, p. 3112.
8. *Fuchs Hearings*, p. 3115.
9. *Fuchs Hearings*, p. 3119.
10. *Fuchs Hearings*, p. 3122.

subject matters of the Wheeler committee's investigations.[11] It was, however, interested in using the group among the staff of the committee to further union organization among employees of the Federal government. As Herbert Fuchs was to say, the "ostensible objective was to organize the Government employees into unions." [12] This was an echo in Washington of the conflict described elsewhere between the American Federation of Government Employees and what eventually became the United Public Workers of America; but although the conflict engineered by Communist elements within the AFGE raged in the lower ranks of the civil service, the unit in the Wheeler committee found itself virtually without program or direction. At the start of the organization created by Fuchs and Gorham, there was difficulty in "finding any significant work to do." [13] Although Arthur Stein was said to be the contact between the Wheeler group and higher circles in the party, the group "received no guidance."

The group met rather irregularly and although it was at first thought that weekly meetings would be feasible, there is doubt that even the biweekly meetings that were common in other units were attained by the unit in the staff of the Wheeler committee. There was the usual distribution of Communist Party literature at the meetings, and dues were assessed by income and collected. At some point, Communist literature became unavailable because too difficult to purchase or too risky to receive, so that it is not clear that even the study functions were carried on throughout.

Fuchs was head of the Wheeler group and, in accordance with the plan of organization described by Gorham, attended other meetings as representative of his group. These were meetings of unit heads who acted as a policy or steering committee, very much like the directory of persons named by Chambers as the seven who comprised the Ware group when he first knew it. The attendance by Fuchs at such meetings was confined to the period when he was with the Wheeler committee — that is, between July 1936 and October 1937 — and ceased when he moved to the National Labor Relations Board. Normally some eight persons attended these section meetings of the Communist Party according to the testimony of Fuchs: Eleanor Nelson from the Department of Labor, Arthur Stein of the WPA, Philip Reno of the Social

---

11. This was indicated in a colloquy between Gorham and the committee counsel: "Mr. Arens: Do you have any information respecting the transmission of any information from the Wheeler committee or its files, into the channels of the Communist Party? Mr. Gorham: Not so far as I know. I do not know that the work of the committee was of particular interest to the party, as a matter of fact." *Fuchs Hearings,* p. 3130.

12. *Fuchs Hearings,* p. 2965.

13. *Fuchs Hearings,* p. 2964.

Security Board, Sidney and Julia Katz, Bernard Stern of the Department of Labor, and Henry and Jessica Rhine.[14] The business of the
section meeting seems to have concentrated largely on lines of policy
to be pursued in trade union affairs. Although there was a higher level
in party organization than the section meeting, and there was doubtless
a link between the section and the next higher level, Fuchs did not
know whether it was inside or outside the government. He thought
the latter, but did not know who the link was.

Gorham corroborated Fuchs about the activity of the Wheeler cell
and supplied more precise detail about some of its affairs. As Fuchs had
said, the major work of the cell was trade union policy, and the organization of "progressive" trade unionism among government employees.
Gorham said that the major responsibility "was to get the ICC union
active and ultimately to move it into the CIO." [15] There was also the
usual internal work of indoctrination — internal, that is, to the unit itself — and efforts were made to get the *Daily Worker* and other Communist publications, and to study and discuss them. Unlike Fuchs and
many others who testified about their experiences in Communist units
in the government, Gorham seems to have engaged in a certain amount
of front activity, thereby risking in some degree the security of the
unit.[16] Although pressed by committee counsel to say in what respects
the unit of the party was able to influence the program of subject
matters of the Wheeler committee, Gorham was unable to say more
than that there were discussions of policy in the unit.[17] He was able
to add two or three names to those supplied by Fuchs, inasmuch as
he stayed on in the Wheeler committee after Fuchs had left it, and
the membership of the Wheeler unit changed somewhat.

Herbert Fuchs made the transfer from the Wheeler committee to
the National Labor Relations Board in October 1937. The employment

14. Eleanor Nelson was active in the affairs of the United Public Workers
Union, and had died at the time of the Fuchs testimony. Stein pleaded self-
incrimination when asked about his part in the cell (*Fuchs Hearings*, p. 3136), as
did Sidney Katz (pp. 3400–3416) and Julia Katz (pp. 3416–3420). There was no
testimony by Bernard Stern or Janet Stern, but other witnesses, like Julia Katz,
for example, refused to say whether they knew them, pleading self-incrimination. Henry Rhine testified and pleaded self-incrimination when asked about
Herbert Fuchs (pp. 3205–3221).

15. *Fuchs Hearings*, p. 3129.

16. When he testified about his transfer to other employment, Gorham said,
". . . I went with the SEC in the fall of 1938 and my recollection is there was
a feeling that I needed a period of, I think, the word was sterilization, because
of my open party associations, and it may very well have been into 1939 before
Mr. Naigles put me into a regular group." *Fuchs Hearings*, p. 3132. Naigles was
identified as Mike Naigles who, according to Gorham, was a member of the
Communist Party working in the Securities and Exchange Commission.

17. See especially *Fuchs Hearings*, pp. 3131–3132.

histories of some party members in the Federal service show manipulation and contrivance in placements, transfers, and promotion, but not all of the movement of party members from agency to agency was the design of hidden operators, and perhaps rather little of it. It may be said again that there was a motion and life in the government service that was quite independent of any contrivance, responding to the restlessness of people interested in promotions, increases within grade, new opportunities, more challenging responsibilities, more interesting jobs; and responding also to the continuous creation of new agencies, and therefore of new chances for interesting and financially rewarding employment. The transfer of Fuchs from the Wheeler committee to the National Labor Relations Board was not, in his opinion, the result of anything more devious than the reduction-in-force that short funds forced on the Wheeler committee.

In a reduction-in-force, it is not unusual to have it fall first among those who can be easily placed in other agencies, and this is what occurred in the Wheeler committee. Fuchs was one of those who could be easily placed, and arrangements were soon made for him to move to the National Labor Relations Board.[18] A graduate of City College of New York and the New York University Law School, Fuchs was not a graduate of one of the schools favored by Nathan Witt, the Secretary of the National Labor Relations Board in 1939. At that time, Mortimer Reimer, who had been executive secretary of the National Lawyers' Guild, quit that organization and applied to Witt for a position as an attorney with the Board. He testified that Witt, whom he knew casually, told him "that the National Labor Relations Board was only hiring lawyers who were graduates of Harvard, Columbia, and he may have mentioned Yale, and preferably those who were on the law reviews of those schools." [19]

Reimer had gone to Syracuse and New York University Law School, but he did obtain a job within two months in a part of the Board not under the control of Witt; and Fuchs, despite the presumed defects of his education, was actually hired by Witt himself. There was no indication that Communist affiliations had any part in the transaction that placed Fuchs in employment with the Board, and he did not think that there was any such consideration.[20] He also testified that when he was employed there was no Communist unit in the National Labor Relations Board, although he was not entirely sure. Whether organized or not at the time of his employment, such a unit was in fact organized

18. *Fuchs Hearings*, p. 2969.
19. *Fuchs Hearings*, pp. 3035–3036.
20. *Fuchs Hearings*, p. 2970.

shortly afterwards when, on the instruction of Arthur Stein, Fuchs said, he made contact with three men, Allan Rosenberg, Martin Kurasch, and Joseph Robison.[21]

Allan Rosenberg had been a member of the staff of the La Follette committee, moving from that spot to the National Labor Relations Board as a lawyer in 1937, shortly after the National Labor Relations Act was declared constitutional by the Supreme Court. He was with the Board until December 1941 when he moved to the Board of Economic Warfare. He was named as a member of the so-called Perlo group by Elizabeth Bentley,[22] and when asked about his knowledge of people in the National Labor Relations Board named by Fuchs, pleaded self-incrimination.[23] Joseph Robison in 1955 said that "I am not now a member of the Communist Party," but pleaded self-incrimination when asked whether he had been a member of the Communist Party when he was a lawyer in Nathan Witt's office at the National Labor Relations Board.[24] A graduate of Rutgers and the Columbia University Law School, Martin Kurasch was with the National Labor Relations Board between August 1937 and 1941 and when called upon to testify after the Fuchs statements, did a considerable amount of sparring with counsel for the House Committee.[25] For example, when merely asked how he obtained employment at the National Labor Relations Board, he objected to the question with remarks about the difference between the political climate of the thirties and the fifties. Like Rosenberg, however, he had come into the Board soon after the Supreme Court had declared the National Labor Relations Act constitutional. Joseph Robison, a schoolmate of Kurasch, had preceded him into the agency. Although he eventually consented to talk about his joining the staff of the Board, the dialogue was often a series of contentious exchanges. He found it "distracting for counsel to walk up and down beside me speaking in a loud voice" and counsel said, "I apologize if I have been discourteous or offensive." [26]

Kurasch served as legal assistant to the Secretary of the Board when

21. *Fuchs Hearings*, p. 2971.
22. Eightieth Congress, Second Session, House of Representatives, Committee on Un-American Activities, *Hearings Regarding Communist Espionage in the United States Government*, p. 512 (hereafter cited as *Hiss Hearings*). The connection between Elizabeth Bentley and Rosenberg is said to have taken place when he was with the Foreign Economic Administration (formerly the Board of Economic Warfare).
23. *Fuchs Hearings*, pp. 3300–3307.
24. *Fuchs Hearings*, p. 3248, for the statement that he was not then a member of the Communist Party, and p. 3249 for the refusal to answer about past membership on grounds of self-incrimination.
25. The testimony of Martin Kurasch appears in *Fuchs Hearings*, pp. 3261–3281.
26. *Fuchs Hearings*, p. 3264.

Witt was the Secretary. He freely acknowledged as associates and colleagues a group of fourteen people, all of whom had been named as Communists, or confessed that they had been. When he was asked whether he had ever belonged to the Communist Party with any of them he declined to answer on grounds of self-incrimination, but presumed to instruct the "chairman and members of the Committee that inferences are not to be drawn from claims of privilege." [27] He also pleaded self-incrimination when asked if any of the testimony of Herbert Fuchs was untrue.

The arrival of Herbert Fuchs in the National Labor Relations Board marked the beginning of a new phase both in his life as a Communist partisan in the government service, and in the establishment of a well-organized center of secret party activity. The Smith committee in 1940 failed to find it because its antilabor animus impaired its ability to discriminate between the fantasy it chased and the fact it ignored.

Saposs and the Smith Committee

The conservative hostility towards the labor board which inspired the Smith committee with remarkable bitterness tended to equate liberalism and revolution. The road to both was presumably opened in 1933 when Section 7a of the National Industrial Recovery Act guaranteed to workers the right to organize for the purpose of collective bargaining or other mutual aid or protection.[28] Except for the temporary arrangements under the War Labor Board in the First World War,[29] and excepting the special case of the railroads,[30] Section 7a of the NIRA was the first serious attempt by the Federal government to create permanent and effective statutory guarantees of the rights of workers to organize and to bargain collectively.

To enforce Section 7a, a board was appointed by President Roosevelt on August 5, 1933, with no more clear or formal statement of its powers than that it was to pass promptly on all cases of hardship or dispute arising out of the President's Reemployment Agreement which set work standards for plants and shops not under the codes of fair competition. The chairman of this board was Senator Robert Wagner of New York, and the other members were William Green, president of the American Federation of Labor, Leo Wolman, and John L. Lewis, president of the United Mine Workers of America, representing the

27. *Fuchs Hearings*, p. 3272.
28. 48 *Stat.* 196 (1933), 15 U.S.C. 701 (1934).
29. See Edwin E. Witte, *The Government in Labor Disputes* (New York: McGraw-Hill, 1932), pp. 246–251, for a brief discussion of the War Labor Board in the First World War.
30. Railway Labor Act of 1926, 44 *Stat.* 577, 45 U.S.C. 151 *et seq.;* Railway Labor Act of 1934, 48 *Stat.* 1186, 45 U.S.C. (1937 Supp.).

labor side; and Walter Teagle, Gerard Swope, and Louis Kirstein from the business community.

Senator Wagner attempted to get Congress to enact an omnibus labor bill in 1934, putting the guarantees of workers' rights on a statutory basis and providing adequate institutions for enforcement, but his effort failed and the Congress instead enacted a joint resolution creating a successor to the National Labor Board.[31] Public Resolution 44 authorized the President to create one or more boards to hear disputes under Section 7a and to hold elections, and in accordance with this authority the President established the first National Labor Relations Board by executive order.[32] The original appointees were Dean Lloyd Garrison of the University of Wisconsin Law School, Professor Harry Millis, and Edwin S. Smith.[33] Joining the legal staff of the new board organized under Public Resolution 44 was Nathan Witt.[34] A revised version of Senator Wagner's 1934 bill was finally enacted after the demise of the NIRA in the Supreme Court in 1935. His proposals had not had strong administration backing before the collapse of the codes, but pressures by unions for statutory protections, and the interest of the administration in salvaging something from the wreckage of the New Deal, aligned the political strength of the White House behind the measure, and the National Labor Relations Act was made law within two weeks.[35]

Although conservative opposition to the mild liberalism of Wagner and the New Deal had failed to prevent the Congress from enacting an abhorrent statute, employers were more successful, for a time, in persuading the Federal judiciary to their view. By early 1937, the work of the National Labor Relations Board was tied up by injunction in a hundred cases in the lower Federal courts,[36] creating a strict strangu-

31. This is Public Resolution 44, 48 *Stat.* 1183 (1934), 15 U.S.C. 702 (a)–(f).
32. Executive Order No. 6763, June 29, 1934.
33. *Fuchs Hearings*, p. 3457.
34. Eighty-third Congress, First Session, United States Senate, Committee on the Judiciary, Subcommittee to Investigate the Administration of the Internal Security Act and Other Internal Security Laws, *Hearings on Interlocking Subversion in Government Departments*, p. 622.
35. The National Labor Relations Act passed the Congress on June 27, 1935, and was signed into law by the President on July 5, 1935. 49 *Stat.* L. (I) 449. In signing the measure, President Roosevelt surely differentiated the new board from the older boards in saying, "It should be clearly understood that it will not act as mediator or conciliator in labor disputes. . . . Compromise, the essence of mediation, has no place in the interpretation and enforcement of the law." For the whole statement, see *First Annual Report of the National Labor Relations Board*, Fiscal Year 1935–1936, p. 9n.
36. The rhetoric of some of the decisions granting the injunctions criticized not only the law but the policy underlying the Act. In *Stout v. Pratt*, it was said, "If his employer bargains with him [a worker] as an individual, as a man, as an American citizen, that is unfair; it is prohibited. The individual employee

lation by papers to be relieved only when the Supreme Court reluctantly loosened the knots.[37] The surrender of the judges to the New Deal occurred in the case upholding the very legislation that embodied the most painful apprehensions of the business community for a welfarist future. With the Jones and Laughlin decision the battle of a half century for the open shop was finally lost.

But while the center had yielded, a campaign of harassment on the flanks promised some recovery of losses, and remorseless and continued hostility to the unions and the National Labor Relations Board fired new pressures from Congress. Within two years or so after the Supreme Court had sustained the National Labor Relations Act, a special committee of the House of Representatives subjected the board to a rushing, wide-swinging attack that required thirty volumes and 7,970 pages to report. The author of the investigation was Congressman Howard Smith of Virginia who had voted against the Act and made a speech about it.[38] He was the spokesman, in introducing his resolution, for that combination of Republicans and Southern Democrats that was to embarrass Democratic administrations thereafter.[39]

The resolution establishing the Smith committee[40] set five goals for the investigation: (1) to ascertain whether the board had been "fair and impartial in its conduct"; (2) to ascertain the effect of the Act on labor disputes, as to whether they had increased or decreased; (3) to ascertain the need for amendments to the Act; (4) to ascertain whether the board had, by interpretation or regulation, modified the intended meaning of the Act; and (5) to ascertain whether new legislative defi-

is dealt with by the Act as an incompetent. The government must protect him even from himself. He is the ward of the United States to be cared for by his guardian even as if he were a member of an uncivilized tribe of Indians or a recently emancipated slave." 12 F. Supp. 864, 867 (1935).

37. *N.L.R.B.* v. *Jones and Laughlin Steel Corporation*, 301 U.S. 1, 57 S.Ct. 615, 81 L.Ed. 893 (1937). Decided at the same time were the cases of a trailer manufacturing company, a clothing manufacturer, an interstate bus company, and the Associated Press.

38. In the House of Representatives, Congressman Smith had said of the National Labor Relations Act: "Mr. Chairman, I am opposed to this bill because it is obviously unconstitutional; because it forbids the courts of the land to consider the controversies arising under it under the usual rules of evidence and procedure pertaining to other litigations; because it abrogates the right to contract; and because I believe it holds out false hopes that cannot be realized under the present constitution and which will lead to strife rather than peace." Seventy-fourth Congress, First Session, *Congressional Record*, June 19, 1935, p. 9692. For a short summary of some aspects of the work of the Smith committee, see D. O. Bowman, *Public Control of Labor Relations* (New York: Macmillan, 1942), and references cited in the index.

39. In the election of 1938, Congressman Smith was one of those on the President's purge list that failed to produce the results intended for it.

40. H. Res. 258, Seventy-sixth Congress, First Session, *Congressional Record*, July 20, 1939, pp. 9592–9593.

nitions of commerce or of employer-employee relations were needed.[41] The report of the Smith committee to Congress found that the board had not been fair and impartial, that the effect of the Act was to increase labor disputes, and that certain amendments to the Act were needed to correct the behavior of the board which had extended the meaning of the statute beyond the intentions of the authors.[42] Since the purpose of the investigation was to validate the implied charges, this outcome is not astonishing. What is absurd is the nature of the hunt; the pursuit chased rabbits while the foxes lay low. The hunters never sighted the Communist presence in the Fuchs cell or the office of the secretary, but they did bring down David Saposs who was in neither, and toasted the kill.

Before the denigration of David Saposs in the Smith committee, he had undergone scrutiny by the House Un-American Activities Committee, where he was attacked by J. B. Matthews, former head of the Communist front, the American League Against War and Fascism. In the course of testimony about Communists he had known, Representative Dies asked Matthews, "Did you in the course of your activity come in contact with Mr. Saposs, who is now on the National Labor Relations Board, and holds a responsible position in that organization?" Saposs was not *on* the board but was head of the economics section, in charge of statistical and other economics research, and an expert witness for the board in cases before it. A left-wing Socialist intellectual, Saposs had written widely, and had been active in the affairs of Brookwood College, a labor school in New York which had gone out of existence by 1938 when Matthews testified. When asked whether Saposs was a member of the Communist Party, Matthews said, "According to my best information, he was not." [43] The worst that could be said of him was that he had been the author of a book titled *Left Wing Unionism* which had been published by International Pub-

41. Seventy-sixth Congress, Second Session, House of Representatives, Special Committee to Investigate the National Labor Relations Board, *Hearings pursuant to H. Res. 258*, pp. 1–2 (hereafter cited as *Smith Committee Hearings*).

42. Seventy-sixth Congress, Third Session, *H. Report No. 1902*. Congressman Smith introduced a bill to carry out the recommendations of the committee which passed the House but was not acted upon in the Senate. For a brief description of the labor the committee undertook, see Bowman, *Public Control of Labor Relations*, pp. 417–418. The plan of operation involved a search of the board's files to ascertain the spirit of administration; an investigation of the docket to see how cases were handled; the mailing of some 60,000 questionnaires "to employers, employees, unions, interveners in cases, police chiefs, and professors of administrative and labor law"; and an analysis of board decisions by the legal staff of the committee.

43. Seventy-fifth Congress, Third Session, House of Representatives, Special Committee on Un-American Activities, Hearings on H. Res. 282, *Investigation of Un-American Activities in the United States*, p. 2173 (hereafter cited as *Hearings on H. Res. 282*).

lishers. Matthews quoted passages from the book.[44] In the same testimony, Matthews, on the afternoon of November 7, 1938, in time for the morning papers the next day — which was election day — put the New Deal in the embrace of Moscow with the remark,

> A complete perusal of the copies of the *Daily Worker* during the current campaign will leave no doubt whatever about the fact that the Communist Party is throwing its full force, whatever that is, behind the candidates in Pennsylvania and Ohio and New York who are running on the so-called New Deal program, with the exception of Vito Marcantonio, who is a Republican candidate.[45]

The only members of the committee present were Dies, who did not need to campaign in his safe district, and a lame duck Democrat, Harold D. Mosier of Ohio, who had been defeated for renomination in an earlier primary, and was not in the campaign at all.[46]

On Valentine's Day in 1940, the Smith committee got around to David Saposs. His work experience and credentials as a labor economist, which were very high,[47] were explored at some length, but the real business was to identify him as an advocate of violent overthrow of the government and the economic system, and this endeavor, although pressed with earnestness, encountered great difficulty.[48] He

44. J. B. Matthews had three passages that he thought enough of to copy and bring to the hearing. The first was, "It is also true that unorganized and particularly immigrant and unskilled workers must develop enthusiasm, solidarity, and understanding through mass action and the strike before they can be interested in becoming dues paying members." The second was, "Propaganda bodies chiefly dedicated to the dissemination of sentiments and ideas may exercise far reaching emotional and intellectual influence with a small membership and little material opulence." The third was, "Communists have been carrying on extensive propaganda among the unorganized, especially immigrants, Negroes, and unskilled workers. At crucial periods they will have their staunch followers strategically placed and when a spontaneous strike or other difficulty arises they are bound to be influential." Perhaps because these statements could have been made by Dies himself, the chairman asked for more quotations from Saposs "in order that we may know what his attitude is towards the Communist Party," but Matthews said that he had not "copied out any more than these." *Hearings on H. Res. 282*, p. 2174.

45. *Hearings on H. Res. 282*, p. 2199.

46. August Raymond Ogden, *The Dies Committee* (Washington, D.C.: Catholic University of America, 1945), p. 86.

47. Saposs came to the board in 1936 as chief economist after taking a competitive Civil Service examination in which 83 applicants participated. Of these, 78 qualified, and Saposs was first on the list. In addition, see his statement of his education, research career, and publications in the questioning by committee counsel, *Smith Committee Hearings*, pp. 3413–3423.

48. In the House of Representatives, Congressman Cox of Georgia made 29 charges against the National Labor Relations Board in the debate on the adoption of legislation to enact the recommendations of the Smith committee. Charge No. 22 went as follows: "I charge David Saposs with the manifestation of a strongly

had been a member of the Socialist Club when a student at the University of Wisconsin, still believed "in various types of reform," believed "that certain types of industries should be owned by the Government," but denied that he "advocated a socialistic form of government in this country as distinguished from the capitalistic and democratic form of government." [49] He insisted that he was a specialist in labor economics and trade unionism, and denied the subversive inferences that the committee counsel wanted to draw, like Matthews eighteen months before, from materials that yielded this conclusion only by force.[50] He favored industrial unionism as an organizing idea, as did John L. Lewis, a Republican supporter of Wendell Willkie in 1940, but Saposs was more vulnerable than Lewis, and when the Smith committee made its final report it singled him out in one of the more pointed affabilities.[51] Although the Congress did not enact the recom-

exaggerated social consciousness. I charge that he was born in Russia; that he was and probably still is a member of the Socialist Party, that he was and still is a member of the Conference for Progressive Labor Action; that he was a member of the faculty of Brookwood Labor College, characterized by the American Federation of Labor as a Communist school; that his writings show that he holds democracy in derisive contempt; that he would destroy capitalism; and that he openly urges labor to destroy capitalism, asserting that the time is now ripe for such destruction." *Smith Committee Hearings*, p. 7726. Previous to this when Saposs had been asked in the Smith committee about his birth and background, he pointed out that he had been born in the Ukraine in the regime of Tsar Alexander II, taken out of Russia during the regime of Tsar Nicholas II at the age of nine, and that he had never been back. *Ibid.*, p. 3417.

49. It was Howard Smith of Virginia who fused capitalism and democracy (*Smith Committee Hearings*, p. 3418), and the committee counsel who thought they were the same in the following exchange: "Mr. Toland: Didn't you also ask that the workers of the middle class destroy capitalism? Mr. Saposs: I advocated the fusion of the workers and the middle class in order to change a great many things in the present system. Mr. Toland: The present system of democratic government that we have? Mr. Saposs: I don't think I was talking about the Government; I was talking about certain economic matters. Mr. Toland: Well, that plays a very important part in the Government." *Ibid.*, p. 3434.

50. One of the principal writings of Saposs that the Smith committee thought pernicious was an article in *Labor Age*, for a time the publication of the Conference for Progressive Labor Action. The article was a report of the International Socialist and Labor Convention held in Vienna in 1931, and the role of Saposs was that of a reporter. The committee persisted in attributing to him his quotations of the positions taken by various speakers at the convention. *Smith Committee Hearings*, pp. 3425–3427.

51. The Committee Report summed up Saposs as follows: "That a person of such definite socialistic leanings as Saposs has demonstrated himself to be in his writings and affiliations should occupy a policy-making position of trust and importance in a government committed to the preservation of the capitalist system of private enterprise appears but another exemplification of indiscreet personnel management by the board as well as furnishing another strong indication that the board's policies are tinged with a philosophical view of the employer-employee relationship as a class struggle, something foreign to the proper American concept of industrial relations." Seventy-sixth Congress, Third Session, *H. Report No. 1902*, p. 36.

mendations of the Smith committee report, the House of Representatives, which had acted favorably on it, made sure that all was not lost by the Senate's inaction. The House Appropriations Committee heeded the recommendation of the Smith committee that Saposs' division of economic research be abolished,[52] cut the appropriation for the division by two-thirds, and recommended that the board abolish the division.[53] After some effort to keep the division under some other name, the board finally acquiesced and the division was destroyed.[54]

As the Smith committee was saving the "capitalistic and democratic form of government" from David Saposs, who was not subverting it,[55] it took sober testimony about the board's operations from some who were. Herbert Fuchs, who, by this time, had succeeded in organizing a cell in the board, testified about the procedure followed by a review attorney in the conduct of a case, with special reference to the use of derogatory slang.[56] Another committee witness was Margaret Bennett Porter. She had worked in the legal division of the Agricultural Adjustment Administration when the Ware group was centered there (1934), written some material for the La Follette committee staff, worked on the staff of the Wheeler committee, and was detailed at one stage by Lee Pressman to Edwin S. Smith to write La Follette committee material — a lady who seems to have had a through ticket on the party line. Her testimony dealt with the relations of a review attorney to a litigation attorney.[57] Allan Rosenberg, at the time legal assistant to the secretary of the board, Nathan Witt, was asked to testify on certain lobbying activities against amendments to the National Labor Relations Act desired by the American Federation of Labor.[58]

Party Influence in the Board

Although the Smith committee had general suspicions about subversive risks, it had no facts; but because it was so concerned with

52. *H. Report No. 1902*, p. 37.
53. Bowman, *Public Control of Labor Relations*, p. 347n.
54. Bowman, *Public Control of Labor Relations*, p. 355.
55. The search of Saposs' writings by the staff of the Smith committee failed to produce any advocacy of revolution or subversion, and he was not accused of being a Communist. Even Congressman Cox of Georgia had to make the delinquency of David Saposs rest on such flaws as an exaggerated social consciousness and the fact that he had been born in Russia.
56. In notes of his own made on the pleadings of certain cases with which he was concerned, Fuchs had labeled company arguments with such sophomoric criticisms as "Nuts." *Smith Committee Hearings*, p. 4179. He had also characterized certain testimony as "baloney." *Ibid.*, p. 4173.
57. For the testimony of Margaret Bennett Porter, see *Smith Committee Hearings*, pp. 1222–1233.
58. For the testimony of Allan Rosenberg, see *Smith Committee Hearings*, pp. 3498–3555 and 4070–4085.

protecting businessmen from the board, it neglected to consider seriously the protection of the board from its parasite faction. There were several significant hints of a Communist presence that were not, however, very strongly followed up and acted upon. David Saposs was the source of one of these but the committee seemed to have assumed that it had caught its limit when it "uncovered" him, and it chose not to be diverted from the main business of pressuring the board to relax the vigorous enforcement of the National Labor Relations Act.

George R. Brooks, the assistant director of the technical service division of the board, working under Saposs, had been called to the office of Congressman Frank Bateman Keefe of Wisconsin to talk with him and Congressman Albert Joseph Engel of Michigan, both being members of the Appropriations Subcommittee who were considering the status of the Saposs division in the National Labor Relations Board. Keefe opened the discussion by saying that he had had several calls from people who had expressed the opinion that Saposs was not a Communist; and he said that he wanted to find out whether this was so, and whether others on the staff of the board were Communists.[59] Brooks suggested that the subcommittee talk with Saposs himself, and this they eventually did. Brooks was asked about a list of people, as to which he said that he had no evidence that those he knew were Communists.[60] As to David Saposs, he was sure that he was not. Congressman Howard Smith, however, did not seem to entertain much doubt about Saposs when he examined Brooks about his conversation with Congressmen Keefe and Engel, making much of selected sentences from another publication of Saposs, "The Role of the Middle Class in Social Development," which had been published in a volume of essays honoring Wesley Mitchell.[61]

Saposs was brought back to testify and, in an unfriendly examination, he was asked about his conversation with Congressmen Keefe and Engel. When Saposs said that Congressman Keefe had asked him about Communists in the board, the following exchange occurred:

> Mr. Toland: Did you ever make the statement, Doctor, not at that particular conference, that the result of what was developed at this committee's hearings and at the hearings before the House Appropriation Committee was that there were people very much pleased at the embarrassment and difficulty that you found yourself in?

59. *Smith Committee Hearings*, p. 6884.
60. George Brooks said that Congressman Keefe had asked about all those named in the list except Marian Bachrach. *Smith Committee Hearings*, p. 6888.
61. The entire article is reproduced in the record at *Smith Committee Hearings*, pp. 3435–3448.

Mr. Saposs: No, sir.

Mr. Toland: Have you ever heard the statement made?

Mr. Saposs: Yes, sir.

Mr. Toland: The tendencies that you state you are opposed to would be the ones that are pleased with the fact that you were being made the goat for the Communists?

Mr. Saposs: I have heard that remark made.

Mr. Toland: Did you ever make that statement yourself, that you were being made the goat for the Communists?

Mr. Saposs: No, sir.

The Chairman: Do you think you are?

Mr. Saposs: I don't know.[62]

Saposs was then asked whether he had not told Congressmen Keefe and Engel that the individuals discussed with George Brooks were believed by him to be "either Communists, to be communistic sympathizers, and/or fellow-travelers," and he said "no." [63] He declined to voice suspicions about subversives and limited his criticism to members of the board staff who had joined such organizations as the National Lawyers' Guild and the American League for Peace and Democracy.

But Saposs was to find vindication if not redress. Over a dozen years later in testimony before the Senate Internal Security Subcommittee he went again over some of the ground that he had covered, but somewhat skimpily, in 1940. By 1953, Nathan Witt had been named as a Communist by Whittaker Chambers, by Nathaniel Weyl, and by his former law partner, Lee Pressman. Of him, Saposs said that he "was undoubtedly the most influential person in the conduct of the affairs of the board." [64] And of Edwin S. Smith who had become a registered agent of the Soviet Union, Saposs said, "Well, Edward Smith was a member of the board, of course, and was always a very close, or sort of buddy or crony of Nathan Witt, and, so far as I was able to observe, as the chief economist of the board, they were the two people that evidently exercised the greatest influence." [65] The chairman of the board, J. Warren Madden, was, according to Saposs, always preoccupied with legal questions — with the principles and problems of the law administered by the board, and governing it, with little time for or interest in the administrative work, "so that in that case both Nathan Witt and Edwin Smith were in the position to actually run

62. *Smith Committee Hearings*, p. 6899.
63. *Smith Committee Hearings*, p. 6900.
64. *Hearings on Interlocking Subversion in Government Departments*, p. 674.
65. *Ibid.*, pp. 674-675. The name "Edward" is either a slip of the tongue or a reporter's error.

the board." When asked whether in fact they did "run the board," Saposs replied, "Oh, yes; no doubt about it. They enjoyed it." [66]

The life of the board in the days of the Smith committee investigation was one of "constant agitation on the part of Communist-front organizations," such as the American League for Peace and Democracy, the League of Women Shoppers, and the Washington Book Shop. Petitions were circulated in behalf of various front causes and donations were solicited during office hours, not unusually but routinely, with the support and approval of Witt and Smith generally understood.[67] Harry Bridges was regarded as "a hero by these people" and Saposs recalled that Edwin Smith had devoted "a lot of time in trying to convince me that Harry Bridges was the greatest labor leader in the United States, and the general sentiment among these people was about the same." Saposs also testified that he was kept "away from preparing any of the material" in important cases involving Bridges' union "because by that time they knew what my point of view was and they knew what my general understanding was of the manoeuvers, the manipulations of the Communists and the fellow travellers." [68]

The Smith committee in 1940 also had significant testimony on the conduct by Nathan Witt of his offices in the National Labor Relations Board which, if pressed closely, might have yielded a more substantial prize than David Saposs. William Leiserson, former chairman of the National Mediation Board, was appointed to the National Labor Relations Board in 1939, and testified in 1939 on his views about Nathan Witt, whom he held in low regard.[69] In its vacuum-sweeping of the files of the board, the committee had turned up a number of memoranda in which Leiserson had complained about the way in which Witt had handled cases.[70] New to the board, although one of the nation's leading experts in labor relations administration, Dr. Leiserson had immediately examined the files and cases pending upon his appointment, and noted his displeasure freely. He had been with the board a short two months only when, according to the minutes of board meetings, he suggested that "Nathan Witt be relieved of his duties as Secretary of the Board." [71] Leiserson felt that Witt was not

66. *Hearings on Interlocking Subversion in Government Departments,* p. 675.
67. *Ibid.*
68. *Ibid.*
69. For the testimony of William Leiserson, see *Hearings on Interlocking Subversion in Government Departments,* pp. 3–141. As the citation shows, Leiserson was the lead-off witness in the extensive committee hearings.
70. See one case Mr. Leiserson declined to participate in because "I think this is another one of those cases in which the Secretary [Witt] has put his fingers and balled it up. . . ." *Hearings on Interlocking Subversion in Government Departments,* p. 25.
71. *Hearings on Interlocking Subversion in Government Departments,* p. 24.

qualified for his position either by training or experience, thought that he lacked understanding of the problems of administration in agencies like the board, and felt no confidence in Witt's "ability to perform his duties impartially as between various parties who appear in cases before the board." Dissatisfaction with Nathan Witt was also expressed by the regional director of the New York office of the board, Elinore Herrick. Witt had sent two men titled "special examiners" into the New York office to investigate it, which they did without providing any information or explanation to the regional director about the standards they were presumably using to judge the work of the office.[72] Mrs. Herrick complained to Chairman Madden in a long letter that carried certain doubtlessly unintended overtones:

> It is the procedure that one might expect from the OGPU, but not from fellow administrators of an agency of the American Government. If this were not such a critical period when the continued existence of the National Labor Relations Act hangs in the balance, I would make an issue of this and fight it to the bitter end. You know that I will do nothing to endanger the statute. Unfortunately certain of your subordinates also know and are taking advantage of this fact. I, therefore, submit under protest to this indecent, destructive, and un-American procedure.[73]

The two special examiners, also called "amateur detectives" by Dr. Leiserson, were Robert Gates and Fred Krivonos.[74]

There were other suggestive facts bearing upon the conduct of the secretary's office, some of which were to be found in various memo-

---

72. *Ibid.*, p. 29.
73. *Ibid.*, p. 30.
74. In another complaint to Chairman Madden about the handling of a board case, Mr. Leiserson said, "Three different people, Witt, B. Stern and Krivonos have handled the case here at different times and have written to the regional office about it. None of them was apparently able to study the documents carefully enough really to know what was involved in the case." *Hearings on Interlocking Subversion in Government Departments*, p. 32. Elinore Herrick in still another case wrote a memorandum to Witt with a copy to Edwin S. Smith complaining about Witt's handling of the Remington-Rand case in which a number of AFL workers were still out of work while strikebreakers held their jobs. The company had failed to comply with a board order reinstating the workers. The material for a contempt citation was ready in June of 1938 but by September Witt's office was still dilatory. When Witt sent Mrs. Herrick a telegram from one of the AFL officials protesting the inaction of the board, she wrote him a memorandum dated September 22, 1938, which said in part, "Personally I think the handling of this matter in Washington has been inexcusably dilatory and careless. I can't imagine why you are pursuing a policy of delay and shilly-shallying. . . ." The conclusion of the memorandum was, "But, for God's sake, don't send me any more silly notes like yours of September 20. I'm sick to death of having you pass the buck to us." *Smith Committee Hearings*, pp. 5182–5183.

randa on pending cases. For example, one of these memoranda, under
date of September 17, 1937, described a meeting in the San Francisco
office of the board, attended by Harry Bridges, Lee Pressman of the
CIO, and the regional director and the regional attorney of the board,
to discuss certain cannery worker cases.[75] Pressman told the group
that he had talked with Edwin S. Smith by telephone that morning;
and that Smith had had Witt telephone Pressman to tell him that the
board was considering a hearing involving the ILWU, Bridges' Longshoremen's Union. The cannery situation was discussed, and the regional lawyer told Pressman and Bridges that their cooperation was
essential in the cases. Bridges agreed to call in all his organizers and
instruct them in the kinds of evidence wanted by the board. It was
not the regional director who was in charge of the matter, evidently,
but Pressman and Bridges, with the cooperation of Smith and Witt.
The influence and access of Pressman, the outsider, to the centers of
board policy were of a superior sort. Not many private lawyers can
tell regional directors of Federal agencies what their superiors are prepared to do and not do.[76]

While the Smith committee was too intent on labor-baiting to draw
the correct inferences from indicative signs of sectarian partisanship,
a fierce struggle for power was actually going on within the board.
William Leiserson put his case for the removal of Witt from his position as secretary on the ground of incompetence, and Elinore Herrick
complained more than once about bad procedures. Whether these complaints were animated as much by ideological suspicions as administrative delinquency it is not possible to say absolutely. The board was
under fire from its enemies outside and internal criticism within the
board was muted in order to avoid giving liberal strength to the conservative attack. Even David Saposs, whose very professional existence
was at stake, was less than open when asked about the possible Communist origin of some of his difficulties.

The socialist journal, New Leader, however, was less inhibited than
the liberals under fire in the board, and in September 1940 clearly
called the play from the sidelines. Even when allowances are made
for a certain partisan exaggeration, the case stated by the New Leader
was difficult to refute. The gravamen of the charge was that the Communist Party was making a bid for complete control of the National

75. *Smith Committee Hearings*, p. 5578.
76. Another example of the close cooperation between Witt and Pressman was
the circulation by Witt to the regional offices of the board of material from
Pressman dealing with the filing of complaints. See exchange of memoranda,
October 3 and October 12, 1938, between Robert H. Cowdrill and Nathan Witt.
Smith Committee Hearings, p. 5707.

Labor Relations Board, the focus of the struggle being centered upon the vacancy created by the promotion of J. Warren Madden to the Federal judiciary.[77] "At present," said the *New Leader*, "the board is the scene of a bitter internal fight between Edwin S. Smith, trusted fellow-traveller and confidante of the Communists, and Dr. William Leiserson, who has the confidence of the bona fide labor movement as loyal to our democratic institutions." [78] Although it did not occur to any congressional investigation committee to refer to the *New Leader* on the matter until 1953, the signs of this tension were even contained in the record compiled by the Smith committee, but, of course, ignored.[79] The upshot of the struggle was that the sectarians of the left lost. Upon the expiration of Chairman Madden's term, his place was taken by H. A. Millis; Nathan Witt shortly thereafter resigned; and Edwin S. Smith was not reappointed when his term expired in August 1941.[80] Witt went with the firm of Leibman, Leider and Witt in January 1941, an office in which Lee Pressman had been a partner, in which he retained certain financial interests, and to which he returned as a partner of Witt's in 1948.[81] A considerable time after his departure from the Board, Smith was questioned about his affiliations. He pleaded self-incrimination when asked to say whether, during his service on the National Labor Relations Board, he had been a secret member of the Communist Party.[82]

77. Bill Harpman, "Communists Plan Tieup of United States War Industries Through Control of National Labor Board," *New Leader*, September 28, 1940.

78. The entire article is reprinted in Exhibit No. 272 in *Hearings on Interlocking Subversion in Government Departments*, pp. 929–931.

79. See, for example, a memorandum from Edwin S. Smith, dated August 11, 1939, in which he said of Leiserson, who had refused to participate in a case characterized by Leiserson as one displaying the "usual irregularities in procedure characteristic of the secretary's [that is, Nathan Witt's] office," "I question whether (1) the Board (i.e., the majority in this instance) should not express condemnation of Leiserson's refusal to participate, or (2) take some sort of action in court to compel him to perform the duties of his office. . . . I think what the Board at least should do is to pass a vote that Mr. Leiserson should do his duty and participate in a decision which requires his voice for determination." *Smith Committee Hearings*, p. 30. The animus of this reaction is scarcely matched in degree by the seriousness of the behavior that presumably provoked it.

80. The board under the National Labor Relations Act had three members appointed for staggered terms. The first three were J. Warren Madden, chairman, Edwin S. Smith, and John Carmody. Carmody resigned in 1936 and his place was taken by Donald Wakefield Smith. He was not reappointed when his term expired in 1938, and Dr. William Leiserson was chosen in his place. At the time of the Smith committee hearings, then, the board was Madden, Edwin S. Smith, and Leiserson.

81. Eighty-first Congress, Second Session, House of Representatives, Committee on Un-American Activities, *Hearings Regarding Communism in the United States Government*, p. 2929.

82. *Hearings on Interlocking Subversion in Government Departments*, p. 548.

An Estimation of the Results

What did the Communist presence in the National Labor Relations Board accomplish? The answer to this varies with the level of activity in view, for Communist activity seems to have occurred at two levels in the staff of the board, a lower and a higher. Herbert Fuchs was the "leader" of the lower level which, like the group he led in the Wheeler committee, only sometimes achieved the fortnightly meetings at which he aimed.[83] The normal organization of a cell was a structure of three officers — the head of the group, an educational director, and a secretary-treasurer to collect dues — but the Fuchs group in the National Labor Relations Board may not have had even this degree of formal organization; at least Fuchs could not recall that it had.[84] His group was limited to lawyers, managed to hold a meeting once a month when it seemed unable to meet oftener, and held the meetings in the homes of the members, which was also standard practice in other such groups. The discussions after the dues were collected and the literature handed out, seemed to concentrate upon cases and issues coming before the board. As Fuchs put it,

> . . . what we discussed were the good solutions and the bad solutions of things, but I don't want to give the impression that we were extralegal in this respect. That is to say, we told ourselves and were told that to be good Communists at the National Labor Relations Board, the better job that we did for the Board and for the Government, that was it. That was the best thing, and to do a good trustworthy job was a good Communist job in that area. Now I know that this doesn't correspond to my present day notions of the Party, but that is the way it was.[85]

According to Fuchs, there was no party line that cases should be decided according to any formula of class conflict or other concept.

Statements by Fuchs illustrate the confusing blur of democratic and dialectical values, to which a form of self-hypnosis contributed. Fuchs said that the members of the group felt that they were performing a patriotic duty by participating in the enforcement of the Wagner Act, and they were zealous in the belief that it was a good thing. But against the indulgent judgment that the Communist members of the group headed by Fuchs thought of themselves as simple industrial reformers is the secret nature of their membership in the party. If Dryden is right, that "Secret guilt by silence is betrayed," the silence of the cell

83. *Fuchs Hearings*, p. 2985.
84. *Fuchs Hearings*, p. 2986.
85. *Fuchs Hearings*, p. 2986.

about its affiliation betrayed the secret guilt that covert membership in the party may have suggested to the sensitive.

While Fuchs was the leader of the board cell of some seventeen members,[86] he ceased to attend the section meetings in which he had been a participant when he was in the Wheeler committee group.[87] When Fuchs left the Wheeler group to join the National Labor Relations Board, Arthur Stein turned him over to Victor Perlo, according to the testimony of Fuchs.[88] Perlo, who was known as "Mike," did not at first attend the meetings of the Fuchs group, and maintained contact with it only through Fuchs. The group knew of "Mike" but did not know that Perlo was Mike. At least one member of the group thought that Nathan Witt was "Mike." [89] Problems that the group itself were unable to resolve were bucked upstairs to "Mike" through Herbert Fuchs.

Perlo was replaced by Arthur Stein as the "higher-up" when he failed to satisfy certain insistent demands of the group. After some undefined time of meeting in each other's houses, exchanging shop-talk about the board and its problems, paying dues, reading "literature" bought for nickels and dimes, the group wanted to act in more public fashion — the secrecy and confinement chafed, and their zeal for causes was frustrated. They protested to "Mike" through Fuchs, and Fuchs could only bring back negative answers. Finally, Fuchs said, he told Perlo that he could no longer satisfy the group with negative answers. Perlo then met with the group, not once but on a number of occasions, and also failed to satisfy as much in person as he had through an intermediary. When he ultimately gave up the attempt to do so, the group was put in the charge of Arthur Stein.[90]

The secrecy of the group was thought to be essential to its security as an organization; and it was under orders — Perlo's and Stein's — to keep under cover. Many of the members of the group felt that they were bureaucratic bookworms, concerned merely with the papers of a job, to the exclusion of a more social kind of activity, and that they were "sterile," when they wanted to be publicly vigorous and productive. And even though there was an interdiction against member-

86. Fuchs named the original four: himself, Allan Rosenberg, Martin Kurasch, and Joseph Robison; and in response to questioning added thirteen others. *Fuchs Hearings*, pp. 2975–2980. Three of the thirteen confessed their membership, although one limited his admission to membership in the group, denying that he was a member of the Communist Party. *Ibid.*, p. 3055.

87. *Fuchs Hearings*, p. 2987.

88. *Fuchs Hearings*, p. 2985.

89. Lester Asher thought that Nathan Witt was "Mike." *Fuchs Hearings*, p. 3050.

90. *Fuchs Hearings*, p. 3004, for the testimony of Fuchs about Perlo and the group.

ship in mass organizations, some of the group had joined the National
Lawyers' Guild. It says something about the security and discipline
of the Fuchs group that the interdiction was eventually lifted, presumably as a result of the constant pressure by the members, and that
after the dispensation, virtually all became members of the National
Lawyers' Guild. Some also became members of the Washington Committee for Democratic Action, an organization created to agitate in
behalf of people expelled from the government for communism.[91]

But the psychology of secrecy was not really impaired by these dis-
pensations, for there was no open declaration of membership in the
party, and secrecy served to contain and center the loyalty of the
group. In the words of Fuchs,

> . . . it seems to me that there is an advantage to the Communists
> and this is the trap of communism in their own illegality, because
> as they are a conspiracy and secret, then every member is involved
> in a kind of trap, potentially a blackmail trap or perhaps only a
> trap with respect to his sentimental desire not to involve other peo-
> ple in trouble. As soon as he has engaged in one or more violations
> of the law, he is in a hostage to this conspiracy to which he perhaps
> altruistically lent himself in the first instance.[92]

For Fuchs, and perhaps for those who insisted upon more public forms
of action, there was no such complete alienation from the society as
characterized those who were not only members of an illegal organization but were in fact doing illegal work. At the time Fuchs and
others in the group joined the party, it was not an illegal organization.
As he said, he was a Communist when he entered the employment of
the government and did not disclose this fact — but then, he had not
been asked to. The evident desire of the group to associate actively in
public front causes indicates, in some degree, that the absolute alienation from the values of the society which makes the dedicated revolutionary did not exist — or not yet. Fuchs thought of himself as a
partisan of agitational goals rather than as an instrument of a long-
range strategy of power.

The choice between dialectical and democratic alternatives was not
forced upon Fuchs, he said, until the end of the war. During the late
thirties and in the war period, "the Communist Party line and American policy were almost exactly identical in many areas, and certainly
in the area in which I worked." [93] He had no problem of loyalty then,

91. *Fuchs Hearings*, pp. 3006–3007.
92. *Fuchs Hearings*, p. 3009.
93. *Fuchs Hearings*, p. 3010.

and the crisis of choices did not confront him until the war was over, at which time he left the Communist Party. It might seem odd that he was able to stomach the change in the line in 1939, and the consequent antagonism to American policy that the Communist Party agitated during the years of the Hitler-Stalin Accord. This was the era of the slogan, "The Yanks Are Not Coming," and there were violent strikes in key industries, stimulated by what the Communists liked to call "progressive" labor leaders. The stated reason for his joining the party in the first place was that he was "genuinely interested in being active in social reform of one sort or another." [94] Others so disposed were knocked right off the party line by the shaking it took when Stalin and Hitler found that their interests were not quite as opposed as Stalin had led the faithful to believe. It was this pact, more than any other single event, that disillusioned thousands whose connection with the party was based on a supposed community of humanitarian ideals.[95] But Fuchs stayed on through it all.

At a higher level in the board than the middle and lower ranks occupied by Fuchs and his group, the opportunity to influence the directions of board policy and practice was manifestly greater.[96] Smith and Witt within the board and Pressman outside occupied three strategic eminences. The essential condition of the struggle for influence in board policy seems — it may fairly be stated — to have been in the control of Pressman, for it was the CIO that provided the dynamism in the unionization of the workers in the mass production industries in the thirties, and he was, of course, the general counsel of the CIO and one, at least, of the principal strategists of the drive, if not its manager. Under John L. Lewis of the Mine Workers and then Philip Murray of the Steel Workers, Pressman was the attorney general of the campaign before the legal agencies of the government — the board and the courts — to extend union organization throughout industry.

94. *Fuchs Hearings*, p. 3011.

95. Fuchs left the National Labor Relations Board in 1942 to join the Denver office of the National War Labor Board, an entirely different organization, concentrating on the settlement of wartime labor disputes. Fuchs not only had not left the party when the Nazi-Soviet Pact was made in 1939; he was active in the Communist cell in Denver during the period of the war. He said that the cell included himself, Martin Kurasch, the regional attorney in the Denver office, John W. Porter and Margaret Bennett Porter, Edward and Lillian Scheunemann, and others. *Fuchs Hearings*, pp. 2995–3002. There were two cells in the Denver office of the National War Labor Board. In 1946 Fuchs returned to the National Labor Relations Board and found his old cell still functioning, with some new members. *Ibid.*, p. 3003.

96. There were two cells in the National Board between 1937 and 1942, according to Fuchs, but he disclaimed knowledge of the second one, saying that although he could speculate about the higher authority to which it reported, he did not have exact and sure knowledge. *Fuchs Hearings*, p. 2998.

He was the moving party, in short, and cases that he brought to the board filled its dockets.

But even when it is conceded that the CIO was the union on the march, using all the new resources of the government to further the goals of union intention, the combination of Smith, Witt, and Pressman produced advantages that neither the statute nor good practice could condone. Mention has already been made of the domination of the San Francisco regional office of the board by Pressman, and the caucus by telephone with Smith and Witt to lay out a campaign among cannery workers with Harry Bridges. Still another example of the same kind of partisanship is the trip to Pittsburgh that Nathan Witt made on June 2, 1937, to design the strategy of attack against Republic, Youngstown, and Inland Steel, three companies against which the Steel Workers Organizing Committee was moving.[97] Witt said that the whole board had suggested his attendance at the Pittsburgh conference, but when he explained this statement it then appeared that it might have been Lee Pressman who telephoned Washington first. It further appeared that it might have been Witt who took the call in which it was suggested that a Washington representative come to Pittsburgh to confer on charges that the SWOC might file against the Little Steel companies, some 60,000 of whose workers were out on strike.[98] Witt talked first with Pressman and then both talked with Philip Murray. No charges had in fact been filed but Pressman, and presumably Murray, were interested to know whether or not a written agreement would be required if the bargaining parties came to an understanding after negotiations, and they wanted a quick decision.[99] Nothing in the statute gave the board jurisdiction to act before a complaint was filed. The case was not like one where a union officer walks into a regional office and talks about a complaint he is going to make. Pressman and Murray wanted a quick decision from the board that a written agreement was necessary after negotiations, and they short-circuited the whole procedure of the statute in order to get the decision they wished. By arrangement, the SWOC demanded exclusive bargaining rights of Inland Steel, were refused, filed a charge under the Act, and Edwin S. Smith authorized the issuing of a complaint in

97. See *Smith Committee Hearings,* p. 897, for the account of Witt's trip to Pittsburgh. And see Bernard Karsh and Phillips L. Garman, "The Impact of the Political Left," mimeo., 66 pp. (n.d.) for a discussion of the influence of Witt and Smith in the National Labor Relations Board.

98. *Smith Committee Hearings,* p. 899.

99. See memorandum from Witt to Charles Fahy, dated June 3, 1937, summarizing the point of the Pittsburgh conversations. *Smith Committee Hearings,* p. 897.

the name of the board.[100] In fact the complaint by the board was prepared before the charge was filed. At the time, Witt was not the secretary of the board but the assistant general counsel.

Harry Bridges supplies still one more example of the cooperation supplied by "progressive" elements in the board to the "progressive" leadership in certain of the CIO unions.[101] In 1937, Harry Bridges demanded that the bargaining unit for longshoremen on the West Coast comprise the entire industry, and the employers' association acquiesced. So Bridges organized a campaign to bring the AFL workers under CIO jurisdiction, and large numbers moved from one organization to the other. Although the AFL had also earlier sought an industry-wide contract, it now argued that representation should be based on the ports, in some of which it could hope to retain bargaining authority for a majority of the longshoremen. Instead of ordering an election to determine the appropriate unit of representation, the board held that the appropriate unit was all of the longshore workers in the Pacific ports of each of the companies in the employers' association, and then certified the Bridges union as the exclusive bargaining representative on the basis of membership cards, and without a formal secret election.[102] Although the AFL took the case to the courts in an effort to get the board decision reversed, it failed to do so.[103]

Of the Communist problem in the prewar years in the Federal government, the evidence supports certain summary statements. First, there does not seem to have been a planned and premeditated "infiltration" of the Federal agencies, certainly not at the start. Second, once the entry into the Federal service by members of the Communist Party took place in the quick expansion of staff that began in 1933, some

100. Smith was the key man in the maneuver to get the quick decision by authorizing the complaint in the name of the board. See *Smith Committee Hearings,* p. 906, for Witt's assertion that Smith was the authorizing officer. Although he continued to say that the whole board knew he was going to Pittsburgh, the critical role in the stratagem played by Smith is evident in Witt's statement: ". . . I didn't do all these things on the direction of Mr. Smith. The full board knew I was going to Pittsburgh. I recall trying to reach the chairman on the phone that morning, and when he wasn't available, I talked to the senior member of the board, who happened to be Mr. Smith." *Ibid.*

101. The close alliance of Harry Bridges and the Communist movement was charged by the CIO itself when, after the war, it purged its constituent unions of Communist leadership. See *Official Reports on the Expulsion of Communist Dominated Organizations from the CIO,* Publication No. 254, September 1954 (Congress of Industrial Organizations), pp. 99–114. See also for an account of the longshoremen's case, Karsh and Garman, "Impact of the Political Left," pp. 55–57.

102. This is Shipowners' Association of the Pacific Coast, 7 *Decisions of the National Labor Relations Board* 120.

103. *American Federation of Labor* v. *National Labor Relations Board,* 103 F. (2d) 933, and 308 U.S. 401 (1940).

members of the party formed in study groups. Third, most of the membership of the party was pretty well scattered in ones and twos here and there, and the total — Chambers guessed about seventy-five — was not large. There were a half million Federal workers in Washington alone. Fourth, there were small concentrations of members of the party in the Department of Agriculture, certain congressional committees, and the National Labor Relations Board. Fifth, the aim of these groups seems to have been the promotion of left tendencies in the development of the public policies of the respective agencies. Sixth, the party groups were not primarily organized for espionage. Seventh, in the three areas discussed — Department of Agriculture, congressional committees, and the National Labor Relations Board — the promotion of left tendencies was not allowed to prevail: there was a "blow-up" in Agriculture, Senator La Follette brought the practice of hiring downtown personnel under restraint, and the bid for control of the NLRB was lost.

With the coming of the war, the Communist problem assumed somewhat more serious proportions.

VI   The Second Front at Home

General Emilio Mola boasted of his Fifth Column in Madrid; and
Georgi Dimitroff, of the Trojan Horse of Communist penetration
that — on some distant dialectical day — would spill out its armed
fighters and take the citadels of reaction from within. During the years
of the Second World War, as the Allies slowly established a second
military front in Europe at great effort and cost, Stalin was served
gratuitously by a second front of his own in the Washington bureaucracy — volunteer groups performing espionage for the Soviet fatherland, most often out of touch with each other, but supplying information to ambiguous superiors by way of pseudonymous couriers.

There is agreement that such an underground existed but disagreement about its extent. Some, like Daniel Bell, have ventured the view
that the work of these groups was exaggerated.[1] Howe and Coser feel
that the infiltration of Communists in the Roosevelt Administration
very probably "has been exaggerated, although there can be little doubt
that Communist spies and agents found their way into the Office of
War Information, the Office of Strategic Services, and the Treasury
Department." [2] James Burnham believes that the penetration was massive, that a veritable web of subversion was woven, and that it had

1. "The *extent* of Communist influence, as revealed in the Mundt-Nixon-Wood-
McCarthy exposures in 1950, is, I believe, somewhat exaggerated. Such influence
was, however, *intensive* in the several agencies where communist cells were able
to gain a strategic position and to seed the agencies with their followers. This
was particularly true in the Department of Agriculture and the NLRB in the
late thirties, and the Treasury Department and the Board of Economic Warfare
during World War II." Daniel Bell, "Marxian Socialism in the United States,"
in Donald Drew Egbert and Stow Persons, *Socialism and American Life* (Princeton: Princeton, 1952), vol. I, p. 358.

2. See Irving Howe and Lewis Coser, *The American Communist Party, 1919–
1957* (Boston: Beacon Press, 1957), p. 398, for a brief account of the effect of the
change in party line on the intellectuals and the counterattack against them in
party organs, and p. 434 for statement of opinion about the extent of espionage
in Federal agencies.

fateful and perhaps even decisive results in the adancement of Soviet interests.[3] The public record supports the finding that there was considerable activity, and that it was not negligible, even if exaggerations are discounted. And the public record is by no means the whole record, which will doubtless never be known. In the decade after the Truman Administration, only one person has stepped forward — Herbert Fuchs — who had not testified at the height of the concern over the issue, between 1948 and 1952.

To read again the public records of one and two decades ago is to recall how much the passion of the debate over the Communist movement — especially the activity of party members in Federal agencies — emphasized much that was contingent, local, and transitory. The sick forebodings of some liberals of the time did not materialize — there are no fascist brigades, white terrors, or book burnings. Professors, poets, sensitive writers, and independent-thinking artisans are threatened more by the diseases of affluence — like boredom — than by the thought police. The vision of imaginary toads in the computer culture of the near future was matched by the inability of many to acknowledge the real toads in the imaginary garden of Soviet-American friendship during the war years. On the other hand, the panic apprehensions of catastrophes of subversion never materialized either — the Union of Soviet Socialist States of America is farther away than ever, the Communist Party USA is in the hands of political receivers like Gus Hall, and consensus rules, not commissars.

In the mass of paper that blizzards of words piled up in the late forties and fifties there is evidence that at least two principal centers

3. James Burnham, *The Web of Subversion* (New York: John Day, 1954). Burnham makes the following statement: ". . . the units of the underground provided the political cover on the American flank for the Soviet Empire's triumphant swallowing of eastern Europe; for the unimpeded Communist conquest of the bulk of the Italian and French trade union movements; for the liquidation, under slogans of reprisal against 'collaborationists,' of tens of thousands of Europe's anti-Communists; for the forced return eastward of hundreds of thousands of anti-Communist war prisoners, refugees and deserters. The underground can take legitimate pride in its clever manipulation of American 'anti-colonial' attitudes in connection with Indonesia, the Middle East and North Africa; its contribution to our continuing paralysis in the face of Guatemala's creeping subjection to Communist rule; its sly use of our genuine concern for civil liberties as a protective shield for its own treachery; its skillful support of the Communist drive into the domestic labor movement; its considerable share in the embittering of relations with our principal allies; and the brain pounding on scientists and policy makers as a result of which the political advantages that could have come to the United States from overwhelming atomic superiority have been so largely sterilized. If we now add the damage from subversion to that from espionage, what sum do we get? The White House, when rejecting the Rosenbergs' plea for clemency, followed Judge Kaufman in estimating the possible future damage from that single espionage action at ten million lives. Have the pleaders of the Fifth Amendment ever faced the probable total?" *Ibid.*, p. 221.

of political espionage were at work in Washington during the war years, and that important sources for the transmission of information to Soviet agents had been established in a number of other places. Not all of the members of this shadow front were members of the Communist Party, but all were aware that they were working for the Soviet Union.

The Companionate Subversion

Aging college professors can testify that the New Deal they knew only yesterday seems as remote to the students they teach as the Populist crusade and the Free Silver movement. For the students, at least, it may be useful to recall the hospitable public attitude towards the Soviet Union that prevailed quite generally during the Second World War among officials and populace alike. The detente does not condone the espionage, nor validate the argument that espionage may be overlooked because friends were spying on friends. (It has been said that a nation has neither friends nor enemies, only interests.) But the pervasive good feeling about our Russian allies, the unfocused and indiscriminating fraternity of the wartime alliance, helped to throw a haze for many over our Slavic partners, to transform the cruelty of the Moscow trials into prescient toughness, and the cynical arrangement with Hitler into admirable realism. Should we not, in reason and charity, recognize our own social defects (what about the Negroes in the South?) and celebrate the kinship of two great nations linked in the service of common goals, indulgently conscious of shared faults but united in basic values?

The party line — a marvel of invertebrate flexibility — changed, with humorless effrontery, in 1939 and then, once again, in 1941, the years respectively of the Nazi-Soviet Pact and the military attack on the Soviet Union by the Germans. In a retreat into isolationism in this Fifth Period (1939–1941), the American Communist Party dismantled the American League for Peace and Democracy and other front organizations of the Fourth Period, and worked, like the America First Committee, Colonel Charles Lindbergh, and Colonel Leonard Wood, to keep the United States from intervening in the war against the Nazis. Trade unions in which Communist policies were salient conducted a series of strikes for political objectives — not the improvement of wages, hours, and working conditions, but the defeat, or embarrassment, of the defense effort.[4] Notable were the strikes in Vultee Aircraft in Downey, California, in November 1940, the North Amer-

4. See Max Kampelman, *The Communist Party vs. The CIO* (New York: Praeger, 1957), chap. iii, p. 25, for a discussion of the CIO, Communists, and the Second World War.

ican aircraft strike in June 1941, and the logging camp and sawmill workers strike in May 1941. But the great grandfather of all such strikes was that in the Allis-Chalmers plant in Milwaukee, a walk-out of seventy-six days after eight months of wrangling during which there were seventeen work stoppages. Kampelman has said of this strike, "No issue of wages, hours, or conditions was at stake." [5]

Louis Budenz, then editor of the *Daily Worker*, wrote that "The workers everywhere do not want their sons to die, mangled scraps of flesh . . . in order to enrich Wall Street. America, keep out of this war." [6] William Z. Foster was later to write of this period,

> Such united front organizations as the American League for Peace and Democracy, National Negro Congress, American Youth Congress, League of American Writers, Southern Congress for Human Welfare, and the like, also went on record against United States participation in the war. When President Roosevelt, therefore, two days after the invasion of Poland, declared that the attitude of the American government toward the war would be one of neutrality, he was undoubtedly supported by the great masses of the people. [7]

Congressman Vito Marcantonio attacked J. Edgar Hoover, Director of the Federal Bureau of Investigation, after the latter's testimony about his office before the House of Representatives subcommittee on appropriations in January 1940, in the following language,

> First, we are preparing a general raid against civil rights, a blackout against the civil liberties of the American people, a system of terror by index cards such as you have in the Gestapo countries of the world; second, we are engendering a war hysteria which is a menace to the peace of the United States. [8]

The Hollywood Anti-Nazi League dropped the "Anti-Nazi" from its title and became the Hollywood League for Democratic Action. The President of the United States was jeered and booed on the front lawn of the White House in February 1940 by his guests, members of the American Youth Congress, when he referred to the Soviet Union as a dictatorship. [9] In June 1940, Israel Amter and Charles Krumbein, chair-

5. Kampelman, *Communist Party vs. The CIO*, p. 26.
6. Howe and Coser, *The American Communist Party*, quoted at p. 390.
7. William Z. Foster, *History of the Communist Party in the United States* (New York: International Publishers, 1952), pp. 386–387.
8. Don Whitehead, *The FBI Story* (New York: Random House, 1956), quoted at p. 171.
9. John Gates, *The Story of an American Communist* (New York: Nelson and Sons, 1958), p. 77. Gates at the time was a leader in the Young Communist League which dominated the Congress. Of the incident, he says, "At a Youth Congress gathering on the White House lawn, at which FDR spoke, the President was

man and secretary respectively of the New York State Communist Party, issued orders to all section organizers to establish peace groups in their sections, branches, and units, the secretaries of other state parties doing the same.[10] The result was the creation of the American Peace Mobilization, which launched a fake pacifist movement.[11] The theme of the APM was that men in high places were dragging America into a war three thousand miles away, and a "perpetual peace vigil" was maintained in front of the White House. On June 21, 1941, the American Peace Mobilization called for observance of a National Peace Week. The next day, the German armies attacked the Soviet Union, nothing was ever again heard of National Peace Week, the American Peace Mobilization changed its name to the American People's Mobilization, what had been a war of imperialist aggression immediately became a people's war, and one's attitude towards fascism ceased to be the "matter of taste" that Molotov had said it was following the Nazi-Soviet Pact of 1939.

Party members became the *ultras* in patriotic striving. In the 1920's they had been a congeries of ethnic factions, in the 1930's they were merely the fellow travelers of a liberal movement, but in the 1940's — during the years of the war, that is — they benefited from the temporary merger of American and Russian military interests, and achieved considerable access to centers of counsel and command. Public signs of the new prestige were at every hand. In the fall of 1940, Earl Browder and others had been arrested for passport violations. Browder was convicted and sent to the Atlanta Penitentiary in March 1941 under a four-year sentence. On May 16, 1942, President Roosevelt freed Browder by commuting his sentence,[12] this act becoming the successful culmination of a nationwide drive by the Communist Party through

booed. The Young Congress could not survive a turn like this. It passed out of existence, and to our shame we were not sorry to see it go. Our slogan was now The Yanks Are Not Coming, and we gleefully sang songs ridiculing President and Mrs. Roosevelt."

10. Seventy-fifth Congress, Third Session, House of Representatives, Special Committee on Un-American Activities, Hearings on H. Res. 282, *Investigation of Un-American Activities in the United States*, vol. XIV, p. 8395 (hereafter cited as *Hearings on H. Res. 282*). This is the testimony of Hazel Huffman, who had been engaged by the Dies Committee to make an investigation of the American Peace Mobilization.

11. The head of the new American Peace Mobilization was the Rev. John B. Thompson of Oklahoma. The other officers were familiar stalwarts in or friends of the Communist Party. For an account of the APM, see Eugene Lyons, *The Red Decade* (Indianapolis: Bobbs-Merrill, 1941), p. 382.

12. Whitehead, *The FBI Story*, p. 351, n. 5. Although arrested on October 23, 1939, Browder was released on bail the next day. Before his trial and conviction, he was free to carry on his campaign as Communist Party candidate for President of the United States. The 1940 election was the last one in which the Communist Party was to run a candidate for the White House.

such fronts as the Citizens Committee to Free Earl Browder, the National Free Browder Congress, and Communist-dominated unions. The theory of the drive was that Browder had been jailed as a political prisoner for disagreeing with the administration over war policy in 1940, that the differences were now resolved, and that the commutation was a necessary gesture for national unity.

In the same month that Earl Browder was freed, Molotov was a distinguished guest at the White House,[13] although no notice was made of it in the press in order to ensure the safety of the Soviet representative.[14] Molotov was in town to argue for a second military front in 1942 for which the Russians pressed from the start, and which, in 1942, would have matched the Nazis at their greatest strength with the allies at their lowest. While in Washington, the code name for Molotov was "Mr. Brown," and although the secret of his visit was kept from the public, it was known to other Soviet representatives in the United States. After Molotov had left, the news was made public in a statement issued June 11, 1942, and shortly afterwards Harry Hopkins made a speech in Madison Square Garden to a Russian war relief rally in observance of the anniversary of the German attack on the Soviet Union. In a context of references to the "unconquerable power of the Soviet people," Hopkins promised a second front and "if necessary a third and a fourth front, to pen the German army in a ring of our offensive steel." [15] The image of the United States shoulder to shoulder with the Soviet Union in the conquest of Nazi aggressors was not only a staple of rhetoric but the exigent fact, which the conferences at Casablanca, Quebec, Cairo, Teheran, and Yalta proved.

Besides the public approval of the Soviet Union expressed by diplomats and other public officials, the people of the country were given encouragement by the newspapers, magazines, radio, and movies to think well of our temporary friends, to overlook their shortcomings, and to appreciate their virtues. The Russian song, "Meadowland," was a favorite on the radio, and among the party members in Hollywood, as Murray Kempton has put it, "there was a false and fevered glow," [16] although nothing like the manipulation of mass moods imagined by the House Committee on Un-American Activities was, or could have been, achieved. Such films as "Song of Russia" and "Counterattack" were later to be closely scanned for subversive dialogue but, although favorable towards the Soviet Union, they could hardly have stirred

13. For an account of the Molotov visit, see Robert E. Sherwood, *Roosevelt and Hopkins* (New York: Bantam Books, 1950), vol. I, p. 139.

14. Sherwood, *Roosevelt and Hopkins*, p. 139.

15. Sherwood, *Roosevelt and Hopkins*, vol. II, p. 174.

16. Murray Kempton, *Part of Our Time* (New York: Simon and Schuster, 1955), p. 199.

the populace to acts of revolutionary folly. The thesis of Chairman J. Parnell Thomas that the Administration encouraged and abetted the production of flagrant propaganda in Hollywood was scarcely supportable; and the only "intervention" that could be ascribed to the production of "Song of Russia" was the delay of Robert Taylor's induction into the Navy while the film was being shot.[17] "Counterattack," written by John Howard Lawson, was a story about a minor Soviet military operation notable chiefly for the saccharine relation between the troops and their superiors.

In 1943, the Soviet Union cooperated in the illusion that permanent bonds of friendship were being forged in the fires of war by abolishing the Communist International,[18] and the American Communist Party a year later abolished itself as a formal party and became instead the Communist Political Association.[19] The action of the Soviet Union was seemingly intended to appear to break that connection with the national parties that the American Communist Party of the Fourth Period always denied existed.[20] The action of the American party in creating the Communist Political Association was based on the assumption of Browder that the wartime partnership would be permanent. His "American exceptionalism" like that of Lovestone fifteen years be-

17. Chairman Thomas was described by an observer at the hearings as "a small, bald, and ruddy man, of a color something between Rose Madder and Vermilion, a color that changes to plum-apple when he is frustrated, which is often. Surprisingly, he is not at all ogreish; he looks and acts Pickwickian, and one could imagine under the circumstances, that the bulge in his coat signifies candy for children." *Life Magazine*, November 14, 1947. Mr. Thomas looked different to another writer three years later: "The blue prison fatigues hung loosely on the weary, perspiring man whose path across the quadrangle was about to meet mine." Ring Lardner, Jr., "My Life on the Blacklist," *Saturday Evening Post*, October 14, 1961. Both Lardner and Thomas were in Danbury prison.

18. William Z. Foster was later to say that "The dissolution of the Comintern was a heavy sacrifice by the Communists for the common cause of victory," a loss especially keen to the CPUSA which owed "a great debt to the Comintern for its own Marxist-Leninist development." *History of the Communist Party*, p. 415.

19. Of the dissolution of the Communist Party in America by the action of Earl Browder, Foster was to charge heresy in the utopian and opportunistic doctrine of Browder that "Capitalism and socialism have begun to find the way to peaceful co-existence and collaboration in the same world." *History of the Communist Party*, p. 422.

20. The Voorhis Act, signed by President Roosevelt in October 1940, required the registration of all agencies and organizations with foreign affiliations. The Communist Party held a special convention in New York on November 16 and 17, 1940, and resolved "that the Communist Party of the U.S.A., in convention assembled, does hereby cancel and dissolve its organizational affiliation to the Communist International, as well as any and all other bodies of any kind outside the boundaries of the United States of America, for the specific purpose of removing itself from the terms of the so-called Voorhis Act." But, as William Z. Foster said, "The Party did not abandon its internationalist position." *History of the Communist Party*, p. 393.

fore was to cost him his leadership of the party when the war ended. Foster had challenged the Browder thesis all along, and it was he who was to prevail when the military collaboration was no longer needed.

During the entire period of this great euphoria, the Soviet Union maintained underground espionage services in Washington and New York, one hand extended in the rough hearty candor of international friendship while the other picked over files and rifled desks. For despite the feeling of many Americans, some of them Communists, that there had been a solid merger of interests because of the war, the Soviet Union acted under no such fantasy, nor did Third Period personalities like William Z. Foster. For them, it was an incorrect estimation of the war alliance to suppose that because Great Britain and the United States had agreed to help the USSR, "they would be trustworthy allies." [21] There *was* no unity of interest. All three powers just happened to be on the same side. Most Americans had yet to learn — or if they knew, to appreciate — the truth expressed by Victor Kravchenko, economic attaché of the Soviet Purchasing Commission from August 1943 to April 1944:

> The Soviet Government has legalized the system of espionage on its citizenry within its own country. This espionage is conducted on a tremendous scale. Why should we think that in America, England, or France, the Soviet Government does not carry on the most active espionage for the furtherance of its military, political, and police aims to the extent which our easy-going attitude and our lack of understanding of the core of Soviet policy permit? . . . Soviet diplomacy is indivisible from the espionage activities of the Kremlin abroad.[22]

In 1943 at the time of one of the great gestures that was intended to reassure the allies of the sincerity of Soviet purpose and intention (the dissolution of the Comintern), Kravchenko and others, on their way to the United States, were being told by their superiors, "You are going to the capitalistic United States. We are allies today because we need each other, but when the war is over and we shall have won the victory — and we are sure we shall win it — we shall again become open enemies." [23] Although the second front against the Nazis was not established until June 1944, the second front of the Soviet Union within

21. Foster, *History of the Communist Party*, p. 413.
22. Eighty-first Congress, First and Second Sessions, House of Representatives, Committee on Un-American Activities, *Hearings Regarding Shipment of Atomic Material to the Soviet Union During World War II*, December 1949 and January and March 1950, testimony of Victor A. Kravchenko, pp. 1175–1194, at p. 1177.
23. *Hearings Regarding Shipment of Atomic Material to the Soviet Union*, p. 1180.

the officialdom of its dominant and indispensable ally had already been flourishing for years.

The Perlo Group

"Is Joe getting all this stuff safely?" This, according to Elizabeth Bentley in sworn testimony, is the question that Victor Perlo asked her when, she said, she first met him in the apartment of John Abt in New York.[24] Victor Perlo, discussed earlier in connection with the Ware group in the thirties, was named by both Whittaker Chambers and Elizabeth Bentley, in separate statements, as the head of a group in the forties which provided information improperly and secretly to agents of the Soviet Union. The principal witness against Perlo was Elizabeth Bentley. The reliability of both sources has been forcefully attacked, and credence to Bentley's account of Perlo certainly requires some toleration of contradiction, invention, and ambiguity. Her book contains inaccuracies, verbatim reports of some conversations she could not have reproduced without stenotype or tape recorder, touches of romantic exclamation, and quick girlish excursions into psychological speculation, desolate either of knowledge or perception.[25] An unwar-

24. Eightieth Congress, Second Session, House of Representatives, Committee on Un-American Activities, *Hearings Regarding Communist Espionage in the United States Government*, p. 692 (hereafter cited as *Hiss Hearings*).

25. Byron Scott, former Democratic member of Congress from Long Beach, California, was counsel for William Henry Taylor, former Treasury official, in the loyalty hearings on Taylor held by the International Organizations Employees Loyalty Board, and because Taylor's name (or rather, a Bill Taylor) was mentioned by Bentley, Scott made a close scrutiny of her testimony, which was given public notice. See Eighty-fourth Congress, First Session, *Congressional Record*, May 24, 1955, Appendix A3591, where Congressman James Roosevelt inserted an article by Murray Marder titled "Fund Official Seeks Bentley Confrontation," which is a reprise in great detail of the Scott memorandum on Bentley's testimony. As to Perlo, the alleged discrepancy that Scott points out is a supposed variance of dates. Scott asserted that she had said that she had collected dues from the Perlo group and turned them over to Jacob Golos, her lover, who was a Communist agent. Scott says that her testimony shows that Golos died four or five months before she met the Perlo group. In *Out of Bondage* (New York: Devin-Adair, 1951), Elizabeth Bentley makes it clear that she met the Perlo group *after* Golos had died (see pp. 236–237). In her testimony before the House Committee on Un-American Activities in the summer of 1948, she made it clear that the material given her by the Perlo group was *not* turned over to Golos, who was dead, but to a new contact who replaced Golos. *Hiss Hearings*, p. 689. In her testimony before the Senate Judiciary Subcommittee Investigating the Institute of Pacific Relations in 1951, Miss Bentley said that Golos had died in 1943 and that she had taken over the Perlo group in 1944. Eighty-second Congress, First Session, United States Senate, Committee on the Judiciary, Subcommittee to Investigate the Administration of the Internal Security Act and Other Internal Security Laws, *Hearings on the Institute of Pacific Relations*, pp. 405–406 and 441 (hereafter cited as *IPR Hearings*). Some of the other alleged discrepancies are of the "It is incredible to think that . . ." sort, and are simply in the realm of whatever you may think it is incredible to think. For a critical study of

ranted use of names led to successful legal actions for redress.[26] Detractors never failed to ridicule Miss Bentley and her story as the
imaginings of a neurotic spinster but, in the main, the account of
espionage she made public in the summer of 1948 has coherence and
no one denies the principal fact, namely, that she was a courier for a
Soviet espionage operation in Washington. Credibility is lent her recital
by the testimony of Chambers at various points, and by certain factors
of circumstance, some negative, like the refusal of Perlo and a dozen
others to deny her charges because of possible self-incrimination, and
some positive, like the statements about Perlo's prewar activities made
by Weyl and Fuchs. Her main disclosures, then, are believable, are
not to be brusquely dismissed as malicious mania, and are still largely
unrefuted.

Jacob Golos, agent of the NKVD, and head of World Tourists, Inc.
until his death from a heart attack in 1943, was the contact and sweetheart of Elizabeth Bentley for five years after she left the open party
and went underground in 1938. Upon his death, it seems that his superiors had not made immediate provision to carry on his work, and
some of the burden fell to Miss Bentley, who took on the responsibility
for two groups: the Perlo group and one headed by Nathan Gregory
Silvermaster. The Perlo group is of unique interest in many ways.
Miss Bentley, in her somewhat cloying style and with more specificity
than most memories permit, described as follows a conversation she
said she had with Earl Browder when she first heard about the Perlo
group:

> Returning from a trip to Washington, just after the New Year, I
> went down to see Earl and show him the material I had collected,
> before passing it on to Bill. He read it through thoughtfully, gave it
> back, then leaned forward in his chair and looked at me appraisingly.
> "I've got another group to be turned over to our friends, but I
> want to be quite sure they're in good hands. Will you take them?"
> "Our friends," I knew, meant the Russians; that was the way Earl
> always referred to them. His trust in me was very flattering, I

the Bentley testimony, see Herbert L. Packer, *Ex-Communist Witnesses*
(Stanford: Stanford, 1962).

26. William Henry Taylor sued the Washington *Daily News* for libel when
it published a statement calling him part of an espionage ring. The newspaper
settled out of court. An adverse judgment against the loyalty of William Henry
Taylor by the International Organizations Employees Loyalty Board was reversed
on January 6, 1956. For a statement about both the reversal and the settlement of
the suit, see *I. F. Stone's Weekly*, January 16, 1956, reprinted in Nathan I. White,
Harry Dexter White, Loyal American (Waban, Massachusetts: Bessie White
Bloom, 1956), pp. 343–344.

thought, but right now I hoped to get out of the undercover business, not get more involved in it. He noticed my hesitation.

"I know you're overburdened already," he said, "and I wouldn't ask you if it weren't absolutely necessary. In the past, they were handled by John Abt and the material passed through me to Golos; now Abt is going to take over a fairly public position and it's too dangerous to continue on that way. They've got to have a new contact." He paused for a moment and then looked at me searchingly. "You know what the Russians are like; I can't give the group over to them. You've got to take them." [27]

By the end of March 1944, Browder had completed arrangements for Miss Bentley to take over the new group, headed, she said, by Victor Perlo.

It is not possible to know what "fairly public position" John Abt was going to take over, since he already occupied a fairly public position as general counsel for the Amalgamated Clothing Workers of America.[28] But the association of Abt and Perlo makes it possible that the group had its roots originally in the Ware cell of a decade before.[29] At least one other member of the original Ware group, besides Abt and Perlo, was a member of the later one, Charles Kramer, so that a third of the Ware group is accounted for in the Perlo group. According to Elizabeth Bentley, Abt ceased to figure as a member of the Perlo group except in a meeting with her in Abt's apartment in New York.[30]

What she called the "Perlo group" had been functioning in an unorganized way for some time; that is, it "had been in a minor way collecting information for some years but not in an organized fashion." [31] Even under Bentley it seems to have continued its work in somewhat

27. Bentley, *Out of Bondage*, p. 237. Although the account is made in direct discourse, there is no evidence that Browder used the exact words that are attributed to him. Miss Bentley did not take the words down, and the attribution must be recollection some time after the event. As has been said, this is a weakness throughout Miss Bentley's book.

28. Lee Pressman is said to have had Abt placed in the ACWA. "Through Pressman, for example, even so anti-Communist a union as Sidney Hillman's Amalgamated Clothing Workers engaged as their general counsel John Abt, 'a member of the Communist Party of long standing.'" Kampelman, *Communist Party vs. The CIO*, p. 19.

29. Although Elizabeth Bentley had had no contact with or knowledge of the Ware group, her recollection of the origins of the Perlo group was that it "was actually an ex-Communist Party unit that I believe had been set up in Washington in the early thirties. . . ." *Hiss Hearings*, p. 511.

30. Miss Bentley testified that she met Perlo twice in the apartment of John Abt to receive information to be turned over to the Russians, and that the rest of the time she met him in the apartment of Mary Price. *Hiss Hearings*, p. 687.

31. *Hiss Hearings*, p. 511.

unorganized fashion, for she reported that she not only received information from Perlo but from other members of the group also.[32] She said she never met Perlo in Washington, although she made periodic trips to Washington to collect information from the Silvermaster unit.[33] Instead, Perlo came to New York and she met him there some seven, eight, or nine times.[34] She collected Communist Party dues from him in New York when she met him, she said, at Mary Price's apartment.[35]

The other members of the Perlo group when she took it over, according to Miss Bentley,[36] were Allan Rosenberg, who had been in the Board of Economic Warfare which later developed into the FEA (Foreign Economic Administration); Donald Wheeler of the Office of Strategic Services; Charles Kramer, then between jobs but on his way to the Kilgore and Pepper committees; Edward Fitzgerald of the War Production Board; Harry Magdoff, employed in the War Production Board from 1941 to 1944, and in the Department of Commerce from 1944 to 1946, when he left the government to go with the New Council of American Business in New York City;[37] Harold Glasser of the Treasury Department; and Sol Lischinsky of the United Nations Relief and Rehabilitation Administration (UNRRA). There was also testi-

32. *Hiss Hearings*, p. 687. Other members of the group from whom she received information, according to Miss Bentley's testimony, were Charles Kramer, Edward Fitzgerald, Allan Rosenberg, and Donald Wheeler.

33. *Hiss Hearings*, p. 689.

34. *Hiss Hearings*, p. 689.

35. John Abt was questioned about the original meeting of Elizabeth Bentley with the Perlo group in his apartment. The question was, "Well, Mr. Abt, in connection with your home, 444 Central Park West, did a meeting take place there some time during the war at which were present Victor Perlo, Elizabeth Bentley, and several other individuals, the purpose of which was to make arrangements for people working in Government to transmit confidential information to Elizabeth Bentley, who was then the head of an espionage ring in Washington?" Abt's first response was, "That is a very long question, Mr. Morris." When pressed to answer he pleaded self-incrimination. Eighty-third Congress, First Session, United States Senate, Committee on the Judiciary, Subcommittee to Investigate the Administration of the Internal Security Act and Other Internal Security Laws, *Hearings on Interlocking Subversion in Government Departments*, p. 645.

36. *Hiss Hearings*, pp. 511–516. In these pages Elizabeth Bentley for the first time in public made known the names of the members of the Perlo and Silvermaster groups.

37. Elizabeth Bentley almost certainly made a mistake in one respect about Magdoff, whom she said she had met only once. *Hiss Hearings*, p. 514. When questioned by committee counsel as to whether she had ever collected Communist Party dues from Magdoff, she said that she had received such dues in New York in collections that included the dues of many. When asked what she did with the dues, she said, "I turned them over to Mr. Golos during his lifetime." *Ibid.*, p. 515. She could not have turned them over to Mr. Golos in his lifetime because she did not get the Perlo group until after Mr. Golos had died.

mony that Miss Bentley, in addition to receiving information from other members of this group besides its putative head, Perlo, received information about matters within the purview of this group from others outside it entirely. Thus, although Wheeler was a presumed source about matters in the Office of Strategic Services, he was not the only one to supply information from the OSS to Miss Bentley. She said that Louis Budenz, managing editor of the *Daily Worker*, also supplied her with information from the OSS provided by Louis Adamic.[38]

The War Production Board (WPB) seems to have provided a number of sources, some of whom were in the Perlo group and others elsewhere. In one such list, Perlo is named along with Fitzgerald and Magdoff.[39] Fitzgerald and Magdoff were both called upon to testify about themselves and their activities in 1953. They had both been mentioned in a top-secret memorandum dated November 1945 which had been made public by Richard Nixon,[40] and both had appeared in executive session before the Senate Internal Security subcommittee the day before their public appearance. By this time Fitzgerald was doing work as a free lance writer and reviewer of books for various newspapers and magazines, and writing fiction for *Confession Magazine*.[41] Fitzgerald disappointed his questioners by refusing to provide any confessions about himself, fictitious or factual. He declined to say whether he was presently a member of the Communist Party on the ground that his answer might tend to incriminate him,[42] declined to say whether he was a member of the espionage ring described in the memorandum of November 1945,[43] and declined to relate the circum-

38. *Hiss Hearings*, pp. 524–525.
39. David J. Dallin, *Soviet Espionage* (New Haven: Yale, 1955), p. 441, contains such a list under the covering sentence (previously mentioned, p. 157): "During the war years the Soviet apparat had its men in at least the following agencies . . . ," and then follows the list of agencies with the names of various individuals attached. The reliability of the list is very dubious, however. The individuals listed for the Department of Agriculture as wartime agents of the Soviet apparat include Harold Ware who was dead, John Abt who was with the Amalgamated Clothing Workers, Nathan Witt who was in private practice, and Lee Pressman who was with the CIO.
40. *Hearings on Interlocking Subversion in Government Departments*, pp. 241–242. This memorandum, prepared by the FBI and circulated in the government, was quite clearly based, so far as Perlo and others were concerned, on the information of Elizabeth Bentley.
41. A list of books reviewed by Fitzgerald was compiled by staff of the Senate subcommittee. The letter from the editor of the *New York Times Book Review*, Francis Brown, said in part, "Our records show that he has reviewed only six times for us and on each occasion his reviews dealt only with fiction of secondary importance."
42. *Hearings on Interlocking Subversion in Government Departments*, p. 245.
43. *Ibid.*, p. 246.

stances leading to his employment by the Federal government,[44] all denials based on the belief that his answers would incriminate him.

In fact, Fitzgerald had come into the Federal government by way of the National Research Project which appears to have functioned as a useful point of entry into the Federal service for several members of the Communist Party, and from which they moved into other agencies.[45] The director of the project was David Weintraub, and the full name of the enterprise was National Research Project on Reemployment Opportunities and Recent Changes in Industrial Techniques of the Works Progress Administration. As a project of the WPA, it lasted until that agency was abolished by the Congress after the third election of Roosevelt, and the main thrust of the national effort shifted from problems of relief and recovery from the depression to those of defense and survival. As Burnham has summed it up, its associate director was Irving Kaplan, and among its members were "Edward J. Fitzgerald, Charles Flato, Jacob Grauman, Harry Magdoff, Harry Ober, Herbert S. Schimmel, and Alfred Van Tassel, who were all in later days to invoke the plea of self-incrimination when asked about relations to Communism and Communists." [46] Although he would not describe the circumstances under which he entered the government — through the National Research Project — Fitzgerald was less reticent about what he did in the project. He worked, for example, on labor market studies in Pennsylvania, Brazil, and Indiana, and on farm-city migration.[47] In the course of this testimony, William Jenner of Indiana, chairman of the Senate subcommittee, contributed comments about squirrel-counting and dog-house building by WPA staff, alleged activities of which he seemed to disapprove.

Harry Magdoff was also a research economist who said, at the time of the hearing, that he was self-employed but declined to say who his

44. *Ibid.*, p. 247.
45. Whittaker Chambers relates that when he decided to break with the Communist Party, he sought some public identification, having been "underground" for years, in order to deter the party or Soviet Military Intelligence from punishing him with reprisals of violence and perhaps even death. He instructed one of the apparatus men in Washington to get him a job in the United States government. Chambers said, "Almost overnight, I found myself employed by the National Research Project. I used the name Chambers. It had been a simple matter for the party to place me in the Government, since one of the national heads of the research project, George Silverman, the research director of the Railroad Retirement Board, for whom the project was making a study, and my immediate boss on the job were all members of the Communist Party." *Witness* (New York: Random House, 1952), p. 40. Hede Massing, when called to Moscow for discipline, also strove to make herself as publicly visible as possible to deter silent reprisals. *This Deception* (New York: Duell, Sloan and Pearce, 1951), pp. 280–283.
46. Burnham, *Web of Subversion*, p. 85.
47. *Hearings on Interlocking Subversion in Government Departments*, p. 248.

clients were on the ground that his answer would tend to incriminate him.[48] He also declined to cooperate with the committee in establishing certain elementary documentary facts. It was shown that he had been the chairman of the editorial board of the *Student Review,* a publication of the Communist National Student League, while he was an undergraduate at New York University in the early 1930's.[49] His first job in the United States Government, obtained in 1936, the year after his graduation from NYU, was also with the National Research Project. He refused, on the familiar grounds, to say how he had got the job, or whether David Weintraub had helped him, or whether he knew Fitzgerald. He stayed with the project until 1940 when he moved to the Advisory Commission of the Council of National Defense and then into the predecessor of the WPB, called in 1941 the Office of Production Management.[50] In 1944 he joined the Department of Commerce and worked in various offices of the department until December 1946.[51] As planning officer in the Department of Commerce, Magdoff was an adviser to Henry Wallace, the Secretary of Commerce. He refused to say whether he had passed any "secret top level Government information" to William Remington when he was in the Department of Commerce or whether he had given any information to anyone about the machinery supplies that the Soviet Union might ask for under Lend Lease.[52] He also declined to say whether he had been loyal to the United States Government during his employment in Federal jobs.[53]

Harold Glasser also entered the service of the Federal government through the Works Progress Administration, but not by way of the National Research Project.[54] He took employment with the WPA in Illinois in 1935 without contrivance or prearrangement. He just walked in and "got the job," helped to make a study of consumers purchases in Minneapolis, and then went to Washington late in 1936 to take a position with the Treasury Department. It was no doubt possible to walk in off the street and get a job with WPA, but the call to Washington to work in the Treasury almost certainly presupposes some sponsorship; and when it is understood that Solomon Adler was in the Treasury at the time, that Solomon Adler had been Glasser's roommate in Chicago in the period from 1933 to 1935, and that Glasser re-

48. *Ibid.,* p. 286.
49. *Ibid.,* pp. 287–288.
50. *Ibid.,* p. 289.
51. *Ibid.,* pp. 290 and 292.
52. *Ibid.,* pp. 292 and 293.
53. *Ibid.,* p. 294.
54. *Ibid.,* p. 53. At the time of the hearings in 1953 before the Senate Internal Security subcommittee, Glasser was a research economist with the Council of Jewish Federations and Welfare Funds in New York City.

fused to talk about Adler on the ground that to do so would tend to incriminate him, the thought may be entertained that Adler may have had something to do with getting Glasser the job in Treasury.[55]

Glasser's rise in Treasury was swift, and in a relatively short time he was working on important tasks. After assignments in the department on questions of foreign trade, he became financial adviser to the Ministry of Finance of the Government of Ecuador in 1940 and stayed in that country for two years. He then went on to other and even more important assignments in Africa, in Italy, England, France, Austria, and elsewhere. According to Whittaker Chambers, J. Peters released Dr. Harold Glasser from the American Communist underground and lent him to the Soviet underground to check on Harry Dexter White, who was said to have been a source for Chambers, although not a member of the Communist Party.[56] When the Chambers account of Glasser was read to the latter by Robert Morris, chief counsel for the Senate Committee on Internal Security subcommittee, Glasser refused to acknowledge the truth of the report, or any knowledge of Chambers, or any question about his relations with Harry Dexter White, with whom he worked in Treasury, on the ground that his answers might tend to incriminate him.[57]

Although it is not possible to know in detail what kinds of information, nor in what quantities information was provided Soviet agents through sources in the War Production Board, there is testimony on one kind of information Elizabeth Bentley says that she received from Perlo. This was a body of secret data on aircraft production, including information about the production of aircraft, the location of engine-making plants, and the location of factories making struts, wings, aircraft armament, B-29 synchronized turrets, automatic computing aircraft gunsights, and so on. It was Bentley's testimony that Perlo turned such information over to her, that she "read through it, and in cases where it was handwritten or cases where it was badly typed" she "recopied it" and turned it over to her Russian contact.

There is also testimony on information said to have been supplied by William Remington, who was employed in the War Production Board. Miss Bentley testified that she collected dues from both Remington and his wife, that she used to meet Remington across from the Willard Hotel or at the National Gallery, and that he would give her slips of paper containing notes of information about original docu-

55. *Hearings on Interlocking Subversion in Government Departments*, pp. 54–57, for questions about the move to the Treasury Department in Washington and the refusal to acknowledge Adler who had been Glasser's roommate.

56. Chambers, *Witness*, pp. 429–430.

57. *Hearings on Interlocking Subversion in Government Departments*, pp. 74–75.

ments that he did not dare take. The information, she said, dealt with internal policy matters within the board, allocations planned for the Soviet Union, aircraft figures, and, on one occasion, "a formula that he had found information on for making synthetic rubber from garbage." Incredulous critics had fun with that one. Eventually, Remington moved to a position in the WPB (at his own request) where the information he was said to have supplied was "of absolutely no use to us," information on the allocation of materials for domestic production.[58]

The Silvermaster Group

Whatever the value of the material Miss Bentley said was supplied by the Perlo group, this was the lesser of the two principal rings with which she operated, the other being the Silvermaster group. The Perlo information was delivered in New York by travelers from Washington to New York. The information provided by sources in the Silvermaster group was collected by Elizabeth Bentley herself on trips made to Washington for the specific purpose.

Like the Ware, La Follette committee, National Labor Relations Board, and other groups, the Silvermaster group as described by Bentley seems to have been an American Communist Party operation. According to her testimony, Earl Browder in July 1941 supplied Jacob Golos, an agent for the OGPU, with the name of "a man working for the United States Government, who was interested in helping in getting information to Russia, and who could organize a group of other Government employees to help in this work." [59] The man, she said, was Nathan Gregory Silvermaster, an employee in the Farm Security Administration of the Department of Agriculture and later, for a short

58. For the quoted references to Miss Bentley's editorial work on Perlo's material, see *Hiss Hearings*, pp. 688–689. For testimony on William Remington, see Eightieth Congress, Second Session, United States Senate, Committee on Expenditures in the Executive Departments, Hearings Pursuant to S. Res. 189, *Export Policy and Loyalty*, pp. 28–35.

59. *Hiss Hearings*, p. 507. The accounts in the Congressional testimony and in the book differ somewhat. In the testimony, as said above, Browder gave Golos the name of a man who wanted to serve as a source and who could organize others. In the book there is no mention of Browder but in a rather stagey account Miss Bentley has Golos receiving orders from the OGPU to get as many trusted comrades as possible into strategic positions in the government where they would have access to secret information that could be relayed to the Soviet Union. *Out of Bondage*, pp. 143–144. The two accounts are not necessarily inconsistent since Golos could indeed have received such orders and Browder could have cooperated with his desire by nominating a source. There is one ineradicable difficulty, however, with the statement in the testimony that Browder in July 1941 gave Golos the name of Silvermaster. Browder was jailed in the Atlanta Penitentiary in March 1941 and was not released until May 1942.

time, in the Board of Economic Warfare.[60] In time, Silvermaster was said to be the center of a group that included William Ludwig Ullman, Solomon Adler, one William Taylor, Harry Dexter White, George Silverman, Frank Coe, William Gold, Sonia Gold, Irving Kaplan, Norman Bursler, and Lauchlin Currie.[61] Although this group was distributed throughout several agencies of the government, there was a core centered in the Treasury Department, as the Perlo group had a core in the War Production Board. The Treasury core was distinguished by the professional quality of its members and the importance of the positions they occupied.

Silvermaster, born in Odessa, Russia, in 1898, arrived in the United States in 1915 and became a naturalized citizen in 1927. A graduate of the University of Washington in 1920, he became a doctor of philosophy in economics in 1932 at the University of California, combining his work for the degree with teaching at St. Mary's College from 1924 to 1930. After some work in relief activities in California, Silvermaster entered upon employment in the Federal government in 1935 by way of the Resettlement Administration, and for the next eleven years held responsible positions in the Resettlement Administration, Maritime Labor Board, Farm Security Administration, the Board of Economic Warfare, and the War Assets Administration.[62] At the time of Miss Bentley's public disclosures in 1948, Silvermaster had been out of the government for about nine months, having resigned in November 1947 from his position as director of the Economic Research Division of the War Assets Administration to become self-employed in Harvey Cedars, New Jersey, building houses.

In a prepared statement which he read before the House Committee on Un-American Activities, Silvermaster said,

> The charges made by Miss Bentley are false and fantastic. I can only conclude that she is a neurotic liar. I am and have been a loyal American citizen and was a faithful Government employee. I am not and have never been a spy or agent of any foreign government.[63]

60. *Hiss Hearings.* The printed record of the testimony has the committee counsel referring to the "Bureau of Economic Warfare," but this is certainly a misprint for the Board of Economic Warfare.

61. *Hiss Hearings,* pp. 507–512, 517–521. It is to be noted that Kaplan is listed in the Silvermaster as well as the Perlo group because it was said that he was giving information through the first and paying dues through the second. *Ibid.,* p. 518. The Taylor listed in the Silvermaster group is the individual on whose identity Bentley did not insist when pressed for clarification by Byron Scott. See above, n. 25. Solomon Adler, although named by Miss Bentley, was not one she had anything to do with directly, since, at the time she said that she took over the Silvermaster group, he was in China. In fact she never met Adler. *Ibid.,* p. 510.

62. *Hiss Hearings,* p. 589.

63. *Hiss Hearings,* p. 590.

Following this vigorous cannonade, Silvermaster, having fired, fell back. Elizabeth Bentley was in the hearing room and was requested to stand. When Silvermaster was then asked whether he knew "Elizabeth T. Bentley, who is standing there," he refused to answer on the ground that "any answer I may give may be self-incriminating." [64] He also thought it might incriminate him to say whether he knew Solomon Adler, Lauchlin Currie, Norman Bursler, Alger Hiss, Frank V. Coe, Edward J. Fitzgerald, Harold Glasser, Sonia Gold, William J. Gold, Victor Perlo, Charles Kramer, Duncan C. Lee, Harry Magdoff, William W. Remington, and others. He pleaded possible self-incrimination in refusing to say whether he had furnished any documents from government files to Elizabeth Bentley, or whether he had any photographic equipment in the basement of his Washington home for the purpose of photographing government documents.

But there was one question he did answer. When asked whether he knew William Ullmann, he said that he did.[65] Ullmann had lived with Silvermaster since 1937, and the latter acknowledged the fact. In this, his behavior was different from that of Glasser who had roomed with Adler, but later refused to acknowledge the relation because he thought that it would incriminate him to do so. When Silvermaster, however, was then asked whether Ullmann was a member of the Communist Party, he renewed his refusal to answer on the ground that his answer might tend to incriminate him.[66]

After the formal refusals to cooperate with the committee in its effort to elicit information about Silvermaster's part, if any, in the events and activities reported by Elizabeth Bentley, Richard Nixon took Silvermaster back to his prepared statement. Since Silvermaster had said that her charges were false and fantastic and that he must conclude that she was a neurotic liar, he was asked on what facts he based his conclusion. Nixon was unable to get Silvermaster to discuss the facts if any that might contradict Bentley, show her charges to be false and fantastic, and prove her to be a neurotic liar.

Silvermaster's detail to the Board of Economic Warfare came under discussion at one point. While still on the payroll of the Farm Security Administration, he was assigned to the Board of Economic Warfare. The Office of Naval Intelligence objected to his employment by the board on the ground that he was a Communist, and urged his removal in a letter which was sent to William T. Stone, assistant administrator of the board having jurisdiction over the division to which Silvermaster was assigned. Stone, according to Silvermaster, showed him the ONI

64. *Hiss Hearings*, p. 592.
65. *Hiss Hearings*, p. 593.
66. *Hiss Hearings*, p. 593.

letter and Silvermaster got in touch with C. B. Baldwin, the administrator of the Farm Security Administration, and with Lauchlin Currie, Administrative Assistant to President Roosevelt, to have them intervene in his behalf. Currie did so, bringing the matter to the attention of the Secretary of War, Robert Patterson. Currie got an exculpatory letter from Patterson for Silvermaster and the latter was allowed to stay with the Board of Economic Warfare, although his tour eventually proved to be short-lived.

The obviously important contacts that Silvermaster enjoyed, the high circles of policy and decision in which he moved, the influence and reputation of the agencies in which his activities were involved — all these elements of circumstance made a dramatic background for the sensational story that Elizabeth Bentley told. Here was a man with enough pull to have White House staff move the Secretary of War to intervene successfully in his behalf against the Office of Naval Intelligence. According to Bentley, the Silvermasters were old friends of Earl Browder, having given him refuge in 1934 in San Francisco at the time of the general strike on the San Francisco waterfront.[67] Silvermaster, she said, also knew Jacob Golos from the early thirties and their relationship, although interrupted several times, was, she thought, "quite a deep one." After she had come to serve as courier for the Silvermaster group, she would make trips to Washington. The Silvermasters were said to have had a basement containing photographic equipment which Miss Bentley claimed to have seen, a place where documents and other papers were copied, some of them, she said, in her presence. At the start of the operations of the Silvermaster group, in 1941 and 1942, some of the films would be developed in the basement. Eventually, however, the number of documents copied photographically became so large that the development was done somewhere in New York from the exposed films Miss Bentley carried.

Unlike the Perlo group which Miss Bentley met for the first time after the death of Jacob Golos, she made the connection with the Silvermasters soon after arrangements were completed to organize the group he headed. But first, she said, she had to be "cleared" by Helen, the wife of Silvermaster, and the daughter of a Russian Baltic baron.[68] When Golos moved to establish Elizabeth Bentley as the intermediary between New York and the Silvermasters in Washington, she was instructed to make a trip to Washington to be looked over.[69] After the

67. *Hiss Hearings*, p. 608. Miss Bentley thought that Silvermaster had known Browder before this time but that Helen Silvermaster did not meet him until he appeared at the Silvermaster house asking for refuge because he was being sought by vigilantes.

68. Bentley, *Out of Bondage*, pp. 151–153.

69. Miss Bentley says of the first meeting with Silvermaster's wife in the latter's

visit, Golos told Miss Bentley that the Silvermasters had reluctantly agreed to accept her as their contact in a chain of connections leading from government offices in Washington to the Russians. Silvermaster was evidently satisfied with the arrangement, but his wife was said to have suspected Miss Bentley of being an undercover agent for the Federal Bureau of Investigation. This story recalls the paranoid distrust of Chambers' superior, Colonel Bykov. When J. Peters turned Chambers over to Bykov, the latter was morbidly upset by the thought that window-shoppers at the RCA building in New York were agents of the *Geheimpolizei.*

But Miss Bentley had a more self-conscious conjecture than paranoia for distrust of her credentials: ". . . looking back on the episode now, I wonder whether Helen didn't have a deeper insight into human nature than all the rest of us. She sensed instinctively that I didn't belong in the Communist movement." [70] Since many at the time Miss Bentley made her disclosures also found it hard to believe that she had ever been a Communist agent, perhaps the incredulity of a noble Russian was less the result of superior aristocratic insight than the striking incongruity — visible even to the ignoble classes — of a simple school teacher working for ferocious goals of world domination.[71]

Miss Bentley was asked about the kinds of information turned over to her by Silvermaster and then given by her to Golos.[72] She said that

----

home off Chevy Chase Circle, "Sitting there bare-legged, in a cotton print dress and red play shoes, she didn't look like a baroness, yet there was an indefinable air of quality in her tone of voice and in the way she held her head." *Out of Bondage*, pp. 153–154. Girlish romantic illusions about baronesses were but one of many anomalies in the dedication of a rather naïve Vassar girl bent on freeing the toiling masses of the oppressions of bloodthirsty capitalistic masters.

70. Bentley, *Out of Bondage*, p. 153.

71. Murray Kempton had a less charitable figure of speech to describe Miss Bentley's involvement with Jacob Golos. She found the OGPU card of Golos and was told that it was a Moscow streetcar pass. He also told her that he loved her and could be happy with her but for the shadow that "lay before them." Says Kempton, "Elizabeth Bentley was, of course, roughly as well equipped to receive this piece of total wisdom as Louisa May Alcott would have been in some similar involvement with Feodor Dostoievsky." *Part of Our Time*, p. 221. Before the Congressional committees could hear Miss Bentley, a New York newspaper "scooped" the disclosures she was to make and represented her in melodramatic phrase as a "beautiful blonde spy queen." This vigorous exercise of freedom of the press did much in the opinion of one commentator at the time to diminish the seriousness in which her disclosures should have been regarded: "She was neither blonde, beautiful, nor a spy queen, but a prim brown-haired courier. That she did not live up to her advance publicity somehow discredited her testimony. When she had testified before the Thomas Committee, the scoffers were ready to cash in on that impression. So, besides becoming 'unconvincing,' Miss Bentley became 'neurotic.' Gregory Silvermaster said so — and so did several prominent liberals known for their opposition to Communism." *New Leader*, August 14, 1948, p. 1 under heading "The Bentley-Chambers Story."

72. *Hiss Hearings*, p. 572.

it was military information, particularly from the Air Corps — information on the production of airplanes, "their destinations to various theaters of war and to various countries, new types of planes being put out, information as to when D-Day would be, all sorts of inside military information." [73] According to Miss Bentley's testimony, she took documents at first, and then photographs when the supply became bulky, and carried it all in a large pocketbook to New York, "or in a knitting bag or a shopping bag or whatever was handy, depending on the size of the collection." The trips to the Silvermasters were said to have been made roughly every two weeks, but the contacts may have been even more frequent because the Silvermasters also traveled to New York where Miss Bentley testified she would meet them in various hotels in or around Times Square, or in eating places in the area. Miss Bentley evidently saw others than the Silvermasters in the group very rarely; she reported that of them only one, George Silverman, ever came to the Silvermaster home while she was there. This efficiency is in contrast with the somewhat haphazard procedures of the Perlo group.

After the death of Golos, Miss Bentley had two other contacts with cover names — "Bill," and the girl who introduced Miss Bentley to Bill, a woman by the name of "Catherine." [74] Although Bill was the contact with Soviet espionage, the material he received from Miss Bentley, she said, was first scanned by Earl Browder who was not interested in the military information but was interested in everything else. After he had scrutinized the material, she would then take the entire package and turn it over to the Russian.

Miss Bentley's testimony about the Silvermaster group on occasion indicated that she was saying as fact what inquiry showed she had simply heard; and that she sometimes talked as though she personally knew people she then confessed she had never met. In at least one instance she had the wrong name. She had said in her original testimony that William Gold and his wife, Sonia Gold, were members of the Silvermaster group and members of the Communist Party also.[75] The

73. Miss Bentley said that the military information came principally from George Silverman and Ullmann. *Hiss Hearings,* p. 525.

74. *Hiss Hearings,* p. 527.

75. The entire testimony on the Golds went as follows: "Mr. Stripling: Any one else? Miss Bentley: William Gold. Mr. Stripling: G-o-l-d? Miss Bentley: Yes. Mr. Stripling: Where was he employed? Miss Bentley: I believe it was then the FEA. I don't recall whether BEW or FEA, but it was that same outfit. Mr. Stripling: Was he a member of the Communist Party? Miss Bentley: Yes. Mr. Stripling: Did he furnish information to your group? Miss Bentley: Yes, he did. Mr. Stripling: Is there anyone else you haven't named? Miss Bentley: Yes; his wife, Sonia Gold. Mr. Stripling: Was she an employee of the Government? Miss Bentley: Yes; in the Treasury." *Hiss Hearings,* p. 517.

Golds immediately asked for permission to appear before the House Committee and did so voluntarily. They denied the accusation that they were members of the Communist Party and part of the Silvermaster group.[76] It appeared that Gold's name was not William at all but Bela, and that he had never used any other. Both the Golds answered questions without resort to the Fifth Amendment, and admitted knowing a number of people who had been named, in contrast to the behavior of Silvermaster himself, for example, who refused to identify all names suggested to him except that of William Ullmann. He in fact refused to acknowledge whether he knew the Golds (the husband was identified as William J. Gold), on the ground that his answer might tend to incriminate him.[77] The committee did not press the Golds, nor cross-examine them, and made no attempt to upset their testimony, but accepted it.

Although the remarks made by the Golds contradicted Bentley's testimony about them, they tended to confirm certain parts of her testimony that others had contradicted. For example, Bela Gold seemed to know Silvermaster quite well, had visited him at his house on numerous occasions to discuss a book that he (Gold) was writing, and had even been in the famous basement. He said that he had not seen photographic equipment there, but did say, "I just knew that Ullmann had, of course, taken pictures because they had pictures hung all over the house that he had taken." [78] It appeared from Gold's testimony that Ullmann was an expert photographer, and that he had at least one camera so complicated that Gold could not operate it successfully when he borrowed it over a week end. Mrs. Gold said that she had never been in the basement of the Silvermaster home although she had visited several times and was impressed by Mrs. Silvermaster, as Elizabeth Bentley had been.[79] For a neurotic woman given to false and fantastic charges, Elizabeth Bentley had shown a remarkable knowledge of the interests and "hobbies" of the people who would not acknowledge her because to do so might incriminate them. The testimony of Bela Gold does not establish the existence of a photographic service operated for the benefit of the workers of the world, but the establishment of the existence in the house of an expert (Ullmann lived with Silvermaster) whose pictures were "hung all over" is to diminish by some degree the elements of falsity and fantasy that Silvermaster's denial said characterized the entire original testimony.[80]

76. *Hiss Hearings*, pp. 906–915.
77. *Hiss Hearings*, p. 592.
78. *Hiss Hearings*, p. 911.
79. *Hiss Hearings*, p. 913.
80. Nathan Gregory Silvermaster died October 7, 1964. *New York Times*, October 15, 1964, p. 39, col. 2.

Mention has already been made of the service that Silverman was said to have provided in getting a cover job for Chambers when he was about to make his break with the Soviet apparatus, although Silverman did not know that he was helping an apostate. At the time Chambers moved from the underground, Silverman was in the Railroad Retirement Board and entrusted, according to Chambers, with the party task of keeping "Harry Dexter White in a buoyant and cooperative frame of mind,"[81] although when Elizabeth Bentley took over the Silvermaster group some four or so years later, Silverman had advanced considerably. It was said that he no longer "had to play underground nursemaid to Harry Dexter White" but had become economic adviser (and chief of analysis and plans) to the assistant chief of the Air Staff in the Material and Services Division of the Air Force.[82]

Whittaker Chambers traced Silverman back to the original Ware group,[83] faulted him for not scrupulously paying his party dues,[84] said that J. Peters had found it hard to get along with Silverman although he (Chambers) managed to do so by treating him as "a highly intelligent child." And, according to Chambers, it was Silverman who introduced Chambers to Harry Dexter White.[85] Silverman was apparently thought well enough of by the Soviet employers of Whittaker Chambers to qualify for one of the Christmas present rugs in 1937, the others going to Harry Dexter White in Treasury, and to Julian Wadleigh and Alger Hiss in the State Department.[86] In the course of a grand jury investigation, the only thing that Silverman would admit, according to Chambers, was that he had had the four rugs in his house.[87]

In the days when Chambers was still working under Colonel Bykov, he said that Silverman was his contact with White. "He would take a brief case of documents from White, which he would later give to me," said Chambers;[88] and then,

They would be photographed in Baltimore and returned to Silverman the same night or the next morning.[89]

In the famous interview with Assistant Secretary of State Adolf A. Berle in 1939 when Chambers first made disclosures about espionage, he omitted two names — those of George Silverman and Harry Dexter

81. Chambers, *Witness*, p. 29.
82. Chambers, *Witness*, p. 69.
83. Chambers, *Witness*, p. 334.
84. Chambers, *Witness*, p. 380.
85. Chambers, *Witness*, p. 383.
86. Chambers, *Witness*, p. 415.
87. Chambers, *Witness*, p. 417.
88. Chambers, *Witness*, pp. 421–422.
89. Chambers, *Witness*, p. 422.

White — because, he later said, he hoped that he had broken them away from the Communist Party.[90] Chambers eventually told agents of the FBI that he had omitted the two names,[91] and he then supplied the information about a pair who were to turn up in Miss Bentley's public charge seven years later.[92]

After Elizabeth Bentley had named Harry Dexter White as one of the sources for the Silvermaster group — although she said that he was not a member of the Communist Party, as did Whittaker Chambers — he appeared before the House Committee and responded to questions. Unlike Silvermaster and Silverman, he did not plead the Fifth Amendment at any point. In fact, he came voluntarily before the committee and said, after stating a creed that drew applause from the spectators, that he was ready for any questions the committee might wish to ask.[93] With seeming candor, he admitted knowing most of the people who had been named by Elizabeth Bentley in her testimony about both the Perlo and Silvermaster groups. He even said that he had been in the famous basement of the Silvermaster house, and had played ping-pong there. Just at this point in his testimony, the chairman of the committee, J. Parnell Thomas, interrupted to comment on a note that White had handed to him. The note said, "I am recovering from a severe heart attack. I would appreciate it if the chairman would give me 5 or 10 minutes rest after each hour." [94] Thomas remarked that for a person with a severe heart condition, White could "certainly play a lot of sports." White replied that he had not intended the note to be read, that the heart attack which had afflicted him had occurred the year before and possibly was the result of having played so many sports and so well, and concluded, "I am speaking of playing ping-pong, and I was a fair tennis player, and a pretty good ball player, many years prior to that. I hope that clears that up, Mr. Chairman." The chairman said, "Yes, sir," and there was applause.

90. Chambers, *Witness*, p. 470. Chambers' statement cannot mean resignation of membership from the Communist Party because White was not a member.

91. For the accounts of the attempt by Chambers to get Silverman and White to break away from the Communist Party, see *Witness*, pp. 67–69. For discrepancies in Chambers' story about the date he talked to the FBI about White, see below, n. 107.

92. Chambers, *Witness*, p. 492. Abraham George Silverman, of course, had an opportunity after Elizabeth Bentley's original testimony, to respond to her assertions but failed to do so, pleading self-incrimination. His formal statement, however, was full of rhetoric and he, like Silvermaster, berated Elizabeth Bentley (he pleaded the Fifth Amendment when asked whether he knew her) in a paragraph that concluded: ". . . I am compelled to conclude that only a mind distorted by fear or greed or deep frustration could construct such an edifice of monstrous falsehood." *Hiss Hearings*, p. 842.

93. *Hiss Hearings*, p. 879.

94. *Hiss Hearings*, p. 881.

As the questioning got back to the basement, he said that he could not recollect whether there was any photographic equipment there. "It might have been; it might not." [95] Like Currie, Harry Dexter White had intervened for Silvermaster when the latter was accused by the Office of Naval Intelligence of being a Communist, and action was started to remove him from the Board of Economic Warfare.[96] White was questioned before Whittaker Chambers delivered the sensational testimony implicating Alger Hiss, and he was asked, as Hiss was later, to say whether he had known Chambers as "Carl," his underground pseudonym, or could even recognize photographs of him in *Time*, *Life*, and the New York *Herald Tribune*. White said that he had seen from five to ten thousand people in the last fifteen years and that although Chambers could have met him, and although White might have chatted with Chambers, he had "no recollection of ever having met him." [97] More specifically, he said that he did not recollect having met any person by the name of Carl in the years 1935 and 1937.

White was allowed to lecture the committee on the Constitution and the Bill of Rights[98] to the applause of the spectators. He thought there was nothing odd or unusual in his having intervened for Silvermaster against the Office of Naval Intelligence, although he had never intervened for anyone else.[99] He had gone no further in testing the allegations of the ONI than to ask Silvermaster if they were true, and he then said of Silvermaster, "I believe he is innocent," at which there was more applause.[100] Nor did White think it strange that of all the people named by Miss Bentley, some ten or so had worked for White, and two others were friends of his.[101] Upon scrutinizing White's testimony before the House Committee, the Earl Jowitt, former Lord Chancellor, was later to say, "As I have said before, it is impossible to form a conclusive judgment merely from a transcript of the evidence, but — having made this point — I must add that I have seldom read the evidence of a witness who struck me so favorably as being a witness of truth." [102] Three days after giving his testimony before the House Committee, Harry Dexter White was dead of a heart attack.[103]

95. *Hiss Hearings*, p. 882.
96. *Hiss Hearings*, pp. 882–883.
97. *Hiss Hearings*, p. 885.
98. *Hiss Hearings*, pp. 892–895.
99. *Hiss Hearings*, p. 897.
100. *Hiss Hearings*, p. 898.
101. *Hiss Hearings*, p. 901.
102. Earl Jowitt, *The Strange Case of Alger Hiss* (New York: Doubleday, 1953), p. 246.
103. One somewhat extreme and speculative suggestion is that the death of White may have been the result of an overdose of sleeping pills, or that he had been put to death in a manner to simulate the appearance of a heart attack, the

If Lord Jowitt admired Harry Dexter White, the Soviet embassy in Washington did also, and its gratitude at one point created a situation comedy worthy of the talents of an Alec Guiness. Harry White, a carpenter living and working in Washington, was astonished one day to find a limousine in front of his humble house, from which stepped a uniformed chauffeur who gave him a package. The package contained caviar and had been sent to Mr. White from the Soviet embassy. Later a case of vodka was delivered, and once, Mr. White received by mail an engraved invitation to attend a social function at the Soviet embassy. Finally a telephone call came to Mr. White. This, however, was not a further attention by the Soviet diplomatic corps but a call from Harry Dexter White, who had located his missing presents. He explained that the Soviet embassy had made a mistake because of the similarity of the names but that since the Assistant Secretary of the Treasury did not want to disappoint the carpenter, he offered to split the gifts with him. The carpenter told a newsman, "I was going to send them all back to him but I thought: 'He's the kind of fellow, that if I send them all back, will still think that I kept half.' So I did." [104]

White's position justified this attention, or at least makes understandable the Soviet esteem for it. For Harry Dexter White was one of the most influential men in international affairs in the 1940's, entrusted by the Secretary of the Treasury, Henry Morgenthau, with vast responsibility and discretion. Beginning his career in the Federal government in 1933, he entered the Treasury, became director of the Division of Monetary Research, Assistant to the Secretary of the Treasury, and Assistant Secretary of the Treasury. In 1941 Morgenthau entrusted to his Assistant to the Secretary full responsibility for all matters of foreign relations in which the Treasury was concerned, and later for all economic and financial matters in which the Treasury was involved with the Army and the Navy. White was "the dominating figure at the Bretton Woods Monetary Conference that launched the International Bank and Fund" [105] of which he was to become the first Executive Director. He had much to do with the Morgenthau plan for the pastoralization of Germany after the Second World War (which was also favored by many American notables) and he was the author of some of the material that went into the "ultimatum" that Secretary of State Hull delivered to the Japanese on November 26, 1941.[106] Even

second of these hypotheses having been suggested by testimony at the trial of the former head of the Russian secret police, Henry Yagoda. Burnham, *Web of Subversion*, pp. 157–158.

104. Chambers, *Witness*, p. 432.
105. Burnham, *Web of Subversion*, pp. 150–152.
106. On November 18, 1941, Secretary Morgenthau sent to the Secretary of State a memorandum drafted by White on the terms that should be presented to

these very few examples of White's responsibilities show that his part in public affairs was of tremendous significance for the national policy.

Elizabeth Bentley said that she did not get to know about White until she became a courier for the Silvermaster group, but Chambers had known him much earlier, as has been indicated. In fact Chambers had left the Communist Party by the time of the events described by Miss Bentley. According to the stories of Chambers and Bentley which supplement each other, Chambers had traffic with White in the thirties and Miss Bentley in the forties. Chambers, as was said, did not tell Berle about White when he made his first attempt to get the government to act, and his memory was uncertain later about the time when he did inform the FBI, assigning different dates on three different occasions.[107] But he was more circumstantial about other details of the relations he said that he had with White, beginning some time about 1936 when he was called to head what he described as a "sleeper apparatus" — an underground group whose principal function was to stand by, existing not to act in the present but to act at some time in the future, to sleep until awakened to perform active espionage.[108] Early in 1937, Colonel Bykov, Chambers' superior in the underground, "began a personal inspection of the sources,[109] and in the course of his encounters met Harry Dexter White.[110] Of his inspection, Chambers said that the meetings were important as they marked the beginning of intensive espionage. He added: "Only in the case of Harry White, I think, did he stimulate any enthusiasm that was lacking before. For, more than any of the others, White, the non-Communist, enjoyed the feeling that he was in direct touch with 'big important people.' "[111] Mention has been made of the alleged procedure for photographing

the Japanese for a settlement of the tensions between Japan and the United States. On November 19, 1941, the White memorandum was revised a little by Maxwell Hamilton, Chief of the Far Eastern Division of the State Department. Hull had the White and Hamilton productions when he drafted the note of November 26. His product contained ten points, of which eight had been supplied by White. See Memorandum by Secretary Morgenthau, November 17, 1941, U. S. Department of State, *Papers Relating to the Foreign Relations of the United States: Japan, 1931–1941* (Washington: Government Printing Office, 1943), vol. IV, 606–613, and Maxwell Hamilton to Secretary Hull, November 19, 1941 (*ibid.*, pp. 622–625).

107. In his testimony before the House Committee, Chambers said that he first told the FBI about White four years after his conversation with Berle in 1939 — that is, in 1943. *Hiss Hearings*, p. 580. In the second trial of Alger Hiss, however, Chambers said that he told the FBI on May 14, 1942. In his autobiography, Chambers said that he told the FBI first in 1941. *Witness*, p. 492. This discrepancy is emphasized in Nathan I. White, *Harry Dexter White*, at pp. 124–125.

108. Chambers placed Alger Hiss and Harry Dexter White in the "sleeper apparatus" Chambers was to activate in 1936. *Witness*, p. 405.

109. Chambers, *Witness*, p. 417.

110. Chambers, *Witness*, p. 419.

111. Chambers, *Witness*, p. 419.

the material supplied to Chambers by White through George Silverman as go-between. Although the output from Alger Hiss, Julian Wadleigh, and others, including White, was said to be high, Bykov complained about the quality of the material. Chambers said that in the early days, out of curiosity he read "Hiss's, White's and Wadleigh's documents," and concluded that political espionage was "a magnificent waste of time" since there was little it could supply that an intelligent man conversant with history, and a student of legitimate sources, could not figure out for himself.

According to Chambers, White was the least productive of the four original sources with whom he worked.[112] He was said to have turned over material on schedule although it was also said that the amount was not great. Of central importance in judging the veracity of the account of Chambers later was his statement that White prepared a regular longhand memorandum every week or two about documents that had come to his attention or events within his notice. Before he finally broke with the party, Chambers collected a sample supply of documents and microfilms to support the disclosures he eventually made. One of these was a memorandum of four pages from Harry Dexter White, which was to turn up ten years after the defection of Chambers and serve as a silent "witness of truth" to contradict the statements that impressed Lord Jowitt.[113] It was such a document that helped to convict Alger Hiss of perjury when he denied the assertions of Whittaker Chambers.

Office of Strategic Services

Although the Perlo and Silvermaster groups were said by Miss Bentley to have been her principal contacts in Washington, her work as a

112. Chambers, *Witness*, p. 429. The four original sources were Alger Hiss, Julian Wadleigh, George Silverman, and Harry Dexter White, according to Chambers.

113. Photostats of the eight sides of the four pages of the memorandum may be seen in White, *Harry Dexter White*, pp. 81–97. The memorandum was disclosed at the time Whittaker Chambers, sued for libel by Alger Hiss, produced documents he had hidden for eight years or so. This was after the death of Harry Dexter White, so that he was never confronted with the memorandum that Chambers had saved. It is suggested by the brother of White that the memorandum was a forgery, or that it was stolen after White's death, or that it was a mere *aide-mémoire*, and not a paper to be given to Soviet espionage agents. But the document was verified by a handwriting expert as the writing of Harry Dexter White, and there is no suggestion as to how four pages written in 1938 could have been stolen from White's effects in 1948. If it were merely an *aide-mémoire*, there would seem to have been no reason for White to keep it for ten years. But even if it were an *aide-mémoire*, if Chambers had received it from White in 1938, a prima-facie case is established for the assertion Chambers made that he was receiving confidential information from White. The confidential nature of the information is admitted by Lord Jowitt, although he argues the

courier involved others also. She was courier for sources working in the OSS, for example. Among those from whom she said that she received information was Duncan Lee, one of the legal advisers to General William J. Donovan, head of the Office of Strategic Services.[114] From him she said that she received information about secret negotiations with governments in the Balkan bloc against the time when the war might end, about operations by the OSS in Hungary and Turkey, and about Donovan's interest "in having an exchange between the NKVD and the OSS." Duncan Lee was not, according to Miss Bentley, a member of the Silvermaster group, and her contact with him was arranged outside the Silvermaster group.

The introduction to Lee took place through one of the women with whom Miss Bentley was in contact as courier. It was Golos who introduced Miss Bentley to Mary Price, said to have been a Communist of many years' standing,[115] a charter member of the United Office and Professional Workers of America, and later secretary to the columnist, Walter Lippmann. Miss Bentley said she received information collected and supplied by Mary Price, and told of one search for material in the files of Walter Lippmann with the help of Mary one week end in Washington when Mr. Lippmann was away.[116] According to Miss Bentley's congressional testimony, Lee had been with the Institute for Pacific Relations in New York, and was turned over to Miss Bentley by Mary Price when he went to Washington to take up duties with the Office of Strategic Services. She was wrong in at least one particular. Lee did not join the Institute for Pacific Relations until 1946 after he had left military service with the OSS. In New York he had been the executive director of Russian War Relief.[117]

Lee acknowledged that he knew Miss Bentley, although he said that he had not known her under that name, but under the name of Helen Grant. He thought that he had met her in October 1943 and was sure that it had been at the home of his friend, Mary Price, in Washington. Lee and his wife knew Miss Bentley for over a year and a quarter, saw her some fifteen times in that period, and enjoyed her company for the first ten months or so. The friendship sickened, however, because the Lees came to the conclusion that Miss Bentley was a "very lonely

---

possibility that the pages were written by White for the information of someone other than an espionage agent.

114. *Hiss Hearings*, p. 529.

115. Bentley, *Out of Bondage*, p. 131.

116. Bentley, *Out of Bondage*, pp. 131–132.

117. Lee had been a member of Donovan's law firm in New York. He was legal counsel to two relief organizations, Russian War Relief and the China Aid Council. He was also with the American Committee for Chinese War Orphans. *Hiss Hearings*, pp. 735–736.

and neurotic woman, that she was a frustrated woman, that her liking and apparent ardent liking for us was unnaturally intense." [118] And so they sought to break off the relationship because Miss Bentley was becoming a nuisance, "an emotional weight around our necks," although when Lee told her that they should not see each other, she protested hard, said that she had to go on seeing them, proposed that they meet in public places, and to this they agreed to get her out of the house.

After that (about October 1944), the Lees saw Miss Bentley once at Martin's Restaurant in Washington, and Lee met her twice in drugstores thereafter. Lee also met with Jacob Golos, the first time in Washington right after he had met Miss Bentley, and the second time, he said, in New York "some months later." [119] Since Lee said that he had met Miss Bentley first in October 1943, and Golos for the first time some weeks after that, he could not possibly have met Golos the second time "some months later" because Golos was dead, having succumbed in November 1943.

Although Lee rose to be a lieutenant-colonel in a counter-espionage agency, where extreme caution was standard operating procedure, his suspicions were not aroused by what he thought was the pressing importunity of a strange woman, whose talk was strongly pro-Communist and who introduced him to a strange man of uncertain connections. Although Lee thought it might be embarrassing to be seen with Miss Bentley because of her outspoken pro-Soviet attitudes, he met her twice in a public drugstore while he was still in uniform. He never suspected that she was a Communist, he said, much less a Soviet agent, and in any case thought that her leftism was a minor consideration in the break he made with her. He did not report any suspicion of Miss Bentley to his superiors in the OSS because he had no suspicions. Although Elizabeth Bentley's charges were privileged when she made them before the House Committee on Un-American Activities and again, in 1951, before the Senate Internal Security subcommittee, she later repeated them in her book, where the charges were not privileged.

Others in the Office of Strategic Services named by Elizabeth Bentley were Helen Tenney in the Spanish and Balkan Divisions of the OSS, J. Julius Joseph in the Japanese Division, his wife, in publicity, and Maurice Halperin, "head of the Latin-American Division Research and Analysis Branch." [120] In later hearings before the Senate Internal Security subcommittee a number of former OSS officials and employees were asked to testify about themselves. The national com-

118. *Hiss Hearings*, p. 721.
119. *Hiss Hearings*, p. 723.
120. *Hiss Hearings*, pp. 530–531.

mander of the Veterans of the Abraham Lincoln Brigade, Milton Wolff, who was with the OSS in Italy, refused to respond on the ground that his answers might incriminate him.[121] Leonard E. Mins, a research analyst with the OSS, wanted to talk about his privileges and the separation of powers but not about his work in the OSS. In the course of his nontestimony he got off such remarks as

Senator McCarran: You are Leonard Mins?
Mr. Mins: Obviously. You are Senator McCarran.[122]

But the real card was George S. Wuchinich who answered the question put by counsel, "Mr. Wuchinich, what is your present occupation?" by saying

Well, Mr. Morris, I have a good answer for that because my occupation over the last 30 years, and it involves my present, has been that of clerk, typist, stenographer, credit manager, export manager, salesman; I have been trained as an engineer; I have been a spy for the United States Government; I have been a paratrooper; I have been a swimmer; I have been everything that my country wanted me to be, but one thing I have been that's common to everybody: I have been unemployed, too, and have been unemployed at a time when I think that most of the American people didn't like that occupation.[123]

Wuchinich was liaison with Communist forces in Yugoslavia but declined to say whether he had been a Communist, either before or after his service with the OSS.

Helen Tenney, one of those named by Miss Bentley, who had served in the OSS as an editorial analyst, declined even to say whether she had been employed by the OSS on the ground that her answer might tend to incriminate her.[124] Irving Fajans, a lieutenant in the Spanish Republican Army in 1937 and 1938 and an official in the Veterans of the Abraham Lincoln Brigade, had been an OSS officer in Italy. He refused to answer critical questions about his connections with the Communist Party or the "Soviet people" on the ground that he might be incriminated.[125]

There is a vast difference between simple testimony in a congressional hearing and firm evidence in a court; but the behavior of the OSS witnesses before the House and Senate committees shows how difficult it is even to get the details of a story straight when those called to

121. *Hearings on Interlocking Subversion in Government Departments*, p. 765.
122. *Ibid.*, p. 685.
123. *Ibid.*, p. 702.
124. *Ibid.*, p. 772.
125. *Ibid.*, p. 787.

testify are bent upon wrecking the proceeding. In the examination of the OSS witnesses before the Senate committee, the behavior of Mins and Wuchinich was so grotesque, and the demeanor of Helen Tenney was so timorous, that the thought was spoken that the former had been sent deliberately to turn the inquiry into the farce it was, and that Helen Tenney had been threatened. The short parade of former officials in a sensitive agency claiming that their answers might incriminate them if they testified about their loyalty doubtless delighted party members who followed the proceedings; but their conduct was a dismaying exhibition of wrecking tactics. It was not the witnesses who were pushed around, but the congressional spokesmen. The witnesses made much of their physical valor, challenging committee counsel and the chairman on their war records, but millions of Americans, as the chairman pointed out, who had shown the same valor during the war, would not, like the witnesses, have said that they might incriminate themselves if they told the truth about their loyalty.

The Bentley-Chambers testimony was not the beginning of the story of espionage in the government during the war but the end of it.[126] When Elizabeth Bentley went to the FBI in New Haven in 1945 to tell her tale, the agency checked its veracity. It thought well enough of it to move J. Edgar Hoover, in a letter dated November 8, 1945, to warn the President of the existence of espionage activities. Among the people named were Harry Dexter White and Lauchlin Currie. A full report of Soviet espionage in the United States was sent to the White House on December 4, 1945. This was a detailed statement of seventy-one pages, reporting the charges against and suspicions of White, Silvermaster, and Ullmann. On January 23, 1946, President Truman nominated Harry Dexter White to the distinguished post of executive director of the International Monetary Fund. In a speech later, President Truman was to say that he first learned of the accusations against White in February 1946. On February 6, 1946, the President had a conference with Secretary of State James F. Byrnes and Secretary of the Treasury Fred M. Vinson to discuss the White nomination. On the same day the Senate ratified the appointment.[127]

126. Elizabeth Bentley died on December 3, 1963, at the age of 55. *New York Times*, December 4, 1963, p. 47, col. 1.

127. For an account and evaluation of the President's course of action in the case of Harry Dexter White, see G. F. Hudson, "The Dexter White Case," *The Twentieth Century*, January 1954, pp. 22–35.

> *There are also those witnesses who share
> the risk of punishment if their evidence
> is pronounced false. These are valid witnesses
> to the fact that an action was or was not done,
> that something is or is not the case. . . .*
>
> ARISTOTLE, *Rhetoric*

VII   *The Department of State*

In its barest bones the Hiss case is the indictment of Alger Hiss by a
Federal Grand Jury in New York on December 15, 1948, for perjury,
the failure of a jury to convict him in a trial that began in May 1949,
his conviction in a second trial in November 1949, his imprisonment
under sentence of five years, and his release from imprisonment in
November 1954. But creative desire has fleshed and plumped out this
meager frame, and imaginations have produced the monster or the
martyr that partisanship requires. Although there had been no joinder
of other parties in the prosecution of Hiss, the American correspondent
for the *Manchester Guardian* thought that it was "a generation on trial"
in the courthouse in Foley Square.[1] A British jurist thought it was a
"strange case," [2] the defendant pleaded for reversal of common judgment "in the court of public opinion," [3] and the incredulous argued
that the trial was an "unfinished story" [4] although no one presumably
prevents the defendant or anyone else from telling it, if it is.

The chief prosecution witness — Whittaker Chambers — lost a
$30,000 a year job as senior editor for *Time* because of disclosures that
were said by his critics to be lies born of malevolence. The FBI had
263 agents at one time or another working in forty-five of the fifty-two
field divisions of the bureau to establish the facts that were said not to
constitute either evidence or proof, although we bet our lives every
day on the nature of circumstances we accept with much less demonstration, like the rationality of drivers on turnpikes.[5] Richard Nixon

1. Alistair Cooke, *A Generation on Trial* (New York: Knopf, 1950).
2. Lord Jowitt, *The Strange Case of Alger Hiss* (New York: Doubleday, 1953).
3. Alger Hiss, *In the Court of Public Opinion* (New York: Knopf, 1957).
4. Fred J. Cook, *The Unfinished Story of Alger Hiss* (New York: Morrow,
1958).
5. Don Whitehead, *The FBI Story* (New York: Random House, 1956), p. 284.
A list of some of the facts whose validity the FBI checked is set out at pp. 284–285.

made a national political career out of the Hiss case;[6] the successful prosecutor, Thomas F. Murphy, became a United States judge in the Southern District of New York; and the defendant, Alger Hiss, served his sentence in the same prison with Douglas Chandler, under life sentence for treason in broadcasting for the Nazis during the Second World War.[7]

Whittaker Chambers died in 1961 of a heart attack at the age of 60, his family maintaining the privacy of a ruined life by withholding the announcement of his death until after the body had been cremated. His last word on the Hiss case was written in the *National Review* in 1959 when he said of Hiss that the latter had not yet paid his penalty "except in the shallowest legalistic sense." Said Chambers further, "There is only one possible payment, as I see it, in his case. It is to speak the truth. Hiss' defiance perpetuates and keeps a fracture in the community as a whole." [8] When Chambers wrote this conclusion, the country had other things on its mind than the tragedy of two actors in a play a decade past. Thirty years before his last word, Whittaker Chambers had translated Franz Werfel's *Class Reunion* from German into English, an event that suggested to Dr. Carl Binger, an alienist for the defense in Hiss's trial, that Chambers had approximately re-enacted the plot of the story in the allegedly mendacious destruction of Hiss. But the denouement in the Werfel book was the discovery by Sebastian that the man before him was not the victim of his reverie. In the dramatic encounter between Chambers and Hiss in 1948 both men were vividly real — it was the plot that seemed unbelievable.[9]

6. During the presidential campaign of 1956, William A. Reuben published *The Honorable Mr. Nixon* (New York: Action Books, 1956) which purported to diminish the role played by Nixon in the Congressional investigation of Hiss. The thesis of the author was that Nixon, contrary to the testimony, and in violation of the canons of decency and fair play, manufactured a destructive conception of Hiss which he sold to the American public, prejudging the verdict of the subsequent trial which, according to the author, failed to substantiate the accusations of Chambers. Thus, Hiss was victimized to promote the political ambitions of Richard Nixon. The decision to follow his judgment that Hiss was a member of a prewar Communist group in the Department of State, as asserted by Chambers, was later described by Nixon as one of the crises of his political life. Richard M. Nixon, *Six Crises* (New York: Doubleday, 1962).

7. There is an account of Alger Hiss in Lewisburg Penitentiary by a fellow prisoner in John O. Staples, "I Knew Alger Hiss in Prison," *Look*, May 18, 1954, pp. 36–37.

8. The quotation from the *National Review* is used in an obituary story in *Time*, July 21, 1961, p. 17. The *Time* summary of the Hiss case is wrong in at least one respect. The date for the sentencing is given as January 25, 1951. The correct date is January 25, 1950.

9. Although Dr. Binger thought that there were extraordinary parallels between the plot of *Class Reunion* and what he assumed to be the facts of the Hiss case, he did not find any analogies "in the child's book, *Bambi*, which Chambers had also translated." Cooke, *A Generation on Trial*, p. 309.

In dealing with the Hiss case as part of the history of the Communist issue in American politics, the problem is to avoid too much recital of familiar detail and yet to provide enough of it to appraise fairly some of the arguments in the highly neurotic public discussion it set off. Until something new shows up to put a whole new light on the controversy, certain facts about the relations between Hiss and Chambers may be regarded as settled. These facts will be summarized briefly. Certain facts about the existence of an espionage operation in the Department of State are also settled, although perception of them was somewhat dazzled by the glare around the two principals. These facts will also be summarized, for some of them are at least as important as the very narrow question of perjury the jury decided.

The Case of Alger Hiss

The indictment on which Hiss was convicted was in two counts, that he had lied when he told a grand jury under oath that he had not turned any documents of the State Department over to Whittaker Chambers, and that he had lied when he told a grand jury that he had not seen Whittaker Chambers after January 1, 1937. The indictment was handed down on December 15, 1948, and was the climax of events that began on August 3, 1948, during the special session of the Congress that President Truman had convened to enact the Republican Party platform adopted shortly before.[10] On that day, Chambers accused Hiss before the House Committee on Un-American Activities of having been a member of the Communist Party with Chambers in the 1930's. Chambers did not accuse Hiss of espionage activity. Two days later Hiss denied the accusation in public session. On August 18 there was a confrontation of Hiss and Chambers in a private session of a special subcommittee of the House Committee in Room 1400 of the Commodore Hotel in New York. At this session, Hiss said he recognized Chambers as a man he had known as George Crosley in the middle 1930's. Hiss challenged Chambers to make his accusations in public without the immunity from libel that statements made in congressional proceedings receive. On August 27, Chambers repeated his accusations on a radio program, *Meet the Press*, and one month later, on September 27, Hiss sued Chambers for defamation in the United States District Court in Baltimore.

10. In the Democratic National Convention of 1948, President Truman told the delegates who had just nominated him, "Now, my friends, if there is any reality behind that Republican platform we ought to get some action out of a short session of the Eightieth Congress. They can do this job in fifteen days if they want to do it." See Jules Abels, *Out of the Jaws of Victory* (New York: Holt, 1959), pp. 94–95. On Turnip Day in Missouri, July 26, Truman called the Congress into special session.

In a pre-trial examination by the lawyers for Hiss in Baltimore on November 17, 1948, Chambers for the first time produced copies of State Department documents that he said that Hiss had transmitted to him. This material, if it proved to be what Chambers said it was, established the complicity of Alger Hiss in espionage activity, an offense of the utmost gravity. More material was given under subpoena to investigators for the House Committee in a lurid nocturnal visit to the Chambers farm where it had been hidden in pumpkins. The new material consisted of rolls of microfilmed photographs of State Department documents that Chambers said Hiss had supplied to him.

Although Hiss had said that he recalled knowing Chambers as George Crosley, a free lance writer, he also said that he had not seen him after July 1, 1936. The internal evidence of the documents Chambers had surrendered made it clear that they referred to events after this time, throughout the year 1937 in fact, and into 1938. Since memory foreshortens the recollection of some events and puts others at an earlier time than was so, Hiss had a toleration of six months in establishing the date of the last encounter with George Crosley. He was certain that he had not seen, and had had nothing to do with, George Crosley after January 1, 1937.

If Hiss was truthful, he obviously could not personally have transmitted documents to Chambers in 1937 and 1938. Contrariwise, if Chambers could show that there was a connection between him and Hiss after January 1, 1937, Hiss would be discredited. Since the documents revealed to the attorneys of Hiss had been typewritten, it became of some importance to decide on whose typewriter they had been written and when. It was certain very early that the typewriter had been a Woodstock, and it soon became known that the Hisses had had a Woodstock table model. It was established that all but one of the Baltimore documents had been typed on the Woodstock typewriter that Hiss had owned.

But although he had once owned it, he had not had it in his possession in a decade. Instead, it had been given to Negro servants by the name of Catlett who had worked in his house. When had they received the typewriter — before January 1, 1937 or afterwards? If afterwards, could it be established that the machine had typed the State Department documents while it was still in the possession of the Hisses? And if it did type the documents while in the possession of the Hisses, who did the typing? The jury that convicted Hiss believed that the machine had not come into the possession of the Catletts until after January-March 1938, which were the dates of the documents. There was some doubt that the Catletts had received the machine even as early as the spring of 1938 since one of them, Perry Catlett, told of taking it immediately to be repaired at a shop that did not in fact open up until September 1938. Although Hiss did not type, the jury believed that the material could have been typed in the Hiss house inasmuch as his wife, Priscilla, had skills sufficient to qualify as "passing" in typing tests she took when a student at Columbia. The case for Hiss was that the typewriter had passed from their possession in December 1937 when they moved from one house to another. The jury believed otherwise.

Now this is by no means absolute proof of the allegations of Whittaker Chambers. The typewriter is the key piece in the puzzle because the documents Chambers had *were* done on the Woodstock, and the Woodstock *was* the typewriter owned by Hiss at one time. But this logically does not connect Chambers with Hiss. It connects both Chambers and Hiss with the typewriter. The jury had to believe other evidence of a close relation between Hiss and Chambers at the dates of the documents, or thereabouts, as to make it most likely that the typewriter was an instrument of unlawful traffic between them in government documents. There was such other evidence, although it was not, either, of iron-clad strength.

Chambers had said that he had been given a loan of $400 by Hiss to buy a car in November 1937. The bank records of Hiss showed that on November 19, Mrs. Hiss withdrew $400 from a meager account, leaving only $14.69 in it. A bill of sale showed that Chambers bought a car four days later for $400. The defense of Hiss was that the money had been withdrawn to pay cash for purchases for a house into which they were to move in December, although Mrs. Hiss had numerous charge accounts in various places in Washington, and there were, by 1949, no cash receipts for such purchases, if there ever had been any. Apart from this, the other evidence, even if all believed, showed not that Chambers and Hiss were close in the first three months of 1938, but that they had been close in 1936, when Hiss "rented" an apartment to Chambers and threw in an old car on the deal, when Chambers gave Hiss a Bokhara rug, and Mrs. Chambers painted the portrait of one of the Hiss children. The jury had to believe that this rather close association continued after the time Hiss said he last saw George Crosley (January 1, 1937) and into the following year and two or three months.

Although the case to support the indictments is not absolute, this is not to say that it is weak. A jury could reasonably believe that Hiss did know Chambers after January 1, 1937, and that he did pass him State Department documents. They could find him guilty of the charges beyond a reasonable doubt and this is what they did. Judge

Goddard, who presided at the second trial, believed that the jury had made "an earnest effort to render, and have rendered, a just verdict."

The typewriter which was so critical in the conviction of Hiss was to figure in two subsequent developments in the Hiss case. The first of these was a motion for a new trial which was made by the attorneys for Hiss on January 24, 1952, on the ground of newly discovered evidence.[11] The alleged new evidence was said to show that a technique of forgery by typewriter existed which was not known about at the time of the trials. The theory of the motion was that the government had forged the Woodstock typewriter — that is, it had made a physical reproduction of the typewriter that was capable of typing exactly like the original, so that material typed on both machines was indistinguishable. There were other elements said to constitute "new evidence" but they were gossamers of presumption, and seem to have been proposed as make weight in the scales that the Hiss lawyers were trying to tip for their client.[12] The big new thing was to be the demonstration that it was possible to forge a typewriter. Even if successful it still would have had to be shown that the prosecution had in fact forged the Hiss typewriter.

There is a story about the earnest eighteenth century religious who described to the *femme savante* the wonder of the decapitated saint who had walked five miles with his head under his arm. Her comment

11. For excerpts from a summary of grounds for the motion for a new trial, see Hiss, *In the Court of Public Opinion*, p. 365.

12. It was said that newly discovered evidence demonstrated that the identification of the Hisses as visitors to Chambers' house was not founded in fact, and that therefore there was no evidence of a close social relationship between the Hisses and the Chambers. But even Hiss had identified Chambers as one with whom he had had more than a passing acquaintance in his testimony before the House Committee on Un-American Activities. It was also said that there was new evidence that Chambers had left the Communist Party before April 1, 1938, and that the conspiracy of which Chambers accused Hiss could not have occurred at the time of the date of the last Baltimore document. But this would not have proved that Hiss did not have traffic with Chambers after January 1, 1937, which was what the indictment charged. It was also said that a former member of the prewar cell had come forward to say that Alger Hiss "was not a member of it." This witness was Lee Pressman who testified on August 28, 1950, before the House Committee on Un-American Activities and confessed his former membership in the Communist Party. But all that Pressman said in this testimony was ". . . I can state as a matter of knowledge, that for the period of my participation in that group, which is the only basis on which I can say I have knowledge, Alger Hiss was not a member of the group." This is a far different thing from saying that Hiss was not a member of the group and, in any case, has nothing to do with the two charges of the indictment under which Hiss was convicted of perjury. For the explanations of the various elements of "new evidence" by Chester T. Lane, the Hiss lawyer on the motion, see Hiss, *In the Court of Public Opinion*, p. 368, for forgery by typewriter; p. 385 for the contradiction of the Chambers' maid; p. 387 for Chambers' break with the Communist Party; and p. 393 for the testimony of Lee Pressman about Hiss and the Ware group.

was, "The first step must have been the hardest." The first step in the demonstration of forgery by typewriter proved to be impassable. After a year of work in the endeavor to produce such a forgery, the effort failed. The characteristics of the original and the duplicate were different from each other, and the difference, although slight, could be detected by experts. Even the affidavits from so-called experts in the detection of typographic and other written forgeries failed to say that the original and the duplicate were identical, and one of them successfully differentiated samples from the two machines without any clue from the Hiss lawyer that it was two machines that had made the samples. A writer in *The Nation* reviewed the efforts of Chester Lane to establish the case for forgery by typewriter several years after the motion for a new trial. He asserted that the experts had said they "would not have suspected that two machines did the typing" had they not been told in advance that this was so,[13] but in an expanded version of the article which was published as a book, he did not repeat the statement. Instead he quoted comments of an "expert" who said it "would be difficult if not impossible to distinguish between two samples from the two machines." [14] He did not quote from the "expert" who, without any clues, had been able to distinguish between the original machine and the duplicate that Lane had had made.[15] The Earl Jowitt, whose review of the evidence of the two trials was sympathetic to Hiss, assumed that no forgery had taken place and accepted the opinion that the Baltimore papers had in fact been typed on the Hiss machine.[16]

There had been no suggestion in either the first or the second trial

13. Fred J. Cook, "Hiss, New Perspectives on the Strangest Case of Our Time," *The Nation,* 185 (8) (September 21, 1957), p. 175.

14. Cook, *The Unfinished Story of Alger Hiss,* pp. 146–147. The "expert" he cited was a woman who had worked with Chester Lane in the effort to produce a duplicate machine.

15. The expert he does not cite was Mrs. Evelyn S. Ehrlich of Boston who had not helped Lane make the duplicate machine but could tell the difference between material typed on the original machine and that typed on the duplicate. For an identification of Mrs. Ehrlich, see Hiss, *In the Court of Public Opinion,* pp. 371–372.

16. Jowitt, *The Strange Case of Alger Hiss.* Although the Jowitt book was published a year after the motion for a new trial was made and argued, there is no mention of it by the author. References to possible forgery by typewriter in the Jowitt book are at pp. 281 and 343. Elsewhere, Jowitt is quite clear that the only alternative to the theory of Hiss's guilt is that "Chambers had at some time got access to the typewriter and had either himself, or by some agent, caused the forty-three documents produced at Baltimore to be typed on that machine." *Ibid.,* p. 271. It is clear in the reference to "forgery by typewriter" that Jowitt means not that someone made a machine that could duplicate the Hiss machine, but that someone typed documents on the Hiss machine to make it appear that Hiss was involved in espionage. To use his typewriter was to forge his connection with the Communist apparatus.

of Hiss that the Baltimore documents were not typed on the Hiss machine. Lloyd Stryker, the defense counsel in the first case, conceded for the defense that the documents Chambers had produced were true copies of State Department originals, and he made something of the fact that it was not the prosecution but one of the lawyers for Hiss, Edward McLean, who had found the Hiss typewriter. Stryker's argument was that the discovery of the typewriter after a number of years, and its production by the defense, were acts not only inconsistent with guilty knowledge, but were indeed the positive acts of a man who had nothing to hide. Claude Cross, counsel in the second Hiss trial, never questioned the authenticity of the documents nor the fact that they were typed on the Hiss typewriter.

Judge Henry W. Goddard, who had presided at the second trial of Alger Hiss, heard the motion for a new trial and denied the motion.[17] He held that the defense had submitted no proof that would support a finding by a jury that the typewriter received in evidence was made by or for Chambers or that the typewriter was not the original machine. Lane filed an appeal from the decision of Judge Goddard in which he said that the judge had predetermined the motion and had abused his discretion, but this appeal failed on January 30, 1953, when the court of appeals upheld the trial judge. The Supreme Court of the United States on April 27, 1953, refused to review the case at all.[18]

The typewriter figured briefly in another development in the Hiss case long after the excitements of the hearings, trials, and appeals. The short sensation was created by a statement in the account by Richard M. Nixon of his part in the investigation of the testimony of Chambers and Hiss in 1948.[19] The grand jury in New York had been sitting for weeks in the late fall of 1948 listening to the case against Hiss,[20] but

17. 107 F. Supp. (S.D.N.Y. 1952). The Hiss case is to be found at *United States v. Hiss*, 195 F.2d 822 (2d Circ. 1950); cert. denied January 27, 1951, 340 U.S. 948 (1951).

18. The motion for a new trial and Judge Goddard's action were discussed in the law journals. For such a discussion see Herbert L. Packer, "A Tale of Two Typewriters," 10 *Stanford Law Review*, No. 3, pp. 409–440 (May 1958). It was Professor Packer's view that even if the defense had been able to prove that the Hiss typewriter had been duplicated, this would not necessarily have exonerated Hiss from either of the two charges in the indictment. The theory of the defense was that Chambers, between September and November 1948, had been able to accomplish what the expert craftsmen employed by the defense had been unable to do in a year.

19. This appears in his *Six Crises*, published in 1962.

20. Indeed the grand jury had served for eighteen months, from June 16, 1947 to December 15, 1948, investigating violations of the espionage laws. In all that time it failed to return one indictment. The indictment it produced against Hiss on the last day of its existence was, as indicated earlier, not for violation of the espionage laws but for perjury.

had failed to return a true bill because it had no other evidence to connect Hiss with the Baltimore documents produced by Chambers than the otherwise unsupported word of Chambers that they were copies of papers that Hiss had unlawfully transmitted to him. In fact there was a strong suspicion that the Department of Justice was prepared to ask the grand jury to indict Chambers and not Hiss. On the last day of the official life of the grand jury, the prosecution brought to the jury room samples of typing done by Mrs. Hiss, two letters written years before and undoubtedly authentic specimens of the work produced on the Hiss typewriter. The characteristics of the typing were the same as those of the Baltimore documents, and the connection was thus established between Hiss and the copies of State Department material that Chambers had received unlawfully. It was this precise fact that led to the ultimate conviction of Hiss.

Because of its bearing on the facts, the FBI had been looking for the Hiss typewriter since November 17, and had failed to find it. Had they been able to produce the typewriter in the grand jury room, they could have demonstrated that the Baltimore documents had been typed on the very machine before the jurors. Failing possession of the typewriter, the presentation of letters that had clearly been written on the machine made the connection between Hiss and the Baltimore documents certain, although somewhat more indirect than would have been the case if the machine itself had materialized. And why had it not materialized? Because the FBI did not have it in December 1948. It was not found by the defense until the following spring.

But in his book, Richard Nixon contradicted this version of the FBI's relation to the typewriter. His account said,

> On December 13, FBI agents found the typewriter. . . . On December 15, the critical last day, an expert from the FBI typed exact copies of the incriminating documents on the old Woodstock machine and had them flown up to New York as exhibits for members of the Grand Jury to see. . . .[21]

This was a devastating statement, flatly opposed to the statement made by the FBI under oath that they did not have possession of the typewriter.

Nixon declined to comment when the contradiction was discovered but a "spokesman for Mr. Nixon" said that the statement in the book had been re-checked and had been found to be an error originating with researchers. The true account, he said, was the one that had been believed for fourteen years:

21. Nixon, *Six Crises*, p. 60.

At the time of the grand jury proceedings in December 1948 —
which were, of course, secret — there were reports to the effect that
the F.B.I. had found the old Hiss Woodstock typewriter. However
the typewriter was not actually found and produced in evidence
until the time of Hiss' first trial for perjury.[22]

The Attorney General, taking notice of the new controversy, issued
a statement:

> The claims made in the past few days by Mr. Hiss and on his
> behalf regarding certain factual matters in connection with his con-
> viction cannot be substantiated.
>
> All the pertinent files and records in the case have been reviewed
> carefully. This review confirmed that the F.B.I. never had possession
> of the disputed typewriter. . . .
>
> Accordingly no further action in this case is contemplated.[23]

The Nixon statements were first cited by Fred J. Cook, author of
The Unfinished Story of Alger Hiss, in an article in *The Nation*,[24]
where he said of the contradiction: "Among the many mysterious aspects of this mysterious case, this is now the most mysterious." Although he had been prepared to accept the theory of the defense in
the motion for a new trial — that someone had created a machine that
duplicated the original Hiss Woodstock — it was not possible to argue
that the Nixon statement now proved such forgery, for the Nixon
statement was inconsistent with the theory of forgery. Mr. Cook went
only so far as to suggest that the secret minutes of the grand jury
should be released to the public to show whether the government submitted samples of the typing from the Woodstock it later denied it ever
had, or whether it did not.

Defenders of Hiss, in taking the new position — that the FBI had
the machine in December 1948 — have argued inconsistently, and it is
not possible to reconcile the theories that the Hiss machine that typed
the fateful documents is an original and a fake at the same time. On
the motion for a new trial the defense "proved" that the machine introduced at the trial was a fake. New type had been soldered on the
old keys, the soldering was inexpert, there were tool marks on the
type, and so on. But if the FBI had the original typewriter on De-

22. *New York Times*, April 2, 1962, p. 1, col. 6.
23. *New York Times*, April 4, 1962, p. 8, col. 3. The defense argued in the motion for a new trial that the FBI had had possession of the typewriter but Earl J.
Connelly, assistant director of the FBI in charge of field operations in the Hiss
case, said in a sworn affidavit that the FBI never had in its possession any typewriter known, believed, or considered to be the Hiss typewriter.
24. Fred J. Cook, "Nixon Kicks a Hole in the Hiss Case," *The Nation*, 194 (14),
April 7, 1962, p. 296.

cember 13, 1948, and even typed up copies of documents for the grand jury on it, why did anyone need to plant a fake where the defense could find it and bring it into court? Since the argument in the motion for a new trial assumed that the Baltimore documents had been typed on the fake machine, the fake machine had to exist before the Baltimore documents were revealed, that is, before November 17, 1948. On December 13, 1948, then, the FBI had both the original and the fake. If the Baltimore documents were typed on the fake, the FBI did not have to wait until December 13 to make sure of the indictment. At any time between the manufacture of the fake and December 13, it could have typed the conclusive documents that moved the grand jury, and made the indictment certain.

Alternative pleading is often the kind of argument that lawyers make when they do not have a case. The defendant was not there; but if he was there, he did not do it; but if he did do it, he was insane; but if he was not insane, he had provocation. Successive arguments of this kind help to keep the Hiss case alive, though no longer lively; and they reflect the feeling of some that Hiss would somehow be exonerated "if the truth were told." It is never quite clear what the truth would look or sound like if it were told, but it would benefit Hiss's reputation, it is believed. The compulsion to disbelieve seems to be stimulated more by the fact that it is Hiss who is involved, than by the supposed deficiencies of the procedure that sent him to jail. If it were otherwise, the clamor for reform of the judicial process would be deafening because every day someone is convicted of crime on evidence quite as convincing as that in the Hiss case.

Wadleigh, Field, and Duggan

The shock of the Hiss case is not limited to the trial for perjury. There was also the disclosure of indisputable evidence of the existence of a spy apparatus that had important sources in the Department of State, an aspect of the whole case that the personal drama overcast and shaded. The authenticity of the documents that Chambers preserved after his break with the Communist Party has not been questioned. They were in fact typewritten and microfilmed copies of actual documents belonging to the State Department and other agencies of the government.[25] As has been said in one of the better summaries of the

25. Although Chambers said that all of the Baltimore papers had been transmitted to him by Alger Hiss, one of them, Number 10, seems to have originated with someone else, Harry Dexter White, according to Chambers at one point. But he later said that it was Hiss who had given him Number 10 also. Earl Jowitt, *The Strange Case of Alger Hiss*, p. 309.

documents,[26] there were three kinds of material: handwritten notes, typed copies, and photographs of documents that could be classified under various headings. Nearly all of the typewritten documents were copies of cables to the Secretary of State from American representatives abroad containing accounts of diplomatic conversations, troop movements, military purchases, and military construction. The photographs (microfilm) were mainly from the internal files of the Trade Agreements Section of the Department of State. Henry Julian Wadleigh was a government economist in the Trade Agreements Section who was described as a source of papers taken from the Department of State and transmitted to Chambers whom he knew under the name Carl Carlson.[27] The papers from the Trade Agreements Section, however, were not, according to Chambers, contributions by Wadleigh but contributions by Hiss,[28] and credence is lent this statement by the fact that at the time Chambers collected documents for his protection — that is, in the spring of 1938 — Julian Wadleigh was out of the country on a diplomatic mission to Turkey.[29] Trade Agreements Section documents were routed to the office of Francis B. Sayre, Assistant Secretary of State and Hiss's superior, where Hiss had access to them, as Wadleigh had had.[30]

Besides sources in the office of Assistant Secretary of State Sayre and the Trade Agreements Section, there is reason to believe that the office of Far Eastern Affairs was also a source of material for the Chambers-Bykov apparatus.[31] One of the Baltimore documents, Number 10, had not been typed on the Hiss Woodstock, but on another

26. Cooke, A Generation on Trial, pp. 161–170.

27. Chambers said that Hiss was his number one source in the Department of State and that Wadleigh was his number two source. Witness (New York: Random House, 1952), pp. 28–29.

28. Chambers makes the statement that the Baltimore documents contained nothing from Wadleigh, in Witness, p. 41.

29. Fred J. Cook has said of Wadleigh's confession that he was a source for Chambers: "This testimony certainly lends weight to the proposition that Wadleigh, not Hiss, may have been Chambers' source for many of the documents, but obviously it is not the complete explanation. Wadleigh's departure for Turkey on March 11, 1938, made it impossible for him to have furnished the later documents dated up to April 1. These must have been supplied either by Hiss or by some other confederate of Chambers inside the State Department. There is no direct evidence that Chambers had such a confederate but the origin of some of the documents in the Far Eastern Section would seem to indicate that he might have had." Cook, The Unfinished Story of Alger Hiss, p. 123.

30. Wadleigh also gave material to one David Carpenter, according to his testimony and the corroboration of Whittaker Chambers. At the time of the Hiss trials, Carpenter was "still a Communist employed by the Daily Worker." Chambers, Witness, p. 781n.

31. The Office of Far Eastern Affairs also figured prominently in the investigation of the Amerasia affair and the Institute of Pacific Relations, which investigations are discussed below.

machine that was never identified.[32] This document was a copy of a
report from the Military Intelligence Division of the War Department. The document was sent to the Far Eastern Division of the State
Department and then to the files. It did not go to the office of Assistant Secretary of State Sayre. It was the theory of the defense in the
second trial of Alger Hiss that there was a "thief" in the Far Eastern
Division[33] and the Earl Jowitt was also of the opinion that the document came from a "third source." [34] If this supposition is correct, there
was another source than Hiss and Wadleigh in the State Department
with whom Chambers was in contact, although this source has not been
identified.[35]

The West European Division of the Department of State was also
involved in charges of espionage.[36] As early as 1938, Noel Field, an
official in the West European Division, had been named as a member
of the Communist Party in proceedings before the House Committee
on Un-American Activities.[37] Under questioning on August 27, 1948,
Whittaker Chambers identified Noel Field as a person he had discussed
with Hiss as a likely prospect for espionage in the State Department,
only to discover, he said, that Field was working for another apparatus.[38] The other apparatus with which Field was said to have been
working was that to which Hede Massing, the former wife of Gerhardt
Eisler, was attached. Hede Massing was not allowed to testify in the
first Hiss trial [39] but she did so in the second trial, identifying Hiss

32. There were 65 sheets in all, 64 of which were typed on the Hiss Woodstock. All the 65 sheets were either copies or summaries of State Department
documents. Of these, 47 were dated in the first three months of 1938 when Chambers said that he gathered the material to serve as a protection against reprisal.

33. The dilemma of the defense in not being able to pin the documents on
Wadleigh, nor to identify the thief in the Far Eastern Division, is commented on
by Cooke, *A Generation on Trial*, p. 322.

34. Jowitt, *The Strange Case of Agler Hiss*, p. 309.

35. Although Chambers was seemingly quite explicit about many aspects of his
life in and out of the Communist apparatus, there are many blanks in the story.
For example, he had a source in the Bureau of Standards whom he was willing
to identify only fictitiously as "Abel Gross." See *Witness*, p. 29.

36. The word "source" is used here in the name sense in which it was employed
by Chambers, as one who "supplied the Soviet espionage apparatus with secret
or confidential information, usually in the form of official United States Government documents for microfilming." *Witness*, p. 28.

37. Eightieth Congress, First Session, House of Representatives, Committee on
Un-American Activities, *Investigation of Un-American Propaganda Activities in
the United States*, vol. III, p. 2172. The witness was J. B. Matthews, who had
turned from Communist enterprises after organizing the League Against War and
Fascism.

38. Eightieth Congress, Second Session, House of Representatives, Committee
on Un-American Activities, *Hearings Regarding Communist Espionage in the
United States Government*, p. 1265 (hereafter cited as *Hiss Hearings*).

39. Although the prosecutor wished to call Hede Massing as a witness in the
first Hiss trial, Judge Irving Kaufman refused to allow her to appear. The news-

as a member of the underground whom she had met when attempting to recruit Field. In fact, as she was later to say in her book, she had gone to Washington especially to meet Field and his wife,[40] and like many of the men she tells of having met in her life, she was impressed by his good looks, thinking that he seemed to resemble "a cross between Anthony Eden and Andre Gide." [41] According to her account, Field one night sang the "Internationale" in Russian from the steps of the Lincoln Memorial, although it is hard to imagine Anthony Eden doing the same.[42]

It is Mrs. Massing's story that the effort of Alger Hiss to recruit Noel Field into his apparatus failed, for reasons that she could not surmise. She was delighted, she said, to have been able to recruit an official in the West European Division of the State Department but her pleasure was not to be prolonged, for Field almost immediately left the Department of State to take a post in Europe.[43] Chambers later said that he had wondered why the parallel apparatus in the State Department (Mrs. Massing's) would let Field leave the department,[44] but the matter was cleared up for him when he was told by General Walter Krivitsky, chief of Soviet Military Intelligence in Western Europe, that Field had been detached from the department on orders from his apparatus to work for Krivitsky. Mrs. Massing's principal connection with Noel Field after his departure from the Department of State occurred in 1938, according to her account, when she was summoned to Moscow for discipline and learned that the Fields had been there for a week without getting in touch with her. It was her conclusion that the Fields had been given orders not to see Mrs.

papers had freely reported that she was prepared to add the only human corroboration of the story of Whittaker Chambers, all the other testimony with the exception of the evidence of the typewriter being the otherwise unsupported assertion of Chambers. The ruling that Mrs. Massing was an inadmissible witness was put on the ground that she had been called as a rebuttal witness on a collateral matter and it was believed by the judge that her testimony, even though relevant, might be merely prejudicial. Judge Goddard in the second trial allowed her testimony, which corroborated that of Chambers.

40. Hede Massing, *This Deception* (New York: Duell, Sloan and Pearce, 1951), p. 165.
41. Massing, *This Deception*, p. 168.
42. This eccentric behavior was intended as a "rare" present from Field to Mrs. Massing, although she did not understand Russian. Her superior in the underground, when she reported the incident to him, was not amused since the incident betrayed an "inclination toward drama" that did not fit his conception of underground work. Massing, *This Deception*, p. 171.
43. Massing, *This Deception*, p. 176. According to Mrs. Massing, Field had been offered a post in the disarmament section of the League of Nations and had thought that he would be more useful to the "cause" there than in the Department of State.
44. Chambers, *Witness*, p. 381.

Massing. She waylaid them in their own hotel, exploited their presence to get an exit visa, and managed thus to secure her departure from the Soviet Union.[45]

Noel Field left the League of Nations and became the director of the European Division of the Unitarian Service. During the Hiss case, Field and his wife, adopted daughter, and brother all disappeared. It was the opinion of Chambers that Noel Field had knowledge about Hiss and others that made it inadvisable to leave him in free Europe or the United States, subject to legal processes.[46] Hiss referred to the disappearance as an arrest "in Poland or Czechoslovakia." [47]

But both the statements of Chambers and Hiss were to be only a pale surmise about the ruddy reality.[48] Although Field worked for Walter Krivitsky, it does not appear that he played more than a minor part in serious intelligence operations while in Switzerland. He was eventually dropped by the Unitarian Service and was in Europe without a job when the Hiss case broke. In May 1949 Noel Field was arrested in Czechoslovakia and taken to Budapest. In August his wife was arrested in Prague and his brother was arrested en route from Warsaw to Prague.

In September 1949, Laszlo Rajk, former Minister of Foreign Affairs and leader of the Hungarian Communist Party, was brought to trial with six other Hungarians and one Yugoslav in a Stalinist purge intended to repress incipient nationalism of the Titoist variety and to purify East European party circles of elements contaminated by contact with the West. All the defendants made the public confessions that characterize such show trials, and freely implicated those whose disgrace or ruin was required by the program. Noel Field was thrust into the role of master American spy and association with him was used to connect some of the defendants with American Intelligence, with Yugoslavia, and with antiparty treachery. In November 1952, Rudolf Slansky, the leader of the Czech purge, was himself brought to trial in Prague on charges of treason and espionage in indictments pungent with anti-Semitism, and Noel Field and his brother again figured as the connections with American espionage that the script required. After the death of Stalin, Rajk was "rehabilitated" — some

45. Massing, *This Deception*, pp. 274–278.
46. Chambers, *Witness*, p. 382.
47. Hiss, *In the Court of Public Opinion*, p. 307. But before the complete disappearance of Field and family, it was possible for Alger Hiss to have a Swiss lawyer interrogate Mrs. Field in Geneva in the summer of 1949.
48. For an extended and intensive account of the European life of Noel Field and his family, see Flora Lewis, *Red Dawn, The Story of Noel Field* (New York: Doubleday, 1965).

time after his execution — and in 1963, Slansky's conviction was post-humously reversed.

Field and his family were in jail for some five years but although he was eligible to return to the United States when release came, he elected to stay on in Hungary. A Candide of Communist catastrophe, he thought that the dictatorship of the proletariat provided greater security for the individual and his family than decayed capitalism.

The Latin-American Division of the Department of State was also said to have been a source for Communist espionage in the person of its chief, Laurence Duggan, a close friend of Noel Field. Although assertedly recruited by Hede Massing, the alleged enrollment of Duggan in the underground seems not to have been easy.[49] Chambers said that on his first day in Washington as a member of the Communist underground he was told by one of his contacts that Duggan must be recruited for the underground because he was "very sympathetic." [50] Henry Collins twice tried to recruit Duggan for the underground, according to Chambers, and presumably failed.[51] Hiss, he said, tried to recruit Duggan,[52] and also seems to have failed. By 1937, Duggan still had not been recruited into the apparatus with which Chambers was connected, but Chambers said that his chief, Colonel Boris Bykov, decided upon still one other attempt. According to Chambers, Frederick Vanderbilt Field, a friend of Duggan's, was consulted by Chambers about the matter, went to Washington to meet with Duggan, and returned to New York the next day to report that he had asked Duggan directly to join the underground and had been told by Duggan that he was already connected with another apparatus.[53]

According to Hede Massing, Duggan was successfully connected with espionage through her apparatus.[54] She was able to meet him through Noel Field, but it took a little while to count him in the fold. According to her story, when he consented to "help" by letting Mrs.

49. Duggan had been in the State Department many years before the sensations of 1948 were exposed. There is mention of him in the diary of Oliver Clubb as a member of a dinner party at the home of the Washington columnist Drew Pearson in 1932. Eighty-second Congress, First Session, House of Representatives, Hearings before the Committee on Un-American Activities, August 20, 1951, *Testimony of Oliver Edmund Clubb*, pp. 2018 and 2019.

50. Chambers, *Witness*, p. 339. The Senate Committee on Internal Security listed Duggan as a member of the underground in Eighty-fifth Congress, First Session, United States Senate, Committee on the Judiciary, Subcommittee to Investigate the Administration of the Internal Security Act and Other Internal Security Laws, *Report No. 131*, Pursuant to S. Res. 58, p. 297.

51. Chambers, *Witness*, p. 341

52. Chambers, *Witness*, p. 381.

53. Chambers, *Witness*, p. 382.

54. Massing, *This Deception*, p. 206.

Massing and her superiors know of "anything of interest," he laid down certain conditions of procedure. He would not hand over any documents but would meet with a contact every second week and give verbal reports on issues of interest. After the agreement to collaborate had been made, according to Mrs. Massing, she then met with Duggan only once more to arrange the connection with the contact, which took place in a parked car on the outskirts of Washington.[55]

This is all there was about Laurence Duggan and espionage at the time of the Hiss trials. There was no further confirmation of Duggan's involvement. Hede Massing was later to testify that the first publisher who was interested in her book, *This Deception*, dropped it because she "was not willing to take out the whole Duggan chapter." [56] Apart from this, the later testimony of Mrs. Massing and that of Whittaker Chambers added nothing to the frugal account they had already made.[57] Duggan's name was mentioned in the closing speeches of the second Hiss trial when Chambers' position on Duggan was clarified by the prosecutor, Thomas Murphy. He said that Chambers had no personal knowledge that Duggan was a member of the Communist Party, and there was no ground for saying that Chambers had ever accused Duggan of such membership. Nor did Hede Massing accuse Duggan of membership in the Communist Party. All other accounts of Duggan's involvement with the underground derive from the statements of Hede Massing and Whittaker Chambers.

Laurence Duggan might conceivably have testified in his own behalf when the sensational exposures of Bentley, Massing, and Chambers were made in 1948. He was questioned by the FBI about his possible connection with espionage but he was so nervous during the inquiry

55. Massing, *This Deception*, p. 209.

56. Eighty-second Congress, First Session, United States Senate, Committee on the Judiciary, Subcommittee to Investigate the Administration of the Internal Security Act and Other Internal Security Laws, *Hearings on the Institute of Pacific Relations*, August 2, 1951, p. 235 (hereafter cited as *IPR Hearings*).

57. The Chambers testimony, which is substantially the same as that in his book, is to be found at *IPR Hearings*, pp. 488–491. There is a curiosity of names in the telling, however. In his testimony on August 16, 1951 before the Senate Internal Security subcommittee, Chambers said that "His name [i.e., Duggan's] was first drawn to my attention, I believe, by one Webster Clayton Powell, who was then an assistant to Harold Ware in a little Communist front. . . . In any case Webster Powell first drew my attention to the name of Laurence Duggan." *IPR Hearings*, pp. 488–489. But in his book Chambers, in describing the same event, refers to "an underground Communist whom I shall call Egmont Gaines" and says, "What I particularly remember is Egmont Gaines sitting on one of the cots, chatting about the possibilities of the underground organization and insisting that we must make contact with 'Larry' Duggan, whom he called 'very sympathetic.' Thus, on my first day in Washington, I heard the name of the late Laurence Duggan, who was then in the State Department, and later became chief of its Latin-American Division." *Witness*, p. 339. Chambers' book was published in 1952. It is a wonder that a real name in 1951 becomes a pseudonym in 1952.

that an arrangement was made to question him further at a later time. The time never came because he died from a fall from his office window in New York on December 20, 1948. Attorney General Tom Clark on December 24, 1948, said that there was no evidence that Duggan had been associated with Communists.[58]

Suspicion about the Latin-American Division of the State Department did not end with Laurence Duggan, its former chief. Maurice Halperin had been chief of the Latin-American Division of the Research and Analysis Branch of the Office of Strategic Services from 1943 to 1945, with power to supervise a staff of about fifty people.[59] On July 31, 1948, Elizabeth Bentley testified that while Halperin was in the OSS she had known him as a Communist, that she had collected party dues from him, and that he had given her both information that the OSS was getting on Latin America and other parts of the world and information from the State Department, to certain of the cables of which the OSS had access.[60] Nathan Gregory Silvermaster declined on grounds of self-incrimination to say whether he knew Maurice Halperin,[61] as did George Silverman[62] and J. Peters, testifying under the name of Alexander Stevens.[63] Halperin was not said by Bentley to have been a member of the Silvermaster or Perlo groups but one of several unattached individuals from whom she received information for the Communist underground.[64]

On March 30, 1953, Nathaniel Weyl, a former member of the Communist Party, testified that Halperin had been a member of the party when at the University of Oklahoma in 1936,[65] and in fact had been accredited as the representative of the Texas-Oklahoma District of the party to the Mexican Communist Party. Halperin's assistant in the State Department, Irving Goldman, testified that he had himself been a member of the Communist Party but that he had broken with it in 1942. About Halperin he said only that he had known him casually when he was with the Office of the Coordinator of Inter-American Affairs and Halperin was with the OSS, that he was assigned to Halperin's office as a soldier at the instigation of Halperin, and that he

58. Jowitt, *The Strange Case of Alger Hiss*, p. 125n.

59. Eighty-third Congress, First Session, United States Senate, Committee on the Judiciary, Subcommittee to Investigate the Administration of the Internal Security Act and Other Internal Security Laws, *Hearings on Subversive Influence in the Educational Process*, March 26, 1953, pp. 664–675 (hereafter cited as *Subversive Influence in the Educational Process*), for the testimony of Maurice Halperin. The statement about his service with the OSS appears at p. 665.

60. *Hiss Hearings*, pp. 530–531.

61. *Hiss Hearings*, p. 593.

62. *Hiss Hearings*, p. 838.

63. *Hiss Hearings*, p. 1273.

64. *Hiss Hearings*, p. 1350.

65. *Subversive Influence in the Educational Process*, p. 714.

first learned that Halperin had been identified as a member of an espionage group when he read about it in the newspapers in 1948.[66]

Although Halperin was accused by Miss Bentley in 1948 and although she repeated her accusation in *Out of Bondage* published in 1951, Halperin seems not to have undergone public questioning by a congressional committee until 1953. He had transferred from OSS to the State Department where he headed the Latin-American Division in 1945 and 1946; and by the time he was called, he had become chairman of the regional studies program in Latin America at Boston University.[67] He refused to say whether he was a Communist on the ground that his answer would constitute testimony against himself. He also refused for the same reason to say whether he had been a member of an espionage group during the war, whether he had been a member of a Communist organization when he was with the OSS or the Department of State,[68] or whether he did any recruiting for the Communist Party among students or teachers at Boston University.[69] He was allowed to insert in the record a statement that argued that his political beliefs as a teacher were outside the power of the congressional committee to investigate, although it is hard to imagine that wartime espionage is one of the truths that the great teacher Socrates died to maintain.[70] Halperin was discharged from his position at Boston University for refusing to appear before a university committee to discuss his case, even though Dr. Harold C. Case, president of the university, had telephoned Halperin in Mexico City offering to pay his expenses to Boston and return.

Dr. Maurice Halperin was to figure in the news on a later occasion. A State Department memorandum in August 1960 said that Halperin and his wife had been on the point of being deported from Mexico in 1958 for Communist activities when they applied to the United States Embassy in Mexico City for passports which the State Department was required to supply, since they were American citizens, under a recent ruling of the Supreme Court that passports could not be denied to Communists or to others because of their political beliefs. The Halperins showed up in the Soviet Union in December 1958 where Maurice Halperin became associated with the Soviet Academy of Sciences. The State Department said that he was serving as an adviser to

66. *Subversive Influence in the Educational Process*, pp. 726–727.
67. From 1946 to 1949 Halperin was an observer and consultant to the Economic and Social Council of the United Nations, first for the American Jewish Conference and later the American Jewish Committee. *Subversive Influence in the Educational Process*, p. 665.
68. *Subversive Influence in the Educational Process*, p. 671.
69. *Subversive Influence in the Education Process*, pp. 672–673.
70. The statement appears *ibid.*, p. 675.

the Soviet Union on Latin-American affairs. Halperin said that he was only making a study of the Latin-American economy from 1945 to 1948, that he was writing a book, and that he was "not working for the Soviet Government any more than Van Cliburn was when he performed in a government-owned concert hall." The State Department replied that the information on which it had based its earlier statement had been supplied by Halperin himself.[71]

Other names of staff of the Department of State during the war years have already been mentioned in connection with espionage or membership in the Communist Party — Carl Marzani,[72] for example — but without multiplying examples, the evidence indicates that an unusual traffic in unauthorized information flourished. The Hiss case, as has been said, has tended to dominate an appreciation of the extent to which there may have been impermissible dissemination of privileged intelligence in the State Department. But there is an incident — "affair," rather — that, by itself, would suggest a favoring ambiance within which such a traffic in information and influence could, and did, prosper. This is the *Amerasia* case.

The Amerasia Case

The *Amerasia* case has been characterized as "one of the weirdest in the history of American criminal jurisprudence." [73] It has also been said, "The *Amerasia* affair was one of the gravest breaches of security in the wartime history of the United States." [74] Even in brief summary, the case is a stunning astonishment. An accidental discovery by the Security Officer of the Office of Strategic Services set in train events that led to the discovery of documents which had been supplied by indiscreet or disloyal employees to the editors of *Amerasia*, a magazine under the control of Communist supporters. The Director of Investigations of the OSS conducted raids that turned up hundreds of classified and unclassified documents which had found their way to the New York offices of *Amerasia* from the OSS, the Departments of State, War, and Navy, and other agencies concerned with measures affecting the security of the United States. General William Donovan, head of the OSS, turned the documents over to the care of Secretary of State

71. See *New York Times*, September 1, 1960, p. 1, col. 1 for the report on the State Department memorandum prepared in connection with legislation on passport controls; *ibid.*, September 5, 1960, p. 4, col. 3 for Halperin's answer, given to newsmen in Moscow; and *ibid.*, September 8, 1960, p. 20, col. 5 for the State Department's reply to Halperin.

72. See above, p. 94.

73. Ralph de Toledano, *Spies, Dupes, and Diplomats* (New York: Duell, Sloane and Pearce, 1952), pp. 134–135, citing a statement by Frederick Woltman.

74. Nathaniel Weyl, *The Battle Against Disloyalty* (New York: Thomas Y. Crowell, 1951), p. 219.

Edward Stettinius, who consulted with Secretary of the Navy James V. Forrestal. The whole matter was then turned over to the FBI, whose surveillance uncovered even more material. As a result of the investigations, six people were arrested, and their prosecution was handed on to the Department of Justice.[75] Of the six arrested, three were never indicted, two got off with light fines, and the indictment against the sixth was nol-prossed. One of those not indicted was John Stewart Service who, by his own admission, had supplied the editor of *Amerasia* with secret military information because the editor was interested in it. Service was cleared by the State Department Loyalty Board of charges of disloyalty, was eventually fired by Secretary of State Dean Acheson, and was reinstated after the Supreme Court held that his dismissal violated State Department procedures.[76]

On February 28, 1945, the security officer of the Office of Strategic Services, Archbold van Beuren, visited the New York office of the director of investigations for the OSS, Frank Brooks Bielaski,[77] and showed him a document prepared in the Research Division of the OSS by Kenneth E. Wells, a Far East analyst. The paper was a statement about and an analysis of conditions in Thailand that had been given a "secret" rating, although less for the content of this single piece than for the significance of the series of which it was a part. The author upon reading an article on British-American relations in Thailand in the January 26 issue of *Amerasia* had had a sudden sense of *déjà vu*. Upon checking the article against his secret report, he discovered that whole paragraphs from the secret document had been reprinted in the public article. Bielaski was given the job of finding the leak, a difficult

75. Perhaps a sign of the strain between the FBI and the Attorney General's office on the case — because of the failure of the Department of Justice to obtain indictments against all arrested — is to be seen in Whitehead, *The FBI Story*. In this paean to the FBI, one might expect some reference to one of the most sensational cases of our time, one in which the FBI had an important part. There is, however, no mention of the case at all, and no reference to any one of the six individuals arrested.

76. *Service* v. *Dulles*, 354 U.S. 363 (1957). Service, a career Foreign Service officer, had been cleared in six security or loyalty proceedings in the Department of State before being fired after the seventh. Congress had given the Secretary the absolute right to discharge anyone in the Department without hearing or other administrative procedure. Instead of relying upon this authority, Secretary Acheson had laid down certain rules within the Department for dealing with cases of security and loyalty. Since the Secretary had laid down such rules, the Court in a unanimous opinion (Clark did not participate) held that he was bound to follow them, which he failed to do.

77. Eighty-first Congress, Second Session, United States Senate, Subcommittee of the Committee on Foreign Relations, Hearings Pursuant to S. Res. 231, *A Resolution to Investigate Whether There Are Employees in the State Department Disloyal to the United States* (hereafter cited as the *Tydings Committee*), Testimony of Frank Brooks Bielaski, pp. 923–967, at p. 924. Mr. Bielaski died in April 1961. *New York Times*, April 6, 1961, p. 26, col. 1.

matter at best since the original memorandum had been distributed to some thirty or so places within the government.

Instead of looking for leads to the leak in some thirty or more government offices, Bielaski decided to go directly to the editorial offices of the magazine itself. On Sunday night, March 11, 1945, five agents and a lock expert from the Office of Naval Intelligence entered the premises. It was not necessary to force an entrance since they were admitted by the assistant superintendent of the building.[78] For a magazine with a circulation (at the time) of only about 1700, and a dealer distribution that had dropped from 550 to 320, approximately, the back room supported a substantial operation in photocopying and photostating. In the course of a search of the other rooms in the offices, Bielaski and his men found dozens of photocopies of government documents, some marked "Top Secret," one dealing with the disposition of units of the Japanese Navy after the battle of the Philippine Sea in the last three months of the previous year, and another concerning the American strategic bombing program for Japan. A prize was a bellows suitcase containing some four hundred or so documents, including four or five OSS documents that the OSS did not know were missing. Although the papers had originated in a dozen places in the government service, they all bore the stamp of the Department of State, showing that the documents had been received there.[79]

Bielaski took a dozen or so of the originals found in the *Amerasia* office to van Beuren, including four or five that had been prepared in the OSS. After a discussion with the Chief of Legal Counsel for the OSS, it was decided to carry the matter immediately to the head of the agency, General Donovan.[80] As indicated, General Donovan then met with Stettinius, and the OSS was out of the case entirely.[81] The search by Bielaski and his agents was in the nature of a preliminary

78. Bielaski was testifying in executive session before the Tydings subcommittee when he gave the account from which this narrative is drawn. When he reluctantly explained how he and the five others had effected entrance, he added, "I would not like to have that known because it might leave them open to some claim by the company." *Tydings Committee*, p. 929. Senator Tydings then said, "That will not go out." The proceedings of the executive session were made public almost immediately.

79. Among the documents were several dealing with Chinese affairs, including discussion of dissensions between Chiang Kai-shek and his generals, and, to quote Bielaski, "the intimate relations between Chiang Kai-shek and Madame Chiang, and that document I assure you was very intimate, and there were about three pages of it." *Tydings Committee*, p. 934.

80. Of the discussion with the Chief of Legal Counsel, Bielaski said, "Major Donigan, when he saw the material and realized the importance of it, nearly fainted — so much so that he couldn't talk." *Tydings Committee*, p. 935.

81. General Donovan advised Stettinius to arrest the staff of *Amerasia* immediately under John Doe warrants, but Stettinius did not follow the advice. *Tydings Committee*, p. 936.

reconnaissance, and the 400 documents in the bellows suitcase were presumably returned. All of the evidence subsequently collected was collected by the FBI.

What was the nature of this small journal which was eventually found to have unlawful possession of more government documents than it had subscribers? The journal was established in 1936 by Frederick Vanderbilt Field and Philip Jaffe, the first a rich young man who has already been mentioned in connection with Laurence Duggan, and the latter a manufacturer of greeting cards.[82] The establishment of the journal coincided with the development of Popular Front tactics in China, but one member of its first advisory board of editors, who was no partisan of the left, said of his enlistment in the venture,

> What Frederick Field and Mr. Jaffe and others connected with *Amerasia* proposed to do was to publish a monthly journal called *Amerasia*, America-Asia, running the two together, which would translate into popular language the learning regarding current affairs in Asia. To me that was a very attractive proposition. I think most of the editors, most of the scholars who agreed to become editors, felt that they were really doing a service to the American people, and doing a service to the schools, doing a service to public opinion, by serving on this *Amerasia*.[83]

At the time he thought that there was no special line in the editorials and features in the magazine in the years 1937, 1938, and 1939, and could detect none when he reviewed the early issues some fifteen years later. A change occurred around 1940, however, and the number of pieces, some printed over his protest, that followed Soviet policy increased. When an agreement with Jaffe that anti-British and anti-Dutch pieces would be balanced by material on the pro-British and pro-Dutch sides was not fulfilled, Professor Colegrove resigned from the board of editors in 1942.[84]

When the FBI entered the case on the evening of March 14, 145, the first thing it did was to establish the identity of the principals in and around the editorial office of *Amerasia*.[85] Philip Jaffe and Kate Mitchell were identified as editors, and it was determined that they were in frequent contact with Emmanuel Larsen of the Department

82. Weyl, *The Battle Against Disloyalty,* p. 221.
83. The witness was Professor Kenneth Colegrove of the Political Science Department of NorthwesternUniversity. *IPR Hearings,* p. 907.
84. He was persuaded to return but resigned a year later for good. *IPR Hearings,* p. 909.
85. An account of the work of the FBI is available in the testimony before the Tydings committee of D. Milton Ladd, Assistant to the Director, and L. B. Nichols, Assistant Director of the FBI. *Tydings Committee,* pp. 1054–1074.

of State, Mark Gayn, a writer for *Collier's,* and with Lieutenant Andrew Roth of the Office of Naval Intelligence.[86] Lieutenant Roth was liaison between the ONI and the Department of State. Within approximately a month, the FBI met with General Julius Holmes, Assistant Secretary of State, and with Mathias Correa, Assistant Secretary of the Navy, and said that it was ready to turn evidence over to the Department of Justice for prosecution. The investigation was continued at the request of the two departments, however, presumably to find out whether other staff in State and Navy were in the unlawful traffic in government secrets, and whether Jaffe was actually obtaining the material for the use of a foreign power.[87] This, at least, was the presumed reason for extending an investigation in a matter in which the FBI had said it was ready to act.

But there were other considerations that led top officials in Navy and Justice and State to slow down and extend and diminish the full and quick prosecution of the case. Secretary of the Navy James V. Forrestal said in his diary for May 28, 1945:

> Major Correa reported to me that the Department of Justice has evidence to the effect that Lieutenant Andrew Roth has been furnishing confidential and secret documents to a man named Jaffe, head of a publication named *Amerasia* in New York City. Jaffe has had intimate relationship with the Russian consul in New York. . . . Major Correa reported that it was proposed that Lieutenant Roth should be taken into surveillance Wednesday. He said that the FBI thought that unless speedy action were taken important evidence would be dissipated, lost and destroyed. I pointed out that the inevitable consequence of such action now would be to greatly embarrass the President in his current conversations with Stalin, because of the anti-Russian play-up the incident would receive out of proportion to its importance.[88]

This caution may also have been inspired by the fact that the San Francisco conference to organize the United Nations was taking place. The most that Forrestal was prepared to do at the moment was to ask Captain James K. Vardaman, Jr., Naval Aide to the President, "to see to it that the President was informed in this matter and I [Forrestal] then called Mr. Edgar Hoover and suggested that he advise Mr. Tom Clark and have him also see that the President is in full information of all the facts in the matter as well as their implications." [89]

86. *Tydings Committee,* p. 1056.
87. *Tydings Committee,* p. 1057.
88. Walter Mills (ed.), *The Forrestal Diaries* (New York: Viking, 1951), p. 65.
89. Mills, *The Forrestal Diaries,* pp. 65–66.

The then Assistant Secretary of State Julius C. Holmes later testified that he was under the impression that Captain Vardaman had
called the Department of Justice from the White House to delay proceedings in the *Amerasia* case[90] but Vardaman said that not only did
he not make such a call, he had never had anything to do with the
Amerasia case and had not even known about it.[91] James M. McInerney,
later Assistant Attorney General in charge of the Criminal Division
of the Department of Justice, eventually found a note he had written
about the *Amerasia* case on May 29, 1945. The note said, "Matter may
be held up by Navy. Mr. Forrestal called Mr. Clark." [92] Mr. Clark,
at that time, was the Assistant Attorney General in charge of the
Criminal Division.

On May 29, 1945, the FBI men met with McInerney to lay before
him the case that they had made against Jaffe, Mitchell, Larsen, Gayn,
Service, and Roth. The FBI had three kinds of information, two of
which it was not possible to introduce in court, and the third, in the
opinion of McInerney, could not have supported a warrant. Of the
inadmissible information there was a recording of a conversation between Philip Jaffe and John Stewart Service which had been obtained
by planting a microphone in Jaffe's hotel room in Washington. The
conversation concerned political and military planning and policy matters[93] in which one of the principal questions was the nature of the
intention of the United States Army to cooperate with local forces
if a landing should be made on the mainland of China.[94] This recording was inadmissible in any trial; and even five years later the FBI
would only provide notes on it to the Loyalty Security Board of the

90. *Tydings Committee*, pp. 1169–1170. Holmes was not able very clearly to recount events in the *Amerasia* case after a lapse of five years, and testimony about
Vardaman was tentative and qualified. But he did say, "The impression that I
have in my mind, of that time, was that the person who had telephoned from
the White House to the Department of Justice was the President's naval aide."
Ibid., p. 1170.

91. *Tydings Committee*, p. 1183.

92. *Tydings Committee*, p. 1057.

93. Service was interrogated about this conversation with Jaffe in proceedings
before the Loyalty Security Board of the Department of State which began on
May 26, 1950. The board did not have an exact transcript of the recording but
told Service in paraphrase and in bits and pieces what the conversation was about,
asking him then to respond to questions as to whether he remembered saying
thus, and whether he recalled so. His recollection was not very clear. For a full
transcript of the Loyalty Security Board proceedings, see *Tydings Committee*,
pp. 1958–2509.

94. One of the issues was whether the United States was committed to cooperate only with the Nationalist forces. Service was of the opinion that the
United States had no such commitment and would cooperate with Communist
troops if they were "the dominant force" at the point of landing. *Tydings Committee*, p. 2458.

State Department when it wanted information about the conversations between Jaffe and Service.[95]

The second body of ineligible material was the fruit of unlawful entry that FBI agents had made in the apartment of Emmanual Larsen on April 6, 1945,[96] the offices of *Amerasia*, and the apartment of Mark Gayn.[97] The Assistant Director of the FBI, L. B. Nichols, later said in extenuation:

> Our chief and immediate concern at the moment was who was getting this information and how to bring a stop to it. Our internal-security function was one of prevention as well as apprehension and prosecution. We put first things first, and we did enter the premises of *Amerasia*, the Mark Gayn apartment, and the Larsen apartment where we observed classified documents emanating from the government.[98]

In addition to the search for classified documents, the agents of the FBI also took a sample of typewriting from a typewriter found in the Larsen apartment. Since these were unlawful searches also, information gained from them would be inadmissible in Federal courts, and arrests made on the basis of such information would be nullified by the first court into which the defendants might be brought. The surreptitious entries were made for the purpose of determining whether a more direct confrontation would avail, and were intended to provide leads for the accumulation of other information on which the prosecution could proceed.

The other material on which the prosecution might proceed consisted of reports of surveillance of the principals in the case, containing information about whom they had seen, what they had carried to meetings, and the length of time spent in each other's company. At best this behavior might support a suspicion, but it could not have established the probable cause that would have justified arrests. And McInerney said, at the meeting with the FBI agents on May 29, 1945,

95. Counsel for Service in the loyalty security proceedings pressed the board for a statement about the source of the board's information. The chairman of the board replied, "I'll say for the record that the board has only the reports of the FBI on which to rely. We do not have the exact texts of these supposed statements. The source, as far as the board is free to reveal, is a confidential source from the FBI. We have nothing further. It is a source which is unavailable for appearance before the board. According to the public press in yesterday's hearing, the actual source of these statements is a recording. As to the facts, the board is unable to make a statement." *Tydings Committee*, p. 2466. The recordings seem to have covered conversations on May 29 also.

96. *Tydings Committee*, p. 1059.

97. *Tydings Committee*, p. 1065

98. *Tydings Committee*, p. 1065.

that he did not think that the FBI had given him enough to work up a prosecution. As he put it,

> I discussed the legal evidence available by that time, and to my mind, it was not sufficient to seek a warrant, because the main evidence, legal evidence at hand at that time was physical surveillances of these individuals . . . but since our experience has always been that we can make a case on an apprehension and search, I authorized the prosecution on May 29.[99]

The procedure, in short, was to develop the evidence that would legally justify the arrests, at the time the arrests were made. Although McInerney had presumably decided to go ahead with prosecution on May 29, 1945, Milton Ladd, Assistant Director of the FBI, said that the FBI was told by McInerney on May 31 that the matter would be held in abeyance.[100] Mr. McInerney's note of May 29, that the matter might be delayed, proved to be prophetic.

Presumably the administration was being saved from embarrassment in dealing with the Russians by officials who had taken it upon themselves to decide what would embarrass the administration. It seems that the last to know how embarrassing it would be to President Harry Truman was President Harry Truman. When officials of the State Department were told on June 2, 1945, that the prosecution was going to be held up, they took steps to get it started. Assistant Secretary of State Julius Holmes went to Acting Secretary of State Joseph Grew and told him the situation. Grew thought that both ought to go to the White House, arranged an appointment with President Truman immediately, and both Grew and Holmes met with the President in his study late in the afternoon of June 2. At Grew's request, Holmes told the President about the state of the matter. The President immediately telephoned the FBI agent who had been in charge of the case (and who had also been told that it would be held up) and directed him to proceed, warning him that if anybody told him to delay, he should not do so without first getting Truman's personal approval.[101]

The FBI immediately advised the Criminal Division of the Department of Justice of the telephone call from President Truman, complaints were prepared against the six defendants, and the FBI was instructed to make the arrests at a time when a search incident to the arrest could also be made.[102] The arrests were synchronized so that

99. *Tydings Committee*, p. 972.
100. *Tydings Committee*, p. 1057.
101. At the end of the conversation, President Truman, according to the account of Julius Holmes, ". . . grinned and said, 'Does that suit you?' And I said, 'Yes, sir.'" *Tydings Committee*, p. 1169.
102. One can only imagine the chagrin and irritation that must have prevailed

they could all be made at about the same time, and the defendants were rounded up on the late afternoon and in the evening of June 6, 1945. The agents found a total of some eight hundred or so documents: about six hundred in Jaffe's office; probably two hundred or three hundred in Larsen's apartment; and about forty-two in Gayn's home.[103] No documents were found on Miss Mitchell, except those in the office of *Amerasia*, which she shared with Jaffe. The FBI agents found no documents on Roth or Service. The documents came from the State Department, Navy Department, Office of Strategic Services, Office of War Information, Federal Communications Commission, Foreign Economic Administration, and the War Department.

The day after the arrests, Robert M. Hitchcock was assigned by McInerney to prepare the prosecution.[104] The warrants for arrest charged conspiracy to violate the Espionage Act. The evidence that the prosecution had was the material picked up at the time of the arrests, the frequent association of the arrested six, and the testimony of Annette Blumenthal, an employee of the Institute of Pacific Relations which had offices in the same building as those of *Amerasia*.[105] She had made typewritten copies of government documents for Jaffe and was able to identify some of them as confidential.[106] It would have been difficult to establish espionage on this basis, since there was no evidence that any of the material had been passed on to the Russians, and such an intent could hardly have been inferred from the facts available. Moreover, there was a basic and besetting weakness in the position of the prosecution in that there had been surreptitious entries to the apartment of Emmanuel Larsen and the offices of *Amerasia* before the arrests. As Hitchcock stated the difficulty,

Nothing is clearer under Federal law than that evidence secured as a result of illegal searches will be suppressed upon the application of

---

among officials of the Department of Justice when President Truman ignored lines of command and other protocol revered by students of public administration to convey notice of his policy in an important matter to them through subordinates in one of the divisions of the agency. Since he had been in office less than two months, perhaps he did not know how mortal is the offense of being bypassed, or perhaps he did not care. There is no mention of the *Amerasia* affair in his *Memoirs by Harry Truman*, vol. I: *Year of Decisions* (New York: Doubleday, 1955).

103. This is McInerney's estimate. *Tydings Committee*, p. 972.

104. Testimony of Robert M. Hitchcock, *Tydings Committee*, pp. 1001–1051, at p. 1003.

105. For the testimony of Annette Blumenthal in the Loyalty Security Board proceeding of the State Department against John Stewart Service in 1950, see *Tydings Committee*, pp. 2102–2109.

106. Under questioning by Senator Millard Tydings of Maryland, Hitchcock summed it up by saying, "I had no evidence then but the report of the seizures, and these associations and the Blumenthal testimony. That is what we had." *Tydings Committee*, p. 1023.

those whose constitutional right to the privacy of their homes, their persons and their effects has been violated. . . . Moreover, evidence obtained as a result of leads secured in this manner will be suppressed. That was our situation with respect to the searches made prior to June 6 in Larsen's home and the *Amerasia* offices.[107]

We hoped that no defendant would learn of these activities.[108]

But one of the defendants, Emmanuel Larsen, while in the custody of one agent, had overheard other agents in his apartment at the time of his arrest telling each other where to look for papers, which made it perfectly clear that the apartment had been entered before.[109] After being let out on bail, he managed to trap the superintendent of his building into admitting that the FBI had been to his apartment "two or three" times before the actual arrest, and his attorney later made use of the news.

There were other weaknesses in the position of the prosecution. The complaints on which the arrests and searches were made were probably faulty in that the affidavits by Justice on which they were based failed to establish probable cause that the offense complained of had in fact been committed. With only the fact of frequent association among the defendants to go on (because the arrest and seizure of material at the place of arrest had not yet occurred), and the exchange of papers that had been observed in some of these encounters, the act seen were consistent with innocent transactions.[110] Moreover the surveillance by the FBI between March 12 when it started (seventy-five men were assigned to the case) and June 6, the date of the arrests, failed to disclose the taking of any paper by any one in an agency, or the transfer of papers from *Amerasia* to anyone else.

The attitude toward the case of James M. McInerney, Assistant Attorney General in charge of the Criminal Division, was somewhat less than eager. It was he whose notice to the FBI on May 31 that the case was to be held up had been reversed on June 2 by President Truman's

107. *Tydings Committee*, p. 1020.

108. Hitchcock added, "This is said with no criticism whatever of the FBI intended. Between March and June of 1945, this Nation was at war, and it seems to me that no reasonable person could have anything but praise for the FBI for utilizing this method to secure proof in a case where there was any basis for believing that the national security was involved. *Tydings Committee*, pp. 1020–1021.

109. McInerney describes the arrest at *Tydings Committee*, pp. 975–976.

110. *Tydings Committee*, p. 979. McInerney testified that in fact Roth and Jaffe were writing books, and some of the encounters could have been held for the purpose of exchanging chapters. This is what was claimed by the defendants, and the prosecution was unable to combat the assertion.

direction to the FBI that the case was to go forward.[111] It was Mc-Inerney's opinion that the case had little substance anyway. He said that he had seen all the documents and he "would say that with respect to all of these documents, that they were of innocuous, very innocuous character." He thought that only about one per cent of them had anything to do with national defense and most were only "a little above the level of teacup gossip in the Far East." [112] And how explain the presence of hundreds of documents in the *Amerasia* office and the apartments of Mark Gayn and Emmanuel? Happens all the time.

Although arrested, the defendants had not been indicted. After the presentation of the government's case to the grand jury, it voted no-bills for Mark Gayn, John Stewart Service, and Miss Mitchell, since somehow the charge was now unlawful possession of government documents and not espionage, since Gayn's offense was minor, and since neither Service nor Mitchell had had such documents at the time of arrest. Indictments were voted against Roth, Larsen, and Jaffe.[113] The grand jury actions were taken on August 10, 1945, and immediately Jaffe proposed that a deal be made with the Department of Justice or, more politely, he "began to make overtures about entering a plea on terms." [114] The overtures were still playing when the production suddenly switched from *passacaglia* to *galop*, which is a lively dance "performed with sliding steps from side to side."

On September 28, the Department of Justice learned that Larsen's lawyer had filed a motion to quash the indictment against his client on the ground that previous entry had been made surreptitiously, that it was this unlawful action that had led the prosecution to make the arrest, and that the papers seized at the time of the arrest were therefore unlawfully seized, and all of the evidence so gained should be suppressed. If Jaffe should hear about Larsen's motion to quash, he would also submit such a motion since his circumstances were like those of Larsen, and the Department of Justice would have no case against anybody. The department's first thought was to return all Larsen's papers to him or leave them out of the case, and proceed against him on the basis of the documents found in Jaffe's place, since Larsen could not complain of an illegal search of Jaffe's office. But even then, if

111. McInerney was Chief of the Internal Security Section of the Criminal Division at the time of the *Amerasia* case. He became Assistant Attorney General in charge of the Criminal Division in January 1950.

112. *Tydings Committee*, p. 974.

113. The grand jury voted 20–0 to no-bill Service; 18–2 for Mitchell; and 15–5 for Gayn. It voted to indict Jaffe by 14–6; Larsen by 14–6; and Roth by 13–7. Twelve votes were required for an indictment. *Tydings Committee*, p. 974.

114. *Tydings Committee*, p. 975.

Jaffe filed a motion to quash, there would still be no case against any-body.

On the same day that Larsen's motion to quash was served on the Criminal Division of the Department of Justice, McInerney telephoned Albert Arent, Jaffe's lawyer, and asked him whether he cared to discuss a plea by Jaffe. The news that the department had been served with the motion was received early in the afternoon, and the call to Arent was made immediately. The Justice men were still talking about their situation when Arent came into the outer office. McInerney then called the clerk of the district court where the motion had been filed, and asked him to keep the news out of the public domain for a few hours so that Jaffe's attorney could not see it. The clerk of the district court said that the news was already in the hands of some news-paper men, although it had not been printed. It was inevitable that when Arent left the meeting with the Justice people and walked out of the office, the papers would be on the streets and he would learn that Larsen had filed the motion to quash.

The Department of Justice then told Arent that it was prepared to discuss Jaffe's plea. In exchange for a plea of guilty, the department would recommend not imprisonment but a substantial fine. It evidently looked like a good deal to Jaffe's lawyer because he accepted after a discussion that lasted four hours. When McInerney was asked later by Senator Lodge why he thought Jaffe's lawyer had consented to the deal, his reply was, "I think now that Jaffe may have been an espionage agent, which information we did not have at that time. We knew him only as the publisher of a magazine." [115] It is perhaps mildly curious that this thought did not occur in 1945 at the time of the case since the FBI surveillance of Jaffe had turned up three or four visits by Jaffe to the home of Earl Browder, and at least one visit to Communist Party headquarters.[116] As Forrestal's memoirs indicated, Jaffe had also been to the Soviet consulate. None of this is enough to demonstrate espionage, of course, but the coloration of the visits is not exactly the same as it might have been if Jaffe had visited Alf Landon three or four times, and spent a few hours at Republican party headquarters.

Arrangements were made to have Jaffe enter the plea of guilty the next morning (even though it was Saturday, McInerney found a judge who would sit). When Arent met McInerney and Hitchcock the next morning in court, Arent, according to Hitchcock, "looked at us and said, 'You sons-of-bitches.' " [117] Despite this derogatory opinion of the

115. *Tydings Committee*, p. 985
116. *Tydings Committee*, pp. 985–986.
117. *Tydings Committee*, p. 1023.

prosecution, Arent nevertheless pleaded his client guilty and the "substantial" fine was set at $2,500. After prolonged negotiation between the Justice officials and Larsen's lawyers, it was decided that Larsen would plead *nolo contendere,* and suffer a small fine, which was set at $500. The "theory" of the prosecution was that Jaffe was the principal, Jaffe had corrupted Larsen, and Larsen should not receive as much "punishment" as Jaffe. Larsen had already lost his job in the State Department. When the fine was fixed, Jaffe paid for Larsen's as well as his own. The proceedings before the judge were very accommodating. The prosecution did not bring in the list of government documents that were stolen nor did it disclose the nature of their contents.[118] Perhaps there was no point when a principal official in the case thought they were "innocuous" and only "teacup gossip in the Far East." It would appear that the Legal Counsel of the OSS who had "nearly fainted" when he saw what Bielaski had brought to him from Jaffe's office had been unduly susceptible. The judge did not know Jaffe's background; the grand jury was not aware of the Communist connections of any of the principal characters. Hitchcock told the court in connection with the proceedings against Larsen, "As I said, Your Honor, in the Jaffe case, there was no disloyalty involved. No element of disloyalty was involved." [119] No espionage, no disloyalty, no element of Communism — just hundreds of — indeed, two or three thousand — documents funneled through the State Department into the offices of *Amerasia,* classified secret and top-secret, for the purpose, presumably, of getting some additional prestige and circulation for a small magazine.

As to Lieutenant Andrew Roth of the United States Navy, he was discharged from the service on June 5, the day before the arrests, and the Navy was thus spared the ignominy of a possible court martial. The indictment against Roth was nol-prossed by the Department of Justice on February 15, 1946 because the Justice lawyers thought that there was no case against Roth. Four or five copies of State Department documents in Roth's handwriting were found in Jaffe's office, and one that had been written on Roth's typewriter, but this was not felt to be enough to convict him.[120] Something might have been made of this evidence if the prosecution had been for conspiracy to commit espionage, but this charge was dropped between the arrests and the indictment of the defendants.

The *Amerasia* case is like the Hiss affair in one respect. Although it

118. *Tydings Committee,* p. 1027.
119. *Tydings Committee,* p. 1029.
120. *Tydings Committee,* pp. 1011–1012.

seemed to be virtually impossible to establish espionage by courtroom standards, there is the silent testimony of the documents themselves. There was either espionage in the *Amerasia* case or the security procedures of the Department of State were so grotesquely lax that the responsible officials should have been disciplined.

Part Three   The Inquest on China

Oligarchies . . . are overthrown when another oligarchy is created within the original one

ARISTOTLE, *Politics*

> *... what a glorious prize is victory!*
> *Therefore be bold; we will be just hereafter.*
>
> *Philoctetes*

VIII   The Red Poppy

On September 22, 1949, after almost a quarter of a century of striving, the Chinese Communist Party assumed powers of government over a half billion people with the establishment of the "Chinese People's Political Consultative Conference." The opening of the conference was attended by Mme. Sun Yat-sen and by several of the former Army commanders of Generalissimo Chiang Kai-shek. On October 2, the Soviet Union recognized the new Chinese People's (Communist) Republic, and severed diplomatic relations with the Nationalist government. The mop-up by the Chinese Red armies went forward, while British troops manned the Hong Kong frontier to take care of refugees. On November 20, 20,000 Chinese Communist troops crossed the Yangtze River and occupied Chungking, the Nationalist capital. On December 7, eight years after Pearl Harbor, the Nationalist government fled the mainland for Formosa where Chiang Kai-shek continued the regime and prepared, with the help of the United States, to organize his forces for the defense of Formosa and possible return to the mainland some day.[1]

There was more than the distance of time between Chiang Kai-shek's acceptance of the post of Supreme Commander of the China Theater[2]

1. The reference to Chiang Kai-shek in as reputable a work as Chambers's *Biographical Dictionary* (New York: St Martin's, 1962) betrays the intensity of feeling aroused by questions of China policy. There it is said that Chiang moved to Formosa "to breathe threats against the mainland which caused more consternation among western politicians than among his enemies" (p. 270).

As early as October and November 1948, the United States Ambassador to China, Dr. John Leighton Stuart, and ranking United States military officers in China were convinced that short of the actual employment of United States troops no amount of military assistance could have saved the Nationalist regime. Franz H. Michael and George E. Taylor, *The Far East in the Modern World* (New York: Holt, 1956), p. 667.

2. For the text of the acceptance, see Department of State, *Foreign Relations of the United States, China, 1942* (Washington: Government Printing Office, 1956), pp. 1-2 (hereafter cited as *China Papers*).

at the invitation of President Roosevelt[3] and his denunciation by Secretary of State Dean Acheson in a White Paper in August 1949.[4] There was also the subjective separation of estrangement, for Chiang had ceased to be regarded as a symbol of China, an American ally in the service of democratic ideals against tyranny, and was now perceived as the head of a reactionary party (the Kuomintang), unable to put into effect a land reform program, intractable in consultation with American authorities about what was good for him, helpless to correct corruption in his own regime. The White Paper was an ex parte argument for the failure of American policy in China, and served as an obituary in August 1949 for the collapse of the patient a month later, and his political demise in December. The *New York Times* said, "This White Paper, an attempt at vindication, is actually a sorry record of well-meaning mistakes." [5]

Not everybody thought that the mistakes were well-meaning, however. The "poppies of Cathay" of Whittier's imagination had been harvest to the sickle of communism, and where the knives had swept, so must there have been hands to move them. Whose hands? Where? The China White Paper pointed out that in the four years after V-J Day, the United States had provided the Nationalist regime with more than two billion dollars in grants and credits, that over a billion dollars of nonmilitary property had been sold to the government for less than a quarter of its value, that 50 per cent of the Nationalist military establishment had been equipped with American materials, that in three months at the end of 1948 Chiang had lost seventeen divisions equipped by the Americans, and that something like 60 per cent of all American military supplies had been captured intact by the Communists. It was odious that we had put up so much money for one regime and had fostered another instead.[6] Secretary of State Dean Acheson was closing

3. President Roosevelt's message of December 29, 1941 to Chiang can be found in *China Papers,* 1941, p. 763.

4. The so-called China White Paper is *United States Relations with China: With Special Reference to the Period 1944–1949* (Washington: Government Printing Office, 1949).

5. *New York Times,* August 6, 1949, p. 16, col. 1. It was said further, "Many of them [the mistakes] are now set down here and those who will can learn their details. If that helps informed critical opinion to aid in preventing some similar mistakes in the future, the White Paper will have served a more important purpose than saving the Administration's face. It can point the way toward a future policy . . ."

6. This was, of course, the first and most spectacular of a succession of failures of this kind. Money and military aid failed to keep Synghman Rhee in power in South Korea, Bao Dai in Vietnam, Prince Boun Oum in Laos, or Fulgencio Batista in Cuba. The difficulty in China was well summed up by former Ambassador Leighton Stuart when he said that the struggle was a clash between two political ideologies for leadership in the Chinese nation, that the activists on both sides were a small part only of the huge, amorphous population, and that a decisive

the account books on a defaulting debtor, no longer eligible for an extension of credit.

But some thought that the accounts should not have been closed. Lieutenant-General Albert C. Wedemeyer, the successor to General Joseph W. Stilwell as commander of American forces in the China theater, made a trip to China in 1947 to report on affairs, and came home convinced that there was indeed corruption in the Chiang regime, that disintegration of the Nationalist forces was proceeding at an alarming rate, and that Chiang did not seem at the moment capable of coping either with the dissolution of his military force or the reasonable expectations of the peasantry for land and other reforms.[7] Nevertheless, he thought that the trend was not irreversible, and proposed that the United States continue aid to the Nationalists on condition that they refer the civil war to the United Nations, ask the United Nations to put Manchuria under five-power guardianship or trusteeship, inaugurate a program of economic and fiscal reconstruction, enact political and military reforms, and accept certain American controls in the administration of aid.[8] This was the last gesture against catastrophe. The State Department did not publish the report.[9]

Why did not the Department of State publish the Wedemeyer Report of 1947? It was presumably not in accord with department policy which was less fraternal towards the Chiang regime than it had been during the war years. The change in United States policy seems to have taken place in the four critical years from 1943 to 1947, and the execution of this change was the work of both events and men. General Wedemeyer, American commander in the China theater from the fall of 1944 to the fall of 1946, and chief of staff to Generalissimo

---

result in our favor would have required a degree of American intervention that neither the American nor the Chinese people desired. John Leighton Stuart, *Fifty Years in China* (New York: Random House, 1954). See also Robert H. Ferrell, *American Diplomacy* (New York: Norton, 1959), p. 470.

7. See Albert C. Wedemeyer, *Wedemeyer Reports!* (New York: Holt, 1958), p. 391. Although he recognized the existence of incompetence, corruption, and economic deterioration in the political and military organizations of the Nationalist government, the emphasis in Wedemeyer's report was on the need to consider these defects in perspective. In particular, involvement with war for almost a decade left little time for internal improvement. *Ibid.*, p. 393.

8. Wedemeyer, *Wedemeyer Reports!* Appendix VI, p. 461, for the detail of the Wedemeyer report. The specific recommendations on policy towards China appear at p. 478.

9. In the course of several visits from Mr. Walton Butterworth, then Chief of the Far Eastern Division of the Department of State, Wedemeyer said that the subject of his report was mentioned only once, and then he was urged to delete certain portions of it. It was suggested to him that the Secretary of State Dean Acheson "might be angry" if Wedemeyer did not accede to his wishes. The Wedemeyer report ultimately appeared, buried in the 600 pages of unindexed annexes of the China White Paper.

Chiang Kai-shek in those two years, had, in that time, four political advisers from the Department of State: John S. Service, John Paton Davies, Raymond Ludden, and John Emmerson,[10] all Foreign Service professionals.[11] In an interview with David Lawrence, printed in 1951, General Wedemeyer expressed the opinion that Communist influence in the departments of the government, including the Department of State, had something to do with the making of China policy, although he was in no way specific,[12] and he had found no disloyalty among the State Department professionals attached to his command. However, he did mention what he described as their "sympathy for the Chinese Communists." [13]

Important to an understanding of the policy of the United States government towards China during the war is the part played by various official actors and by private groups with access to the State Department and to its officials. But it is also important to appreciate the harsh nature of the strife between Chiang and the Chinese Communist Party and the irrelevance of formulations about it that rest upon western concepts of party competition. The curve of tendency in China, upon which the United States rode only a very small arc, began its rise almost three decades before the political and military defeat of Chiang in 1949.

The Struggle for Power

Chiang Kai-shek, in a summing-up of his life at seventy, said that there were three phases in the development of relations between Soviet communism and China, although four would fit the history more accurately.[14] The first period, from 1924 to 1927, was the period of

10. Eighty-second Congress, First Session, United States Senate, Committee on the Judiciary, Subcommittee to Investigate the Administration of the Internal Security Act and Other Internal Security Laws, *Hearings on the Institute of Pacific Relations,* August 2, 1951, p. 776 (hereafter cited as *IPR Hearings*).

11. The general outlook of this group may not improperly be inferred from a few excerpts in a memorandum by John S. Service to General Stilwell, General Wedemeyer's predecessor, "Our dealings with Chiang Kai-shek apparently continue on the basis of the unrealistic assumption that he is China and that he is necessary to our cause. It is time, for the sake of the war and also for our future interests in China, that we take a more realistic line. . . . We need not fear the collapse of the Kuomintang government. . . . Any new government under any other than the present reactionary control will be more cooperative and better able to mobilize the country. . . . We need not support Chiang in the belief that he represents pro-American or democratic China." The full text of the Service report to General Stilwell is printed in *IPR Hearings,* pp. 785–787.

12. "How Policy Was Influenced," *United States News and World Report,* September 14, 1951.

13. See below, chap. ix, n. 13.

14. Chiang Chung-Cheng (Chiang Kai-shek), *Soviet Russia in China* (New York: Farrar, Straus and Cudahy, 1957), Part One.

close collaboration between the Chinese Communist Party and the Kuomintang, or National People's Party.

In June 1920, eight years after the revolution led by Sun Yat-sen, Gregori Voitinsky, chief of the Eastern Division of the Communist International, arrived in Shanghai to arrange for the formation of a Chinese Communist Party.[15] In July 1921 Mao Tse-tung and eleven others founded the Chinese Communist Party in Shanghai at about the same time a Chinese Communist group was being organized in France, which included Chou En-lai and Li Li-san. Despite Lenin's theses on the colonial question,[16] a majority of this first meeting were unwilling to support Sun Yat-sen and the Kuomintang, but they were to be induced to do so by Soviet suggestions. On January 26, 1923, Sun Yat-sen issued a joint statement with Adolf Joffe, representing the Soviet Commissariat for Foreign Affairs, in which an accord was arranged between the Russian Communist Party and the Kuomintang, the Soviets promising to support the efforts of Sun to unify China.[17] Michael Borodin arrived in China as adviser to Sun Yat-sen from the Third International in 1923 and the first period really began.

In May of 1923 the Executive Committee of the Communist International sent instructions to the Third Congress of the Chinese Communist Party, making it clear that the revolution for which the party must work was a bourgeois-democratic revolution in which the peasant question was to be uppermost.[18] That is to say, the party was

15. Jane Degras (ed.), *The Communist International, 1919–1943, Documents,* vol. I: *1919–1923* (London: Oxford, 1960), p. 5.

16. Lenin was principally responsible for the theses and statutes of the Third International, adopted by the Second World Congress in Moscow, July 17 to August 7, 1919. Among the theses on national and colonial questions was the dictum: "The Communist International must establish temporary relations and even unions with the revolutionary movements in the colonies and backward countries, without, however, amalgamating with them, but preserving the independent character of the proletarian movement, even though it be still in its embryonic state." Eighty-fourth Congress, Second Session, House of Representatives, Committee on Un-American Activities, House Report No. 2242, *The Communist Conspiracy,* Part I, Section C: *The World Congresses of the Communist International,* pp. 69–70.

17. It is to be noted that Sun Yat-sen was not committing himself to the Soviet way or view of affairs. The joint statement said in part, "Dr. Sun Yat-sen holds that the communistic order, or even the Soviet system, cannot actually be introduced into China because there do not exist the conditions for the successful establishment of either communism or sovietism." For the complete paragraph, see Helmut G. Callis, *China: Confucian and Communist* (New York: Holt, 1959), p. 244.

18. *The Communist International, 1919–1943, Documents,* p. 25. The Second Party Congress of the Chinese Communist Party in June and July 1922 had "decided definitely that the Chinese Communist Party belonged to the world Communist movement, and final steps were taken for joining the Communist International." Robert C. North, *Moscow and Chinese Communists* (Stanford, California: Stanford, 1953), p. 63.

to promote agrarian agitation, and endeavor to effect a union of peasant and worker forces through membership in the Kuomintang. In accordance with the decision of the International, the Third Congress of the Chinese Communist Party voted to enter the Kuomintang,[19] stated that "We enter the Kuomintang but preserve still our own organization," [20] and adopted a series of resolutions on policy and program, the first of a number of such blueprints for the achievement of a Chinese Communist state.[21]

Although there was close collaboration between the Kuomintang and the Chinese Communists between 1924 and 1927, the strains that split them apart appeared at the outset, and moved irreversibly towards the break. Within six months after the election of the First Central Executive Committee in January 1925, according to North, proposals to impeach the Communist Party were brought by right-wing dissidents in the Kuomintang, charging that the Communist members of the party were acting as a caucus under the direction of the Central Committee of the Chinese Communist Party.[22] Chiang Kai-shek puts the first protests against the operations of the party-within-a-party a year earlier, with the impeachment of dual-party members for disruption brought by the Canton City Headquarters of the Kuomintang.[23] It does not seem that the Chinese Communists at first sought to

19. The China White Paper of 1949 brushed over this decision with the statement that the Communists decided to enter the Kuomintang "and create a 'united front' against the northern militarists." *United States Relations with China*, p. 42. This statement fails to give adequate weight to the tactical aspects of the decision.

20. C. Martin Wilbur and Julie Lien-ying How (eds.), *Documents on Communism, Nationalism, and Soviet Advisers in China, 1918–1927* (New York: Columbia, 1956), p. 85. The documents in this collection are translations of papers seized by Kuomintang forces in a raid on the Soviet embassy in Peking, April 1927.

21. Among the documents seized in the 1927 Peking raid was *A Brief History of the Chinese Communist Party*, written in Russian by an unidentified author, believed by one expert to have had the use of a first draft in Chinese written by Li Ta-chao, one of the founders of the Chinese Communist Party and the first to join the Kuomintang with the understanding that he would "retain his Bolshevik allegiance." North, *Moscow and Chinese Communists*, pp. 70–71. For an account of the origins of the "Brief History," see Wilbur and How, *Documents on Communism, Nationalism, and Soviet Advisers in China, 1918–1927*, p. 38. The resolutions of the Third Congress in June 1923 are set out in the "Brief History" at Wilbur and How, pp. 66–69.

It has been pointed out that the relation between Borodin and the Chinese on the one hand and Moscow on the other was ambiguous, both the Kuomintang and the Soviets claiming that he was a mere private citizen without official credentials. North, *Moscow and Chinese Communists*, p. 73. Documents found in the Peking raid suggest, however, that he was, indeed, sent to China by the Soviets, but that the connection with Moscow was to be denied, for tactical reasons.

22. North, *Moscow and Chinese Communists*, pp. 82–83.

23. Chiang Kai-shek, *Soviet Russia in China*, p. 33.

control the Kuomintang as a whole but they did work to manipulate it, first by infiltration and then by division, categorizing the members of the Kuomintang as leftists, centrists, and rightists,[24] and making common cause with the first two. At a meeting of the Fifth World Congress of the Communist International in July 1924, a Chinese delegate said that by joining the KMT (Kuomintang), the Communists hoped to correct its false attitude and to get the leadership into their hands.[25]

The fissures within the Kuomintang which appeared in 1924 were deepened and widened by the death of Lenin in 1924, and by the death of Sun Yat-sen in 1925, removing in each case the dominant figures in the Russian and the Chinese revolutions, and creating a shortage of commanding influence which factional rivals then maneuvered to fill. For a while the most influential leader of the Chinese seems to have been the Russian, Michael Borodin,[26] although his influence was largely operative through others.

Chiang came to the fore with the help of Borodin. In Canton, Borodin created a triumvirate consisting of Chiang, Hsu Chung-chih, the commander of the Kuomintang armies (and therefore Chiang's military superior), and Wang Ching-wei, the civilian head of the party. This arrangement was not to last. Not the least of the difficulties was the fact that the Russians distrusted Hsu. In September 1925, Chiang, with the support of Borodin and with the help of his Whampoa cadets and Communist strikers, executed a coup in which he removed his military superior from his command and was made commander in chief in his place.[27] In February of 1926, taking advantage of Borodin's absence from Canton, Chiang executed another coup which resulted in the arrest of all of the Communist political workers attached to units under his command, including many of Wang's left-wing followers. Wang fled to Europe, and a friend of Chiang's was installed as the chairman of the Central Executive Committee of the Kuomintang.[28]

24. Chiang Kai-shek, *Soviet Russia in China*, p. 32.
25. *The Communist International, 1923–1928, Documents*, p. 157.
26. The China White Paper indicates that Chiang Kai-shek became "the leading figure in the Kuomintang" immediately upon the death of Sun, but more scholarly accounts differ. *United States Relations with China*, p. 43. For an account of the role of Borodin in the months directly after the death of Sun, see North, *Moscow and Chinese Communists*, pp. 85–89.
27. Callis, *China: Confucian and Communist*, p. 251
28. North suggests that the coup was based on a claim by Chiang that he had discovered a conspiracy against him among the officers of a warship anchored off Whampoa. *Moscow and Chinese Communists*, p. 86. Of this incident, Chiang himself has said, "I sensed a Communist plot. At the time, however, all that I suspected was that they intended to stage a revolt to harm me. Only after it was all over did I learn of their plan to seize me on board the *Chungshan* when I was

The coup of March 20, 1926, caused consternation among the Russians,[29] and in a mood of self-criticism, General Stepanov, Russian adviser to the First Army, sought for the answers in errors of the Russian advisers and in the personality of Chiang Kai-shek.[30] Both Stalin and Borodin were totally unprepared for the Chiang action, and a resolution on the Chinese situation adopted later in the year by the Executive Committee of the Communist International did not have one word to say about the incident.[31]

The coup was followed by a policy of conciliation which produced an agreement between Chiang and Borodin on the restriction of Communist Party activity within the Kuomintang,[32] and the acquiescence of Borodin in a military campaign from the south against the war lords of central and northern China, which he had formerly opposed. Members of an older generation will recall the prominence of "war lords" in the news of China in the 1920's, the phrase itself imparting a journalistic glamor to a condition of near anarchy. The campaign against the northern war lords began on July 9, 1926, and was a remarkable operation, the way being prepared by Communist-trained propagandists and political agitators who organized strikes and peasant revolts behind enemy lines.[33] The relations between Chiang and the Communists were closely cooperative in this military operation. The very success of the Northern Expedition seems to have stimulated the confidence in intrigue that led the Communists to overreach themselves, and to have provided the anti-Communist Chiang with the occasion and the means for bringing the conjuncture of the Kuomintang and the Communists to an end.

---

to take it to go back to the Military Academy at Whampoa from Canton. They would then send me as a prisoner to Russia via Vladivostok, thereby removing the major obstacle to their scheme of using the National revolution as a medium for setting up a 'dictatorship of the proletariat.' " *Soviet Russia in China*, p. 39.

29. The immediate reaction by the Comintern was to deny that the incident had occurred. North, *Moscow and Chinese Communists*, p. 87.

30. Among the errors of the Russians, Stepanov listed excessive supervision of the Chinese by Russian generals, and failure to follow rules of Chinese etiquette. The Chinese Communists had pushed too hard, he thought, in an effort to control Kuomintang organs. The correct policy for the situation created by Chiang was to conciliate him, to satisfy his desire for power and glory, and to make political concessions to him as a price for his cooperation. Wilbur and How, *Documents on Communism*, p. 219, for editors' summary, and pp. 248–265 for a translation of Stepanov's reports.

31. *The Communist International, 1923–1928, Documents*, p. 338.

32. Wilbur and How, *Documents on Communism*, Document 25, dated June 3, 1926, "A Report to Moscow from Soviet Russia's Central Military Organ in Peking on Strife within the Southern Government Centered Around Chiang Kai-shek," pp. 266–270.

33. North, *Moscow and Chinese Communists*, p. 89.

The split came on April 12 when Chiang turned upon the left wing, the Chinese Communists, and their Soviet associates in a series of violent actions in Shanghai, dissolving all their organizations, raiding their premises, arresting the members, and executing hundreds of them. Three days later he established his government at Nanking, rival to that dominated by the left elements in Wuhan. By July all of the Soviet advisers had been sent back to the Soviet Union, including the master of the three-year adventure, Michael Borodin, and the collaboration between the Kuomintang on the one hand and the Soviet and Chinese Communists on the other begun by Dr. Sun Yat-sen came to an end.

Certain aspects of the first period merit emphasis. First, the Communist movement in China was not an affair of rural romantics bent upon improving the lot of the peasant, but a phase of what the Communist ideology thinks is the class struggle. That is to say, the Chinese Communist Party was organized soon after the Russian Revolution and became a functioning part of the Communist International. Second, the Communist Party grew in influence in the 1920's because Sun Yat-sen invited the collaboration of the Soviet Union in the struggles of the Chinese Revolution for national unification and social development. If it can be said that he invited a disaster that he did not fully comprehend, it can also be said that the Americans, British, and French at the time were largely more interested in concessions, extraterritoriality, and other forms of privilege than they were in the promotion of Sun's program. Third, the actual numbers of Kuomintang and Chinese Communist members engaged in revolutionary politics was small, the Communist Party numbering not more than a few thousand in a country of hundreds of millions, while the Kuomintang itself was only a minute fraction of the population. Fourth, although Chiang did not accept the Communist program for widespread social revolution that was being promoted behind the public effort at national unification, he did accept Soviet army and party organization. If the Chiang regime is a "dictatorship" — as it was frequently referred to when the Department of State abandoned its policy of support — it was so because Michael Borodin had built it on the Soviet model. And fifth, the Comintern-Chinese Communist policy towards the peasant was greatly confused. Although there was agitation among the peasantry, and tough words were spoken in Moscow about joining the worker and peasant in a proletarian whole, the surge of the peasants seemed to be a dialectical embarrassment and both Stalin and the Chinese Communists thought it necessary policy to slow the peasant uprising to permit the prior organization of a proletarian base for the party in the cities. It was to be Mao's contribution to party development to establish a mass base among the peasants and to organize them as a class militia against the middle class coalition of Chiang without waiting for the organization of a proletariat.

Chiang Kai-shek referred to the years 1932–1945 as the second period of a three-stage development in "peaceful co-existence" between the Soviet Union and China,[34] but these thirteen years comprise two separate intervals of tension and balance. The first was the period between 1928 and 1936, starting with the ejection of the Russian Communists by Chiang and ending with the kidnapping of Chiang by Chang Hseuh-liang in December 1936. The second began with a degree of forced cooperation between Chiang and military and Communist elements against the Japanese and ended with the start of Chiang's collapse as leader of China, and the eventual triumph of the Communist leadership.

By 1928, certainly, Russian leadership in the Communist movement in China had been discredited. Borodin had left, urging the Chinese Communists, as he did so, to go underground to resist the capitalist regime of Chiang.[35] The year before, documents discovered in raids on the Russian embassy in Peking showed that Borodin had been taking orders literally from Moscow, in the furtherance of designs for the sovietization of China.[36] The debacle of the Soviet policy in China became one of the talking points in the power struggle between Stalin and Trotsky. Trotsky had argued at the Fifteenth CPSU conference in September 1926 that the policy towards the Kuomintang had been wholly opportunist, that the Chinese Communist Party should not have entered the KMT, and that it should have acted as an independent proletarian party, although perhaps with a bloc relation to the KMT.[37] After the coup of Chiang Kai-shek in October 1927, Trotsky wrote that "The cruel massacres of the Chinese proletariat . . . and the general weakening of the position of the Comintern and the Soviet Union, the party owes principally and above all to comrade Stalin." [38] The

34. Chiang Kai-shek, *Soviet Russia in China*, p. 9. The irony of the reference to "peaceful coexistence" is extended in the opening words of the book: "The Chinese Communist Party is not indigenous to China. It is an outgrowth of Soviet Russia and the Communist empire. . . . Its aim was to set up in the course of China's wars of unification and independence a Soviet puppet regime and to create the first satellite in Asia." *Ibid.*, p. 11.

35. Callis, *China: Confucian and Communist*, p. 254. Borodin was accompanied out of China by some Communist sympathizers and collaborators with the Soviet Union, including Madame Sun Yat-sen.

36. Callis, *China: Confucian and Communist*, p. 254. See nn. 20 and 21 for reference to the seized documents and citation of source. The authenticity of the documents has been questioned, but Zinoviev is said to have told Trotsky that the documents were in part forged and in part true. For comment on the question of authenticity, see *The Communist International, 1923–1928, Documents*, p. 363.

37. *The Communist International, 1923–1928, Documents*, p. 336.

38. *The Communist International, 1923–1928, Documents*, p. 392.

Executive Committee of the Communist International in July 1927 criticized the leaders of the Chinese Communist Party for their mistakes.[39] The debate in party councils was a preview of one to occur in the United States two and a half decades later on the same subject, "Who Lost China?"

After the debacle of 1927, according to Edgar Snow, the activities of the Comintern in China were almost nil.[40] As he put it, "Russian organs in China were closed, Russian Communists were killed or driven from the country, the flow of financial, military, and political help from Russia ceased, and the Chinese Communist Party was thrown into great confusion, and for a time lost contact with the Comintern." [41] But although it may have been small, the Soviet influence was certainly not absent, and names that were to become publicly familiar later are connected with activity in China in the years right after Chiang's triumph. Among these are Gerhardt Eisler, who later served as Comintern leader in the United States, and Richard Sorge, who was to meet execution at the hands of the Japanese for sensational espionage activity as a supposed Nazi in the German embassy in Tokyo. Hede Massing, the former wife of Gerhardt Eisler, placed Eisler as a Comintern agent in China in 1930,[42] and the Fourth Section of the Red Army (Intelligence) was represented by Richard Sorge and others.[43] According to statements attributed to Richard Sorge at the time of his arrest and examination by the Japanese authorities in 1941, he said of Eisler:

I chanced to meet Gerhardt [Eisler] in Shanghai and renewed our old acquaintance, but our work was absolutely unrelated. Gerhardt's duty, or rather that of the political branch, was to act as a spokesman for the political policy with respect to the Chinese Communist Party

39. *The Communist International, 1923–1928, Documents*, p. 395.
40. Edgar Snow, *Red Star Over China* (New York: Random House, 1938), p. 378.
41. Snow, *Red Star Over China*, p. 378.
42. Hede Massing, *This Deception* (New York: Duell, Sloan and Pearce, 1951), p. 96. In fact she thought that the experience in China produced a change in Eisler's personality. "Gerhardt," she said, "was a different Gerhardt. Today, I know that people become toughened by experience, that they take on habits, expressions, and mannerisms that life imposed on them. But Gerhardt used to be so smart and observant! He would size up a situation in a flash and act accordingly. It was so very unlike him to be rude and a show-off. His modesty was gone and with it his interest in other people. I was shocked by his display of being in the know and his poorly veiled indications of how important a job he thought he had done." *Ibid.*, p. 97.
43. Eighty-second Congress, First Session, House of Representatives, Committee on Un-American Activities, *Hearings on American Aspects of the Richard Sorge Spy Case*, August 9, 22, and 23, 1951, p. 1175 (hereafter cited as *American Aspects of the Richard Sorge Spy Case*). See also Major General Charles A. Willoughby, *Shanghai Conspiracy, The Sorge Spy Ring* (New York: E. P. Dutton, 1952).

decided upon by the Comintern general conference. It also acted as an intermediary for the exchange of information between the Chinese Communist Party and the Comintern and submitted reports concerning all the social problems involved in the labor movement in China.[44]

Eisler stayed in China until it became too precarious for him to do so after the arrest of two Comintern agents, and he returned to Moscow.

Although the Comintern was to maintain operations centered in Shanghai in the six years after 1928, and to seem to exercise nominal influence and apparent control of the Chinese Communist Party, these were the years in fact in which the composition of the party changed and local Chinese leadership rose to power, which from a developing mass base came to challenge Chiang and eventually overthrow him. The development of autonomous indigenous strength was aided by further miscalculations by Moscow. At the Sixth Congress of the Third International in 1928, Stalin, having disposed of Trotsky and his thesis of permanent revolution, laid out a program of armed insurrection in China which, under the leadership of Li Li-san, was to be pressed forward in 1929 and to failure in 1930.[45] Li was removed from leadership of the Chinese Communist Party in 1931, which was then vested in the hands of the "Returned Students," a group of recent graduates of Sun Yat-sen University in Moscow, under the guidance of Pavel Mif, a Russian specialist in China. Li Li-san, in Moscow where he was to stay many years before returning to China, admitted errors and remained to pursue Marxist studies, but in the course of his account of his leadership he also expressed the resentment of Chinese comrades about Russian domination of Chinese affairs which they did not understand, and to which they brought racial prejudices.[46]

Edgar Snow is of the opinion that the movement to establish soviets in China and the creation of the Chinese Red Army began spontaneously under Chinese leadership in the years soon after 1928.[47] Another source has also said that it was in the time after the fall of Li Li-san and the advent of Mif and the Returned Students that the peasant composition of the Red movement achieved recognition and that Mao Tse-tung gradually increased his power.[48] And still elsewhere, the period is described as the one in which the peasant composition of the Communist movement in China received recognition, rural soviets were

44. *American Aspects of the Richard Sorge Spy Case*, p. 1187.
45. Robert C. North, *Kuomintang and Chinese Communist Elites* (Stanford, California: Stanford, 1952), p. 32.
46. North, *Kuomintang and Chinese Communist Elites*, p. 34.
47. Snow, *Red Star Over China*, p. 378.
48. North, *Kuomintang and Chinese Communist Elites*, p. 34.

drawn together under a central government, and Mao Tse-tung with his Red Army increased in influence. Unfortunately there are such gaps in the Chinese Communist record in these years that it is difficult to be specific about the changes that did occur in the nature and the thrust of the Chinese Communist Party, although by 1934 it was clear enough that they had taken place.

The invasion of Manchuria by the Japanese in 1931 led to the reestablishment of diplomatic relations between China and the Soviet Union in 1932, but Chiang's policy to suppress the Chinese Communists was not abated by this act. In fact he stepped up a series of extermination campaigns, the first of which had been turned back in November 1930 by the Chinese Red Army, and the second in April 1931. In both these campaigns against Red Army forces fighting guerrilla battles in the mountain regions, the Chinese Red forces perfected their skills, developed their tactics, and augmented their supplies from the attacking forces. The third campaign of the Nationalist regime of Chiang Kai-shek began in July 1931 against the soviets in the province of Kiangsi. By October, although the Communists were taken by some surprise, Chiang had withdrawn and the Chinese Red Army was again the gainer in ammunition, guns, and equipment.

So far did the forces of Mao succeed in establishing soviets among the peasants in the wake of the Red Army that the First All-China Soviet Congress was convened in Juichin, Kiangsi, on November 7, 1932, the anniversary of the Bolshevik revolution in Russia. This first Chinese Soviet Congress drafted a constitution for a Central Soviet Government, based (in the Marxist jargon) not on the democracy of the bourgeoisie, but upon the democracy of workers and peasants. The constitution and resolutions produced by this Congress were quite clearly modeled on Russian examples, although tailored in some respects to suit particular Chinese conditions. Of some importance for events sixteen or so years later were the plans adopted between 1931 and 1934 that laid down the basic agrarian policy of the Chinese Soviet Republic. Two of these adopted plans became part of the program in 1950 for land reform in the Chinese People's Republic.[49]

Chiang again launched an attack against Communist troops in the autumn of 1932 — his fourth campaign in the Chinese civil war — but the Japanese renewed their attack through a mountain pass in the Great Wall of China and it became necessary to meet this crisis. When it was over, a fifth campaign was pressed against the Communists in Kiangsi which succeeded so well that, by October 1934, the Juichin Republic had either to flee or face annihilation. The first Chinese Soviet Republic fell when the Red Army began the Long March out of

49. North, *Moscow and Chinese Communists*, pp. 153–154.

Kiangsi on the night of October 15, 1934, and traveled 6,000 miles into the provinces of Yunnan, Szechwan, and Shensi.[50]

The slogan of the "two Chinas" may have special application to events after the forces of Chiang had been driven from the mainland in 1949, but two Chinas had in fact emerged by 1931. The nominal jurisdiction of the Kuomintang over the whole of China was belied by the fact that Chiang's control was largely located on the coast north and south of the Yangtze and up the river a distance. In some of the farther reaches of the country, he depended upon the uncertain allegiance of generals with armies of their own, and in some of the areas, authority was in fact in the hands of a hostile "state," namely, the Communists and the Red Army. In his report to the Second All-China Soviet Congress on January 22, 1934 (before the collapse of the Juichin Republic), Mao crowed about the development of the Soviet movement throughout China which was to bring about a "bright, happy new socialist society, following the example of the workers and peasants of the Soviet Union." This was a "Soviet regime" with control over "Soviet areas" under a "Soviet government," that is, a state within the territory claimed by the Kuomintang, complete with all of the apparatus of governance and the symbols of socialist legitimacy.[51] Although this Soviet regime was basically peasant in character, the rhetoric of revolution made it necessary to avow it in the name of the proletariat and the urban workers, as well as the peasants. While denying the pretense to legitimacy of the Communist soviets, Chiang himself recognized their de facto status in his account of the Fifth Campaign. It was the "Communist area in five provinces" (Hunan, Kiangsi, Hupeh, Honan, and Anhwei) which he said had been reduced by the summer of 1934 to "less than 2000 square kilometers." This territory was "only one-fiftieth of what the Communists had under their control in 1932," he said.[52] Even by Chiang's figures, then, the area under Communist control in 1932 would have been some 62,500 square miles, the equivalent of the states of Pennsylvania, New Jersey, and Maryland, or all of New England.

50. Accounts differ as to where the forces went on the Long March and how many made it to the end. Callis, *China: Confucian and Communist*, says that Chu Teh led the Red Army to Shensi in the northwest and that 20,000 completed the trek out of 80,000 who started (p. 279). Chiang Kai-shek on the other hand says the troops went into the three provinces mentioned in the text and that "there were only some 5,000 armed Communists left." *Soviet Russia in China*, p. 65. Snow indicates that the main march was into Shensi, although there were troops in the other two provinces and that less than 20,000 survivors reached their destination on October 20, 1935, over a year after their departure from Kiangsi. *Red Star Over China*, p. 194.

51. Conrad Brandt, Benjamin Schwartz, and John K. Fairbank, *A Documentary History of Chinese Communism* (Cambridge, Mass: Harvard, 1952), p. 229.

52. Chiang Kai-shek, *Soviet Russia in China*, p. 64.

By 1932 the struggle in China was no longer one between two factions of the same party, nor even one between two parties, the Kuomintang and the Communist, but between two regimes for control of the same territory, each with its own army, its own police, and its own political institutions. Seen in this light, the conflict between Chiang and the Communists is a war between two governments, not a scuffle for party advantage between Far East versions of Republicans and Democrats. Mao and the Communists regarded Chiang as the "enemy" who "has been bent on its efforts to effect destruction and oppression of the Soviet areas." Chiang regarded the Japanese and the Communists both as the "enemy," as equal threats to the only established and lawful regime in China, recognized by both the United States in 1928 and by the Soviet Union in 1932. In this view of the struggle of Chiang and the Communists as a war between two regimes, neither of which controlled the entire country, some of the later policy suggestions emanating from the United States Government and elsewhere seem peculiarly irrelevant to the reality to which they were presumably addressed. Coalition for Chiang would have to be as difficult as coalition for Korea or Germany, and as fruitless of harmony and good faith and efficacy. As well expect Thaddeus Stevens and Jefferson Davis in the same government, with the Confederate Army intact and aggressive.

By the time the Red Army had reached Shensi Province in northwest China at the end of the Long March, the policy of the Comintern had changed again, and the time of the Popular Front had arrived. Leaders of the Long March had been out of touch with events for months and the news of the Dimitroff speech at the Seventh Congress of the Communist International proclaiming the new tactic was received with surprise. But Communist propaganda began immediately to press for a "united front" with the Kuomintang. From the time of the Japanese invasion of Manchuria in 1931, the Chinese Communist Party had called for resistance to it by an alliance of anti-Japanese groups, although it had never been quite clear before 1935 whether it was including the Kuomintang in the invitation.

The thrust of these considerations acquires sharp point in the Sian Incident of December 1936[53] when Chiang was kidnapped by two of his generals, Chang and Yang, and eventually released after some agree-

---

53. Chiang Kai-shek, did not ascribe the kidnapping to the Communists. The most that he was prepared to say was that "there had even been reports that both Chang and Yang had formed ties with the Chinese Communist Party," that "these two men must have acted under the strong influence of the Chinese Communists," and that six months earlier "Chang was already in an advanced state of collusion with the Communists." Nowhere does he state that the Communists were responsible for the Sian affair. *Soviet Russia in China*, pp. 73–75.

ments with his captors on the conduct of the war with the Japanese. It was because of "Communist influences with the mutineers" and the personal mediation of Madame Chiang and her brother, T. V. Soong, however, that Chiang was released on December 25, 1936.[54] The Tungpei army officers (Chang's army) were unwilling to release Chiang at all and had demanded his death, but, according to W. H. Donald, Chiang's Australian adviser, Chou En-lai "was actually the one man who enabled Chiang to depart unharmed from the 1936 Sian kidnapping." [55]

One measure of the importance attached by the Soviet Union to the "united front" policy in China was the decision of the Seventh World Congress of the Communist International to reorganize the Executive Committee of the International so as to provide equal representation to members from China and the Soviet Union. The Chinese members were Ch'en Shao-yu (Wang Ming), Chou En-lai, Chang Kuo-tao, and Mao Tse-tung. Ch'en Shao-yu was elected a member of the Presidium of the Executive Committee along with Stalin and seventeen others, and the Chinese and Soviet Union delegations were the largest among all of the Communist parties of the world [56] on the Executive Committee of the Communist International.

The United Front in China

With the establishment of an entente between the two revolutionary powers on the territory of China, the third stage began in their struggle for supremacy. Although there was no formal treaty of alliance between the Chinese Communists and the Kuomintang, there was a series of parallel documents put out by both sides on which the alliance was assumed to rest.[57] In March 1937, the Kuomintang laid down terms

54. Callis, *China:Confucian and Communist*, p. 264.

55. The quotation is taken from the report prepared in 1945 by the Military Intelligence Division of the War Department under Brigadier-General P. E. Peabody, titled "The Chinese Communist Movement," and classified as "Secret." The classification was removed in 1949, and in 1952 the report was reprinted in Eighty-second Congress, Second Session, United States Senate, Committee on the Judiciary, Subcommittee to Investigate the Administration of the Internal Security Act and Other Internal Security Laws, *Hearings on the Institute of Pacific Relations*, Part 7A, Appendix II, p. 233. (This intelligence report will be hereafter cited as *The Chinese Communist Movement*.) The State Department, however, was later to say that "The Chinese Communist Party, whose representatives were called to Sian immediately after his capture, at first favored the execution of the Generalissimo but, apparently on orders from Moscow, shifted to a policy of saving his life." *United States Relations with China*, p. 47.

56. *The Chinese Communist Movement*, p. 2329.

57. The character of the Communist Party-Red Army combination as a political state capable of making a "treaty" is suggested by the observation of Edgar Snow reporting an interview with Mao Tse-tung in 1936, "In the beginning of July 1936, I entered Soviet territory in Northern Shensi to seek interviews with

for the submission of the Communists in a united front.[58] The Red Army was to be abolished as a separate organization and it was to be incorporated into the Kuomintang Government's Central Army under direct control of a National Military Council. The other terms demanded dissolution of the Chinese Soviet Republic, cessation of Communist Party propaganda, and suspension of the class struggle.[59] The Chinese Communists accepted these terms on March 15, 1937, with the approval of Moscow.

The united front was not a merger but an alliance, and in the course of a relatively short time the conditions of the alliance were compromised in several ways helpful to the Communists. There was no overt repudiation of the terms, and throughout the Second World War Chiang was referred to by the Communists as the leader of the nation in arms against the Japanese. But the Communists conducted two main lines of counter-policy within the framework of the agreed conditions. First, they expanded their areas of military control, and within these areas established their own version of a united front based upon the "Soviet democracy of the toilers." Second, they exerted the utmost pressure upon the Kuomintang and upon the people in areas controlled by the Kuomintang to introduce democracy in the western sense of the word — the broad representation of groups, the procedures of consultation and consent, and so on, policies that favor the influence of a cohesive and hard-working minority.[60]

In the areas devoted to the "democracy of the toilers," members of the middle classes were allowed to vote, and non-Communist parties were permitted to exist in the border regions under Communist control so long as they conformed to Communist Party policies as carried out through the party-controlled border governments. The Kuomintang was permitted to function in the border regions but it could not establish itself as a party competing with the Chinese Communist Party. Individuals who voiced their opposition to the Communists and attempted to work against them were outlawed. The Communist line

leading Chinese Communists and to observe for myself the kind of regime furnished by the Soviet government and the Red Army. . . . The present Soviet regions are the biggest single territory ever occupied by the Red Army." Eighty-fourth Congress, Second Session, House of Representatives, Report No. 2243, *Strategy and Tactic of World Communism*, Part I: *Communism Outside the United States*, Section D: *Communist Activities Around the World*, p. 490.

58. This account of the establishment of the entente is taken from *The Chinese Communist Movement*, p. 2331.

59. Five days before the opening of the Third Plenary Session of the Fifth Central Executive Committee of the Kuomintang on February 15, 1937, the Central Committee of the Chinese Communist Party addressed a telegram to the session offering terms like those that the Kuomintang laid down. See *United States Relations with China*, p. 48

60. *The Chinese Communist Movement*, p. 2344.

was the Stalinist line, and Trotskyite Communists were classed with traitors, spies, and Japanophiles.

But in the Kuomintang areas matters were differently arranged. When the Central Government was in Hankow in 1938, having been driven out of Nanking by the Japanese, a resolution of the Kuomintang Congress granted free speech and association, whereupon the Communists began to establish mass organizations like those in their guerrilla areas in North China. Within a few weeks there began to appear such Communist-sponsored organizations as the "Wuhan Youth National Salvation Corps," "The National Emancipation Vanguards," and "The Ant Society." These mass organizations were looked upon with alarm by the Kuomintang because they presaged the creeping domination by the Communists which similar front groups had assisted in North China, and because they threatened the development of the San Min Chu I Youth Corps, a mass organization sponsored by Chiang to stimulate popular support for the Kuomintang. The first crack in the united front appeared when the Hankow-Wuchang Defense General Headquarters ordered the dissolution of the three Communist-sponsored mass organizations.[61]

In both the military and the political sectors the united front was merely a device of convenience in the prosecution of the war against Japan, and not a merger, nor even a subordination of the interests of the two principal Chinese powers. It was the war against Japan that prevented the contenders from renewing the open civil war of a few years earlier. The pretense of unity was maintained in Chungking, which became the capital after the Central Government was driven by the Japanese out of Hankow, but even the pretense tended to disappear in the provinces. In the summer of 1939, the Chungking government began to enforce a military blockade against the Shen-Kan-Ning Border Region, dominated by the Communists, in order to prevent infiltration of the non-Communist areas to the west and south, and to close off overland routes between the Communist bases on the one hand and Sinkiang and Soviet Russia on the other. In the guerrilla areas of East China, frequent fighting occurred between the forces of the two Chinese powers. It became apparent that the Chinese Communists considered it within their right to expand into any war area of eastern China without permission of the commander-in-chief, Chiang, and without consultation with the National Military Council or the war-zone commanders appointed by the Central Government. As an American Military Intelligence estimate of 1945 said of the earlier period,

> While the regular Central Army forces were distributed in the various front sectors according to the plan of the High Command in

61. *The Chinese Communist Movement,* pp. 2343–2344.

Chungking, the Communist forces moved anywhere they liked according to plans laid down in Yenan. And wherever they went, they set up their own guerrilla bases and their own type of democratic united front governments which were linked up with Yenan instead of Chungking.[62]

The Central Government on several occasions asked the Communists to establish a clear demarcation of defense zones so as to avoid the great confusion caused by the intrusion of Communist forces into the defense zones of the Central Government. It finally offered the Communists all of North China above the Yellow River (except Southern Shansi) as their defense zone, provided that they withdrew the New Fourth Army to North China.[63]

The offer was accepted, and in the latter part of 1940 forces of the New Fourth Army began to cross the Yangtze, presumably on their way north in accordance with the agreement. By the end of 1940, three-quarters of the troops were across the Yangtze, that is, on the north bank instead of the south, and were proceeding north. It seemed to the Central Government, however, that the New Fourth was literally dragging its feet, and an order of the National Military Council specifically directed the New Fourth to abandon its positions on the lower Yangtze region and join with the Eighth Route Army in Hopeh. Instead of proceeding forthwith, both the New Fourth and the Eighth Route armies were pressing their campaigns in North Kiangsu and South Shantung against government troops for possession of bases.

Thereupon Central Government forces launched an attack on the headquarters of the commander of the New Fourth Army on January 6, 1941, and on January 12, 1941, the Central Government ordered that the New Fourth Army be disbanded. The scale of the attack drew protests from the Communists and from non-Communist elements in Kuomintang China, and attracted the notice of the world press. Negotiations were started at Chungking to resolve the controversy over the New Fourth Army affair amid claims and counter-claims and charges and refutations, but the breach made in the relations between the Kuomintang and the Chinese Communists was not closed and eventually ruptured into open warfare.

To sum up matters in China when the United States entered the Second World War: first, the United States was to become involved only in the last act of a struggle that had been going on at least since June 1920 when Gregori Voitinsky arrived in Shanghai from Moscow to found the Chinese Communist Party. Second, in both the 1920's and the 1930's the center of the struggle was the effort of the Chinese

62. *The Chinese Communist Movement*, p. 2348.
63. *The Chinese Communist Movement*, p. 2349.

Communists to bring China under domination and to establish a Chinese Soviet Republic according to Marxist-Leninist principle, and as close to the Soviet Russian model as Chinese circumstance would allow. Third, the policy line, military program, and diplomatic orientation of the Chinese Communists generally followed those of the Soviet Union and the Communist International. And fourth, in the thirties and the forties, the Chinese Communist movement was not merely the activity of a political party. It was represented by a regime virtually uncontrollable by Chiang Kai-shek, a separate Chinese power exercising de facto independence, with territory, people, government, law, armies, and money.

For twenty years the official American policy had been noninterventionist in the internal affairs of China. The imperatives of war brought the internal affairs of China within the ambiance of American military and political concerns, and carried with them a responsibility for decisions about these affairs that have consequences still to unfold.

IX *Missions of Mistrust*

One extensive study of American policy in China from the attack on
Pearl Harbor to the mission of General George C. Marshall is called
The China Tangle.[1] The title accurately characterizes six years during
which the United States — much of the time — worked for military
results through political means, and the Chinese, both Nationalist and
Communist, worked for political results through military means. In
the course of these years the United States was represented in Chungking by three different ambassadors; the top military command was
first in the hands of General Joseph Stilwell, who did not get along
with Chiang, and then Albert E. Wedemeyer, who did get along with
Chiang; and there were three special missions, the first headed by Vice
President Henry A. Wallace, the second by General Patrick J. Hurley,
and the third by General George Marshall. The outcome of all this
busyness was that the Japanese lost the war, Chiang lost China, notables
lost reputation, and Washington suffered shock and convulsion in the
aftermath of the debacle. The Department of State did not release its
secret and long-controversial China papers of 1943 until nineteen years
later.[2] So sensitive were some apprehensions even at that late date that
Everett F. Drumright, Ambassador to Chiang Kai-shek on Taiwan,
resigned from his post as envoy to Nationalist China, presumably because he opposed publication of the China papers.[3]

Angry critics of the fortunes of war in the United States Senate
rejected explanations of helpless inevitability, and were not content
with the thought that we could not have succeeded anyway. Secretary
of State Dean Acheson had said in transmitting the China White Paper
of 1949 that,

1. Herbert Feis, *The China Tangle* (Princeton: Princeton, 1953).
2. Department of State, *Foreign Relations of the United States, China, 1943*
(Washington: Government Printing Office, 1956) (hereafter cited as *China
Papers*).
3. *New York Times,* March 21, 1962, p. 2, col. 3.

The unfortunate but inescapable fact is that the ominous result of the civil war in China was beyond the control of the government of the United States. Nothing that this country did or could have done within the reasonable limits of its capabilities could have changed that result; nothing that was left undone by this country has contributed to it. It was the product of internal Chinese forces, forces which this country tried to influence but could not. A decision was arrived at within China, if only a decision by default.[4]

Opposed to his pessimistic judgment was the feeling of some, as has been said, that the victim had died not by accident but by design, and that Communists and their supporters working within the Department of State had encompassed the ruin of Chiang. There is no doubt that the traditional American policy of nonintervention in Chinese internal affairs did change with the Marshall mission to one of active mediation. The new policy was designed to achieve political stability but it failed to do so because the necessary condition for stability demanded by each of the adversaries was the complete subjugation of the other.

Stilwell, Chiang, and the State Department

The United States joined the war effort in China — which had been struggling against the Japanese for over four years — when General Joseph W. Stilwell was assigned by the Pentagon to Chiang Kai-shek's combined staff in January 1942. At the time the only entrance to China was by the back door, that is, through Burma, and thence to Chungking; and in order to get to Burma, it was necessary for Stilwell to fly from New York to Miami to Brazil to Africa to India. Stilwell was put in command of Chinese troops in Burma, and as early as March 1942 found himself in disagreement with Chiang Kai-shek over the use of these troops, with Stilwell favoring immediate attack and Chiang less willing.[5] Although Stilwell had command of the Chinese Fifth and Sixth Armies, he complained to his journal that his control was weakened by Chiang who kept in close touch with the subordinate Chinese commanders, sending directions, suggestions, cautions, and advices,

4. *United States Relations with China: With Special Reference to the Period 1944-1949* (Washington: Government Printing Office, 1949), p. xvi.

5. Joseph W. Stilwell, *The Stilwell Papers* (New York: William Sloane Associates, 1948). After an early meeting with Chiang on military plans, Stilwell wrote in his journal, "What a directive. What a mess. How they [Chiang and his staff] hate the Limeys. And what a sucker I am. Well, at least, Chiang Kai-shek is sticking to one part of the agreement. Never before has a foreigner been allowed any control over Chinese troops" (p. 55).

with Stilwell in the dark about many of them.[6] By May of 1942, the Japanese had succeeded in outflanking the Chinese in Burma and they were forced to withdraw to India. The Burma Road to China was cut, and Stilwell was required to retreat through the jungle in a depressing and taxing effort of three weeks. The strength of Japanese arms was the principal cause of the disaster but Stilwell was bitter about the many contributory causes, including, he felt, the interference of Chiang Kai-shek in matters of command.

From the late spring of 1942 until the early winter of 1944, it was Stilwell's principal task to prepare for the reconquest of Burma, a matter of plans and projects, of conferences and negotiations, and an entanglement in political intrigue. The grand design called for a push by the Chinese into Burma from the east, where it bordered the province of Yunnan; for a thrust by the British into South Burma from India; and for a drive into northwest Burma from Assam, in India, with a joint Chinese-American force. To effect this plan, Stilwell was also put in charge of the supply, training, and leadership of Chinese troops.

There were other difficulties besides the normal ones of inadequate supplies, confused command, and imperfect communications. One of General Stilwell's most bitter critics was another American general in the China-Burma-India theater — Major-General Claire Chennault, who first headed an American Volunteer Group — the "Flying Tigers" — which fought under contract with the Chinese government. It was dissolved in July 1942, some of the members being absorbed into the Tenth Air Force which was under Stilwell's command. Chennault thought that Stilwell did not fully appreciate the possibilities of China-based air power, and openly and frequently expressed his low opinion of Stilwell's military judgment. Chennault was much admired in Chiang's circle, and did all he could to have his own ideas about things known in Washington.[7]

American military authorities in Washington were a second source of difficulty not only for Stilwell but for Chiang. With responsibility for campaigns in Europe and Africa as well as that in the Far East, the Pentagon tended to neglect and skimp the second for the first, which had priority in the master plan of the war. In late June 1942, it was thought necessary in the Pentagon to divert air strength from the Far East to the Middle East to guard Alexandria against the threatening Rommel, a decision that led Chiang to lay down an ultimatum with

6. Of these commanders Stilwell wrote, "I can't shoot them; I can't relieve them; and just talking to them does no good. So the upshot of it is that I am the stooge who does the dirty work and takes the rap." *The Stilwell Papers*, p. 77.
7. Feis, *The China Tangle*, p. 40.

hinted threats of Chinese defection if it were not met.[8] Chiang's minimum requirements were three American divisions; five hundred planes; and at least five thousand tons of monthly supplies over the Hump. The requests were refused. Instead, a special envoy was sent to Chiang to discuss the critical turn that relations had taken.[9]

The special envoy was Lauchlin Currie, administrative assistant to the President. A letter to Chiang from President Roosevelt dated July 4, 1942, assured the Generalissimo that Currie "has my complete confidence, has access to me at all times, and has quietly and in the background been active on all phases of Sino-American relations. . . ." [10] Currie had a dozen talks with Chiang Kai-shek which were said to have been helpful in soothing feelings and in stimulating the flow of help to China.[11] He also talked with Stilwell whose journal indicates that the general thought that he had found a receptive and willing ear.[12] One of Currie's recommendations upon his return to the United States was that Stilwell ought to be relieved. It may be said that throughout Stilwell's assignment in China, the main support at home for the supposedly pro-Communist general came from Henry Stimson and George Marshall; while the New Dealers — Corcoran, Hopkins, Wallace, and, as we have seen, Currie — were for Stilwell's recall and his supersession by Chennault or Wedemeyer. This fact makes it even harder to support the conspiratorial thesis later pushed by critics of the China policy in the forties.

While General Stilwell was struggling like Laocoon with the serpents of a dozen tangled relationships, there was a steady flow of official communications between the Department of State in Washington and several persons in the field whose names were later to become prominent in congressional committee rooms. Among these were the four people mentioned at the beginning of the previous chapter —

8. Feis, *The China Tangle*, p. 44.

9. On May 31, 1942, Mme. Chiang had written to Lauchlin Currie asking that Harry Hopkins be sent to China immediately to discuss the Chinese situation, and suggesting that Currie might accompany him. Currie addressed a memorandum to President Roosevelt the next day suggesting that Hopkins be sent, adding that if Hopkins did go, Currie's presence would not add a lot, but expressing willingness to go if Hopkins should be unavailable. This was followed up on June 3 with an estimation of what such a mission might accomplish. *China Papers*, 1942, pp. 60–63.

10. *China Papers*, 1942, p. 95.

11. Feis, *The China Tangle*, p. 44.

12. For example, Stilwell's notes for July 23 say, "Long talk with Currie. He did not dream the mess was as bad as it is. Primed him on the intriguing, lying, etc." *The Stilwell Papers*, p. 129. The notes on the next day report, "Wrote up dope for Currie and took it down to him. He's getting educated. Talking about the iron hand in the velvet glove." *Ibid.*, p. 130.

Davies, Service, Ludden, and Emmerson. It was Stilwell himself who requested State Department staff to help him with diplomatic connections, and he specifically asked for John Paton Davies, Jr.,[13] who was officially assigned to Kunming as Consul, designated as Second Secretary for temporary duty at Chungking, and detailed to General Stilwell for liaison duties.[14] Although there is no mention of Davies in Stilwell's published papers, there is a record of communications from Davies to Stilwell in the State Department's China papers. Davies was an early critic of Chiang and his regime, and his views fitted in with the increasing irritation and contempt engendered in Stilwell by his personal frustration in dealing with Chiang. One of the Davies communications dated July 7, 1942, only a few months after Stilwell's arrival in China, passed on complaints by Chou En-lai and other Communist leaders about the blockade of Communist troops by Kuomintang troops in Ningsia, Shensi, and Shansi; the expectation of these leaders that if war broke out between Russia and Japan, the Central Government would seize the opportunity to attack, not the Japanese, but the Chinese Communist troops; and their suggestion that the Central Government was conserving its strength out of domestic political considerations.[15] Davies also reported a conversation with a former Chinese ambassador to Moscow in which the latter warned that lend-lease to China should be closely monitored lest supplies be

13. *China Papers*, 1942, p. 12. Davies seems not to have liked much the encroachment in the fields of intelligence information and analysis by new agencies like the Board of Economic Warfare, the Office of Strategic Services, and the Office of War Information, all of which had field agencies in Chungking and New Delhi. As Davies said in a memorandum requesting the assignment of four Foreign Service people to General Stilwell's staff: "As a Foreign Service officer somewhat anxious over the encroachment of new Government agencies in the field of foreign affairs, I feel not only as the General does — that the detail of the four officers requested will be of very real assistance to him in his tremendously difficult and delicate task — but also that the five of us working in close coordination under the guidance of the Ambassador at Chungking and Chief of Mission at New Delhi can give some political direction to this program and forestall errors which representatives of the new agencies might otherwise commit." See *China Papers*, 1943, pp. 60–62. At the formal request of the Secretary of War to the Secretary of State, Stilwell got Ludden, Service, and Emmerson (*ibid.*, p. 68) and they were retained as advisers when General Wedemeyer took command in the fall of 1944.

General Wedemeyer thought that the four advisers had been very helpful to him, although he was later to say that he "was too preoccupied with my military duties . . . to have time to evaluate fully the reports of my political officers — Davies, Service, Ludden, and Emmerson. Their sympathy for the Chinese Communists is obvious in their reports and in their recommendations that we back the Communists instead of the National Government." (See Albert C. Wedemeyer, *Wedemeyer Reports!* [New York: Henry Holt, 1958], p. 312.)

14. *China Papers*, 1942, p. 18.
15. *China Papers*, 1942, pp. 98–102.

diverted from their intended purpose and hoarded by the Central Government for civil warfare.[16] In a memorandum to the State Department dated July 31, 1942, Davies considered it axiomatic that the objectives of the Chinese government were to ensure "its own perpetuation and domestic supremacy," and to come to the peace table as militarily strong as possible.[17]

Davies also passed on to Stilwell information said to have been supplied by "two persons close to General Chou En-lai and the Communist headquarters here in Chungking." [18] The "information" was a medley of statements on a number of aspects of the war, with a strong concentration of derogatory suspicions of the Central Government. It had been said, Davies reported, that there was a natural ideological affinity between the Chiang regime and the Nazis; that there was a pronounced admiration in the Central Government for the success of German arms; and that the only Germans confined to a camp in Chungking were three Jews. Mr. Davies was also the bearer of personal messages from Chou En-lai to Lauchlin Currie.[19] One of these warned the American government to watch lend-lease arrangements lest such supplies "be hoarded for use after the war in maintaining the position of the ruling faction," a message of remarkably close similarity to warnings Davies had passed on to Stilwell. Chou En-lai also thought that representatives of the American government — army officers, possibly — might visit the Communist-controlled areas, and that Chiang could reasonably be requested to grant permission for such a tour. Despite unchanging protestations of submission to the central direction of the Central Government that these messages indicate,[20] the Chinese Communists continued to behave like governors of an independent regime, though temporarily restricted in their range of free movement, with access through John Paton Davies to the White House itself.

Another figure of importance in the flow of communications between the field and Washington was John Carter Vincent who, in 1942, was counselor to the American Embassy in Chungking, in continuous touch with Washington on Chinese affairs. After the diversion of planes from Burma to the Middle East in the late spring of 1942, Vincent argued in a memorandum to the Secretary of State that the sug-

16. *China Papers*, 1942, pp. 115–116.

17. *China Papers*, 1942, p. 129.

18. The memorandum, dated July 10, 1942, was titled "Conversation with Two Leftists." *China Papers*, 1942, p. 207.

19. *China Papers*, 1942, pp. 226–228.

20. In a report to Stilwell of still another of his conversations with Chou En-lai, Davies said (October 11, 1942), "He [Chou En-lai] proclaimed his loyalty to General Chiang, declaring that the Generalissimo was not the leader of one party or faction but of the whole people." *China Papers*, 1942, p. 247.

gestion given Stilwell by Chiang and Mme. Chiang that continued Chinese resistance depended upon Allied aid was not to be taken seriously; nor was the further hint by Mme. Chiang that the Chinese might come to terms with the Japanese.[21] Like Davies, Vincent also had conversations with Chou En-lai, in the course of one of which Chou supplied Vincent with an estimation of the strongest elements in the Kuomintang under Chiang, the civilians among whom were said to cherish strongly conservative views,[22] including paternal monarchism. But what was reported as Chou's opinion on May 6, 1942, was then reported as Vincent's opinion on July 22,[23] and the remarks of both Chou and Vincent on the power structure of the Kuomintang are much the same. The analysis written by Vincent was not unfriendly to Chiang, however, and he said of the Generalissimo that he was not a dictator, that the political elements he led were held together by the personal force and political acumen that he exercised, and that his leadership was subject to modifications by influential elements within the party and the government.

In the troubled year of 1942, John Stewart Service was Third Secretary of the Embassy in China. The State Department in the early summer of 1942 wanted a brief description of the chief propaganda, psychological warfare, and morale agencies operating in Free China. In a brief not-well-written account of some of the propaganda agencies and their output, Service, unlike Vincent, referred to the Chiang regime as the "Kuomintang dictatorship," and thought that the breakdown in the "united front" had led the Kuomintang to devote attention to the promotion of an anti-Communist line, with subsequent deterioration of the vigor and vitality of anti-Japanese propaganda.[24] He dated the breakup of the united front from 1938 when the government moved from Hankow to Chungking, and attributed it to the apparent jealousy of "the growing influence of the Communists." The Kuomintang, he said, subjected the "Communists and the left-wing to a growing repression which, culminating in the clash with the New Fourth Army, has led to the present situation of suspicion and near hostilities."[25] Raymond P. Ludden by the end of 1942 was Consul in Kunming and also was contributing to the stream of military information preceding offensive operations to recapture Burma in 1943.[26]

21. *China Papers,* 1942, pp. 105–109.
22. *China Papers,* 1942, p. 198.
23. Memorandum to Ambassador Christian Gauss. *China Papers,* 1942, pp. 212–226.
24. *China Papers,* 1942, pp. 202–206.
25. *China Papers,* 1942, p. 204.
26. *China Papers,* 1942, pp. 182–185, for a dispatch to Ambassador Gauss, dated December 16, 1942.

It can be seen from these dispatches in 1942 that critics of Chiang gave voice early to their reservations about his contribution to the war effort, and their skepticism about the priority of two of Chiang's goals — defeat of the Japanese and defeat of the Chinese Communists. Since the Japanese were the obvious and active enemy, there was a tendency to diminish the threat of the other. Were not both the KMT and the Communists on the same side after all? Better reporting might have pointed out that the breakup of the united front was created by elements somewhat less subjective than Chiang's jealousy or hateful repression by the Kuomintang, which had no independent authority in Communist-held areas.

Throughout the year 1943, the military effort in the China-Burma-India theater was a long series of uncertain plans, frustrations, half-promises, failures to deliver, assurances of improvement, hesitations, unclear communication, growing exasperation, increasing doubts, and cynical suspicion. On the American side the principal decisions were being made by the Pentagon and the White House, not by the Department of State, and although it can be said that concern for global strategy understandably limited the support that could immediately be given to the China theater, this imperative was small solace to the Chinese. On the other hand, it was a widespread American view that the Central Government was capable of doing more for itself than it was in fact doing. In one form or another, the thought formulated by Feis represented the opinion of many American observers, military and civilian, public and private:

> . . . the Chiang Kai-shek regime wanted to be sure that it would survive in power. It was convinced that the maintenance of its position was essential for an orderly and unified China after the war. Hence it was afraid to take military chances; the loss of the capital, Chungking, might mean the end of the government, no matter what victories might be won elsewhere. It was afraid of making demands which might cause local military commanders and politicians to desert; and afraid of offending elements within the Kuomintang by radical measures of reform. Never out of mind was the knowledge that up north the Communists were waiting their chance to extend themselves and gain power; the government was determined they should not get it.[27]

It was also felt that Chiang was following a course that might defeat the very struggle of the regime to survive; for he was failing to use American help to build and train a military force of the kind and strength that would ensure eventual political influence and power.

27. Feis, *The China Tangle*, pp. 74–75.

Not everybody was quite so critical. Although he acknowledged that Chiang's military policy was conservative and cautious, General Albert C. Wedemeyer thought it understandable why it should be so.[28] The Chinese had been fighting the Japanese for four years before the United States ever entered the war, and they were exhausted. In fact they had fought battles at Shanghai and Nanking that rivaled the carnage of Verdun in the First World War, and this during a time when the United States was a source of war material for the Japanese. The attack upon the Chinese by the Japanese had been launched to prevent the unification of China under the Central Government, and Chiang had not lost sight of the goals of unification and independence for which so much sacrifice had already been made. Throughout the years after 1937, the Japanese had made several offers of peace which were always rejected, and the zeal to stay steadfast and not to capitulate was unmoved. Chiang, in any case, was receiving relatively little direct military aid from the United States and had to husband what he got. If he had had firm assurances of postwar backing from the United States against the Communists and both British and Russian imperialists, he might have been more willing to throw all of his best into attacks upon the Japanese in Burma and in China.

During the dragging months of military exasperation in 1943, and amid a general disappointment at numerous failures — to build adequate roads for military supply, to get on with the training of troops, to develop the Fourteenth Air Force under General Chennault to the point where it could operate as a full offensive arm — efforts were made by Chiang Kai-shek to negotiate differences with the Chinese Communist Party. In fact these efforts had continued from 1941 after the incident of the New Fourth Army,[29] sometimes in the face of suspicion in the Communist camp that elements of the Kuomintang would seize any convenient opportunity to attack the Chinese Communists.[30] Chiang Kai-shek had a conference on June 6, 1943, with General Lin Piao, Communist Party representative from Yenan, and Chou En-lai, Communist representative at Chungking, at which Chiang offered terms.[31] The Communist Party was to be given legal status as a *party*, on condition that it give up its border government in Yenan and the district governments under its control. It was also stipulated that the

28. Wedemeyer, *Wedemeyer Reports!* pp. 279–282.
29. *United States Relations with China*, p. 53.
30. This suspicion was reported more than once in the dispatches circulated in the State Department. See mention of the possibility of a resolution of the Central Executive Committee of the Kuomintang advocating the use of force against the Communists. *China Papers*, 1943, p. 117.
31. See the telegrams from the Chargé in China (Atcheson) to the Secretary of State in late June and early July 1943 for a report of these terms. *China Papers*, 1943, pp. 257 and 275.

Communists would have to place their army under the command of
the Central Government. The Generalissimo was reported to have
told the Communists that his views had not changed regarding the
differences between them. They would have to give up their independent governments and their army, after which they could join the
Kuomintang, or become like any of the other minority parties already
existing in Free China. His terms in short were an affirmation of the
agreements of 1937.

Nothing came of the negotiations since the Communists, as a rival
regime on the China mainland, were more interested in obtaining recognition of some independence and separate status in the conduct of
military affairs. In the year 1943, some of the views of the Communists in this respect were given notice in the dispatches and memoranda
of John Paton Davies, Jr., John Stewart Service, and John Carter
Vincent. Davies in a dispatch dated March 16, 1943, reported that he
had sounded out Chou En-lai on the possibility of "our drawing in
Communist intelligence regarding enemy activities," and that Chou
had instead repeated his proposal of the previous summer, that American military observers be assigned to the Communist areas.[32] Three
months later Davies was in Washington advocating that the United
States abandon its hands-off policy in the dispute between the Kuomintang and the Communists, and that it prepare to intervene.[33] As a
first step in the formulation of a policy of intervention, he thought
it necessary for the United States to have its own sources of official
information in the Communist area, which was Chou's thought too.
He also suggested that Chiang might not like the idea but that our
bargaining position with him was stronger than we realized, since
Chiang could not desert the Americans although the Americans could
defeat the Japanese without his aid. Because it would be useful to have
accurate information about Communist military strength, according to
Davies, he proposed that we should send a military mission to the Communist areas. John S. Service in a memorandum of September 14, 1943,
lent support to the repeated proposal for an American military mission
to the Chinese Communists in a report he made of a meeting between
General Stilwell (to whose staff he had been attached) and General
Teng Pao-shan, Commander of the Central Government's 22d Army,
with headquarters in Shensi Province, a man identified by Service as
"of liberal tendencies and as sympathetic toward the Communists." [34]
John Carter Vincent as Chargé in China also passed on Chou En-lai's

32. *China Papers*, 1943, p. 214.
33. The proposals were set out in a memorandum by the Second Secretary of
Embassy in China (Davies), temporarily in the United States, dated June 24,
1943. *China Papers*, 1943, pp. 258–266.
34. *China Papers*, 1943, pp. 331–332.

suggestion that American military and civilian observers be sent to the guerrilla areas.[35]

But as the view was being pressed by some of the officers of the State Department that the United States ought to have a more active policy with respect to the Chinese Communists, there were others in the department who argued a different line. The Chief of the Far Eastern Division of the State Department, Maxwell D. Hamilton, in a summary statement dated February 11, 1943, took notice of widespread rumors about the morale and attitudes of the Chinese.[36] He pointed out that the active phase of Sino-Japanese hostilities had ended some two and a half years before, and that since that time the Chinese had held their lines against the Japanese and were pinning down some 600,000 out of approximately two and a quarter million Japanese troops. While the Chinese themselves had some two and a half million troops of their own, only a comparatively small portion of them was adequately armed. Without "general military assistance on a considerable scale," it did not seem possible that the Chinese could continue to contain the Japanese, especially if the Japanese should launch a concerted effort to advance. Chinese morale was adversely affected not only by the lack of military aid but by diversions of aid allocated, and by failure on the part of the Americans to fulfill promises of aid.

Stanley K. Hornbeck, the Department of State's Adviser on Political Relations, reported a conversation in Washington with T. V. Soong, the Chinese Foreign Minister, in August 1943.[37] In the course of this conversation Hornbeck mentioned rumors that "the American and the British Governments were urgently pressing upon the Chinese Government a course of action regarding the Communists." Hornbeck told Soong that there was nothing to the rumor, that the American position had always been one of hope that civil strife would be avoided "but we have scrupulously refrained from urging upon the Chinese Government any particular course of action in connection with or in regard to matters of Chinese international [sic] politics." He later reviewed the policy of the Soviet Union in the Far East, and with considerable accuracy (in August 1943) predicted the entry of the Soviet Union into the war in its late stages and before the capitulation of Japan.[38] Suspicious of the Soviet Union, he nevertheless thought that, for the time, the Soviet Union would continue its policy of expedient stability in its relations with Japan and would maintain "at least openly a neutral attitude between the Chinese Communists and the Kuomin-

35. *China Papers,* 1943, pp. 230–231.
36. *China Papers,* 1943, pp. 4–9.
37. *China Papers,* 1943, pp. 96–100.
38. *China Papers,* 1943, pp. 317–320.

tang." Late in October 1943, Hornbeck defended the Chinese against the increasing charge that they were apathetic about the war with Japan, pointing out that the Chinese could also with some justice say that the Americans and the British showed a general tendency to pay too little attention to the China theater and its potentialities.[39]

Two incidents outside the government touched upon the Department of State in its relations with the Chinese Communists and the Kuomintang in late 1942 and in 1943. The first incident was created by Earl Browder, the General Secretary of the Communist Party, USA, who said in the *Daily Worker* of October 4, 1942, that reactionary officials in the Department of State were encouraging Chiang Kai-shek to keep his best armies out of the war with Japan with a view towards liquidating the Chinese Communists. He also charged that the State Department had informed Chungking that our government would be displeased if complete unity were established between the Kuomintang and the Chinese Communists, and that we had told Chungking that "it must continue to fight the communists if it wishes United States friendship." [40] This pressure by the CPUSA on the State Department drew the formal denial it was presumably planned to elicit. The State Department prepared a memorandum of denial of all the points charged and on October 12, 1942, no less a personage than Sumner Welles, the Under Secretary of State, gave the disclaimer to Earl Browder.[41] The day after the statement was issued, Earl Browder wrote to Welles thanking him for "the frank and helpful character of the cooperation you have shown us, which we feel will add to the effectiveness of our work for the victory." [42] Browder was later to testify that the CPUSA was fully satisfied with the policy of the State Department between 1942 and 1946 as expressed in the Welles memorandum.[43]

39. *China Papers*, 1943, pp. 152–153.
40. See Memorandum Prepared in the Department of State, dated October 3, 1942, referring to Mr. Browder's "intended statement," no copy of which, however, was to be found in State Department files. *China Papers*, 1942, pp. 243–244.
41. Although no copy of the Welles statement is available in the files of the Department of State, the department printed in *China Papers*, 1942, the copy of the statement as it appeared in the *Daily Worker* of October 16, 1942. See *China Papers*, 1942, pp. 248–249.
42. *China Papers*, 1942, p. 249.
43. Browder said, ". . . in 1942, it became unnecessary any longer to bring . . . pressure upon the Government of the United States, because the officially declared policy, from that time until 1946, was the United States pressed upon China the coalition of the Kuomintang, the Communist, and all the democratic mass forces in one united government. From 1942 to 1946 that was the official policy of the American Government, and it was therefore no occasion for the Communists — I would say from 1942 to 1945, the only period of which I can speak — there was no occasion for the Communists to press for a change of policy in the United States Government at that time." Eighty-first Congress, Second

The other incident was the suspension by the Chungking Vice Minister of Information in July 1943 of Gunther Stein, correspondent for the Institute of Pacific Relations and the *Christian Science Monitor*. Stein was suspended as a correspondent for the IPR but not as correspondent for the *Monitor*. The occasion was an article in *Far Eastern Survey* (one of the IPR journals) written, not by Stein, but by T. A. Bisson of the secretariat of the IPR in which it was said that there were two Chinas, Feudal China, which was the Kuomintang regime, and Democratic China, which was the Communist establishment.[44] Chiang Kai-shek later said that after this article, "international Communists worked overtime to turn American public opinion and American diplomacy against the Republic of China and Chinese Government."[45] In October 1943, however, the American Ambassador to China, Christian Gauss, was to write to the Secretary of State that American press criticism of China was fairly widely approved by liberal elements in China, who felt that an article by Pearl Buck (to a great extent) and those by Hanson Baldwin and T. A. Bisson (to a lesser degree) had had a salutory effect on the Chinese government.[46]

It was suggested by the ambassador that the articles had probably led to the adoption by the Central Executive Committee of the Kuomintang in Plenary Session in September 1943 of resolutions for the political reorganization of the regime. At this session of the CEC feeling against the Communists by "Kuomintang die-hards" ran high and there was talk of liquidating them by force.[47] But cooler counsels prevailed, and the CEC instead adopted revised articles of the organic law of the National Government on September 10, the chief provision of which was the constitutionalization of the authority of Chiang, who was then elected president.[48] At the September meeting of the CEC, Chiang gave specific instructions that the Chinese Communist problem should be handled peacefully, that "we should clearly recognize that the Communist problem is a purely political problem and should be solved by political means."[49] The alarm that civil war might break out in 1943 was thus allayed.

Session, United States Senate, Subcommittee of the Committee on Foreign Relations, Hearings Pursuant to S. Res. 231, *A Resolution to Investigate Whether There Are Employees in the State Department Disloyal to the United States*, pt. 1, p. 682 (hereafter cited as the *Tydings Committee*).

44. See *China Papers*, 1943, p. 79, for report of suspension of Atcheson, Chargé in China, to the Secretary of State.

45. Chiang Kai-shek, *Soviet Russia in China* (New York: Farrar, Straus and Cudahy, 1957), pp. 111–113.

46. *China Papers*, 1943, pp. 148–150, at p. 149.

47. *China Papers*, 1943. The Chargé in China (Atcheson) to the Secretary of State, September 17, 1943, p. 340.

48. For the revisions adopted, see *China Papers*, 1943, p. 333.

49. *United States Relations with China*, p. 54.

Two other events in 1943 were foreboding. First, Chiang seems to have made up his mind, tentatively at least, to ask for the replacement of General Stilwell, and was evidently deterred from doing so only by the intervention of Mme. Chiang Kai-shek and her sister, Mme. K'ung.[50] Although Stilwell's notes reek of his contempt for the Generalissimo, to whom he often referred as the "Peanut," and whom he described as a "crabbed little bastard," [51] the difficult relationship was to endure for another year. Second, the Soviet Union by the end of 1943 was finally free of the threatening disaster of the German invasion of Russia, was getting stronger, and was beginning to look towards the pattern of positions when the war should end. With respect to China, this meant among other things expression of concern — for the first time during the war — for the Chinese Communist Party. In August 1943 it was reported from Moscow that for the first time since the beginning of the Sino-Japanese war, the Soviet press was emphasizing the role of the Communists in the struggle against Japan, and was openly supporting their cause.[52] In 1943 the Allies finally gave high public attention to Chiang Kai-shek by inviting him to the Cairo Conference in November where he was given flattering assurances about the postwar settlements and a solid commitment for the recovery of Burma in 1944.

With the sense widespread in 1944 that the end of the war was in sight, both the military and the political tempos in China increased. The speed and force of the first were raised by two offensives, that by Stilwell in Burma and the other by the Japanese in East China. Stilwell, with what more conservative commanders thought was unpardonable verve and unsound procedure, took the field himself, and from January to July 1944 led the Chinese troops he had trained in India through the jungle across North Burma to victory over the Japanese at Myitkyina, which fell in July. Stilwell in a letter to his wife called it the "first sustained offensive in Chinese history against a first-class enemy." [53] Even Chiang was impressed by the feat and contributed troops at the request of Stilwell. One consequence of the victory was a decision by Roosevelt to try to persuade Chiang Kai-shek to make Stilwell the commander in chief of the Chinese armies; and he sent

50. For Stilwell's account of the episode in October 1943, see *The Stilwell Papers*, pp. 231–237.

51. Stilwell, *The Stilwell Papers*, p. 229.

52. Eighty-second Congress, Second Session, United States Senate, Committee on the Judiciary, Subcommittee to Investigate the Administration of the Internal Security Act and Other Internal Security Laws, *Hearings on the Institute of Pacific Relations*, Part 7A, Appendix II, p. 2382. (This Intelligence Report is hereafter cited as *The Chinese Communist Movement*.)

53. *The Stilwell Papers*, p. 313.

Patrick J. Hurley, Oklahoma oil man, and Donald Nelson of the War Production Board to handle the delicate negotiations. Nelson was presumably to discuss lend-lease matters in any new arrangement that might be negotiated.

The second great offensive, however, was Japanese, not Chinese. The success of sea raids by American planes against the Japanese drove the Japanese to launch a massive campaign against bases in East China from which the planes were launched. The offensive against the forces of the Central Government almost split East China in two. By September 1944 the Japanese were approaching the great American military center at Kweilin. Signs of military disintegration that had appeared among the Chinese in the spring, and multiplied in the summer, threatened disaster in the fall. The attack upon Kweilin was pressed relentlessly to victory by the Japanese; the military center fell on November 12, and with it the entire East China front. It was possible that the Japanese could have continued on to Chungking and to the "vitally important American base at Kunming." [54]

These ominous developments, and the success of Stilwell in Burma were the factors that led Roosevelt to propose his appointment as commander in chief of all the Chinese and American forces, not only once but twice.[55] The pressure from the President created a final crisis of policy, and of face, for Chiang. He was being crowded to put a foreigner in control of all the armies, and to use Communist troops if this should be feasible, as Roosevelt urged. He first agreed in principle to the appointment of Stilwell, and then he failed to appoint him. On September 22, General Stilwell reported to the Chief of Staff in Washington that Chiang "believes that our advance in the Pacific will be swift enough and effective enough to spare his further effort, and he would like to avoid the bitter pill of recognizing the communists and putting a foreigner in command of the army. . . ." Four days later, Stilwell reported to Washington that "I am now convinced that, for the reasons stated, the United States will not get any real cooperation from China while Chiang Kai-shek is in power." [56] On September 24, Chiang demanded the recall of General Stilwell. On October 13, Stilwell was still waiting for Roosevelt's decision on Chiang's request

54. *United States Relations with China*, p. 66.
55. The original suggestion was made in a communication dated July 7 and repeated in another of August 23, 1944. In the second message, Roosevelt also said, "I do not think the forces to come under General Stilwell's command should be limited except by their availability to defend China and to fight the Japanese. When the enemy is pressing us toward possible disaster, it appears unsound to reject the aid of anyone who will kill Japanese." *United States Relations with China*, p. 67.
56. *United States Relations with China*, p. 68.

for his removal and noted in his journal, "Some indications F.D.R. will get tough but I don't trust politicians." [57] On October 19, he received a radio message from General George Marshall that he had been recalled, and that General Albert C. Wedemeyer was to command the troops in China.

The Wallace, Hurley, and Marshall Missions

Before a discussion of the Hurley mission and the bearing it had on American policy, mention should be made of the mission of Vice President Henry A. Wallace in June 1944. Roosevelt had asked Wallace to go to China to see what he could do about consolidating the Chinese war effort against Japan. John Carter Vincent, by now chief of the Division of Chinese Affairs in the State Department, accompanied Wallace on the trip and took notes of the three days of conversations between Wallace and Chiang Kai-shek.[58] The record shows that Owen Lattimore, whose name was to become more familiar than it was at the time, sat in on the conversations on two of the three days and helped in the translating on one of them.

In the course of the conversations, Wallace told Chiang that President Roosevelt had assumed that, inasmuch as the Communists and the Kuomintang were all basically friends, "nothing should be final between friends," which was certainly a remarkable testament of ignorance of history, the Chinese civil war, and human nature.[59] In the course of some lengthy exchanges about the Communists in China, Chiang told Wallace that the notion that they were agrarian democrats was false; and he said further that they were part of the international Communist movement, and that they were more communistic than the Russians. Vincent's notes at one point say, "Mr. Wallace referred to the patriotic attitude of the Communists in the United States and said that he could not understand the attitude of the Chinese Communists, as described by President Chiang." [60] In the course of the conversations, Chiang finally agreed to the proposal that had been discussed in State Department dispatches for some time — to send Americans as observers to the Communist areas. He stipulated only that they go under the auspices of the National Military Council and not the United States Army, and added that Chinese officers would have to go with them. Wallace had received a message from Roosevelt while he was in Chungking advising him to press Chiang to permit

57. The Stilwell Papers, p. 343.
58. These notes are available in United States Relations with China, pp. 549–559.
59. Wallace also told Chiang that Roosevelt had said that a friend might be called in to mediate, and that he might be that friend. United States Relations with China, p. 549.
60. United States Relations with China, p. 553.

the dispatch of an Army observer group to the Communist areas. When the terms of the understanding were being discussed, General Ferris and his aide, John Stewart Service, participated in the discussions.

In his messages for President Roosevelt, at the end of the visit by Wallace, Chiang said that the Chinese Communist question was an internal political problem but that he would welcome the intervention of the President "if the President, after mature consideration, decides he would like to give his help." He also warned him against thinking that the conflict between the Central Government and the Chinese Communists was like that between capital and labor in the United States. In a message to Chiang after the Wallace mission, President Roosevelt, after the amenities, suggested again the desirability of reaching an agreement between the Central Government and the Chinese Communists for effective prosecution of the war against Japan in North China.

The pressure from the United States to get Chiang to resolve "differences" with the Chinese Communists was resented by Chiang, who felt that there was great misunderstanding among the Americans of the nature of the problem, and thought that pressure should also be applied to the Chinese Communists to resolve their differences with the Central Government. Ambassador Gauss wrote to the Secretary of State on August 31, 1944, summarizing Chiang's position. The increasingly repeated request that China meet Communist demands "is equivalent to asking China's unconditional surrender to a party known to be under a foreign power's influence [the Soviet Union]." [61] Chiang said that the American attitude was only intensifying the recalcitrance of the Chinese Communists and that very serious consequences for China might result.

Ambassador Gauss told Chiang that the United States Government was not interested in the cause of the Communists but that it did want to see a solution of an internal problem "which finds the armed forces of China facing one another instead of facing and making war upon Japan, and, in the present critical period of the war this is of outstanding importance." Gauss also made it clear that the United States Government was not proposing that the Central Government "yield to the demands of the Communists," but was interested only in the dissipation of the existing critical situation and in the unification of China. Gauss thought that some contribution to these ends might be made if there were wider participation by "special groups or parties" in responsible war planning and in carrying out of such plans, although not necessarily in representation of the Communists in the government.

61. *United States Relations with China*, pp. 61–63.

In his reply Secretary Hull on September 9 noted that the suggestion that the United States press the Chinese Communists to accede to the Central Government had been made by Chiang to Wallace also, and that the repetition of the notion "would indicate a discouraging lack of progress in the Generalissimo's thinking." [62] The observer group in North China should not be asked to press the Communists in the matter since its function was military and not political, but Hull suggested that Gauss through Chiang might arrange a meeting with the Communist representative at Chungking in order to urge him to have the Chinese Communists come to terms with the Central Government. Hull was pleased that Gauss had mentioned the possibility of "a coalition council as described by you," and authorized him to tell Chiang that Hull and Roosevelt both felt that the "suggestion is timely as well as practical, and worthy of careful consideration."

By September 1944, then, American policy towards the Central Government seems to have modified somewhat. Although it was unremitting in its support of the government, it no longer assumed the aloof stance of detachment from the internal affairs of China. It had slowly come to be modified in at least two respects: first, the command of the armies of China should be placed under an American, with the clear implication that he would arm and supply the Chinese Communists and utilize them in the war effort; and second, the planning and administration of the war effort under the Central Government should be broadened by the inclusion of other parties and groups in a war council or some other administrative form of coalition. These suggestions were reinforced by the alarm felt in both American military and civilian circles that the Central Government might collapse before the Japanese offensive, and by the reports by the military observers and John Stewart Service in the American observer mission in the Communist areas.[63]

The two most important missions in the general debacle of China policy were the Hurley mission and the Marshall mission. Hurley, as has been said, had been sent to China by the President to promote harmonious relations between Chiang and Stilwell, to perform certain duties with respect to military supplies, to represent Roosevelt to the Generalissimo, and to keep in touch with Ambassador Gauss. Almost immediately Stilwell was out of the picture; and Ambassador Gauss had resigned. Hurley was then appointed ambassador to China and he redefined his mission as follows: to prevent the collapse of the Central Government; to keep Chiang in power as president of the Republic and as Generalissimo of the armies; to harmonize relations

62. *United States Relations with China*, pp. 63–64.
63. For comment on the Service reports, see Feis, *The China Tangle*, p. 175.

between Chiang and the American commander; to promote production of war supplies and prevent economic collapse; and to unify all
military forces in China for the purpose of defeating Japan. Hurley
had no clear instructions as to how he was to deal with the Chinese
Communists, nor any directive that it was American policy to keep
the Chiang regime in control of the government of China.[64] Although
Hurley's definition of his mission was a substantial modification of
American policy, he was never contradicted in his assumptions.

Hurley went to China by way of Moscow where he had conversations with Molotov, the Foreign Minister of the Soviet Union, who
told the believing Hurley that the Soviet Union had had no responsibility for various happenings in China in recent years, that Moscow
should not be associated with the Communists in China, that because
of poverty, the Chinese Communists called themselves "Communists"
as a form of protest against their condition, and that they were related
to communism in no way at all.[65] Incredible though they were, Hurley
took these statements to be literally true about both the Chinese Communists and about the relation between the Chinese Communists and
the Soviet Union. Upon arrival in China, Hurley immediately com-
municated to Chiang the stimulating news he had received from Molotov. Being of the opinion that the unification of all military forces
for the defeat of Japan depended upon the unification of the Chinese,
Hurley then set about the task of mediating the differences between
the Kuomintang and the Communists (now, remarkably, not really
Communists at all), and thought, in December 1944, that he had convinced Chiang that the Chinese Communist Party was not an instrument of the Soviet Union,[66] which — to whatever degree true in 1944
— was a statement that only the history of the previous twenty-four
years could put in proper perspective.

On November 7, 1944, Hurley went to Yenan, conferred with the
Communist representatives for two days, and came up on November 10
with a Five Point Draft Agreement, signed by Mao Tse-tung as chairman of the Central Executive Committee of the Chinese Communist
Party. The second of the five points provided both for the establishment of a coalition war council and for the establishment of a "coalition National Government" embracing representatives of all anti-
Japanese parties and non-partisan political bodies. Point 5 provided
that "The coalition National Government of China recognizes the
legality of the Kuomintang of China, the Chinese Communist Party,
and all anti-Japanese parties." It is of some interest that here for the

64. Feis, *The China Tangle*, p. 179.
65. *United States Relations with China*, pp. 71–72.
66. *United States Relations with China*, p. 73.

first time a responsible American spokesman, with a mandate from the President, acting as his personal representative, endorses a coalition government as a practical plan for the settlement of the issues between the Kuomintang and the Communists. Even Hurley's admirer, General Wedemeyer, found this hard to take, and suggested that Hurley was either misled by the warmth of his reception by the Chinese Communists, or had thought he was "attempting a task no more impossible to achieve than arbitration between a trade union and management in a labor dispute." [67]

The Central Government understandably rejected the Five Point Draft Agreement and proposed instead that it would incorporate the Communist army into its own and recognize the Communist Party as legal, the Communists consenting to give over control of all their troops, and to accept membership in the National Military Council. There was no mention of coalition government. On December 16, 1944, Chou told Hurley that the fundamental difficulty in coming to agreement was the unwillingness of the Kuomintang to forsake one party rule and accept "democratic coalition government." [68] Then ensued a month of jockeying back and forth on a meeting of Yenan and Kuomintang representatives which eventually took place late in January in Chungking. The Chungking spokesmen added to their previous three points the proposal that a war cabinet with Communist representation in it be established, and that an American might command the Communist troops for the duration of the war after the Communist army had been incorporated into the national forces with the help of a three-man military group containing one Central Government, one Communist, and one American military officer.

On March 1, 1945, Chiang announced that a People's Congress to inaugurate constitutional government in China would be convened on November 12, that upon the inauguration of constitutional government all political parties would have legal status and would enjoy equality. He noted parenthetically that the Central Government had offered to give legal recognition to the Communist Party as soon as it should agree to incorporate its army and local administration in the National Government. The date of the statement is significant for, although the fighting had not yet stopped, the postwar period had in effect begun. That is, the prime problem was not now the organization of unified forces to beat Japan. The problem was the struggle for postwar position. The Chinese Communists reacted sharply against the Chiang statement, insisting that it showed merely that the Kuomintang was not sincerely interested in the establishment of "democratic re-

67. *Wedemeyer Reports!* p. 310.
68. *United States Relations with China*, p. 77.

forms," and that it had left no basis on which negotiations between "the Communist Party and the other democratic parties and the Kuomintang Government" could be continued.

Hurley's preposterous comment on the negotiations was that "two fundamental facts are emerging: (1) the Communists are not in fact Communists, they are striving for democratic principles; and (2) the one party, one man personal government of the Kuomintang is not in fact fascist, it is striving for democratic principles." [69] Hurley returned to the United States in the month of March, among other reasons to discuss the then recently concluded Yalta Conference, which he had not been invited to attend. He held a press and radio conference in the State Department on April 2, 1945, in the course of which he was asked questions about the Communists in China. He described the conflict in the following words:

> All the demands that the Communist Party have been making have been on a democratic basis. That has led to the statement that the Communist Party in China are not, in fact, real Communists. The Communist Party of China is supporting exactly the same principles as those promulgated by the National Government of China and conceded to be objectives also of the National Government. . . .
> Q. Could you tell us what is the divergence between them? How do they differ?
> . . . . .
> A. Well as a matter of fact, the divergence between the parties in China seems to be not in the objective desired because they both assert that they are for the establishment of a government in China that will decentralize authority and conduct itself along democratic lines, employing democratic processes. The divergence between them is the procedure by which they can be achieved.[70]

In testimony before the Senate Foreign Relations Committee on December 6, 1945 (after Hurley's resignation as ambassador to China), he asked his questioners please to "distinguish between them [the Chinese Communists] and the Union of Soviet Socialist Republics, because they are different, and all of this Marshal Stalin and Commissar Molotov had been telling me, and throughout the entire period of the vicissitudes through which we passed so far as I know they have kept their

69. *United States Relations with China*, p. 86.
70. Reported in Eighty-second Congress, First Session, United States Senate, Committee on Armed Services and Committee on Foreign Relations, *Hearings to Conduct an Inquiry into the Military Situation in the Far East and the Facts Surrounding the Relief of General of the Army Douglas MacArthur from his Assignments in that Area*, p. 2896 (hereafter cited as *The Military Situation in the Far East*).

word to me, that . . . Russia . . . does not recognize the Chinese armed Communist Party as Communists at all." [71] It is possible that Hurley did more damage to Chiang by statements like these than all the Foreign Service critics in the field.

Hurley resigned as ambassador to China on November 26, 1945, his mission concluded, if not accomplished. For by that time the war had ended in Europe and Asia, and there were new elements domestic and international to influence the course of events in China. The Yalta Agreements had introduced the Soviet Union as an active belligerent in Asia, and were to put Soviet armies into the scales of the military balance that had oscillated little from the horizontal on the land mass of China for four years. If it had been Soviet policy for much of the war to promote common causes with the Kuomintang, the military necessity to do so after V-J Day was lifted. Although Hurley may have been miffed that he had not been invited to Yalta,[72] how much more so should Chiang Kai-shek, who was not consulted at all about the disposition of Chinese affairs? A Treaty of Friendship and Alliance between the Soviet Union and China was signed on August 14, 1945, pledging mutual respect for respective sovereignties and non-interference in internal affairs. The Soviet Union promised to supply aid and support only to the "National Government as the central government of China" and recognized Chinese sovereignty in Manchuria.[73] And from these beginnings the confused course of United States policy towards China was to unfold to its end in sorry and bitter frustration.

While Hurley was proceeding with his assignment in China, he felt that he was being opposed by foreign service officers in the field and by State Department staff in Washington.[74] As was said, he had come

71. *The Military Situation in the Far East*, p. 2895.

72. Feis suggests that when Hurley left Chungking for Washington on February 19, 1945, "There may also have been in his mind a tinge of feeling that he ought to have been present at the Yalta Conference. He had traveled to Moscow before coming to China in order to prepare the way for an agreement between the Chinese and Soviet governments. He had kept the President reminded of its utility. It would have been natural for him to think he should have been called on to advise on China's situation and needs, especially since he did not know of the rapid march of plans for Soviet entry into the war, which crowded Roosevelt into the Yalta accord in the Far East." *The China Tangle*, p. 225.

73. *United States Relations with China*, p. 117. Hurley, in reporting to the State Department a conversation with Chiang about the treaty (he was "generally satisfied" with it), said that "Yesterday he [Chiang] thanked me for the basis I had helped him lay for the approchement with the Soviets." *Ibid.*, p. 120.

74. In December 1944, Hurley had complained to Roosevelt, without informing General Wedemeyer, that members of Wedemeyer's staff had been undermining Hurley's efforts to secure Communist troops for use against Japan. One of these was General Robert McClure, Wedemeyer's Chief of Staff. General McClure and two other officers had framed exploratory plans for the use of Chinese Communist troops with the full knowledge and consent of General Wedemeyer.

to regard it as his mission to maintain the Chiang regime in power, and he had not been contradicted in this by the Secretary of State. This was not the view of State Department critics of Chiang, however. They felt that maintenance of the existing regime should not be confused with support because any regime might be replaced some day, transformed into a constitutional system, or otherwise changed in composition and orientation. The critics then were therefore not greatly apprehensive about the possible consequences to the regime from any improvement in the position of the Chinese Communists. And there were some who actively disliked the Chiang regime, felt that it needed to be reformed, and counseled steps that would force reform. A score of the memoranda from some of the foreign service officers between 1943 and 1945 illustrate these opinions with clarity.[75]

These communications showed an awareness that the intentions of the Soviet Union with respect to the Far East, including China, were aggressive.[76] They indicated that the Chinese Communists had a "background of subservience" to the Soviet Union but felt that nationalism was an influence modifying this dependency. There was feeling that the Communists were a dynamic force challenging the Kuomintang for control of the country and that the KMT and the National Government were disintegrating. Possible civil war between the two powers in China could have the effect of hampering the war against Japan, pressing the Chinese Communists back into the arms of the Soviet Union, and risking American-Soviet involvement in the struggle. There was more belief than the facts might have justified that the Communists would win such a civil war, although it is true that the Communists were stronger than they had been in the early 1930's and Chiang had not then been able to exterminate them.

What then to do, assuming the truth of the foregoing? American policy, it was thought, should attempt to avoid civil war by the adjustment of new alignments of power in China, through peaceful processes. The desirable way was to encourage the reform of the government by broadening the representation of other groups than the Kuomintang — that is, by establishing a coalition. Failing this, it should be American policy to limit our involvement with the Kuomintang, and to commence some cooperation with the Communists, the force destined to control China, in an effort to influence them further into an independent position friendly to the United States. All this should

Wedemeyer Reports! pp. 305–306. Wedemeyer felt that Hurley had "unjustly impugned the loyalty of my Chief of Staff, General McClure."
75. *United States Relations with China*, pp. 564–576.
76. The principal themes of the reports are summarized in *United States Relations with China*, at pp. 64–65.

be done before the Soviet Union entered the war and invaded China.

By January 1945, the lines seem to have been clearly drawn in the State Department between those who argued that military aid to the Chinese Communists would help the war against Japan and would force Chiang into more active effort, and Hurley's view that the United States should work only through Chiang. Hurley told the Secretary of State at the end of January that "In all my negotiations with the Communists, I have insisted that the United States will not supply or otherwise aid the Chinese Communists as a political party or as an insurrection against the National Government. Any aid to the Communist Party must go to that party through the National Government of China." [77] And General Wedemeyer followed this political line also.[78]

In March 1945 there was a showdown in the State Department on the policy question that divided Hurley and some of the members of the Foreign Service staff. While Hurley and General Wedemeyer were in Washington for consultations, a telegram was prepared by John Stewart Service on the basis of reports by Raymond P. Ludden, and on the suggestion of George Atcheson, Counselor of the Embassy, and sent to Washington on February 28.[79] It was a proposal that the United States get tough with Chiang. He was to be told that military necessity required that we supply and support Communist and other suitable groups who could aid in the war against Japan, and that to accomplish this end, "we are taking direct steps." Chiang would be assured that we would not reduce our assistance to the Central Government. The United States would be prepared to continue to lend good offices to promote the unification of China, and it was felt that public notice of this would itself exert pressure upon Chiang to make the necessary concessions required for unity and to put his own house in order. Service later said, "At Atcheson's instructions, this telegram was shown by me to Wedemeyer's Chief of Staff General Gross, who was then in acting command, and he gave it his hearty endorsement." [80]

77. Feis, *The China Tangle*, p. 266.
78. In a press conference in Chungking on February 12, 1945, General Wedemeyer said that he had required every one of his officers to sign a statement that he understood Wedemeyer's position on political matters. "My policy," he said, "is this, that we will not give assistance to any individual, to any activity or any organization within the China Theater, we American officers, we American people . . . I am ordered to support the Central Government and I am going to do that to the best of my ability . . ." Quoted in Don Lohbeck, *Patrick J. Hurley* (Chicago: Henry Regnery Company, 1956), p. 342.
79. *Tydings Committee*, p. 1974. The origin and preparation of the telegram are explained in the course of a long personal statement by John Stewart Service which is reprinted in the Tydings Committee hearings. A paraphrase of the telegram itself is to be found in *United States Relations with China*, pp. 87–92.
80. *Tydings Committee*, p. 1974.

Acting Secretary of State Joseph Grew passed it on to the White House with the suggestion that there were signs of a need for more flexibility in United States policy towards China.[81] On March 5, 1945, there was a meeting between Hurley and the State Department staff on the proposals of February 28, and the matter of policy was vigorously argued. There were later conversations between Hurley and top State Department, War Department, and military officials and the matter was discussed by Hurley with the President. The President sustained Hurley in the controversy.

As a result of Hurley's insistence, General Wedemeyer's staff from the State Department was dispersed. John Paton Davies, Jr. was recalled by the State Department and subsequently transferred to Moscow. Wedemeyer tells of the painful scene on the occasion of the departure of Davies when Hurley accused him of being a Communist and of failing to support the Chinese Nationalists.[82] John Stewart Service was transferred to the Department of State in Washington, and soon became involved in the public agitation over the *Amerasia* affair.

Hurley went back to China after the confrontation of views in March in an effort to advance the negotiations for unification but without much success. President Truman asked Hurley to stay on as ambassador to China but by October of 1945 Hurley was ready to resign and did so on November 26. In his letter of resignation he said in part:

> . . . it is no secret that the American policy in China did not have the support of all the career men in the State Department. The professional foreign service men sided with the Chinese Communist armed party and the imperialist bloc of nations whose policy it was to keep China divided against herself. . . .
>
> I requested the relief of the career men who were opposing the American policy in the Chinese Theater of war. These professional diplomats were returned to Washington and placed in the Chinese and Far Eastern Divisions of the State Department as my supervisors.[83]

There was much else in the letter of resignation. He claimed that he had made progress towards the unification of the armed forces of China, that he had prevented the civil war between the rival factions, and that the leaders of the rival parties had been brought together for peaceful discussions — all statements of doubtful accuracy.

81. Feis, *The China Tangle*, p. 271.
82. *Wedemeyer Reports!* pp. 318–319.
83. *United States Relations with China*, pp. 581–584, at p. 582.

It is not the purpose of this discussion to recount the steps by which the eventual debacle of our China policy was reached, moving from one frustration of intent to another in a confusion of counsels and plans. But mention may be made of a final effort to mediate the civil conflict in China which relentlessly moved into open warfare and the eventual defeat of Chiang. The day after Hurley's resignation, President Truman appointed General George C. Marshall as his special representative in China, and after over a year of effort to get the Kuomintang and the Chinese Communists to unify "by peaceful, democratic methods," Marshall gave up, and was recalled by President Truman on January 6, 1947. At one stage, he thought that the mission would be strengthened if he could have the support and assistance of Dr. J. Leighton Stuart, President of Yenching University of Peiping, so he recommended Stuart's appointment as ambassador to China and President Truman complied with the request, the Senate confirming the nomination July 11, 1946. On October 1, 1946, General Marshall told Chiang that unless a basis of agreement was reached for terminating the fighting "without further delays of proposals and counterproposals," he would ask Truman to call him home and end the effort of mediation.[84] When the National Government offered a temporary end to the fighting and the declaration of a truce, Marshall asked the State Department to inform Truman of the fact and of Marshall's decision to withdraw the recommendation for his recall. Thereupon the Communists rejected the truce proposal. Marshall came to feel that he was being used by both the National Government and the Chinese Communists — that the first had wanted American mediation as a shield for its military campaigns, and that the Communists, by the end of 1946, at least, did not want mediation at all. Marshall felt repugnance at being used by either party and thought that Communist rejection of all government overtures played directly into the hands of Kuomintang die-hards, from whom his chief opposition had always come. The Marshall mission failed. The basic premise on which it operated was probably faulty — namely, that the solvents of patience, tact, discussion, sincerity could reduce the implacable determination of the Chinese Communists to destroy the regime of Chiang Kai-shek and the cold determination of the leadership of the National Government to exterminate the Communists.[85]

Reasons for the rise of China policy to a political issue of great magnitude and passion are, in general, the same that made the issue of

84. *United States Relations with China*, p. 189.

85. See also Robert C. North, *Moscow and Chinese Communists* (Stanford, California: Stanford, 1953), p. 228, for a similar expression of view. North points out that it may have been determined as a matter of Communist policy as early as the autumn of 1945 not to cooperate with the Kuomintang.

Communists in government so explosive in the years preceding the Republican presidential victory of 1952, and as such will be discussed in the chapters that follow. Here it is enough to say that the translation of a problem into an issue can never be explained simply by reference to the objective facts, however disturbing these facts might be. "Fall-out" with its potential threat to the present and the future of mankind has never really become a political issue in the United States, despite the dogged efforts of Adlai Stevenson in 1956 and many scientists before and since to make it one. The Rosenberg case never became an issue in the United States although for several months it dominated the front pages of many European and Asian newspapers. Indochina fell and was partitioned without important political repercussions. Klaus Fuchs, Burgess and McLean, and Bruno Pontecorvo were exposed as Communist agents, but neither the treachery nor its consequence has seriously aroused the British people as did the threat of "McCarthyism" three thousand miles away.[86]

The creation of a political issue of first rate magnitude involves the interaction of an objective situation with a complex of other factors including, at least, the existence of a group interested in developing and reiterating the essentials of the potential issue, the accidental inclusion or the adroit manipulation of social and political symbols which tradition and temper have made meaningful and moving to a broad audience, the state of the confidence of the people in their governors, and the number and thrust of other problems with comparable potential as issues competing for the public attention at a given time. Thus, in December 1945, the Senate Foreign Relations Committee heard all that Hurley had to say about his "betrayal" in the State Department, and the news caused scarcely a ripple. But, with the same information, he was one of the stars in the proceedings of the Joint Committees on Armed Services and Foreign Relations of the United States Senate when the recall of General Douglas MacArthur was under scrutiny in 1951.

Before considering the attack upon the Department of State begun in February 1950 by Senator Joseph R. McCarthy of Wisconsin and continued with force and some skill by the Senate Committee on Internal Security in the hearings on the Institute of Pacific Relations in 1952, mention should be made of certain changes that occurred in the organization and staffing of the State Department in the summer of 1945. Dean Acheson had been Assistant Secretary of State from February 1, 1941. With the end of the war he wished to return to the private

86. For an account of these cases, see Alan Moorehead, *The Traitors* (New York: Harper and Row, 1963). See also Rebecca West, *The New Meaning of Treason* (New York: Viking, 1964).

practice of the law, and to concern himself with the affairs of family and relations. He received a "Dear Dean" letter from Truman and left the scene where he had been active for more than four years.[87] Almost immediately after leaving the State Department, Acheson received an invitation to become Under Secretary of State in place of Joseph Grew. This offer was part of a general shake-up in the department that brought James Francis Byrnes to the post of Secretary of State in place of Edward Stettinius. Byrnes was to be Secretary from July 1945 until his resignation January 20, 1947. Acheson went to Grew's office and said, "I suppose you know why I am here," to which Grew replied that he did indeed know. Although Acheson was pleased to have the new position he did not want to push Grew out against the latter's possibly strong feeling that he should stay. But Grew did not want to stay. In a letter to the author, he said,

> The circumstances of my retirement from the Department and the Foreign Service in 1945 were quite simple although I am sorry to say that a good many myths have grown up around them. The facts are, and I so told the then Secretary of State, Mr. Byrnes, that having served as a member of the Foreign Service for 41 years and having passed the legal age of retirement, with the war being over, I did desire to retire at that point in order to return to other activities. Mr. Byrnes did ask me to continue but he did not press the point. I knew at least that my advice and recommendations were not then being accepted and I did not find it possible to develop with Mr. Byrnes the same close relations that I had enjoyed with some other chiefs. In spite of published comments, largely from left-wing sources that I had been pushed out, I did not myself feel this to be so, especially since my retirement came at my own urgent request.[88]

Under Secretary Grew thought that "while our policy in China may have been closely associated with this move, I think the circumstances arose largely in view of my efforts to retain the Emperor of Japan." On this subject, he said, "there was definitely a policy split among Far Eastern office personnel."

With the accession of Dean Acheson to the office of Under Secretary of State, there were quick changes and shifts of personnel. Eugene Dooman was replaced by John Carter Vincent, and Joseph C. Ballantine and Stanley Hornbeck were also replaced. According to Acheson, these changes were his idea, not that of Secretary Byrnes,

87. The information about the appointment of Acheson and the reorganization of the State Department staff he effected is drawn from notes of an interview with Dean Acheson, July 18, 1957, at his law offices in Washington, D.C.

88. Letter: Joseph C. Grew to Earl Latham, July 31, 1957.

President Truman, or anyone else, and they were made not for the purpose of getting any particular views represented in the Far Eastern Division but because of what Acheson thought were the special rigidities and personalities of the men being forced out. The men who came in had the confidence of Acheson because he thought they were fresh, original, and creative.[89] John Carter Vincent agreed that it was Acheson who was responsible for ousting Hornbeck, Dooman, and Ballantine.[90] Vincent also acknowledged that there were real policy differences between him and Dooman on Japan, and between him and Hornbeck on China.[91] Vincent and Acheson argued for a strong and coercive reorganization of the Japanese government and economy,[92] and Dooman's view, like that of Joseph Grew, was for a more moderate line. Vincent did not agree with the view he attributed to Stanley Hornbeck, that Chiang should be supported and that nothing derogatory should be said about the regime. It would seem from the foregoing that the personnel changes effected in August 1945 showed some consistency in the perspectives of those removed, and of those ousted; and Vincent agreed that this was so, although he pointed out that the sweep was not entirely complete. Vincent retained as head of the China Division Everett Drumright, who was more sympathetic to Chiang than his chief.

Still one other change was made that was to draw the unfavorable attention of critics of the State Department, the reinstatement of John Stewart Service by the new Under Secretary of State. Senator McCarthy attacked Service in connection with the *Amerasia* case and in the course of a statement about Service said that Joseph Grew "who had insisted on his prosecution, was forced to resign," and that two days after Acheson took over, Service was reinstated in the department and put in charge of placements and promotions.[93] Although it

89. Interview with Dean Acheson, July 18, 1957.

90. Joseph C. Ballantine, who had been Chief of the Division of Far Eastern Affairs in 1943.

91. Interview with John Carter Vincent, Cambridge, Massachusetts, August 21, 1958. For Dooman's version, see Eighty-second Congress, First Session, United States Senate, Committee on the Judiciary, Subcommittee to Investigate the Administration of the Internal Security Act and Other Internal Security Laws, *Hearings on the Institute of Pacific Relations,* pp. 714–715.

92. Acheson told the author that the replacement of Dooman by Vincent on the Far Eastern subcommittee of SWINK (an inter-agency coordinating committee in Washington) changed the line that was being agitated there by the State Department in 1945. Acheson had been a strong advocate of a Draconian peace for Japan — throw out the Mikado, occupy the country, reform it by tough action. These views did not prevail. Vincent has told the author that the tough line laid down in "United States Initial Post Surrender Policy for Japan" had already been laid down in the document during Dooman's membership on the subcommittee.

93. *Tydings Committee,* p. 1555.

is true that Service was brought into the fold again by Acheson, Grew was to tell Service that he had not insisted upon Service's prosecution (he had ordered the arrest of five persons unknown to him, on information he credited, one of the unidentified persons being Service), that he had been shocked to learn that Service was one of them, that it was a relief to him when Service had been no-billed by the grand jury, and that it was with great satisfaction that he had seen him reinstated in the department.[94]

94. Letter: Joseph C. Grew to John Stewart Service, April 17, 1950, at *Tydings Committee,* p. 1277.

*A speech has two parts —
you must state your case and
you must prove it.*

ARISTOTLE, *Rhetoric*

X Autopsy of Failure

Senator McCarthy's charges against the State Department in 1950 launched him on the public career that was to stamp his name on a certain political style, split the intellectual and governmental communities into desperate factions, temporarily destroy the morale of the State Department, eventually offend the United States Senate, and throw him into oblivion as fast as he had shot out of it. His admirers and his detractors have written books about him, and these may be consulted for reference by any who may still be interested in the polemics.[1] He is of interest at this point because of the nature of the charges he first made and the credence to be given them.

In brief, 1950 was a year of trial, and McCarthy was the prosecutor of the theme that the Department of State was one of the centers of a Communist conspiracy to influence American policy in China, the haven of men who consciously and traitorously worked to advance the cause of international communism against the interests of the United States. The framework of inquiry created by both the charges and by the setting of the first of two inquests on possible subversion and China policy[2] — the Tydings Committee inquiry — were such, however, as to tend to defeat clarity and discovery. Although it was

1. See, for example, William F. Buckley, Jr. and L. Brent Bozell, *McCarthy and his Enemies* (Chicago: Henry Regnery Company, 1954) by two supporters of McCarthy against his critics; and Richard H. Rovere, *Senator Joe McCarthy* (New York: Harcourt, Brace, 1959) for the negative.

2. The second inquest, that of the Senate subcommittee of the Committee on the Judiciary, Eighty-second Congress, First and Second Sessions, *Hearings on the Institute of Pacific Relations*, 1951–1953, was conducted more as a systematic research investigation than were the hearings of the Tydings Committee. Although the IPR Hearings were organized on assumptions that the testimony was expected to demonstrate, they *were* organized. The Tydings Committee was in the thick of a sensational battle that involved the White House, the Department of State, members of Congress, the press, and journals of opinion and comment, subject to the vagaries and shifting pressures of political warfare.

the theory of McCarthy's attack that there was a pattern of conspiracy, the accusations centered less upon the supposed pattern than upon the identity and personal characteristics of specific individuals; while the strategy of the Tydings committee, which had charge of the inquiry, was chiefly designed to meet these specific assertions, and to ignore the more general issue.

The Tydings Committee Hearings

After Senator McCarthy had said in a routine Lincoln Day speech in Wheeling, West Virginia, on February 9, 1950, that he knew the names of a number of Communists working in the State Department, events moved swiftly.[3] The political air was already tense with shock and suspicion because of the climax, in the previous month, of events that had been unfolding since the summer of 1948. Alger Hiss was found guilty of perjury and sentenced to five years; and the Secretary of State, Dean Acheson, had avowed that he would "not turn his back on Hiss." [4] This seemed to suggest jaunty bravado or, at least, pernicious impenitence about delinquencies that some felt had mortal significance. The passion of the storm then broke loudly in an atmosphere sultry with resentment and anxiety. Although it thundered for months, it failed to bring cool airs when it was done; because it did not really pass on, but merely abated.

The Truman Administration, which had been on the defensive about security and loyalty since the Eightieth Congress, took a stand against the McCarthy charges which had been repeated on the floor of the Senate on February 20 and 22.[5] Scott Lucas, the Senate Majority Leader, introduced Senate Resolution 231 (adopted February 22, 1950) to authorize study and investigation "as to whether persons who are disloyal to the United States are, or have been, employed by the De-

3. Buckley and Bozell, *McCarthy and his Enemies*, in chap. v of their examination of the McCarthy charges, agree that McCarthy's estimation of the number changed from time to time, and that in some 38 instances he was guilty of exaggeration in that fellow traveler became Communist and alleged pro-Communist became pro-Communist (see p. 60). It is clear that McCarthy did not have new or original information, that he was asserting as a fact what on the most favorable reading could only have been an inference, and that the inferences were drawn from files of the House Committee on Appropriations two years before. *Ibid.*, p. 57.

4. See *New York Times*, January 22, 1950, p. 1, col. 8; January 26, 1950, p. 1, col. 1; and January 26, 1950, p. 14, col. 2.

5. McCarthy's accusations may be found at Eighty-first Congress, Second Session, *Congressional Record*, February 20, 1950, pp. 2043–2071; February 21, 1950, pp. 2104–2110; February 22, 1950, pp. 2168–2169 and 2173–2195. Subsequent Senate Resolution 231, McCarthy attacked the State Department again on February 28, 1950, pp. 2485–2486 and 2523–2524, and on March 2, 1950, p. 2678.

partment of State." [6] A subcommittee of the Senate Committee on Foreign Relations was appointed to conduct the inquiry under the chairmanship of Millard Tydings of Maryland, and the hearings began on March 8 with Senator McCarthy as the first witness. By the time the hearings began, Acheson had been called before the Senate Foreign Relations Committee to clarify his stand on the Hiss case[7] and Judith Coplon of the Justice Department and her Soviet sweetheart in the United Nations, V. A. Gubitchev, had been convicted of conspiracy to misappropriate classified papers.[8]

In the various formations of his major theme between the original charges and the Tydings hearings, the number of McCarthy's "cases" changed from time to time. When the committee was ready to proceed, the number had settled at eighty-one. The hearings began in a peculiarly disorderly way. Senator Tydings would not give McCarthy a chance at the outset to make a sequential statement but crowded him to say whether a functionary referred to in Case 14 was elsewhere specifically dealt with as one of the eighty-one cases or had merely been mentioned to substantiate accusations about Case 14.[9] This was a matter, one would suppose, of somewhat less than shattering concern to the substance of life, or the procedures of the subcommittee, and Senator Henry Cabot Lodge of Massachusetts and Senator Bourke Hickenlooper intervened to permit McCarthy to tell his story in his own way, which he was finally allowed to do.[10]

Or rather he was allowed to start his story again, for soon there was another scuffle over procedure — as to whether the names McCarthy was about to submit should be offered in public session or in executive session. McCarthy's position was, "I have the documents. The names appear on the documents very clearly. If the committee wants to go into executive session and take this testimony, that is entirely up to the committee." [11] He also said, "I personally do not favor presenting names, no matter how conclusive the evidence is. The committee has called me this morning, and in order to intelligibly present this in-

6. Eighty-first Congress, Second Session, United States Senate, Subcommittee of the Committee on Foreign Relations, Hearings Pursuant to S. Res. 231, *A Resolution to Investigate Whether There Are Employees in the State Department Disloyal to the United States*, p. 1 (hereafter cited as the *Tydings Committee*).

7. *New York Times*, March 1, 1950, p. 1, col. 6.

8. *New York Times*, March 8, 1950, p. 1, col. 6.

9. *Tydings Committee*, pp. 2–3.

10. It was Tydings' thought in pressing for an answer from McCarthy, he said, to get the name of the "high State Department officials" referred to so as to "clean out any subversive elements in the State Department" right away. *Tydings Committee*, p. 5.

11. *Tydings Committee*, p. 16.

formation, I must give the names. I think this should be in executive session. I think it would be better." [12] Tydings told McCarthy he could proceed as he saw fit, and that if he wanted to give names in executive session, "we will be very glad to have your wishes acceded to." But McCarthy had already given names to the press in a prepared statement before the opening of the hearing, and he continued in open session. The whole argument was a piece of gamesmanship. McCarthy knew that the hearings were expected to be open. Tydings knew that it was for the committee, and not McCarthy, to decide whether the hearings should be public or executive. A majority of the committee had decided to make them public. Although the hearings were open there were many occasions to go into executive session for short periods of time, and most of the eighty-one "cases" of Senator McCarthy were never named at all.[13]

The printed record of the Tydings Committee hearings is 1,484 pages long, in addition to which there is an Appendix of 2,509 pages containing numerous exhibits. One might imagine that all this print would pretty well cover the subject of the inquiry — "whether persons who are disloyal to the United States are, or have been, employed by the Department of State" — but such is not the case. The hearings fell into three parts, although to say even this is to impart grace and form to the welter that appears in the record. The first part is the public identification by Senator McCarthy of six persons and the presentation of some documentation to support his view that they were disloyal or security risks or both and should be investigated further. Second, there is an inquiry into the *Amerasia* affair and the case of John Stewart Service; and third, there is the special attention paid to two individuals (of the nine named), Philip Jessup and Owen Lattimore. These categories overlap and cut across each other somewhat but they have separate centers. The rest of the testimony is procedural or ancillary to these three subjects. Thus, there is testimony by Attorney General Howard McGrath on the inviolability of the files of the Department of Justice,[14] and testimony by J. Edgar Hoover on FBI procedures.[15] There are also descriptions of State Department security procedures and of the work of the Civil Service Loyalty Board

12. *Tydings Committee*, pp. 17–18.

13. For a special instance, see the reference to an unnamed individual with a police record of arrest for sexual perversion, who had been a member of the State Department staff until 1948, and who had left for unspecified reasons to take a position with the Central Intelligence Agency "where he now holds an important and high-paying position." *Tydings Committee*, pp. 128–130.

14. *Tydings Committee*, p. 315.

15. *Tydings Committee*, p. 327.

by officials of those agencies. Of the nine people charged by McCarthy, all were invited to respond, and six made appearances before the subcommittee to defend themselves. All had counsel.

Of the nine persons mentioned, six had no connection with China policy. The first was Dorothy Kenyon, a New York lawyer and former municipal judge who had been appointed in 1947 by the Department of State as American delegate to the United Nations Commission on the Status of Women, but whose term had ended some two months before the hearings.[16] The "case" against Miss Kenyon by McCarthy was that she had been a member of twenty-eight Communist-front organizations. "Someone so naive," he said, "is a bad security risk, so naive that they would sponsor twenty-eight." [17] Miss Kenyon's answer to the accusation was, "I am not and have never been disloyal. I am not and have never been a Communist. I am not and have never been a fellow traveller." [18] As to the front organizations, she had not known as Communist those that may later have been shown to have been, she joined some in company with numerous other public persons of impeccable credentials, and some of the organizations she did not know about at all. In fact only four of the groups cited by McCarthy as Communist fronts were so designated on the Attorney General's list.[19] Miss Kenyon introduced in her own behalf an article in the *New York Times* reporting an attack upon her by the Russians for "endeavoring to conceal her reactionary stand" against a Soviet position at a meeting of the United Nations Commission on the Status of Women.[20]

The second of McCarthy's "cases" was that of Haldore Hanson, appointed in 1948 executive director of the Secretariat of the Interdepartmental Committee on Scientific and Cultural Relations, after he had spent a little time in junior positions in the Far Eastern Affairs Division of the State Department.[21] At the time of the Tydings hearings, he was Chief of the Technical Cooperation Projects Staff, an activity

16. *Tydings Committee*, p. 18.
17. *Tydings Committee*, p. 31.
18. *Tydings Committee*, p. 176.
19. Buckley and Bozell point out that McCarthy was in error to say that nine of the twenty-eight had been put on the Attorney General's list, but suggest that the Communist-front character of such organizations is not determined by their appearance on the list, since the procedures for citing them are slow. *McCarthy and his Enemies*, p. 81.
20. *Tydings Committee*, pp. 185–187.
21. Hanson had been a teacher in Chinese colleges from 1934 to 1937, a press correspondent in China from 1936 to 1939, a staff writer from 1938 to 1942 when he joined the State Department. From June to November 1948, he was Acting Chief of the Far Eastern Area, Public Affairs Overseas Program Staff. *Tydings Committee*, p. 75.

connected with the Point Four program. The case against him was the substance and tone of a book that Hanson had written in the 1930's from which McCarthy read numerous excerpts expressing admiration of the Chinese Communists, and which he offered as evidence of "pro-Communist proclivities." [22] Mr. Hanson denied past and present membership in the Communist Party, membership in any organization declared subversive or Communist-front by the Attorney General, knowing association with an espionage agent of a foreign power, advocacy of the Communist form of government for anybody, anywhere, at any time, or any act of disloyalty.[23] Most of his testimony after his initial statement was concerned with what he said and what he meant when he was twenty-eight years old.[24]

Senator McCarthy adduced certain military intelligence and other documents on Gustavo Duran, a naturalized American of Spanish origin, who had been an officer in the Spanish Republican Army and, for a time, head of the Madrid Zone of the Military Intelligence Service. The documents were said to show that Duran had been a Communist but Duran, in a sworn written statement to the Tydings Committee (he did not testify personally), denied all of the derogatory allegations.[25] Duran had been with Spruille Braden in Havana in 1943 when Braden was ambassador to Cuba, and had gone to Washington with Braden when the latter was made Assistant Secretary of State for Latin American Affairs. After Senator Wherry of the Senate subcommittee on appropriations for the State Department had urged the department in August 1946 to discharge Duran as a bad security risk, and a department security check in September cleared him as a security risk, Duran resigned from the department in October 1946. He had not been in the department for four years at the time he became one of McCarthy's cases.[26]

Senator McCarthy also asked the Tydings Committee to investigate further into the background and status of Esther Brunauer, Assistant Director of Policy Liaison of the UNESCO Relations staff of the State Department, largely because of asserted associations with front

22. *Tydings Committee*, p. 74.
23. *Tydings Committee*, p. 342.
24. Buckley and Bozell felt that the "State Department was justified in clearing Hanson, security-wise, *as of the time McCarthy leveled his charges*" (emphasis theirs), although they also say that it does not follow that McCarthy was unjustified in questioning Hanson's loyalty. *McCarthy and his Enemies*, pp. 95–96.
25. *Tydings Committee*, p. 110 for the introduction of Duran's name by Senator McCarthy and p. 1865 for Duran's written statement. At the time of the Tydings investigation Duran was a member of the staff of the United Nations.
26. This does not mean that he was not within the competence of the Tydings Committee to investigate, since Senate Resolution 231 authorized inquiry about disloyal persons who "are, or have been, employed by the Department of State."

groups,[27] and into the matter of Professor Harlow Shapley of Harvard and Professor Frederick Schuman of Williams College, neither of whom had ever been employees of the State Department.[28]

The accusations by Senator McCarthy against Philip Jessup were largely made on the floor of the Senate. He did not use the Tydings Committee hearing to establish the case he thought he had against Jessup and in fact no mention of him at all was made by McCarthy in the hearings outside of two passing references.[29] But in the United States Senate on March 30, 1950, McCarthy said of Jessup that he showed "an unusual affinity for Communist causes," and that he was a "well-meaning dupe of the Lattimore crowd." [30] Ambassador-at-Large Philip Jessup flew back to Washington from Pakistan to testify. In the Senate, McCarthy had linked Jessup to a group in the State Department he said had "delivered China to the Communists," but while he thus had Jessup's interest — and that of a stunned country — McCarthy also hinted at fresh sensations. He was going to give to the Tydings Committee, he said, the name of a person alleged to be the "top U.S.S.R. espionage agent." [31] The meeting of the Tydings Committee on March 21, 1950, was in executive session and to it McCarthy divulged the name of Owen Lattimore who, he said, was "one of the top espionage agents," "the top Russian spy," "the top of the whole ring of which Hiss was a part." [32] The subcommittee saw the file of the FBI on the man accused as the "top U.S.S.R. spy," and for the Monday newspapers, March 27, 1950, Owen Lattimore was publicly revealed to be the person denounced by Senator McCarthy as the "chief Soviet espionage agent in the United States." [33] He had already

27. *Tydings Committee*, p. 84 for the introduction of Mrs. Brunauer's name by Senator McCarthy, and p. 293 for her personal testimony in rebuttal. Buckley and Bozell say of the Brunauer case that on the whole, apart from data cited from her loyalty file, the evidence "must be set down as weak and inconclusive." *McCarthy and his Enemies*, p. 133.

28. For mention of Shapley, see *Tydings Committee*, p. 125, with his written statements at pp. 1870–1873. On Schuman, see p. 142 for introduction of his name, and pp. 1873–1874 for his statement. Both of the professors had on occasion lectured for the State Department.

29. *Tydings Committee*, p. 28 and p. 100.

30. Eighty-first Congress, Second Session, *Congressional Record*, March 30, 1950, p. 4464. See newspaper account in *New York Times*, March 21, 1950, p. 1, col. 8; June 3, 1950, p. 1, col. 4. The second statement made on June 2, 1950, followed the Declaration of Conscience presented by Senator Margaret Chase Smith of Maine and six other Republicans, scoring both the tactics of Senator McCarthy and the lack of leadership imputed to President Truman. *New York Times*, June 2, 1950, p. 1, col. 6. The statements of Senator McCarthy on June 2 are to be found at Eighty-first Congress, Second Session, *Congressional Record*, June 2, 1950, p. 8109 *et seq.*

31. *New York Times*, March 22, 1950, p. 1, col. 7.

32. *Tydings Committee*, pp. 277–292.

33. *New York Times*, March 27, 1950, p. 1, col. 8.

been characterized by McCarthy as "one of the principal architects of our far eastern policy." [34] Both Jessup and Lattimore had full opportunity to reply.

The "affinity for Communist causes" was said to appear in Jessup's connection with five Communist fronts,[35] his connections with the Institute of Pacific Relations, and various positions he had publicly taken on public issues. Among the latter was a letter to the *New York Times*, February 6, 1946, of which Jessup was one of the co-signers, urging that the production of atomic bombs be stopped and that essential atomic ingredients be dumped into the sea. In the Tydings Committee hearings, Jessup said that he had changed his mind about the matter, that in view of the policy of the Soviet Union not to cooperate in plans for the international control of atomic weapons, the suggestions he joined in making in 1946 were no longer tenable, and he repudiated them now. Jessup had been a character witness for Alger Hiss in the latter's trial for perjury, and Senator McCarthy made something of this.[36] As to the front organizations, Jessup said that he had been a faculty advisory board member of the American Law Students Association and that his last contact with it had been in March 1940; that his name had been used as a sponsor of the meeting of the National Emergency Conference in Washington in May 1939, but that he did not recall attending the meeting, did not remember the organization, and did not know that it had been cited as subversive; that his name had been listed as a sponsor of the National Council for Democratic Rights in 1940 but that he did not recall the organization or that he had participated in its activities; that he had sponsored two dinners of the American Russian Institute in 1944 and in 1946, although he had not been a sponsor of the Institute, and that he had declined invitations to speak at its dinners in 1948 and 1949.[37]

Although these affiliations were presented by Senator McCarthy as

34. *Tydings Committee*, p. 92.

35. Four of the groups had been either cited or designated as fronts: the American Russian Institute, the National Emergency Conference and its successor the National Emergency Conference for Democratic Rights, the American Law Students Association, and the American Council of the Institute of Pacific Relations. The citation against the American Council was withdrawn in 1951. Buckley and Bozell disagree with the Tydings Committee conclusion that Jessup had affiliations with only two fronts, in both cases prior to the time they were cited as fronts. *McCarthy and his Enemies*, p. 101.

36. Eighty-first Congress, Second Session, *Congressional Record*, March 30, 1950, p. 4405.

37. See Eighty-first Congress, Second Session, Senate Report No. 2108, Report of the Committee on Foreign Relations Pursuant to S. Res. 231, *State Department Loyalty Investigation*, July 20, 1950, pp. 37–43 (hereafter cited as *Tydings Committee Report*), for a summary of the accusations against Jessup, his answers, and the committee's conclusions.

noxious associations sufficient in themselves, the weight of the suggestion that Jessup was sympathetic to Communist enterprise was carried by his activity in the Institute of Pacific Relations, with which he had been connected for many years. He was a member of the board of trustees of the Institute from 1933 to 1946, chairman of the American Council of the Institute in 1939 and 1940, and of the Pacific Council of the Institute from 1939 to 1942. In addition, he had at various times been a member of the Executive Committee of the Institute and in 1944 was Chairman of the Research Advisory Committee. The suggestion of sinister fellowship in this dry recital of offices must necessarily depend upon the character and coloration of the Institute of Pacific Relations, which will be discussed further presently. It is enough at this point to remark that Senator McCarthy thought the Institute to be a damnable nest of unclean birds with whom Jessup had flocked, and that the Tydings Committee thought that Jessup's connections with the Institute did not in any way reflect unfavorably upon him "when the true character of the organization is revealed," although it did not elaborate on its nature.[38]

Senator McCarthy argued that Jessup had responsibility for the contents of *Far Eastern Survey*, one of the journals of the Institute of Pacific Relations (over which he had "absolute control"), which, he said, promoted views favorable to the Chinese Communists and hostile to Chiang Kai-shek ("the smear campaign against Nationalist China and Chiang Kai-shek"), as a matter of deliberate policy. The Tydings Committee said that it could not find any evidence to support the allegation that Jessup was in control of the *Far Eastern Survey* or that the magazine took part in any "smear campaign" against Chiang Kai-shek.[39] T. A. Bisson's article on the two Chinas had appeared in 1943 and McCarthy dated the development of the anti-Chiang position from that time, but the committee concluded that Jessup was only shown to have been chairman of the Research Advisory Committee in 1944, after the asserted campaign had started, said that the *Far Eastern Survey* was a reputable publication, and held that the evidence in support of "the so-called 'smear campaign' is non-existent."

Jessup in his own behalf entered into the record accusatory statements made against him by the Chinese Communist and Soviet presses, statements he made to the Security Council of the United Nations and elsewhere opposing Soviet and other Communist policies, and testimonials from General George Marshall and Dwight D. Eisenhower, affirming Jessup's "opposition to all Soviet or Communist attacks or pressures" and his "devotion to the principles of Americanism." Sen-

38. *Tydings Committee Report*, p. 41.
39. *Tydings Committee Report*, p. 42.

ator Henry Cabot Lodge of Massachusetts who stated "individual views" at the end of the Tydings Committee report did not mention Jessup at all, and even two of the most skeptical critics of the committee later concluded that Jessup was not a security risk in 1950.[40] While the hearings were going on and before any final report had been made by the Tydings Committee, President Truman announced that Jessup would continue indefinitely as Ambassador-at-Large.[41]

The controversy over Jessup was renewed a little over a year later, however, when President Truman nominated him to represent the United States as a member of the United States delegation to the Sixth General Assembly of the United Nations.[42] Senator McCarthy, the first witness, opposed the nomination, and went over the ground he had traversed in his Senate speeches during the Tydings Committee hearings. The principal difference now was the availability to him of material gathered by the Senate Subcommittee on Internal Security which was in the process of conducting a full-scale investigation of the Institute of Pacific Relations. The principal new matter was information about a conference of experts that had been called to discuss policy in the Far East.[43] This information was amplified by Harold Stassen, who had originally supplied it to the McCarran committee investigating the IPR, and who appeared before the nominating subcommittee and expatiated at length.[44] During the conference on Far Eastern Affairs held in the State Department October 6–8, 1949, there had been discussion of numerous policies that the United States did not follow, such, for example, as the recognition of Red China, the government of which had just been established. Jessup's unfitness for appointment was thought to lie in the fact that he had called the conference, and might have agreed with some of the discussion, although he did not say so. In fact he said that his role was to chair the meeting, and not to state opinions.[45] The upshot was that the Senate subcommittee refused to approve Jessup's nomination on October 18, 1951, by a vote of three to two. Two of the Senators declared that they had confidence in Jessup's loyalty but opposed his nomination because he did not have public confidence. President Truman then (October 22) gave Jessup a

40. Buckley and Bozell, *McCarthy and his Enemies*, p. 123. This conclusion is shadowed by the qualifier that the judgment is made "under the prevailing understanding of the reasonable doubt standard," and that a preferable standard would be one that did not presume the innocence of the accused.

41. *New York Times*, March 28, 1950, p. 1, col. 6.

42. Eighty-second Congress, First Session, United States Senate, Committee on Foreign Relations, *Hearings before a Subcommittee on Nomination of Philip C. Jessup* (hereafter cited as *Jessup Nomination*), p. 1.

43. *Jessup Nomination*, pp. 51–58.

44. *Jessup Nomination*, p. 686 et seq.

45. *Jessup Nomination*, p. 618.

recess appointment to the General Assembly meeting in Paris and Jessup accepted it. Ten years later President Kennedy appointed Jessup to the International Court of Justice as the American representative on that distinguished tribunal.

The most sensational of the accusations made by Senator McCarthy, however, was that against Owen D. Lattimore, Director of the Walter Hines Page School of International Relations at Johns Hopkins University. McCarthy said of the Lattimore case, "I am willing to stand or fall on this one." And further, "If I am wrong on this, I think the subcommittee would be justified in not taking my other cases too seriously." [46] He told the subcommittee, "If you crack this case, it will be the biggest espionage case in the history of the country. That is my own personal thought on it." [47] He was soon to say on the Senate floor, "I fear that I may have perhaps placed too much stress on the question of whether or not he had been an espionage agent. . . ." [48] The conclusion of the Tydings Committee was, "We find no evidence to support the charge that Owen Lattimore is the 'top Russian spy' or, for that matter, any other sort of spy." [49]

But there were other accusations. If not the top Russian spy, then he was a policy and security risk in the State Department. McCarthy said, "I don't know when he has been on the payroll of the State Department. I understand that he has very free access to a desk there and access to all the files, and comes in whenever he cares to." [50] It soon appeared that Owen Lattimore was not an employee of the State Department or, as the Tydings Report put it, "We find that Owen Lattimore is not now and never has been in any proper sense an employee of our State Department." [51] His connection had been "peripheral" and "sporadic" at the most.

He had, however, been active in various employments in Far Eastern affairs, in all of which the State Department had been intensely in-

46. At another place, McCarthy told the subcommittee, "I am telling you that this is the one case in which I think we can easily have a determination by this committee as to whether or not my charges are well founded or not. I think for the balance of the investigation you should know that. If I am completely mistaken on this case, then you can assume that many of the other cases. . . . Senator Tydings: This is the key? Senator McCarthy: Yes, sir; . . ." *Tydings Committee*, p. 285.

47. *Tydings Committee*, p. 278. Richard Rovere is of the opinion that when McCarthy first talked about Lattimore as the "top espionage agent," the Senator "hadn't the slightest notion which unfortunate name on his list he would single out for this distinction. I also believe that he sensed almost immediately that he had made a rather foolish mistake in picking Lattimore." *Senator Joe McCarthy*, p. 151.

48. Buckley and Bozell cite this statement. *McCarthy and his Enemies*, p. 154.

49. *Tydings Committee Report*, p. 72.

50. *Tydings Committee*, p. 278.

51. *Tydings Committee Report*, p. 72.

terested, and with respect to which he had reasonably close working relations with the department. For example, he had been chosen in 1941 by President Roosevelt to serve Chiang Kai-shek as a personal political adviser, and had functioned as such until the end of 1942. From 1942 to 1944, he was head of Pacific operations for the Office of War Information, which clearly had to place him fairly closely in touch with State Department activity in China. We have seen that Lattimore accompanied Vice President Wallace to China in 1944. The year following he was a member of the Pauley Reparations Mission to Japan. In short, although not a member of the staff of the State Department, Lattimore was in the thick of China affairs and in positions of close cooperation with the State Department.

Was Lattimore a Communist? The McCarran committee that investigated the Institute of Pacific Relations in 1951 did not say so. What it did say was that "Owen Lattimore was, from some time beginning in the 1930's, a conscious articulate instrument of the Soviet conspiracy." [52] Louis Budenz, who testified before the Tydings Committee, did not say Lattimore was a Communist. What he did say was ". . . Jack Stachel advised me to consider Owen Lattimore as a Communist, which to me meant, because that was our method of discussing these matters, to treat as authoritative anything that he would say or advise." Bella Dodd, a former Communist, attacked Budenz and said that his statement about Stachel was "laughable to anyone who knows the party" inasmuch as Stachel's work was with trade unions at the time Budenz said he was giving him names to remember and instructions about Lattimore.[53] Budenz did not know Lattimore personally, and had never seen him.[54] In response to a question, he said, "Outside of what I was officially told by the Communist leaders, I do not know of Mr. Lattimore as a Communist." [55] Freda Utley, like Budenz, also a former Communist, said that McCarthy was wrong in his statement that Lattimore was the Soviet government's top espionage agent in America, said she did not know "whether Mr. Lattimore is a member of the Communist Party," and thought that he "may not be the 'architect' of the disastrous China policy pursued by the administration." [56] But she did feel that there was no reasonable doubt that the Far Eastern policy advocated and to a large degree followed by the administration

52. Eighty-second Congress, Second Session, United States Senate, Committee on the Judiciary, Report No. 2050 Pursuant to S. Res. 366, *Institute of Pacific Relations*, p. 224 (hereafter cited as *McCarran Committee Report*).

53. *Tydings Committee*, p. 492 for the Budenz statement and p. 637 for the statement of Bella Dodd.

54. *Tydings Committee*, p. 491.

55. *Tydings Committee*, p. 527.

56. *Tydings Committee*, p. 768.

"was inspired by Mr. Lattimore and his disciples, protegés, and friends"; and that the phrase "Judas cow" was a fit appellation for Mr. Lattimore since "his function has been to lead us unknowingly to destruction."[57] His work was more important than espionage, she thought: "To suggest that Mr. Lattimore's great talents have been utilized in espionage seems to me as absurd as to suggest that Mr. Gromyko or Mr. Molotov employ their leisure hours at Lake Success, or at international conferences, in snitching documents." Earl Browder, former General Secretary of the Communist Party, USA, also said that he did not know Lattimore, had never seen Lattimore, to his knowledge, had never heard reference to Lattimore when he (Browder) was in the Communist Party, never discussed Lattimore with anyone in the Communist Party, and had never known of Lattimore as a member of the Communist Party.[58]

Lattimore's testimony in his own behalf was extensive, covering some 189 pages of the published record. He was accorded deference and sympathy by his interrogators. He was accompanied by counsel and his counsel was allowed to participate to some extent in the proceedings, an unusual privilege.[59] Lattimore denied that he was or had ever been a Communist,[60] said that he had had no connections with the State Department except for his appointment to the Pauley Reparations Mission to Japan for three or four months, his participation in a panel discussion of China problems at the State Department in October 1949, and a lecture at the State Department. He was paid for his services as a member of the Reparations Commission and as a lecturer. "Other than this I have never been a consultant for the State Department or on its payroll."[61]

The final report of the Tydings Committee cleared Lattimore of all of the accusations that had been made against him, although it did have one curious paragraph of soft chiding,

> Some of Mr. Lattimore's friends, associates and contacts have been identified before us as Communists. On the other hand many of his intimate associates are people of the highest repute. Certainly the former connections, when taken with the latter, are not such as to conclude that he is a Communist on the theory that 'birds of a feather flock together,' even were we prepared to accept such a theory under the circumstances. Perhaps in many of his contacts, Mr. Lat-

57. *Tydings Committee*, p. 768.
58. *Tydings Committee*, pp. 673 and 676.
59. Abe Fortas and Paul Porter were listed as counsel for Lattimore but it was Fortas who seems to have been active. See, for example, *Tydings Committee*, pp. 507, 531, and 580, where counsel was allowed to function in the proceedings.
60. *Tydings Committee*, p. 424.
61. *Tydings Committee*, p. 421.

timore has not exercised the discretion which our knowledge of communism in 1950 indicates would have been wise, but we are impelled to comment that in no instance has Mr. Lattimore on the evidence before us shown to have been knowingly associated with Communists. The convenient theory suggested to us that *he must have known* [committee emphasis] has not yet become the criterion for judging a private citizen in this country.[62]

The Tydings Committee Report did not, however, end the Lattimore case; it merely concluded that part of it that Lattimore was to title the "ordeal by slander." [63] There was more to come in the McCarran committee investigation of the Institute of Pacific Relations with which Lattimore, like Jessup, had been closely connected for many years.

Before a consideration of this second of two extensive inquiries into the China policy of the 1940's, some observations about the Tydings Committee investigation are pertinent. First, The Tydings Committee investigation was called a "whitewash" by its critics, and Senator Lodge thought that the probe had been superficial,[64] although the committee report was adopted by the Senate, albeit in a strictly partisan vote.[65] One observer a dozen years later thought that the epithet "whitewash" was undeserved, if the term means "a willful blindness toward available evidence that would tend to support the conclusion that Lattimore was a Communist agent." [66] Within the range of McCarthy's often repeated intention — that he was not "proving" anything but was merely bringing to the attention of the committee certain cases that he thought it should investigate further — the committee in fact did look further. The whole hearing was a "further" investigation in that all of the accused had a chance to explain and most did, and in one instance there was even an unprecedented disclosure of FBI files. On the order of President Truman, J. Edgar Hoover, director of the bureau, prepared a summary of the FBI files on Lattimore for the information of the committee, and Tydings told Lattimore that there was nothing in them to show that he was either a Communist or an espionage agent.[67]

On the other hand, the Tydings Committee certainly had partisan

62. *Tydings Committee Report*, p. 73.

63. Owen Lattimore, *Ordeal by Slander* (Boston: Little, Brown, 1950).

64. *New York Times*, July 18, 1950, p. 1, col. 1.

65. *New York Times*, July 21, 1950, p. 1, col. 3; July 22, 1950, p. 1, col. 1; July 25, 1950, p. 1, col. 2. The vote in the Senate was 45 to 37.

66. Herbert L. Packer, *Ex-Communist Witnesses, Four Studies in Fact-Finding* (Stanford, California: Stanford, 1962), p. 157.

67. Packer, *Ex-Communist Witnesses*, p. 128, where the disclosure was called "precedent-shattering." See also *New York Times*, April 7, 1950, p. 1, col. 8, for reference to the Tydings statement and April 11, 1950, p. 1, col. 8, for Lodge statement dissociating himself from the Tydings statement.

ends to serve. The Democratic administration was under attack by the Republican Senator McCarthy and the hearings, more or less expectedly, were in the nature of a defense against the attacks, in which it was important to show that the government had been alert to the menace of communism all along, that it did not harbor subversives, and that its loyalty and security procedures were efficient. The indisposition of a Democratic committee to expose a Democratic administration was perhaps not entirely without warrant when it is considered that McCarthy had not really prepared much of a case, relying on old files already processed and information at secondhand, some of it concerning individuals who had not been in the department for several years, or who had never been employees, or who were clearly not what he said they were. With better information to work with, other Democratic committees in the Truman years showed no reluctance about exposing mink coat chiseling and deep freeze corruption in the President's administration.

Second, under the circumstances of the inquiry, it may be wondered whether an *ad hoc* congressional committee, defending an administration under attack by the opposition, would have been capable of making a long calm patient re-inquiry. Senator Lodge did not think so, and he and Senator Hickenlooper failed to sign the report. In the course of the investigation, Lodge offered a bill to appoint a bipartisan commission of twelve members, four to be named by the President and four each by the House and the Senate, to conduct an impartial inquiry, and he renewed the suggestion, somewhat revised, in his separate statement in the Tydings Committee Report.[68] Congressional committees, he thought, were inadequate to the task because of lack of time, lack of technical expertness, the inadequacy of the tools available to Congressmen for the execution of the task, and the inescapable political considerations which infuse committees representing party majorities and minorities.

Third, because of the concentration of concern on identities and personalities, the broader question of policy splits on China in the Department of State was not developed. Nor was the alleged existence of Communist conspiracy with the department at the center explored, although this assumption was implicit in the accusations about the loyalty of individuals mentioned as has been said. Neither of these

---

68. *Tydings Committee Report*, p. 28 of "Individual Views." Towards the end of the deliberations of the subcommittee, Senator Lodge in the course of conversation about procedure with other members of the committee said to Senator Tydings: "In all the years I have been here, I have never been on a committee where people worked harder and where a more sincere effort was made. . . . I have never been on any other committee where the members put in more time and worked harder." *Tydings Committee*, p. 2517.

fundamentals was considered because no one seemed to be particularly interested, so exciting was the farrago of shock and fright of the melee.

The Chorus of Comment

In the *Poetics*, Aristotle said that the "chorus should be regarded as one of the actors," and the drama of the Tydings hearings is certainly better appreciated if notice is taken of two choruses in the background, one swaying left and the other right, chanting interpretations of the action on the Senate stage. *The Nation* and the *Washington Post* were supporters of the Tydings Committee and the Washington *Times-Herald* was a critic of both the Tydings Committee and the State Department. The position of the *New Leader* was that there was a serious problem of Communist influence in the State Department to investigate, but that it was not being investigated very well. Although these four journals (now three, since the *Post* has absorbed the *Times-Herald*), by no means comprise the Press, they did state and exploit the central themes of critical comment.

In late February 1950, in commenting on McCarthy's "refusal" to name those on his list of "card-holding communists" in the State Department or to turn the list over to the FBI, *The Nation* wrote that "none" of the four persons who had up to then been named by the Senator, "presumably, were ever shown to have been Communists. These samples make it clear why the Senator is not eager to reveal any more names. As long as he can keep facts out of the picture he can make political capital, but once he acts in the open he is in the position of the late Jimmy Walker when that waggish politician complained to a friend, 'Another good story ruined by eyewitnesses.' " [69] *The Nation* maintained this attitude in succeeding issues. It did not dismiss the possibility that McCarthy might uncover some Communists in the State Department, but it rejected his charges as a whole as a political maneuver. About a week after the hearings began, for example, *The Nation* said:

> Senator McCarthy is on the loose with a blunderbuss. If he succeeds in bringing down just one authentic specimen of a Communist in the State Department — he started out by saying there were fifty-seven card-holding comrades in that agency — he will be sitting pretty, and the Republican Party will have some fine fuel to fire their electoral campaign. If he fails to bag any game at all, the G.O.P. will take no responsibility for the fiasco and McCarthy himself will have suffered no serious loss, his reputation as a statesman being negligible to begin with.[70]

69. "The Shape of Things" (editorial), *The Nation*, February 25, 1950, p. 167.
70. "McCarthy's Blunderbuss" (editorial), *The Nation*, March 18, 1950, p. 243.

To *The Nation*, McCarthy's general "charge that the State Department has fifty-seven card-holding Communists in its employ" was "grotesque." [71]

The Nation carried its skepticism into its discussion of the *Amerasia* case also and devoted to it three of its eighteen articles on the Tydings hearings. Two articles by Willard Shelton reviewed the case and another by Freda Kirchwey attacked the testimony of Emmanuel S. Larsen before the Tydings Committee, in particular those portions of it which dealt with Andrew Roth, who was then (1950) on the staff of *The Nation*. It was one of Shelton's first conclusions that "some aspects of the *Amerasia* case still need clarification. It is not yet known who passed all the documents to Jaffe." [72] In his next article, however, Shelton called the "uproar about *Amerasia* . . . a political and journalistic disgrace," and continued:

> The cure for what happened in the *Amerasia* case is to recognize that in this particular matter the investigators helped blow up the prosecution and that our laws protecting government papers were, and still are, lax. This is what the Hobbs committee reported; this is what the Tydings committee should report. We need an Official Secrets Act carefully enough drafted to protect legitimate classified material without depriving the public of the facts it must have to judge policy.[73]

Kirchwey dubbed Larsen's accusations against Roth during the Tydings hearings as "slander masked as testimony." [74] She held that the *Amerasia* case should be taken out of the hands of Congressional committees and given to a "non-political, non-partisan committee of eminent citizens." [75] Unlike the *New Leader*, which was hostile to most of the people named by McCarthy, even when it expressed reservations about the Senator's "methods," and his specific charges, *The Nation* was sympathetic toward McCarthy's main "targets." For example, it claimed that Dorothy Kenyon had made "mincemeat" of the Wisconsin Senator's accusations;[76] it criticized the recall of John Stewart Service from his overseas mission to answer charges; and it defended Roth, who had been implicated in the *Amerasia* case.

However, *The Nation* paid most attention to Owen Lattimore. Shel-

71. "The Shape of Things" (editorial), *The Nation*, March 25, 1950, p. 261.

72. Willard Shelton, "The *Amerasia* Case," *The Nation*, June 18, 1950, pp. 590–592.

73. Willard Shelton, "The *Amerasia* Case II," *The Nation*, June 24, 1950, pp. 613–615.

74. Freda Kirchwey, "The McCarthy Blight," *The Nation*, June 24, 1950, pp. 609–610.

75. *Ibid.*

76. "The Shape of Things" (editorial), *The Nation*, March 25, 1950, p. 261.

ton called Lattimore's testimony before the Tydings Committee a "magnificent performance" in which he had "succeeded in turning the caucus room into a hall for the discussion of both American foreign policy in the Far East and the principles of free speech." [77] According to Shelton, after his original charge against Lattimore, McCarthy "retreated" to "a new line — a non-libelous charge that Lattimore's views 'paralleled' the view of the Cominform." [78] The testimony of Louis Budenz regarding Lattimore was simply "hearsay" knowledge.[79] *The Nation* seemed to have little doubt of Lattimore's "innocence," although in a review of *Ordeal by Slander*, Philip Mandel — with an explicit reference to the embarrassment of liberals in the Hiss case — introduced what seemed to be a note of caution:

> This is the case history of a man who was suddenly singled out as the target for the smear campaign of a publicity-seeking demagogue. . . . A book like this cannot satisfy those who are looking for conclusive proof of Lattimore's innocence — Lattimore did not write it as a document of defense — but it succeeds completely in dramatizing the menace of McCarthyism to intellectual freedom and the vitality of the American system.[80]

The Nation approved the majority report on the investigation. Its final evaluation of McCarthy's charges was summed up in an editorial criticizing Senator Lodge for opposing the committee majority's decision to end the investigation: "Lodge has had access to the evidence proving McCarthy a brazen demagogue who never lets exposure of false 'facts' stop his repetition of them and a political slanderer unmatched in our recent history." [81]

The *New Leader*'s comments during the Tydings hearings reflected views that the periodical had been expressing long before McCarthy made his charges. The following quotation is an example of the tone and substance of material found in almost every issue of the *New Leader* in the early weeks of 1950:

> Today, as Mao sits closeted in Moscow with Stalin, the Far Eastern Division of the State Department — a division of misinformation ever since Henry Stimson left State — is the last refuge of the Henry Wallace-Owen Lattimore type of "progressive" — the abode of John

77. Willard Shelton, "McCarthy's Vicious Retreat," *The Nation*, April 15, 1950, pp. 341–342.
78. *Ibid.*
79. "Dementia Unlimited" (editorial), *The Nation*, April 29, 1950, p. 388.
80. Philip Mandel, "Review of Owen Lattimore, *Ordeal by Slander*," *The Nation*, August 19, 1950, pp. 170–171.
81. "The Shape of Things" (editorial), *The Nation*, July 8, 1950, p. 21.

Davieses, Fulton Freemans and Walton Butterworths, if not of Alger Hisses. The Far Eastern Division still emits the pungent stench of the John Carter Vincent-Institute of Pacific Relations days, and if you sniff real hard, you can detect the odor of the *Amerasia* spy case.[82]

In the same editorial it called for a congressional investigation of the State Department: "The blame for the betrayal of China must fall on all shoulders. But no forthright policy on Asia can be expected in the future until the Far Eastern Division is completely fumigated. Congress's first duty is a thorough and hard-boiled investigation of the Far Eastern Division."

Given its often expressed views on Communist or pro-Communist influences in the national government, it is not surprising that the *New Leader* took McCarthy's charges against the State Department seriously. The various authors published by the *New Leader*, however, drew somewhat varied inferences from the material brought out in the course of the Tydings hearings, as some brief quotations will indicate. In March, Jonathan Stout wrote that McCarthy had *failed* to support his charges and that this would have some "unfortunate" results: "Those who agree with Senator McCarthy's basic thesis that innocents and fellow-travellers often can prove more dangerous in objective fact than the bona fide Communist party member, cannot be grateful to the Senator for the carelessness with which he prepared his case." [83] Two weeks later Eugene Lyons claimed that the Communists were in "luck" when "McCarthy was cast in the role of Hercules cleaning the Augean stables of the State Department" since the Senator was not "fully prepared" for the task; but "the hooting and whistling in the press and on the air should not be permitted to drown out the fact that those stables need cleaning." [84] Other passages in the Lyons article reflect so well the general tone of the *New Leader* that they are worth quoting at greater length:

> Observers in Washington with a trained nose for Moscovite aromas have long known that the odor was especially acrid in the State Department. They find it hard to forget how Bullitt, Berle, Grew and others who took a relatively realistic view of Soviet Russia were driven out by pro-Stalinist elements. They recall the distressing facts of the *Amerasia* espionage scandal, still visible through the coats of

82. "Thunder Over Asia" (editorial), *New Leader*, January 1, 1950, p. 1.
83. Jonathan Stout, "McCarthy by the Numbers," *New Leader*, March 18, 1950, p. 3.
84. Eugene Lyons, "Communists Lucky to be Investigated by Dies, McCarthy," *New Leader*, April 1, 1950, pp. 1, 6.

whitewash. When Acheson refuses to "turn his back" on a convicted Soviet agent, they are reminded of an earlier occasion when
the same Acheson, then Assistant Secretary of State, refused to turn
his back on one Harold Glasser, who resigned under fire and was
subsequently named by Elizabeth Bentley as a member of her Soviet
"apparatus." . . .

Too much is at stake in foreign policy just now to justify smugness,
against this distressing background, on the issue of Kremlin infiltration of the State Department. The motives and manners and skills
of a Senator are utterly irrelevant to that basic menace. Whatever
the Tydings inquiry reveals or conceals, we should not permit the
problem itself to be shoved out of sight. The kind of comment that
limits itself to derogation of McCarthy is mischievously shallow.[85]

In mid-April David Dallin developed his variation of the general theme:
Senator McCarthy was "bound to lose his case" because the "Soviet
conception of espionage has never been accepted in the West. . . . He
promised a cavalcade of spies, top spies, key spies, master spies. Instead
he presented 'just' fellow-travellers, public figures, and college professors." [86] As a final example of the *New Leader's* general orientation,
in late April Stout approved Chairman Connally's plan to divide the
Foreign Relations Committee into subcommittees to deal with the
areas of the State Department's main divisions and to watch over their
policies, and he commented (with a certain mixture of metaphor): "If
the hand of the Kremlin is creeping through the State Department, as
McCarthy has said, and some still think, the close examination of
policies and, as a natural consequence, their makers, must inevitably
expose and frustrate any conspiracies that exist in actual fact." [87]
The *New Leader* devoted one of seventeen articles on the Tydings
hearings entirely to a review of the *Amerasia* case (the case was also
mentioned briefly in a number of other articles). The final paragraphs
of the article indicate the weekly's views on this subject:

According to Congressman Dondero, the grand jury which considered the cases of Service, Gayn and Miss Mitchell [persons implicated in the case] heard only a small portion of the evidence the
FBI had collected. Moreover, U.S. Attorney Robert Hitchcock, in
the case against Jaffe, "told the court there was no element of disloyalty in connection with the case."

85. *Ibid.*
86. David J. Dallin, "More Harmful Than Spies," *New Leader*, April 15, 1950,
p. 2.
87. Jonathan Stout, "State Department Policy, Not Personnel, Main Concern of
Senate Committee," *New Leader*, April 22, 1950, p. 3.

Since grand jury proceedings are secret, it is hard to tell how and why the Government dropped the *Amerasia* case. But J. Raymond Walsh, the fellow-travelling radio commentator, gave a strong hint on August 13, 1945, when he declared that John Service's arrest "brought some exceedingly powerful people within the Government to his defense." [88]

The *New Leader* showed little sympathy for most of the people who were named by McCarthy during the Tydings hearings. Lyons wrote that McCarthy "certainly betrayed strategic limitations in choosing Judge Dorothy Kenyon as his initial exhibit," but added that both Kenyon and Jessup "have had a peculiar weakness for joining crypto-communist causes" and "they have remarkable gall in insulting a legislator who alludes to their undisputed fellow-travelling proclivities. His mistake in supposing that they are friends of Stalin is minor compared to their mistake in supposing that Communist fronts were liberal parlor games." [89] Anatole Shub was similarly critical of persons named by the Wisconsin Senator: "Liberals," he wrote in early April, are as "skeptical of the charges against Owen Lattimore, John Service, John Carter Vincent, Haldore Hanson, Esther Brunauer and the rest as they were of Whittaker Chambers' original allegations against Alger Hiss, Lee Pressman, Nathan Witt, Harry White, *et al*." [90]

But the *New Leader*'s favorite villain was Owen Lattimore; seven articles were devoted almost entirely to the Johns Hopkins professor, and most of these were extremely hostile to him. For example, Dallin wrote: "Owen Lattimore as a professor is doing more harm than as an adviser of the State Department." [91] And Lyons, in his review of *Ordeal by Slander*, wrote that "vital facts have been revealed since the book's publication and others seem certain to come out. Those who now weep publicly over his distress may yet be as embarrassed as they were when the Hiss case was clarified." [92]

In general, most of the *New Leader* writers (Granville Hicks, perhaps, less than others), if mildly critical of McCarthy, apparently were so because they felt that his kind of accusation distracted the public from the real dangers posed by certain individuals in the State Department and in public life who might not be Communists but who

88. "The Mystery of *Amerasia*," *New Leader*, April 1, 1950, p. 6.

89. Eugene Lyons, "Communists Lucky to be Investigated by Dies, McCarthy," *New Leader*, April 1, 1950, pp. 1, 6.

90. Anatole Shub, "Three Myths Help Confuse Liberals," *New Leader*, April 1, 1950, p. 7.

91. David J. Dallin, "More Harmful Than Spies," *New Leader*, April 15, 1950, p. 2.

92. Eugene Lyons, "Lattimore: Dreyfus or Hiss?" Review of Owen Lattimore, *Ordeal by Slander*, *New Leader*, September 2, 1950, pp. 16–19.

were for various reasons "incapable," as Dallin put it, of "fighting communism with the same devotion, fire, dynamism they had developed against Nazism a short while before." [93]

In fifty-seven editorials the *Washington Post* provided a running commentary — in some periods almost on a daily basis — on the McCarthy charges and the Tydings investigation. The paper insisted throughout that the charges were nothing but "extravagances" [94] and "inflamed imaginings" [95] of the Wisconsin Senator.

The first reaction of the *Post* to McCarthy's statements was an editorial titled "Sewer Politics." After noting the changing numbers of allegedly Communist State Department employees used by McCarthy in his various February speeches, the editorial stated that "rarely has a man in public life crawled and squirmed so abjectly." [96] Ten days later, after the Senator's charges had led to the creation of the Tydings Committee, the *Post* maintained that McCarthy's "animus" centered mainly on "those persons who had intelligence and understanding in reporting on the China situation. Their sin, in his view, it would seem, was that they were prematurely right about a foregone conclusion." [97] Shortly before the committee began its hearings, the *Post* contended that while the State Department had once had "security risks" it had "purged these people long ago," and it urged the Tydings group to "expose Senator McCarthy without exposing innocent persons whom he has tried to victimize." [98]

During the five months from the beginning of the hearings to the release of the subcommittee's reports, the *Post* continued to belittle McCarthy's charges about Communists and Communist sympathizers in the Department of State and it defended most of the individuals named by the Senator. It noted with approval Seth Richardson's report that in three years of screening, the Loyalty Review Board had not revealed a "single case" of espionage among government employees.[99] It attacked Senator Robert Taft because he had criticized President Truman for "assuming the innocence" of persons accused by McCarthy.[100] In late May, the *Post* approved the State Department's rebuttals to Senator McCarthy's charges: "It is high time. For the McCarthy attempts to make the department a pariah could easily result both in the

93. David J. Dallin, "More Harmful Than Spies," *New Leader,* April 15, 1950, p. 2.
94. "McCarthy's Reds," *Washington Post,* February 24, 1950, p. 22.
95. "For Want of a Code," *Washington Post,* March 22, 1950, p. 12.
96. "Sewer Politics," *Washington Post,* February 14, 1950, p. 10.
97. "McCarthy's Reds," *Washington Post,* February 24, 1950, p. 22.
98. "Guilt by Reiteration," *Washington Post,* March 2, 1950, p. 12.
99. "No Spies," *Washington Post,* April 8, 1950, p. 6.
100. "Assuming Innocence," *Washington Post,* April 14, 1950, p. 20.

paralysis of foreign policy and in an establishment manned by timid second-raters." [101]

A small number of the *Post*'s editorials dealt largely with the *Amerasia* case, admitting that some aspects remained unclear but also minimizing its current (1950) significance. In early May the paper called on the Tydings Committee to "clear up the mystery of the *Amerasia* case" — explicitly mentioning, as part of the "mystery," the reasons for the arrest of Service and the reasons for the "casual" disposition of the "guilty." [102] However, in late June the paper argued that since the case had been "studied" by two grand juries and two congressional committees, "the country had better forget about it and pass on to more pressing current problems." [103] The *Post* said it did not want a "whitewash" but "neither do we wish to see anyone black-washed for the mere satisfaction of the sensation seekers." [104] After the Tydings hearings were closed, the *Post* noted Senator Lodge's criticism of the way the *Amerasia* case had been handled by the government in 1945, but it did not discuss the substance of the issue and contended simply that the *Amerasia* problem had been "tangential" to the Tydings subcommittee's field of investigation.[105]

As to John Stewart Service, the *Post* insisted that Service's relations with *Amerasia* and his work in China must be kept separate: his work in China was "patriotic as well as meritorious." [106] In late June it noted with approval Service's sixth clearance by the Loyalty Security Board of the State Department.

Unlike the *Times-Herald*, the *Post* paid more attention to Lattimore than to any other individual called before the Tydings Committee, and it never doubted his "innocence":

> The error of both cases [Lattimore and Haldore Hanson, also named by McCarthy] is the same. They were right about a foregone conclusion — that Mao Tse Tung was a comer. . . . The mere fact that they used their eyes and exercised their brains is regarded as circumstantial evidence of guilt, and Senator McCarthy passes on to the Tydings subcommittee the task of finding chapter and verse to prove it.[107]

When Lattimore was revealed to be McCarthy's "top Soviet spy," the paper commented "if his volumes are merely fronts for Soviet Russia,

101. "Fighting Back," *Washington Post*, May 20, 1950, p. 8.
102. "*Amerasia* Case," *Washington Post*, May 6, 1950, p. 8.
103. "Blackwash," *Washington Post*, June 20, 1950, p. 10.
104. *Ibid.*
105. " 'A Fraud and a Hoax'!" *Washington Post*, July 18, 1950, p. 12.
106. "What Service Did," *Washington Post*, June 24, 1950, p. 8.
107. "Communist Circus," *Washington Post*, March 14, 1950, p. 10.

hundreds of scholars will be rated as dunces." [108] And also: "But whatever sections may be torn out of the context of his writings, whatever joinings he has indulged in, we feel confident that he will be able to divest himself of the atrocious label that Mr. McCarthy has pinned on him." [109] The paper later said that a memorandum prepared by Lattimore in 1949 for the State Department as part of a panel on Far East policy organized by Jessup was his "guide in the conduct of the cold war with Russia in a sort of neo-Churchillian framework." [110] Still later, the *Post* discounted Louis Budenz's testimony against Lattimore as "casuistry" and said that "Senator McCarthy's star witness contributed to yesterday's circus proceedings nothing more than the plain acknowledgement that he had never seen Dr. Lattimore and that he had no first-hand knowledge of any party affiliations on Dr. Lattimore's part." [111] Early in May, the *Post* published somewhat of a summation of its views on the Lattimore case, which also contained a significant passage on its view of the function of congressional investigations. Among the "facts" of the case, according to the *Post*,

> One is that it can prove nothing whatever about the validity of Senator McCarthy's charges that there are 205 or 57 or 81 Communists in the State Department. The other is that the Senate of the United States has no business conducting a trial and passing judgment on the "loyalty" of a private citizen. Of course, if this involves the crime of espionage, then such a case should be referred to a grand jury. However, Senator McCarthy has apparently abandoned this charge. . . .
>
> [The Tydings subcommittee] is now under obligation, as a matter of elementary justice, we think, to give Dr. Lattimore a speedy and unequivocal vindication, and in view of the wide mischief and alarm that have been caused, to make a ringing declaration in behalf of the freedom of inquiry which has been gravely threatened by the Lattimore case.[112]

In a long editorial published in mid-July, the *Post* approved without reservations the report on the investigation signed by Tydings and the two other Democratic Senators. While the report was "angry and indignant," it seemed "essentially judicious and just." [113] The paper said that neither McCarthy's own information, nor the FBI files, nor the "witnesses called at his behest revealed the presence in the State

108. "The Man at the Top," *Washington Post*, March 28, 1950, p. 10.
109. *Ibid*.
110. "Memo on China," *Washington Post*, April 4, 1950, p. 12.
111. "Tangled Web," *Washington Post*, April 21, 1950, p. 22.
112. "The McCarthy Record," *Washington Post*, May 2, 1950, p. 10.
113. " 'A Fraud and a Hoax'!" *Washington Post*, July 18, 1950, p. 12.

Department of a single employee who could reasonably be called a Communist, or an agent of the Soviet Union, or even a security risk." It was "unfortunate" that Senator Lodge did not sign the majority report and his own report was "inconclusive in the extreme."

Even before McCarthy's Wheeling speech and the formation of the Tydings subcommittee, the *Times-Herald* was giving considerable attention to the issue of communism in the government and, like other conservative voices, it frequently said that there were both Communists and pro-Communists throughout the government service, and particularly in the State Department.

Shortly before the Tydings subcommittee was formed, the paper approved J. Edgar Hoover's request for an expansion of the FBI and commented that Hoover "should be encouraged in his efforts to find the Soviet master spy who STILL is hidden in the works of the Truman Administration. . . . Who is that man?" [114] The same theme appeared in the *Times-Herald*'s first comments on the formation of the Tydings subcommittee: The paper hoped that Tydings would "do an honest job" and not, "as so many times before, use the occasion to smoke-screen the real facts." The paper suggested what these facts might be: "Everyone knows good and well that Communists have done this country terrible damage and that they have got in some of their most tremendous blows in the State Department." [115] In the first editorial it published after the hearings began, the paper seemed to modify its position somewhat: McCarthy, it wrote, says he has information *"tending to show* disloyalty in 81 cases. The Senate committee headed by Tydings was selected to find out *if* there is anything in McCarthy's charges" [emphasis added].[116] But this wait-and-see attitude was only a passing phase. On March 23, it said that "the known failures of high officials of the State Department in dealing with subversion, pinkos and Communist agents have destroyed public confidence in this important branch of the government." [117] Later it insisted that the Tydings Committee must find "the Communists who *are* and *have been* wrecking American foreign policy from within the State Department." ". . . Communists are still where they always were and the disaster to the United States is obvious to every man, woman and child." [118] The *Times-Herald* belittled Acheson's claim that the State Department had

114. "He's Still Here," Washington *Times-Herald*, February 21, 1950.

115. "Where Spies Hurt Us Most," Washington *Times-Herald*, February 28, 1950, p. 10.

116. "Whitewash — Again!" Washington *Times-Herald*, March 9, 1950, p. 18.

117. "Is That Presidential Bee," Washington *Times-Herald*, March 23, 1950, p. 22.

118. "Is Tydings Man or Mouse?" Washington *Times-Herald*, April 2, 1950, p. 12.

"honorable, loyal and clean-living employees." [119] It claimed, when Earl Browder testified before the committee, that his testimony "confirms the existence of a Communist-New Deal working relationship which has long been obvious to anyone willing to recognize it." [120]

Five of the *Times-Herald*'s thirty-one editorials on the Tydings hearings dealt almost entirely with the *Amerasia* case, and it was mentioned in a number of others. It was a persistent suggestion of the paper that the case had been "fixed" by the government in 1945, and that it was being "whitewashed" by the Tydings group in 1950. The case, wrote the paper, is "a scandal of major proportions," and "the Truman gang is trying to hide the record from the public." [121] The paper "dared" Tydings to call J. Edgar Hoover to testify: Hoover's public testimony "could close the question once and for all." [122] It called the testimony of Emmanuel S. Larsen "part of the New Deal's game of cover-up." [123] For the individuals named before the committee, the *Times-Herald* had little or no sympathy. As to Dorothy Kenyon, it maintained that McCarthy's use of the Kenyon case was to show the "kinds of people" cleared by loyalty boards.[124]

The *Times-Herald* commented more extensively on Jessup than on Lattimore (presumably because Jessup was identified with the "internationalists" who were perennial targets of Colonel McCormick). The *Times-Herald* first expressed its opinion of Jessup in an editorial titled "Self-Portrait of an Internationalist." The editorial argued for a sort of objective guilt, claiming that "all of the internationalists [Jessup among these] who successfully clamored for American entry into World War II, thereby insured the destruction of Germany and Japan as the only brakes on Soviet expansion. The result is Russia's rise to world power." [125] Jessup aided the "internationalist policy of Roosevelt and Truman" and, consequently, the paper maintained, "if he had been a card-carrying member of the Communist party, he could never have served Stalin anywhere nearly as effectively." In a later editorial, after a review of Jessup's "record," the *Times-Herald*

119. " 'Honorable' Americans: II," Washington *Times-Herald*, April 28, 1950, p. 18.
120. "Browder and Roosevelt," Washington *Times-Herald*, May 5, 1950, p. 14, Sec. I.
121. "Some Teacup," Washington *Times-Herald*, June 1, 1950, p. 22.
122. "Let Hoover Talk," Washington *Times-Herald*, June 6, 1950, p. 12.
123. "What the *Amerasia* Record Shows," Washington *Times-Herald*, June 21, 1950, p. 18.
124. "The Company You Keep," Washington *Times-Herald*, April 10, 1950, p. 6.
125. "Self-Portrait of an Internationalist," Washington *Times-Herald*, March 24, 1950, p. 14, Sec. I. In fact, Jessup had been a supporter of America First, the isolationist organization that resisted involvement in the war in Europe.

concluded that "if he is the best we can get, heaven help the country, for its days are numbered." [126]

The *Times-Herald* discussed John Stewart Service as part of the *Amerasia* issue. It said the Tydings Committee should check to see whether Service really had had authority to declassify documents and make them available to newsmen as background. Even if he did have such authority, the paper asked, why should Service have provided material to a "pro-Soviet" magazine of small circulation? Also, photoengraving equipment on *Amerasia* premises indicated that it was "serving a spy ring." [127]

The *Times-Herald* was cautious in its comments when McCarthy first accused Lattimore of being the "chief Soviet agent" in the United States. But it said that Lattimore "has exerted a very considerable influence on the formation of State Department policy governing the Orient" and that "some" of his writings sound "suspiciously like the prevailing party line." [128] The only other significant discussion of Lattimore occurred in July, in an editorial which referred to him as the "principal architect of America's disastrous policy in China and Asia" but did not mention McCarthy's original and more serious charges against Lattimore.[129]

The *Times-Herald*'s views on the Tydings investigation were summed up in a full-page editorial published on July 19. Most of the editorial was a violent attack on the "New Deal" and the current Democratic administration and on the characters and motives of the three Democratic senators on the Tydings Committee. The majority report, it said, was a "whitewash" that "nobody believes." [130] Three days later, the *Times-Herald* "agreed" with Senator Lodge that the Tydings Committee had "no evidence" that Communists were then in the State Department, but the reason, it said, was that the committee did not do its job, which was "to find out who is or has been doing Stalin's work in the State Department."

Although it may not be astonishing that these journals showed unchanging patterns throughout the Tydings hearings, it is remarkable. That is, it is worthy of being remarked that these members of the press, which is sometimes said to write the first draft of history, closed the books as soon as the first page was turned. There may have been

126. "Dr. Jessup and Mr. Hyde," Washington *Times-Herald*, July 10, 1950, p. 6.
127. "Tydings Trapped," Washington *Times-Herald*, July 13, 1950, p. 20.
128. "Judge Them by Their Works," Washington *Times-Herald*, March 29, 1950, p. 14.
129. "Dr. Jessup and Mr. Hyde," Washington *Times-Herald*, July 10, 1950, p. 6.
130. "The Herring Is a Little Higher Now — The Report Nobody Believes," Washington *Times-Herald*, July 19, 1950, p. 18.

two reasons for this. The first is the obvious commonsense explanation
that the positions of the journals were not so much based on "facts" as
on their interpretations of "facts," with all that this implies for the
operation of values, judgments, and even ulterior motives. The material that constituted the agenda of McCarthy and the Tydings Committee simply provided the journals with illustrations for definitions
of reality to which commitments had already been made. Second,
assuming that the views of the journals *could* have been modified by a
Congressional investigation, the Tydings Committee failed to do so
because it was not an "authoritative" body whose findings would be
generally respected by all sides to the controversy. But then it may
be, that nobody whose findings failed to please one of the camps
would ever be regarded as "authoritative."

The Institute of Pacific Relations

The theory of the Internal Security subcommittee of the Senate
Judiciary Committee, commonly known as the McCarran committee
from the name of its chairman, that persons of pro-Communist orientation *did* have something to do with helping Mao and hurting Chiang
was given full test in the hearings on the Institute of Pacific Relations.
The McCarran committee was empowered by Senate Resolution of
December 21, 1950, to inquire into various aspects of internal security,
including the extent, nature, and effects of subversive activities besides
espionage and sabotage. It was under this general authority that the
investigation of the IPR took place, to determine whether it was
influenced or controlled by Communist agents; whether and to what
extent these agents and their "dupes" worked through the IPR "into
the United States government to the point where they exerted an
influence on United States far eastern policy"; and whether or to what
extent they "led or misled American public opinion, particularly with
respect to far eastern policy." [131]

The investigation started off in sensational fashion when staff of
the subcommittee raided a barn in Lee, Massachusetts, and seized records of the Institute of Pacific Relations stored there by Edward C.
Carter, former secretary-general of the Pacific Council of the organization.[132] This episode was very melodramatic, but the records were

131. *McCarran Committee Report*, pp. 1-2.
132. Alan Barth, *Government by Investigation* (New York: Viking, 1955), p.
97. See also testimony of William L. Holland, secretary-general of the Institute
of Pacific Relations, Eighty-second Congress, First Session, United States Senate,
Committee on the Judiciary, Subcommittee to Investigate the Administration of
the Internal Security Act and Other Internal Security Laws, *Hearings on the Institute of Pacific Relations*, p. 1172 *et seq.* (hereafter cited as *IPR Hearings*) for
mention of the interest of the FBI in the files. They were made available to the
FBI in the summer of 1950 as a consequence of the McCarthy charges and the
Tydings committee investigation.

already well known to the Federal Bureau of Investigation, they had
previously been made available to the FBI, and agents of the bureau
had taken some few papers they had thought useful and departed.
The files were seized early in February 1951 and for five months
thereafter staff of the McCarran committee prepared the case that they
expected to illustrate through the testimony of witnesses.[133]

The inquiry conducted by the McCarran committee differed from
the Tydings hearing considerably. It was not a helpful colloquy conducted by friendly senators, with generous toleration of counsel for
the witnesses, but a kind of trial with many rough passages in which
witnesses were put on the defensive, sometimes not allowed to finish
their statements, and throughout denied permission to engage the
lawyers in the proceedings who accompanied their clients to the hearing room.[134] Senator James O. Eastland of Mississippi was the chairman
of the subcommittee of the Senate Judiciary Committee investigating
the Institute of Pacific Relations, and the other members were Pat
McCarran of Nevada and Homer Ferguson of Michigan. The special
counsel of the subcommittee was Robert Morris who was subsequently
to have a disappointing political career in New Jersey, and the director
of research was Benjamin Mandel who had for years assisted public
officials and others in the investigation of Communist activity. The
hearings began on July 25, 1951, and lasted until June 20, 1952; and
the printed record of the proceedings alone totaled over 5,000 pages.

The Institute of Pacific Relations was an association of national
councils in ten countries having an interest in Far Eastern affairs — in
1950 these were the United States, Canada, Australia, New Zealand,
Philippines, France, Britain, India, Japan, and Pakistan. It was organized in 1925 to conduct a program of research, publications, and conferences for which it obtained money from its national councils and
from foundations. Although the national councils were autonomous,
they came together in the Pacific Council (where each had representation) which carried on the program of the Institute through a
small international secretariat located in New York. From 1925 to

133. The McCarran committee estimated that it took testimony from 66 witnesses, 28 of whom had some connection with the Institute of Pacific Relations.
McCarran Committee Report, p. 2.

134. See *IPR Hearings*, p. 2902, for the peremptory and overbearing manner of
Senator Homer Ferguson of Michigan in dealing with Owen Lattimore as the
witness tried to get into the first paragraphs of his opening statement. See also
p. 2898 for Senator Eastland's tough attitude towards Abe Fortas, counsel for
Lattimore before the McCarran committee as he had been in the Tydings committee proceedings: "The *Chairman:* . . . I did tell you privately and I will tell
you now on the record that you will be permitted to remain here. You will not
be permitted to testify and you will not be permitted to suggest answers to questions. . . . *Mr. Fortas:* Thank you, Senator. May I ask whether I am permitted to
object to questions? The *Chairman:* No, sir."

1950 the average annual budget of the Institute was $100,000, to which American sources contributed some 77 per cent. The American Council of the Institute, as an autonomous member, also had a budget averaging about $100,000 a year in the twenty-five years of the Institute's existence, the funds coming from membership subscriptions, gifts from individuals and corporations, and grants by foundations.[135]

The McCarran committee in conclusions published at the end of the long hearings said, "There is no evidence that the large majority of its members supported the IPR for any reason except to advance the professed research and scholarly purposes of the organization." [136] This is virtually the only reasonably friendly thing the McCarran committee had to say about the Institute. It concluded that IPR activities were made possible largely through the financial support of American corporations, industrialists, and foundations, the majority of whom were not familiar with the inner workings of the organization. Further, most members of the Institute and of its board of trustees were inactive and obviously without influence over the policies of the organization and the conduct of its affairs. Control of the organization was in the hands of a small core of officials and staff members and the "small core of officials and staff members who controlled the IPR were either Communist or pro-Communist."

The McCarran committee did not say that the Institute of Pacific Relations was a Communist organization. It did not say that it was a Communist-front organization. It did say that "The IPR has been considered by the American Communist Party and by Soviet officials as an instrument of Communist policy, propaganda and military intelligence." [137] It was the committee's position that the Institute had been used by some persons said to be Communist or pro-Communist as a vehicle for promoting the interests of the Soviet Union in the United States, for the advancement of international Communist interests, and for the affectation of American interests adversely. This it was said they had been able to do by allegedly publishing false information and by working to set up active cooperative and confidential relationships with persons in government involved in the determination of foreign policy and by achieving "close organic relations with the State Department through the interchange of personnel, attendance of State Department officials at IPR conferences, constant exchange of information and social contacts." The result, according to the committee, was that a "group of persons operating within and

135. T. Coleman Andrews, Commissioner of Internal Revenue in 1955, removed the Institute from tax-exempt status. Because of the financial burden this act imposed, the Institute left New York for Vancouver, B.C. at the end of 1960.
136. *McCarran Committee Report*, p. 223.
137. *McCarran Committee Report*, p. 223.

about the Institute of Pacific Relations exerted a substantial influence on United States far eastern policy." In particular, "Owen Lattimore and John Carter Vincent were influential in bringing about a change in United States policy in 1945 favorable to the Chinese Communists." [138]

The extensive testimony taken by the committee amply shows that some of the officials of the Institute enjoyed a remarkable degree of access to the highest reaches of the United States Government, and there is considerable evidence of the activity of individuals in the organization who were named under oath as either Communists or fellow travelers.[139] The McCarran Committee Report listed the names of eighty-seven persons in the IPR with alleged Communist affiliations, of whom forty-seven were said to have been identified as members of the Communist Party by one or more persons.[140] Of this number, ten denied under oath that they were or had been members of the party, and eleven refused to answer the question on the ground that a truthful answer might tend to incriminate them. Of those charged by one or more witnesses under oath of being Communists, who neither denied nor pleaded the Fifth Amendment, twelve were either out of the country or otherwise unavailable by subpoena, and four had died. Among those not charged by anybody (according to the committee's list) with being members of the Communist Party were Edward C. Carter, former secretary-general of the Institute, and William L. Holland, the secretary-general at the time of the hearings. In both instances the nature of the alleged Communist affiliation was connection with other groups. Carter was said to have been affiliated with *Amerasia*, the American Russian Institute, and Russian War Relief; and Holland was said to have been affiliated with *Amerasia* and the China Aid Council. In at least one instance a man who had been

138. *McCarran Committee Report*, p. 225.
139. In the Tydings committee investigation, Frederick V. Field, employed by the Institute from 1928 to 1940 as executive secretary of the American branch during the last six years of that time, pleaded the Fifth Amendment when asked whether he was or had ever been a member of the Communist Party. *Tydings Committee*, pp. 710–711. Of Field, whom Lattimore knew in the Institute, he said, "He is frequently and publicly listed as a Communist, though so far as I know he has neither admitted nor denied party membership. He strikes me as an individualist who has gone over so far to the left that there is nobody else there except the Communists." Lattimore, *Ordeal by Slander*, pp. 135–136. After resigning as secretary in 1940, Field served as a trustee and member of the executive committee of the board. When called before the McCarran Committee in executive session, he also pleaded the Fifth Amendment. In the public session, the chairman said, "Today, the committee does not intend to adopt a harsh attitude toward you." *IPR Hearings*, p. 75.
140. *McCarran Committee Report*, pp. 151–159. Many of those named in the list, however, seem to have had only a very marginal connection with the IPR, according to William Holland. See *IPR Hearings*, p. 5684.

a member of the Communist Party (as he later confessed) was listed merely because he had been proposed as a delegate to an IPR conference in 1944. This was Lee Pressman, at the time general counsel for the CIO.[141]

The principal publications of the Institute of Pacific Relations were the *Far Eastern Survey* and *Pacific Affairs*. To determine if possible the ideological line of these journals, staff of the committee had the Legislative Reference Service of Congress make a content analysis.[142] Legislative Reference Service calculated the percentages of material contributed by Communists, those who might be regarded as anti-Communist, and those who fell into neither category and were characterized as "neutral." The three groups were labeled P (pro-Communist), A (anti-Communist) and N (neutral), and both the number of pages and the frequency of contributions in the years surveyed (1931–1951) were counted and arrayed in various ways. An estimation of the share of the three groups in the number of contributions showed that the P group had 30.33 per cent, the A group 12.64 per cent, and the N group 57.03 per cent of the *Far Eastern Survey* in the two decades covered. In *Pacific Affairs*, the share of the P group was 15.71 per cent, that of the A group 15.81 per cent, and that of the N group 68.47 per cent. The distribution of the number of pages among the three groups in the two decades roughly corresponds with the distribution according to the number of items. Much of the space in the magazines was devoted to highly technical discussions of economic and social problems,[143] which accounts for the large percentages of the N group, but even so, the distribution may not be utterly without significance.

Owen Lattimore was editor of *Pacific Affairs* from 1934 to 1941 during which the proportion of contributions by the P group showed a marked rise. In 1931–33 the P group contributed 6.32 per cent of the items, the A group 6.56 per cent and the N group 87.11 per cent. In the next seven years the P group went from 6.32 to 22.83 per cent, the A group from 6.56 to 17.25 per cent, and the N group dropped to 59.92 per cent. Although the A group increased in this period over the earlier one, the increase in the P group was almost fourfold (3.7) as against an increase of twofold and a half (2.6) for the A group.

141. *IPR Hearings*, p. 2809.

142. The work was done by the Legislative Reference Service of the Library of Congress, and transmitted to the subcommittee on June 16, 1952 in response to its request of April 3, 1952 by Ernest S. Griffith, Director of the Legislative Reference Service. *McCarran Committee Report*, pp. 99–105. All of the material in the text is taken from the subcommittee summary of the statistical report.

143. Buckley and Bozell, *McCarthy and his Enemies*, p. 106, discuss the significance of the percentages and say "such an analysis is inadequate for it fails to reveal how much of the material submitted by each group had any *political* [emphasis theirs] significance."

The McCarran committee found these distributions to be of some significance in determining the political tendency of the journals under the editorship of Owen Lattimore, but Lattimore presented a compilation of his own in testimony, the burden of which was to show that in *Pacific Affairs* "we published at least 94 contributions that were definitely to the right of center, which means about seven times as much right-wing material as there was left wing views or information." [144] One trouble with this testimony is that, like much else Lattimore said, it proves too much. On his count of pieces in *Pacific Affairs* the journal must have been favorite reading by subscribers strongly hostile to the liberal progressivism with which he was widely identified and which he, by his account, would seem to have muted as editor in favor of views he rejected. However, since the Legislative Reference Service used an objective criterion for the P group (one or more identifications under oath of affiliation with Communist-controlled organizations, or documentary evidence to the same effect) and Lattimore's categories of left of center, right of center, and neutral are otherwise undefined, it is not possible to compare the two compilations.

The testimony of IPR officials themselves established the existence of a Communist presence in the organization. William Holland, the secretary-general of the IPR, thought that he would be able "to say that there are possibly three or four people whom I can think of whose subsequent actions suggest to me that they may have been Communists. . . ." [145] These were Chi Ch'ao Ting, a research associate, Y. Hsu, also a research associate, and Israel Epstein, a writer. Other former officers of IPR were more expansive in their estimate. Raymond Dennett, who was secretary of the American Council of the Institute of Pacific Relations from approximately March 1944 to December 1945, felt that there was a bias favorable to the Soviet Union among the staff of twenty-four with which he worked, although he said that he was not in a position to judge whether any of the staff was a Communist, nor did it occur to him at the time. [146] He did say that "I think it was generally assumed by everyone that Frederick Field was, if not a Communist, at least a fellow traveller." [147] Professor David Rowe of Yale, a member of the board of trustees of the IPR from February 1947 to the early part of 1950, resigned from the board and declined to return because he did not like the leftist ideological bias he felt pervaded much of the work of the IPR. [148] As for Lattimore, Professor Rowe said, "I have for a number of years labeled Lattimore

144. *IPR Hearings*, p. 2981.
145. *IPR Hearings*, p. 3899.
146. *IPR Hearings*, pp. 950 and 948.
147. *IPR Hearings*, p. 954.
148. *IPR Hearings*, pp. 3970–3972.

as a fellow traveller." [149] *Amerasia* was closely linked with the IPR through Frederick Field who was owner of 50 per cent of its stock, and, for a time, both chairman of its editorial board and executive secretary of the American Council of the IPR. Regulars of the IPR like Lattimore and Chi were on the board of editors of *Amerasia*, and articles and writers were shunted back and forth among the *Far Eastern Survey*, *Pacific Affairs*, and *Amerasia*.[150] Professor Kenneth Colegrove (mentioned previously in the discussion of the *Amerasia* case), a member of the Institute and a member of the advisory board of editors of *Amerasia* from 1937 to 1942 when he resigned, had been asked to join the board by Frederick Field, and he thought that the issues during 1937, 1938, and 1939 were well balanced. It was later that he thought a pro-Communist line began to intrude, especially in the writings of Chi.[151] He expressed shock over a letter from Owen Lattimore to Edward C. Carter dated July 10, 1938, in which the writer said,

> For the general purposes of this inquiry it seems to me that the good scoring position for the IPR differs with different countries. For China, my hunch is that it will pay to keep behind the official Chinese Communist position — far enough not to be covered by the same label — but enough ahead of the active Chinese liberals to be noticeable.[152]

It was Professor Colegrove's conclusion that "This shows behind the front the Institute of Pacific Relations was nothing else than a propaganda organization supporting a line," which he then said was "the Communist line." [153] The "inquiry" was a $90,000 research undertaking into the issues of the Sino-Japanese war.[154]

The McCarran committee adduced enough information to show that there was a Communist enterprise within the Institute of Pacific Relations, that there were party-liners in active roles, and that the journals of the Institute showed a sympathetic regard for both the Soviet Union and the Chinese Communists, especially in the late thirties and the 1940's. But it made more than the evidence seems to justify out of the fact that the Soviet Union had formal membership in the Institute of Pacific Relations. In 1934, the secretary general of the Institute, Edward C. Carter, and other Americans pressed for the organization of a Soviet Council and its admission to the Institute of Pa-

149. *IPR Hearings*, p. 3984.
150. *McCarran Committee Report*, p. 71.
151. *IPR Hearings*, pp. 906–907.
152. *IPR Hearings*, p. 916.
153. *IPR Hearings*, p. 916.
154. See testimony of Edward E. Carter, *IPR Hearings*, at p. 36, and at pp. 39–41 for the full text of the letter.

cific Relations, but it is hard to share the sense of ominous significance that the subcommittee attached to this action. Like many other foundations, the IPR was interested in pushing its activity, expanding its program, borrowing the prestige of others to enhance the reputation of its own organization and the status of its bureaucracy, puffing its wares, its services, its acceptability, its name-dropping connection with the great, the near-great and the merely-swollen of the international political world — in short, like advertisers generally, to create the need that it was established to satisfy. The Soviet Union obviously has been a Pacific power; in 1933 the United States recognized the Soviet Union, and what passes for normal relations with the Russians were established between Washington and Moscow. A Russian scientific society, the Pacific Institute, was admitted to the IPR in 1934 as a national council. It is of some note that although the Russians had representation in the Pacific Council of the Institute, they were never active, except in 1936, and after 1939 took no part whatsoever in the Institute's program, neglecting even to answer routine correspondence. Between 1935 and 1939, the IPR received contributions from its Soviet constituent, and after 1939 none.[155] This does not mean that the relationship was entirely inert, for there is information about trips to the Soviet Union by officers and staff of the IPR, the exchange of books and manuscripts, and meetings with Soviet officials after 1934. The records show considerable foolishness, even by the standards of the 1930's, in Edward C. Carter's estimation of current events in the Soviet Union, like the purge trials of 1936 and 1937 which he thought had a bad reputation in America, in part because of Trotskyite clamor.[156]

But what of the transaction from the other side? What did the Soviet Union have in mind when permission was granted to establish the Soviet Council? It is entirely possible that Military Intelligence thought of the Institute of Pacific Relations as an organization through which it could establish useful intelligence operations, under cover, in areas in the Far East where the Soviet Union did not have normal diplomatic relations. It is quite conceivable that contacts with foreign members of the Institute, especially those already flattered to be seemingly accepted by the Soviet Union, would be utilized for intelligence and propaganda purposes, and that through them, witting or not, there would be a flow of news out from Moscow as well as in to Moscow.

There was some testimony about Soviet intelligence activity in the IPR but it was somewhat tenuous. Alexander Gregory Barmine, a

155. See statement inserted in the record by William Holland, *IPR Hearings*, p. 1225. Many pages of the *McCarran Committee Report* (pp. 13–54) are devoted to the relations between the IPR and the Soviet Union.

156. See letter from Carter to William Holland, dated March 5, 1937, at *IPR Hearings*, p. 3932.

former Soviet general, mentioned a conversation he had in 1933 with General Berzin of Military Intelligence in which the latter suggested that the military might want to hide arms in China under cover of an export corporation Barmine headed. When Barmine said that the affair would require trusted men, Berzin was said to have mentioned Owen Lattimore and Joseph Barnes among others. Later Barmine said he was told that they would be more useful in the plans for the building up of branches of the IPR that could be used as a cover for military intelligence work in the Pacific area.[157] (Joseph Barnes was secretary of the American Council and served on its staff from 1931 to 1934, later becoming foreign editor of the *New York Herald Tribune*.) Barmine said that in 1937 he had another conversation, this time with General Walter Krivitsky, also of Military Intelligence, after the latter had fled the Soviet Union. Barmine asked him whether he knew Lattimore and Barnes, was told that Military Intelligence had a "flourishing" operation in the Institute of Pacific Relations, and that Lattimore and Barnes "are working within the Institute of Pacific Relations and they are still, what he said, 'they are still our men.' "[158]

Lattimore rebutted these statements by pointing out that Barmine had written a book, *One Who Survived*, which had appeared in a French and an English version, and that there was no mention of a General Berzin under whom Barmine was supposed to have worked for fifteen years. He said also that General Krivitsky, too, had written a book and testified before the House Committee on Un-American Activities in 1938, and failed to mention Lattimore, Barnes, the Institute of Pacific Relations, or either Barmine or Berzin. Lattimore suggested that Barmine was making up his story.[159] There was no corroboration of Barmine's story. Bogolepov, who described the use made by Litag (literary agitation) of the channels of the Institute, could only say that he had once seen Lattimore in the IPR building in Moscow and that he heard a functionary suggest the name of Lattimore as one who might write a book on Mongolia.[160]

The sum of the evidence in the long hearings was added up in the

157. *IPR Hearings*, pp. 201–202.
158. *IPR Hearings*, pp. 208–209.
159. *IPR Hearings*, pp. 3103 and 3704–3705.
160. *IPR Hearings*, pp. 4516 and 4519. Igor Bogolepov was a former counselor in the Soviet Foreign Office. He was also a colonel in the Russian retreat to Leningrad in August 1941, when he decided to go over to the Germans. He operated a transmitter broadcasting propaganda for them until his station was shut down as a consequence of a struggle between cliques of Nazis. He found it impossible to work with the Germans. "It was not that the Nazis were too bad," he said in testimony. "When I came over and [*sic*] knew they were no good. But I didn't know the Germans were so silly as they are." *IPR Hearings*, p. 4487.

committee's final report.[161] The conclusions about the influence that
the Institute was thought to have had upon United States foreign
policy in the Far East were stated with the tightness of a lawyer's brief,
but some of them were merely argumentative and some were insinu-
ated inferences from the established facts. For example, Lauchlin
Currie, the administrative assistant to President Roosevelt, and special
adviser on Far Eastern affairs, by reason of his important office was the
center of a great deal of traffic in policy and attempted policy. He
seems to have first recommended the appointment of Lattimore as an
adviser to Chiang when Chiang asked President Roosevelt to nominate an adviser to him.[162] On June 18, 1941, before there was public
announcement of Lattimore's appointment, he and Edward C. Carter
had lunch with Constantine Oumansky, the Soviet ambassador to the
United States. Or, as Carter put it in a letter at the time, he (Carter)
had lunch "with Oumansky in Washington on Wednesday. We talked
for a couple of hours. I was fortunate in getting Lattimore over from
Baltimore, as I thought it was pretty important for him to have a long
talk with Oumansky, in view of his job and the evolving world situation. It was a most illuminating two hours." [163] The committee report
does not say what conclusion is to be drawn from this information.[164]
Even if nothing more devious than fellowship is suggested by the meet-

161. Following his testimony in February and March 1952, Owen Lattimore
was indicted on seven counts of perjury by a Federal grand jury. Lattimore on
December 19, 1952, pleaded not guilty to charges that he committed perjury in
the McCarran hearings when he denied (1) that he had promoted communism
and Communist interests; (2) that he did not know that the pen name of a
writer for the IPR concealed the name of a known Communist; (3) that he had
published articles by known Communists when he was editor of *Pacific Affairs;*
(4) that he had entered China in 1937 with the aid of the Communist Party; (5)
that he was told that a certain Chinese official was a Communist; (6) that he
took over the White House correspondence during the absence of an administrative assistant; and (7) that he met former Russian ambassador Constantine Oumansky during the period of the Hitler-Stalin Pact. On May 2, 1953, Federal Judge
Luther W. Youngdahl dismissed the first four counts of the indictment, and
said that there were "serious doubts" about the validity of the other three. On
August 24, 1953, the Government asked the Court of Appeals to restore the four
counts. On July 8, 1954, the Court of Appeals restored two of the counts but on
June 28, 1955, the Attorney General ordered all charges dismissed.

162. Stanley Hornbeck was privately told by Currie that he had recommended
Lattimore. Hornbeck testified that he objected to the making of the nomination
without consultation with the Secretary of State, and that he had not thought
Lattimore suitable for the assignment. *IPR Hearings*, pp. 3209–3210.

163. *IPR Hearings*, p. 3264.

164. In fact it merely insinuates the conclusion it does not adopt, in the statement that "Lattimore could give the subcommittee no reasonable explanation as
to why he should confer with the Ambassador of a country that had an alliance
with both Germany and China's enemy, Japan, and was at political war with the
United States." *McCarran Committee Report*, p. 179.

ing with the Soviet ambassador, it does establish amiable concourse and fraternization with a top Soviet representative by officials of the IPR at an extremely critical time. There is no record that Carter had Lattimore to lunch with the Japanese ambassador, who also would have had an interest in the new mission and with whose country we were officially at peace.

In late November 1941, the possibility of a modus vivendi between the United States and Japan was considered, with agreement for a ninety-day truce while negotiations continued. On November 26, Secretary Hull rejected the idea and twelve days later the Japanese attacked Pearl Harbor. While the American decision on the modus vivendi was in the balance, Harry Dexter White, then Under Secretary of the Treasury, asked Edward C. Carter to come to Washington from New York to lobby against it. Lattimore wired Currie to advise the President of Chiang's opposition to the modus vivendi. Carter reported a meeting he had with Currie on November 28 in which he expressed the feeling that Currie had probably had an anxious time the previous week. These are all of the statements in the McCarran report on the activity of Americans on the modus vivendi. There is no conclusion as to what we are to make of it. There is no evidence of policy influence here. There is evidence of attempted policy influence in the useless trip Carter made to New York (the issue was settled before he arrived), and there is a presumption that people as highly placed in the government as Currie and White could possibly exercise some degree of policy influence, although there is no demonstration here that they did. We have seen earlier that White did in fact provide Hull with a memorandum that figured in the final diplomatic exchanges with the Japanese but even this does not demonstrate IPR influence, which was the subject of the McCarran investigation.[165] It is true that the Soviet Union was relieved to have Japan involved in a war with the United States, but so were Chiang Kai-shek and Winston Churchill.[166]

The McCarran committee report is on firmer ground when it details the activity of various persons around the White House, some of whom had close connections with the Institute of Pacific Relations. Currie served as a high adviser to officials of the Institute. Currie admired Lattimore and allowed him to use a small office in his suite in the State Department building when he (Lattimore) returned from China in

165. See above, p. 177.
166. This section of the *McCarran Committee Report* contains what would seem to be an entirely irrelevant series of statements about Elizabeth Bentley's testimony on George Silverman. It does not seem to connect with the title of the section which is "Institute of Pacific Relations Personnel Worked to Prevent United States-Japanese Truce." *Ibid.*, pp. 179–181.

February 1942. Carter attempted to use Currie to shape Far Eastern policy, or rather, it should be said, Carter obviously thought that his chances of influencing Currie were so good that he could consider making an effort to do so. Even here, however, the record is slim, consisting in the main of telegrams about arrangements for short meetings of five minutes, ten minutes, and so on; and a letter to Chi for advice on the advisability of sending a cable to Currie (then in China) about some publicity on a meeting between Currie and Chou En-lai to allay rumors about a split in Chinese unity.[167] Carter in 1942 worked to get an Army commission (in Intelligence) for Frederick Field, who had resigned as secretary of the American Council of the Institute to become executive secretary of the American Peace Mobilization, a Communist agitation group. Field thought that it was possible that Currie had endorsed him through the intervention of others, but he was not sure.[168]

Lattimore was succeeded as managing editor of *Pacific Affairs* in 1941 by Michael Greenberg. Elizabeth Bentley testified that she had recruited Greenberg into her espionage ring[169] and Professor George Edward Taylor, a trustee of the Institute, said that Greenberg was so blatant in his beliefs that he was surprised to see him turn up in the White House. On November 9, 1942, Greenberg was appointed to a position with the Board of Economic Warfare and was assigned to and shared an office with Lauchlin Currie. All of this certainly suggests the existence of a small group of people, more or less connected with the IPR, centered at the White House, sharing a generally leftward perspective on policy, at least one of whom, perhaps, even engaged in espionage (if Bentley's account is credited). Even if espionage is discounted, substantial evidence remains of frequent effort to influence the courses of policy in the Far East by people like Carter and Lattimore.

The Institute was responsible for two triennial conferences during the war years, which the McCarran committee report thought significant. The first was at Mont Tremblant, Canada, in December 1942, and the second was at Hot Springs, Virginia, in January 1945. At the Canadian conference the American delegation numbered twenty-six. The report said that William W. Lockwood, the secretary of the American Council of the Institute, conferred with Lauchlin Currie on the conference; that seven of the twenty-six were accused of being Communists in the course of the McCarran hearings; that Currie, Alger Hiss, Joseph Barnes, Jessup, Edward Carter, and Lockwood were in

167. *IPR Hearings*, p. 429.
168. *IPR Hearings*, p. 426.
169. *IPR Hearings*, p. 108.

varying degrees involved in the selection of conferees; that IPR persons on the inside closely controlled the program arrangements; and that State Department policy-makers who attended the conference had no organizational role. It is not entirely clear why it should be notable that IPR insiders should control the program of an IPR conference, nor why State Department people attending the conference should have any organizational role at all.[170] None of this information supplies any evidence of influence on Far Eastern policy by the IPR conference. In fact there is no information in the report as to what the program of the conference was.

The material on the Mont Tremblant conference does indicate further, however, the ambition of the IPR leadership to cut a wide swath in public affairs. There is a great busyness of letters, telephone calls, conferences, and caucuses, and the sense of joy in the sharing of association with high level people is evident in some of the correspondence. There is evidence also that a small cluster of people persistently identified under oath as Communists show up here as they do in some other associations. Although the conference is made to seem sinister, it can scarcely be viewed as a conspiracy or even as a very safe vehicle for the cultivation of propaganda. In this regard there is an interesting point in the testimony of Elizabeth Bentley who said that she had once asked Jacob Golos why he did not take over the Communists within the IPR as a unit, and he said, "No; they are operating much too loosely." [171] By that he "meant that they were operating so much in the open and they were making so many blunders that it would be a mercy if the FBI didn't get them."

The Hot Springs conference in January 1945 was a kind of preface to the United Nations conference in San Francisco, and was attended by many delegates from countries other than the United States on their way to found the United Nations. Lauchlin Currie played some part in the selection of delegates and was consulted by Raymond Dennett (at that time secretary of the American Council) twice on arrangements for the conference. Currie suggested that Acheson, John Carter Vincent, and Eugene Dooman be the government delegates from the State Department; Will Clayton, Harry Dexter White, and possibly Frank Coe from other agencies; and Rupert Emerson from the Foreign Economic Administration.[172] Philip Jessup submitted approximately thirty names as delegates of whom ten were accused by

170. There are some seeming irrelevancies in this section of the report also. For example, there is information about Alger Hiss and his opinion of Ludwig Rajchman, who eventually turned up as a leading member of the Polish delegation at the United Nations. *McCarran Committee Report,* p. 183.
171. *IPR Hearings,* p. 412.
172. *IPR Hearings,* p. 981.

various witnesses of Communist connections, and six of these were among the seven who had gone to Mont Tremblant. There were twenty-eight members in the full delegation.[173] They caucused before the conference to discuss the possibility of getting discussion on the internal affairs of China, and in the conference itself Lattimore irked the French, British, and Dutch delegates by attacking colonialism.[174]

This section of the report is open to the same criticism as that on the Mont Tremblant conference. It ends with the assertion: "Thus did the IPR continue to establish pro-Communist influence at the Hot Springs International Conference. Thus were the various influential non-Communist delegates from the United States and foreign governments exposed to this influence." [175] No influence is demonstrated. If the British, French, and Dutch delegates resented attacks on colonialism by Lattimore and others, the resentment would at least indicate that they were not being brainwashed. All of the delegates who were going to San Francisco were under instructions from their governments, and it may be doubted whether anything that they heard at Hot Springs led them to disobey them. It could be that the chief function of the two IPR conferences was to enhance the prestige of the IPR, and to make it new friends. In any case, no influence on anyone was established by the McCarran committee report on these conferences and none was pointed to.

A section of the McCarran committee report on the production and circulation of IPR pamphlets[176] fails to supply information on the policy influence of IPR members on the government. The evidence is that there was a circulation of IPR reports and manuscripts, the works of Lawrence K. Rosinger being particularly suspect. He was accused of Communist connections by three witnesses at the McCarran hearings and pleaded the Fifth Amendment when he testified himself.[177]

In three important sections of the McCarran committee report attention leaves the IPR and turns instead to the reports of Foreign Service officers in the field, the Wallace Mission to China, and the Marshall Mission, the whole being introduced by some conclusions about the conveyance of Chinese Communist wishes to American officials. The opening lines are:

All during this period, 1941–45, it was the publicly expressed and clearly defined official policy of the United States to aid the Government of Nationalist China. It was also United States policy to keep

173. *IPR Hearings*, pp. 995–996, for a list of names and identifications.
174. This is in the testimony of Raymond Dennett (*IPR Hearings*, p. 994).
175. *McCarran Committee Report*, p. 195.
176. *McCarran Committee Report*, pp. 184–186.
177. *IRP Hearings*, p. 2475.

the armies of that Government fighting the common enemy. But, during this period there developed a distinct undermining of this policy.[178]

The best that the report can do to document this "publicly expressed and clearly defined" American policy is to refer to the testimony of General Albert Wedemeyer.[179] But the testimony of General Wedemeyer reversed the order of priority in which the committee cast its statement. General Wedemeyer said, "At that time, the American policy as I interpreted it, was to keep China in the war and to support the Chinese Nationalist Government." Instead of finding a clear-cut policy to follow, General Wedemeyer said, "There were no clear-cut American policies enunciated, insofar as I can recall, pertaining to China or any other area of the world." He said that theater commanders in remote areas oftentimes had to conjecture what was desired "in a broad sense." However, he felt that his job in China "was to continue China in the war" and, "as I stated, also to support the Chinese Nationalist Government which our own Government recognized as sovereign in that area."

It may also be pointed out that the mission of Wallace and the directive of General Marshall can hardly be described as "a distinct undermining of this policy." When officials at this level of government undertake missions directly under the supervision of the President, they are making policy, or changing policy, but can hardly be described as undermining policy, since this is the level at which policy is made. The same might also be argued in the case of the Foreign Service officers, since it is the duty of the FSO to report his recommendations and criticisms of existing policy in his area. The picture of policy-making supposed by the report is a curious one if the Vice President, and the President's special representative, and the FSO's, can all be described as "undermining policy."

Contacts between Chou En-lai and representatives of the State Department and the White House have been alluded to earlier. The committee spoke of some of these contacts as evidence of the dovetailing of Communist and American demands on the Nationalist Government. The critical opinion of Chiang held by some officers was, however, no secret. The reports of both Service and Vincent to the department on their conversations with Chou En-lai and Lin Piao at least remove any tinge of clandestinity from their meeting with these Communist leaders.

The reports from FSO staff in the field showed, as has been indi-

178. *McCarran Committee Report*, p. 186
179. *IPR Hearings*, p. 777.

cated above, a growing impatience with the stalemate of Nationalist forces, the failure of Chiang to put all of his troops against the Japanese, his stubborn appraisal of the intentions of the Chinese Communists, and his unwillingness to accept them on their professed terms. The selections from these reports in the McCarran committee report, as well as a similar selection in the China White Paper of two years earlier, illustrate the difference of opinion within the State Department that resulted in the showdown in February 1945 in which the Hurley view of policy prevailed. It is difficult to assess the assertion in the committee statement that the Service-Davies reports exaggerated the weakness of the Nationalists, the degree of internal unrest, and the economic instability of the regime in China. These difficulties, it seems, were very pronounced, and could have been stated strongly without being "exaggerated." However, there does seem to be little basis for assertion by Foreign Service officers that the Communists were the real fighters against the Japanese.

On the other hand, while there was some equivocation in the various reports about the degree of the attachment of the Chinese Communists to the USSR, such attachment was acknowledged and frequently brought into the reports in warnings about what the situation would be if we did not take such and such steps to demonstrate our friendliness to the Communists, to wean them away from the Kremlin, or to prevent their permanent adherence to Moscow. The accusation that field advices favoring more democracy in China were pretexts for vitiating the authority of the Nationalist Government, is an oversimplification of the matter. It is possible that some who urged democratic reforms on Chiang sincerely believed in the superiority of democracy as a form of government, realized that this might institutionalize Communist representation, but felt that democratic elements would be strong enough to hold control of affairs.

The tendency of the reports from the CBI theater was to leave open the question as to which of the two factions we should support. After 1949, of course, the question could not even be asked. If the total impact of the reports was to create or maintain a question as to which faction we should support, then one would presumably have to describe them as very influential. On the other hand, throughout the long period of civil war in China, in the thirties and the forties up to the advent of the Cold War in Europe in 1948, the United States was not really committed to keep Chiang in power. Up to the Hurley and Marshall missions the policy (an historic one) was nonintervention in internal affairs. After the defeat of the Japanese, Marshall's role was that of *impartial* mediator and President Truman refused in 1947 to make an unequivocal declaration of support for the Nationalist cause.

These acts, as well as the arms embargo, are consistent with the concept of an American policy aimed not to promote communism but to create pressure to get unity.

If the reports were influential, they were influential through the normal channels of government, and they emanated from members of the regular Foreign Service. If they showed lack of comprehension of the character of the Chinese Communists, they share this failing with General Joseph E. Stilwell, General Patrick J. Hurley, and General George C. Marshall. Until and unless conscious pro-Communist bias can be demonstrated, then the recommendations fall into the bulging category of foreign policy errors, not into the category of subversive influences on foreign policy. The McCarran committee did not seriously attempt to establish Communist Party membership, or disciplined fellow-traveling, with respect to the Foreign Service staff, although it worked harder on Service than on others because of his connection with the *Amerasia* case. It was argued instead that there was correspondence between the views and recommendations of the FSO staff and the Chinese Communist or international Communist line, and that the objective effect of these views was to strengthen the Communists. No special link is shown between the Institute of Pacific Relations and Davies, Ludden, or Emmerson, nor is there a close connection shown between Service and the IPR until a later date than the reports. The inclusion by the McCarran committee of the material on the FSO's in a report on the IPR serves by its conjunction to confuse the question of subversion with which the committee was primarily concerned.

In the committee report John Carter Vincent is regarded as one of those who steered Wallace along Communist lines, although the report does not square this judgment with the fact that Vincent supported Wallace's recommendation that Stilwell be removed, and that Wedemeyer be given command. There is nothing in the record to connect Vincent with the Communist Party except the cryptic testimony of the former Communist Budenz who, when asked whether John Carter Vincent was a member of the Communist Party, replied, "From official reports that I have received, he was." [180] If Vincent had made the statements in the China conversations that Wallace is quoted to have made, committee counsel could only have regarded them as a bonanza. The most foolish ones made by Wallace were omitted from the report and even in the hearings.

After the shakeup in the Department of State in the summer of 1945, which has been described, it was Vincent's function to operate at the highest levels in the formulation of the directives of the Mar-

180. *IPR Hearings*, p. 625

shall mission. The Chinese Communist Party in May 1945 adopted resolutions calling for an "independent, free, democratic, unified, strong, and prosperous China" with coalition government to include Communist representation. Owen Lattimore sent a letter to President Truman on June 10, 1945, urging a coalition government in which the Communists would have strong but minority representation. The directives prepared in part by Vincent instructed Marshall to strive for the unification of China through his good offices. Vincent had urged that the basis of the Chinese government be broadened to include other political elements. His outline of proposals urged that the United States not make a "military intervention in an internecine struggle." The committee report by juxtaposition implies that each of these successive acts was the cause of the next. Thus Mao speaks, Lattimore writes, Vincent acts, and Truman sends Marshall to "bring to bear upon the Chinese National Government the pressure of United States influence."

Apart from the fact that juxtaposition does not establish cause, it should be noted that the official subject of the report is the Institute of Pacific Relations. One of the subtitles is "Lattimore and Vincent of the IPR were Influential in Bringing about a Change in U. S. Policy in 1945 Favorable to the Chinese Communists." It is true that Vincent was an active member of the IPR but the influence described in the body of the report was that of the chief of the Far Eastern Division of the State Department. Although the point has minor substantive importance, to say that "Vincent of the State Department" was influential in making United States policy has entirely different import and effect from the statement that "Vincent of the IPR" was influential in making United States policy. However strongly one might disagree with Vincent's recommendations and analyses, one can hardly find it curious that the director of the Far Eastern office should have an effect on United States foreign policy in the Far East, or improper, or noteworthy.

On the committee version of events it is assumed that Lattimore so influenced Truman that he personally brought about changes in personnel in the State Department, which change in turn precipitated the change in policy. We know that this is not the case. It was Acheson who brought about the personnel changes, and the President, so far as can be ascertained, had nothing to do with Acheson's appointments. Furthermore, since everybody seems to agree that Byrnes had no interest in Far Eastern policy, it is unlikely in the extreme that Byrnes appointed Acheson to promote any particular point of view on Far Eastern policy.

The hearings of the McCarran committee on the Institute of Pacific

Relations and China affairs show something less than subversive conspiracy in the making of foreign policy, and something more than quiet routine. The thesis of conspiracy, even if hypothetically provable, is not proved. Foreign policy is not determined alone by field officers and the bureau chiefs over them but is an affair in which many others share — the top organization of the State Department, for example, with assistant secretaries, deputy secretaries, under secretaries, and the Secretary of State, most of whom would have had to connive in complicity to make the thesis of conspiracy tenable. And if Hull, Stettinius, Byrnes, and Marshall are imagined to be accomplices of subversion, knowing or not, there are still others to reckon with — the Pentagon and the White House itself — for they were making foreign policy in the forties quite as much if not more than the Department of State. Even in the relatively lowly work of gathering intelligence, John Paton Davies, Jr. complained about the encroachments of new agencies on what he thought was the jurisdiction of the old line State Department.

The hearings do show that pro-Communist and fellow-traveler attitudes abounded in the overlapping circles of groups, official and unofficial, that buzzed and swarmed in constant movement around the State Department, and that there was public agitation — like Browder's pressure in 1942 — and private agitation — like Carter's trip to Washington in 1941 and Lattimore's letter to President Truman in 1945 — to affect the course of policy. There was unwarranted access to impermissible information originating all over the government and channeled to the Department of State through the *Amerasia* operation. There were private links between the Soviet Embassy and the State Department through Edward C. Carter; and informal channels of communication between Chou En-lai and both the State Department and the White House through John Paton Davies, Jr. and Lauchlin Currie.

The security procedures of the State Department in the forties seem to have been sadly lax. We have the word of the State Department itself that it flushed out hundreds of security risks once it undertook to look into the situation intensively. The thought of Service checking in with Jaffe on his return from the field is unsettling. The speculation as to whether it was Wadleigh, Hiss, or somebody else who was taking papers from the desk of Sayre stirs wonder both about anonymous actors and about the lighting on the stage which conceals the cast. The later record of the first Eisenhower Administration, however, should diminish the expectation held out by programs that aim at total security. In the first three years of experience with a hard line policy on security, almost half of the people discharged by the Eisenhower Administration were people who had been hired by the Eisenhower Administration.

An extensive account of the wartime policy of the United States, or of the policy towards China, or even of the roles played in both by the Department of State and its staff, is beyond the scope of these pages. It may be said, however, that the simple finding of those conducting the inquest on the China policy — namely, that conspirators in the State Department gave China to the Communists — is not only untenable, but tended to detract from a true appreciation of the influence of serious handicaps in the conduct of our first major venture in ideological politics around the world. In the simple matter of gathering information abroad, for example, the United States lacked a seasoned, centralized, trained corps of intelligence officers, and the intelligence function was performed by at least five agencies — the FBI, the State Department, the Office of Naval Intelligence, Army intelligence, and the Office of Strategic Services (there were doubtless more), some in competition with the others. In some respects the structure of the State Department was better suited to the quiet days of the 1920's than to the requirements of a modern foreign office, and during the war years, the Bureau of the Budget constantly pressed State to rationalize its administrative disorder. The economic aspects of modern warfare were in the charge of a succession of *ad hoc* agencies of uncertain jurisdiction, like the Board of Economic Warfare, the Foreign Economic Administration, and the United Nations Relief and Rehabilitation Administration, none of which was more than loosely jointed to the main conduits of foreign policy presumably manned by the State Department.

In the 1940's and 1950's there was confusion, to be sure, as was suggested in Chapter VIII, about the nature of the Communist movement and the civil war in China. There were differences of opinion as to whether the Chinese Communists were linked with the International, or whether it was important if they were; whether they were indigenous radicals without Soviet connections, as Molotov told Hurley was the case; whether they were democratic reformers as T. A. Bisson said in his article on the two Chinas in 1943; or whether they were like a competitive party on the American model, as Wallace suggested to Chiang during his mission to Chungking. In addition to these confusions, there was also incompetence, bad judgment, and romanticism, as the record has shown.

At the center of difficulty, however, lay the special intractability of the world ideological struggle with which we had just begun to contend, and with which we are still contending. American prescriptions for the "unification" and "democratization" of China were all irrelevant to the stubborn fact that we were not involved with just one political system with two principal parties, but with two one-party systems. Two independent and adversary regimes could not be unified and democratized since they did not constitute one system. Chiang knew this all along — his invariable condition for cooperation with the Communists was the surrender of the Red Army, its incorporation with the Nationalist force, and the acceptance by the Communist leaders of a *party* role within the structure of Kuomintang political institutions. We would better have appreciated how difficult it was to save China if we could only have known how difficult it was going to be to save South Vietnam, and why.

Part Four The Politics of Hysteria

*In dealing with prejudice, one class of argument
is that whereby you can dispel
objectionable suppositions about yourself. . . .
Another way is to meet any of the issues directly:
to deny the alleged fact; or to say that
you have done no harm, or none to* him,
*or not as much as he says;
or that you have done him no injustice, or not much;
or that you have done nothing disgraceful enough to matter:
these are the sort of questions
on which the dispute hinges. . . .
Or you may admit the wrong, but balance it
with other facts, and say that, if the deed
harmed him, at any rate it was honorable;
or that, if it gave him pain,
at least it did him good; or something else like that. . . .
Another way is open when your calumniator,
or any of his connexions, is or has been subject
to the same grounds for suspicion. Yet another,
when others are subject to the same grounds for suspicion
but are admitted to be in fact innocent of the charge:
e.g. "Must I be a profligate because I am well-groomed?
Then so-and-so must be one too." . . .
Another way is to return calumny for calumny
and say, "It is monstrous to trust the man's
statements when you cannot trust the man himself."*

ARISTOTLE, Rhetoric

*Hysteria: A psychoneurosis characterized by
emotional excitability and often by a great variety of other
symptoms, as partial losses of memory. . . .*

WEBSTER's New International Dictionary

The Plot in fact should be
so framed that, even without seeing
the things take place,
he who simply hears the account of them
shall be filled with horror
and pity at the incidents . . .

ARISTOTLE, *Poetics*

XI Chairman McCarthy

In 1954, Dwight Macdonald said, "Like Gogol's Chichikov, McCarthy is a dealer in dead souls. His targets are not actual, living breathing Communists but rather people who once were or may have been but were not but may be made to appear to have possibly once been Communists or sympathizers or at any rate suspiciously 'soft' on the question," [1] and he regretted the passing of "the idyllic era of the Hiss case when tangible evidence was frequently produced," and where "each day used to bring its startling vindication of some fantastic charge by Bentley or Chambers." It is a fact — already mentioned — that after the confession of Lee Pressman in 1951, there was only one other former Communist to come forward — Herbert Fuchs — to provide solid information about the extent and incidence of Communist activity in the Federal government, and this occurred after Macdonald's remarks.[2]

1. "McCarthy and His Apologists," a review of *McCarthy and His Enemies* by William F. Buckley, Jr. and L. Brent Bozell, 21 *Partisan Review* 418 (1954). Macdonald lays emphasis on the 34 "inaccuracies," "exaggerations," and "misstatements" that the authors "grimly admit" McCarthy made, which he labels "lies," and which he says would be doubled in number if one were to include the 38 instances out of the 81 cases before the Tydings Committee in which the authors say that McCarthy was guilty of exaggeration. The tone of the review may be gathered from Macdonald's statement that the Buckley-Bozell book "defends a coarse demagogue in an elegantly academic style replete with nice discriminations and pedantic hair-splittings, giving the general effect of a brief by Cadwallader, Wickersham, and Taft on behalf of a pickpocket arrested in a subway men's room."

2. Macdonald's judgment about the Tydings Committee hearings was that "its Democratic majority seemed no more genuinely interested in whether in fact there were security risks still in the Department than McCarthy himself." Dwight Macdonald, "McCarthy and His Apologists." In the partisan clash of claims that continued for years after the hearings, recollection often seemed to be shaped and pointed by predilection. Thus in an article titled "The Secret of Political Success" eight years after the Tydings Committee, Elizabeth Churchill Brown could say that Tydings "astounded all concerned when he ruled that the hearings

The modicum of firm information about the nature of the Communist enterprise in the Federal government (only apostates seemed capable of supplying it to congressional committees) stimulated a rash of accusations in which conjecture, implication, and inference became imposters of knowledge, bearing only partisan credentials. The Communist problem, in short, became the Communist *issue*, which was essentially an appeal to portions of the anatomy considerably further south than the head. This is not to say that there were no partisan strivings in 1948[3] nor that after 1952 there were no new facts, but in the mixture of fact and rhetoric there was more solid information in the earlier period, and more invention in the second.

Even before the partisan cleavage over the Communist issue had been slashed open by the Tydings investigation of 1950, the investigation of American communism had begun to embrace the whole range of human activity. Eventually, university professors, trade unions, "a generation of Far Eastern experts," Jews, atheists, liberals, socialists, and "non-conformists" all, from time to time, took themselves to be the chief targets of "professional anti-Communists" and congressional committees. Chairmen of these committees saw themselves as martyrs to a "left-wing" press — a concept that occasionally seemed to include virtually the entire press[4] — bent upon sabotage of their efforts to oust Communists through smear, misrepresentation, and deliberate lies. Scholars and publicists of unquestionable loyalty foresaw the death of our liberties at the hands of congressional inquisitors.[5] Numberless articles attacked congressional committees and loyalty programs as creators of an atmosphere in which no one dared attack congressional committees and loyalty programs. Headlines were given to statements

would be open, thus giving none of the suspected a chance to clear themselves privately. McCarthy was obliged to name the cases in public." *Human Events*, XV (34), August 25, 1958.

3. In fact the sensational disclosures of the summer of 1948 were not an issue in the 1948 presidential election, as will be discussed further below.

4. Senator McCarthy, for example, attacked for distortion and card-stacking against him: the St. Louis *Post-Dispatch*, *New York Post*, Milwaukee *Journal*, *Washington Post*, Associated Press, United Press, and International News Service. Senator Joe McCarthy, *McCarthyism, The Fight for America* (New York: Devin-Adair, 1952), p. 3. James Wechsler of the *New York Post* was attacked by McCarthy in hearings that presumably concerned the books in overseas libraries of what was then called the International Information Service but which concentrated considerably upon Wechsler's opinions and those of the paper under circumstances that convinced Wechsler that the paper was the prime object of attack. James A. Wechsler, *The Age of Suspicion* (New York: Random House, 1953), p. 298.

5. See, for example, Robert K. Carr, *The House Committee on Un-American Activities, 1945–1950* (Ithaca: Cornell, 1952); Telford Taylor, *Grand Inquest* (New York: Simon and Schuster, 1955); and Alan Barth, *Government by Investigation* (New York: Viking, 1955).

impugning the loyalty of a President who, in his turn, had tried to dismiss the Hiss hearings as political diversion.[6]

A Borean blast from rostrum and press blew hard upon the mind and ear. Perhaps one irony of this screeching abuse is that, in general, the spokesmen for the rightist groups had regarded communism for a longer time more nearly as it was to be commonly perceived later — that is, as a totalitarian movement, destructive of diversity of individual values, intellectual independence, and freedom of political action.[7] This judgment may be tempered, however, by the realization that many doubtless thought that social security legislation was the same as the liquidation of the Kulaks, so that hostility was a product of general animus against any social reform and not specifically of libertarian anxiety.

The Republican victory in the presidential and congressional elections of 1952 moved McCarthy from the ranks of the opposition to the headquarters of what he called "the fight for America." No longer in the minority he was to have authority in his own hands to summon witnesses, issue subpoenas, push for contempt citations, refer matters to the Department of Justice, probe, press, pry, push, and expose the "evil" which had been the theme of so many speeches, clangorous and foreboding. He would now presumably wrench the truth from the dark pockets of concealment that Democratic officials had guarded, and drag it forth. With Republicans in the majority in both houses of Congress, and in control of the executive branch, the Communists at home were going to experience a little of that "massive retaliation" that the new Secretary of State, John Foster Dulles, promised would be the lot of the Communist abroad.

The new platform on which Senator McCarthy was to perform was the Senate Committee on Government Operations, of which he became chairman, and its Permanent Subcommittee on Investigations, of which

6. Two days after the first charges by Whittaker Chambers against Alger Hiss, President Truman at a press conference dismissed the congressional investigation as a political red herring, designed by the Republicans to distract public attention from their failure to control inflation. See Eric Goldman, *The Crucial Decade* (New York: Knopf, 1956), pp. 101–102.

7. A further irony is the fact that the posture of anticommunism did not necessarily suppose, or require, any understanding of or interest in communism as philosophy, program, plot, conspiracy, movement, policy, creed, or racket. James Rorty tells of an incident that illustrates this: "Then and later [at the time of the hearings of the Voice of America] I found myself astonished by how little ideological interest McCarthy had in either communism or anti-communism. Once, in a taxi hurrying from his office to his hotel, I asked him what kind of a Voice program he would ordain if he could have what he wanted. He looked blank; obviously he had never thought about it." This appears in Rorty's review of Richard H. Rovere, *Senator Joe McCarthy*, under the title "Leave Him to the Ages" in *New Leader*, August 3–10, 1959, p. 26.

he was also the chairman. William Jenner of Indiana succeeded McCarran of Nevada as the chairman of the Internal Security Subcommittee of the Senate Committee on the Judiciary, which had the principal jurisdiction in the Senate to make investigations of matters involving loyalty and security; and Senator Jenner had what he thought was an understanding with Senator McCarthy that the Internal Security Subcommittee would have priority in subversion probes.[8] Earl Mazo has said that he was told by Richard Nixon that the latter had never "shared the belief of some in the Eisenhower administration that 'Communism was to McCarthy a racket,'"[9] but the Vice President was quite aware that there could be a split in the Republican party over the Wisconsin Senator whose understanding with Jenner was not to last long. As Mazo describes it,

> A few nights after Eisenhower's election McCarthy was invited to Bill Rogers' home. Nixon and Jerry Persons, of Eisenhower's staff, also were there, and it was a fine friendly evening. McCarthy agreed that perhaps he had been a little extreme in some things he had said and maybe even a bit irresponsible at times. He explained also that he believed seriously in what he was doing. Nixon and the others applauded and said that they did not want him to take his eye off a single Communist. In the interest of promoting the anti-Communist cause, they urged that he cooperate with fellow Republicans in the White House.
>
> This aura of peace and good will lasted for almost a month after the Republican administration was inaugurated.[10]

Although he had full investigative powers and a substantial budget and staff of investigators, Senator McCarthy made no effort in the two years he was in charge of the Committee on Government Operations and the Permanent Subcommittee on Investigations to prove the original charges that had launched him into public notice. In fact, he never even made reference to the earlier assertions about the numbers of Communist risks he said should be investigated.[11] Instead he launched investigations into the Voice of America, the information centers conducted abroad by the State Department, the Government Printing Office, and the United Nations. With the acquiescence of the Secretary of State, he wrought, with brute brilliance,[12] a catastrophe

8. *New York Times*, January 31, 1953, p. 7, col. 2.
9. Earl Mazo, *Richard Nixon* (New York: Harper and Brothers, 1959), p. 144.
10. Mazo, *Richard Nixon*, p. 145.
11. "McCarthy: A Documented Record," *The Progressive*, 18 (4), April 1954, p. 33.
12. This phrase is attributed to Philip Graham, publisher of the *Washington Post*. Wechsler, *The Age of Suspicion*, p. 272.

of sick apprehension in the Department of State, and the destruction of its morale.

The Voice of America

The public hearings on the Voice of America began on February 16, 1953, short weeks after Senator McCarthy took the control of the Permanent Subcommittee on Investigations. The Voice of America, like the information centers, was a source of news and propaganda operated by the International Information Administration which, at the time, was a part of the Department of State. The Voice maintained a substantial radio transmission to more than fourscore countries in an effort to reach the minds of peoples abroad with information about American policies, institutions, culture, and perspectives — to counteract the rigid stereotypes of Marxist invention that Soviet transmitters were purveying. The overseas libraries were centers for the display and offer of books, papers, periodicals, and other writing conveying the same message about an America with faults and flaws that were not denied, but an America of democratic philosophy and program, with an eternal commitment to human rights and individual values.

Although the formal hearings began on February 16, a publicity build-up had preceded it, of a kind to convince newspaper readers that the Voice harbored an anti-American conspiracy and that the infiltration of the agency by subversives was "appalling." [13] The hearings that followed were less in the nature of a fact-finding inquiry than a show trial to validate the headlines that went before. In the printed record of the hearings there is no indication of any resolution or reference to the committee to conduct the inquiry, nor any preliminary statement of the purpose of the proceeding, nor any word about the subject to be searched.[14] The hearings simply started with the calling of the first witness, Lewis J. McKesson, who had been an engineer with the Voice from December 1949 to November 1952.

13. Martin Merson, *The Private Diary of a Public Servant* (New York: Macmillan, 1955), p. 11. Merson refers specifically to the headlines and stories that were carried by the *Chicago Tribune*, Washington *Times-Herald*, and *New York Daily News*, the papers owned by Colonel Robert R. McCormick and his sister, Alicia McCormick Patterson.

14. Eighty-third Congress, First Session, United States Senate, Committee on Government Operations, Permanent Subcommittee on Investigations, Hearings Pursuant to S. Res. 40, *State Department Information Program — Voice of America* (hereafter cited as *State Department Information Program — Voice of America*). The hearings on the overseas libraries that followed those on the Voice of America have the same citation, except they are titled *State Department Information Program — Information Centers*, which is the way they will be cited hereafter. It is of interest that the resolution that presumably supported the investigation into the State Department information program was titled, "A Resolution Authorizing the Committee on Government Operations to Employ Temporarily Additional Personnel and Increasing the Limit of Expenditures."

The principal argument for the proposition that an anti-American conspiracy must have existed in the Voice was the controversy over the location of two powerful transmitters, called Baker East and Baker West, the first to be built at Cape Hatteras, North Carolina, and the second, at Seattle, Washington. The target of Baker West was Manila, a relay station for broadcast into the Far East, and the target for Baker East was Munich, Germany, for rebroadcast throughout Europe. There was a difference of engineering opinion about the efficacy of the proposed locations, with McKesson asserting that if the stations were moved south — from Seattle to southern California, and from Hatteras to southern Florida — the wattage required for broadcast from the southern areas would be only 10 per cent of that required farther north.[15] The reason was said to be the presence of the auroral absorption belt — an area of magnetic storms about a thousand miles above the earth in the high northern latitudes. McKesson said that it would save about $18,000,000 to move the transmitters south.[16] The next day the work on Baker West was suspended, and on March 20 the Baker projects were abandoned by Dr. Robert L. Johnson, former president of Temple University, who had been appointed head of the International Information Administration on February 24.[17]

In the hearings on the Bakers, Senator McCarthy pushed the suggestion into the mouth of the lead-off witness that the proposed locations would make it easier for the Russians to jam our radio signals.[18] The chairman asked Mr. McKesson what other significance — than waste of resources — he would attach to the proposed locations of Baker East and West, and the witness, missing his cue, responded that the location of the Baker West would reduce the effectiveness of the Voice of America to the relay stations and beyond, into Iron Curtain territory on the mainland of Asia. But this was not the answer, and in the following colloquy, the preferred answer was elicited socratically:

> The Chairman: Let us put it this way: Let us assume we have a good Voice of America, a voice that is really the voice of America. Assume I do not want that to reach Communist territory. Would not

15. *State Department Information Program — Voice of America*, p. 5.
16. *State Department Information Program — Voice of America*, p. 4.
17. Martin Merson, who was Dr. Johnson's assistant, denied, in a bitter book about his short experience in the International Information Administration during the investigation by McCarthy, that testimony before the McCarthy committee had anything to do with the decision to cancel. *Private Diary of a Public Servant*, p. 51. But he offered no explanation for the cancellation. The closest he came to an explanation was his statement that the contracts had already been suspended, and that Johnson felt pressure to accommodate himself to Budget Bureau cuts. *Ibid.*
18. *State Department Information Program — Voice of America*, p. 9.

the best way to sabotage that voice be to place your transmitters within that magnetic storm area, so that you would have this tremendous interference?

Mr. McKesson: I would agree with you one hundred percent, sir.

The Chairman: The same applies to the east coast, also?

Mr. McKesson: Yes, sir.[19]

In a report of the hearings a year later, Senator McCarthy said that "this report will be confined to marshalling the evidence of waste, mismanagement, and the mislocation of key broadcasting stations which made them useless to the extent that one very competent radio engineer (L. J. McKesson) referred to the mislocations as sabotage." [20]

The McCarthy committee created an appearance of furtive conniving in the testimony it adduced on the steps by which the decision was reached on the location of Baker East and West. It was made to appear that the Bureau of Standards was not consulted when in fact the Bureau of Standards prepared a report on the technology of transmission. Dr. Newbern Smith, chief of the Central Radio Propaganda Laboratory of the United States Bureau of Standards, testified for a few minutes on the subject. In answer to the question, "Is it a fact that the Voice never contacted the Bureau of Standards when they were considering the location of Baker East and Baker West?", Smith replied, "That is correct. We were never formally contacted." [21] However, on April 17, 1951, the Central Radio Propagation Laboratory did submit a thirty-nine-page report on data concerning possible locations at the request of the Voice.[22] The evidence is that not only the Bureau of Standards but the research laboratories of the Radio Corporation of America, the Signal Corps of the United States Army, and the Research Laboratory of Electronics of the Massachusetts Institute of Technology were involved in the choice of location.

Quite apart from the merits of the decision to locate the transmitters in Seattle and the Cape Hatteras region (it was thought generally that better service would be provided despite the difficulty with the auroral absorption belt), there was not, as lawyers used to say, one scintilla of evidence that the decision was in any way achieved through the influence of Communists, pro-Communists, fellow travelers, Reds, pinks,

19. *State Department Information Program — Voice of America*, p. 8.
20. Merson, *Private Diary of a Public Servant*, p. 52, for comment on the claim. See also, Eighty-third Congress, Second Session, United States Senate, Committee on Government Operations, Permanent Subcommittee on Investigations, *Annual Report*, S. Rept. 881, January 25, 1954.
21. *State Department Information Program — Voice of America*, p. 11.
22. "McCarthy: A Documented Record," pp. 34–35. This account of the Bureau of Standards incident also refers to letters in the files of the State Department discussing studies made for the Voice of America by the Bureau of Standards.

or any of the other rubicund tones. The testimony failed in every respect to uphold the sensational promise of the headlines that Marxist marplots were garbling the Voice of America by strangling its signals.

But there were other charges against the Voice of America. Senator McCarthy had the assistance of an unknown number of spies and informers in the Department of State whose confidence he encouraged.[23] This "American Underground" fed information, rumors, gossip, spite, and malice to the Senator and his staff, and thereby maintained a state of high neurotic tension. A transmission belt of faceless volunteers, devious and administratively disloyal, subversive of the good order of the agency, provided much of the agenda for the hearings on the Voice of America by keeping the subcommittee supplied with many hot tips and remarkably few cold facts.

There was a sensation in the French Service of the Voice of America. A witness who had been fired from her position in the French Section was encouraged by the chairman to say that she had been let go because she had reviewed *Witness* by Whittaker Chambers, but then it appeared that she had had full approval to review the book in a radio broadcast.[24] It also appeared that she had not got along very well with people, either at the Voice or at a college where she had taught briefly.[25] There was testimony that one of the script writers had said disparaging things in a French broadcast to Europe about Texas and

23. See Merson, *Private Diary of a Public Servant*, p. 92, for a reference to a personal experience. David Schine, one of McCarthy's staff whose name was to figure in the Army-McCarthy controversy, told Merson that he had seen a classified document from Bradley Connors, the chief of policies and plans in the IIA. This had been smuggled to him by an informer working under Merson. After his talk with Merson, Schine telephoned one of his associates, calling him out of a meeting, to tell him the names of others at the meeting, which was a "conference on a sensitive matter." It was Merson's opinion that the purpose of this kiddish stunt was intimidation. On the activity of Senator McCarthy's spies and informers in the Voice of America, see Philip Horton, "Voices Within the Voice," *The Reporter*, July 21, 1953.

24. *State Department Information Program — Voice of America*, p. 172.

25. In fact she did not cooperate very clearly with the chairman either. He supplied her with lines she did not reproduce very well. Thus, the chairman asks "Is there any doubt in your mind today that you were fired because you favorably reviewed Chambers' book?" The witness answers, "Well, it is not such a simple — it is difficult for me to state. The fact is this. To my knowledge — and I am not sure of this — I do not believe that any other use besides my own was made by the Voice of America of this book, which is a natural propaganda item." The chairman returned to his theme — "I am going to ask you a very simple question. Do you think you were fired because you favorably reviewed Chambers' book?" To which the answer was, "I think, Senator, that I was fired because of the reasons that made me review the book, and that that was just the last — " The chairman: "And the reason that made you review it is that you were anti-Communist; is that right?" In assent, the witness answered, "Yes. I felt that the program should have dignity and purpose." *State Department Information Program — Voice of America*, p. 176.

Texans, but then it appeared that it was actually Edna Ferber who had perpetrated this anti-American outrage, and the script writer had said, "Miss Ferber knows the Texans well, whatever the Texans may say to the contrary." [26] When this discussion was concluded, Senator McCarthy had the following to say,

> Chairman: Let me ask you this. If I were a member of the Communist Party, and I wanted to discredit America and further the Communist cause, could you think of any better job I could do helping out the Communist cause than by beaming to Europe the type of material you have just described?
>
> Mr. Horneffer: No, sir. Not possibly.
>
> Chairman: In other words, you feel we are doing a great service to the Communist cause in beaming this material out in the so-called fight against communism?
>
> Mr. Horneffer: Yes, sir.[27]

It did appear that one speech by Jacob Malik, Soviet representative in the United Nations, was broadcast by the Voice without comment, although the "beginning of the speech, which was just a diatribe against America," was shortened. After the testimony of the witness on scripts and broadcasts, the chairman asked the witness to say whether he thought "this discrediting of America and forwarding the cause of communism" was done through stupidity and incompetence, or whether "it is deliberately being done." [28] The witness said that he had first thought it was stupidity and incompetence, but then he started having "very, very grave doubts about it, oh, a year or even two years ago." [29] This would have dated the initiation of sinister design some little time after the Tydings investigation and the beginning of the IPR inquiry when the State Department was under constant scrutiny, which would seem to be an unlikely time to hope to sneak furtive asides to millions of European listeners, unnoticed. It was Senator McCarthy's suggestion to the witness that the Voice of America (in the French Section, at least) was really the Voice of Moscow, but the witness topped this with the thought that it might appropriately be called the Voice of International Communism. The record does not say whether anybody laughed.

There was trouble in the Latin-American division also. The acting assistant chief of the Latin-American division, Stuart Ayers, testified that he had encountered no opposition in the transmission of short-

26. *State Department Information Program — Voice of America*, pp. 179–180.
27. *State Department Information Program — Voice of America*, p. 182.
28. *Ibid.*, p. 184.
29. *Ibid.*, p. 185.

wave broadcasts about America, but that he had had difficulty in the production of suitable recordings, to be broadcast by local radio stations in Latin America (called platter programs).[30] The complaint was that "programs we felt would be in the national interest were somehow not produced, and others we felt were rather fragile or not of anti-Communist content were produced to be sent to the field." The platters were prepared by the Overseas Services branch, which also controlled the budget for such activity. The chief of the Overseas Services branch was one Robert Bauer, and it seems that he and others had disagreed about a series, "The Eye of the Eagle," which originated in the Overseas Services branch and which some of the area division officials did not like. "The Eye of the Eagle" was a serial for juveniles. Ayers thought that juvenile serials had only a minor place in propaganda when budgets were limited and low, and that there was not enough direct anti-Communist material in the scripts. Mr. Ayers was asked by Senator McCarthy whether he thought the "individuals responsible for the type of material put out were loyal to America," and the answer was, "I do not believe that I can say that these people were subversives, because I have no proof of that, but I do feel that there are many ways of gauging what you think is the truth about a country." [31] Senator Jackson of Washington asked whether the witness thought that there was "some sort of a conspiracy" to make broadcasts ineffectual, and Mr. Ayers answered, "No, there is no such conspiracy in our Division." [32] But he did say that there were individuals he felt had been responsible for misdirecting output, and he had mentioned names in executive session which were not disclosed in the public hearings.[33]

Mr. Bauer asked to be heard after the testimony of Ayers, and introduced photostats showing the concurrence of the Latin-American division in the use of "The Eye of the Eagle." [34] He testified that the series had been initiated jointly by his division and the Latin-American division,[35] demonstrated the degree to which the original scripts contained anti-Communist material and the approval they had received in notices from the field,[36] and led Senator Mundt of South Dakota to suggest that "we are wasting a lot of our committee time trying to arbitrate an argument between drama critics, which happens all over the country." Senator Mundt had made some inquiries of his own about

30. *Ibid.*, p. 80.
31. *Ibid.*, p. 91.
32. *Ibid.*, p. 93.
33. *Ibid.*, p. 94.
34. *Ibid.*, p. 524.
35. *Ibid.*, p. 531.
36. *Ibid.*, pp. 536–538.

the fuss and was fully satisfied about the good faith, competence, and credentials of Mr. Bauer and the value of the program as seen from the field. He suggested that "until we can get something more specific in the record, I would like to lay this one on ice, and see if we cannot find something a bit more important." [37]

There was trouble over an order to suspend broadcasts in Hebrew to Israel. Dr. Sidney Glazer, chief of the Hebrew Service of the Voice of America, and his superior, Gerald Dooher, acting chief of the South Asian and African Near East division of the Voice, both complained of the order suspending the service which was issued on December 5, 1952, after it had been determined by the IIA Program Allocations Board that budget considerations made the elimination of the Hebrew broadcasts to Israel necessary.[38] Before the order was issued, the Voice in New York cabled Reed Harris, acting administrator of the International Information Administration, to inquire whether consideration had been given to the timeliness of the order. There had been recent disclosures in the Slansky trial in Czechoslovakia of strong anti-Semitism in the Communist Party, and the suggestion of the Voice was that this was an important theme to be exploited in the Hebrew broadcasts to Israel. The decision to suspend was confirmed, however, and the formal order was issued on December 9, 1952. This was then appealed to the head of the Voice, Mr. Alfred Morton, who was in Europe, and through him to Dr. Compton, the head of the IIA, who was also in Europe, and the Voice received authority to continue the broadcasts until further notice. What, in one of the communications, was referred to as the "public relations problem" involved in shutting off Hebrew broadcasts to Israel was more sharply appreciated by Congressmen than by the Programs Allocation Board of the IIA. When word was spread that the broadcasts might be shut off, "various members of Congress made formal protests to the State Department," [39] and the Hebrew Language Service was allowed to continue.

Although there had been no evidence or testimony that Communist sympathizers were choking the life out of the Hebrew Language Service, Senator McCarthy supplied the necessary implication by putting words into the mouth of one of the witnesses:

The Chairman: Let me ask you this, also. Do you feel that if Harris' order had been followed, you would have been performing a great service to the Communist cause?
Mr. Dooher: I feel so, sir.
The Chairman: In other words, see if this is correct. You feel that

37. *Ibid.*, p. 539.
38. *Ibid.*, p. 195.
39. *Ibid.*, p. 198.

here you had a real counter-propaganda weapon; that international communism had proved that they would not respect the rights of religious and racial minorities, contrary to what they had been preaching for so long, and you felt this information was of tremendous interest to the world, not only to the Jewish world, but to the entire world, because today it might be the Jewish people who were being hung, and tomorrow it is another minority group?

Mr. Dooher: That is true, sir.[40]

And then Dooher added that he had thought the suspension would have been tragic to the people of Israel, when they really needed the Voice of America to show them that we were fighting the same battle against the Communist enemy. He also volunteered the view in a colloquy with Senator Charles E. Potter of Michigan that the suspension ordered was "exactly what the Soviet Union wanted to happen."[41] The chairman at a later point entered more of his own testimony in the record through the lips of the witness:

The Chairman: Am I correct in this, that you feel that the reason why the Hebrew language desk was being discontinued was because it was doing a good job of combatting communism?

Mr. Dooher: Again, sir, I don't want to go into the thinking of the people who gave the directive, but the result was the same.

The Chairman: Let us put it this way: If I had been in a position of power, if I were an ardent member of the Communist Party, would I not have taken the same action that was taken to discontinue the Hebrew language desk, at a time when Communist Russia became openly anti-Semitic, at a time when we had this great counter-propaganda weapon?

Mr. Dooher: I believe so, sir.

. . . . .

The Chairman: . . . you feel that the action would have been the same had they been representing Joe Stalin?

Mr. Dooher: That is correct, sir. . . .[42]

It is of interest that the same logic led Martin Merson, deputy administrator of the International Information Administration, to the same conclusion about Senator McCarthy and Roy Cohn, counsel to the subcommittee. After McCarthy had influenced the closing of the two Bakers, shutting off powerful transmitters for the broadcast of the American message to the world, Merson wrote: "I couldn't help asking

40. *Ibid.*, p. 198.
41. *Ibid.*, p. 199.
42. *Ibid.*, pp. 205–206.

myself: If McCarthy and Cohn were themselves Communists, could they be doing a more skillful job of sabotage? Or if not themselves subversives, were they unwitting tools in the hands of fiendishly more clever minds?" [43]

Although the decision to suspend the Hebrew broadcasts had been made by the Program Allocations Board of the IIA, the finger of implied accusation was pointed at Reed Harris. The examination of Reed Harris started with his career at Columbia University as a student in the early 1930's. He was an editor on the school paper, *The Spectator*, and he had written a book called *King Football* which was basically an attack upon commercialism in college sport, but which wandered over a considerable area of commentary in which distaste was notable for the Daughters of the American Revolution, the American Legion, and other symbols of liberal rejection. He had been suspended by the school (and then reinstated) for leading campus protests against college policy on faculty dismissals. He subsequently resigned. He had been questioned in executive session before the public hearing, like other witnesses in the investigation, and was then put on the stand to explain by way of radio and television that he was sorry he had written the book twenty-one years before, that he disavowed most of the callow opinion he had then expressed, that he believed in marriage, and that he did not now think that Communists and Fascists should be allowed to teach. There was somewhat aimless reference to what the personnel files on him might show, but no assertion that he was a Communist, had ever been a Communist, or had been, at any time of his life, other than loyal. Although there was some testimony on the Bakers, the committee never got around to the suspension of the Hebrew language broadcasts. Reed Harris resigned his position as deputy administrator shortly afterwards, having acted in the interregnum between Wilson Compton and Dr. Robert L. Johnson of Temple University. Two months after the public hearings on the Voice of America, Dr. Johnson canceled the Hebrew language broadcasts to Israel. No one accused him of doing Stalin's dirty work.

Although the committee had failed to establish conspiracy, or for that matter much more than the usual inefficiency and accompanying waste of time and effort in the operations of the Voice in the French and Hebrew language broadcasts, the platter program in Latin America, and the matter of the two Bakers, it did question witnesses who pleaded the Fifth Amendment when asked about Communist connections. One of these was the author, Howard Fast, who, before his break with the Communists, had been somewhat of a literary hero in the Soviet Union. It was true that he was not employed by the Voice

43. Merson, *Private Diary of a Public Servant*, p. 55.

of America, had never been employed by the Voice of America, and had never held any Federal job except a short connection with the Office of War Information in 1942. His name came up, however, in connection with a policy guide signed by Bradley Connors, assistant administrator for Policy and Plans of the Department of State. The memorandum of instructions for the use of the Voice of America and other staff of the IIA gave permission under certain circumstances to use the works of Howard Fast. The language of advice was, "Similarly, if — like Howard Fast — he is known as a Soviet-endorsed author, materials favorable to the United States in some of his works may thereby be given a special credibility among selected key audiences." [44] This was doubtless a memorandum that one of the informers detested by Martin Merson had secured for the subcommittee staff.[45]

Fast was first asked whether he was Howard Fast, the author, and then immediately, whether he was a member of the Communist Party. He said "I am" to the first question, and declined to answer the second question on Fifth Amendment grounds.[46] Instead of being interested in what he had done in the Office of War Information,[47] the chairman concentrated on how much money Fast had made in Federal employment.[48] It turned out to be a relatively small amount, and nothing was made of the sum, one way or the other.

Two other witnesses were called before Bradley Connors, the principal figure, was put on the stand. One was Dr. Kwant Tsing Wu, from the Library of Congress, who had translated part of the confession of a Chinese Communist made before he was executed by the Nationalist Government. The confession, which had been made part of the record of the McCarran committee hearings on the Institute of Pacific Re-

44. *State Department Information Program — Voice of America*, p. 97.
45. See above, n. 23.
46. *State Department Information Program — Voice of America*, p. 98.
47. Fast was asked whether he had known members of the Communist Party working with the OWI when he was with it, but he refused to answer this question on Fifth Amendment grounds. *State Department Information Program — Voice of America*, p. 99.
48. There was one line of questioning by Senator Potter of Michigan that gave Fast some trouble. He was asked whether he would, if drafted, serve in the "fight against communism in Korea," and he refused to answer the question directly. He kept saying that he would "accept the service of my country if I were drafted," shying each time from the direct question whether he would fight Communists or communism. At length, Senator Potter asked, "Why are you so nervous when we say fighting Communists?" To which Fast answered, "I am not nervous; angry, but very calm. Don't tell me I'm nervous." *State Department Information Program — Voice of America*, p. 109. Howard Fast was in fact so highly regarded by the Soviet Union as a "progressive" author that he was awarded the Stalin Prize. He later broke with and left the party, as he reveals in *The Naked God* (New York: Praeger, 1957).

lations,[49] said that at the time (1947) certain persons in the United States embassy in China were "fundamentally dissatisfied with the Nationalist Government," and further, "Wittingly or unwittingly, they leaked out diplomatic secrets which were transmitted through the embassies of third countries into the ears of the Soviet intelligence personnel." [50] One of the persons charged with being the source of leaks was Bradley Connors who had been an information officer in the embassy. The confessor did not accuse Connors of being a Communist. The other witness was John C. Caldwell, who had been with the State Department from 1945 to 1947, and from 1949 to 1950, and had been chief of the China branch in the State Department information program in 1945 and 1946, the Washington counterpart of John K. Fairbank in China. He did not get along very well with Connors, recited what he thought were his personal shortcomings, and said that he had heard him criticize the Nationalist Government but had not heard him criticize the Communists. But he also said that he had never had reason to doubt the loyalty of Connors and "would never dream that Mr. Connors is a Communist." [51]

When Connors was put on the stand he said that he was not an authority on the Communist movement, that he had never read any of the works of Marx, Engels, Lenin, or Stalin, and that he had never studied a history of the Communist movement, or the operations of the Communist movement. But he denied that his mind was "pretty much of a blank as far as the workings of the Communist movement" were concerned. The void of personal knowledge was filled by the Department of State which supplied him with information on "the propaganda lines and the actions that the Communist Party is planning." [52] With great agility he led his questioners into the traps, deadfalls, and blind alleys of administrative routine — no, he did not write the directive, it was prepared under the direction of Dr. Compton; yes, he had signed it (in answer to a question whether he agreed with it)

49. The confession, which had appeared in the *Central Daily News* (Shanghai) on September 3, 1950, was translated in part by John K. Fairbank, and read into the record of the McCarran committee proceedings. Eighty-second Congress, First Session, United States Senate, Committee on the Judiciary, Subcommittee to Investigate the Administration of the Internal Security Act and Other Internal Security Laws, *Hearings on the Institute of Pacific Relations*, pp. 3786–3790 (hereafter cited as *IPR Hearings*). He was not required by the committee to read the names of the two other persons besides himself who had been mentioned in the confession as witting or unwitting sources of leaks that eventually came to the Communists through other embassies. *State Department Information Program — Voice of America*, p. 121.

50. *State Department Information Program — Voice of America*, p. 115.

51. *Ibid.*, p. 123.

52. *Ibid.*, p. 127.

334 THE POLITICS OF HYSTERIA

because he had been informed that Dr. Compton had personally approved it; the directive did not actually authorize the use of Howard Fast's materials; well, yes it did, but only under very restrictive conditions; a later directive canceled an earlier directive; well, it did not specifically cancel it but it set up different criteria; he had not taken steps to cancel an order for the procurement of Fast's books (which were on a permitted list); he was not present at a meeting when Fast's books were discussed; and so on. Although he was not informed about communism, and although he disclaimed responsibility for many bureaucratic procedures and decisions mentioned to him, he too had a familiar colloquy with Senator McCarthy about the two Bakers:

> Q. Let me ask you this: If I were in your Department and I were a member of the Communist Party attempting to sabotage the Voice program, would it not be wise for me to try and locate the stations within that magnetic storm area so that they would be subject to jamming by Communist Russia and so that we could not hit the target area with radio signals?
> A. Yes, sir.
> Q. Would that not be the logical thing, if I were a Communist, to do?
> A. Yes, sir.[53]

But Mr. Connors would not say whether the alleged mislocation of the two stations was the result of stupidity or of a deliberate attempt to sabotage the Voice of America.

He had been press officer for both Generals Marshall and Wedemeyer during their separate missions in China after V-J Day, denied that he had wittingly or unwittingly leaked any news to anyone, denied the allegations of the confession that he had done so, said that he was not a member of the Communist Party and had never been, nor of any fellow-traveler organizations listed by the Attorney General, and agreed that "there is considerable feeling not of the best nature" between Caldwell and him.[54] He also denied Caldwell's statement about his critical attitude towards the Nationalist Government and said that he "was in full sympathy with the Nationalist Government," that he felt that there were certain reforms that could have been made, but that he was unalterably opposed to the Communists. This was all there was to the suspicion that the directive which mentioned the works of Howard Fast would lead to the disclosure of a Communist conspiracy in the Voice of America, or to the operation of a very efficient operation of any kind, for us or against us.

53. *Ibid.,* pp. 135–136.
54. *Ibid.,* p. 141.

There were other alarms that failed to locate fires, and what was thought to be smoke in some cases turned out to be fog. Dr. John Cocutz, acting chief of the Rumanian Service of the Voice of America, reported that many of the writers and editors on the European desk of the Voice did not seem to know very much about communism, that he had proposed that they be given training sessions, that he had submitted a memorandum to Voice officials to establish such a training program which had been ignored, and that he had given a copy of his program to the staff of the subcommittee.[55] It appeared that he disagreed with Dr. Wilson Compton, former head of the IIA, about the shape that the Voice programs should take; the hearings gave him the opportunity to say how he thought the agency should be run.

His sensation was the remark that the policy director of the Voice had told him (Cocutz) that he (the policy director) had told someone else that the man who headed the religious desk was an atheist.[56] Cocutz had met the head of the religious desk a few times but had never talked with him about his views. Roger Lyons, the director of Religious Programming of the Voice of America, appeared soon after his name had been mentioned by Dr. Cocutz — in fact on the afternoon of the day in which Cocutz had testified in the morning. Although Mr. Lyons did "not belong to any affiliated church organization," and it seemed ominous that he had written a thesis at Columbia University, "Toward a Clearer Criterion of Moral Value," without expressing an opinion as to whether he believed in God, it turned out that he was not an atheist nor an agnostic, that he did believe in God, and that he would not have accepted the position of religious director of Religious Programming unless he did so.[57] Edwin Kretzmann, the policy adviser of the Voice of America, and the alleged author of the statement that Dr. Cocutz had repeated, found himself almost immediately in a discussion of Bertram Wolfe, a gifted writer and noted anti-Communist, who was once a member of the Communist Party. Senator McCarthy seemed to think that the question was still open in 1953 whether Wolfe who had broken with the Stalinists in 1929 was still a Communist, despite years of opposition.[58] The remark about Lyons' religious belief was garbled in the telling by Dr. Cocutz. Kretzmann said that a superior in the Department of State had asked him the specific religious sectarian belief of Roger Lyons. Said Kretzmann:

55. *Ibid.*, pp. 228–233.
56. *Ibid.*, pp. 234–235.
57. *Ibid.*, pp. 298–299.
58. *Ibid.*, pp. 306–307. Senator McCarthy started the discussion by asking Kretzmann whether Kretzmann knew that Bertram Wolfe "admits having belonged to the Communist Party?" Kretzmann's answer was "Yes, sir; that is why we hired him."

My answer was that that was not a pertinent question for him to ask; and laughingly I added, "For all I know, he may be an atheist."

This I knew not to be a fact because I had talked to Mr. Lyons previously.[59]

A woman on the staff of the Voice of America said that she had had conversations with Roger Lyons between 1944 and 1946, and that she did not think he believed in God then.[60] And a producer-announcer testified that he had had an argument with Lyons a month before about a sentence in a script titled "Back to God" — a documentary, he called it.[61] Although the producer-announcer could not exactly say that Lyons objected to the sentence because it referred to a divine being, he was able to say that "I am a Roman Catholic, and to my perhaps myopic view, I did not think he was very religious." [62] The woman was recalled for a question as to whether she had "been going with" Lyons at the time of her conversations with him about religion, and she said that she had been. She said, "Oh, no" when asked whether her testimony was colored by the fact that "he did not go out with you any longer." She summed it all up by saying, "I am not disgruntled; no." [63]

The hearings on the Voice of America produced a great chaff of spiteful suggestion by numbers of people who had lost arguments with superiors over policy, had lived in a rivalry of hateful tensions over rank and assignment, or who were likely to lose jobs because of administrative decisions. Tomorrow's witnesses could see today's testimony on television; and the public could read all about it in the headlines that featured the accusations but not the denials, which did not have the same value as news. The atmosphere of the proceedings was such as to stir rootless anxieties, and to settle a miasma of choleric depression over the staff of the State Department, which could not look for support from the Secretary of State.

The Information Centers

It was in the investigation of the overseas information centers that the State Department most sorely needed the support of the Secretary of State, but had it least. At the time the Eisenhower Administration took office in January 1953, there did not seem to be any particular problem connected with the choice of books for overseas libraries. The

59. *State Department Information Program — Voice of America*, pp. 307–308.
60. *Ibid.*, pp. 320–321.
61. *Ibid.*, pp. 322–323.
62. *Ibid.*, p. 323.
63. *Ibid.*, p. 324.

basic line in the use of books by Communist authors had been recommended by the United States Advisory Commission on Educational Exchange, a group whose membership included J. L. Morrill, chairman, president of the University of Minnesota; Mark Starr, educational director of the International Ladies Garment Workers Union; Harold W. Dodds, president of Princeton University; Martin R. P. McGuire, professor at Catholic University of America; and Edwin F. Fred, president of the University of Wisconsin.[64] On December 4, 1952, this commission set a policy as follows:

> The Commission by motion unanimously adopted and endorsed this latter resolution and recommendations — that the criterion for determining the availability of books for inclusion in collections of the USIS libraries abroad be based on content without regard to authorship.[65]

The commission's policy had been based upon a recommendation from its own subcommittee — the Committee on Books Abroad — and was intended merely to lay down a general line.[66] The thought seems to have been that works or portions of works of Communist authors might sometimes conceivably promote American ends. Thus some of the early works of Howard Fast were thought to be in this category, although not later ones, which were rejected for agency use. But this was a Truman administration group and a new line was begun with the advent of the Republicans. On January 30, the first of the directives on new policy was issued and sent to the field offices on February 3, 1953, as Policy Order No. 5. This was the order which Bradley Connors had signed and to which the subcommittee gave some attention, as has been indicated. In the whole context of the order, however,[67] the phrases about Howard Fast, which were by way of illustration, were intended generally to implement the master policy laid down on December 4, 1952.

Frightened by the antagonism of Senator McCarthy and his staff to the order of February 3, the Assistant Secretary of State for Public

64. *Ibid.,* p. 130.
65. *Ibid.,* p. 131.
66. The Committee on Books Abroad was made up of the following people: Martin R. P. McGuire of Catholic University of America, chairman; Charles P. Brett, president of Macmillan and Company; Cass Canfield, chairman of the board of Harper and Brothers; Robert L. Crowell, president of Thomas Y. Crowell Company; and Keyes D. Metcalf, director of libraries for Harvard University. *State Department Information Program — Voice of America,* p. 131.
67. For the full text of the order, see *State Department Information Program — Voice of America,* pp. 144–145.

Affairs, Carl McCardle, canceled it ten days after it was issued, and a new policy was substituted. The new policy, sent to the field on February 19, 1953, banned the books, music, and paintings ". . . of any Communists, fellow travellers, et cetera," and it ordered that "librarians should at once remove all books and other material by Communists, fellow travellers, et cetera, from their shelves and withdraw any that may be in circulation." It was difficult enough to know exactly who was a fellow traveler but it was impossible to guess what an "et cetera" might be. All works that might possibly fall under the new order were proscribed, and the consequence was the removal from the shelves of the overseas libraries of the writings of Bert Andrews, head of the Washington Bureau of the New York *Herald-Tribune;* Joseph Davies, former ambassador to Moscow; Vera Micheles Dean of the Foreign Policy Association; as well as works that seemed to come more clearly within the ban.[68] The directive on "Communists, fellow travellers, et cetera" applied also to the Voice of America, but Alfred H. Morton, chief of the Voice of America in New York, wired Washington that he would continue to "quote Stalin, Vishinsky, Gromyko and other Communists to the extent that the use of such material advances our cause." Washington told him that the February 19 policy was binding on him.

It was Francis P. Flanagan, the predecessor of Roy Cohn on the McCarthy subcommittee as chief counsel, who told the Under Secretary of State for Administration about Morton's telegram, an example of the efficiency of the spy network operating to benefit the subcommittee. It was the subcommittee view that Morton was in defiance of the February 19 directive, although there is no evidence that he did not obey the answer to his telegram. He was suspended from his job by Under Secretary of State Walter Bedell Smith on February 24, and then reinstated within a day, but the news of the firing was page one in the *New York Times* of February 25, while the news of his reinstatement was page thirteen the following day.[69]

It was Secretary of State Dulles who had ordered the February 19 directive and after appeal for clarification it was Dulles, through McCardle, the Assistant Secretary of State for Public Affairs, who told the then new head of the International Information Administration, Johnson, what the new line would be. It was the same as before, although the phrase "et cetera" had been dropped. For clarity in the

68. See Merson, *Private Diary of a Public Servant*, pp. 14–15, for a fuller list (from which these names were taken), and for an account of the purge of the overseas libraries.

69. *New York Times,* February 25, 1953, p. 1, col. 2; and February 26, 1953, p. 13, col. 1.

enforcement of the policy the field libraries needed an *Index Librorum Prohibitorum*, and the IIA in fact asked the State Department Security Office for such a list, which was never supplied.[70]

This was the situation, then, when the hearings on the Voice of America were finished in the third week of March 1953. There was nothing conclusive about the end of the hearings. They just stopped. The investigation of the overseas information centers began when Roy Cohn and David Schine of the subcommittee staff made a quick tour of Europe, presumably to investigate the centers. The story of this pair of peripatetics on tour in Europe is a tale of farce and fright; and need not be recounted to make the connection between it and the relation it was thought by them to bear to the discovery of Communist influences in the Federal service. The conclusion they reached was that there were books by Communists on the shelves of the overseas libraries, that they should not be there, and that there were not enough anti-Communist books and magazines. Cohn also came back with the name of one Theodore Kaghan, a public affairs officer for the United States High Commission for Germany, who had described Cohn and Schine to a newspaperman as "junketeering gumshoes."[71]

The purpose of the hearings on the information centers was presumably to determine the extent of Communist influence in these centers. The method was to examine a parade of witnesses whose books were in the libraries of the centers. Inevitably the inquiry was an investigation into the connections between these authors and the Communist movement, where such a connection existed, as it did for some. The authors were not civil servants in the employ of the United States but private citizens whose writings were on the shelves of the overseas libraries.

Louis Budenz, former managing editor of the *Daily Worker*, was put on the stand to testify about Communist authors generally.[72] Books, he said, are regarded as part of psychological warfare, Communist officials exercise a strict control over authors under discipline, authors are required to follow the party line, and to introduce it in their works where possible. Where this is not possible, the author under discipline lends himself to Communist causes, plays a part in some front, and gives sums of money to the party. International Publishers was identified as one of the publishing houses of the Communist Party in the

70. Merson, *Private Diary of a Public Servant*, pp. 16–18, from which the account in the text is drawn.

71. Richard Rovere, *Senator Joe McCarthy* (New York: Harcourt, Brace, 1959), p. 204. Rovere provides an account of the whole trip of Cohn and Schine at pp. 199–205.

72. *State Department Information Program — Information Centers*, p. 41.

United States. At the request of the subcommittee, Budenz examined
a partial list of some authors whose books were currently being used
in the information centers and he said that he had found some seventy-
five by Communist authors. It was also said by Senator McCarthy for
the record that none of them had been purchased since the advent of
Dr. Johnson as head of the IIA, that is, after the orders of late February
and March 1953, and before the subcommittee began its inquiry into
the information centers and the contents of their libraries.[73]

Then followed a number of writers and artists whose works were
still in the information centers and who refused to testify on Fifth
Amendment grounds about alleged Communist affiliation, most of them
on television. Among these were Lawrence K. Rosinger,[74] a writer on
Far Eastern affairs; Dashiell Hammett,[75] the writer of mystery novels
who had served a term in prison for declining to answer a question as
to whether he was a trustee of the bail bond fund of the Civil Rights
Congress; Helen Goldfrank,[76] author of children's books; Dr. Bernhard
J. Stern of Columbia University,[77] a sociologist, who said that he was
not a member of the Communist Party, but declined on Fifth Amendment grounds to say whether he ever had been; Miss Gene Weltfish,[78]
an anthropologist; Herbert Aptheker,[79] identified by a witness as an
instructor at the Jefferson School of Social Science, and the author of
books "which are used as the official Communist Party line in relation
to the Negro question in the United States";[80] Philip S. Foner,[81] who
refused on Fifth Amendment grounds to say whether he was a teacher
"in a Communist school, the Jefferson School of Social Science"; William Gropper[82] and Rockwell Kent,[83] well-known painters; Richard
O. Boyer,[84] a writer for magazines for the most part; Edwin Berry

73. *Ibid.*, p. 44.
74. *Ibid.*, p. 59.
75. *Ibid.*, p. 83.
76. *Ibid.*, p. 90.
77. *Ibid.*, p. 97.
78. *Ibid.*, p. 115.
79. *Ibid.*, p. 374.
80. *Ibid.*, p. 368. The witness was Harvey Matusow, who later asserted that he
had deliberately given false testimony on a number of occasions, including the
1952 trial of Communist leaders, the McCarran committee hearings on Owen
Lattimore and the Institute of Pacific Relations, and the trial of a Texas labor
leader accused of filing false affidavits under the Taft-Hartley Act. As to Lattimore, he said, "I climaxed my testimony with the dramatic assertion that Owen
Lattimore's books were used as the official Communist Party guides on Asia.
Once again, I told a complete falsehood." Harvey Matusow, *False Witness* (New
York: Cameron and Kahn, 1955), p. 104.
81. *State Department Information Program — Information Centers*, p. 386.
82. *Ibid.*, p. 388.
83. *Ibid.*, p. 417.
84. *Ibid.*, p. 422.

Burgum,[85] author and literary critic; Doxey Wilkerson,[86] former research worker with the President's Advisory Committee on Education in 1938–39, employee of the Office of Price Administration in 1942 and 1943, and a witness for the eleven Communist leaders in the pre-trial proceeding on the alleged discriminatory character of the jury system; Arnold d'Usseau,[87] a playwright and author, who thought that the South Koreans had attacked the North Koreans; and Eslanda Cardoza Goode Robeson,[88] the wife of Paul Robeson.

Edwin Seaver,[89] Langston Hughes,[90] and Grace Lumpkin[91] all testified freely, did not take the Fifth Amendment, and said that they thought that works of theirs now on the shelves of the overseas libraries, written when they were close to the Communist movement, should not be used by the information centers. Leo Huberman,[92] a non-Communist Marxian and co-editor of *Monthly Review*, said that he had never been a member of the Communist Party. At some points he did talk about the First Amendment and complained that he was being examined as to his political opinions, but in the course of the inquiry he made a rather full exposition of his political opinions, in part with the help of a statement that he was allowed to read. The position of Harvey O'Connor was somewhat different.[93] He objected to the jurisdiction of the subcommittee to inquire into his political opinions on the ground that the First Amendment protected this right. O'Connor said that he had not known until the moment of the hearing that any of his books was in overseas libraries, that he did not think that his answers would tend to incriminate him, but that he was not answering anyway because he thought his freedoms under the First Amendment were being invaded. His examination took a few minutes, he was asked to step down, he was later cited for contempt in refusing to answer, and was convicted.[94] By the end of the inquiry into the information centers, the chairman of the subcommittee, the staff, and Senator Mundt of South Dakota were no longer talking about the suspected enormities of the State Department as it was, but about the delinquencies of "the old Acheson State Department" that had been responsible for putting offensive matter in the overseas libraries.

85. *Ibid.*, p. 433.
86. *Ibid.*, p. 441.
87. *Ibid.*, p. 464.
88. *Ibid.*, p. 473.
89. *State Department Information Program — Information Centers*, p. 71.
90. *Ibid.*, p. 73.
91. *Ibid.*, p. 155.
92. *Ibid.*, p. 483.
93. *Ibid.*, p. 484.
94. O'Connor was fined $500 and sentenced to a one-year term in prison. The jail sentence was suspended. *New York Times*, November 19, 1954, p. 10, col. 4.

In the course of the examination of the authors, there was no demonstration, as there could have been none, that they were employees of the government, or that they had had anything to do with putting their writings into the information centers overseas. The chairman of the committee and the staff tried to make a tenuous connection between the writers and some legitimate interest that the subcommittee might have in the great world of books by talking about money. The books were bought, there were royalties presumably, the authors were then in receipt of United States moneys, they could be asked about themselves and their writings, and questioned as to whether they were Communists at the time they wrote their books. This line of inquiry produced no information whatever about the existence of possible conspiracy in the State Department to effect purposes contrary to the interests of the United States. It was the theory of the subcommittee, however, that the cause corrupted the man, and that the identification "Communist" vested all of the works of the defending witness with opprobrium, a moralistic and somewhat unrealistic opinion in the view of the original Advisory Commission of Educational Exchanges which had recommended that the content of books, not the authors of them, supply the answer to the question whether they would serve the objectives of the United States.

One of the examinations stood out from the others — that of James Wechsler of the *New York Post*, which was different from that of the other authors because Senator McCarthy seemed to have a personal interest in what the *New York Post* had been saying about him. This inquiry took Wechsler back to the time when he was a student and a member of the Young Communist League, and the author of a couple of books — *Revolt on the Campus* and *War, Our Heritage* — that were Communist tracts. Wechsler had joined the party in 1934 under the name Arthur Lawson, and stayed in until 1937. By 1938 he had left the party, some fifteen years before the investigation, and had shown himself as editor of the *New York Post* and in other writing to have been sincere in his break. He had been called ostensibly to discuss his books, but he was never told in the course of the examination which books he was supposed to be discussing. In fact the contents of his books were of small interest to the subcommittee although the contents of the *New York Post* were of great interest to Senator McCarthy.[95]

Cohn and Schine had been to Germany in their rapid inspection of the overseas information centers, and the trip, brief as it was, supplied part of the agenda of the subcommittee. James Aronson[96] had been

95. *State Department Information Program — Information Centers*, p. 253. For an account of his experience with Senator McCarthy, see Wechsler, *The Age of Suspicion*.

96. *State Department Information Program — Information Centers*, p. 395.

employed by the Office of War Information and then by the War Department in Germany, had been a member of the staff of the *New York Post*, on leave of absence during his wartime service, had joined the *New York Times* in the fall of 1946, and left it to work for a journal which he refused to identify on Fifth Amendment grounds. He refused to say on the same grounds whether he worked for the *National Guardian*, and declined to say whether he had been a Communist when he was with the *Times*. His job in Germany some seven years or so before the subcommittee hearing had been to license papers which would be allowed to publish during the Occupation, and in a speech a month before the hearing he had said that he had had the responsibility for licensing what he described as "democratic" papers. He also declined to say whether he was "a member of the Communist Party as of today."

Cedric Henning Belfrage was also called to testify about the licensing of newspapers in the immediate period after the collapse of Germany and the occupation by the Allies.[97] A British subject, Belfrage had been living in the United States for sixteen years as a resident alien, and declined to say on Fifth Amendment grounds whether he was a member of the Communist Party or whether he believed in the overthrow of the government of the United States. He also declined to say whether he had been a Communist at the time he served as a press officer in Germany with responsibilities similar to those of Aronson, where he was employed at the time of the hearing, and whether he knew Elizabeth Bentley.

Through these two witnesses the subcommittee did throw a little light on events in Germany in 1945 and 1946 in the licensing of newspapers. It is certainly of some interest that two so employed by the American Military Government were shy about Communist connections, and the possibility that there might be others equally shy was piquant. The subcommittee, however, had turned up no such individuals in the investigation of the Voice of America or the information centers (which was the subject of their inquiry) and those that they had turned up in the Military Government licensing program had left Germany years before, and were presently working for journals they would not identify.

There remained one other person to be examined — the man who had attracted the unfavorable notice of Roy Cohn, Theodore Kaghan,[98] the acting deputy director of the Office of Public Affairs of the United States High Commission in Germany who had been first mentioned in the hearings on the Voice of America.[99] Kaghan said

97. *Ibid.*, p. 407.
98. *Ibid.*, pp. 171 and 221.
99. *State Department Information Program — Voice of America*, p. 214.

that he had never been a member of the Communist Party, that between the years 1935 and 1940 he had attended meetings that were run or controlled by Communists, that he had lived for a year with a roommate who he assumed was a Communist, that he had signed a nominating petition for a Communist candidate for councilman in New York "to support his attempt to get on the ballot," and that he had thought of communism in those days as a political party and not as a political conspiracy. He was reminded that he had referred to Cohn and Schine as "junketeering gumshoes," that he had written a number of plays that he admitted were, by and large, acceptable to the Communists although perhaps not in detail. He said that he had come to think of communism as a menace in 1945 or thereafter when he had to work with the Russians in Vienna. He had a letter from the Austrian Chancellor Figl praising him for his anticommunism.

There was some discussion in the subcommittee with Kaghan about the interpretation of some of his plays. He acknowledged that one of them had been put on by a Communist front theatrical organization, said that it had probably aided Communist causes in the thirties because it was about the Abraham Lincoln Brigade, and was then presented with the names of a number of people about some of whom he was able to make some comment. He did not plead any of the amendments, and was quietly eased out of his job in Germany when the McCarthy committee was through with him. In a television interview in June, Senator McCarthy said that anyone who invoked the Fifth Amendment when asked about Communists obviously was one.[100] But, as in the example of Kaghan, this rule of thumb obviously did not work the other way.[101]

Two witnesses, Freda Utley[102] and Karl Baarslag,[103] had visited in-

100. *New York Times*, June 22, 1953, p. 9, col. 5.

101. It is curious, although there may be some explanation which is not obvious, that *The Progressive* in its bill of particulars against Senator McCarthy did not mention the Kaghan affair. See "McCarthy: A Documented Record."

102. For the testimony of Freda Utley, see *State Department Information Program — Information Centers*, pp. 129 and 212. Miss Utley had testified before the McCarran committee in the investigation of the Institute of Pacific Relations against Owen Lattimore. Although critical of those who had seemed to think that the Chinese Communists were something less than Communist, Miss Utley as late as 1939 and 1940 was writing that "Communism in China having become almost entirely an agrarian movement, had by 1935 been transmuted by the logic of history into a movement of peasant emancipation." And of the Chinese Communist Party, ". . . its aim has genuinely become social and political reform along capitalist and democratic lines." For these and other quotations of similar import from her writing in the period, see *IPR Hearings*, pp. 3705–3706.

103. Baarslag had been research director of the National Americanism Commission of the American Legion, and was to join the staff of McCarthy's subcommittee in the summer of 1953. For his testimony on the books in the information centers abroad, see *State Department Information Program — Information Centers*, p. 159.

formation centers abroad and said that they had found books by Communists. Miss Utley said that she felt that the selection of books in the information centers she visited did not provide a true picture of American life, that the catalogues were not set up so that it would be easy to find anti-Communist books, there were not very many anyway, that a book by Ilya Ehrenburg was listed in one of the catalogues although she did not actually see the book, and that there were books by several authors she said were Communists or pro-Communists. She could not find Toledano, *Seeds of Treason,* but she did see Barth's *Loyalty of Free Men,* evidence she thought that the bookshelves were ". . . loaded up with what you might call anti-anti-Communist material, not fellow-traveller or Communist-sympathizer material but people who are extremely anti those who are doing anything against the Communists." [104]

When Baarslag was asked whether he had paid "particular attention to the magazines and periodicals which were stocked in the State Department information centers," he said that he had "got into that, Mr. Counsel, only indirectly, at Frankfort," where someone had told him that you could not find any anti-Communist books or magazines in any of the USIS libraries or in the Army Special Services libraries. So he checked the USIS information center in Frankfort and he found books by some of the people who were to appear before the subcommittee to testify about their possible Communist connections, but he had also found anti-Communist books. He then went to Munich and found books by undesirable authors, but he had also found books by Whittaker Chambers, Kravchenko, Koestler, Eugene Lyons, James Burnham, Fulton J. Sheen, and other anti-Communist writers. This news was somewhat contrary to the line being developed by Mr. Cohn, but the conversation switched to magazines and periodicals, and things ran smoothly again. Baarslag had looked for the *American Legion Magazine,* could not find it, and said ". . . I am not naive. I was rather shocked, nevertheless, to find that they had never heard of it." They had also never heard of the *National Republic.* He had asked for the *Freeman* and learned that "they had never heard of that." There were no anti-Communist magazines, although he said that he could find *The Nation* and the *New Republic* in all the centers he examined. When it appeared that "they" had also never heard of the McCarran committee or the House Committee on Un-American Activities, it developed that "they"

were, of course, the girls on the floor in charge of the publications. I must make it clear that they were not the chief librarians or the

104. *State Department Information Program — Information Centers,* p. 137.

people in the front office, so called. I just walked in as an ordinary visitor.

Q. But they were American citizens?

A. I would have no way of knowing. They all spoke very good English, and my information is that most of them were Germans, or, in the case of Paris, French, but whether they were citizens or not, I wouldn't know.[105]

After having made it clear that there were German girls in the German centers and French girls in Paris, Baarslag concluded,

> The presence of these pro-Communist, pro-Soviet books in these libraries was one thing: that somebody put them there. But that is only half the picture. What I was interested in, and I have tried to point this out in my testimony, was the absence of the books on our side, because that also implies conscious knowledge of what is an anti-Communist book, and conscious activity in keeping them out of libraries.
>
> Now, presumably even innocents or dupes or uninformed people who could have put a pro-Communist or pro-Soviet book on those library shelves, also innocently would have put the other side on the shelves. I leave that inference with you.
>
> Q. Apparently, then, it was by design.
>
> A. That is the only inference that any reasonable man could draw, that if pro-Soviet books by notorious Communists like Mandel and others found their way onto the shelves, books on our side would also have found their way there. But, as I said, the books were there, but the magazines were totally absent. . . .[106]

The investigation of the information centers was remarkably inconclusive, and the results were remarkably insubstantial. In its report on the centers a half year later, the subcommittee could do little more than say that there were books by Communists in the centers, that under the "old State Department" there had been inadequate use of anti-Communist materials, that under the "old State Department" officials had been negligent in the advancement of American ideas in the struggle against communism, and that the personnel departments of the information centers should be put under men with strong anti-Communist attitudes.[107] But the excitement caused by the investiga-

105. *Ibid.*, p. 161.
106. *Ibid.*, p. 163.
107. Eighty-third Congress, Second Session, United States Senate, Committee on Government Operations, Permanent Subcommittee on Investigations, *Report on State Department Information Program — Information Centers*, S. Rept. 879, January 25, 1954.

tion among the staff of the State Department, in the Republican administration itself, and in the press, was in inverse ratio to the substantiality of the charges, and as the television cameras recorded the play between committee and witness, and sensational statements pulsed in the headlines, the tension of anxiety tightened the more, in that it had less to grasp. The search for facts became a competition of symbols.

One of the symbols was the burning of the books. Following the panic directives of February and March 1953 from the headquarters of the International Information Administration, information centers abroad began clearing the shelves of forbidden books. Some books were in fact burned — Secretary Dulles set the number at eleven.[108] The actual number burned was of no consequence — nor the reason for the burning of any, such as that they were no longer useful, or that they could not be returned, stored, or given away. The act itself was reminiscent of the Nazis who made *Walpurgisnachten* of the destruction of books by fire. President Eisenhower said at Dartmouth College on June 14,

> Don't join the book-burners. Don't think you are going to conceal faults by concealing evidence that they ever existed. Don't be afraid to go in your library and read every book as long as any document does not offend our own ideas of decency. That should be the only censorship.[109]

One Republican writer on the first Eisenhower administration later said that the matter of the books was discussed at a cabinet meeting on June 26.[110] Dulles explained to his colleagues and the President that the burnings had been the independent acts of librarians overseas and not the order of Washington, and that they had been animated "either by fear of or out of hatred for McCarthy." The President asked for a policy statement on books by the date of the next cabinet meeting.

On June 26 also, President Eisenhower wrote a letter to the American Library Association which was holding a convention in Los Angeles in which he criticized zealots who would suppress information and ideas. The convention adopted a resolution threatening to with-

108. *New York Times*, June 16, 1953, p. 1, col. 2.

109. For an account of the debate over the burning of books, see Goldman, *The Crucial Decade*, pp. 252–254. Goldman says that the words about the burning of books got into Eisenhower's address because he had overheard a discussion of the matter by three other recipients of honorary degrees at the commencement: John J. McCloy, Judge Joseph M. Proskauer of New York, and Lester B. Pearson, then Secretary of State for External Affairs in Canada. *Ibid.*, p. 252.

110. Robert J. Donovan, *The Inside Story* (New York: Harper and Brothers, 1956), p. 92

draw its support of the overseas library program unless the integrity and effectiveness of the program were assured.[111] On July 8, 1953, the administration made public through Robert Johnson, the head of the International Information Administration, the content of a new policy.[112] Among other things, the statement said that the yardstick for choosing books should be their usefulness in meeting the needs of a particular area, that conceivably books by Communists and Communist sympathizers might be included in special instances if the authors had written something which affirmatively served the ends of democracy, and that under no circumstances should a book be burned. Said the statement,

> The burning of a book is a wicked symbolic act. There is no place for book-burnings in an American library, let alone a library operated by our government. We don't deal with ideas we dislike by imitating the totalitarian techniques we despise. The burning of a book is not an act against that book alone; it is an act against free institutions.[113]

The matter was discussed again in the Cabinet meeting of July 10. The new policy statement was considered and the thought prevailed that it represented a practicable solution to the problem, although Secretary of Defense Charles Wilson suggested that the government should get out of the business of maintaining libraries abroad, and Secretary of the Treasury George Humphrey and Secretary of Health, Education, and Welfare Oveta Culp Hobby proposed that the overseas libraries be limited to the presentation of Americana.[114] Thus the controversy came full circle, and the policy finally reached was the one with which the controversy started, namely, the order of February 3 which had implemented the general policy of December 1952.

On July 9, 1953, McCarthy sent a telegram to Dr. Johnson demanding to know from Johnson the names of those Communists whose writings he thought would serve the ends of democracy, an estimate of the amount of the taxpayers' money he would like to have appropriated to purchase and maintain the works of Communists which serve the ends of democracy, and the appearance before him of the individual or individuals responsible for the decision to continue the purchase of books by Communist authors. Johnson replied to Senator McCarthy immediately, explaining and defending the new policy of

111. "McCarthy: A Documented Record," p. 42.
112. Donovan, *Inside Story*, pp. 92–93.
113. Donovan, *Inside Story*, pp. 92–93. See also Merson, *Private Diary of a Public Servant*, pp. 123–127, for an account of the writing of the initial statement in the IIA which was added to by the White House.
114. Donovan, *Inside Story*, p. 93.

July 8. By this time, Dr. Johnson had submitted his resignation as head of the International Information Administration and, presumably feeling freer than before to act independently in an administration that was easing him out, issued a White Paper on July 15, without clearing with Dulles, in which he explained the work of the IIA, and criticized some of those who he said were in the forefront of the fight against communism but were damaging the action programs that do battle against it. Senator Hennings of Missouri perhaps summed it all up best in a speech in the Senate on July 10, 1953, in which he said of the policy statement of July 8:

> The confusion generated in the last five months by some eleven directives issued to those in charge of the Overseas Libraries should now be dispelled. It is unfortunate that the State Department, in this period, departed from its sound and well-considered policy and undertook to readjust its program to meet each vicissitude of Congressional investigations.[115]

The Government Printing Office

During the last two weeks in August 1953, hearings were held in the matter of Edward Rothschild, a bookbinder at the Government Printing Office, who had been cleared by the agency loyalty board four times, and then pleaded the Fifth Amendment when asked by the subcommittee about possible Communist associations. Rothschild was suspected of being a Communist and of having stolen secret documents from the GPO, although it was not possible to establish the alleged particulars. Quite apart from the foolish exaggerations of McCarthy with respect to the Rothschild case — possibly "worse than the Alger Hiss case" — enough was disclosed about operations within the GPO to establish the probability of Communist activity, and perhaps espionage.[116]

One of the principal witnesses was Mrs. Mary Stalcup Markward, who had been an agent of the FBI in the Communist Party from

115. Merson, *Private Diary of a Public Servant*, pp. 132–133. Merson also describes an encounter at the same time over a statement made by Karl Baarslag (who became research director for the McCarthy subcommittee) to a Scripps-Howard reporter about the absence of anti-Communist books in the overseas libraries. Johnson sent a stinging rebuttal which specified the facts, Baarslag then said that he had meant magazines, McCarthy said that the reporter had messed up the story, a Scripps-Howard editor said that McCarthy's statement was false, and the White House gagged Dr. Johnson who wished to reply further. *Ibid.*, pp. 139–150.
116. For the testimony in this matter, see Eighty-third Congress, First Session, United States Senate, Committee on Government Operations, Permanent Subcommittee on Investigations, Hearings Pursuant to S. Res. 40, *Security — Government Printing Office* (hereafter cited as *Security — Government Printing Office*).

1943 to 1949.[117] She had previously been used by the government in the trial of eleven Communists for violating the Smith Act, and testified before the McCarthy subcommittee about Mrs. Rothschild, with whom, she said, she had had party associations a dozen times, and whom she identified in the hearing room. Mrs. Markward had held a number of offices in the Communist Party (later the Communist Political Association) in the Washington area, and testified that she had known Mrs. Rothschild as a member of the Thomas Jefferson Club of the Communist Political Association. The Thomas Jefferson Club was a white-collar organization whose members were thought to be important enough to the party to warrant special security precautions. They were not to identify themselves publicly with Communist causes, but were otherwise to serve the party as faithful members. In this they benefited from a kind of class separation within the clubs of the Communist Political Association in the Washington area, for the lower paid and less important members of the organization were under no such security protection.

The meetings of the Thomas Jefferson Club, according to Mrs. Markward, were held at a Communist print shop in northeast Washington. The print shop had been employed by the GPO to do various jobs, none secret — work for the Treasury, Veterans' Administration, Navy, Coast Guard, Post Office, War Department, General Accounting Office, Department of Agriculture, Selective Service, and Reconstruction Finance Corporation. Meetings of the Thomas Jefferson Club were also held at the home of the owners of the print shop, and at a home in Montgomery County, Maryland. The testimony of Mrs. Markward was that Mrs. Rothschild had been active in steps that were subsequently taken to turn the Communist Political Association back into the Communist Party.

Unlike other McCarthy hearings, the GPO investigation was one in which counsel for the witnesses were allowed to submit questions which were then put by the subcommittee to Mrs. Markward. A number of the questions submitted by counsel for Mrs. Rothschild had to do with the way in which Mrs. Markward reported to the FBI, how soon she had reported after one of the meetings mentioned in testimony before the subcommittee, whether the reports were in writing, whether she had seen them since, and so on. Others dealt with addresses and the dates she had met with Mrs. Rothschild, what she did with the money she collected as dues from Mrs. Rothschild, whether she kept a list of the sums and the numbers of persons paying such dues, whether she turned such a list over to the FBI, and the source of her income when she was a member of the Communist Party

117. *Security — Government Printing Office,* p. 1.

and at the (then) present time. Where she was unclear in her answers counsel for Mrs. Rothschild were allowed to say so and the sub-committee required Mrs. Markward to respond.

But Mrs. Markward did not identify Mr. Rothschild, who was in the Navy at the time she knew his wife. In fact she had never met him. James B. Phillips, however, a binding machine operator at the GPO, who said that he had known Rothschild since 1938 or thereabouts, testified that he attended a Communist Party meeting with Rothschild in 1939 which had been called to plan the formation of a cell in the GPO. Later, he said, he was asked by Rothschild and another man to join the party cell in the GPO, he asked for two months to think it over, and then went to the Dies Committee to testify,[118] after which he was not invited again to join the Communist Party. The production manager for the GPO testified that the GPO handled secret and top secret documents for the Air Force, Navy, Army, and State Department and other agencies, and Rothschild himself, in executive session, said that he had had access to secret and confidential material.[119]

The man known to Phillips in 1939 only as "Fred" was identified by him as Frederick Sillers who took employment with the Government Printing Office in 1938 or 1939, first as a chemist and then as foreman of the metals section. He was at the GPO for four years before moving to another position in the Bureau of Standards, then to the Bureau of Mines, first in Washington and then in Rolla, Missouri. He declined on Fifth Amendment grounds to answer whether he had been a member of the Washington Bookshop or the American League for Peace and Democracy, and whether he had ever been a member of the Communist Party or of the United Public Office Workers of America, which was expelled from the CIO because it was Communist-controlled. On the same grounds he refused to answer whether he knew Edward Rothschild, although in executive session he had said he knew both Rothschild and his wife and had visited with them at their home.[120] When Rothschild testified, he refused to answer any questions whatever, including the question whether he was working for the GPO, basing his refusal on the Fifth Amendment. A Mrs. Gertrude Evans, Executive Secretary of the Progressive Party of the District of Columbia, appeared at the request of the Rothschilds (ac-

118. Phillips was 22 years old when he testified before the Dies Committee in executive session on October 9, 1939. He did not know Rothschild by name then and could not supply the name to the committee. The man with Rothschild when the two approached Phillips about joining the Communist cell he could identify in 1939 only as "Fred." Seventy-sixth Congress, Third Session, House of Representatives, Special Committee on Un-American Activities, Hearings on H. Res. 282, *Executive Hearings*, pp. 69–76.

119. *Security — Government Printing Office*, p. 38.

120. *Ibid.*, p. 58.

cording to the chairman of the subcommittee) but when she was put on the stand she pleaded the Fifth Amendment and refused to answer any questions about Communist associations. Mrs. Rothschild was also put on the stand and, like her husband, declined to answer questions that had anything to do with Communist associations.

Counsel for the Rothschilds were permitted to put specific questions — through the chairman — to the chief of the Employee Relations Section of the GPO who had some of the responsibility for the loyalty clearance procedures of the agency. It appeared that the board had cleared Rothschild as late as July 1953, although the FBI information given to the loyalty board contained the identity of a witness who had worked next to Rothschild and who had claimed to have seen him steal classified documents.[121] The director of personnel of the GPO, who was also the security officer for the agency, explained that under the loyalty program first established in 1947 it was the prevailing rule that mere membership in the Communist Party was not enough to bar a worker, that the FBI information was not evaluated by the FBI, that the loyalty board members were not trained in the evaluation of evidence, and that they did the best they knew how. In one instance, the agency loyalty board had recommended the separation of a woman employee as a loyalty and security risk and had been overruled by the then security officer, the Deputy Public Printer. Shortly afterwards the woman was caught stealing secret documents. She was then discharged. The testimony of both the chief of the Employee Relations Section and the personnel officer of the agency raised questions as to the efficacy of the loyalty and security programs of the GPO.

There was other testimony about loyalty procedures in the GPO, and a few witnesses were brought forward to testify about their relations with the Rothschilds, or about their own possible connections with the Communist Party, who declined to answer on Fifth Amendment grounds. A former assistant to Rothschild, however, in a sworn affidavit that was read into the record, said that she had seen him take classified documents, including a secret code of the Merchant Marine, and that she had reported it to the foreman and then to the FBI.[122] Of all of the time spent by the McCarthy subcommittee from February through August 1953, when the Government Printing Office hearings ended, most of it seemed to be wasted — the most substantial indication of the existence of an active Communist group, and of possible espionage, was that turned up in the GPO inquiry.

The GPO hearings led to some inquiry into the matter of the Com-

121. *Ibid.*, p. 87.
122. *Ibid.*, pp. 110–112.

munist associations of United States citizens in the United Nations, and although United Nations affairs were primarily a responsibility of other committees of the Senate, the Permanent Subcommittee on Investigations went ahead with a short investigation. The interest in the United Nations problem was said to have issued from the discovery that the Government Printing Office had been turning out material for the United Nations, a rather remote connection, perhaps, but one for the investigation of which clearance had been made by McCarthy with his colleagues on the Internal Security and Foreign Relations committees.

The principal witness was Julius Reiss, a documentation clerk with the Polish Delegation to the United Nations, an American citizen, identified by Paul Crouch and John Lautner as a man they had both known in the Communist Party under the name, Joel Remes.[123] Julius Reiss refused to answer questions about possible Communist associations on Fifth Amendment grounds.[124] John Lautner said that Joel Remes was a member of the Communist Party, a functionary in the National Committee of the Communist Party, and an associate editor of *Political Affairs*, the theoretical organ of the American Communist Party. Lautner also identified Abraham Unger and David Freedman, law partners, as party members, both having worked as counsel for the defense in the Smith Act prosecutions, in which they had employed Julius Reiss to do research. Both Unger and Freedman refused to co-operate with the subcommittee when questioned, Unger's behavior being particularly obstructive to the good order of the proceedings.[125]

123. Eighty-third Congress, First Session, United States Senate, Committee on Government Operations, Permanent Subcommittee on Investigations, Hearings Pursuant to S. Res. 40, *Security — United Nations* (hereafter cited as *Security — United Nations*)

124. *Security — United Nations*, p. 9.

125. Unger was first examined in executive session on September 15, 1953, at which time he asked for an extension of time to supply information on the employment of Julius Reiss. The meeting was held in the United States Court-house, Foley Square, New York, with Senator McCarthy presiding. The other Senators of the subcommittee were not present, although the administrative assistants of Senators Potter and Dirkson attended, as well as staff of the sub-committee. Unger made no objection to the fact that only Senator McCarthy was present from the subcommittee on September 15. At his request, the whole group stayed over in New York two days to get his further testimony. On September 17, 1953, Unger appeared and consumed the time with unresponsive and ex-tended arguments about the lack of a quorum of the subcommittee, and the lack of authority of the subcommittee to question him about communism or his connection with the Communist movement. He would not say yes or no or plead the Fifth Amendment. He avoided answer at all. On September 18, 1953, he appeared as required at the public hearing, and when it was evident that the public hearing might be a repetition of the executive hearing, Unger was removed from the room. See *Security — United Nations*, p. 36, for the removal of Unger; pp. 69–80 for the testimony he gave at the first executive session; and pp. 40–55

McCarthy as Chairman

Senator McCarthy as chairman of the Permanent Subcommittee on Investigations succeeded in transforming serious questions of fealty and public policy into an obsession with self. In the investigation of the Department of State programs of overseas information, he reached the height of his influence — he had the volunteer services of a number of informers inside the department; he had his own agent, Scott McLeod, strategically placed as security officer in the department; and even the Secretary of State cooperated with him and his committee in his attacks upon the agency. The investigations of the Voice of America and the information centers turned up no evidence of conspiratorial design. The short hearings on the Government Printing Office showed some evidence of possible espionage but the information was already known to the Federal Bureau of Investigation, and McCarthy contributed nothing to the national security in his handling of the material. The hearings as a whole seem to have served little other purpose than to enable McCarthy to pay off grudges, his own and those of his staff and informers in the Department of State. If there was subversion in the agencies of the Department of State he investigated, he did not find it.

The proceedings, however, served to fix the lineaments of his public personality, and to intensify the emotions of his supporters and detractors. His supporters saw him as a champion, a rough fellow, to be sure, but a great fighter against communism and all its works, a battler for Christian ideals, a purger and a cleanser of intellectual vice, a true believer, a dedicated foe crusading against moral delinquency in high places. For others, the hearings reinforced their conviction that McCarthy was a paradigm of wickedness.

Some of the distaste for him was undoubtedly esthetic — however attractive he may have been to close friends and political allies, in his official role he was heavy, graceless, saturnine, contemptuous, and tough. But the concern he created among political liberals was more than artistic wincing. Other political figures have been coarse and overbearing, loud and rude, without exciting the anxiety McCarthy generated. There was something else in his manner — a latency that yielded more meaning than the sum of his words, a sense of willingness to perpetrate gross assault without decency or restraint if it served

---

for his testimony at the second executive session. Provocative tactics had also been used by Unger in the trial of the Dennis case in 1949 before Judge Harold Medina in an effort to break up the trial — without success. For an account of his personal experiences with the tactics of the defense and their supporters in and out of the court room, see Harold R. Medina, *The Anatomy of Freedom* (New York: Henry Holt, 1959), chap. i.

his ends. He could literally unhinge the timid because he wrenched them from their confidence in the normal barriers that protect the personality from violation — courtesy, respect, and the due process of custom and law. McCarthy's power, "like a desolating pestilence," sickened the first two years of the first Eisenhower administration and, like the pox, left ineradicable pits and scars.

. . . constitutions . . . are destroyed
both by not being pushed far enough
and by being pushed too far.

ARISTOTLE, *Rhetoric*

XII   The Stress of Government

Did Attorney General Robert Kennedy in the summer of 1963 leak information that forced the British permaturely to disclose the identity of H. A. R. Philby, a former British diplomat, as a Soviet spy? Did not the disclosure help the Soviet Union by making public the news that the British knew that Philby was a Soviet agent? Did John A. McCone, head of the Central Intelligence Agency, tell a woman guest at a dinner party in Washington one evening that a big spy case was about to break in Britain, and thus tip off the ever vigilant agents of the Soviet Union?[1] Although these were interesting questions and though they involved security in the highest reaches of the Federal government, few seemed to care, there was no excitement about loyalty and security, and no demand to have the officials named appear before a congressional committee to testify about their credentials. Things had been different short years before when Americans in the Chinese Embassy in 1947 who were accused of having talked loosely about Chiang Kai-shek were investigated suspiciously. But — it may be said — there was no excitement about Robert Kennedy, former member of Senator McCarthy's staff,[2] and John McCone, Republican friend of Richard Nixon, because they were respectable officials, an argument of merry inconsequence in the heyday of the investigations. And in certain respects, it was an argument of no value in 1963, either, for

1. The suggestion that Attorney General Kennedy and John A. McCone were the Americans responsible for forcing the disclosure was made by a reporter for the *New York Times* in a general article. See *New York Times*, July 18, 1963, p. 2, col. 2.

2. The exasperated Martin Merson said, "On any weekday one was almost certain to find McCarthy, Cohn, and Schine, and, if they were in town, Surine, Juliana, Robert Kennedy, son of Joseph P. and brother of Senator John, an assistant counsel of the McCarthy subcommittee . . ." The place of which he was speaking was the Carroll Arms Hotel, which is behind the Capitol. Martin Merson, *The Private Diary of a Public Servant* (New York: Macmillan, 1955), p. 98.

one of the disclosures in a rash of spy cases was the identity of Colonel Stig Wennerstrom, the Swedish Defense Ministry official, an air attaché in Washington from 1952 to 1957, a charming man who confessed that he had been an agent of the Soviet Union for fifteen years — including the time he was in Washington — and who had obtained information from at least one indiscreet American military officer as to which military sites in the Soviet Union were of particular interest to the United States.[3] Everybody loved Colonel Wennerstrom. Nobody cared.

Nor was the excitement generated by news abroad much greater. China went to the Communists in 1949 in an uproar of hateful philippics, but much of Indo-China went quietly to the Communists in 1954. It was President Eisenhower who said, in words thought traitorous short years before, that the United States was trying to reach a modus vivendi on Indo-China.[4] Fulgencio Batista — in a parallel bearing close resemblance to some aspects of the Chinese civil war — was abandoned by the Republican administration, which welcomed his Communist successor as an agrarian reformer. In April 1959, Fidel

3. A central case in the number of spy disclosures in the spring and summer of 1963 was that of Oleg Penkevsky. Penkevsky, a Soviet official who had been working for the West, was given a summary trial in Moscow in May, and executed almost immediately. He had been deputy head of the Foreign Department of the State Committee for the Coordination of Scientific Research, a position that gave him wide access within the Soviet Union and the Soviet bloc. He confessed that he had sold secrets over a period of 17 months to a British businessman, Greville Wynne (who was also tried and sentenced to eight years in prison) and to United States Embassy officials. See Hanson Baldwin, "A Flurry of Spy Cases," *New York Times*, July 29, 1963, p. 3, col. 5. In a conviction upheld by the Federal High Court of West Germany, three West Germans who spied for the Soviet Union were said to have passed about 15,000 documents to the Russians and to have betrayed 95 West German agents to the Soviet Union. *New York Times*, July 24, 1963, p. 1, col. 1. In this country, a Russian couple, Ivan D. and Aleksandra Egorov, both at the United Nations, were indicted for espionage. *New York Times*, July 17, 1963, p. 3, col. 1. Indicted with them were a Washington, D.C., couple, Robert K. and Joy Ann Baltch. *New York Times*, July 23, 1963, p. 3, col. 2.

For an account of interrogations of the Swedish colonel, see Eighty-eighth Congress, Second Session, United States Senate, Committee on the Judiciary, Subcommittee on Internal Security, *The Wennerstroem Spy Case* (Washington: Government Printing Office, 1964).

4. William Costello, *The Facts About Nixon* (New York: Viking, 1960), p. 121. The modus vivendi is also discussed in Robert J. Donovan, *The Inside Story* (New York: Harper and Brothers, 1956), p. 267. With more sense of recent history than some of the Congressional Republicans showed, President Eisenhower's answer to the comment that the administration would be accused of doing nothing if it did not offer military help to the French: "Well, they've said that before. They said it about the Democrats during the Chinese situation in the forties. And they said it about Stimson when the Japanese invaded Manchuria in the early thirties." Sherman Adams, *Firsthand Report* (New York: Popular Library, 1962), p. 127.

Castro made a spectacular visit to the United States (and Canada) during which he lunched with Christian A. Herter (who was soon to replace Dulles), visited with Vice President Richard Nixon at his home, met with members of the House Committee on Foreign Affairs and the Senate Committee on Foreign Relations, spoke to newspaper editors and to the Press Club, was received by Mayor Robert Wagner of New York, and appeared at a rally of 30,000 people in Central Park. If Mao Tze-tung ever visited Vice President Wallace at *his* home, there is no public record of the event.

The contrast between what was thought to be news in 1953 and in 1963 is striking but it did not really take a whole ten years for the tension about Communists and their activities in Washington to subside and dissipate. The remarkable thing is that the tension seemed to vanish with the condemnation of McCarthy by the United States Senate in December 1954. Before this time he was front page news; after this time mention of him and of his activities was to be found on the inside pages near the shipping notices. What had he lost? Not his seat in the United States Senate, for there was never any thought that the Senate would expel him from the club. Not any committee positions, for he retained all he had had, except for the chairmanship of the Permanent Subcommittee on Investigations which the Republicans lost in the elections of 1954. Could he have been diminished by the fact that he could no longer run a committee? It does not seem likely when one recalls that he had never had a committee to run in 1950, 1951, and 1952 — years of strife and rage.

Did the tension relax because the Republicans were now in office and could be trusted to root out Reds, so that people might now turn their attention to other matters, confident that security had been won? To attribute the disappearance of the Communist issue to the appearance in power of trustworthy Republicans is to ignore two contrary indicators: first, the condemnation of McCarthy by the Senate was primarily the work of the Republicans in the executive and legislative branches (how could the exposure of Communists be assisted by the public condemnation of the champion of crusaders?), and second, of the three principal congressional actors in the agitation over communism, the most vocal and public at least — Martin Dies, Pat McCarran, and Joseph McCarthy — two had been Democrats, and they had been in the business longer than the Republicans were going to control the Congress.

It is one of the astonishments of politics that the deflation of McCarthy should have proceeded so completely and abruptly, and it will be one of the tasks of this chapter and the next to suggest an explanation. There is important political meaning in the fact that it was Congress that showed the most concern about domestic communism. It was not a concern equally shared by the executive establishment. Congress was the active agency in Washington officialdom from Dies to McCarthy in this matter and, as the issue originated there, so did it abate there. The alignment of Congress and the executive establishment in adversary stance created a stress of government that could have led to more serious disablement than the stultification of the Truman program had it not been relieved. But Congress was only the instrument through which the stress was laid on, not the force which pushed it, force which moved the executive too little and the legislature (in the opinion of some) too much. Before proceeding to a discussion of the collapse of communism is an *issue*, however, something will be said in summary about the *problem*, and about the role of Congress in dealing with it.

The Communist Problem: A Summary

In numbers the Communists in the United States have never even remotely achieved anything like a mass party, as earlier pages of this book have said. Even Senator McCarthy, certainly not one to keep the figure unnecessarily low, said at the opening of hearings in 1954 to determine who was lying in his dispute with the Army that there were only 54,714 members in 1950 and approximately 25,000 members in 1954.[5] It is true, however, that the numbers themselves are not an exact gauge of the possible influence of the membership, that a small tightly disciplined cadre can wield commanding leverage sometimes in larger organizations of which it is a part, that the establishment of controlled fronts can create an unstable but massive augmentation of the voices that guide them, and that — in the past, at least — it was possible for many to confuse Communist and liberal values, and thus to afford spurious credentials to real impostures.

Although the influence of Communists in labor unions is not the concern of this book, it may be said that the greatest success achieved by them was in fact won in the unions — for a time, that is, until the expulsion of Communist elements by the CIO in the postwar 1940's.

5. Eighty-third Congress, Second Session, United States Senate, Committee on Government Operations, Special Subcommittee on Investigations, *Special Senate Investigation of Charges and Countercharges Involving: Secretary of the Army Robert T. Stevens, John G. Adams, H. Struve Hensel and Senator Joe McCarthy, Roy M. Cohn, and Francis P. Carr, Hearings* (hereafter cited as *Army-McCarthy Hearings*). Most of the hearings, which came to 2,986 pages of record and took six weeks to compile, had nothing to do with the Communist movement but a great deal to do with questions of fact and assertion about McCarthy and his staff by Army spokesmen and about the Department of the Army by Senator McCarthy. The testimony on the size of the Communist Party was made by McCarthy as the opening witness.

The victories of the Communist elements in a number of unions came through discipline, financial strength, skill, and ruthlessness, and the successes came to pass, it may be said, partly through the valuable opposition of antiunion, antiliberal, and anti-New Deal forces which persisted in labeling popular programs with pejorative spleen as "Communist." [6]

Whatever might be said in extenuation of many of those who joined the party in the thirties out of liberal impulse, those who stayed in the party in the forties, or joined it then, could not be excused on grounds of amiable ignorance of the power aims of the Soviet Union or of the connection between the American party and the Soviet Union, especially after the Nazi-Soviet Pact of 1939 and the change in the party line in June 1941. The disavowal of communism for some preceded the pact, and for some, perhaps, occurred soon afterwards and progressed swiftly, but it was inevitable for any whose original attachment to the party was soluble in the candor and skepticism of reason working upon objective facts of public notice. Not all such attachments were soluble, however, and the Communist party continued to receive support from the willfully faithful.

Enough to constitute a "problem" remained in employments in Washington, in some instances encouraged and protected by comrades in petty complicity, or tolerated by superiors who gave them the benefit of doubts, or who went merely undiscovered by lax, clumsy, and inefficient security procedures in the charge of untrained and overworked functionaries. As compared with the freedom to act in labor unions, however, the latitude permitted Communists in government employment was narrow. Infiltration was not difficult, but what of "control"? Making policy in an agency is more like making a movie than directing a ballet — a movie for which there are several illegible scripts, three stars competing for the lead, two directors who hate each other, and trouble at the bank. And when the movie finally gets to the screens, there are a thousand critics who could have done it better. Communist party members were a source of income to the party treasury, and they can doubtless exercise marginal influence on policy, but the final product has to accord with the broad sense of what the opposition and the critics think is probably about right, else the departure from this standard will be rejected. In the McCarran hearings on the Institute of Pacific Relations much was made of the reports to Washington from Foreign Service officers in the field, but it was not demonstrated that the reports of dissatisfaction with the weaknesses of the Nationalist regime were objectively wrong, or even exaggerated.

6. This is the opinion also of Morris L. Ernst and David Loth, *Report on the American Communist* (New York: Holt, 1952), p. 41.

And although John Carter Vincent had a great deal to do with the final directives for the Marshall mission, his work had to be done in concert with others in the Department of State and the White House. Difficult as theft of classified material may be, it is probably easier to steal secrets from a major agency of the United States Government than to control its policy. It is of interest in this connection that the only hard information about Communist activity in Washington from 1948 to 1954 — provided by recusant Communists — concerned espionage, not policy influence.

There is a contrary view, namely that the achievements of espionage were trifling and that the principal accomplishments of Communists and their partners in government office were in the making and administration of policy. Chambers, it will be recalled, thought that the information provided by cooperative sources in government was relatively poor. By imaginary contrast to the poor pickings for spies, there is the veritable Golconda for the party policy entrepreneur to exploit. Harry Dexter White pushes for the pastoralization of Germany after the war, and State Department functionaries work to get Chiang to share his government with the Chinese Communists. But Germany was not pastoralized and Chiang did not share the power his enemies took by violence. Communists wanted the United States in the war against Japan in 1941 but, as has been said, so did Chiang and Churchill. It is not unfair to conclude that in the great questions of policy, the Communist position either accorded with an already prevailing conception of desirable American policy, or it was defeated. The China affair is no exception to this generalization. The United States did not enter the war against Japan in 1941 to save Chiang, or even China, but to save itself. And when it had done so, there was no strong urge to tarry then on the mainland of Asia. Even the occupation of Japan was limited to a few years.

But whether espionage or policy was the more important Communist activity in Washington in the thirties and the forties, and whatever the value of either, Communist activity was not insubstantial. The evidence establishes that there were at least five centers for the collection and transmission of information to the Soviet Union. The complicity of an Assistant Secretary of the Treasury, Harry Dexter White, was charged under oath and, although the charge was answered in a book after White's death, troublesome questions remain.[7] At least one person in the Department of Justice passed information to a Soviet agent as the trial of Judy Coplon made clear. Her conviction was re-

7. Two writers think that there is no question about the charge. James Rorty and Moshe Decter, *McCarthy and the Communists* (Boston: Beacon Press, 1954), pp. 5–6.

versed not because the prosecution had failed to prove the accusation but because it had used impermissible means to establish the principal facts. The complicity of a White House administrative assistant, Lauchlin Currie, was also charged under oath, but although he did meet the charge, many questions were unresolved. There was Communist activity in the Department of Agriculture, set in motion by Harold Ware.

It is established that persons in the Department of State were engaged in the transmission of papers to the Communists. In the *Amerasia* case, the evidence suggests that the magazine had access through the Department of State to a large number of classified papers originating in that department and in other agencies. The Institute of Pacific Relations was not a Communist organization, nor a Communist-front organization, but there were members of the Communist Party among its officials and it did have a close relationship with the Department of State.

There was Communist activity in the Government Printing Office. There was Communist activity in the Office of Strategic Services. There was a brisk Communist enterprise in the National Labor Relations Board. It is also clear that there were active members of the Communist movement in such other agencies of government as the Board of Economic Warfare, the International Monetary Fund, the staffs of certain Senate subcommittees, and elsewhere in officialdom. It is not necessary to add to the detail of the preceding pages to conclude that there was a substantial Communist activity in the Federal government, that it consisted in part in the procurement of classified information for the use of the Soviet government, and that the members of it were fully aware of the reprehensible nature of their undertaking.

Congress Presses the White House

The employment of Communists in the government service posed a problem about which the executive agencies were less quick than Congress to act extensively or very decisively, although they were not indifferent. Rules on the subject were initiated by Congress in 1938.[8] It is usually assumed that the Hatch Act of 1938 was the first

8. Eighty-fourth Congress, First Session, United States Senate, Committee on Government Operations, Subcommittee on Reorganization, Hearing on S. J. Res. 21, *A Joint Resolution to Establish a Commission on Government Security* (hereafter cited as *Government Security Commission Hearings*), for an extensive inquiry into the loyalty and security program of the Federal government. With the loss of the Republican majority in the 1954 elections, the chairmanship of the Committee on Government Operations fell to Senator John L. McClellan of Arkansas, with Senator McCarthy the ranking member of the minority. The chairman of the Subcommittee on Reorganization was Senator John F. Kennedy of Massachusetts, but the hearings were conducted by Senator Hubert Humphrey

regulation on loyalty and security, but concern for these matters dates back to the Civil War.[9] Civil Service Commission investigations before 1939, however, were limited to character and competence, and political affiliation was not questioned.[10] In February 1940 a question was added to the standard application for government employment that embodied the language of the Hatch Act, Section 9A of which forbade "membership in any political party or organization which advocates the overthrow of our constitutional form of government in the United States" to employees of the Federal government. Later, the standard question was whether the applicant advocated, had ever advocated, or belonged to or had ever belonged to any organization advocating the overthrow of the Government of the United States by force or violence. Early in 1942, President Roosevelt issued War Service Regulation II which disqualified for civil service examination or appointment to the Federal service any person whose loyalty to the United States Government was in reasonable doubt. Congress in 1940 and 1942 gave the Secretaries of War and Navy and the Coast Guard the power to remove summarily any employee thought to be a risk of the national security, and in 1946 this authority was extended to the Secretary of State, and later, to the Secretaries of Defense and the Air Force.

Congress in 1941 voted $100,000 for the investigation by the Department of Justice of disloyalty complaints against Federal employees, the department to report its findings to the Congress and to the heads of the departments involved. The investigations were conducted by the FBI which was advised by Attorney General Francis Biddle that membership in the Communist Party, the German-American Bund, or seven other organizations would constitute questionable loyalty. But

---

of Minnesota as Acting Chairman. As a result of the subcommittee's investigation, an *ad hoc* Commission on Government Security was appointed — four members by the President and four each by the President of the Senate and the Speaker of the House of Representatives — to investigate and report on the need for revision of the loyalty and security procedures of the Federal government. The commission was aided by a Citizens' Advisory Committee, and it submitted its report on June 21, 1957, which was printed as a public document as *Report of the Commission on Government Security, Pursuant to Public Law 304, Eighty-fourth Congress, as Amended* (hereafter cited as *Report of the Commission on Government Security*).

9. *Report of the Commission on Government Security*, p. 5.

10. The same limitation did not apply to FBI investigations. For an interesting account of the authorization arranged for the FBI to conduct general investigations into subversive activities in 1936, see Don Whitehead, *The FBI Story* (New York: Random House, 1956), pp. 158–160. Taking advantage of a quirk in the Appropriation Act under which the FBI operated, President Roosevelt arranged for the Department of State to request the Attorney General to make the necessary investigations. What the FBI got was a secret directive from President Roosevelt through Secretary of State Cordell Hull.

although there were plenty of regulations — the Hatch Act, War Service Regulation II, the Attorney General's list — there was no strong desire in the agencies to proceed very far or fast with loyalty checks. The Attorney General's report to Congress on September 1, 1942, contained figures that demonstrated this sharply. The FBI said that 1,597 cases containing derogatory information had been supplied to the heads of departments and agencies for advice as to whether investigation should be conducted. After three months, only 193 cases had been authorized for investigation; 254 had been returned with the notation that no investigation was desired; and the receipt of the remaining 1,150 cases was not even acknowledged by the agencies. In view of this, the Attorney General told the employing departments and agencies on October 21, 1941, that he had instructed the FBI to proceed with investigations of this kind without reference to the employing agency at all.[11]

In April 1942, the Attorney General created an Interdepartmental Committee on Investigations which almost immediately expressed its unhappiness about its responsibility and its reluctance to serve. In a report on June 30, 1942, it objected to the duty laid upon it, thought that investigations had produced little result commensurate with the resources invested, and said that the agencies were inexperienced in security work, that FBI agents were being diverted from wartime employments, that membership in Communist fronts was not a crime, and that although there was some evidence of irresponsibility among some Federal workers, it was not often a cause for disciplinary action.[12] The Interdepartmental Committee deprecated general personnel investigations and suggested that inquiries be limited to instances of serious suspicion of delinquency.

By 1943 there were two different standards of loyalty for Federal employees.[13] The Interdepartmental Committee was using the standard of membership in organizations declared to be subversive by the Attorney General in accord with congressional desire. The Civil Service Commission was using the standard of "reasonable doubt." A subcommittee of the House Civil Service Committee reported in July 1946 that the existence of two standards was causing confusion, and recommended that the agencies adopt a uniform and consistent policy. One trouble was that persons rejected by one agency on loyalty

11. *Government Security Commission Hearings*, testimony of Assistant Attorney General William F. Tompkins, p. 82.

12. "A Report to the Honorable Francis Biddle, Attorney General of the United States, From the Interdepartmental Committee on Investigations, Pursuant to Public Law No. 135, June 30, 1942," reprinted in *Government Security Commission Hearings*, pp. 83–90.

13. *Report of the Commission on Government Security*, p. 8.

grounds were being accepted by others. On the subcommittee of three, the Democrats of course had two members, since the Democrats were in the majority in Congress. The minority member was Edward H. Rees, Republican, of Kansas, who filed a minority report that was considerably sterner than that of the majority in that it called for a far-reaching enforcement of loyalty procedures in the Federal service, said that the criterion of decision should be "reasonable doubt" of loyalty, and urged that all doubts should be resolved in favor of the government. The importance of this statement lies in its timing. It represented a widespread Republican view in Congress in the summer of 1946 that a substantial effort to ascertain the loyalty of Federal employees had never been really made, that it should be made, and that the Republicans, if they should win a majority in Congress, would see that it was made.[14]

The election of 1946 was an odd one in that the professional leaders of the Democratic party, whose chief was President of the United States, seemed more embarrassed than pleased that it was Harry Truman. Or, to put it more directly, President Truman seemed to be more of a liability than an asset. A national poll disclosed that only a quarter of the people asked thought that he was doing a satisfactory job. In October he went back to Independence, Missouri, so as not to remind too many that he was President (presumably), and instead of having him put on one of his vigorous whistle-stop campaigns for the Democrats, the chairman of the Democratic National Committee played old Roosevelt records on the radio instead. The Republicans for the first time since 1928 succeeded in winning majorities in both houses of the Congress.[15]

The election took place on November 5. On November 25, 1946, President Truman issued Executive Order 9806 establishing a temporary Commission on Loyalty, with one representative each from the Departments of Justice, State, Treasury, War, Navy, and the Civil Service Commission, and he directed it to give consideration to the findings and recommendations of the House Civil Service subcom-

14. Ralph S. Brown, Jr., *Loyalty and Security, Employment Tests in the United States* (New Haven: Yale, 1958), pp. 22–23, briefly describes some of the circumstances presumably leading to the establishment of the Truman loyalty program — the collapse of the wartime alliance with the Soviet Union and the beginning of the Cold War — but omits any reference to the domestic political situation, which was the efficient cause.

15. Brown at another place does argue that loyalty and security tests are, in some sense, political in character although not as an issue between Republicans and Democrats. It is a "political" decision to define politics in such a way as to exclude Communist activity, on the assumption that communism is a struggle for power which, if it should succeed, would eliminate those very liberal democratic procedures for the making of policy that we normally think of as "politics." *Loyalty and Security,* pp. 10–11.

mittee. The temporary commission heard witnesses from various agencies and from Congressmen Rees and J. M. Combs of Texas, the latter having been chairman of the House Civil Service subcommittee. The commission concluded that the employment of disloyal persons was more than a contingent and remote risk to the government, although it was not able to say how serious it was. It did say, however, that certain events constituted evidence that the threat existed, among them the report in Canada in June 1946 of the disclosures of Igor Gouzenko, a clerk in the Soviet Embassy in Ottawa, whose testimony, and the evidence of documents he had taken, led to the conviction of Klaus Fuchs in England and of the Rosenbergs in the United States for transmitting atomic secrets to the Soviet Union.[16]

The pressure on the Administration from Congress led to the promulgation of Executive Order 9835, which set up the first comprehensive and systematic effort to screen Federal employees for subversive connections. The report of the temporary commission was made public the day after the promulgation of Executive Order 9835. The standard for refusal of employment on loyalty grounds was that, on all the evidence, "reasonable grounds exist for the belief that the person involved is disloyal to the Government of the United States." [17] Loyalty investigations, mandatory for all new employees, were to be completed within eighteen months of entry upon service; and all incumbents were to be given investigations, with a right to administrative review of adverse determinations, and ultimate review by a Loyalty Review Board set up in the Civil Service Commission. Although the basic executive order was later amended for improved clarity, the fact is that there was no very clear standard for the agencies to follow.[18] A study of the loyalty program made by an Interdepartmental Committee of the National Security Council in cooperation with the Civil Service Commission recommended, on April 29, 1952, that the

16. Early works on the subect are Alan Moorehead, *The Traitors* (New York: Harper and Row, 1952, 1963) and Oliver Pilat, *The Atom Spies* (New York: G. P. Putnam's Sons, 1952). Both, it will be noted, were originally published in 1952. The Moorehead book was reprinted in 1963 with a new preface. For an exposition of the view that there was no atomic secret and no atom spy plot, and that the whole affair was the manufacture of militarists, politicians, and financiers fighting against peace, see William A. Reuben, *The Atom Spy Hoax* (New York: Action Books, 1955). For an exposition of the view that the Rosenbergs were "framed," that they were political victims of the Cold War and convenient scapegoats for the Korean War whose deaths were to be a symbolic warning to terrify and silence all liberals and dissenters, see John Wexley, *The Judgment of Julius and Ethel Rosenberg* (New York: Cameron and Kahn, 1955). The most recent account of atomic espionage is Ralph de Toledano, *The Greatest Plot in History* (New York: Duell, Sloan and Pearce, 1963).

17. *Report of the Commission on Government Security*, pp. 9–10.

18. For a review of the problems of the Truman loyalty program, see Eleanor Bontecou, *The Federal Loyalty-Security Program* (Ithaca: Cornell, 1953).

standard be changed to "reason to believe that the employment or retention of the individual in a sensitive position would be prejudicial to the national security." [19]

One of the chief difficulties in the administration of the Truman loyalty program had been the rigidity of the loyalty test itself. As one of the witnesses before the security commission put it,

> Only when it was clearly demonstrated that an individual was presently disloyal was any action generally taken under that program. The standard used for refusal of employment, namely, "reasonable grounds for belief" that the person involved was disloyal, was found to be inadequate to cover the security aspect of our government.[20]

But when one considers the responsibility of the agencies to make the loyalty program work, sight should not be lost of the authority vested in many of the agencies by Congress to cut through the complexities and ambiguities of the order to remove summarily any person whose continued employment was not in the national interest or involved or threatened national security. And in removing employees for these reasons, it was not necessary for the department head to present reasons or hold a hearing. Had such summary dismissals taken place throughout the government, there doubtless would have been a storm of protest by worried critics who found much to disapprove in the program as it was.[21]

Still another committee was appointed by President Truman to make sense out of the tangle of regulations, statutes, orders, procedures, and practices that had become the lacework of Federal rules on loyalty. A committee headed by L. V. Meloy of the Civil Service Commission with members supplied by five agencies began to work in October 1952 on the formulation of a consistent set of rules that would cover loyalty, security, and suitability proeedings but it never finished its work because of the change in administration after the election of 1952. Disbanding in February 1953 it did get far enough to propose a new executive order that would have suited the requirements of the government with fairness to the employee or applicant.[22]

President Truman had forestalled the enactment by the Republican Congress of harsh and coercive legislation in 1947, and he anticipated

19. *Report of the Commission on Government Security*, p. 11.

20. *Government Security Commission Hearings*, p. 91.

21. For example, see "The Loyalty Order — Procedure Termed Inadequate and Defects Pointed Out," a letter signed by four professors at the Harvard Law School and published in the *New York Times*, April 13, 1947.

22. For a list of 16 factors bearing upon the suitability of the employee or applicant for Federal employment, see *Report of the Commission on Government Security*, pp. 15-16.

the revision of the loyalty-security system that the Eisenhower administration was to effect. But, in both instances, he just barely managed to act in time. Indeed, he was almost overtaken by Congressman Rees of Kansas who continued to push for congressional regulation of loyalty and security affairs despite Executive Order 9835. Congressman Rees convened the House Committee on Post Office and Civil Service in June 1947 to consider the enactment of H. R. 3588, a proposed Federal Employees Loyalty Act, which required investigations of all Federal employees to determine their loyalty, first by the Civil Service Commission and then, upon the discovery of derogatory information, by the Federal Bureau of Investigation. A Loyalty Review Board within the Civil Service Commission would have been set up to review all reports of loyalty investigations by the FBI, and it would have been empowered to enforce all adverse decisions. That is, all agency heads would have been required to refuse employment to or to discharge any person judged disloyal by the board. This would have taken the removal power away from the executive branch in matters of loyalty and security, and objection was laid against the bill by the Attorney General and the Civil Service Commission on the ground of possible unconstitutionality.[23]

On April 27, 1953, President Eisenhower issued Executive Order 10450 which shifted the standard of eligibility for employment in the Federal service from loyalty to security, that is, the test of suitability (apart from competence, experience, and other personal qualifications) was "whether the employment and retention in employment of any civilian officer or employee . . . is clearly consistent with the interests of the national security." [24] Three sets of criteria were established for the determination of security suitability which accord closely with the recommendations made by the Meloy Committee in February

23. In the case of *U.S. v. Lovett,* 328 U.S. 303 (1946), decided the year before the Rees bill, the Supreme Court had held unconstitutional an attempt by Martin Dies of Texas, with the support of the Congress, to force the removal of three men he charged with being loyalty-security risks. The sanction was to forbid the payment of any United States moneys to the three unless the President sent their names to the United States Senate for confirmation. The proviso was attached as a rider to the Urgent Deficiencies Act of 1943. President Roosevelt did not comply with the requirement of Senate confirmation. The men were not paid; they remained on their jobs and sued the United States in the Court of Claims for the salaries they said were owed them. Although there was no forced removal by Congress in this case, and the ground of the decision was violation of the ex post facto clause of the Constitution, it did constitute an interference by Congress with the presidential power of removal and, in this aspect, was in accord with previous decisions protecting the presidential power from invasion.

24. For a collection of pertinent statutes, executive orders, and regulations on security, see the appendixes to *Report of the Special Committee on the Federal Loyalty-Security Program of the Association of the Bar of the City of New York* (New York: Dodd, Mead, 1956).

1953 before it went out of existence. Executive Order 10450 also extended to all agencies the power to separate summarily those whose employment constituted an unacceptable security risk. The later review of the Federal loyalty-security program conducted by the Commission on Government Security, however, urged a return to the loyalty standard as the guiding principle in loyalty-security proceedings instead of the format of Executive Order 10450.[25]

Many of those who were separated from Federal employment on security grounds in 1953 and 1954 were found unsuitable because of personal traits that did not involve loyalty, but in the publication of such figures by the Civil Service Commission, the unwary could have concluded that the Eisenhower administration had discovered coveys of Communists and fellow travelers left over from the Truman administration. Three weeks before the election of 1954, Vice President Richard Nixon got the Civil Service Commission to announce figures on separations under the new security program. It was reported that 6,926 Federal employees had been dismissed or had resigned under the new program, and that of these, 1,743 had had data in their files indicating some degree of some kind of subversive connection. It was disclosed well over a year later that 41.2 per cent of the dismissed or resigned security risks had actually been hired after the Eisenhower administration took office.[26] The exact number of dismissals under the Truman and Eisenhower programs from 1947 through 1956 is greatly speculative, but it has been estimated that the total number of Federal service employees dismissed (not counting those in Federal employments in private service) was 3,900.[27]

Although the tension between Congress and the executive establishment over loyalty and security programs in the Roosevelt and Truman administrations was to relax in the Eisenhower years, Republican spokesmen until the election of 1954 continued to make something of the lack of diligence they said had characterized the Truman effort, and the most sensational of these accusations was that of Attorney General Herbert Brownell in November 1953. Speaking before the Executives' Club in Chicago, Brownell revived the almost forgotten case of Harry Dexter White, charging that President Truman had appointed White (then Assistant Secretary of the Treasury) as executive director of the International Monetary Fund despite knowledge of the FBI report that accused White of spying for the Soviet Union.[28]

25. *Report of the Commission on Government Security*, pp. 41–46.
26. Earl Mazo, *Richard Nixon* (New York: Harper and Brothers, 1959), p. 156.
27. See the tabulation of Brown, *Loyalty and Security*, pp. 487–488.
28. *New York Times*, November 7, 1953, p. 1, col. 8. See also chap. VI, n. 113, above, for a brief account of the accusations against White and the defense of him written after his death by his brother.

Brownell had discussed making public his information with Sherman Adams and James Hagerty, the President's press secretary, before mentioning it to President Eisenhower.[29] When he discussed it with Eisenhower, the President did not go into the details of the case — he was later to say that he was even vague about who White was — but trusted his Attorney General's judgment about making the charges.[30] This conversation was enough presumably to justify Hagerty's assertion that the Brownell speech on White had been cleared with the President.[31]

Chairman Harold Velde of the House Committee on Un-American Activities immediately subpoenaed former President Truman, former Secretary of State James Byrnes, and former Attorney General (and now Associate Justice of the Supreme Court) Tom Clark to appear before the committee to testify on the White case.[32] Like the frog in the fable who tried to inflate himself to the size of the envied ox, Chairman Velde strove to match the enormity of Senator McCarthy, but he was not alone in wishing to give McCarthy some competition. According to Sherman Adams, Brownell thought that his sensational accusation "would take away some of the glamour of the McCarthy stage play." [33] Congressman Francis Walter, former chairman of the House Committee on Un-American Activities, expressed the view that Velde's move was just a spurt in a race for headlines between the House committee and the Senate Internal Security subcommittee, now under the chairmanship of Senator William Jenner of Indiana.[34]

Eisenhower gave Velde and Brownell little support at his next news conference when he said that he would not have subpoenaed Truman or Clark, that it was inconceivable that Truman would knowingly do anything to damage the United States, and that he, the President, had left the decision on the White disclosure to Brownell.[35] James Byrnes refused to honor the subpoena on states' rights grounds;[36] Truman refused to honor the subpoena on constitutional grounds;[37] and Justice Clark followed suit.[38] The White House acted to dissociate the President from the White controversy when Hagerty said that Eisenhower had only briefly discussed the Brownell speech with the Attorney General on November 2, that the President had not seen nor approved

29. Adams, *Firsthand Report*, p. 139.
30. Adams, *Firsthand Report*, pp. 139–140.
31. *New York Times*, November 7, 1953, p. 11, col. 6.
32. *New York Times*, November 11, 1953, p. 1, col. 8.
33. Adams, *Firsthand Report*, p. 140.
34. *New York Times*, November 11, 1953, p. 19, col. 3.
35. *New York Times*, November 12, 1953, p. 1, col. 8.
36. *New York Times*, November 12, 1953, p. 19, col. 1.
37. *New York Times*, November 13, 1953, p. 1, col. 8.
38. *New York Times*, November 14, 1953, p. 1, col. 7.

an advance copy of the speech, and that no clearance had been sought, which was somewhat different from the earlier assertion that clearance had been obtained.[39]

Former President Truman defended himself with asperity in a national address broadcast by radio and television. He charged that Attorney General Brownell had lied in saying that Truman knew that White was a spy when he appointed him to the International Monetary Fund, that the Attorney General had lied again in attempting to impugn his loyalty, and that Brownell had deceived President Eisenhower about his plans before the Chicago speech was made.[40] With Velde knocked out in the political roughhouse, members of the Senate jumped into the melee. Senator McCarthy undertook to answer Truman — also on radio and television — because Truman had said that the Eisenhower administration had embraced McCarthyism for political ends, and since he had been mentioned, the junior Senator from Wisconsin asked for and got time to reply. The burden of the answer was that the White case was not an isolated instance of the failure of the Truman administration to oust Communists from government, and the prediction was made that the issue would be an important one in the 1954 elections.[41] This was poor prophecy.

The weight of the Senate assault, however, was carried by the Internal Security subcommittee under the leadership of Jenner of Indiana.[42] Attorney General Brownell and FBI director J. Edgar Hoover both testified before the subcommittee. Brownell said that Truman had been warned by the FBI in 1945 and 1946 of spy rings operating within the government and, although he denied charging

39. *New York Times*, November 17, 1953, p. 1, col. 6.
40. *New York Times*, November 17, 1953, p. 26, col. 1.
41. *New York Times*, November 25, 1953, p. 1, col. 5.
42. For a summary account of the proceedings before the Internal Security subcommittee, see the following references in the *New York Times:* November 18, 1953, p. 1, col. 7; November 18, 1953, p. 1, col. 8. In October 1953, the Permanent Subcommittee on Investigations had held hearings into the transfer to the Soviet government in 1944 of plates for the printing of occupation currency. The testimony of Elizabeth Bentley was that she had obtained copies of the currency for reproduction by the Soviets, that they had been unable to make good copies, that pressure had then been put on Harry Dexter White by instruction of her superiors in espionage to have the United States officially supply the Soviets with the currency plates. In the course of the hearings, the names of former government employees who were alleged to have engaged in espionage — and who had been mentioned in the original Hiss hearings — were mentioned again. The subcommittee anticipated by a month, then, the revival of the name of Harry Dexter White. See Eighty-third Congress, First Session, United States Senate, Committee on Government Operations, Permanent Subcommittee on Investigations, *Hearings on Transfer of Occupation Currency Plates — Espionage Phase;* and *Transfer of Occupation Currency Plates — Espionage Phase, Interim Report*, S. Rept. 837, December 15, 1953. For a summary account of the subcommittee interim report, see *New York Times*, December 16, 1953, p. 29, col. 3.

Truman with disloyalty, he did insist that the former President and
his staff had been unwilling to recognize the perils of Communist espionage in government. Hoover testified that memoranda on White
had been sent to the White House on November 8, 1945 and thereafter, certainly before Truman nominated White for the post with
the International Monetary Fund in January 1946. What seems clear,
as related earlier in the discussion of the White case, is that Truman
found out about White too late to have his name withdrawn before
the Senate confirmed the appointment.[43]

The White affair was a sudden flash — bright, hot, and brief — in
a number of small fires that Republican investigators were patiently
blowing on without much success, not for lack of wind but for lack
of fuel. Even the White case was five years old. The Jenner committee thought that the Canadian spy case might be good for another
try and asked the Department of State to request the Canadian government for permission to question Igor Gouzenko.[44] Although the
Canadian Prime Minister replied that Gouzenko had no new information, a note was sent to Secretary of State Dulles to permit members
of the Internal Security subcommittee to question Gouzenko, but only
under Canadian auspices in conformity with Canadian procedure, and
only if no evidence were published except with Canadian consent.
These conditions were certainly discouraging to investigators who
expected more of a show, and the whole enterprise seemed to collapse
when Gouzenko said that he did not want to be interviewed by the
subcommittee because he had no new data anyway, and the safety of
his family might be jeopardized. The Internal Security subcommittee
then did the next best thing — if they could not make a show of
Gouzenko, they could make a show of some of Gouzenko's data. Accordingly, the subcommittee published secret FBI material that had
been supplied by Gouzenko charging that a Soviet agent in the office
of Fleet Admiral Ernest J. King may have given data on the proximity
fuse to the Soviet Union in 1945. The alleged spy was identified as
"X." But then the subcommittee decided to accept the Canadian terms
after all, and Gouzenko agreed to be interviewed. Senators Jenner and
McCarran of the Internal Security subcommittee conferred with

43. Although he gives this fact a partisan twist, even Sherman Adams confirms
the statement that Truman, after conversation with Byrnes, ordered one of his
staff aides to call the Secretary of the Senate, "only to find out that the Senate
had already approved the nomination." Adams, *Firsthand Report*, p. 141.
44. For a running newspaper account of the Internal Security subcommittee and Gouzenko, see *New York Times*, November 20, 1953, p. 1, col. 2;
November 22, 1953, p. 1, col. 5; November 26, 1953, p. 1, col. 1; December 1,
1953, p. 2, col. 4; December 2, 1953, p. 1, col. 2; December 3, 1953, p. 1, col. 3;
December 11, 1953, p. 1, col. 2; January 1, 1954, p. 8, col. 4.

Gouzenko in Canada, quietly, without fuss, and without the knock-about fun of hearings in one of the rumpus rooms of the Senate.

The Politics of Prescriptive Publicity

To summarize at this point — congressional concern about possible disloyal activity sharpened in 1938 as the passage of the Hatch Act and the establishment of the House Committee on Un-American Activities attest. Administration representatives did not seem to regard possible subversive activity in the government as seriously as did critics in the Congress; and it was not until the war was over, and the administration had lost its majorities in the House and Senate, that it undertook a comprehensive loyalty-security program throughout the government, under pressure from Congress. For at least nine years, then, from 1938 to 1947, the line of tension over subversion and security found Congress on one side in the active, and even offensive posture, and the administration on the other, in an attitude of guardedness and wary assurance, convinced in its impassivity that the motives of congressional critics were largely impure in that they contained elements of personal ambition, partisan antagonism, and historic hostility, fixed in the constitutional separation of powers and fed by rivalry to control the courses of statecraft. Were these in fact the reasons for the increasing stress of government in the late forties and early fifties? Let us look first at the element of personal ambition in the committees of Congress.

Ambition, of course, played a strong role in the stimulation of the controversy over communism in Washington, although it can have played only a collateral part, since Congressmen after 1954 were presumably still ambitious but none could make great political capital out of the issue. Congressmen in charge of sensational investigations enjoyed a notoriety which for some, doubtless, had rich psychic compensations, and there was always the prospect of political reward. The prospect was always better than the reality, however. Martin Dies, whose example was followed by a dozen grand inquisitors, withdrew from politics in the face of increasing risk of loss in his congressional district. J. Parnell Thomas, who succeeded him as chairman of the House Committee on Un-American Activities in the Eightieth Congress, went to jail. Congressman John Wood of Georgia, who succeeded Thomas, and Wood's successor, Harold Velde of Illinois, laid no foundation for substantial political careers. On the Senate side, McCarthy was condemned by the Senate (and thereby ruined politically) and William Jenner of Indiana eventually yielded his seat to a Democratic newcomer. Francis Walter of Pennsylvania, Pat McCarran of

Nevada, and Karl Mundt of South Dakota stayed within their competences and doubtless would have been re-elected even if they had never headed important investigations. Of the ten or a dozen principal investigators between 1938 and 1954, the only one who was able to make his success lead to higher political office was Richard Nixon. But however much or little the investigators exploited their positions for psychological or other personal advantages, ambition alone cannot account for the prominence given to the Communist issue. However these chanticleers may have flapped their wings and crowed, it was not they who made the red sun rise.

Second, party identification does not explain the vigor of the congressional investigations either. From 1938 to 1947, it was the Democratic Martin Dies and a committee with a Democratic majority that investigated possible subversion in a Democratic administration. From 1949 to 1953, it was the Democratic Pat McCarran with a Democratic committee that investigated the suspected delinquencies of the Democratic administrations of the 1940's. The Democratic Francis Walter was no less fervent a chairman of the House Committee on Un-American Activities than the Republican J. Parnell Thomas. The Republican Senator Joseph McCarthy gave the Republican administration of President Eisenhower trying times in the investigations of Fort Monmouth and the Department of State, and in the controversy over the Department of the Army. It was the lame duck Republican Eighty-third Congress that condemned McCarthy. Great majorities from both parties regularly voted funds to continue the investigations. The only partisan investigation — in which the Democrats and the Republicans were on opposite sides — was the Tydings inquiry in 1950, when the Democratic Tydings defended the Democratic Department of State from accusations by McCarthy.

Third, personal ambition and partisan identification, although not without significance to an understanding of the Communist controversy, do not adequately explain the fervor and persistence of the congressional inquiries of sixteen years. What, then, of the separation of powers? It may be said, provisionally, that the separation of powers accounts for the *form* that congressional inquiries into communism took, but it is first necessary, in order to appreciate most accurately the significance of this question of form, to state analytically the systematic elements within which it takes on importance. It appears in the struggle with the Executive over the control of the President's own administration; in the historical congressional claim of a constitutional right to force from officials of the administration papers and other information, a claim which Presidents since George Washington have always rejected when they thought it necessary to do so, or when it was inconvenient to comply; in the development of such institutions as senatorial courtesy, which is a limitation on the presidential power of appointment; in the practice that excludes the presence of the President in the houses of Congress unless he is invited; and so on. Although Woodrow Wilson when President did not always act as though he thought the center of government was located in Congress, he once wrote that it was; and Congress, although it knows that one end of Pennsylvania Avenue represents an America of millions, is equally sure that the other end represents the millions of America, with coordinate authority.

Except for contempts of Congress, the legislative branch has no independent power — nor, indeed, any power — to see that the laws are executed. It can supervise the manner in which the Executive performs this constitutional function, and of course does so regularly in the consideration of estimates of appropriation, and upon other occasions when the circumstance seems to warrant it. It can reorganize all of the agencies of the executive branch; it can abolish all of the agencies of the executive branch, and of the judiciary (except the office of Chief Justice) if it so desires; it can vest the appointment of all inferior officers of the government in the President, the heads of departments, or in the courts; it can refuse appropriations for any agency; it can prescribe the rules of procedure that all of the quasi-judicial agencies must follow — it can do all of these things, and yet it cannot enforce the law or administer the programs that it sees fit to entrust to the Executive. This is the executive power, and under the Constitution of the United States it is the President who sees that the laws are faithfully executed.

The three branches of the Federal government are political agencies of public control. Together they constitute a system of interlocking institutions by which this control is made legitimate. Each of the branches has a function of its own in the process by which legitimacy is ascribed to rules, regulations, acts, orders, decrees, and other commands intended to have the characteristic of officiality. Each of the branches has a ritual of its own by which notice of this intention is made public.

The special function of Congress may be stated in the following propositions: that Congress is an agency for making public control legitimate through the negotiation of alternatives of policy; that this negotiation occurs for the most part among publicly-oriented voluntary associations and political parties which provide vital links between the government and the citizenry; that while Congress mediates the negotiation, it also enters into it as a party in interest to serve values which are broader than the sum of the immediate stakes; and that one of these values is the corporate interest of Congress as a public institution. The Federal legislature is a miniature and inaccurate reproduction of the social structure with which it deals, being skewed in its representativeness in favor of white, Protestant, nonurban, better-off elements, economically and educationally. However, it tends to correspond remarkably well in its goal and value orientations with the most stable, enduring, and politically significant (i.e., influential) sectors of the society.

Congress follows certain procedures — "rituals" — in performing its functions which are less formalistic and rigid than either those of the Executive or the courts. A hearing, for example, can be virtually what a committee wishes it to be as to agenda, tempo, breadth of participation, and appeal. The Senate has unlimited debate — it makes and unmakes rules as it goes along, as when it suspends the rules to do something that the "rules" forbid. The rituals of Congress are characterized by accessibility, flexibility, mutability, and sociability, these being attributes that support its role as negotiator among the manifold groups that make up the society.

The normal result when Congress performs its legislative function according to the proper ritual is *prescription*, that is to say, a rule of action, authoritatively defined.

The special function of the Executive may be stated in the following propositions: that the Executive is an agency for making public control legitimate by acts to obtain compliance with the prescriptions of Congress, under conditions in which the enforcement of the rule is either voluntarily acknowledged as valid by the individual or group against which it is applied, or is said to be valid by the courts. There are other functions vested in the Executive besides enforcement but this is central. For example, the President has some portion of the function of prescription when he proposes legislation, supports the claims of groups pressing for new rules from Congress, vetoes bills submitted to him, and so on. In addition, he has other activities that engage him,[45] but the distinguishing characteristic of the Executive is his command of force.

The rituals of the Executive that validate its authority are more formal and rigid than those of the Congress, but are less formal and rigid than those of the courts. There are two limiting influences that produce greater rigidity in the rituals of the Executive as compared with those of the Congress. The first is that the executive function applies to prescriptions already established — its authority to invent prescriptions is narrow. Second, the custom of the culture which refuses

45. See Clinton Rossiter, *The American Presidency* (New York: Harcourt, Brace, 1956) for an exposition of the many roles of the office.

validity to some executive action without the approval of the courts has brought the judges into a share of the executive function. They sometimes refuse validation unless the Executive modifies its behavior in accordance with judicial specifications. In an extreme case, like that of the quasi-judicial agencies, the only ritual tolerated by the judges is that which imitates the judicial mode.

The normal result when the Executive performs its enforcing function according to the proper ritual is *proceeding*.

The special function of the Courts may be stated in the following propositions: that the Courts are an agency for making public control legitimate by validating the enforcement of prescriptions. To some extent the judges share the legislative function in that judges make prescriptions without recourse to the legislature. When they do so they act in the absence of those conditions that secure acceptability for congressional acts — public hearing, debate about alternatives, and open votes. An example of judge-made prescription is the invention of the segregation formula in 1896 and its rejection in 1954.

The rituals of the Courts are the most formal and rigid of all the branches of the government. The forms of address are austere and distant, on some benches the mode of dress is different from that of other functionaries of the government, the forms of pleading and argument are stiffly conventional, the utmost care is taken to prepare a "record," the rules of evidence limit the nature of testimony which judges and juries may heed in making decisions, and so on. These rituals are historically hallowed, and represent a conscious and studied effort to symbolize deliberation, solemnity, and objectivity.

The function of validation performed by the Courts is *judgment*.

Government as a system of public control then establishes legal status for new norms through the cooperative action of three principal interlocking institutions, each of which has its special function in the process, and a suitable ritual by which it is performed. The normal products of these functions, and the sequence in which, analytically, they occur, are prescription, proceeding, and judgment. The formalizing of new norms is always accompanied by a certain amount of tension among the groups that stand to lose or gain by the rule, for a prescription distributes both rewards and deprivations. It is in the nature of such a norm that while it serves and augments the values of some groups, it may work changes in or adversely affect those of others. All the agencies of government are concerned with the equitable balance of these values — with the adjustment of conflicts of principle. The group tension is verbalized in a clash of claims about the importance to the society of the values enhanced and the values modified.

Four points may be made about the special function of Congress, which is prescription: (1) that Congress has a social organization and a corporate interest; (2) that the role of Congress as legislator may be discussed in terms of the principal parts into which the process of prescription may be divided — ascertainment, deliberation, and enactment; (3) that Congress sometimes employs a procedure that may be characterized as *prescriptive publicity*; and (4) that the value conflicts stirred by the exercise of prescriptive publicity show some pattern.

As to the element of corporate interest, it may be said that the behavior of Congress shows status and role patterns and rituals that tend to reinforce the self-perception of Congressmen as the "people's tribunes," "guardians of the national interest," and so on. Forms of discourse, such as the "gentleman from Massachusetts," "the distinguished Senator from Vermont," the habitual third person reference to other members in face-to-face relations on the floor, the requirement that addresses to individuals be channeled through the presiding officer, the practice of seniority, the domination of committees by chairmen — all of these customs have as one of their objects the assertion and reassertion of a unifying feeling of community among Congressmen which transcends their specific constituencies. Senator McCarthy's condemnation occurred only when he refused to acknowledge by the proper signs his acceptance of the corporate as distinguished from the constituency identification.

It may be said also that the attitudes, postures, and forms of speech which celebrate the corporate unity of the Congress are not merely symbolic of normal group feeling, but that they are in fact necessary to the performance of the very functions of Congress. As an agency for the mediating of social conflict and for the establishment of authoritative rules, Congress is exceptionally vulnerable to the divisive stresses of party and group antagonism. Without a moderating conception of the transcendent unity of the institution, within which the cross-pull of adversary maneuvers may occur safely, the very organization of this key institution would be threatened, and its function would be vitiated. The ceremonials of the group symbolize the unity which contains and tolerates the pressures of faction, and civilizes them. There is in short an integrative purpose served by these attitudes, postures, and forms of speech.

The coherence of in-group feeling then is sustained by ceremonials born of functional necessity, and maintained by custom. This feeling is often tested, and strengthened, in the relations between Congress and the other agencies which inhabit the universe of social groups and individuals within which Congress dwells and does business, particularly the Executive. Some of the tensions between the two "policy" branches of the government occur at the margins where the corporate interests of the Congress and the Executive collide, as when Congress insists that it has a right to the possession of information in the control of the Executive, which the latter refuses to yield.

The ceremonials for the process of prescription may be further classified as follows: ascertainment, deliberation, and enactment. *Ascertainment* is the process by which members of Congress, committees, and the separate houses of the national legislature collect and appraise the evidence for and against the establishment of new authoritative rules. There are many ways of ascertainment, some more formal than others. The most public is the formal hearing in which Congressmen exercise the power to compel the presence of witnesses and the production of books and papers. But Congressmen "ascertain" such evidence in other ways also. The presentations and solicitations of pressure groups and lobbies, letters from constituents, polls of constituent opinion, telephone calls from influential citizens, research, and other inquiries made by the Congressman or his staff on their own initiative — all of these are forms of ascertainment.

Altogether, these notices, advices, and independent discoveries comprise a structure of communications through which the relation between government and the citizenry is mediated. As a structure of communications, these intersecting and overlapping lines of information sometimes transmit clearly and sometimes not at all. Various impediments mar the clarity of the signals. The letters from home are "canned," the poll was biased and distorted, the hearing was badly prepared, the witnesses refused to cooperate. Among the impediments of transmission must be counted the selective perception of the Congressman himself, who brings to his tasks the usual baggage of bias, prejudgment, goal and value orientations, prejudices, and preferments. These tend to magnify some signals and diminish the intensity of others. He responds to some kinds of appeal more accurately and faithfully than to others. Thus some will hear the chant of the churchmen where others are deaf; and some will be able to hear the whisper of the dairyman more clearly than the shouts of a million consumers of milk. The corporate interest of Congress affects the process of ascertainment at critical points. Congress forbids certain kinds of appeal — like bribery — because the integrity of the institution would be threatened by its widespread use.

Analytically, *deliberation* follows ascertainment, although both ascertainment and deliberation may occur in the same area of inquiry, and at the same time. The most public and formal mode of deliberation is debate on the floor, of which a public record is kept. But deliberation occurs also in the cloak rooms, in the caucuses, in the offices of

Congressmen, in the committee rooms, and elsewhere. The object, and the usual result of deliberation is *alignment* or *commitment*. That is to say, the active elements for and against the enactment of new social norms at this critical stage work to commit the support and to align the votes of members of Congress.

Enactment, or a decision against enactment, is the form which successful deliberation takes. Enactment is the ceremony by which prescription is made public. It embodies the new rule of public control and is the chief symbol of legitimacy. The normal expectation when Congress acts as legislator is that ascertainment is the preliminary to deliberation, and that both will result in enactment — or not — depending upon the pattern of commitments and alignments. Stated another way, Congress in the popular conception is playing its role as "legislator" when it exercises the most public form of ascertainment for the purpose of writing legislation. This most public form of ascertainment is also called "fact-finding," and the courts in the past have suggested that the justification for fact-finding is that it will lead to deliberation, and possibly enactment, as was said in the McGrain and other cases. Among the many examples in which this most public form of ascertainment did lead to deliberation and enactment are the Teapot Dome investigation, and the many investigations in the 1930's into banking, holding company control of utilities, stock market operations, and the like.

Congress successfully plays its role as legislator (in the sense that it meets the average of expectations for it) when two conditions are present. The first is that there exists generally throughout the country or among strategic publics a significant feeling (both in incidence and intensity) that prescription is desirable, and even necessary. The second is a significant consensus that the ceremonials that lead to prescription have been observed, since they symbolize the officiality of the result. These conditions are met when Congress after hearings, for example, makes it a crime to transport kidnapped persons across state lines, or enacts legislation that prohibits the harmful adulteration of food products sold in interstate commerce. Kidnappers and sellers of rotten food will be widely regarded as violators of norms of conduct believed to be desirable. There will be a significant consensus that kidnapping and adulteration of food constitute punishable behavior.

Where the questionable behavior is not the threat to the security of the person but to the security of the state — where it is subversion that is to be regulated — there are many areas of prescription where the two conditions have been met. Such are statutes forbidding espionage, incitement to mutiny in the armed forces, sabotage of physical properties, theft of documents from government sources, organization of paramilitary cadres and squads, and conspiracy to perform any of these forbidden acts.

Congressional concern for these matters dates at least from 1919 when the Senate Judiciary Committee in the Sixty-fourth Congress, and thereafter, conducted long hearings on the new Soviet regime and its propaganda, and on radical activities in the United States. In the hearings of the Fish committee in 1930–31 and the McCormack-Dickstein committee of 1934–35, Communist Party witnesses, as has been said, were still testifying that force and violence would be used to subvert the state if nonviolent methods failed. In all of these instances, the ceremonials of ascertainment, deliberation, and enactment were in train, although a general statute to control advocacy of subversion did not result. The logical fulfillment of the trend of these hearings, however, was reached in the Smith Act of 1940 which was the expected and foreseeable prescription. Subversion and even the advocacy of subversion were brought under Federal penalty.

The change in the Communist Party line in 1935 had two consequences for the development of the Federal law on subversion. First, while the open party could still be more or less clearly distinguished, its many ancillary points of support in all phases of American life sank from sight. The promotion of causes that were auxiliary to the unyielding goals of overthrow and subversion blurred the line between revolutionary ambition and mere nonconformity. Second, the conventional and customary procedures of outlawry by legislation seemed to some to be inadequate to meet the exigencies of the new threat posed to established institutions. That is to say, prescriptive legislation, enacted after hearing and debate, seemed to be an inept instrument for the control of subversive influence through fronts like the American League for Peace and Democracy, the influence of subversive elements in trade unions and schools, and other activity of subversive intent but without immediate physical consequence.

Congressional committees then proceeded to develop a new form of outlawry that stopped short of enactment, and was therefore not fully ritualized. This new form of control may be called *prescriptive publicity*, by which is meant a form of public notice intended to instruct, and deter. In the words of the House Committee on Un-American Activities in its report of August 27, 1948, the committees considered it to be their function "to permit American public opinion . . . an . . . opportunity to render a continuing verdict on all of its public officials and to evaluate the merit of many in private life who either openly associate with and assist disloyal groups or covertly operate as members or fellow-travellers of such organizations."

The sanction of prescriptive publicity was social disapproval and whatever personal consequence (like loss of employment) that might follow public exposure. The Supreme Court was wrong in the Watkins case to speak of this as exposure for exposure's sake. It was intended to have certain punitive consequences. But punitive consequences have been generally thought to be legitimate only after all three stages in the development of social control by government — prescription, proceeding, and judgment — had been gone through. Prescriptive publicity employed the most public form of ascertainment and stopped short of enactment. Prescriptive publicity was a mode of governance which normally required the cooperation of the branches of Federal officialdom but was in fact being wielded by Congress without the participation of Executive or Courts.

One of the main lines of attack by critics of prescriptive publicity was the proclamation of new values — that is, it was argued that the ceremonials of proceeding and adjudication should characterize ascertainment, although these ceremonies had not been thought applicable before. Prescriptive publicity grew out of the most public form of ascertainment, and it reflected most of the functional attributes and qualities of the Congress itself — mutability, flexibility, accessibility, and absence of rigid procedure — qualities that serve to effectuate the congressional function, which is mediation of social claims and the institutionalized negotiation of conflicting group demands. For critics of the committees, however, the virtues of plasticity, accommodation, and adaptability became vices.

Critics argued, as will be shown presently, that congressional hearings should be like court proceedings. It was said that the ceremonials that govern the use of judicial sanctions were applicable to the exercise of prescriptive publicity, and that courtroom rights should be accorded to witnesses in congressional proceedings. Hence the disputation over the right of witnesses to present statements, the assumption that a hearing was an adversary proceeding, the right to counsel, the right to cross-examine witnesses, the right to the full disclosure of the identity of informants, and the use of the Fifth Amendment.

Critics also argued for the recognition of new values of personal security, and urged their incorporation into the conduct of congressional hearings. Among these were freedom from "guilt by association." In this respect, the demand urged a species of right that even defendants in a courtroom do not have. The associations of witnesses, for prosecution and defense, have always been regarded as of evidentiary value in determining such matters as credibility, for example.

Expulsion, ostracism, and outlawry for the security of the state are not political novelties, born of local circumstance in mid-century America; nor is the demand for public testimonials of commitment to

whatever is the predominant morality. For example, Greek ostracism
— a form of physical expulsion — was designed to rid the community
temporarily of persons who appeared to menace its welfare.[46] A device
invented by Cleisthenes to guarantee the security of the democratic
faction after the civil war between the democrats and the Pisistratids,
ostracism made it possible to remove from the community, leaders of
the aristocratic faction who might be dangerous to the domination of
the democrats — subversive, that is. Established in 508 B.C., it was
not used at all until 487 B.C., and in the whole of Athenian history
only ten persons were ever ostracized.

The ceremonial of Greek ostracism resembled prescriptive publicity
in some respects. The formal procedure for ostracism was a kind of
hearing at an appointed time each year. At the prescribed time, the
question on the agenda of the Ecclesia was whether a special plenary
assembly should be called to vote an ostracism. If the answer was
affirmative, such an assembly was summoned. This procedure transferred to the popular assembly the most important political function
of the Areopagus — a court-like council, with power to enforce criminal justice — "that of guarding the constitution and protecting the
state from tyranny." Critics of Congress were to say it, too, came to
exercise functions like those of prosecution and judgment.

Political ostracism was not entirely new in Washington in the forties
and fifties. A simple example of its normal use, that is, as a procedure
of expulsion from the community for violation of the basic values of
the community, is the deportation of aliens — which is actual physical
removal. It is history that the anxieties about communism and subversion after the First World War — justified or not — led to the
physical expulsion of many suspected persons, an enactment of the
ritual of ostracism. For most of the hearings, however, from 1938 to
1954, the expulsion was largely symbolic, although here too there were
physical separations, as in dismissal from employment in the Federal
government.

Other cultures have supported similar institutions. Lazarsfeld and
Merton mention certain rituals that resemble the procedures of the
congressional investigators, rituals first described by Malinowski in
his studies of the Trobriand Islanders.[47] Among the latter no organized

---

46. On the institution of ostracism, see Florence Mishman, "Ostracism," *En-
cyclopedia of the Social Sciences* (New York: Macmillan, 1930); J. B. Bury, *A
History of Greece* (New York: Modern Library, n.d.), pp. 248–249.

47. Paul F. Lazarsfeld and Robert K. Merton, "Mass Communication, Popular
Taste, and Organized Social Action," in Lyman Bryson (ed.), *The Communica-
tion of Ideas* (New York: Harper and Brothers, 1948), pp. 95–118. Reprinted in
Bernard Rosenberg and David Manning White, *Mass Culture* (Glencoe, Illinois:
Free Press, 1957), pp. 457–473.

social action was taken against personal behavior that violated deeply-held beliefs about what is right and wrong (called "social norms") unless there was a *public* announcement of the deviation. This was not merely a matter of letting the individuals in the group know the facts. Indeed many could have known privately of delinquent behavior, such as incest, much as in our own society many may know of business or political corruption through private experience, and the information remains private. Among the Trobriand Islanders, however, the public exposure of aberrant conduct begot tension between what was privately tolerable and what was publicly acknowledgeable.

Private toleration of the behavior of others was undisturbed up to the point where one must take a public stand for or against the social norm. Publicity was the enforced acknowledgement by members of the group that impermissible behavior had occurred, whereupon each individual had to commit himself one way or the other — align himself with the nonconformists, and thereby attest that he too repudiated the social norm and was outside the moral framework of the society, or, whatever his private preference, go with the majority. In the words of Lazarsfeld and Merton,

> Publicity closes the gap between "private attitudes" and "public morality." Publicity exerts pressure for a single rather than a dual morality by preventing continued evasion of the issue. It calls forth public reaffirmation and (however sporadic) application of the social norm.[48]

This closely characterizes what the investigators sought to do in the forties and fifties. Publicity created pressure for a single morality on communism and made it difficult to maintain a dual morality by continued evasion of the issue.[49]

Congressional investigators, like Malinowski's primitives, invariably pressed for overt and public evidence that private attitudes and behavior, once idiosyncratic, had changed to conform — that those once affiliated with Communist organizations knowingly had in fact broken with them, and come to accept the common values of the public morality about communism. The conception of McCarthy as to how rigorous such evidence had to be in order to be convincing was less generous than that of Senator Henry M. Jackson of Washington. In the questioning of James A. Wechsler about his membership in and departure from the Young Communist League, McCarthy said:

48. *Ibid.*
49. On the part necessarily played by the press in such publicity, see the critical remarks in Wallace Carroll, "The Seven Deadly Virtues," *Michigan Alumnus Quarterly Review*, LXI (21) (August 6, 1955), 329–338, and Saxon Graham, *American Culture* (New York: Harper and Brothers, 1957), p. 333.

I would suggest that if during that 15-year period [the time since the break with the Young Communist League] you have ever taken an active part in exposing, obtaining the conviction or deportation of an individual Communist, that would be very, very strong evidence that my evaluation of your activities is wrong.

If you merely place in the record general statements against communism, any logical person, I believe, would assume that regardless of whether you have broken or not would be the sort of thing you would do.[50]

But Senator Jackson would not accept this rule for the test of recantation. He told McCarthy,

Mr. Chairman, I would disagree with you on the statement about the deportation illustration. The only thing I can go by — I cannot look into a man's brain — is whether his behavior is inconsistent with the policies and programs of the Communist Party.

And in a colloquy with Wechsler, Senator Jackson indicated that he thought the witness had clearly established bona fides:

Q. . . . If my interpretation of the record is correct in this case, Mr. Wechsler has taken a stand publicly contrary to the aims and views of the Communist Party on every major turn of the party line. Is that a fair statement?
A. That is correct. Let me interpolate that if the Communist Party is for more public housing, I am not going to be against it. I think in the realm of foreign policy, where the issues have been clearly drawn, I have taken positions that are unequivocally hostile to Communists throughout this period.
Q. I understand you have never indicated an unwillingness to cooperate with Government agencies when you have been approached by such agencies with reference to your past connections with the Young Communist League or during that period of 1934 to 1937; is that correct?
A. That is correct.
Q. As I understand it, you made a voluntary statement back in 1948 to Mr. Nichols of the FBI?
A. That is correct.
Q. Giving him at that time all the information you had?
A. That is, all the information he requested. I want to make clear

50. Eighty-third Congress, First Session, United States Senate, Committee on Government Operations, Permanent Subcommittee on Investigations, Hearings Pursuant to S. Res. 40, *State Department Information Program — Information Centers,* p. 312.

that he did not at that time ask me for a list of these dimensions [a list that McCarthy had requested]. . . .

Q. I do not know just what a person should do in a case like this to more clearly indicate his position as compared with his earlier position when he was a member of the Young Communist League. I just wonder what a person is supposed to do in a case like this above and beyond what the record discloses here.[51]

Investigators like Dies, Thomas, McCarran, and McCarthy wielded the powerful instruments of prescriptive publicity but they were certainly not the first to do so. Senator Hugo Black of Alabama said it all for McCarthy and McCarran when he was the scourge of the holding companies in the 1930's:

There is no power on earth that can tear away the veil behind which powerful and audacious and unscrupulous groups operate save the sovereign legislative power armed with the right of subpoena and search. . . . Witnesses have declined to answer questions from time to time. The chief reason advanced has been that the testimony related to purely private affairs. In each instance with which I am familiar, the House and Senate have steadfastly adhered to their right to compel reply, and the witness has either answered or been imprisoned. . . .[52]

He could have been talking about the scores of witnesses who refused to testify in the congressional investigations of communism, but he was not. In the Watkins case in 1957, he was with the majority which set aside a conviction for refusal to answer questions.

Senator Black in 1936 was the kind of legislator Justice Black had no use for twenty years later. In 1936 Senator Black said further, in discussing congressional investigations:

Public investigating committees, formed from the people themselves or from their public representatives . . . have always been opposed by groups that seek or have special privileges. The spokesmen of these greedy groups never rest in their opposition to exposure and publicity. That is because special privilege thrives in secrecy and darkness and is destroyed by the rays of pitiless publicity.

Prescriptive publicity — that is, the publicity that destroys, and is intended to destroy — was a familiar and well-liked instrument of more liberal goals in an earlier time.

In the years 1950–1954, the exercise by Congress of the power of

---

51. *State Department Information Program — Information Centers*, p. 313.
52. Hugo L. Black, "Inside a Senate Investigation," *Harper's*, 172 (February 1936), 273.

prescriptive publicity set off an ardent debate between critics and supporters of the far-reaching sanction. *The Nation* quoted with approval the remark of Alan Barth that the incurable defect of the congressional investigations was the "concept that Congress may properly punish, by publicity, activities which it cannot constitutionally declare criminal." [53] An unsigned statement in *The Nation* in February 1953 referred to the investigations as "the perversion of the judicial process through the attempt to punish political beliefs, opinions, and attitudes as crimes against the state." [54] With appropriate references to Madison and Macaulay, J. R. Wiggins of the *Washington Post* wrote in *The Nation* that the committees were "performing essentially judicial functions," [55] and "in many cases" were performing legislative, executive, and judicial functions although he did not say that the press was cooperating with the "tyranny" he detested by printing each malicious charge. Carey McWilliams, later editor of *The Nation*, suggested that no nicety of procedure would make tolerable proceedings which were basically a "witch hunt," having as their object the "lynching" of witnesses. [56] Don Riddle thought that rules for congressional inquiries could not save freedom, and refused to think that the inquiries of the thirties (those of Senator Black, for example) were like those of the late forties and fifties. [57] The earlier ones, it was said, were concerned with the *activities* of witnesses, not their political or other *beliefs*.

Writers in the more moderate *Reporter* also expressed concern about prescriptive publicity. Two lawyers felt that prescriptive publicity was not limited to investigations of communism but that other investigations (in 1953 and before) had resembled combined prosecutions and trials with one purpose to serve, the "prosecution and punishment of gamblers, subversives, influence peddlers, and dishonest or misguided government officials." [58] Congressman Jacob K. Javits thought that some reform of procedure would curb excesses[59] and Congressman Peter Frelinghuysen, Jr., thought so too.[60]

53. "The Incurable Defect" (editorial), *The Nation*, November 1, 1952, pp. 398–399.
54. "Perjury or Heresy?" (editorial), *The Nation*, February 28, 1953, pp. 179–181.
55. J. R. Wiggins, "Freedom of the Printed Word," *The Nation*, May 30, 1953, p. 457.
56. Carey McWilliams, "Gentleman's Agreement," *The Nation*, March 6, 1954, pp. 191–193.
57. Don Riddle, "Rules for Inquiries Cannot Save Freedom," *The Nation*, March 24, 1954, pp. 234–235.
58. William H. Berman and Walter F. Hoffman, "Lawmakers as Judges," *The Reporter*, February 17, 1953, pp. 20–23.
59. Jacob K. Javits, "Some Queensberry Rules for Congressional Investigations," *The Reporter*, September 1, 1953, pp. 23–25.
60. Peter Frelinghuysen, Jr., "A G.O.P. Congressman's Views on Security Investigations," *The Reporter*, March 16, 1954, pp. 25–27.

Writers in the *New Leader* were less critical of the way in which the committees conducted grand investigations, and one of them, Richard L. Walker, called investigation "one of their primary functions." [61] Granville Hicks said that the congressional investigations were "one of the ways by which an informed public opinion can be created" and that "Communism is a subject about which the public must be informed," but hoped that an improvement in methods might make them more effective.[62]

The *Freeman*, by way of contrast with *The Nation*, did not think that any substantive or procedural limits should bind Congress. With the arrival of the Eisenhower administration, it felt that the real show would now start. It opposed the judicialization of procedure and felt that the processes of the courts were not adequate as the first line of defense against Communists.[63] It scoffed at what Bertrand Russell called the "reign of terror" and Justice William O. Douglas called the "black silence of fear," and it advocated more and better "red-baiting" — that is, "in the sense of reasoned, documented exposure of Communist and pro-Communist infiltration of government departments and private agencies of information and communication." [64] One of the most detailed discussions in the more conservative journals of the validity of prescriptive publicity was that by C. Dickerman Williams in the *Freeman* of September 21, 1953, under the title, "The Duty to Investigate." [65] He supported a broad-based power in Congress to oversee the Executive, and to perform what he and Woodrow Wilson called the "informing function." Although he recognized that there were occasional lapses from propriety in the conduct of the hearings, he thought that it was widespread publicity that led to the formation of a forceful public opinion. As to the consequences of publicity, "One may sympathize with those whose mistakes have been exposed, but it can hardly be suggested that Congress should refrain from performance of its most important functions because people regret what they are shown to have done." [66] Nor did he accept the argument that the committees were performing judicial functions. What seemed like ju-

61. Richard L. Walker, "Lattimore and the IPR," *New Leader*, March 31, 1952, Sec. II (special sec.), pp. S1–S16, at p. S5.

62. Granville Hicks, "Recent Congressional Witness Backs Plan to Investigate the Investigators," *New Leader*, April 15, 1953, pp. 21–22.

63. "More Light" (editorial), *Freeman*, January 12, 1953, pp. 260–261.

64. "The Necessity of 'Red-Baiting'" (editorial), *Freeman*, June 1, 1953, pp. 619–620.

65. C. Dickerman Williams, "The Duty to Investigate," *Freeman*, September 21, 1953, pp. 917–920.

66. Williams, "The Duty to Investigate," *Freeman*, September 21, 1953, pp. 917–920.

dicial procedure was merely the reporting by committees of the facts that they had found.

A switch on a familiar theme was the statement of Congressman Gordon H. Scherer in the *American Legion Magazine* that it was the Congressmen, and especially the members of the House Committee on Un-American Activities, who were being pressured by publicity. The plain fact, he said, about the HUAC is that it has "been pretty much intimidated by the continuous vilification." [67]

The argument *ad hominem* was freely used in the strident babel of the "black silence of fear," and most of it was pretty unedifying. In *The Nation*, M. R. Werner praised Alan Barth for saying that the investigators were more interested in enforcing conformity with their own forms of conservatism than in "protecting us from the evils of communism." [68] *The Nation* said that McCarthy was a candidate for the presidency, Kit Clardy was a junior McCarthy who was looking for headlines to help his campaign for Congressman in 1954, and McCarthy's aim was "to seize total power." [69] Roy Wier, Congressman from Minnesota, thought that Velde, McCarthy, and Jenner all wanted to be President.[70]

Senator Allen Ellender of Louisiana was mentioned in *The Reporter* as one who thought that it was professional investigators who started investigations, or that they were started by "someone who comes to us and sells us an idea." [71] Another *Reporter* note quoted the opinion of a colleague of Harold H. Velde of the Un-American Activities Committee that Velde "is drunk with power." [72] William H. Hessler wrote that some ambitious Congressmen "sink new shafts almost at random when a pay lode gives out, in order to make work for a committee on which their political careers may depend." [73] Benjamin Ginzburg, who denounced the "tightening chain" of security regulation (just about the time it was beginning to relax), said that the Dies Committee had not been created by an aroused or inflamed public

67. Gordon H. Scherer, "I Was the Target," *American Legion Magazine*, April 1954, pp. 20–21, 54–56.
68. M. R. Werner, "Loyalty vs. Freedom," review of Alan Barth's *The Loyalty of Free Men*, in *The Nation*, January 27, 1951, p. 88.
69. C. L. Barker, "Kit Clardy — Junior McCarthy," *The Nation*, February 13, 1954, pp. 132–133.
70. Roy W. Wier, "Why He Voted 'No'," *The Nation*, April 10, 1954, p. 305.
71. "The Reporter's Notes — Career Investigator" (editorial), *The Reporter*, March 31, 1953, p. 3.
72. "The Reporter's Notes — Inquisitor from Illinois" (editorial), *The Reporter*, April 14, 1953, p. 2.
73. William H. Hessler, "Our Baffled Neighbors to the North," *The Reporter*, March 2, 1954, pp. 26–28.

opinion; it was the committee that had aroused and inflamed public opinion.[74]

Although *The Nation* had thought that the congressional investigations suffered from an "incurable defect," remedies to control prescriptive publicity were offered or criticized in its pages. Leonard Boudin opposed the bill to give the Attorney General power to grant immunity from prosecution to witnesses before grand juries, courts, and congressional committees.[75] *The Nation* editorially suggested that Senator McCarran's investigation of the Institute of Pacific Relations should be investigated, with special reference to the veracity of Budenz.[76] *The Nation* supported a long list of changes in procedure that would have had the effect of transforming a committee room into a court room,[77] and two writers argued that frequent claims of privilege under the Fifth Amendment were "a sure sign" that committees had departed from their constitutional role and were attempting to usurp the judicial function. They said,

> The McCarthy, Jenner and Velde type of investigation is becoming a trial to such an extent that efforts to introduce some aspects of court procedure into it are being seriously discussed. That the privilege [of the Fifth Amendment] should be used to curb this judicial role is entirely proper. . . . The tendency of the Fifth Amendment to impede the development of trial by committee is one of its most important virtues.[78]

The notion that the congressional investigators were acting like judges — or rather, attempting to perform the judicial function — was frequently voiced in the liberal journals. Merlo J. Pusey in *The Reporter* referred to the committees as "mighty seats of judgment," [79] and suggested that "old-fashioned ideas about the rights of privacy have been sharply modified" because the committees were putting individuals under subpoena as well as public officials, although the heroes of some of the important investigations of the past — Jay Cooke, John Brown, Harry Sinclair, Edward Doheny, Frank Costello, J. Pierpont Morgan, and Greasy Thumb Guzik — were private persons without office in the government. Two writers in *The Reporter*, like two writ-

74. Benjamin Ginzburg, "Loyalty, Suspicion, and the Tightening Chain," *The Reporter*, July 6, 1954, pp. 10–14.

75. Leonard Boudin, "The Fifth Amendment: Freedom's Bastion," *The Nation*, September 29, 1951, pp. 258–260.

76. "The Shape of Things" (editorial), *The Nation*, October 20, 1951, p. 317.

77. "Runaway Inquiries" (editorial), *The Nation*, March 28, 1953, pp. 259–260.

78. Laurent B. Frantz and Norman Redlich, "Does Silence Mean Guilt?" *The Nation*, June 6, 1953, pp. 471–477.

79. Merlo J. Pusey, "Congressional Investigations — the Fact vs. the Smear," *The Reporter*, March 20, 1951, pp. 14–16.

ers in *The Nation*, thought that congressional committees should give individuals the same degree of protection that they get in a court of law.[80] William H. Hessler in *The Reporter* contrasted Canadian and American styles in investigation, pointing out when the Canadian government really believed that it was dealing with spies, it was tougher than the American government and more indifferent to the ordinary rights of citizens, but that Canadians were appalled "by the indiscriminate hurling of charges in public, by the smearing of individuals simply because they refuse to answer questions, and by the *pitiless publicity* [emphasis added] given those persons marked out as targets." [81]

Neither the *New Leader* nor the conservative journals generally were much aroused by the procedures of the committees. William Bohn in the *New Leader*, unlike writers in *The Nation*, characterized Budenz as a "straightforward, decent and honest man," [82] and he argued the case for televising sessions of Congress but not congressional committee hearings, on the ground that the latter were dull anyway, for the most part, and those that dealt with various sorts of wrongdoing mingled the innocent and the guilty in a stream of witnesses that onlookers would tend to condemn in a body.[83] Richard L. Walker thought that the McCarran investigation of the IPR was milder and fairer than newspaper accounts would indicate but suggested nevertheless that it would be useful to develop a code of fair investigative procedure.[84] Peter Meyer, reviewing the Ernst and Loth book on American Communists in the *New Leader*, reproved the authors for proposing to halt public congressional investigations, and said that critics could not have it both ways; "raise a cry about 'star-chamber proceedings' if a case is heard in executive session, and about 'sensational publicity' if it is heard in public." [85]

On Fifth Amendment pleas, Zechariah Chafee, Jr. and Arthur Sutherland of the Harvard Law School said, "Certainly the fact that disclosure of present or past association with the Communist Party will cause trouble for the witness with his church, his lodge, his union,

80. Berman and Hoffman, "Lawmakers as Judges," *The Reporter*, February 17, 1953, p. 22.
81. Hessler, "Our Baffled Neighbors to the North, *The Reporter*, March 2, 1954, p. 28.
82. William E. Bohn, "The Truth, the Whole Truth," *New Leader*, January 7, 1950, p. 2.
83. William E. Bohn, "Let's Televise Congress," *New Leader*, April 16, 1951, p. 6.
84. Walker, "Lattimore and the IPR," *New Leader*, March 31, 1952, p. S16.
85. Peter Meyer, "Report on the Marginal Communists," review of Ernst and Loth, *Report on the American Communist*, in *New Leader*, January 26, 1953, pp. 24–25.

his employer, or his university does not excuse him from answering questions about it when subpoenaed before a competent body." [86] This language was underlined by the editors of the *New Leader*. Norman Thomas chided liberals who passionately denounced the methods of McCarthy but showed no equivalent concern for individual rights when the New Dealers controlled the machinery of congressional inquiry.[87] And Robert Gorham Davis, in a review in the *New Leader* of Burnham's *Web of Subversion*, said in the same vein:

> Among intellectuals who are critical of the committees — and certainly there is plenty to criticize — it is uncommon to find someone who has read extensively the transcripts of the hearings, though this would seem to be a first requirement before making a judgment. Such reading may strengthen criticisms of the committees, but it almost always results in a rather dramatic decrease in sympathy for the non-cooperative witnesses.[88]

In the rhetoric of the argument about prescriptive publicity, this technique of governance was clearly enough perceived by both liberals and conservatives for what it actually was — the exercise by Congress of an authority that it was normally expected to share with the other branches in a political system of constitutionally separated powers. Despite strong rationalizations on both sides of the tension, the difference between them was basically one of a priori commitments. Both tended to favor a double standard. As Norman Thomas observed, liberals had one for McCarthy and another for New Deal investigators. Those it would be fair to assign to the conservative side were early objectors to committee tactics — Mally S. Daugherty got to the Supreme Court with his argument that the Senate was usurping judicial functions by undertaking to "try" him; Harry Sinclair also got to the Supreme Court with his objection to answering certain questions when he voluntarily appeared before a committee. Senator Black was sure in 1936 that complaints about the committees, like Samuel Johnson's definition of patriotism, were the last refuge of scoundrels. It was greedy groups that never rested in their opposition to exposure and publicity.

The New Deal investigations and those of the 1920's have been distinguished from those of the late forties and fifties on the ground that the first dealt with activities and the later ones with beliefs. This classi-

86. Zechariah Chafee, Jr. and Arthur E. Sutherland, "Self-Incrimination: When and How," *New Leader*, February 3, 1953, pp. 14–15.

87. Norman Thomas, "The Threat to Freedom," *New Leader*, March 1, 1954, pp. 3–5.

88. Robert Gorham Davis, "A Machiavellian Views Subversion," *New Leader*, May 10, 1954, pp. 16–18.

fication is not entirely apt, especially for the later hearings. When a witness is asked whether he joined the Communist Party, or passed papers to a courier, or attended a meeting, he is being asked about what he did. It may be improper for some other reason (like self-incrimination) to press these questions, but not because they do not deal with activities. It is also true, however, that many witnesses were pushed around by inquisitors, not because they *did* anything but because they believed something. This happened, for example, in the Smith committee hearings on the NLRB. But even with these qualifications, the classifications of belief and activity are only moderately serviceable. The later uses of prescriptive publicity became so closely associated in public discourse with the name and personality of Senator McCarthy that the derogatory noun "McCarthyism" was coined to describe it, although McCarthy was not the only one to employ the technique (even in the later period) and McCarthyism is a concept of somewhat broader scope than prescriptive publicity, as the next chapter will consider.

The Frustration of Political Change

The increasing stress of government in the years which this study has covered has been ascribed to the Cold War, to the virulence of isolationist sentiment, and to the uneasiness created by the Korean war — a rag bag of references to current events without analytical structure. The Korean war is an especially plausible explanation of McCarthyism to some because (to borrow the language of one statement) Communists were killing American boys in Korea in 1950 and the United States (for reasons that few people understood) was not striking back with full force. Here was a situation filled with agony and frustration and ready-made for demagogic exploitation, making it possible to transform McCarthy's crusade from an eccentric sideshow into a popular movement and give it contact with millions of Americans. McCarthy, of course, was a sensation before the outbreak of the war in Korea, the inquiries never concerned themselves with the killing of American boys by Communists in Korea, and incredible as it may seem, the Stouffer study (discussed in the next chapter) indicates that McCarthy's crusade made little or no impression at all among the generality of the populace, although it was a torment in governmental, professional, and literary circles. As for isolationism, the nation in 1945 committed herself to a permanent policy of international involvement through the United Nations, the Truman administration challenged the Russians in Berlin in 1948 with the support of the country, the Marshall Plan and NATO were economic and military pledges of inextricable international association, and the gravamen of the complaint about Korea was not that we should not be there but that we were not doing enough.

To appraise fully the whole nature of the McCarthy phenomenon requires more space than is available here. The remaining pages of this book, then, can only suggest some considerations that might be taken into account in some definitive treatment of the matter. These suggestions must begin with a question: Why did the Communist issue arise when it did — after 1948 — and assume the swollen proportions into which it grew after 1950?

In considering the appearance of the Communist "issue," great weight must be given to the presidential election of 1948, for the American political system in that year failed to provide for and facilitate a decisive change in office for which the impulse had been building for a decade. It may be fairer to say that the failure was not a failure of the system so much as it was a failure of the electorate decisively to make up its mind. If it had been able to do so, the system would have recorded the result. But whether the shortcoming was in the system or in the electorate, there was no settling decision. All of the presidential votes in the election of 1948 were negative ones — more people actually voted against Truman than voted for him; more people voted against Dewey than voted for him; and more people voted against Henry Wallace and Strom Thurmond than voted for either of these candidates for the White House. There was no popular majority for President in the year 1948. The significance of this fact is heightened by the behavior of the electorate in the ten years preceding the election of 1948.

If Franklin Roosevelt had thought more of the so-called third term tradition than he did, he probably would not have run for office — at least not for the presidency — in 1940. The Republicans in their own convention and conservative elements in the Democratic party — the Garners, the Farleys, and their like — would have therefore enjoyed a kind of, not vogue, and not endorsement, but respectability, perhaps, which events were to deny them. The conservative faction in the Democratic party would have had an opportunity at least to attempt to nominate a candidate more to their liking (whether he would have won or not) and the conservative perspective might have won through in the Republican party. Roosevelt's decision to run for a third term suppressed the conservative element in the Democratic party, and moderate Republicans beat the more conservative faction in the 1940 convention as they were to do in every succeeding convention until 1964. The third term, then, and the fourth term of the war years closed the normal outlets of political expression to the conservatives, and increased their anxieties in the adulation extended to the Soviet

Union. Preceding pages have already dealt with the latter of these two circumstances. The first needs further clarification.

The record of elections from 1938 to 1946 shows a rise in conservative preference. As the following figures indicate, the Democratic proportion of the two-party vote for President declined from 1936 to 1944. In 1932, the Democrats had 57.4 per cent of the two-party vote; in 1936, they had 60.2 per cent; in 1940, 53.8 per cent; and in 1944, 51.6 per cent. There is an interesting result in the 1940 elections. The Democrats received 27,476,000 in 1936 and 27,243,000 popular votes in 1940, just about holding their own. The change in the percentages of 1936 and 1940 occurred because about 5 million more voters came out to vote for the Republicans and against Roosevelt in 1940, the increase moving from 16,679,000 to 22,304,000, while the Democratic vote remained about the same in the two elections.

The change in the composition of both the House and the Senate in the same period reflects the same trend. The Democrats had 69 seats in the Senate in 1934; 76 in 1936; 69 in 1938; 66 in 1940; 58 in 1942; 56 in 1944; and 45 in 1946. In the House, the Democrats had 319 in 1934; 331 in 1936; 261 in 1938; 268 in 1940; 218 in 1942; 242 in 1944; and 188 in 1946. Although the Democrats did a little better in each presidential year than they had in the biennial election just preceding, there is a straight decline through 1936, 1940, and 1944, and a straight decline through 1938, 1942, and 1946.

The next chapter concludes with a short analysis of the politics of social change so as, more accurately, to locate McCarthyism in the historic swing between periods of conservative and liberal predominance in Washington. Here it is enough for the moment to point to the swing without explaining the dynamism that gave it energy. Since 1896, every President has been able to count on a second term in office except William Howard Taft and Herbert Hoover. The political budget has normally been balanced between the parties in intervals of eight or twelve years, the latter figure representing the terms of the Republican candidates Taft and Hoover as extensions of eight preceding years of Republican tenure in the White House. The change from one party to the other has occurred as a function of the accumulation of resentments and disappointed expectations. People tend to vote against rather than for, which is one of the reasons that Roosevelt in effect ran against Herbert Hoover four times. The periodicity of this swing was upset and frustrated by the third term and then the Second World War that made the fourth term inevitable. The balancing of the political budget by 1948 was long overdue and a transfer of power, normal for the pattern of half a century, was expected. Not without significance in these expectations was the record of congressional elections which for over sixty years had forecast with some reliability changes in party incumbency in the White House. The victory of the Republicans in 1946 was generally assumed to forecast victory in 1948, since similar out-party successes had forecast change in the White House in 1930, 1918, 1910, 1894, 1890, and 1882, by the loss of one or both houses by the party represented in the White House.

Communism was not a strong issue even though the Communist Party was actually riding pretty high in 1948. Although the highest membership of the party had been reached some ten years before, the year 1948 was to be the year of the party's greatest political — certainly electoral — influence. The candidate it supported was Henry Wallace and its agency was the Progressive Party which polled a million votes.[89] Communist elements took control of the American Labor Party in New York City early in 1948, and in January endorsed Wallace for President. Ten days later the annual convention of the Progressive Citizens of America also endorsed Wallace. The move by Communist elements to line up labor unions behind Wallace failed, however. On February 2, 1948, the executive council of the AFL denounced Wallace as the "front, spokesman, and apologist" for the Communist Party and rejected his third party bid for the presidency. Lee Pressman worked to get the CIO to endorse Wallace, failed, and then resigned as general counsel for the CIO when its executive board on February 6 refused to support Wallace and the third party ticket.

The Communist issue figured lightly in the duel between Thomas Dewey and Harold Stassen for the Republican nomination. On April 10, Dewey in Nebraska said that he thought the Communist Party ought not to be outlawed. Stassen challenged him to debate the matter and on May 17 the exchange took place by radio. Stassen had counted on a tough anti-Communist line to help him in the Oregon primary, but he lost it nevertheless.

Democrats shared the opinion of Dewey and Republican leaders that their time had come in 1948. Mention has been made of the embarrassment that Truman seemed to create among the professionals in 1946. The loss of the congressional majorities in that year confirmed the feeling that he was a drag on the ticket and that he should not be the candidate in 1948. Jake Arvey, the Democratic leader from Chicago, hoped to get Truman off the ticket in the party convention in July and many worked to give the nomination to General Dwight D. Eisenhower, including leaders of the newly formed Americans for Democratic Action. On July 15, 1948, the convention nominated Harry

89. David A. Shannon, *The Decline of American Communism* (New York: Harcourt, Brace, 1959).

S. Truman, and in September Elmo Roper stopped polling the electorate because it was so obvious that Dewey would win. *Life* magazine
printed a picture of Dewey on a ferry in San Francisco and referred
to him as the next President.

As soon as he was nominated, however, Truman challenged the
Republican party to enact the platform of the party which he thought
was a piece of hypocrisy, and he called the Congress into special
session to achieve this end. With a little of the sense of history he
claims for himself, Mr. Truman might have been reminded of the
disastrous action of Herbert Hoover when he called Congress into
special session in the spring of 1929 to enact farm legislation. Instead
of dealing with the matter it was convened to deal with, the Congress
enacted the worst tariff in the history of this sorry legislation, the
Smoot-Hawley tariff. The Republican Congress Truman called into
special session, of course, did nothing about the Republican party
platform. Instead, it proceeded to investigate communism. On July 30,
Elizabeth Bentley testified. On July 31, she testified again, naming
Lauchlin Currie and Harry Dexter White. Whittaker Chambers on
August 3 named Alger Hiss, and the next day Elizabeth Bentley named
Nathan Gregory Silvermaster. On August 5, Truman said that the
hearings were intended to distract attention from the failure of the
Congress to enact the Republican party platform, and on August 7
the special session adjourned.

Although Congress had adjourned, the genie let out of the bottle
in a short session could not be put back. On August 17, Chambers
and Hiss confronted each other in New York and Hiss said that he
recognized his accuser. On August 20, Pressman, Witt, and Abt refused to testify about possible Communist connections. On August 30,
Chambers named J. Peters, and on September 27, Hiss sued Chambers.
Although the Republicans seemed to have a ready-made issue with
which to attack the Democrats, the fight over the Communist issue,
such as it was, was waged not by the principals but by the secondaries.
The House Committee on Un-American Activities, to be sure, was in
the fray, and the administration countered the committee with the
Department of Justice. On September 29, spokesmen in the department
accused the committee of seeking election-year publicity. On September 30, acting chairman McDowell of the committee accused the
department of having drawn the indictment against the eleven Communist leaders (eventually convicted) in such a way as to ensure their
acquittal. On October 1, the United States attorney for the southern
district of New York asked McDowell to appear before the grand
jury in New York to prove his contention. On October 8, McDowell
said that he had never said what he was said to have said, and the

district attorney then cancelled his request for an appearance before the grand jury.

Despite all this, it may be repeated that communism was not a very great issue in the election of 1948. It had a certain amount of verbal salience but lacked deep political impact. It was a make-weight in the scales against the administration but not the heavy balance. It was on the fringes of the contest, not at the center. It was a controversy between Dewey and Stassen and between the Department of Justice and the House Committee on Un-American Activities. It was not an issue between Truman and Dewey. The Communists were not helping the administration in the election, and there could be no confusion about the direction of their support. The main issue of the campaign was whether the Democrats had not forfeited their license to remain in office because of the accumulation of petty and great grievances that long tenure had fostered. Most people wanted some kind of change but they were not clear what it should be, and the election failed to produce it. All it did was to register the indecision. Instead of the change forecast, Truman was to remain in the White House for four more years.

The failure of the electorate to effect a change of government in 1948 with such opportunity as the political system might permit for the release of antiwelfarist ambitions, under conditions of some political responsibility for the outcome (which inevitably would have tempered and moderated policy), produced a political compression that exploded in McCarthyism. The corking of tensions laid an immediate and heavy stress on the whole governmental system — in domestic matters at least — in which the White House was to be countered and frustrated at almost every turn. First, in domestic affairs, the country was leaderless, despite Mr. Truman's famous zest for action. The celebrated Fair Deal was little more than Truman's 1949 message to a *Democratic* Congress which the Congress refused to enact. Second, effective political control over domestic public policy passed from 1600 Pennsylvania Avenue to Capitol Hill where it was wielded by a coalition of Republicans and southern Democrats. Since the party system had failed to deliver the responsibility for such policy to the more conservative elements in the two parties, they would take it themselves. If they could not win the White House they could control the Congress. And, as has been indicated, Congress took up the special sanction in prescriptive publicity which it could wield all by itself, and which did not depend for its justification upon any action by the President or his agencies.

There is continuity in the control of the Communist issue which Truman inadvertently placed in the hands of Congress when he called it into special session in July 1948. Despite some changes in the composition of the committees and even in their party majorities, there is a sense in which it is true that the special session did not disband for at least six years. Although the members went home from time to time, the investigation of Communists did not cease to be the business of the Congress until the issue disappeared.

And what made the issue disappear? It was the change in the administration in 1952 which was already four years overdue, for the issue was symbolic of pressures to put the government into new hands, if only temporarily. Senator Robert A. Taft showed a certain partisan realism for which he was to be strongly castigated when he said of McCarthy's reckless attacks, "If one case doesn't work, then bring up another." By 1952, the electorate was no longer indecisive. The awaited change occurred when the Republicans took both houses of Congress and the presidency. There was no great new information for the committees to find, but some of the Republican Congressmen wanted to keep things going and even to step up the tempo.

XIII   The Meaning of McCarthyism

Upon the access of the Republicans to office in 1953, with majorities in both the House and the Senate, there should have been an easy and natural relaxation of the tensions of the previous half decade. The frustration of twenty years had been eased. Although it had seemed desirable and even necessary for the more aggressive and less liberal Republicans, when they were out on the sidewalk looking in, to throw rocks at the house they hoped to occupy, they were now inside and had an interest in keeping the property intact. But McCarthy was inside also and, although he was no longer throwing rocks, he was breaking up the furniture. We have seen that the Secretary of State indulged McCarthy in the investigations that were so painful to sections of the Department of State.

The recklessness of McCarthy gradually drew the leadership of the Executive establishment into a posture of defense against him, and a series of slow braking actions was begun in 1953. This is not to say that the enclosure and constraint of McCarthy was a smooth, single-minded, and efficient operation. There were too many cross-pressures of opinion within the Republican party to make this possible, some confusion of motives, and frequent failures of nerve. But the record shows a gradually insistent intention to bring matters to a climax.

On March 6, 1953, Eisenhower said that he would intervene if congressional inquiries threatened the international relations of the United States. On March 10, 1953, Harold Velde, the new chairman of the House Committee on Un-American Activities, announced that he would institute an investigation of Communist infiltration of American churches, and pressure forced him to abandon the plan. On March 15, J. P. Warburg told congressional committees to stop their infringements upon the powers of the Executive and the judiciary, and to confine themselves to the preparation of legislation. On March 27,

Eisenhower said that although congressional committees undoubtedly had the power to investigate, abuse of the power could endanger the country. Early in April, Congressman Kenneth Keating of New York conceded that committees had abused their powers and supported the adoption of uniform rules for the conduct of investigations. In July, J. B. Matthews in the *American Mercury* charged that the largest single group in the United States backing the Communists was the Protestant clergy. Eisenhower expressed his disapproval of this accusation and pressure forced Senator McCarthy to fire Matthews from his staff.

The events of 1954 brought the climax of release. Although McCarthy's committee was voted a $214,000 budget almost unanimously, McCarthy's report of the previous year's activity of the Subcommittee on Investigations was signed only by him. On February 27, the Senate Republican Policy Committee unanimously voted to study rules for the conduct of investigating committees. (The congressional Republicans, however, quietly killed all proposals to curb the behavior of the committees, leaving it up to the chairmen whether they would improve their deportment.) On February 28, Eisenhower told Republican Senate leaders that he wanted the other Republicans on McCarthy's committee to attend the hearings and to exercise a restraining influence upon the Senator from Wisconsin. On March 3, the chairman of the Republican National Committee rebuked McCarthy for his controversy with Secretary of the Army Stevens. The next day Eisenhower said that he would not tolerate the humiliation of employees of the executive branch by congressional committees.

The Senate Condemnation

The real leadership against McCarthy, however, was taken by Senator Ralph Flanders of Vermont, a man invulnerable to reprisal because of his years, his economic independence, and his credentials as a Vermont Republican. On June 12, 1954, he introduced a motion in the Senate to have McCarthy ousted from his chairmanships. On July 17, Flanders asked for McCarthy's censure by the Senate. On August 3, the Senate passed the resolution of Senator William Knowland to send the Flanders motion to a select committee of three Republicans and three Democrats for consideration, and Vice President Nixon appointed Senator Watkins of Utah as chairman.

On the day that Senator Watkins opened public hearings on the Flanders motion, the Mundt committee that had heard the charges between McCarthy and the Army reported that although McCarthy had not intervened directly to obtain preferred treatment for G. David

Schine, he had known that Roy Cohn had done so, and had condoned it. The reports also found that the Army had wanted to bring McCarthy's investigation of Fort Monmouth to an end.

There was no television in the hearings of the Watkins committee and the chairman made it clear at the start that he would not tolerate diversions, abruptly recessing the hearings at one point after lecturing McCarthy on decorum, an act that drew from McCarthy the deathless line, "This is the most unheard-of thing I ever heard of." The Watkins committee was stern and decorous in its procedures but it was selectively indulgent in some of the judgments it reached on the merits. One series of charges accused McCarthy of contempt of the Gillette-Hennings subcommittee of the committee on privileges and elections which, in 1951, had looked into accusations against McCarthy brought by Senator Benton of Connecticut. The subcommittee had called on McCarthy to discuss certain funds collected for anti-Communist activities which, it was alleged, had been diverted to personal uses. Instead of cooperating with the subcommittee, McCarthy abused its members, failed to appear before it at all, although called many times, and issued a press statement in which he said of one of its members, Senator Robert C. Hendrickson of New Jersey, that he was "a living miracle in that he is without question the only man who has lived so long with neither brains nor guts." The Watkins committee did not think that this was a very nice thing to say and recommended censure. Nor did it condone McCarthy's telling Senators Hayden and Guy Gillette that he thought the subcommittee was "guilty of stealing just as clearly as though the members engaged in picking the pockets of the taxpayers and turning the loot over to the Democratic National Committee."

The judgment of the Watkins committee was more compassionate about what the civil service prose of the committee counsel described as "incidents of encouragement of United States employees to violate the law and their oaths of office or Executive orders." McCarthy had repeatedly told "two million Federal employees that I feel it is their duty to give us any information which they have about graft, corruption, communism, treason," and he had said that there "is no loyalty to a superior officer which can tower above and beyond their loyalty to their country." Untold but doubtless large numbers of Federal employees had responded to this invitation to administrative sabotage, and the staff of the Permanent Subcommittee became a confessional for informers.

Although the morale of several agencies had been impaired by suspicion of undermining, including sections of the State Department, the Watkins committee let Senator McCarthy off with a soft impeachment, preferring instead to maintain the futile theoretical position that the Congress has and should have unlimited access to Executive information, an argument that no President has honored, beginning with George Washington. The committee also let McCarthy off on the charge that he had received and used classified information wrongfully taken from an Executive department. The charge grew out of an incident in the Army-McCarthy hearings when McCarthy produced a two-and-one-quarter-page paper purporting to be a letter from J. Edgar Hoover to Major General Bolling, Assistant Chief of Staff, G-2, about security arrangements at the Fort Monmouth Laboratory. Mr. Hoover said that there was no such letter but that information in the doctored fake had been lifted from a fifteen-page memorandum from the FBI to Army Intelligence. McCarthy offered the purported letter to the Mundt subcommittee which discreetly placed its contents beyond public discussion. Although it was a possible violation of espionage laws for McCarthy to have had even a false document containing real information bearing on security, the Watkins committee found that he had been "under the stress or strain of being tried or investigated by the subcommittee," and that this was a mitigating circumstance.

The Watkins committee also condoned McCarthy's abuse of Senator Ralph Flanders of Vermont although it had found that his abuse of Senator Hendrickson was censurable. There was, the committee thought, a difference between the circumstances in the two cases. On June 11, 1954, Senator Flanders had walked into the Senate caucus room where McCarthy was testifying coast to coast on television in the Army-McCarthy hearings, and had informed him that he was about to attack the junior Senator from Wisconsin on the floor of the Senate. The appearance of Flanders *had* been a little startling. After the incident, McCarthy was asked by the press to make a statement about the intended speech, and he said, "Senile — I think they should get a man with a net and take him to a good quiet place." Although the Watkins committee thought that McCarthy's crack about Flanders was vulgar and base, it was not censurable because Flanders had been provocative.

The Watkins committee was tougher on McCarthy for his treatment of General Ralph W. Zwicker who had been a witness in McCarthy's investigation of security at Fort Monmouth in February 1954. The immediate issue was military responsibility for the promotion of Captain Irving Peress to the rank of major and his honorable separation from the Army after he had taken the Fifth Amendment in earlier proceedings before McCarthy's subcommittee. McCarthy accused the General of arrogance, evasiveness, and contempt, and told him that he was unfit to wear the uniform and should be removed from command. The committee recommended that McCarthy be censured for his treatment of General Zwicker.

It also recommended that he be censured for contempt of a Senate committee but the debate on the recommendations and on Senator Flanders' original motion to censure was put off until after the November elections so as to permit the Senate, in the words of Knowland of California, to act "in an atmosphere free from pre-election tensions."

On November 10, pre-election tensions having disappeared, Senator Knowland of California, the majority leader in the Senate, moved to have the Senate consider S. 301, the resolution to censure Senator McCarthy, and, in a last stand, McCarthy's defenders spoke for the record.[1] Senator Butler of Maryland, whose successful campaign against Millard Tydings had been assisted by Senator McCarthy, said a word for him or, rather, said a word against the Watkins committee report recommending censure. Butler thought that committee chairmen in the future might be penalized merely for losing their tempers, as he said McCarthy had done when he had had General Zwicker before him. Bricker of Ohio said that it would be vindictive to censure McCarthy; that when he called Senator Hendrickson a "living miracle, without brains or guts," McCarthy was only using a kind of language that others had used against McCarthy. Bricker saw the censure action as part of the "life-or-death struggle with the Communist conspiracy." The thesis that the meaning of the attack upon Senator McCarthy was to be found in his championship of anticommunism was a staple of McCarthy's friends.

Senator Barry Goldwater of Arizona was one of these. The genesis of the anti-McCarthy drive, he said, was Communist. If it might seem strange that the movement was being led by men of impeccable political credentials, this circumstance was deceiving. Communists had skillfully shifted the leadership of the movement to sincere anti-Communists. McCarthy was being singled out for punishment because he had been so effective in his investigations. McCarthy was being shut up by the men who were responsible for soft policies towards the Soviet Union from 1941 to 1946. Censure would weaken the united front we should show to foreign nations on the Communist issue. Senator Goldwater warned, "Do not think that the 'trust Stalin' people of the war and Yalta period all had a change of heart when we went into the cold war. . . . They went into the storm cellars. They put on the anti-Communist label so that they could survive as a political and journalistic force." [2] How could one know who these people are? They

1. Eighty-third Congress, Second Session, *Congressional Record*, p. 1592.
2. Eighty-third Congress, Second Session, *Congressional Record*, p. 16005.

spend their time abusing such people as Walter Winchell, Fulton Lewis, David Lawrence, and George Sokolsky; and they hurl vitriol at the American Legion, the Veterans of Foreign Wars, and the Daughters of the American Revolution.

Senator Jenner of Indiana was another friend who saw McCarthy as the victim of a Communist attack upon Congress. He said that the Communists had been notably successful in the past in scheming against the Congress. They were responsible for the 1938 "purge" of the Democratic party under the leadership of Earl Browder, who came and went from the White House by a side door so that the people could not know who their enemies were. The most pathetic victim of the purge, according to Senator Jenner, was O'Connor of New York, who as chairman of the Rules Committee of the House had had much to do with the defeat of Roosevelt's proposal for reorganization of the Federal agencies. It did not seem to have altered Jenner's perception of the facts that it was Roosevelt who thought that he needed more reliable supporters than those who had deserted him on the Supreme Court and reorganization bills; or that the "purge" was largely a failure. So insidious was Communist influence in the opinion of Senator Jenner that he proposed a Senate bureau of investigation to probe Communist influence over Senators, their staffs, and nominees sent to the Senate by the Executive for confirmation. Jenner inserted into the *Congressional Record* an article on McCarthy's achievements which had appeared in an ultra right publication,[3] and made a final speech on December 2, 1954, in which he renewed his interpretation of the unfolding event as an aspect of the cold war in which subversives were undermining the United States.

McCarthy's friends outside the Senate also contributed to the discourse, and the Senator from Wisconsin chipped in himself. As the debate moved on, an organization headed by Lieutenant General George Stratemeyer called "Ten Million Americans Mobilizing for Justice" launched a drive for ten million signatures to urge rejection of the censure resolution. The theory of the "Ten Million" was that the "Communists and their un-American cohorts, by vicious propaganda, and through willing stooges and blind but innocent dupes," had "victimized certain members of the U. S. Senate," and that Communist influence was responsible for both the Watkins committee and its recommendations. A communion breakfast of Catholic War Veterans in New York was told that $5,000,000 had been collected to oust McCarthy from the Senate, and that the ouster was sought because of McCarthy's "Catholic ideals." The day after this news, McCarthy distributed excerpts from the *Daily Worker* to all Senators to show that

3. Eighty-third Congress, Second Session, *Congressional Record*, p. 16109.

the Communist party backed his censure. He later put material into the *Congressional Record* in which he blamed Communists for his plight in that they had made the Watkins committee an "unwitting handmaiden" and an "involuntary agent" of his ruin. He also said that he could show that the Watkins committee had imitated Communist methods in its proceedings.

On December 2, 1954, the Senate voted to "condemn" McCarthy for contempt of the elections subcommittee, abuse of its members, and insults to the Senate during the censure proceedings. There was nothing on General Zwicker. All forty-four Democrats voted for the condemnation, and the Republicans split twenty-two to twenty-two. Wayne Morse, then an Independent, voted for condemnation.

Comment on the Senate Action

Although McCarthy had filled the headlines for five years, there was relatively little effort in the journals after the condemnation to evaluate the meaning of McCarthyism, but there was some. Peter Viereck said that in 1793, the Jacobins had purged persons for upper class sympathies; in the McCarthy period men were purged for lower class sympathies, that is, for leftist tendencies. Actually many of those who had been attacked — such as Lodge, Bohlen, and Stevenson — did not have lower class sympathies, but the reason for the attacks upon them was that the suddenly enthroned lower classes were proving that they were upper class by tearing down those whom they knew to be America's real aristocracy. In Viereck's words, ". . . McCarthyism is actually a leftist instinct behind a self-deceptive rightist veneer." [4] Another historian, Eric Goldman, thought there was nothing new about McCarthyism,[5] but the concept was made broad enough to include middle class fears about socialism at the end of the nineteenth century, anxieties about Bolshevism after the First World War, anxieties about communism after the Second World War, and the rise of the middle class out of the feudal structure of the middle ages.

Liberal journals took little note of the fall of McCarthy. It was mentioned in *The Nation* that the rapport between McCarthy and his successor, McClellan, as head of the Committee on Government Operations might mean no lessening of anti-Communist investigations,[6] and months later it was suggested that McCarthyism still endured in the form of test oaths, subversive lists, and committees whose procedures

4. Peter Viereck, "The New American Radicals," *The Reporter*, December 30, 1954, p. 41.
5. Eric Goldman, *The Reporter*, September 14, 1954, p. 26.
6. *The Nation*, January 15, 1955, p. 43.

were still unreformed.[7] Without much excitement the *New Republic* observed that McCarthy, although condemned by the Senate, had not been removed from any committee, and that if the Republicans should win in 1956, McCarthy would be back in business.[8]

The Catholic journal, *Commonweal*, had followed all the events of 1954 closely. It rejected the notion that there was a Catholic position on McCarthy,[9] took a position of opposition to the junior Senator from Wisconsin,[10] rebuked Dewey, Brownell, and Hall for echoing McCarthy's charge against the Democrats that they had perpetrated "twenty years of treason,"[11] said that democracy is a procedure without the substantive content that creates political orthodoxies,[12] and concluded that the McCarthy crusade was an "essentially know-nothing attempt to gain personal power by playing on the very real fears of his fellow-citizens."[13] In April 1955, in some comments on Homer Capehart, it was remarked, "Senator McCarthy has faded away quite satisfactorily, but the inanities to which he gave his name still find their voice in the United States Senate."[14]

McCarthy died in May 1957, and this occasion might have invited reflection upon the meaning he held for the time of his triumph, but few accepted the invitation to do more than note his passing. A letter to the *American Legion Magazine* thought that "the posthumous honor accorded him to lie in state in the chamber of his own execution is suggestive of the guilty conscience of the gutless Senators who voted to censure him."[15] *The Nation*, which had earlier apprehensions about the continuation of McCarthyism, said,

Senator Joseph McCarthy is dead. So quickly does malevolence rise and vanish in American life that the news of his death, which would have incited sensational interest two years ago, may now be noted in a paragraph, sealing as it does a verdict then returned. The junior Senator from Wisconsin left a squalid political estate with few legatees or claimants. His single contribution was the addition of the

7. "The McCarthy Era," *The Nation*, August 27, 1955, p. 65.

8. *New Republic*, January 24, 1955, p. 2.

9. "Catholics, Non-Catholics, and Senator McCarthy," *Commonweal*, April 2, 1954, p. 639.

10. "What is *Commonweal*? Some Notes Towards a Definition of This Magazine and Its Role in the Catholic Press," *Commonweal*, February 5, 1954, p. 443.

11. "The Limits of Partisanship," *Commonweal*, February 26, 1954, p. 513.

12. John Cogley, "Question of Method," *Commonweal*, March 12, 1954, p. 570.

13. "The Same McCarthy," *Commonweal*, March 26, 1954, p. 616.

14. "The Senator and the Economist," *Commonweal*, April 1, 1955, p. 669.

15. *American Legion Magazine*, July 1957, p. 5.

word McCarthyism to the American language. The best that can be said of him was that his idea of American patriotism, which we hope he was sincere about, is not one that *The Nation* shared while he was living and could, of course, never accept now that he is dead.[16]

Eric Sevareid essayed a slightly more general appraisal of the meaning of McCarthyism. He thought that McCarthyism died with the censure of Senator McCarthy, that McCarthy had been "a sudden rocket in the sky, enrapturing some, frightening others, catching millions in a kind of spell that dissipated only when the rocket itself, as a rocket must, spluttered, went cold, and fell." Circumstance was largely responsible for his vogue for "it was pure chance that shot him to fame in 1950 as Communist Hunter No. 1." [17] Writers in the *National Review* saw McCarthy as an instrument of the Western will in the war against communism; the "very essence of Western civilization"; a fighter for the truth that man has free will to choose between good and evil.[18] *Commonweal* merely noted the death of McCarthy and said that the wounds in the society which he had created were just then beginning to heal.

Explanations of McCarthyism

McCarthyism was regarded by thousands as a disturbance of domestic tranquillity of oppressive weight and pain, especially by workers and officials in government, politics, and the professions; and, indeed, rather generally throughout the articulate and better educated circles of the society. The evidence of a substantial study of communism, conformity, and civil liberty by Samuel Stouffer, however, was that the vast masses were largely unconcerned with the turmoil. In 1954 the number of people who said that they were worried either about the threat of Communists in the United States or about civil liberties was less than one per cent.[19] Nearly one-third of the population could not name a single Senator or Congressman who had taken a leading part in the investigation of communism,[20] not even the name of Senator McCarthy. Among those categorized in the sample as "less interested" a total of 50 per cent failed to name a single Congressman or Senator. The same survey showed that 68 per cent of a national cross-section

16. *The Nation*, May 11, 1957, p. 401.
17. *The Reporter*, May 16, 1957, p. 2.
18. "The End of McCarthy," *National Review*, May 18, 1957, p. 462; William Schlamm, "Across McCarthy's Grave," p. 469; Frank S. Meyer, "McCarthy's Unforfeited Word," June 8, 1957, p. 548.
19. Samuel A. Stouffer, *Communism, Conformity and Civil Liberties* (Garden City, New York: Doubleday, 1955), p. 59.
20. Stouffer, *Communism, Conformity and Civil Liberties*, p. 86.

favored forbidding a Communist the right to make a speech in their communities.[21]

But depressing though it is to be reminded in numerous polls of the relatively small part that liberal values, or any kind of political concern, plays in the lives of most Americans, the real wonder in McCarthyism is the nature of the phenomenon itself. Political scientists have been especially remiss in failing to treat it as a political problem of high consequence, and most of the writing on the subject has been contributed by sociologists, historians, and literary people. The basic political question is whether McCarthyism was a flash of stunning but temporary impact, associated with a demagogue of great force and fire; or the surface appearance of more serious strains in the social and political system which must find ease, or threaten ruin. Opinions have differed. There are at least five kinds of explanations in the literature contributed by liberal and neutral commentators, and a common theme presented by conservative writers in varying degrees of sophistication.

The first explanation by writers of liberal or neutral perspective is that McCarthy was a demagogue, one of many who have appeared in American history to stir discontents, most of whom have been of only passing significance and who have disappeared from the public scene without regret or lasting effect. Viewed so, McCarthyism is simply the behavior of Senator McCarthy, and with the departure of McCarthy the "problem" of McCarthyism disappears. A twist to this explanation was provided by Will Herberg who argued that McCarthyism was the logical fulfillment of a political style made popular by Franklin Roosevelt — direct appeals to the people against their elected representatives — a species of government by rabble-rousing in which the rabble was urged to take instant action against their duly chosen officers.[22] Any good result accomplished by the committees was only incidental to "their primary *political* function" which was to rouse the masses and keep them in turmoil. The difference between Roosevelt and McCarthy was that Roosevelt, like Pericles, was a gentleman, and McCarthy, like Cleon, was a clod.

Second, there is the view that McCarthyism was incipient totalitarianism. One should exclude from this category those who merely used such words as "totalitarian" and "authoritarian" as terms of abuse in the rhetoric of dissent. These apart, there were writers who thought that there were strong resemblances in philosophy and program between McCarthy and the twentieth century totalitarian leaders of

21. Stouffer, *Communism, Conformity and Civil Liberties,* p. 41.
22. Will Herberg, "Government by Rabble-Rousing," *New Leader,* January 18, 1954, pp. 13–16.

Europe. For example, Marya Mannes, in a report on the Army-McCarthy hearings, described the pattern of McCarthy's behavior as totalitarian in structure and psychology. Said she,

> When you come down to it, slowly, reluctantly, but inevitably, the real horror of these hearings has been in this: that the pattern of the protagonist was totalitarian. Senator Potter got closer to it when he said, "We have all been through a brainwashing here." For here were all the dread familiar methods: the relentless, interminable breaking down of the witness; the repeated statements of unverified fact; the assumption of guilt without proof; the deliberate evasion of the basic issues; the constant diversionary moves to obscure them. Here were the totalitarian clichés, the inversions of Communist labels: "Pentagon Politicians," "Fifth Amendment Communist," "Leftist Press." Here, most appalling of all, was the open admission and condonement of a spy-and-informer system within our government — the "Loyal American Underground." Here, finally, was the radical attempt to wreck the Executive Branch of the United States Government.[23]

Miss Mannes thought that the hearings symbolized a grave and desperate division among Americans, sharpened into an antagonism not far from civil war.

Two others, arguing from different grounds, also represent the view that McCarthyism was considerably more than the eccentricity of a politician on the make. Richard Hofstadter in "The Pseudo-Conservative Revolt" [24] suggested that authoritarianism was the key to many of the most zealous followers of McCarthy, although this goes little beyond a literary appreciation of the psychology of authoritarianism (the essay depends strongly on Adorno and others on the authoritarian personality) without empirical demonstration of the supposed authoritarianism of some of the most zealous of McCarthy's followers. For Hofstadter, the "pseudo-conservative" was impossible to identify by class "for the pseudo-conservative impulse can be found in practically all classes in society." [25] Carey McWilliams tended to write of McCarthyism as a form of American reactionism fostered by the classical Right of progressive prophecy. When Senator Flanders of Vermont introduced the resolution in the United States Senate to condemn McCarthy, McWilliams wrote that "McCarthy is only a symbol; the movement he represents would not vanish if his power were utterly

23. Marya Mannes, "Did or Did Not . . . ," *The Reporter*, June 8, 1954, pp. 40–41.
24. *The American Scholar* (Winter, 1954–55), pp. 9–27.
25. *The American Scholar*, p. 11.

destroyed." And what was this movement? It was the reaction of the right, and although it might have seemed as strange to progressives as it had to Senator Goldwater that the champion of the right should be under attack by a conservative New England Senator, there was an explanation. For "McCarthy is now being attacked from the right in an effort to preserve the movement which he helped to bring to maturity." [26] Goldwater was sure it was Communist cunning.

Third, there is the thought that McCarthyism was a kind of midcentury Populism, and several writers have accepted this view in whole or in part. Hofstadter, Lipset, and Parsons work with this notion, for example. Another statement of it is that of Leslie Fiedler in an essay titled "McCarthy and the Intellectuals." For Fiedler

. . . McCarthyism is, generally speaking, an extension of the ambiguous American impulse toward "direct democracy" with its distrust of authority, institutions, and expert knowledge; and, more precisely, it is the form that populist conviction takes when forced to define itself against a competing "European" radicalism.[27]

And elsewhere,

The emergence of McCarthy out of the wreckage of the LaFollette Progressive movement in Wisconsin is a clue to what he represents. He inherits the bitterest and most provincial aspects of a populism to which smooth talking has always meant the Big City, and the Big City has meant the Enemy.[28]

Statements of this kind, however, help more to explain than to understand, for even if it is conceded that a provincial populistic distaste for smooth-talkers, mincing accents, Harvard degrees, wealth, effete culture, and New York lent vigor to McCarthy's attacks, it does not explain the abnormal tensions of McCarthyism.

It is true that the small-town rural outlook is the one that has tended to dominate the committees. It is Southerners who have come to the chairmanships when the Democrats have a majority, and it is rural or small-town mid-Westerners who have come to dominate the committees when the Republicans have a majority in the houses of Congress. The committees then tend to reflect the small-town rural skepticism of the cities and other urban areas. The attitude is likely to be anticosmopolitan as well as antimetropolitan but this does not establish the propo-

26. "Double Exposure — Woltman on McCarthy," *The Nation*, July 31, 1954, pp. 85–87.
27. Leslie Fiedler in *An End to Innocence* (Boston: Beacon Press, 1955), pp. 46–87, at p. 57.
28. Fiedler, *An End to Innocence*, p. 77.

sition that the tension over subversion and security was basically a revolt of the American interior against eastern seaboard intellectuals and the polyglot cities with their enthusiasm for social security, modern art, communism, coffeehouses, poetry, high taxes, Zionism, and education. It may only be that these hostilities gave zest and a self-consciousness of doing good in a context of opportunity created by other influences.

During the New Deal era, the Roosevelt programs seemed to many to have more in common with Populism than with the later Progressivism, although Populism lost its seal of literary approval and became a word of opprobrium as a result of the "shock of the encounter with McCarthyism." C. Vann Woodward has shown that there is a considerable difference between the contemporary conception of the Populism of the nineteenth century and the historical reality.[29] The assumption has been widespread that Populism was historically a Western affair, that Wisconsin was the "seed-bed of the movement," and that the elder La Follette was its principal champion. None of these assumptions is true. In fact Populism had "negligible appeal in the Middle Western states," and was most attractive in the South where the Populists were more often the victims than the authors of thought control, racism, and the lynch spirit. Populism was neither class politics nor "status politics" (to be discussed presently) but more like interest politics in the familiar manner. As to racialism, the anti-Semitism of the historical Populists was (although not innocent) largely rhetorical, and Professor Woodward is of the opinion that perhaps the most remarkable aspect of the whole Populist movement was the resistance its leaders put up in the South against racism and racialist propaganda. As to the supposed element of isolationist feeling, the South was perhaps the least isolationist section of the country in the foreign policy crisis before the Second World War.

Fourth, a set of attitudes and behaviors called status politics is thought by some to be the key to McCarthyism, and Daniel Bell (building on certain theses stated by Lipset and Hofstadter) has explained McCarthy as a catalyst of these tensions in "Status Politics and New Anxieties."[30] Sectional politics, class politics, and interest group politics are all incapable of helping us to "understand the Communist issue, the forces behind the new nationalism of, say, Senators Bricker and Knowland, and the momentary range of support and the intense emotional heat generated by Senator McCarthy."[31] Even after one allows for the Korean war and the emotional reaction against Chinese

29. C. Vann Woodward, "The Populist Heritage and the Intellectual," *American Scholar*, 29 (Winter, 1959–60), pp. 55–72.
30. Daniel Bell in *The End of Ideology* (Glencoe, Illinois: Free Press, 1960), pp. 94–112.
31. Bell, *The End of Ideology*, p. 100.

and Russian Communists that carried over to domestic Communists, the discovery of Communists in high places in the Federal government and the existence of espionage rings in Washington, and the Canadian spy investigations — even "after the natural effects of all these are taken into account, it is difficult to explain the unchallenged position so long held by Senator McCarthy."

McCarthy's targets, however, are presumed to provide important clues to a "radical right" that backed him and to the reason for that support. The groups in support were "soured patricians," the "new rich," the rising middle class strata of various ethnic groups especially Irish and German, and a small group of intellectuals "some of them cankered ex-Communists, who, pivoting on McCarthy, opened up an attack on liberalism in general." What do these groups have in common? They have status anxieties in common. The central notion is that groups that are on their way up in wealth and social position are "often as anxious and politically feverish as groups that have become *declasse*." Groups on their way up and groups on their way down seek to impose upon all groups the basic values of the society. Status issues characterized the politics of prosperity; economic class and interest group issues characterize the politics of depression periods.

It is possible, however, that this explanation accounts for a single instance and then only imperfectly. If it explains McCarthyism before December 1954, what about the immediate loss of vogue he suffered after the condemnation? Did the groups on their way up stop climbing or, still climbing, did they stop being anxious? One would have thought they should be even more anxious with the political decapitation of their totem. Did the groups becoming *declasse* stop worrying about their loss of status? If neither of these changes occurred, it is possible that the collapse of McCarthyism after 1954 is connected with the disappearance of some other kind of tension that in fact generated it in the first place, and the sweats of the old rich and the new rich are irrelevant — or, at most, collateral — to the phenomenon of McCarthyism.

The suggestion is also dubious that McCarthyism is one of the diseases of affluence — that status anxieties and the issues they create occur in prosperous times and that economic class and interest group issues characterize the politics of hard times. There were two occasions before the McCarthy era when subversion was a pressing question of real or imaginary importance — in the time of the Palmer raids directly after the First World War, and in the time of the Alien and Sedition Acts. These were not times of prosperity but of economic decline, temporary in each case, but marked in each case. Now it may be said that although there was an excitement about subversion and an insistence upon conformity in these two periods, this was not status politics as defined, but something else. It might be said in answer that the phenomenon of McCarthyism was not status politics either, but something else. In both periods there was social mobility, up and down — in the earlier one the Federalists were on the decline and the Jeffersonians were on the rise, each of them roughly representative of different class concentrations; and in the later period, lower class immigration was on the point of being stopped, and the rise to middle class status of those already here was about to begin. But the whole history of the United States has been one of movement of social classes, so there may be nothing especially peculiar about such change in the late forties and early fifties. The status politics interpretation of McCarthyism, then, fails to fit the McCarthy period because tensions both preceded and followed the McCarthy era without producing McCarthyism; because notable tensions over subversion in the past appeared in the absence of the necessary conditions (prosperity) which are supposed to supply the reason for status anxiety; and because the issue of subversion did appear under conditions that are supposed to beget economic class and interest group activities, not status anxiety.

Fifth, there is the suggestion that McCarthy's strength was really Republican strength, that he had a vogue where the Republicans were strong and had no vogue where the Republicans were not strong, that he had no substantial personal following at the polls independent of the party and unique to him, and that he was not responsible for beating Benton and Tydings in Connecticut and Maryland.[32] Such a statement usefully supports the notion that McCarthyism is to be explained primarily in political terms, but while explaining what McCarthyism was not, it does not get far into an explanation of what it was.

The theory of McCarthyism that has been presented by writers with a conservative identification has appeared in three versions of increasing sophistication. First, there is the simplistic notion that "McCarthyism" was an invention of those who did not want to see communism exposed, attacked, and uprooted — that it was merely an organized slander. The reasons for anti-anti-Communist rejection of McCarthy and his works were various — fear of discovery, toleration of communism as a philosophy, refusal to regard communism seriously as a mortal threat to American institutions, pro-Communist bias, an amiable and ignorant relativism which refuses the priority that right can claim over wrong, and a soft compassion for the brutal defendant which forgets the crime. As John T. Flynn said in an article titled "What Is Joe McCarthy Trying to Do?" there was no mystery about Joe Mc-

32. Nelson Polsby, "Towards an Explanation of McCarthyism," *Political Studies*, October 1960, pp. 250–271.

Carthy, who was actually "the most obvious person in Washington." [33]
He "just doesn't like Communists."

One variation of this theme was that of William F. Buckley, Jr. in
"The New Conformity," a chapter in his defense of McCarthy against
his enemies.[34] The argument is that there are basic value preferences
in every society, an orthodoxy of outlook on fundamentals, that anticommunism is the American orthodoxy, and that McCarthyism is
simply the hardening of that orthodoxy. The tension between liberals
and conservatives is a dispute about the fundamentals of the society
and the debate over McCarthyism is a skirmish in a conflict that covers
a much broader front.

The most thoroughly developed of the conservative statements about
McCarthyism is that of Willmoore Kendall in "McCarthyism: The
Pons Asinorum of American Conservatism." [35] There it is said that the
American people, like other free peoples in the late 1930's, had to make
a decision of fateful consequence: to choose whether or not it would
allow totalitarian movements to emerge in its midst. The American
consensus rejected totalitarian movements of both right and left: the
leader of the Nazi Bund went to jail, the Smith Act of 1940 outlawed
subversive activity and the advocacy of subversive activity, and there
were later prosecutions of a parcel of fringe radicals of the right, such
as the Silver Shirts, and of the left, such as the Trotskyites of Minneapolis. The central cases against the Communists were the prosecutions against Eugene Dennis and ten other defendants for violation of
the Smith Act.

Consensus is incomprehensible unless it is taken to exclude ideas that
are contrary to itself. The rejection of totalitarianism is incomprehensible if totalitarianism is to be condoned and tolerated. The thought
that even in an "open society" some questions are closed and that not
every first principle is forever arguable counters much supposition to
the contrary. It is said to be a characteristic of the liberal view of
politics to suppose that nothing is settled, that all is flux, that every
idea has a license to compete for custom in the market places of thought
and discourse, and that this is the basic American political theory. But
what is this notion but an "orthodoxy" of its own? It thus appears that
liberals like conservatives have "first principles" that are not arguable
and that the statement of this "first principle" falsifies its very purport,
namely, that there are no closed questions. The dispute between con-

33. John T. Flynn, *American Mercury*, March 1954, pp. 69–72.
34. William Buckley and Brent Bozell, *McCarthy and His Enemies* (Chicago:
Regnery, 1954), pp. 308–340.
35. Willmoore Kendall, *The Conservative Affirmation* (Chicago: Regnery,
1963), pp. 50–76.

servatives and liberals is, then, at bottom, a struggle of orthodoxies. Anti-McCarthyites "got mad" at McCarthyites over opposing claims about the basic nature of the American society. Disputation over the "methods" of McCarthy is a trifle over procedure when one compares it with the more profound rift over the fundamentals of politics.

This is a very free rendition of the rationale of the division between the two camps — the liberal and the conservative — as seen in conservative expositions, but it is intended to be close and not just remotely approximate. It is a casuistical argument in the literal meaning of the adjective — a set of inferences about conduct drawn from moral principles. The conflict is thus viewed as one of heresy, in which each side thinks the other heretical. The logic of this position is to support both prosecution and persecution, and regret was expressed that McCarthyism was no longer an issue, and that it was put to an end in the middle fifties.

McCarthyism and the Politics of Social Change

What are we to make of the numerous speculations about the meaning of McCarthyism, some of which are contradictory? We certainly touch hands with history to be told that McCarthyism has something in common with the rise of the middle class out of the feudal system; or paradoxically, that McCarthy was really a leftist looking right, the same kind of fellow as Robespierre except that Robespierre looked left and acted left; or that McCarthyism is really later-day Populism or would be if later-day Populism were like McCarthyism; or that he is to be explained by anxieties about status in a country of fluid social change which has never had a rigid class system and in which everybody is an immigrant or the descendant of one.

Apart from certain shortcomings in each of the principal explanations, none gives much weight to the existence of political elements in the problem. Despite the paradox that McCarthy may have been a "leftist," he was a member of and a spokesman for a position that came to be identified with the Republicans. Although his position had adherents in the Democratic party also, it was as a Republican that McCarthy came into office, stayed in office, made his first attacks upon the Administration, acquired the full authority of a chairmanship, and lost his influence when he attacked the leadership of his own party. It is true that he started his political career as a Democrat, and that he was thought by many to be the stereotype American Catholic — a man with only surface commitments to democratic values.[36] But this

36. John Cogley, "Two Images of One Man," *Commonweal*, June 3, 1955.

socio-religious aspect of the McCarthy experience is collateral to the main fact that he was a Republican spokesman in a time when the Republicans were, most of the time, out of office.

Most of the conservative explanations of McCarthy are as difficult to accept as those of the liberal commentators but for different reasons. If the liberal commentators are sometimes short on the history they invoke, many of the conservative commentators tend to confuse religious truth with political conviction. It is a confusion of religion and politics to import into political discourse such constructs as the freedom of the Western will, the "gargoyles of Anti-Christ," absolute choices between good and evil, and the like. The antiliberal orthodoxy that proceeds to purge the liberal heresy in the name of democracy makes democracy — which is a procedure — the vessel of substantive religious truth which, in its way, is as reprehensible as the familiar Communist tactic which would use the procedure of democracy to end democracy. There can be no such thing as a political heresy in a democracy because there can be no such thing as a political orthodoxy.[37] Heresy and orthodoxy are the concerns of theologians.

McCarthyism may have been more than a political phenomenon — but it was at least a political phenomenon. McCarthy acquired his vogue and most of his meaning from the immediate political circumstance which begot him, and for which he was the temporary instrument. But the political roots of McCarthyism are to be found in the past, and the branches stretch into the future.

The industrial revolution after the Civil War created an economic system of marvelous productivity, a true wonder of the world, and brought to dominance new elites of economic enterprise whose very success made them the cultural idols of the society, to whom deference was expected and was accorded, who left the imprint of their taste and interest on every aspect of the society. They constituted a new system of power over the wealth and the material resources of the land. There were critics of the new order but they were not destined to prevail any more than did the machine-smashers and barn-burners of England when the industrial revolution took hold there. In the years after the Civil War, what may be called the "conservative consensus" became fixed in the structure of American social values, and there was to be, thereafter, no major challenge to the domination of the economy by private business enterprise.

The new business oligarchy came to wield presiding influence in the affairs of the Republican party. As Malcolm Moos, a biographer of the Republican party, has said,

37. John Cogley, "Question of Method," *Commonweal*, June 3, 1955.

For Grant, a man who could never make a success in business, those who had become so fabulously successful seemed to have almost a fatal fascination. But it was more than merely appointments and special favors that went to business — it was the Republican party. And as the party became the champion of capital, it did so with the hearty approval of a great mass of American people. . . . Nor was it an unnatural alliance, this new combine of politician and capitalist. As business looked to Washington for support, aid and comfort, the businessman looked to the politician as a broker — albeit a broker who sometimes had a little bet on the side.[38]

The party of Grant was not the party of Lincoln, for the principal energy was no longer provided by moral concern for the human condition but by concern for the gospel of free enterprise, for the protection and advancement of an economic philosophy which tended to equate the public interest with the well-being of the managers of the economy.

The President of the United States, in this conception of the public policy, was merely the minister of the desire of the Congress, the agent charged by the Constitution to see that the laws (of Congress) were faithfully executed, a conception that has characterized the conservative perspective throughout American history, as Wilfred Binkley has observed. The weak-President model of the Executive office is congenial to an economic philosophy in which the major decisions are to be left in private hands. In practical effect the fracture and decentralization of the public power that this model entails works to the advantage of the business community in two ways: it makes governmental regulation of the business community more difficult; and it favors the enactment of promotions, subsidies, tariffs, and other tangible benefits that may be negotiated through bargain and compromise among legislators who are responsive to the separated constituencies that Congressmen represent. In short, it tends to favor Congress over the Executive as the center of Federal authority.

There seems to operate in democratic politics something like a presumption of continuous office. In the absence of strong doctrinary alternatives, the case has to be made *against* incumbents. As Eugene Burdick has his protagonist instructor say in *The Ninth Wave*, people tend to vote often for negative reasons, that is, out of dislike, hatred even, and fear. The sum total of the statements made in a political campaign is likely to be a minus. Political campaigns take on some of the aspects of a public ligitation, with all the narrowness and distortion that special pleading involves. By contrast, the sum total of statements

38. Malcolm Moos, *The Republicans* (New York: Random House, 1956), p. 135.

made in business competition is a plus. By the common law and by many statutes, there are certain forms of destructive statement and action against business competitors that will not be tolerated in the courts. The political competitor will make much of the rascality of the opposition. The business competitor is required to confine himself to superlatives about himself. When all political campaigners plead the venality of each other and all businessmen argue which of them is the more virtuous, it may be supposed that stereotypes become fixed in the public consciousness (or unconsciousness) of the politician as a suspicious character and that of the businessman as a praiseworthy fellow, although some might be more praiseworthy than others. Working in favor of incumbents, then, is their tenure — if only because a case must be made for throwing them out. But the presumption of continuous office can be rebutted. It will generally be rebutted when there is a sufficiently large and onerous accumulation of grievances to impel the people at the polls to act.

With the domination of the economy and of the commonwealth by business influence after the Civil War, the presumption of continuous office favored unlimited tenure. But the regimes of Grant and his successors could and did forfeit their right to rule in the gradual accumulation of grievances that a narrow and sectarian view of the public interest and public policy produced. Resistance, in the first instance, took such forms of political self-help as the Granger movement in the states, when farmers lobbied and pressured state legislatures for political relief from economic disadvantage, and even ruin. The depression of 1873, which the manipulations of Jay Cooke and others in the stock market helped to create, produced widespread social unrest. Among the railroad workers, this led to blind and leaderless protest as in the spontaneous strike actions of 1877. Among other workers, it led first to the development of the Knights of Labor and then to the American Federation of Labor when the principle of organization of the Knights proved to be so vulnerable in the 1880's.

The experience of the farmers in Illinois and other states of the Middle West in the 1870's and 1880's showed that political relief could be had through coalitions of the disaffected. As the potency of the symbol of the "bloody shirt" faded with the advent of a new generation to whom the tensions of the Civil War were relatively less strainful than the painful economic urgencies of the present, the Democratic party began to win seats in Congress. Although the capture of the White House by the Democrats had been frustrated in 1876, the portent of the election of 1882 for the presidential election of 1884 was unmistakable. The businessman-Republican party alliance had become like a corporate management that the creditors can force into bankruptcy. They continue to own the enterprise but the referees in bankruptcy liquidate some of their assets to pay claims that have been defaulted.

It was the historic function of the Democratic party in the 1880's to serve as the people's referee to redistribute some of the assets. The Grange, the Alliance, the Wheel, the 700,000 members of the Knights of Labor, the railroad strikes, the Haymarket riots, the rise of the American Federation of Labor, the organization of the Pinkerton Detective Agency to conduct industrial espionage — many elements in this great social ferment of the ninth decade of the nineteenth century were material to be organized into a coalition of the disaffected, capable of obtaining political compensation for economic disadvantage through welfarist and social benefit programs. This was the historic role of the Democratic party in 1912 and 1932 and it might have been realized in 1884.

But in 1884, Cleveland misconceived the role of the party. It is true that he had to contend with a Republican Senate, but he had trouble with the Democratic House also. The root difficulty was his conception of what he was doing. So firmly stuck was the notion that free enterprise had some of the organic authority of the Constitution of the United States (a view that the Supreme Court in the 1880's was busy promoting) that he acted as though the chief function of government was to apply "business principles to public affairs." With respect to the farmer, Cleveland took the narrow view of Federal authority favored by the Republicans and their business constituency, and he vetoed a measure to supply free seed. Even when he returned to the White House in 1892, after losing the election of 1888, he refused inflationary formulas for the relief of agriculture, supported the gold standard, and thereby alienated the West. His view of the powers of the Federal government was not so narrow, however, that he could not send his Attorney General into the Pullman strike of 1894, to break it, which he did with the injunction. It took almost forty years to undo the effects of this unhappy intervention, in the Norris-La Guardia Act of 1932.

Since the grievances of farmers and workers and other casualties of the new industrialism of the eighties and the nineties were evidently not on the agenda of the two major parties, disaffected groups sought political compensation for their economic disadvantage in the formation of separate political movements like the Alliance and the Populists, which scored great successes. Although the protest parties never won the presidency, they had victories in the Congress, both in the capture of seats and in influencing the enactment of measures like the Sherman Antitrust Act of 1890, the income tax law of 1890, the Silver Purchase

Act of 1890, and other progressive measures. Populist sentiment was counteracted and frustrated by the courts which voided the income tax law, made a nullity of the Interstate Commerce Commission Act of 1887, and reduced the scope of the Sherman Antitrust Act; while the business world helped itself to substantial portions of benefit through the tariff. But the force of the Populist crusade had far-reaching effects. It won electoral votes, captured state governments, frightened southern whites into programs of racial restriction, and provided lessons for all to learn of the value of political organization. It spent its force in the nineties, and the grievances that set it in motion were assuaged with returning prosperity. Although class tensions were rife in the election of 1896, the Republican party succeeded in putting together support from city workers and western farmers that was strong enough to prevail.

By 1912, however, the Democrats under the leadership of Woodrow Wilson understood their historic role. As V. O. Key has said, "If a party is to govern, it must bring into mutually advantageous alliance an aggregate of interest powerful enough to win a presidential election. If it is to govern for long, it must see that the loaves and fishes are divided in a manner to command popular approbation." [39] The alliance contrived by McKinley and Hanna and continued by Theodore Roosevelt got power to govern for a considerable period. It could not solve the problem of the loaves and the fishes, however, because important sectors of the society were not content to wait until the benefits of the new enterprise trickled slowly down to the multitude, with the government confined to the role of auxiliary to the businessman as strikebreaker, policeman, and customs collector. Theodore Roosevelt's gestures towards reform were often verbalisms with a political function rather than an operational effect. Wilson seized the leadership of the disaffected and made it clear that the business community was finally to be challenged, for the first time, effectively, since the days of Andrew Jackson. The election was a split among three candidates and Wilson won largely because the Republicans were divided between Roosevelt and Taft, but the total votes for progressive reform were greater than the total votes for the *status quo.*

By 1920, the country had had enough of reform (the discontents of the disaffected had been appeased for that matter after the first Wilson election and he almost lost the second), and the country was returned to the control of the business managers who succeeded, after a decade, in producing a real bankruptcy. The persistence of the Cleveland myth — that the national Democratic party was really just like the Repub-

39. V. O. Key, *Politics, Parties, and Pressure Groups* (New York: Thomas Y. Crowell, 1964), p. 178.

lican, only a little less so — was revived in 1924, and it offered a conservative candidate with remarkably good credentials in the world of business affairs, and little appeal to the groups concerned with liberal action. John W. Davis was the 1920's counterpart of Alton B. Parker who had also failed to move multitudes with his promises to be like the Republicans. As in 1892, when Cleveland was so strongly promoted by business groups, there appeared in 1924 a third party, the Progressives of La Follette, but it failed to run again in 1928. The Democrats perpetrated a political debacle in 1928 with Alfred E. Smith who, although more liberal than Davis, was not much more so, as his subsequent attacks upon the New Deal and his membership in the American Liberty League were to attest; and who, moreover, was, for most of the country, a caricature of the East Side with whom it was difficult to make any kind of personal identification.

The party of General Grant, Rutherford B. Hayes, Chester Alan Arthur, William McKinley, William Howard Taft, Warren Gamaliel Harding, Calvin Coolidge, and Herbert Hoover found it difficult not only to get into the White House after 1932 but to get its candidates nominated for the presidency. Herbert Hoover was shunted to one side in 1936, Vandenberg (before his conversion to internationalist causes) was defeated by Wendell Willkie, John Bricker of Ohio lost it to Dewey in 1944, Taft lost it to Dewey in 1948 and to Eisenhower in 1952. Like the Democratic party of Cleveland, Parker, and Davis which imitated the Republicans, the Republicans between 1936 and 1964 made no frontal assault upon the programs of the New Deal but only a collateral harassment, promising to keep the social gains (although not to add to them) while administering programs more economically and efficiently. There was no restoration in 1940, as there had been in 1920, following the political adjustment of creditor claims, and the prevailing leadership in successive Republican national conventions did not seem capable of obtaining it.

The decline of the New Deal after 1936 as measured by the gradual loss of Democratic seats in the House and Senate and the shrinkage of the popular margins in the presidential elections of 1940 and 1944, presaged the expected change in 1948 which did not take place. Eager for office, disappointed by frustration, the Republican party with the help of conservative Democrats took control of the Congress in 1950, found a storm leader in McCarthy, developed the technique of prescriptive publicity as a formidable weapon of political harassment, and with an assist from the timorous and defensive leadership of the Administration managed to achieve in 1952 the victory they had been denied for two decades, which the politics of eighty years promised and, according to which, was overdue.

McCarthyism in this view of the party movements of almost a century was the agent of a fundamentalist conservatism that was prepared to yield public policy to the reformers for the relatively short periods required to satisfy grievances but which expected to recover predominance when these intervals were over. McCarthy had no social program of his own and in this respect was the perfect instrument for the realization of the social aims of those who were to benefit from his attacks, for the restoration which a third term and a war had denied. The Communist issue was the cutting edge for the attack. The Communist problem lent itself to quiet and nonsensational solutions before the late forties and after 1954. When McCarthy and the Communist issue had served their purposes, they both disappeared.

The fundamentalist conservatism that McCarthy served has been an enduring aspect of the American system since the Civil War and has not been dissipated. It believes with profound faith in free enterprise, reacts to symbols that seem to threaten it, is suspicious of welfarism and other social reform, tends to stand pat, and is moved only by exigency. The stronghold of this faith in the Republican party has been centered in the Middle and Rocky Mountain West and it has not been satisfied with the moderate conservatism of the eastern states. It regards itself as the heart and soul of the Republican party, uncorrupted by the liberalism that has softened the eastern wing, and is determined to recover the conservative spirit of the 1920's and earlier times. It is pre-New Deal in its mentality. It came to office if not to power with the help of McCarthy in the three years after 1950, and may some time surge again in an effort to hold time still, and perhaps even turn it back a little.

It has been said that the tyrant with the sword is followed by the historian with the sponge, but no erasure has softened the image of former Senator Joseph R. McCarthy of Wisconsin since his condemnation by the United States Senate on December 2, 1954, for unsenatorial behavior. Although he was to serve a short-run goal in a short span of years, he has achieved permanent prominence of a sort. The clamors of that anxious time have guaranteed that McCarthy's name, like that of Pope's Cromwell, will be "dam'd to everlasting fame."

Appendix Sources for Survey of Press Comment on Tydings Investigation

(ALL DATES ARE 1950)

The Nation

1. n.a., "The Shape of Things" (editorial), February 25, p. 167.
2. n.a., "McCarthy's Blunderbuss" (editorial), March 18, p. 243.
3. n.a., "The Shape of Things" (editorial), March 25, p. 261.
4. Freda Kirchwey, "Appeasement's Tragedy" (editorial), April 8, pp. 312–313.
5. Willard Shelton, "The New Irresponsibles," April 8, pp. 313–315.
6. Willard Shelton, "McCarthy's Vicious Retreat," April 15, pp. 341–342.
7. n.a., "Dementia Unlimited" (editorial), April 29, p. 388.
8. Willard Shelton, "The McCarthy Method," May 6, pp. 417–418.
9. Willard Shelton, "Ananias in Washington," May 13, pp. 437–438.
10. n.a., "The Shape of Things" (editorial), May 20, p. 462.
11. n.a., "The Shape of Things" (editorial), June 10, p. 559.
12. Willard Shelton, "The *Amerasia* Case," June 17, pp. 590–592.
13. Freda Kirchwey, "The McCarthy Blight," June 24, pp. 609–610.
14. Willard Shelton, "The *Amerasia* Case, II," June 24, pp. 613–615.
15. n.a., "The Shape of Things" (editorial), July 8, p. 21.
16. n.a., "McCarthy to Trial," July 29, pp. 99–100.
17. Philip Mandel, Review of Owen Lattimore, *Ordeal by Slander*, August 19, pp. 170–171.
18. n.a., "The Shape of Things" (editorial), October 28, p. 373.

The Reporter

19. John Hoving, "My Friend McCarthy," April 25, pp. 28–31.
20. Max Ascoli, "The G.O.P.'s Choice" (editorial), June 6, p. 4.
21. William H. Hessler, "Ordeal by Headline," June 6, pp. 5–7.
22. n.a., "Reading Lattimore," June 6, pp. 13–15.
23. Jean Jacques Servan Schreiber, "How It Looks from Europe," June 6, pp. 15–17.
24. Douglass Cater, "The Captive Press," June 6, pp. 17–20.

New Leader

25. Jonathan Stout, "McCarthy by the Numbers," March 18, p. 3.
26. Eugene Lyons, "Communists Lucky to be Investigated by Dies, McCarthy," April 1, pp. 1, 6.
27. Miles McMillin, "The Man Behind the State Department Probe: Who Is Joe McCarthy?" April 1, pp. 1, 7.
28. n.a., "The Mystery of *Amerasia*," April 1, p. 6.
29. Anatole Shub, "Three Myths Help Confuse Liberals," April 1, p. 7.
30. David J. Dallin, "More Harmful Than Spies," April 15, p. 2.
31. Rodney Gilbert, "Mr. Lattimore's Latest" (review of Owen Lattimore, *Pivot of Asia*), April 15, p. 8.
32. Jonathan Stout, "State Department Policy, Not Personnel, Main Concern of Senate Committee," April 22, p. 3.
33. Granville Hicks, "Owen Lattimore and Louis Budenz," May 6, p. 15.
34. David J. Dallin, "Writings of Owen Lattimore Reflect Pro-Soviet Views," May 13, p. 11.
35. Robert Muhlen, "The Hysteria of the Hisslings," May 13, pp. 16–18.
36. n.a., "The Hards and the Softs" (editorial), May 20, pp. 30–31.
37. Elmer Davis and Granville Hicks, "Lattimore and the Liberals" (debate), May 27, pp. 16–18.
38. n.a., "A Lady Speaks Out" (editorial), June 10, p. 30.
39. Granville Hicks, "McCarthy and the Homosexuals," June 17, p. 9.
40. William Henry Chamberlin, "Lattimore Views the Soviet Scene: Purges = Democracy, Dalstroi = TVA," July 1, p. 19.
41. Eugene Lyons, "Lattimore: Dreyfus or Hiss?" (review of Owen Lattimore, *Ordeal by Slander*), September 2, pp. 16–19.

Washington Post (editorials only)

42. "Sewer Politics," February 14, p. 10.
43. "McCarthy's Reds," February 24, p. 22.
44. "Guilt by Reiteration," March 2, p. 12.
45. "Loyalty Files," March 6, p. 8.
46. "McCarthy's Arrow," March 9, p. 10.
47. "Mrs. Acheson's Mite," March 10, p. 20.
48. "Communist Circus," March 14, p. 10.
49. "Case in the Flesh," March 15, p. 12.
50. "The Aberrants," March 17, p. 22.
51. "Access to Files," March 18, p. 8.
52. "The Case of Dr. Jessup," March 21, p. 8.
53. "For Want of a Code," March 22, p. 12.
54. "Diplomatic Blues," March 25, p. 10.
55. "Loyalty Files," March 26, p. 4B.
56. "The Personal Equation," March 28, p. 10.
57. "The Man at the Top," March 28, p. 10.
58. "FBI Files," March 29, p. 10.
59. "Private Eye," March 30, p. 10.
60. "Investigation," April 1, p. 8.
61. "McCarthy's 'Evidence,'" April 2, p. 4B.
62. "Investigator Wanted," April 4, p. 12.
63. "Memo on China," April 4, p. 12.

64. "Sen. McCarthy's Sources," April 6, p. 12.
65. "A Man Stands Up," April 7, p. 20.
66. "No Spies," April 8, p. 6.
67. "Lattimore 'Clearance,' " April 12, p. 14.
68. "Kohlberg's Klan," April 13, p. 12.
69. "Assuming Innocence," April 14, p. 20.
70. "Tangled Web," April 21, p. 22.
71. "Acheson Hits Back," April 24, p. 10.
72. "Imposter Witness," April 27, p. 10.
73. "Mr. Browder's Contempt," April 28, p. 20.
74. "Mud on Tuesday," April 30, p. 4B.
75. "Files on Parade," April 30, p. 4B.
76. "Contempt Citations," May 1, p. 8.
77. "The McCarthy Record," May 2, p. 10.
78. "Barbarian Invasion," May 3, p. 12.
79. "Point of Fact," May 4, p. 10.
80. "*Amerasia* Case," May 6, p. 8.
81. "The 81 Files," May 7, p. 4B.
82. "Mr. Chavez's Reply," May 14, p. 4B.
83. "Fighting Back," May 20, p. 8.
84. "The Road Back to America," May 22, p. 10.
85. "Four Horsemen," June 2, p. 20.
86. "*Amerasia*," June 3, p. 8.
87. "An Issue Above Party," June 9, p. 20.
88. "Under the Bed," June 10, p. 8.
89. "Self-Incrimination," June 15, p. 14.
90. "McCarthy on 'Payoffs,' " June 17, p. 8.
91. "Blackwash," June 20, p. 10.
92. "Essential Test Case," June 23, p. 20.
93. "What Service Did," June 24, p. 8.
94. "Loyalty to Employes," June 30, p. 22.
95. " 'A Fraud and a Hoax'!" July 18, p. 12.
96. "Censuring McCarthy," July 21, p. 18.
97. "Bury It," July 23, p. 4B.
98. "Congressional Immunity," July 30, p. 4B.

Freeman

99. Isaac Don Levine, "*Plain Talk* and *Amerasia*," October 2, pp. 20–22.
100. John Chamberlain, "A Reviewer's Notebook" (review of Owen Lattimore, *Ordeal by Slander*), October 16, pp. 57–58.
101. Robert Morris, "Counsel for the Minority — A Report on the Tydings Investigation," October 30, pp. 78–81.
102. Ralph de Toledano, "The Liberal Disintegration — A Conservative View," November 13, pp. 109–111.

Mercury

103. "Judge Kenyon Meets the Press" (excerpts from NBC radio broadcast), June, pp. 700–708.
104. "Louis Budenz Meets the Press" (excerpts from NBC radio broadcast), July, pp. 90–99.

105. "A Former OSS Agent Meets the Press" (excerpts from NBC radio broadcast), August, pp. 199–207.
106. Frederick Woltman and Victor Lasky, "The Mystery of the *Amerasia* Case," September, pp. 274–284.
107. "Senator McMahon Meets the Press" (excerpts from NBC radio broadcast), September, pp. 320–326.
108. Benjamin Stolberg, "Lattimore: Master of Omission" (review of Owen Lattimore, *Ordeal by Slander*), October, pp. 489–498.

Washington *Times-Herald* (editorials only)

109. "Where Spies Hurt Us Most," February 28, p. 10.
110. "Whitewash — Again!" March 9, p. 18.
111. "Vote of Confidence," March 22, p. 16.
112. "Is That Presidential Bee," March 23, p. 22.
113. "Self-Portrait of an Internationalist," March 24, p. 14, Sect. I.
114. "Judge Them By Their Works," March 29, p. 14.
115. "It's There, Find It," March 30, p. 20.
116. "The Elite," March 31, p. 15, Sect. I.
117. "Is Tydings Man or Mouse?" April 2, p. 12.
118. "Lord Vansittart and Mr. Stimson," April 3, p. 6.
119. "The Company You Keep," April 10, p. 6.
120. " 'Honorable' Americans: I," April 26, p. 18.
121. " 'Honorable' Americans: II," April 28, p. 18, Sect. I.
122. "Browder's Nest Mates," May 1, p. 6.
123. "Who's Irresponsible?" May 4, p. 22.
124. "Browder and Roosevelt," May 5, p. 14, Sect. I.
125. "Why Tydings' Nerve Has Snapped," May 14, p. 16.
126. "Look Who Deplores Witch Hunting," May 29, p. 6.
127. "Some Teacup," June 1, p. 22.
128. " 'Don't Make a Move,' " June 3, p. 20.
129. "Let Hoover Talk," June 6, p. 12.
130. "McGrath Can't Alibi This," June 8, p. 20.
131. "The Decline and Fall of Public Morals," June 9, p. 14, Sect. I.
132. "So Files *Can* be Opened When Truman Pleases," June 20, p. 12.
133. "What the *Amerasia* Record Shows," June 21, p. 18.
134. "What's the Game, Senator?" June 24, p. 22.
135. "Just a Service, Says Mr. Service," June 26, p. 8.
136. "Dr. Jessup and Mr. Hyde," July 10, p. 6.
137. "Tydings Trapped," July 13, p. 20.
138. "The Herring Is a Little Higher Now, — The Report Nobody Believes," July 19, p. 18.
139. "Hold It, Senator," July 22, p. 10.
140. "Harry, the Spy Hunter," July 29, p. 12.

Index

Abt, John, 159, 163n, 397; and Ware group, 107–110 *passim*, 117, 119, 120; with La Follette subcommittee, 121; and Perlo group, 161, 162n

Acheson, Dean, 204, 220, 221n, 293, 308, 313; and 1945 State Dept. reorganization, 265–268, 313; on China, 220, 221n, 239–240; support of Hiss, 270, 271, 288

Adamic, Louis, 163

Adams, Sherman, 370, 372n

Adler, Solomon: and Glasser, 165–166, 169; and Silvermaster group, 168, 169

Agents, foreign: registration of, 37; recruitment for Communist espionage, 82, 85

Agricultural Adjustment Administration (Dept. of Agriculture), 73; nucleus of Ware group in, 107–111, 117–121, 137

Agriculture, U.S. Dept. of, 42; Communist members in, 101, 102–123, 150, 151n, 163n, 362; Soil Conservation Service, 109; Consumers Counsel, 109–110, 119, 120

Air Force, U.S., 174; Dept. of, security powers, 363

Aircraft production: secret data on, 166, 172; strikes in, 153–154

Alien and Sedition Acts, 413–414

All-China Soviet Congress: First, 231; Second, 232

Almond, Gabriel, *The Appeals of Communism*, evaluated, 59–60

ALPD. *See* American League for Peace and Democracy

Amalgamated Clothing Workers of America, 161, 163n

Amerasia, 299; case of, 2, 9, 195n, 203–216, 263, 267, 272, 312, 314, 362; press comment on case of, 285, 287, 288–289, 291, 294, 295; and IPR hearings, 302

America First Committee, 153

American Civil Liberties Union: and Fish hearings, 30, 33–34; and CPUSA, 1930's–1940's, 34n; and Gastonia strike, 38

American Coalition, The, 35n, 41

American Committee for Chinese War Orphans, 18on

American Committee for the Struggle Against War, 67n

"American Exceptionalism": Lovestone on, 20n; Browder's, 157

American Federation of Government Employees, 87–88, 90, 127

American Federation of Labor, 136n, 137; government unions in, 87, 88; Third Period party line on, 22–23; Communists in, 44; split, 1935, 49; Remington-Rand case, 141n; vs. Bridges on union representation, 149; rejection of Wallace, 1948, 396; growth of, 419, 420

American Federation of State, County, and Municipal Employees, 88

American Fund for Public Service (Garland Fund), 34

American Jewish Committee, 202n

American Jewish Conference, 202n

American Labor Party, 89, 396

American Law Students Association, 276

American League Against War and Fascism, 50–51n, 67, 68n, 134, 196n. *See also* American League for Peace and Democracy

American League for Peace and Democracy, 8, 139, 140, 154, 351; discussed as a front organization, 66–71; dismantled, 153; Fifth Congress of,

Matusow, Harvey, 340n
Mazo, Earl, 322
Medina, Harold, 89, 354
Meloy, L. V., committee on loyalty and security, 367, 368–369
Merson, Martin, 324n, 326n, 330, 332
Merton, Robert K., 383, 384
Metcalf, Keyes D., 337n
Meyer, Peter, 391
Mif, Pavel, 230
Military Intelligence Service, Madrid Zone, 274
Millis, Prof. Harry, 132, 143
Mink, George, 85, 86, 106
Mins, Henry F., 86
Mins, Leonard E., 182, 183
Mitchell, Kate, 206, 208, 211, 213, 288
Mola, General Emilio, 151
Molotov, V. M., 105n, 155; statement on China to Hurley, 2, 257, 315; visit to U.S., 1942, 156
Mont Tremblant, Canada, IPR conference at, 307–308, 309
Monthly Review, 341
Moos, Malcolm, 417–418
Morgenthau, Henry, 177
Morrill, J. L., 337
Morris, Robert, 166, 297
Morse, Sen. Wayne, 406
Morton, Alfred, 329, 338
Mosier, Rep. Harold D., 135
Mundt, Sen. Karl, 111, 115n, 374; and Voice of America hearings, 328–329; and overseas information centers hearings, 341
Mundt committee, 401, 403
Murphy, Raymond, 108n
Murphy, Thomas F., 185, 200
Murray, Philip, 94, 147, 148
Murray Special Committee on Small Business, 121, 122

Naigles, Mike, 128n
Nation, The, 190, 193, 345; on McCarthy charges, *Amerasia* case, and Tydings committee hearings, 284–286; on congressional investigations, 387, 388, 389, 390–391; on McCarthy, 406, 407–408
National Association for the Advancement of Colored People, 25
National Council for Democratic Rights, 276
National Emergency Conference, 276
National Emergency Conference for Democratic Rights, 276
National Free Browder Congress, 156

National Industrial Recovery Act, Sec. 7a, 131, 132
National Labor Board, 73, 131–132
National Labor Relations Act, 132, 141; and Smith committee hearings, 133–134, 137, 138; steel unionization and, 148–149
National Labor Relations Board, 15, 73, 110, 117; Communist activity in, 1, 95, 124, 129–131, 138–143, 144–150, 151n, 167, 362; Fuchs in, 127, 128–129, 131; court cases concerning, 132–133; investigation by Smith committee, 9, 134–138
National Lawyers' Guild, 129, 139, 146
National Maritime Union, 106n
National Military Council, Chinese, 235, 236–237, 254, 258
National Negro Congress, 154
National Recovery Administration (NRA), 75, 109, 114, 117, 120, 126
National Republic, 31, 41
National Research Project (of WPA), 164, 165
National Review, 408
National Student League, 81n, 165
National War Labor Board, 147n
National Youth Administration, 110, 117, 120
Nationalism, Communist party line on, 47–48
Navy, U.S. Dept. of, 203, 207, 211, 363
Nazi party, 20, 45, 46n, 52, 185; and McCormack-Dickstein hearings, 34–35, 36; Davies on Chiang regime and, 244
Nazi-Soviet Pact. *See* Soviet Union
Negro Zionism, 23
Negroes: Communist party line on, 23–26, 41, 66, 71, 78; membership in Communist Party, 30, 33; union problems, 88–89
Nelson, Donald, 253
Nelson, Eleanor, 127, 128
Nelson, Rep. John E., 28–29n, 30, 31, 33, 34, 43, 44
New Deal, 6, 15, 105, 115, 135; lessened electoral support, 7; as exponent of liberal tradition, 19; changing Communist Party policy toward, 26–28, 41, 48, 52; growth of bureaucracy during, and need for employees, 72–73, 75–76; attractions of, 76–77; and labor statutes, 132–133; investigations during, compared to 1940's, 392–393; Republican reaction, 422
New Leader: on NLRB, 142–143; on McCarthy charges, State Dept., and